CW01637801

Sweet Magnolias
&
English Lavender

ALSO BY JAMES O'DONALD MAYS

The Splendid Shilling
A Social History of an Engaging Coin
(Awarded the Lotka Memorial Prize by
The Royal Numismatic Society)

Mr Hawthorne Goes to England
The Adventures of a Reluctant Consul

TOKENS OF THOSE *TRYING TIMES*
A Social History of Britain's 19th Century Silver Tokens

The New Forest Book
An Illustrated Anthology

Produced by Hobbs the Printers, Southampton

(Didn't they do well!)

Sweet Magnolias
&
English Lavender

An Anglo-American Romance

James O'Donald Mays

James O'Donald Mays

NEW FOREST LEAVES
Burley, Ringwood, Hampshire

© James O'Donald Mays, 2008

All rights reserved. Except for brief quotations in a review, this book, or any part thereof, may not be reproduced, stored in a retrieval system, or transmitted in any form or by any means (electronic, mechanical, photocopying, recording or otherwise) without the prior written permission of the copyright owner.

British Library in Publication Data: A CIP catalogue record for this book is available from the British Library.

2 4 6 8 10 7 5 3 1

Paperback ISBN 978 0 907956 07 5
Hardback ISBN 978 0 907956 08 2

This book is for a half-dozen of the best (grandchildren)

Anna and Daniel
Gilbert and Arthur
Georgia and Flavia

Acknowledgements

Foremost I must thank those national institutions, agencies and officials, American and British, who generously gave permission for use of their photographs. Credits will be found in the captions to illustrations, but are repeated below to emphasize my gratitude: US Department of Defense (wartime illustrations); US Information Agency; US State Department; National Aeronautics and Space Agency; National Portrait Gallery, London, and Ronny and Michael Schwartz and the Bernard Lee Schwartz Foundation (the Bern Schwartz portrait of Constance Applebee); Alastair Arnott and the Southampton City Heritage Services (wartime illustration).

British newspapers also have kindly allowed inclusion of several photographs that were important in documenting both wartime and post-war subjects featured in this work. The *Daily Express* and the *Sunday Express* happily gave permission to reproduce two of Giles' famous Second World War cartoons relating to the shipment of GI Brides to the United States. Southampton's *Daily Echo* generously allowed permission to reproduce a wartime ambulance operation and the Portsmouth *Evening News* permitted reproduction of a Scouting photograph. In addition, Peter Newark's Pictures provided likenesses of Presidents Eisenhower and de Gaulle and Eleanor Roosevelt.

For use of some photographs from Finland I am indebted to Aira Laitinen and Lehtikuva, U.A. Saarinen, Kristian Runeberg, and MTV3.

I am indebted to several friends who read the typescript of this work in draft form, offering many suggestions for improvement. They include Rosemary Brinton, Carol Smith, Mike Oliver and my daughter, Angela. Anne Blackman kindly helped with the bibliographic entry. My sister-in-law, Betty Rudd, provided valuable information about the Roberts and Houghton families. My granddaughters, Georgia and Flavia, also made significant contributions during their brief visits to me during their school holidays.

In the United States Rose Mays and my sister Hope located old family photographs to help document events in the lives of my parents and grandparents. Jane Hagner kindly gave permission for inclusion of her mother's recipe for making authentic Maryland Crab Soup.

I also owe thanks to my photographer friend, Gerry Beauchamp, who laboured long to make the most of the illustrations. Finally, it is impossible for me to thank sufficiently two "workhorses" who laboured hard and long to make this work possible – Annie Ratford, my faithful typist-cum-editor and Nick Palmer who has helped with the IT requirements.

In a work spanning the lifetime of a nonagenarian there may well be some errors and omissions; for these I ask the readers' forgiveness. In a few instances I have not used the real names of people.

J.O.M.

Contents

PART I
Growing up in Georgia
1918-1942

PART II
The Allies win a war and I win a bride
1942-1946

PART III
In search of my destiny: My South or my world?
1946-1956

PART IV
Flying the flag
1956-1970

PART V
Idylls of the New Forest
1970-1986

Preface

Every mortal, someone once said, has a story to tell. If by accident or achievement a person becomes famous, there are many waiting to read the notable's story.

I cannot lay claim to either of these reasons for putting pen to paper. On the contrary, I was born under quite ordinary circumstances on a cotton farm in the Deep South state of Georgia. I began a career as a journalist only to have it interrupted by the Second World War. I then went on to represent the United States abroad in several diplomatic assignments and retired to Britain to combine my love of history with a small publishing enterprise.

My youth, spent in an American South still deeply scarred by memories of the lost cause of the Confederacy, was also influenced by the subsequent agrarian poverty that seemed to be our destiny. When the Great Depression came, members of our family experienced acute hardship in common with millions of others in the South and elsewhere.

Yet, even in those trying times when we did not know from one day to the next if there would be bread to eat, we developed a fierce loyalty to family and a fierce pride in our community. These would sustain us until President Franklin D. Roosevelt's "New Deal" began to make our lives more tolerable.

Going to university, on the face of it, was well nigh impossible for children of low income families like mine. Outright grants were virtually non-existent and families without means could contribute little or nothing towards their childrens' higher education costs. But there was one route that permitted millions of students to obtain degrees from American universities in those difficult days: "working one's way through college". It was a small miracle that most American universities helped untold numbers of students obtain degrees by providing part-time jobs to defray some of their costs. My room mates and I were among those lucky ones.

If my years at university increased my formal learning and opened my eyes to new hope for our impoverished South, it was the Second World War that accelerated my growing interest in national and international affairs. I was lucky to be assigned to an Army unit in southern England where I could observe the launching of the Normandy invasion, arguably one of the most crucial events of the 20th century. From my vantage point in Southampton I saw the logistical miracle of D-Day and the frantic build-up phase that followed.

Those years in uniform were also the "marrying years" for my generation, that is, the time when young people are most attracted to matrimony. Thus it was that I met and married Mary. Our union was to produce three wonderful children and, in time, a bevy of equally fabulous grandchildren.

My working life has been a mixture of conventional journalism and government service, the latter principally as press attaché at several American diplomatic posts. These assignments took me to Tel Aviv, Paris and Helsinki with additional brief postings to Tehran and Geneva.

All of these took place during the Cold War when, like it or not, the United States was obliged to react against any threat, real or perceived, by the Soviet bloc. Frustratingly, the governments of Israel, France and Finland then had delicate relationships with the United States: Israel, because it was constantly in fear of losing American economic and military assistance; France, because de Gaulle's "force de frappe" (an independent French military capability) had serious knock-on effects for NATO and the United States; and Finland, obliged to nurture its delicate East-West posture so as not to offend the powerful Soviet Union next door.

Though never a principal player in those tense times, I was close enough to events to share both the joys and disappointments that came America's way. The war in Vietnam and the American Civil Rights struggle were undoubtedly the most traumatic events of my diplomatic career. The one ray of sunshine during those tumultuous times came when substantial progress was made towards nuclear disarmament.

Retirement to Britain enabled me to realise a long-dormant interest in publishing, fed in part by my journalistic background and in part by a love of history and literature. At first my wife and all three children assisted me in this challenging enterprise. Then, one by one the children went their separate ways. At the peak of our publishing venture Mary was struck down with Alzheimer's Disease. Her passing was a blow from which I have never completely recovered. Although millions suffer from this disease, many people remain unaware of its symptoms, characteristics and development. With a view to promoting a broader understanding of Alzheimer's, I have deliberately detailed several aspects of Mary's illness.

With the one exception that follows, I have mainly refrained from philosophising about the good and evil I have observed in my 20th century world. I do believe it is within the capability of civilised people to retain much of what is good, to eliminate a great deal that is bad and to bring a higher standard of living to those living in underdeveloped areas.

Despite its many problems and critics, the United Nations, in my view, remains the best hope for preventing wars and providing succour for the world's needy. I have long felt that the UN needs a permanent rapid reaction force to deal with disasters such as famines, floods and earthquakes, and with small-scale military interventions when UN Security Council backing can be obtained. Under such a plan the world's most prosperous countries could earmark military units that could be despatched quickly anywhere in the world to administer aid programmes using previously designated stocks of food, clothing and medicines. Likewise, lightly armoured units could be deployed quickly to trouble spots, hopefully preventing major outbreaks of fighting.

That the UN has become a cumbersome, sometimes unwieldly body is beyond doubt, but this is a condition which good management can put right. In the final analysis, the UN will be only as effective as is its intake of able people, adequate finance from member nations and support of the general public. It remains our last, best hope and we must ensure that it succeeds.

Finally, a point on a personal level. I believe that the preservation of the conventional family is crucial to halting the breakdown of moral and ethical standards in both society and government. Communities of closely knit families, it seems to me, are better positioned to promote a strengthening of personal identity and an enhanced sense of caring – two qualities that should be instilled into our lives from the earliest days.

PART I

Growing up in Georgia

1918-1942

1
Hard slog for them: Pure joy for me

Grandfather Mays was a remarkable man. The son of a Scots-Irish emigrant from Ulster, he was gifted with the same zeal that enabled many of his peers to seek their fortunes in the southern United States during the latter half of the 19th century.

"Grandpa", as we grandchildren called him, was born in the small town of Millen, at the junction of two railroads: the Central of Georgia running from Atlanta to Savannah (General Sherman's route on his famous march to the sea), and the Georgia Railroad, which ran from Augusta to Millen. His father, on arriving in America, had immediately headed south, settling first in neighbouring South Carolina and later in Millen where he worked for the Central of Georgia line.

Although by now a second generation Irish-American, Grandpa had lost little of his Irish accent, humour and love for the occasional sip of whiskey. Most of all he was determined to succeed in farming, his chosen career. His first task was to acquire land, which he did by small increments, and next a wife who would bear him numerous sons and daughters to assure his future on the land. In those days agriculture reigned supreme in the United States and farmers were expected to have large families to enable their sons to marry daughters of nearby farmers and their daughters to become wives of their neighbours' sons.

So Sarah Jane Hillis (Sally) knew what the score was when she accepted his proposal of marriage. Over her two decades of child-bearing age she bore him an even dozen children, half of them boys and half girls. My father, Floyd, was next to the youngest. It wasn't long before he displayed a love of all things technical – electrical, mechanical – and by the time he was a teenager his services on the farm were already proving invaluable to Grandpa. In time he helped install and maintain a small Delco-Remy electric plant for the farm. When the poorly built reapers broke down, he got them to work again.

But my grandparents knew that education was also important to success in the New World. After all, one son, Robert, had gone to Mercer University in Macon where he graduated from the School of Medicine. So my father was also sent off to Mercer, but unable to bear the enclosed halls of learning and hourly classes, he left after only a week and returned to the farm.

Of medium height, handsome and athletic, my father no doubt cut a dashing figure among the circle of young ladies he knew. He and my mother probably would never have been married had it not been for a fever epidemic at the State Normal College (later to become the University of Georgia's College of Education). My mother's father was James M. Lutes, a lifelong educator who at one time was Headmaster of Louisville Academy, the high school from which I was later to graduate. "Professor Lutes", as he was called, was in no doubt that his pretty, vivacious daughter Kathleen should also follow the teaching profession and so enrolled her at the State Normal.

When an epidemic of contagious fever broke out in mid-term, the school's administrators cancelled classes and ordered all students home until the doctors could give the all clear for their return. Kathleen arrived home restless and aimless – but not for long. My father, having heard of the hiatus in her higher education, knew he had to act fast if he were to capture his prize. At that time he owned one of the first Harley Davidson motorcycles in the area. With its mesmerising purr, the Harley Davidson and its dashing driver must have been impossible for my mother to resist.

Following a whirlwind courtship, they were married on September 8th, 1917 at Hurst Chapel, the nearby country church attended by my grandparents and their children. As it was a scorching hot day, someone suggested the marriage ceremony take place outside the church amidst the surrounding rows of cotton. No one objected, for had not St. Chrysostom proclaimed "When one or two are gathered together in my name, there am I." As a child I often gazed at their wedding photograph and marvelled at the thought that a couple could be married anywhere if they loved one another.

Both of my parents were just 20 years old. It was my Uncle Robert who was called upon to deliver me nine months later. As my father's services were much in demand to maintain all the equipment on the farm, it was taken for granted that he and his new bride should live there for as long as they wished. That understanding allowed me to spend my early years under the most idyllic circumstances imaginable for a small boy.

One day I was taken by my mother and shown shotgun pellets embedded in the baseboard of her bedroom. "See those?" she asked. "Well, they were originally intended for me." I didn't understand. Then she explained how my father, proud possessor of a new shotgun, had just explained to her some of its finer features. Finishing his description, he placed his finger on the trigger and aimed the gun at my mother.

"Don't point it at me!" she shouted. My father grinned and assured her the gun was not loaded. Complying with her request, however, he aimed at the baseboard and pulled the trigger. The blast resounded throughout the house and was heard in the nearby fields. Family and workers came running from all directions. When they rushed to the bedroom, they found a deeply remorseful young husband trying to console his distressed wife.

Although Grandpa Mays had cows, pigs and chicken for family consumption and a small acreage of grain to feed them, cotton was his main crop – as it was for most farmers throughout the South. King Cotton remained so until the arrival of the insidious boll weevil. This insect devoured the heart of the cotton bolls before they could mature. The result was catastrophic. Grandpa, like many prosperous farmers, had installed a cotton gin for processing his cotton and that of nearby small planters. Suddenly the gin became redundant as the quantity and quality of cotton plummeted. They were not to know that the arrival of the boll weevil was a blessing. It vividly showed Southern farmers the folly of relying on a single crop; thus the practice of crop diversification was adopted.

As a child growing up on my grandfather's farm I was not always aware of these perilous economic issues. I did, however, remember a few years when so much cotton was produced that the income did not cover the cost of production. This led to a popular song of the time which began:

"Eleven cent cotton and forty cent meat,
How in the world can a poor man eat?"

In my mind the farm was my "world" and the farmhouse my "capitol". Those youthful years, though often difficult for the grown-ups, were some of the happiest of my life.

Almost from birth I was aware how hard my grandparents worked and how nature ruthlessly dictated their daily life. Simply put, prompt execution of chores was essential to their existence. It was still dark when Grandpa rose at 4.30 every morning to build a fire in the kitchen stove for Grandma. That done, he immediately went out to milk the cows. Grandma, meanwhile, went to the kitchen and soon the smell of frying bacon and percolating coffee wafted throughout the farmhouse, foretelling the hearty breakfast that was to follow.

That old kitchen range baked the best cakes I have ever tasted. No one worried about cholesterol then, so each cake contained generous quantities of eggs and butter. Grandma's basic cake recipe called for several layers topped by the chosen icing of the day. Chocolate or caramel covered with pecan or walnut halves were my favourites.

We had no refrigerator but there was a massive "ice box" that had to be constantly replenished with fresh ice. Its main purpose was to preserve the family's milk and butter and any meat that might be left over. Several shelves held large, shallow pans on which rich cream formed from milk obtained from the Jersey cows. Every two or three days the cream would be skimmed off and made into butter. My grandparents kept a watchful eye on the amount of ice that remained in the ice box each day, for all of the family's perishable foods would be at risk if the last of the ice melted. In towns there was no problem, for the ice-man made daily rounds. But my grandparents' farm was several miles from the nearest town, Sardis, so they were obliged to go there once or twice weekly, depending on the weather, to top-up the lump of ice that remained. I don't remember a time when they let the ice melt completely.

At one end of the farmhouse's L-shaped enclosed porch was a double washstand – a necessity in a house with many children. We were allowed only "top and tail" washing. Complete baths were taken at weekly or longer intervals. When it was my time for a bath, a corrugated tub was brought into my grandparents' bedroom and placed in front of the fireplace. After filling it with hot water, my mother tossed me in, scrubbed off the farm dirt and then dried me. I became quite fond of these baths, especially during cold weather when I enjoyed the warmth of the open fire.

The toilet, or privy as we called it, was outdoors at the far end of an enclosed chicken run, some thirty yards from the farmhouse. Of all the unpleasant sensations a human can experience, surely none can compare with the soft squish of hot chicken droppings between one's toes on a summer's day. As a small barefoot boy, I experienced this unique sensation countless times on mad dashes to the privy.

That was the hazard of getting to, and leaving from, the privy but there were other perils within. It never happened on Grandpa's farm but it was fairly common practice for neighbouring pranksters, after lying in wait for some family member to arrive at the privy, to creep stealthily from his hiding place and topple the privy with the unfortunate occupant still inside.

Grandpa's privy was a two-seater, necessary because of his large family. It simplified things when anyone was faced with the reality of "If you have to go, you have to go".

Cleaning oneself afterwards was a delicate art. If you were a man and up to it, there was a basket of rough corn cobs (shelled ears of maize). Their length made it easy to grasp, but their coarse surface could make piles enjoyable by contrast. A better means was to use shredded newspapers. These, however, often were too thick. Best of all were the thin pages of last season's Sears and Roebuck catalogue. The Sears catalogues have become part of American folklore for bringing every imaginable article of everyday use to rural America, but chroniclers seldom mention the soothing after-glow these pages produced when used on one's backside. The Sears catalogues were thick – a single issue would easily last a family several months.

An apocryphal story tells of a farmer who, having heard about a new-fangled invention called "toilet paper", wrote to Sears and asked that a roll be shipped to him COD ("Collect on Delivery", a once familiar postal practice.) Sears wrote back saying if the farmer would order by catalogue number, his request would be promptly fulfilled. The irate farmer quickly fired back: "If I had your gol-darned catalogue, I wouldn't need your toilet paper."

The privy must have been the most frequented of the outbuildings, but there were other useful ones. The "barn" was actually a complex of sheds, a lean-to, stables and a hayloft. The latter was the favourite place for hens to lay their eggs. At first Grandma took me with her to collect the eggs, but after I got to know the favoured nests, I did the chore myself. The hens were clever, using only corners of the haylofts where they knew they were most secure. Not so, however, for Grandma's guinea fowl which notoriously found different places every day for depositing their eggs. I never understood why this should be, unless they were more feral by nature than their more popular poultry cousins. I think there must never have been a time when we found all the eggs laid daily by the guinea fowl.

The shed where the ears of corn (maize) were shucked and shelled always fascinated me. Removing the outside shucks by hand was often difficult for my small hands, but there was no problem turning the handle of the shelling machine. Once the flywheel was spinning, an ear of corn was dropped into the open slot and – "whoosh!" – it was shelled instantly. The grains fell into a waiting bag while the discarded cobs went into a basket later taken to the privy, or to the kitchen for starting fires in the stove.

I was much intrigued at how the steel teeth of the shelling machine magically removed every grain in seconds. Anxious to see how this was done, I turned the wheel gently and inserted my hand into the mesh of metal teeth. What happened next was seeing my hand chewed up and all my fingers badly lacerated. I ran screaming to the farmhouse where a quick inspection by Grandma revealed no broken bones. That was my first and last exploration into the mysteries of the moving parts. For certain I had not inherited my father's technical genes.

A large shed housed the heavy farm equipment. A smaller one boasted the farm's Delco-Remy "light plant" that provided electricity for the farm and its outbuildings. It was in these two sheds that my father spent most of his time. Two other buildings, one containing the syrup boiler and another an abandoned country store, became favourite haunts of mine.

Interspersed among these buildings were numerous trees, my favourites being the pecan, black walnut and the peach and the pear. The pecans were distinguished mainly by the thickness of their shells – hardshells and papershells. We also had "hog pecans". Always round and hard-shelled, their meat lacked the distinctive flavour of the other varieties. I wondered if hogs actually liked them.

Grandma Mays, in common with most housewives of her generation, did a huge amount of "canning" (preserving) food. Most of it went into the popular Mason jars with their unique two-piece pressure lids. Pears and peaches, whether as pickles or as preserves, were my favourites. Grandma's famous layer cakes were prepared from Madeira-like recipes and were interlaid with rich milk chocolate or caramel and then topped with pecan or walnut halves. I have never eaten a commercially produced cake whose flavour was equal to one of Grandma's.

My grandmother involved me at an early age in simple aspects of homemaking. My favourite was the weekly butter-making which I learned in time to do on my own. Milk from the family's Jersey cows, a breed producing a high butterfat content, was always kept in large, wide pans in the ice box. After a day or two, a thick coat of cream appeared. I learned to ladle this cream into a large glass churn, removing as little milk as possible in the process. Once the churn was filled, I clamped on the lid and started churning. It took only a few minutes for the rich cream to congeal into lumps of butter. With a few more turns of the handle, the churning became more and more difficult. Eventually a great blob of butter formed and further churning was impossible. At that point, Grandma took over, removed the butter, squeezed out any remaining milk and sprinkled it with salt. Once the desired degree of firmness was reached, she patted the butter into wooden moulds which produced blocks of butter with beautiful floral designs. They were then wrapped in greaseproof paper to be taken to the family grocer who accepted them in exchange for salt, sugar and other food items not produced on the farm.

Meanwhile, as my reward for churning, Grandma allowed me to consume the whole of the buttery milk left in the churn. This "grandoldbuttermilk", as a famous Georgia country editor (Louis Morris) always spelled it, is my culinary treat of all time. Chilled and drunk on a hot summer's day, there is nothing to equal the soothing milk with its tiny lumps of Jersey butter – granules that invariably got jammed between my tiny teeth, thereby giving a lingering, delicious aftertaste. In America today one may buy commercially produced buttermilk but it is a distant relation of the real thing.

Many years later my friend Louis Morris was asked to dedicate a newly built bridge across the Savannah River connecting Georgia and South Carolina. He proudly did so, christening it with a bottle of grandoldbuttermilk. Another reason Louis always took great pleasure in writing about grandoldbuttermilk was because it took up almost an entire line of type in his newspaper columns!

2
Pleasing the stomach

Other than churning butter, making ice cream was another chore I readily volunteered for. The reason was simple: the tasty reward that awaited me at the end.

Our ice cream churn was the standard type used all over America between the world wars. A stout wooden cask held a steel cylinder, over which a handle for churning was placed. The space between the cylinder and the cask was filled with broken ice and large grains of salt which hastened the melting of the ice. The cylinder, which had a lid fitted at the top, contained the ingredients: whole milk with cream, sometimes butter, sugar and, in season, fresh fruit. At first the churn did not turn easily, so tightly packed were the chunks of ice in the cavity between the lining of the cask and the steel drum. Sometimes I had to find the offending piece of stubborn ice and either punch or remove it, to allow the cylinder to rotate. Eventually the churning went smoothly until suddenly there was a resistance to the blades turning inside the cylinder. That meant the ice cream was ready. Although my small hands ached, I did not mind. My reward was near at hand.

I shouted for Grandma and she hurried over with a large, shallow pan. First we took off the handle, then the lid of the container. Then came the difficult part: removing the blades. It was important to Grandma not to remove too much ice cream in the process. But it was important to me that the blades had enough ice cream still attached to have made my churning worthwhile, for licking the blades was my reward.

Somehow Grandma always found the happy medium. With a knife she scraped away the large formations attached to the dasher blades, but was careful not to punch out the bits between the blades. The dasher was then laid carefully in the large pan and, aided by a teaspoon, I was transported to ice cream heaven. In this way, I could both start and end my Sunday meal with ice cream.

Another sweet treat which could appear at any meal, but most commonly at breakfast, was syrup and biscuits. While the grownups were feasting on ham and biscuits, we small fry had our own way of extracting the best from the famous southern biscuit.

Grandma vowed the best biscuits were made with buttermilk and we agreed. The southern biscuit is a “food vehicle” for something else: ham, sausage or simply syrup or molasses.

When I was small, my little finger was just the right size to punch a hole in the side of one of Grandma’s biscuits. This I did the moment the biscuits landed on the table, piping hot from the oven. Sometimes they were so hot that my finger got burned, but it didn’t matter. The trick was quickly to fill the hole, first with rich Jersey butter and, then after it had melted and soaked into the biscuit, with syrup. The timing was crucial to obtain that glorious, sublime taste: a mixture of cane syrup, country butter and hot biscuit in just the right proportions.

Syrup was consumed the year round, so it was important that the pantry was kept well stocked with this energy-giving food. Row upon row of gallon buckets were stacked there to satisfy our appetites. The pantry also held lard, coffee, spices, dried peas and beans, jars of pickles and preserves made by Grandma, as well as condiments and other essentials for feeding a large household. Together they gave the pantry that rich, distinct aroma reminiscent of country general stores.

Thanks to Grandma’s intervention, late one summer I was allowed to be present at the climax of the annual syrup-making. That was a great privilege, for the process had gone on for several days and now I could see the end to this complex logistical operation.

First, the sugar cane had to be cut in sufficient quantities each day to feed the cane mill. Then wagons and labour were organised to move the cane from the fields to the mill. The mill was powered by a pair of mules, which walked in circles for hours. One mule worked while the other rested and was fed. The juice was taken from the mill to the boiler where it was attended by a master-craftsman, the syrup-maker.

It seemed as if I had slept all night when I felt Grandma’s gentle tugging at my bedclothes. A moment later I was fully awake, eagerly anticipating the night’s adventure. Helping me into a warm coat to guard against the night chill, she led me from the house in pitch-darkness, except for the beam of her torch. Soon I could hear excited voices urging one action or another and then I saw men scurrying all round the syrup-making shed. A powerful light shone on the boiler so that the consistency of the syrup’s texture could be carefully monitored at all times.

Grandpa now spotted our approach and came to welcome us. He led me immediately to the great open-top boiler where I saw the golden syrup erupting in thousands of miniature volcanoes. He explained that the longer the boiling continued, the smaller the quantity of syrup. The trick, he said, was to get it just right. Some families wanted a lot of syrup and didn't mind it being somewhat "watery". Other people, and Grandpa and Grandma were among them, liked their syrup somewhere between thin and molasses consistency. Frequent sampling was essential for the desired quality to be achieved.

Throughout the course of the boiling two men skimmed a white foam from the surface and ladled it into a small keg. By now the keg was almost full. I was told that the contents of the keg, if kept for a while, would produce a powerful drink similar to rum. I asked for a taste but, at that stage, it was no different from ordinary syrup.

Much more palatable was the pure sugar cane juice. Almost since I could remember anything, I had used a pocket knife to cut sugar into "joints" and then strip them before chewing to extract the succulent juice. The lower down the stalk, the sweeter was the juice. By the time I had cut, stripped and chewed an entire cane, my jaw would be aching.

Now, from the mouth of the cane mill, came a steady stream of juice, flowing like a small stream down the spout into the waiting barrel. The trick was to dart to the mill between the rounds of the mule and fill my dipper with the pure juice. It didn't take long to realise that one could soon tire of good things. What was more, Grandma cautioned, too much juice could have a laxative effect.

I was fascinated by the mill. It was a simple affair: two metal cylinders mounted on four stout legs about a man's height. Above was a long arched trunk of a tree whose centre was attached firmly to the cog that turned the two cylinders. One end of the trunk was pulled by the mule, the other, the heavier end, served as a balance. Adjacent to the mill was a huge pile of sugar cane, freshly cut from the fields. The mill attendant constantly walked to this pile, picked up an armful of stalks and brought them to the mill.

There he fed the stalks into the jaws of the revolving cylinders, sometimes two or three at a time. The juice then flowed into the barrel until it was full. The squeezed canes fell to the ground on the far side of the mill and occasionally had to be removed when the pile grew too large. One or more barrels of juice were needed for each new batch of syrup, the process repeated until all of the juice had been used.

By now the juice that had been boiling when I arrived had turned into syrup and there was a hectic rush to pour it into the tin buckets before it thickened further. I moved as near to the huge boiler as I dared, without getting in anyone's way. Already the first bucket was being poured. I knew it was good syrup, for the aroma from the boiler was exactly like that of the newly-made syrup placed on the dining room table. Bucket after shining bucket was hastily filled, wiped clean and stacked on the side. At last the boiler was empty and everyone relaxed. Then someone poured several pails of water into the boiler so the cleaning process would not be too difficult.

The night's work was now almost over. The two mules were returned to the barn for feeding and resting. The men who had helped, all black and living in houses on Grandpa's farm, gathered round to take their allotted buckets of syrup to their families. Grandpa thanked them all, then they all said goodnight and disappeared into the darkness. Grandma and Grandpa took several buckets each, turned off the lights and we slowly made our way back to the farmhouse.

The magic of the night had been overwhelming and I slept soundly until late the next morning. No doubt I had sweet dreams.

3
The house where I was born

I remember, I remember,
The house where I was born,
The little window where the sun
Came peeping in at morn.

I remember, I remember,
Where I used to swing,
And thought the air must rush as fresh
To swallows on the wing.

These lines from Thomas Hood's "I Remember, I Remember" remind me of my grandparents' home – and especially the majestic sycamore tree which stood near its front entrance.

It was easily the most loved object (and "love" was the operative word) at the farm. It held two attractions for the young generation. One was the swing that hung from its lowest limb. Here my numerous cousins and I rushed when we had just arrived for our annual school vacations. Here "small fry" were pushed to dangerously high arcs by their older cousins, some enjoying the thrill and others scared out of their wits.

The second pleasure the sycamore gave was not physical but spiritual. Many pairs of initials had been carved into the soft bark of the tree by my father and his brothers and sisters as each, in turn, found their mates. It was thrilling to find the pairing made by Uncle Robert or Uncle George, or those in which the initials of Aunt Edna or Aunt Florence appeared.

I did not then know the meaning of romantic love, but the sight of my parents' initials on that old tree signified a kind of magic that told me my parents' love was deep and would last forever. Perhaps I also saw in those initials my future happiness firmly anchored within the family circle.

Even as a small boy, I could not escape the strong impression that the farm had once been a place ringing with joy and laughter as its young people grew up, went courting and got married. A player-piano, the principal feature of the living room, was the main testament to this bygone era. It had been so much the centre of amusement that most of its music-rolls were badly mauled and unfit for playing. Nonetheless enough usable ones remained to allow me to marvel how the old piano could still ring out with poignant romantic tunes of long ago. How the girls – and maybe the boys too – must have gloried in their "playing skills" to impress their respective beaux and belles.

How all my uncles and aunts managed to ring their respective sweethearts I can only imagine, for even in my time the telephone was constantly busy. Almost all of Grandpa's calls were related to his duties as County Commissioner.

He was not, however, always able to use the phone when he needed to. In those days only "party line" telephones were available in rural Georgia. This usually meant three (but sometimes more) farmers shared the same number, so they were obliged to listen carefully for 'their ring' – once, twice or three times.

Not all Grandpas' neighbours were as busy as he but there was a constant problem of finding the phone free to use. The problem lay with the wives of the other farmers on Grandpa's party line. They called each other, often several times a day, to exchange news and gossip. When Grandpa interrupted to ask them to end their conversations, they insisted they had as much right as he to use the line.

It was common practice for someone in each household on a party line to listen in when other families had incoming calls. Sometimes you could even hear the breathing or the wheezing of the eavesdropper. Grandpa, who could recognise all his neighbours' voices, often had to interrupt a conversation by saying something like: "Mabel, I know it's you. Would you mind letting me make a quick call? I'll take only a few minutes; then you can come back on the line." But Mabel could be stubborn and insist on knowing why Grandpa had to call just then. So he had to explain that a scraper was needed urgently for a country road that had become impassable because of overnight rain. Only when she heard this would Mabel relent.

The heart of my grandparents' home was their bedroom. For one thing it boasted the only fireplace in the house. Above the fireplace was a wide mantel where a large clock stood. Propped up in front of the clock were slips of paper – notices of meetings, invitations to functions and anything else that told Grandpa he had to be some place at a certain time.

When the clock struck the hours, the sound echoed throughout the downstairs rooms. As I lay on my bed in the adjacent room, the sound of those soft, soothing notes told me it was the end of another day and that all was right with the world.

4
Doodle bugs and “rabbit tobacco”

County government in most of the rural South during my childhood was administered by a board of commissioners. The chairman of our county's board when I took my school vacations on the family farm was my Grandpa Mays. I quickly realised he was a Very Important Person in our county.

I never knew the range of Grandpa's responsibilities, but I would have been blind not to know he had a lot to do with the county road system. Rural roads were the life blood of farmers, for without them there was no way of getting cotton to gins and other farm produce to markets. People were constantly visiting or telephoning Grandpa to demand that roads in their respective districts be improved.

Most rural roads in middle Georgia were not paved then and, being pure clay, became as slippery as ice with the slightest rainfall. Consequently, a small army of men operated road scrapers, heavy duty trucks and other maintenance equipment. Even so, the road repairers found it difficult to keep up with the dire driving conditions of a prolonged rainy season.

My Uncle George, a road scraper for the county at that time, sometimes arranged his work to turn up at the farmhouse at mealtime. People who didn't know any better may have accused Grandpa of nepotism in putting his son George on the county payroll. But George was both industrious and efficient and left potential critics no grounds for complaint.

I remember being in the front yard one day when he arrived on his scraper just before lunch time. Parking the scraper in front of the house, he took off his hat and started picking blackberries for his dessert. After a few minutes the hat was full. Then he strode to the dining room, just as the mid-day meal was being served, quickly ate, and then proceeded to enjoy his bowl of blackberries, sugar and cream. Without a word, he then went on his way again, scraping the roads in our district. Later, Uncle George made his career as agent for John D. Rockefeller's Standard Oil Company in our county seat, Millen.

Grandpa Mays, despite his strict standards, could be kind and compassionate. Frequently on my arrival at the farm to spend summer vacations, he would present me with his latest “toy”. These were not children's toys in the usual sense, but sturdy, scale models of road scrapers and earth movers presented to Grandpa by salesmen who hoped to persuade him to buy the real thing. These working models did everything demanded of their full-sized counterparts; the front wheels turned and the scraping blades could be lowered, raised or tilted. In short, a small boy could instantly create his own “road network” in the vast expanse of the farmyard or in the playing area beneath the farmhouse.

The area beneath the house, originally designed to keep away snakes and floods, provided me and the other grandchildren with a marvellous all-weather playground. Our favourite pastime was enticing to the surface the doodlebugs, the popular name for the larvae of the ant lion which live about an inch deep in the sand. It was easy to find the doodlebug "house", for he marked his home by creating a small circular pit just above it. Woe to the ant, fly, moth or other insect who stumbled into the pit. Instantly the doodlebug pierced the surface and grabbed the intruder.

To make the doodlebug emerge from his conical pit, we children thought it was necessary to chant "Doodlebug, doodlebug, where are you?" while gently stirring the depression with a twig or one finger. What we didn't know was that the little ditty was unnecessary. Unfailingly, the doodlebug emerged, only to be disappointed when he found human trespassers. We would then leave him to recreate his little crater trap and burrow once more out of sight.

It was also in this play area that one of my cousins and I learned a lifelong lesson about good health, although we did not realise it at the time. In some parts of the rural South there was a plant which we children called "rabbit tobacco". Its leaves were much like those of real tobacco. My friends, I and my peers naively believed it to be the real thing. All we had to do, we thought, was to gather some leaves, make crude cigarettes and then smoke like the grown-ups.

One summer day one of my male cousins and I decided to try it out. We gathered a few leaves, tore some pages from the Sears catalogue in the privy, and took a box of matches from the kitchen and we were ready for business. Stealthily we crept beneath the house and set about rolling our cigarettes. Then came the moment we had been waiting for: we would know the thrill of smoking! Solemnly we struck the matches and watched the paper and the tobacco leaves catch fire.

Then we took our first draws. As we knew nothing about the effects of inhaling, within a few minutes our heads seemed to start spinning. Was this, we wondered, what smoking was about? We carried on for another few minutes hoping the dizziness would go away. Instead it got worse. At that point we panicked, threw down our cigarettes and rushed to get away. In our befuddled condition our heads banged repeatedly against the beams supporting the floorboards of the house. Groggy and bleeding, we eventually emerged into the light of day.

We stared in amazement at each other's blood-stained faces. Then we surreptitiously crept to the washbasins and cleaned ourselves up. Relieved that we had not been spotted, we then and there decided smoking was not for us. To this day smoking has not interested me.

With so many exciting places to play, trees to climb and woods to explore, it was inevitable that Grandpa and Grandma Mays should be constantly ministering to our many cuts, bruises, burns and other assorted injuries. I never remember a doctor being called, for there seemed to be a home remedy for almost everything. I recall once developing a severe sore throat one night. Grandma immediately put me to bed, saying she had just the thing to make me fit by morning. She disappeared, but returned in a moment with a tablespoon of sugar saturated with kerosene oil. "Lick it slowly", she ordered. I balked at the thought of swallowing kerosene, which I supposed suitable only for lamps and heaters. "Go ahead", she said, "lick it!" I did, slowly as she had asked, and found the mixture both soothing to my throat and pleasing to the palate. Grandma then tucked me in and, with the pain in the throat now eased, I was asleep in a flash. Next morning, just as Grandma had said, there was no trace of the soreness.

5
Growing cotton and dodging lightning

Grandpa and Grandma knew they had produced 12 children but I doubt if they ever kept count of their grandchildren.

Most of my first cousins were from nearby Georgia towns, but some lived in South Carolina, Tennessee and Kentucky. Almost all shared my love for the "old home place" and we eagerly looked forward to our annual visits. As competition for the available number of weeks was great, our grandparents were obliged to develop a roster, usually with two cousins coming at the same time. That was not always easy, for personalities differed and inevitable clashes occurred.

My brother Floyd and I never clashed, but our imaginations and antics must have left our grandparents feeling they were constantly on the brink of disaster. I was never able to figure whether it was Floyd or I who brought on the wrath of Grandpa, but I do know it took only a minute after our arrival at the farm for things to go wrong.

Our first such misadventure happened late one summer when the cotton was being picked. Grandpa stored the cotton in his disused country general store until there was enough to justify a trip to the gin. The old store was spacious and convenient to the nearby fields of cotton.

Floyd and I, in search of excitement, came upon the store with its unlocked door and saw that it was packed to the ceiling with inviting, soft cotton. We hesitated briefly, for we thought we vaguely remembered that Grandpa had said we should never trample on the stored cotton. But the fluffy white mountain was more than twice our height and seemed to be begging us to plunge its depths. Repeatedly, Floyd and I took running starts and dived headlong, completely disappearing from view. The sensation of being able to run at full speed and land unhurt in the downy pile was irresistible. Again and again we repeated the antic, throwing caution to the wind and shouting with glee.

Then, to our horror, we heard steps at the door just as we buried ourselves in the cotton after one particularly glorious plunge.

"I know you are in there!" came Grandpa's booming voice.

Without moving the rest of our bodies, Floyd and I tilted our heads slowly until we could glimpse, through the cotton, Grandpa standing in the doorway. He stood defiantly, but we did not make a sound. Perhaps, we dared to hope, he would conclude we weren't there after all and go away.

That pipe-dream lasted only seconds, for the next thing we knew Grandpa marched to the corner of the storeroom and picked up one of the over-sized pitchforks used for shovelling the cotton. He now addressed the cotton pile.

"I'll count to 10," he shouted, "and if you aren't out by then, I'm coming after you with this pitchfork!"

Almost at once he shouted "One!"

Floyd and I had no need to confer. We hastily dragged ourselves from the cotton, brushing off bits that had become caught in our hair and on our clothes. As we faced Grandpa, he delivered a stern lecture on the sorry plight of cotton farmers. He reminded us, to our chagrin, of his earlier warning and asked how we expected him to provide us with bread and meat if we caused him to receive less money for his cotton.

We were shattered and, feeling like villains, burst into tears. Needless to say, we were never to invade Grandpa's cotton store again.

Picking cotton was one farm chore always "available" to me in season, but it was one I neither relished nor performed well. Some of the black farm workers picked several hundred pounds of cotton in a day, enough for an entire bale.

At first, the picking seemed easy, but it wasn't long before I realised I had hardly covered the bottom of my huge bag. The intense heat, perspiration and insects did not help, but I suppose the most demoralising aspect was the speed with which the pickers in the adjacent rows filled their bags, emptied them onto ground sheeting, and returned to their picking.

On such downcast occasions Grandma would suddenly emerge from the kitchen, having spotted my lack of progress through the window, and in a matter of minutes would pick several aprons full and dump them into my bag.

Grandpa Mays, like most other farmers in the South at that time, was a one-crop man, and that crop was cotton. Although his farm was small (about 200 acres) by old plantation standards and only about half a dozen black families lived on the place, at the height of his prosperity he acquired a cotton gin – the mill that separated the seed from the cotton.

He was regarded as being one of the most efficient farmers in the county. One year the local newspaper, *The Millen News*, wrote: "Mr. E.O. Mays takes the front rank among the best farmers of our section, and makes full proof of his progressive views by curtailing his crops, cutting down his expenses and running the farm on a strictly cash basis."

In good years he made a reasonable profit but after the boll weevil appeared, he and many other farmers experienced disaster. Even in my boyhood his cotton gin had become unprofitable. When the Great Depression came and forced the closure of many local banks, untold numbers of Southern farmers became bankrupt overnight.

During the peak of the cotton-picking season, Grandpa thought it more efficient to offer the workers a hot meal at the farm house. This meal was eaten just outside the kitchen door on a wooden patio. The signal to leave off work was the tolling of the farm bell, mounted on a post on the patio. It rang about 10 minutes before the meals were brought out, so the food would still be hot when they sat down.

There was an understanding among our neighbours that the farm bell should ring only at midday for meals. At any other time, the bell signified either a fire or a dire emergency. This unwritten code, impeccably respected, enabled many farm buildings to be saved from destruction by fire, for whenever a neighbour's bell was heard, everyone downed tools and rushed to the scene to help.

I do not remember a fire at my grandparents' farm, but it was always uppermost in the minds of all farmers as an ever-present peril. Rural fire-fighting services did not exist in our part of the world then and a raging fire, if unchecked in the first few minutes, usually meant the loss of a wooden farmhouse or barn.

Cigarettes were not then a danger, but fire from bolts of lightning were much feared – especially in the summer and autumn. Some farmers in the South had their kitchens built as separate annexes, connected to the main houses by ramps. The theory was that a fire was most likely to originate in the kitchen and, if it did so, the annex would be sacrificed while all efforts would be concentrated on watering down the main house. All too often, the wooden ramp joining the two units caught fire as well, leading to the destruction of the farmhouse.

My grandparents, in common with more of their neighbours, had lightning rods erected on the high points of the farmhouse roof. The rods were grounded by cables running down the sides of the house into the ground. The travelling lightning rod salesman was a well known figure on farms before and after the First World War. He always had a great store of jokes but was also the subject of stories told by others. In these accounts the farmer's pretty daughter invariably was the object of his attention. When romance threatened the salesman was quickly seen off the premises by the irate father.

I had vivid proof of the effectiveness of lightning rods one night when visiting my grandparents. Asleep in my bed, I was awakened by an almighty crash and a simultaneous flash of lightning that made my bedroom brighter than it had ever been on a summer's day. Almost at the same time there was a great splitting sound in the direction of the towering oak in the front yard. An acrid smell akin to that of an electrical fire was everywhere.

Then followed other crashes, not quite as loud and near as the first; then torrential rain. Grandma sat on my bed comforting me, saying the worst was over. Next morning I saw that the dear old oak tree, Grandpa's pride, was no more. There it stood, forlorn, rent from top to bottom. What had been a century-old living creature was now split, denuded and dead.

6
Grandpa is almost zapped

Our most infamous encounter with Grandpa arose by sheer accident. The upper floor of the farmhouse consisted of two large rooms. One had been finished years ago, lived in by one or another of our grandparents' children. The second, on the left of the stairs, was more exciting. It had no inside walls – and there was no ceiling – only the bottom side of the roof. There were no cupboards, no refinements – only the bare floor and a double bed with mattresses.

Floyd and I had long wanted to sleep in this room. Its austerity and the window overlooking the great pecan tree and the fields beyond made it by far the most desirable sleeping place in the house. We debated whether we should ask Grandma for permission to sleep in the upstairs room. We knew it was no good asking Grandpa first; he would refuse us, just on principle.

Eventually we mustered enough courage to ask Grandma. We found her in the kitchen and put the crucial question. The moment we saw the twinkle in her eye we knew we had carried the day. Why was it, we wondered, that Grandma always seemed to be young at heart? Come to think of it, had Grandpa ever been a boy?

"You may sleep in the room," Grandma said softly, "provided you go to bed early and don't make a lot of noise. You know how tired your Grandpa is after a day of hard work on the farm."

Good old Grandma. She then took us to the linen cupboard and gave us sheets, pillowcases and a couple of light blankets.

"Better open the window," she said, "The room hasn't been aired for ages."

We dashed upstairs, overcome with joy. We could hardly believe our good luck. But what if Grandpa found out and overruled Grandma? No, we concluded, Grandma would surely persuade him.

Quickly Floyd opened the window and a welcome gush of fresh air swept into the room. Then together we put the bed clothing on the bed. We could not resist trying out our new luxury. Stretched out, with our hands behind our heads, we gazed at the unfinished ceiling, then around the simple, unfurnished room. Why, we had the whole of the upstairs to ourselves – it was sheer paradise!

At supper Floyd and I eyed Grandpa uneasily. Had Grandma told him of our plan, we wondered. We gulped down our food, almost without realising what we were eating. During all this time Grandma sat quietly. Then, just as we were finishing the meal, she turned toward Grandpa and said:

"The boys are sleeping upstairs tonight in…"

"Upstairs? *Upstairs*?" Grandpa interrupted. "What's wrong with the room they've been sleeping in?"

Grandma put her hand gently on Grandpa's arm and smiled. "They thought it would be fun, a kind of adventure – they'll be in that unfinished room on the left. It'll be something like camping. They'll have an exciting time up there on their own."

Grandpa muttered something unintelligible and gave Floyd and me a sharp look, as if to say we had pulled one over on him. But when he voiced no objection Floyd and I exchanged looks of relief and quickly excused ourselves from the table.

We went to our old room and gathered up our pyjamas and suitcases, for we assumed we could remain in our new-found "castle" for the rest of our summer vacation. We gave no thought of baths; there was far more important business at hand. In minutes we stripped, changed into pyjamas and leapt into bed.

The open window was enticing and every few minutes we would get up and admire the peaceful view outside. By now the chickens had gone to their roosts and the birds had fallen silent. Then the sounds of the Georgia countryside on a summer's evening began to set in. There were the ubiquitous crickets with their constant chirping. Occasionally a mosquito would come in through the open window with its high-pitched singing. Neither of these disturbed us.

But as night came on, we began to have doubts about sleeping alone in a strange part of the house. Almost as far back as we could remember we had slept downstairs in the bedroom adjacent to Grandpa's and Grandma's room. It had always been comforting to hear their voices discussing the achievements of the day and what needed to be done on the morrow. Then Grandma would come in to make sure we were well tucked in and to say goodnight. After that we were aware only of the ticking of the old clock on the mantelpiece in our grandparents' bedroom. The ticking was just audible, but it somehow symbolised security and continuity of life – two qualities Floyd and I now began to doubt we had in the upstairs room.

Without our grandparents' reassuring voices and the familiar old clock, we were left to the mercy of the nocturnal noises that increasingly wafted in through the open window. Before long an owl arrived in the pecan tree outside the window and let fly a series of chilling hoots. There are few things so blood-curdling, so calculated to strike fear into the hearts of small boys as the mournful hooting of an owl on a dark night.

Floyd and I sat up, all thought of sleep gone. Our new sleeping quarters may have been attractive enough during the daytime, but now they seemed distinctly unsafe. Visions of ghosts and other threatening creatures took over our imaginations. We suddenly realised there was nothing to bar an intruder from getting into the house and making straight for our room. But what could we do?

At length I had an idea.

"Floyd," I said, "why don't we rig up a burglar alarm? Then we can go off to sleep and if anyone tries to get into our room, we'll be awakened by the alarm."

Floyd readily agreed, but wondered what we could use for a burglar alarm without looking for materials downstairs and disturbing Grandpa. We turned on the light and looked round the almost bare room.

We crept to the other bedroom across the hallway. It contained only another ancient double bed, with springs but no mattress. Then our eyes lit on the bed slats supporting the springs.

"I've got it!" I whispered to Floyd. "We can take a couple of those slats, connect them with string and if anyone comes up the stairs in the dark, he'll walk straight into our trap and the slats fall with a great bang."

Together we lifted the bedsprings and pulled out two slats. We took them to the head of the stairs and tried to stand them on end. We saw that the lights were still on downstairs and so moved gingerly.

To our dismay, the two slats would not remain upright. Either they had been sawn unevenly or the floor itself was not even. We tried reversing the ends, but with the same result. Eventually we just managed to balance them and joined them with a piece of string.

"This string is just long enough to go round the two slats and reach the knob of the door of our bedroom," Floyd said.

Just then Grandpa appeared at the foot of the stairs. Fortunately he was not looking our way but was talking to Aunt Gertrude and Uncle Joe Miller whose room was at the bottom of the stairs.

To our dismay, we now found the slats wouldn't stay upright. The only solution was to tilt them slightly towards the stairs and then tie the string firmly to the door knob. At last we achieved the perfect balance. We stood back and admired our handiwork. Yes, it was impossible for anyone coming up the stairs to miss the slats. We would surely sleep soundly now. Rubbing our hands with glee, we tip-toed towards our room lest we attract Grandpa's attention.

Floyd grabbed the doorknob and yanked open the door.

"The string!" whispered Floyd, in a panic. "I forgot it was attached to the doorknob!"

Too late, we realised we were setting off our burglar alarm! At first there was a kind of swish and a scraping noise, as the two slats skidded to the floor. First one slat, then the other teetered at the top of the staircase. The first one then became overbalanced and started down the stairs.

Grandpa had heard the fall of the slats on the floor, but by the time he looked up the stairs the first slat was already hurtling down and gaining speed. He may have been of Irish descent and no doubt had danced many a jig in his youth. But he hardly could have been expected to dance a jig that evening. Although not given to swearing, when he saw the speeding slat zooming straight at him, he shouted "Good God Almighty!" and gave a mighty leap. His timing was perfect, for the slat passed beneath him and hit the wall with a resounding "Zap!" By now the second slat was also streaking down the stairs. Grandpa had barely landed on his feet when he spotted the second missile arriving. Unable to get completely airborne, he only managed to lift his left leg as the slat shot beneath and slammed into the wall with another mighty whack.

Grandpa didn't have to tell us he could easily have suffered broken ankles. While we knew he was lucky to have escaped, Floyd and I couldn't help thinking how effective our alarm would have been against a real burglar. We tried, with straight faces, to explain this to Grandpa but he would not listen. Minutes later we were marched off to our original bedroom where, no doubt, he hoped he would be safe from our machinations.

Floyd and I relaxed beneath the bed covers, listening once more to the soothing sound of the old clock above the fireplace in the next room. Our grandparents were talking as usual. Occasionally we heard Grandpa raise his voice in a heated reference to us.

The excitement of the evening was too much for us. As we yawned sleepily, Floyd turned to me and said:

"Gosh, but did we ever make Grandpa jump!"

In fairness to Grandpa, he seemed an ogre only when we grandchildren were bent on mischief-making – which was often. Given the trouble we caused him, it was a wonder he could be kind to us on other occasions.

He once took me to his little cabinet in the hallway and extracted a perfect arrowhead found on the farm when he was a young man. It belonged, he said, to some member of the Creek Indian tribe that originally inhabited a large area of Georgia. Eventually they were forcibly removed to Oklahoma by the white man. Enduring great hardship along the way, their trek became etched in American history as "The Trail of Tears."

Grandpa's arrowhead was a vivid reminder of a bygone era when native Americans had lived peacefully in the very surroundings in which Floyd and I now cavorted.

7
The magic of RFD (Rural Free Delivery)

During my childhood the lack of good roads in rural Georgia was not only a hardship but travelling on them in wet weather was downright terrifying. Virtually all roads had long since lost their top soil. They now consisted of red clay – so red that the creeks and rivers ran red for weeks after a good rain.

The terror in trying to drive over slippery clay roads was as real for grown-ups as for young people. Imagine the relief in finally reaching the peak of a difficult hill, driving carefully in the two deep ruts developed by previous cars. You pray there will be no car coming up the other side of the hill so you can have a safe run down it. Then, on reaching the crest, you see a driver – like yourself – speeding and struggling to reach the top of the hill before getting mired. There is only one set of ruts and both are deep. Who is going to yield, and even if one or the other does, can it be done before colliding head-on? And once a car leaves the ruts in such a situation, the driver knows there is only a 50-50 chance of staying on the road.

The magic of RFD (Rural Free Delivery)

Once I was riding in the back seat of my grandparents' car when Grandpa lost control because one of the ruts was not deep enough to hold the tyres. The car swung across the road and pitched into a deep ditch. Like most others in the 1920's, it was built of heavy gauge metal and suffered no damage, but Grandpa was cut on the face and Grandma and I were badly shaken up. Yet, so terrifying was the ordeal of the driving before the crash, the accident itself came almost as a relief.

Happily, despite our isolation and the perilous roads, there was one reliable link with the Great Outside World. That was the institution – there's no other word for it – of Rural Free Delivery. "RFD", as it was lovingly called, was the first of three blessings to come to American farmers; the other two were paved roads and rural electrification.

The RFD system began in 1896 with the aim of serving virtually all the nation's farms with daily postal service. In the midwest, where farm population was dense, there was a rural postal route for about every 1200 people; in the South and West, however, it took nearly twice that population to establish a rural route.

In a typical rural county, each road leading out of the county town was given a number – Route 1, Route 4 etc. The US Post Office itself did not operate the route, but let out tenders for each route when there were vacancies. The person who won the contract was called a "mail carrier" and some remained in the job for many years and became folk heroes of a sort.

Our mail carrier was Claud Sullivan and he was a great friend of children. The famous slogan of the US Postal Service about its determination to get mail delivered despite sleet or snow should have included a reference to the red clay hills of Georgia, for this peril was a very real one – even for Claud Sullivan. He was delayed on many occasions, but if he ever missed a day's delivery I never heard of it.

Long before he was due, I peeled my eyes for the sight of his familiar car. When at last I saw it approaching, I sprinted to the metal mail box on the side of the road in front of the farmhouse. Some people had no letters to post and unless the little metal "flags" on their mail boxes were turned up, the mail carrier passed them by. The upraised flag meant that the carrier should stop, either to pick up outgoing mail or to sell stamps or a money order.

Claud Sullivan always arrived smiling, asked how I was, how Grandpa and Grandma were, and if anything exciting had happened since his previous delivery. All the while he was extracting letters, magazines, newspapers and circulars from the great leather strap which held the mail. At last he would hand me a hefty pile. Seldom was there anything for me. But I was not to be disappointed, for he would then reach into the glove compartment and pull out a pack of Juicy Fruit chewing gum and give me a stick. Then this genial man would wave good-bye and continue on his way to the other farms.

For the grown-ups in the farmhouse – my grandparents and my Uncle Joe Miller (still working on the farm) and his wife, Gertrude – Rural Free Delivery meant both convenience and wonder. It brought us the county newspaper every Friday which, by general consent, was the most important day of the week. On that day we learned all the news in the county, as well as who was ill, away on vacation, or whatever, in the paper's "Personals" column.

Grandpa, as Chairman of the County Commissioners, received many glossy circulars picturing gigantic earth-moving equipment; these he seldom looked at, but always found me an enthusiastic recipient. There were several farm journals and bulletins, one of which carried free advertisements for every conceivable product of a farm. For example, someone in the adjacent county had duck eggs for sale, while another farmer in north Georgia offered "barefoot root", reputedly a cure for rheumatism when soaked in whiskey.

When we wanted to order something by mail, the carrier sold us a money order. His job, thus, was not merely to deliver mail, but to provide virtually all the services available at the county seat post office.

Interest in what Claud Sullivan might bring to the farmhouse peaked twice a year when the Spring and Summer, or the Fall and Winter catalogues of Sears, Roebuck and Company arrived. This interest was universal: I was just as keen to see it as my grandparents or Uncle Joe Miller and Aunt Gertrude. Being small fry I was usually last in the pecking order, for Grandpa may have been waiting to see the latest range of horse- drawn Florence wagons, while Aunt Gertrude might be in need of a new dress.

Much is made of today's vices – smoking drinking, drug addiction – but we had a vice in the 1920s too. It would have been called Temptation, had there been a name for it, and it would have been inspired by those wonderful Sears Roebuck catalogues. Few who spent hours poring over those thousands of items in the mail order emporium could put down the catalogue without ordering something. The Sears catalogues were also great educators, for they brought knowledge about new inventions and conveniences to those of us otherwise cut off from population centres. They also helped to standardise our agricultural language, for farmers in north and south Georgia (or other parts of the South) sometimes had different names for the same implement.

My primary interest in the latest Sears catalogue lay in the newest title in The Rover Boys series of books written by one "Arthur M. Winfield". My best friend, George Franklin, and I were thoroughly hooked on the adventures of Dick, Tom and Sam Rover, and we could be sure there would be new titles, for Winfield (his pen name) had been churning them out in great numbers since 1899. In later life I was disillusioned to learn he had contracted other writers to produce some of the Rover Boys books on the condition that they bore his (Winfield's) name. His real name (Edward Stratemeyer, as I discovered) wasn't nearly as impressive as his pen name.

George and I could not afford to buy the several new volumes of The Rover Boys published annually but we developed a plan whereby we could be sure to read every new issue. As we received gifts from our parents on our birthdays and at Christmas, we stipulated to them precisely which titles we wanted. By lending our books to each other, we managed to read every new title published. From this childish scheme we both developed a lifelong interest in reading.

8
Dinosaurs!

After Floyd and I invented our burglar alarm – one that came close to crippling Grandpa - we were separated and new vacation partners assigned us. I was paired with my favourite cousin, Virginia. We saw eye-to-eye in all things. That she was a girl never occurred to me, for she could run as fast and climb any tree that I could. We never had a disagreement and if we found little to amuse us at the farmhouse, we simply went further afield.

One summer day Virginia and I decided to go exploring. We walked as long as it took to find a place where we had never before ventured. It didn't matter, we said, if we got lost, for that, too, would be exciting.

Through field after field we plodded in the hot sun. Eventually we left the cultivated fields and entered a scrub area filled with an assortment of bushes and stunted trees. This gave way to a beautiful pine forest, not planted in formal rows but one that had developed naturally over the years. Whether we were still on Grandpa's land we had no idea.

As we marvelled at the thick coat of pine needles on the forest floor, we thought we were sharing some of the excitement of those intrepid explorers of long ago. We wandered ecstatically through this sylvan paradise, the only sound being that of the gentle breeze among the pines and the occasional "Bob White" call of the quail. Then suddenly we stumbled into a large depression, almost like a crater. We stood amazed at the sight before us: a huge quantity of monstrous bones, white with age, protruding everywhere above the blanket of brown pine needles. Virginia and I could not believe our good luck, for we instantly knew what they were.

"Dinosaurs!" we exclaimed at the same time.

We fell to our feet to examine the find. Yes, the bones had been blanched white with age. They had to be several million years old, at least. How long ago was it, we wondered, when dinosaurs roamed America?

Brushing aside the pine needles, we made out what appeared to be giant ribs, some still joined together. Others had fallen off, no doubt from the ravages of time.

"Look what I've found!" suddenly exclaimed Virginia from another part of the crater. I rushed over. There, partly embedded in the soil was – yes, there was no doubt – a dinosaur skull! We tugged gently, for we did not want to damage our precious discovery.

With the aid of a sharp stick found nearby, we managed to dig away enough soil to loosen the skull. When it was free of obstructions, we together lifted it gently out of the pit onto level ground.

We admired our handiwork. Surely there was no finer dinosaur skull anywhere. Virginia, oddly, did not share my enthusiasm. Instead, she looked puzzled.

"What's wrong?" I asked.

"Aren't dinosaurs huge, huge monsters?" she asked.

I pondered the impact of her question.

"Yes," I said, recalling the photographs I had seen of reconstructed dinosaurs in museums. "But there must be dinosaurs of all sizes – large and small, grown ups and babies, just as there are with humans."

Virginia thought that made sense, and her excitement returned.

"Then what we have here is the skull of a baby dinosaur," she said confidently.

We now turned our thoughts to how we could get the skull back to the farmhouse without damaging it. After all, what museum would want a bashed dinosaur skull.

It was too large for one of us to carry, for we were miles from the farmhouse and the undergrowth was almost impenetrable in places. We set about examining the skull more closely and discovered that a pole would just pass through the two eye sockets, allowing us to carry it suspended.

After discarding several rotten poles, we eventually fashioned one from a newly fallen branch which was sound enough to support the skull's weight.

We started off spiritedly, but our walking caused the skull to bounce up and down and we feared we would either break the pole or, worse still, fracture the eye sockets of the skull itself. So we slowed our pace and managed to wriggle through the endless blackberry bushes and shrubs that barred our way.

Our conversation now turned to Grandpa and what his reaction would be. We knew beyond doubt he would be pleased when he heard that dinosaur remains had been found on *his* land. Why, he would become the most famous farmer in all Georgia, maybe the whole of the United States. Indeed, once the news of our discovery got out, the farm probably would be besieged by photographers and reporters, and perhaps even a team from the *National Geographic*!

Such happy thoughts eased the hardship of the long tramp back through the woods and fields. Thorn scratches, insect bites, the blazing sun – none of these dampened our spirits. On and on we plunged, by now soaked with perspiration – and exhilaration.

Our vision of glory for ourselves and Grandpa was rudely interrupted by a noise that sent chills down our spines. We thought it was a rattlesnake, just to our right. Freezing in our tracks, we peered into the thick undergrowth but could see nothing. We imagined the snake was there, very close – perhaps even close enough to strike.

Without speaking, Virginia and I remained motionless for what seemed ages. Was it our imagination, or had there been a rattler there? Slowly our confidence returned and we stepped forward gingerly, looking right and left. No sight or sound anywhere. Vastly relieved, we resumed our trek, increasing our pace but looking carefully at every step. At last the familiar farmhouse hove into view. As we got nearer, I saw Grandpa in the farmyard cleaning tools.

"What a surprise he'll be in for!" whispered Virginia to me, with a twinkle in her eye.

"Look what we've got!" she shouted, as we approached.

"A dinosaur skull!" I added, majestically.

Grandpa had never told us he was an expert on dinosaurs, but he must have been, for his reaction shocked us.

"What have you brought that old horse head here for?" he shouted. "Just take it back to the burying ground as fast as you can!"

Exhausted and thirsty, we dared not ask for a moment's respite. Wearily we set out to retrace the several miles to the animal burying ground, a place – Grandma later told us – that had been used to dispose of dead animals for as long as she could remember. Virginia and I said nothing for a long time, for the disappointment and humiliation rested heavily on our youthful hearts.

At length Virginia turned towards me with a wonderful smile.

"I guess," she said, "we aren't meant to be famous yet."

9
The joy – and sadness – of family reunions

Even though most of my childhood memories are associated with my Grandpa Mays' farm, there were also visits to my mother's maternal home, the old "Lovett house" in adjacent Screven County. The two storey building of indeterminate age, but probably dating back to the 1800s, had a kitchen annex connected to the main house by a narrow, covered ramp of the type commonly incorporated into homes of this period.

The Lovett house, although originally built of sturdy wood, creaked mightily during high winds and I feared its collapse at any moment. It had no heating (except for fireplaces) or plumbing. My father recalled – while staying overnight in the dead of winter during his courtship of my mother – having to open his bedroom window and break icicles off the eaves to obtain water for shaving.

Family ties were strong during my youth and the Lovetts often staged family events during good weather months. One of my earliest memories is of a family "fish fry" at nearby Jacksonboro Bridge. Here some 20 or 30 family members assembled one fine Saturday afternoon, the men to catch fish and the women to do the frying. Trees lined the bank of the creek which, although only a few feet deep, seemed to me a great river. The children had the best of all worlds, being obliged neither to fish (though some of us would have liked to) nor help with the cooking. Instead we waded and swam to our hearts' content. It was here that I learned to float on my back.

Meanwhile the men soon landed their first fish, mainly perch or catfish – the two commonly found species in many small streams of the American South. Within minutes they were scraped of their scales, gutted, coated with spiced cornmeal and tossed into frying pans of bubbling lard. While the fish were cooked, other frying pans were filled with "hush puppies", those delectable balls of cornmeal, flour, eggs and onions. Cooked to a crisp, in the fish-flavoured fat, they were perfect companions to the fish which, once consumed, were washed down by countless glasses of iced tea.

Even more memorable than the fish fries were the Lovett family reunions, always held alfresco, in late summer. On these occasions anyone who could claim the slightest kinship to a Lovett turned up, so great was the reputation of the Lovett ladies for providing the best food in Screven County.

One long table was formed of many small ones, some brought from nearby homes for the day. Tablecloth upon white tablecloth appeared, but not the best family silverware or china. Energetic children and enthusiastic adults could put these valuable items at risk.

It was an unwritten rule that no one could take a mouthful until grace was said. Even we children knew this, so we waited impatiently for the designated grace-sayer to speak his piece. If no Lovett present was a preacher, deacon, or recognised pillar of the church, then someone volunteered for the occasion. He was sensible enough to know a certain feast awaited him, but he also knew that anything longer than two or three minutes might cause him to be overlooked for the next year's reunion. Short and sweet was the correct formula. Once he uttered "Amen" there erupted a hundred other "Amens" and everyone pitched in with vengeance – each determined to be the first to try Miss Betsy's chocolate layer cake, Uncle Henry's smoked sausage, or some other specialty for which they had waited an entire year.

The choices were endless; a selection, sadly, was the only sane way to approach eating. Boys and girls, unfortunately, did not know this, and each year there would be some upset stomachs among the younger generation. After all, how does one choose among several shoulders of hickory-cured hams, plates of coarse-cut country sausage made with each family's secret recipe, heaped platters of fried chicken, a roast turkey, barbecued spare ribs, Brunswick stew, a pork roast, meat loaves, as well as family variations of other meat dishes?

Beans, peas and other seasonable vegetables were there in abundance. My favourite, the sweet potato, was present in all its delectable forms: candied (especially good with roast pork), baked, soufflé with rows of white marshmallows on top, and the crowning glory – sweet potato pie.

It was in desserts that the ladies excelled. The ingredients that went into the layer cakes would raise eyebrows of those concerned about their figures today, but we never gave a passing thought to such things. Taste was what cakes were all about, and no wife worth her salt would attempt a cake without plenty of butter and eggs.

And what variety a small boy had to choose from! Where to begin – or end! Angel's Food, Caramel, Chocolate (with or without pecan icing), Date, Devil's Food, Marble, Orange, Pineapple-Upside-Down (one of my favourites), Pound, Spice - and many more. The only way to do justice to the occasion, I soon learned, was to take a small slice of each. Homemade pies took second place to the cakes, but only just. Most popular were apple, lemon meringue, cherry, chocolate, egg custard, pecan and sweet potato. One of the best, however, was made from fresh fruit – the Georgia freestone peach – still found on menus in the American South today. Accompanying the cakes and pies was an assortment of homemade ice creams – peach, vanilla, walnut, strawberry – all churned on the spot and served straight from the churn.

Iced tea and ice-cold lemonade were the two most popular drinks. Beer was unheard of in the South during my boyhood and in any case would have been illegal at family reunions in those Prohibition days.

Once appetites were sated, family groups drifted off to exchange news with other family branches. Then came photographs – one large one of everyone present, and others made of several family branches. The picture-taking was an emotional occasion, for some of the older ones present, in their 90s or just over 100, knew this could be their last reunion – although they would never admit it.

When saying good-byes, tears came to their eyes. I realised, too, how time moved on when some of my older cousins would come back the next year married – sometimes with an infant in tow. And how amazing it was, looking back on those reunion photographs, to find four or five generations alive at the same time. This happened when girls from successive generations married at 15 or 16 and immediately started their families.

For a small boy these reunions were a mixed experience. Gastronomically, the annual reunion was the event of the year – looked forward to eagerly from one summer to another. But by the time we started home in our separate cars the pleasures of the palate began to give way to the realisation that I had probably seen some of those elderly beloved family members for the last time.

I was not the only one moved by the strong family bonds of those days. Before she died, my mother asked that her remains be interred in the Lovett family cemetery situated within sight of the old home place.

10
I get into deep trouble

As immigrants poured into the United States during the 1800's, new villages and towns sprang up everywhere. Often these new places bore the surnames of their founding fathers.

One such village, Hiltonia, was named after the Hiltons, a prominent family with many branches in South Carolina and Georgia. It was to Hiltonia, a stop on the Augusta – Savannah railway, that my parents moved when I was four.

Even such a small place was a new world for me, fresh from my grandparents' farm. My father was attracted to Hiltonia because it possessed nothing to do with automobiles – by now his obsession. It had only a few hundred residents, two or three general stores, two churches and, of course, my father's automobile shop. He sold the inhabitants new cars of any marque, petrol and oil and carried out general repairs. He installed a small Delco-Remy electric generating power plant which was sufficient to provide for all the needs of our house and the nearby shop. Fellow citizens of Hiltonia begged him to install a larger plant to serve the entire hamlet, a move that would have made him well off if not, in time, wealthy. He turned a deaf ear to these appeals, however, for cars were to be his lifelong interest.

It was in Hiltonia that I was introduced to man's best friend, a dog named Rover. He was a beautiful, intelligent and loving Collie bought by my parents to be my companion. One day I was playing with Rover in the middle of the main road, an unimproved track that ran in front of our house. I was oblivious to a fast approaching car, but Rover had seen it bearing down upon us. With instinct and skill that I have many times since marvelled upon, he literally pushed me out of the path of the speeding vehicle.

My grief at Rover's death soon afterwards can hardly be imagined, especially since I was the cause of it. I was playing with a set of wooden ABC blocks that my parents had given me when I discovered that Rover liked retrieving any block that I tossed to him. Soon it became a game and I gleefully threw one block after another several feet away, then to see him pick them up and return them to me. Then, with Rover standing a few feet farther away I tossed another block – this time near his feet. It landed, point downwards, on his left paw and he instantly toppled over, dead.

The vet came quickly but it was no use. The sharp point had hit a vital nerve and Rover had died without uttering a sound. My only friend, who so gallantly had saved my life only a few days before, now lay dead by my own hand. My parents tried to persuade me it was an accident and not my fault, but I was too young to understand their reasoning and for a long time I grieved over Rover.

On another occasion I was to bring unspeakable agony to my parents. As there was no public water supply in Hiltonia each home had its own deep well. My father had built a "well house" over our well, roofed to keep away surface water and walled on three of its four sides. Around the three walls he kept an assortment of boxes, crates and a collection of tools mounted on pegs.

The open well had a wooden surround about my height and a timber frame supporting a pulley and its pail which my parents let down whenever they needed water. Many times I was cautioned not to get near the well and particularly never to try and climb up onto the surround. This caution made the well a great fascination for me and I was determined somehow to find out how deep it was. One day, spotting a large "monkey" wrench among my father's tools, I grabbed it and, with no thought of the consequences, pushed it up over the edge of the surround and into the well. To my great joy, it seemed ages before it hit the water. When it did so, there was an almighty splash. If my mother had not been in the kitchen at that moment with her window open, the incident might have ended there with only remorse on my part for having lost one of my father's most useful tools.

But my mother, who vaguely knew I had been playing near the well, heard the splash and immediately assumed the worst. When she started shouting my name, I ran and hid behind the crates. As I didn't dare own up to throwing my father's wrench into the well, I decided to keep quiet in the hope they would be prepared to forget about the missing tool after a time.

My young mind did not at first comprehend my mother's concern for me. She ran for my father and within minutes he returned with several other men and a long rope used for towing disabled cars. They quickly tied the rope to the well's overhead frame. Meanwhile, my mother stood wringing her hands and shouting "My little boy!"

Only then did the reality of my mischief dawn on me. They thought that I had fallen into the well! As one of the men tied one end of the rope around his body and prepared to mount to the surround and be lowered into the well, I could stand it no longer. I rushed from my hiding place crying, as my mother stared first in disbelief – then in joy. Although I tearfully owned up to my crime, neither my father nor mother ever reproved me.

Although my family did not leave Hiltonia until I was six, several other events are etched in my memory of those early days.

One was a spectacular train wreck a few miles away where the railway line passed over Briar Creek. When my father heard the news, he immediately scooped me up and we sped to the scene. It was difficult for me to imagine how those giant "car boxes", as we called the freight wagons, could be toppled from their tracks, but sure enough, there they were – some to the right, some to the left and some even piggy-banked on top of others. Fortunately no one was killed. The rescue crew with its enormous crane had not yet arrived, so my father and I, along with hundreds of others, freely roamed and marvelled at the sight. Briar Creek was the scene of a major battle in Sherman's March through Georgia, but in my mind the stream will always be associated with that glorious mangle of metal.

I get into deep trouble

The "quilting bee" is one of those beloved American institutions renowned for bringing a rural community together to do serious work, but in a party atmosphere. Commemorated in song and verse, they allowed a woman in need of extra "cover" for the coming winter, to achieve that aim in a single day through clever planning. She would notify her friends well in advance of the proposed date so they had time to dig out all the remnants from their sewing boxes. As most women made their own clothes in those days, a colourful variety of "patches" emerged when these ladies revealed what they had brought.

First, though, came the simple but exacting task of building a square or rectangular frame which would be mounted on the backs of chairs of equal height. Husbands or sons would have been prevailed upon to fetch the four necessary slim wooden pieces. My mother's planning had reached this stage when her friends had gathered, helping to steady the wooden pieces as she nailed them together.

I remember that quilting bee, not for its purpose and gaiety, but because of my mother's "miss-hit" of a nail on one corner of the frame. It flew directly to her mouth, just missing the flesh but neatly breaking off a sizeable chunk of one tooth. I heard her screams and came running, but was relieved to see her more frightened than injured. Work recommenced and when the backing was tied to the frame, the ladies began in earnest to cut their squares and start sewing. When completed, the quilt was a joy to behold. Homemade quilts of this type often were star exhibits in county and state fairs.

Another memorable Hiltonia event was a man-and-wife "performing act". As we were only a small town, the couple must have been very hard up indeed to think they could drum up a paying audience there. But days ahead of the event, posters appeared in the shops and on the appointed day the couple's tent was filled with paying customers. It turned out that the woman's husband did all the promotion, planning and other work while his wife was the performer. But instead of displaying acts of magic or agility, the lady instantly gained our sympathy when we saw she had no arms. With a pen held between her toes, she wrote our names almost as legibly as if she had fingers. Everyone there happily paid a few cents for these souvenir cards.

Perhaps more dramatic than the train wreck was another Hiltonia event – one that evoked drama, mystery and the threat of violence. Three houses away from our home lived a man, given to strong drink, who regularly beat his wife. I was sometimes deeply affected by her screams until my parents assured me she was not being killed. Then one night, without any prior hint, my parents took me into the front yard where we had a clear view of the offending man's house.

Signalling me to remain quiet, they rested their hands on my shoulders while one car after another arrived in front of the house – clearly destined for some purpose – but what, I wondered. While awaiting the last of the cars to arrive, the drivers of the other cars emerged, remaining silent. I saw to my surprise that they were dressed all in white - gowns covering their bodies and pointed white hoods on their heads. When the number of cars had reached 10 or 15, all the drivers got inside their cars. Without saying a word, they started up their engines and began driving round in a large circle in front of the wife-beater's house. This with headlights full on and horns blaring. It was like an immense Catherine Wheel of vehicles and its sight and sound was both thrilling and frightening.

The effect it had upon the wayward husband could only be imagined but my parents assured me later he had instantly repented. Not until some days afterwards did I learn that the men in white were all members of the dreaded Ku Klux Klan.

11
Heavy drinking – but not for long

My father, convinced that his – and America's – future would be dictated by the automobile, decided to set up a business in Millen, our county seat, just as I was starting primary school at the age of six.

He had a grand scheme to supply the burgeoning number of car owners with all their needs: petrol, spare parts, repairs and, most exciting of all, new cars. He obtained the dealership for Chrysler, a marque that survives to this day. This meant I spent a great deal of time around cars, although I entirely lacked my father's technical genius.

One day I witnessed an incident which was to illustrate the monetary value of technical knowledge. Millen's mayor, a well known lawyer, brought his car to my father, complaining it was badly leaking oil from its underside. My father quickly saw the oil pan had become loose – probably from hitting a stone – and the oil was gradually being depleted. He picked up a wrench, tightened the faulty bolt and – hey, presto - the leak stopped.

"How much are you charging me for that?" asked the lawyer.

"Twenty five cents" replied my father.

(Allowing for multiple inflation rises, 25 cents would amount to several dollars today.)

"What!" exclaimed the lawyer, "25 cents just to tighten one bolt?"

My father answered calmly.

"That's 5 cents for tightening the bolt and 20 cents for knowing which bolt to tighten."

Millen was an important stop on the Central of Georgia railway, the state's longest and most famous line. As in many another American town in the prosperous era of railroads, Millen's main street faced the railway and it was here that the principal shops were built.

The early years in Millen were happy, learning ones during which Floyd and I were joined by a sister, Hope, and another brother, Harold. I remember little about my first year of school except that we all looked forward to the visit of the itinerant school photographer who took our pictures, not in class groups, but individually at our desks. The word DIXIE appeared at the bottom of every print, attesting to the fierce spirit of regionalism that pervaded the Southern states at the time. Thanks to my parents, this first school picture, showing a decidedly cross-eyed boy, survived our many subsequent moves during the Great Depression, and eventually fell into the hands of my wife who considered it one of her prized possessions. Was she amused by my crossed eyes? Or perhaps intrigued that the picture was made at almost the same time she was born.

My eye condition, after several visits to a specialist in nearby Augusta, revealed there was no sight in my left eye except for light and colour perception. The specialist told my parents and me that I would never be able to see or read with the left eye and that I should take great care in sports and other outdoor activities not to damage my good (right) eye, lest I become totally blind. That dire prospect was to affect my participation in team sports later, as well as my medical classification in the Second World War.

My parents were kind and loving as they struggled to provide us with the bare necessities of life. We never complained and, as most of our playmates were in similar circumstances, we had no grounds for envy. My childhood memories up to the Great Depression are centred largely on happy vacations on my grandparents' farm and numerous adventures with my brother Floyd. One came close to taking his life at the early age of five. After a violent storm had brought down the electric cable in the street in front of our house, he picked up one end of the live wire to see what would happen. Instantly the high voltage shot through his body, tossing the cable across one shoulder where he was unable to remove it. I heard his screams and so did, fortunately, the lady across the street. She rushed to the telephone, called the town's electric generating plant, and demanded that the power be turned off instantly. Although there were two small hospitals in Millen at the time with the possibility that one or both had operations in progress, the town's electrical engineer did as told and Floyd emerged with no more than a large scar on his shoulder.

Floyd's other close call was domestic, but nonetheless a dramatic one for our family. Many an American child must have been tempted to put the small one-cent coin into his or her mouth and swallow it. Floyd, so tempted, accomplished the feat before my shocked mother could stop him. Once he managed to pass the coin through his wind-pipe, he seemed none the worse for the experience and continued to smile and play. A hurried call to the doctor resulted in advice no doubt gleaned from previous such incidents.

"Bake several sweet potatoes and feed them to him at every meal. The potato is coarse and eventually will collect the penny and pass it through the body."

My mother did as she was told and poor Floyd had one potato after another stuffed into him. Each time he had to relieve himself we all gathered in the bathroom to see if the offending penny would emerge. After several disappointments, it eventually passed from his body with a distinct clink. Southern cookbooks devote many pages in praise of the sweet potato but I have never seen one that cited it as a sure-fire dislodger of a swallowed coin.

Floyd and I didn't know it, but we had already adopted a practice to guarantee regular bowel movements. At that time advertisements appeared in all our daily and weekly papers, as well as in magazines, for that "elixir of healthy living", California Syrup of Figs. The reader was offered a free sample for the price of a five-cent stamp. So I sent away my stamp and duly received a small bottle, which I shared with Floyd. We decided that was the best five cents worth of fruit juice we had ever drunk and were determined to have more.

Even at our age, we knew the sample was meant to encourage us to buy the full-sized bottle from the local drug store. We had no intention of doing so, for we would never have the necessary money. Eventually we decided we could afford to order a bottle every two weeks using different names. Fortunately both of us had two "given" names, so there were several permutations open to us. As soon as we accumulated the required five cent pieces (not easy in those days), we sent off for the samples.

We hoped the California Syrup of Figs people did so much business they wouldn't notice all those requests coming from so many people at the same address in a little town called Millen.

As it turned out, our downfall came when my mother began to notice how frequently we needed to visit the bathroom and that our stools were decidedly on the liquid side. Under severe questioning we owned up, and were told we risked injuring our stomachs if we continued our bouts of heavy drinking. Silently we consumed our last hidden bottle together, savouring every sip in the knowledge there would be no more.

12
The kiss that produced nothing

Our primary school principal was "Fesser" Brinson. What his academic credentials were I never knew, but he had long since become a favourite of "The Little People" because of his love of singing. To our great joy he insisted on giving over the major part of our weekly school assemblies to the singing of his favourite tunes which quickly became our own.

Although the torch of the Confederate cause had been extinguished at Appomattox Courthouse half a century earlier, its memory still burned bright in our young hearts. Nowhere was "Dixie" sung more lustily; nowhere was "Tenting Tonight" voiced more poignantly than in our school assembly.

Through these Civil War songs we relived the hope and the agony of our grandfathers and great-grandfathers who had given their lives. And yet "Fesser" led us, just as enthusiastically, in the singing of anti-slavery songs like "Old Black Joe" and "Darling Nellie Gray". Whether he was trying to be fair, or merely liked the tunes, I never learned.

For me the most moving of the Civil War songs was "Just Before the Battle, Mother". We youngsters always liked singing it, but when we came to the chorus, there was not a dry eye among us. We were right there with that young soldier, fully aware that he probably would never see his loved ones again:

"Farewell, Mother, you may never
Press me to your heart again;
But, oh, you'll not forget me, Mother
If I'm numbered with the slain."

Another "tear-jerker" began:

"In my prison cell I sit, thinking mother dear of you
And our bright and happy home so far away;
And the tears they fill my eyes, spite of all that I can do
Though I try to cheer my comrades and be gay."

My schoolmates and I resented the Yankees in the North and vowed that it would be different "next time". It would take many years, and much travel and study, before we could know that the reasons for the war were far more complex than we imagined.

But it was impossible not to be constantly reminded of the war in my youth. The UDC (United Daughters of the Confederacy) was a powerful influence in most Southern towns. On Confederate Memorial Day it organised events to mark the memory of the lost cause, including the decoration of soldiers' graves in cemeteries throughout the South. It also sponsored essay competitions on General Robert E. Lee and other heroes of our homeland.

The most unforgettable link with the war, at least to us young people, was the annual "parade" of the last remaining Confederate soldiers on these occasions. At first, there must have been a dozen or more old soldiers in their upper seventies or eighties. Thereafter the numbers dropped dramatically to only two or three and then suddenly, there were none. They hobbled slowly, painfully to the Confederate War Memorial (there is one in virtually every Southern county seat), there to place, with great feeling and tenderness, a wreath in memory of their fallen comrades.

"Fesser" Brinson's repertoire of songs was by no means limited to those invoking nostalgia for our lost cause. We also sang popular tunes of the day (many of which have passed into oblivion), and he was likewise quick to take advantage of school talent. One of our younger playmates, Billy Edenfield, made a kind of banjo-mandolin out of an old cigar box and piano wire. He had a high-pitched voice that could carry a tune well and he was not the least shy.

The kiss that produced nothing

When Billy learned the words of a contemporary hit tune, "Yessir, That's My Baby", "Fesser" was so impressed he pulled him out of his class, led him by the arm to every other classroom and had him perform. More than one dedicated teacher, in the midst of explaining some difficult point, was interrupted by the smiling principal with little Billy in tow. By the time Billy finished we pupils were in hilarious uproar, and even our serious teachers broke into smiles.

Sometimes we had guest speakers at our weekly school assemblies. The one I remember most was William D. Upshaw. He later became a candidate for President of the United States, representing the Prohibition Party, one of many small parties (he received 82,000 votes). Upshaw's anti-drink stance was well received by most of our parents.

Upshaw rightly said, when he began his talk, that we might not remember a word he uttered that day, but we would remember what he would do next. Reaching into his pocket, he took out a new silver dollar, held it up for all to see, drew back his arm and, with a quick thrust, bounced it off the stage floor into the midst of the startled pupils. A dollar was then more than a day's wage for many men, so there was a mad scramble for the coin. At last, one pupil got his hands on it, to the envy of the rest for he was allowed to keep it. We thought it a pity Upshaw did not do better in the balloting, and an even greater pity that he visited us only once.

Another school visitor was a kilted Scot who arrived with bagpipe to perform during school recess. This was the era of Sir Harry Lauder's popularity in America and other Scottish performers quickly jumped aboard the bandwagon. I don't remember the name of our visiting piper or the airs he played, but several of my school friends and I were so moved by the marching tunes that we fell into step behind him. He was good-natured enough not to object.

My sweetheart at the time, blissfully unaware of the esteem in which I held her, was Ruth Newton, a sweet, petite lass. School meals had not yet arrived, so we had the choice of bringing our lunch, or - if we could do so in the allotted time – go home to eat. Ruth lived a few miles outside Millen and brought her lunch to school; I lived only 10 minutes away, and so had a hot meal at home each day.

One day the desire to demonstrate my affection for Ruth overwhelmed me. I was only seven or eight years old and not experienced in the etiquette of making romantic overtures. Should I tell her outright, or write a note? The first I didn't have the courage to do, the second somehow seemed a feeble gesture.

I knew a kiss symbolised love but what if she refused me? After pondering this weighty problem for several days I came up with a solution that appeared to meet all necessary criteria. My strategy called for giving Ruth a kiss without saying a word. That way, I calculated, she would unmistakably know my feelings for her. A polite "conversation" beforehand, I concluded, wasn't really necessary. No, stealth and speed – above all, speed – were essential if the plan were to succeed.

I had observed that Ruth always had her lunch in the same place: on the ramp of a disused school garage. Fortunately for my scheme, this was on the direct route to my home. After failing to muster the necessary courage for several days, I at last became confident enough to show Ruth I loved her.

On the chosen day I nervously awaited the lunchtime bell. I managed a sideways glance at dear, gentle Ruth on the other side of the room as she extracted her lunch box from the desk. Ah, I thought, she is blissfully unaware of the kiss I am soon to implant. I could already imagine the softness of her sweet face. I was startled out of my dreams by the lunchtime bell and the pupils' mad scramble to rush outdoors.

Restraining myself to allow Ruth time to get to the ramp, I ambled slowly along the path – pausing occasionally to look right and left to use up time. At last I could see that she had seated herself and was opening her lunch box. Now she had a sandwich in her hands and was about to eat. For me, it was now or never.

I started jogging casually, as any pupil might do en route for home. Then, with only a few yards remaining, I broke into a sprint, lowered my head as I neared Ruth, gave her a resounding smack on the cheek, and dashed away at top speed. I risked looking back only once, just in time to see dear Ruth raising herself from the floor of the ramp where I had knocked her. She wasn't looking at me but for her sandwich. While this wasn't quite the result I had in mind, I prayed that she might appreciate my kiss enough to forgive the sudden, rough manner in which it had been bestowed. Then remorse set in. Had I upset the one person in the world I most loved? Would she ever forgive me?

Half a century later I recounted the story to Ruth, then on the staff of Millen's library. To my surprise, she had no memory of it. Apparently my daring deed had made no lasting impression on her.

13
My cross-eyed heroine

The school days in Millen were not without high drama. One day an old man who lived in a house opposite the school was found dead on the sidewalk a few yards from his home. He had been shot in the back sometime the night before.

Although the body had been removed by the time we children arrived the next morning, the blood-splattered sidewalk had not been cleaned and remained in its gory state until heavy rains did the job some days later. Everyone spoke openly about the murder and how the victim, out for his usual evening stroll, had been cut down by someone who knew his habits well.

The circumstances pointed directly to one well known person who stood to gain by the man's death, but in the absence of witnesses or evidence, I believe no one was ever brought to trial. My school friends and I thought this a great injustice. In our ignorance of the necessity to have more than mere suspicion, we were left to lament "This is not right".

Millen was not one of the old towns of Georgia and possessed few graceful "colonial" homes, such as are found in nearby Washington and Madison. The town owed its original prosperity to the managers of the Central of Georgia Railroad who saw its future as an important stop. Because a first class highway system was still years away, Georgia's railways in the 1920's carried not only freight but passengers. My friends and I came to the railway depot – not to travel – but to see those wonderful trains with names like the 'Nancy Hanks' which maintained speeds averaging 40 to 50 miles per hour over the Atlanta – Savannah run.

Nancy Hanks was a legendary Georgia Revolutionary War heroine who was cross-eyed. When two British soldiers invaded her home she seized her rifle and pointed it in the general direction of the pair. Not being sure which one she was aiming at, both men dropped their weapons and became Nancy's prisoners. Having been born cross-eyed myself, I naturally placed Nancy among my favourite Revolutionary War figures.

Millen's population at the time was around two thousand souls, of whom approximately one-third were blacks. The whites had Baptist, Methodist and Presbyterian churches; the blacks had their own Baptist-oriented congregations. The only three "foreigners" in Millen were business people, and that exciting discovery made it possible for me to approach them for help with my fledgling stamp collection.

My fascination for stamps, which became life-long, derived from a keen interest in geography and history and the accidental discovery of a discarded envelope with a French stamp portraying a graceful woman sowing grain. Never seduced by the monetary value of stamps, I was instead awed by these little pieces of coloured paper that had originated in faraway places where, in most cases, people spoke other languages and followed customs both fascinating and strange to me. My imagination took hold and I had to have maps, encyclopaedias and, as well, history and language references to supply answers to the questions the stamps raised in my young mind.

There was no such thing then as a weekly allowance for my friends and me, for we all knew our fathers were hard-pressed to make ends meet. Thus the thought never crossed my mind that I could buy stamps for my collection. In any case, it was much more exciting to search out people who had either been born abroad or who had relations there. A great plus was that they could tell me something about the person or place depicted on the stamps from their home countries.

The foreigner who lived nearest to our house was Charlie Lee, operator of an immaculate Chinese laundry on a side street. I had to pass his sweet-smelling shop every time I went to Millen's business district and I fear I must have been almost a daily pest. His family in China were regular correspondents and Charlie kindly apportioned his stamps among a few other young collectors and me.

Millen's sole bakery was run by the Fischer family whose ancestors were German. They made glorious bread and pastries, and the most delightful aroma wafted daily from their premises into the street outside. I had never been in the bakery, but had been told the Fischers were Catholics.

Except for the prevailing notion among us children that they – like the damnyankees – might have horns, I had no idea what a Catholic might look like. As I had no German stamps in my collection, the time came when I was obliged to approach Mr. Fischer to see if he occasionally received letters from the old country. I was amazed to find a large, quiet-mannered man behind the counter who smilingly told me that if I cared to come around about once a month, he would save a few German stamps for me. Perhaps it was Mr. Fischer's kindness that stirred within me my first ecumenical instinct.

The only restaurant in Millen at the time was owned by a Greek, Nick Economos. I shall associate grapefruit with Nick to my dying day. When my mother was in labour with my sister, Hope, my father took me to Nick's for a meal. Nick placed the entrée, half a grapefruit, in front of me. I must have been about eight at the time, but had never seen a grapefruit before. To me it looked like a giant orange. Oranges I liked, so I dug out a generous spoonful and gulped it down.

Unlike some of the sweet or semi-sweet grapefruit of today, mine was the Original Acid Product. I shouted, clutched my throat and shoved the plate away. It took my father several minutes to demonstrate that a slight sprinkling of sugar could make a sour grapefruit quite acceptable.

Perhaps Nick, too, never forgot that incident, for he was eager to give me stamps of his native Greece – some showing the Parthenon in Athens and the famous Corinth Canal. Little by little, I became aware of the world beyond Millen, Georgia and the United States. I learned there were other lands, other people (who were as nice as anyone I knew), and other languages. From the stamps I gleaned a few words in French and other languages, and wondered if one day I might be lucky enough to travel to some of the exciting places represented by my stamps.

My best friend in primary school was George Franklin whose home was at the nearby Birdsville Plantation. The stately old home was one of few to survive Sherman's march to Savannah – in part because it was used to billet some of his army. But another reason, according to family legend, was that the mistress of the house stubbornly refused to leave when Sherman's men announced they intended to burn it to the ground.

Birdsville was another world - the American colonial period - to me. In front were stately columns and clusters of sweet magnolias so celebrated in Southern literature and song. In the rear was an elegant staircase and porch crafted in wrought iron. Inside was a splendid four-poster bed in which George's mother kindly allowed me to sleep during my frequent visits. Some of the furniture and family silver came from

England. There was a vast cellar, at one time used to store some of the food needed to maintain the large household. There was also a coach house with the family coach intact, though by now worse for wear. At the rear of the home there was an aged tree, allegedly scarred by a cannon ball from one of Sherman's guns.

On the Birdsville plantation was a large body of water known locally as Duke's Pond. Although not deep, it never dried up and during a normal year covered several acres. The pond later became the focus of attention for national and state public health officials who sought an explanation for the high incidence of malaria fever in our county. Every child in our school was tested for malaria and a considerable number, including myself, proved positive.

Those affected were immediately required to take heavy doses of quinine. These caused unforgettable high-pitched ringing in our ears, but, happily, the dreaded disease was nipped in the bud. Acting on the precedent of the Panama Canal experience, in which marshes were eliminated to curtail the mosquitoes which caused malaria and yellow fever, public health officials ordered Duke's Pond to be drained. When this was done, new cases of malaria dropped dramatically.

14
Early American media

The printed page, whether in a book or newspaper, fascinated me from an early age. So I was thrilled when my father bought me a typewriter at about age seven on condition that I type all his customers' invoices for automotive services. I jumped at the offer, for I knew I could write letters and, who could tell, even a book!

Although I did not know it at the time, this budding interest in the media would lead to a lifetime love of newspapers, radio and, much later, television. Particularly exciting was our local weekly paper whose every issue had news about all the people around me with whom I was in daily contact. It was also interesting to learn about people and events in more distant cities like Augusta and Atlanta.

But there was another paper we received, *Grit*, that then touched the heartstrings of Rural America. Founded in Williamsport, Pennsylvania, by Dietrick Lamade and his family, it circulated throughout the United States thanks to a network of young boys and girls who received an assortment of prizes for their sales. Lamade's personal maxim, "Difficulties show what men are", was constantly reflected in *Grit*'s monthly house magazine which became an effective introduction to salesmanship for tens of thousands of American boys and girls.

I joined this happy band of peddlers and soon learned to give no credit, to delete anyone who had promised to take the paper but changed his mind at the point of delivery, to salt away every penny earned in an interest-bearing account and to forego luxury items that my better-off friends might have. I also learned the value of reliability for, like the postman, the boy or girl who delivered *Grit* had to work willingly and cheerfully in fair weather and foul.

Grit's circulation eventually exceeded a million copies weekly. Its appeal to rural and small-town America lay in its folksy approach to news, editorials and features. It also incorporated a magazine with serials, stories and a philosophical column by one of the paper's best-loved characters, "Faraway Moses". Old Faraway somehow had the knack of making his readers' many faults seem both excusable and curable.

My favourite feature was the pen-pal section on the youth page. Over a period of several years I formed close friendships with boys and girls of my age throughout the United States. We swapped not only letters about ourselves and our home towns, but also snapshots and mementoes. For example, the first slide-rule I ever saw was given to me by Royce Staves of Rome, New York, whose father was employed in an engineering firm there.

As I delivered copies of the paper year after year during my boyhood, I secretly harboured the dream of visiting *Grit* printing works one day. The Great Depression of the 1930s prevented me from going anywhere; the Second World War saw me going great distances but I had no say as to where. Subsequent work took me to various points overseas, but Williamsport was never on the way to any of them.

Not until my retirement was I able to make my dream come true. Then, in the company of my wife, I at last made my way to the attractive Pennsylvanian city of 40,000 on the west branch of the Susquehanna River.

When we arrived at the *Grit* plant, the editor gave us a warm welcome and promptly assigned a member of the staff to take us around the premises. Everywhere we met enthusiastic employees determined to achieve the founder's ideal: "Make every issue of *Grit* ring the joy bells of life". The guide later reeled off a list of famous men who had distributed *Grit* as boys, among them the poet Carl Sandburg; Gene Autry, the cowboy film star; and William Rogers, a man I came to admire as an American Secretary of State.

As thrilled as I was with the printed word, it was the radio that most stirred my imagination and brought distant places into our home. Our first radio in Millen was a large, plain set with a simple tuning dial, another for volume, and an off-on button. Although some of the early stations had powerful transmitters, this did not prevent them from becoming overridden by adjacent stations on the imprecise tuner. Thus, it was a constant battle to keep a station tuned in without interference, either from another station or, worse still, static.

More often than not, during those early days of radio, we would gather round the set to hear a favourite programme or sporting event, only to have the signal fade away completely and leave us in a quandary over the outcome. My father, with his knowledge of electricity, usually managed to manipulate the tuning and, when necessary, replace a faulty tube.

The early American radio industry was personalised to a remarkable extent. Government regulations then were lax and almost anyone with money could start up a station. Although there was a maximum limit to transmitter power, some monied interests evaded this restriction by building powerful transmitters just across the border in Mexico from which they could reach the whole of the United States. In Georgia the strongest signal came from Atlanta's WSB, the letters standing for "Welcome South, Brother".

Local stations then were obliged to start their call letters either with a "W" or a "K". Thus it was that one entrepreneur in Shreveport, Louisiana, W.K. Henderson, opened a station embodying his initials in its call letters, KWKH.

American supermarkets, especially the Great Atlantic and Pacific stores, were sweeping the land and many a small grocer was forced out of business. Henderson took up the cause of the small town grocer along with other popular grievances of the time and asked the public to contribute to his "battle fund". Money poured in and Henderson, finding he had more than enough for his causes, set about using some for his own purposes. He was found out and investigated, but the Shreveport station carried on with Henderson's initials in its call letters.

Two types of programmes from those early days of American radio stand out in my memory. One was the broadcasting of heavyweight boxing championships; the other, the popular Saturday night feature, the Grand Old Opry.

Heavyweight boxing titles nowadays have become largely an all-American affair, but in the 1930s they had an international flavour with the German Max Schmeling, the Italian Primo Carnera, and other foreign fighters taking part. Millions of Americans were glued to their unreliable radio sets on those championship nights.

The fights of that period that most interested Georgians were those in which a native son, W.L. ("Young") Stribling took part. Stribling was from Macon and was managed by his father who could always be heard over the radio encouraging his son by shouting, "Come on, W.L."! Young Stribling went from strength to strength and, at last, on 3 July, 1931 was matched against Max Schmeling for the world heavyweight title in Cleveland.

That fight was memorable for going to the 15th round when Schmeling won over Stribling by a knockout. We did not know it, but Stribling's boxing career was all but over for he died not long afterwards from injuries sustained in a motorcycle accident.

By far the most popular radio programme in the South of my childhood was the Grand Old Opry, an American country music institution to this day. The ballads, fiddle tunes and love songs that had heretofore been confined to the Southern Appalachian Mountains were now given a national voice over station WSM in Nashville, Tennessee. Each Saturday night for about four or five hours, many famous performers appeared on the show under the direction of the much loved emcee, George D. Hay.

It was largely because of Hay that the Grand Old Opry developed into a national institution. If the performers lacked colourful names or costumes, he suggested something to blend with the programme's goal of reflecting the best of what was then called "mountain music".

Eventually WSM increased its transmitter strength and was able to beam its signal over the whole of the United States. Soon the Grand Old Opry came into its own and laid the foundation for Nashville's reputation as "Music City, USA" With their universities, symphonic orchestra and other cultural assets, old Nashville families at first were reluctant to see their city become the capital of what came to be known as country music. This reluctance eased slightly with the development of the "Opryland USA" complex which brings millions of visitors from all over the world to Nashville every year.

Today's country-and-western music is a far cry from the Grand Old Opry of the 1920's. Rock-and-pop influences had not then infiltrated what was essentially a world of English, Scottish and Irish folk tunes, together with some colonial American off-shoots.

Many great names, among them the legendary Carter family of Virginia, appeared on the Grand Old Opry, but my childhood favourite was "Uncle Dave" Macon, perhaps the most popular banjo player of all time. I would sit enthralled when Uncle Dave, accompanied by his son, rendered such Appalachian favourites as "Grey Cat on the Tennessee Farm", "Take Me Home, Poor Julia", "Rabbit in the Pea Patch" and "Go 'long, Mule".

One of Macon's "tricks" was a song with a chorus about the best known American chewing gum, Juicy Fruit. In this he sang the words "Juicy Fruit" several times, each time slightly softer. At an almost indiscernible point, he introduced the strings of the banjo sounding exactly like the words "Juicy Fruit". So cleverly did he mingle human voice with banjo that only with intense listening could one detect when one stopped and the other began.

15
Making whiskey in the bath

Reading, stamp collecting and being transported to the ends of the earth through the magic of radio fired my youthful imagination of far away places and people. But it would be many years before I was to see much of Georgia and my native South. A notable exception was our annual trip to Savannah to visit Aunt Julia.

Savannah was settled by England's James Edward Oglethorpe in 1733 and thus became the first capital of Georgia. It, together with Charleston, South Carolina, has a grace and charm unrivalled in the Colonial South. As I was intensely interested in history at the time, I eagerly looked forward to these annual pilgrimages to what I considered the most exciting city in the world. There was the Savannah River with cargo ships from round the world and even a regular ocean passenger service between New York and Savannah. How I longed to make that short voyage! There was also a marker at the very spot where Oglethorpe first set foot in Georgia and was welcomed by the Indian Chief, Tomichichi.

Usually we would visit the seaside at nearby Tybee Island at least once during our stay with Aunt Julia. In those days it had a huge wooden pier, built partly over the beach and partly over the sea. We took a picnic lunch and spent most of the day wading, swimming or simply just lolling in the sun. Every so often I stopped to take in the vast expanse of the Atlantic Ocean. I could see the world was round because ships dipped below the horizon. But I could not see where they were going. In my juvenile mind I determined that one day I would find out.

There was little housing development then and much of the area between Savannah and Tybee was woodland and field. Once we managed to capture a wild turkey and bring it back to Millen – only to have a neighbour steal it the following week. We were no doubt punished for removing the bird from its natural habitat.

Apart from the chance to see some new historical site in Savannah, I looked upon these visits to Aunt Julia with both eagerness and trepidation. She had two lovely daughters, a few years older than myself, and an old-fashioned Victrola record player with an assortment of popular discs of the period. Within five minutes of arriving, I had started using the player. My favourite was "I Wish I Was Single Again", whose chorus ran:

"When I was single, my pockets did jingle,
Oh, I wish I was single again."

I never visited Aunt Julia without fear that everyone in the household (including us visitors) would be sent to the county penal institution, popularly known as "The Brown Farm". The reason: Aunt Julia's husband had deserted her years before, leaving her to support two daughters by "illicit endeavours".

Even before the break-up of her marriage, Aunt Julia knew about her husband's fondness for other women. One night she devised a plan that would both show her disgust and cause her husband great pain. When he returned home after spending several hours with a girlfriend, he fell into bed and was soon sound asleep. Aunt Julia quietly got out of bed, went to the kitchen and picked up a tin of red pepper. Tip-toeing back to the bedroom, she found her husband's underpants and sprinkled the pepper generously inside. Then she returned to her bed and soon was sound asleep.

The next morning her husband arose and, in due course, began to put on his clothing. After a few minutes he experienced a burning sensation in the region of his genitals. He immediately thought he had picked up a venereal disease from one of the several women he had been visiting. Aunt Julia kept a straight face as her husband complained of sharp pains in his groin and quickly left to see the family doctor.

It did not take the GP long to diagnose the problem. While the joke may have given the doctor a hearty laugh, Aunt Julia's husband did not take it well. As the marriage was already heading for the rocks, this incident served only to speed up the process.

Aunt Julia, although pleased to be rid of her womanising husband, had no training for a trade or profession and decided the only way to provide for her children was to make bootleg whiskey. Aunt Julia did not consider making and selling whiskey dishonourable; she was a teetotaller herself and her craft was simply a means of making ends meet.

What put her at risk were the prohibition laws, violation of which could mean heavy fines or, worst of all, imprisonment at the notorious Brown Farm.

Aunt Julia made her whiskey in the bath of her Savannah apartment. The bath was convenient and sanitary but its greatest attribute for Aunt Julia was the ease with which she could get rid of the evidence should "the law" suddenly arrive. A procession of apprehensive men climbed the stairs to Aunt Julia's apartment, there to be scrutinised through a peep-hole. She knew her regular customers, but there was no way of telling if a newcomer was a genuine buyer or a sting buyer operating for the police. When Aunt Julia was ready to gamble on the authenticity of a visitor, she quickly filled a fruit jar with whiskey, put it in a paper bag and exchanged it for a dollar bill at the door.

Meanwhile, I waited in the adjacent room for the sound of the siren and the sheriff's men, but they never came – at least not in my time. Aunt Julia was constantly cautioning her daughters to be careful about their speech and actions in public lest "we all wind up on the Brown Farm". During our visits I took that "we" to include my parents and myself.

Enjoyable as were the visits to Savannah, I always heaved a huge sigh of relief when we departed Aunt Julia's apartment for home. I don't believe she was ever apprehended. Surely the sheriff must have learned about her moonshine. Why was she not arrested? Most likely, he took pity on an enterprising mother struggling to provide for her two young girls.

Apart from those exciting visits to Savannah and the occasional trip to nearby Augusta, our family did little travelling during my boyhood. My mother was busy adding to her family and my father devoted all his time to cars.

However, there was one occasion – when I was nearly nine – when history came to Millen.

That took the form of Colonel Charles A. Lindberg, the first person to fly solo across the Atlantic. Lindberg made his epochal flight on 20-21 May 1927, leaving from Long Island's Roosevelt Field and landing at Paris' Le Bourget Airport. The flight took 33 hours and 32 minutes, about 10 times longer than that taken by Concorde, but it demonstrated to the world that civil aviation had arrived.

In the weeks following his historic flight Lindberg was feted both in Europe and the United States. Later in the year he flew the plane in which he had crossed the Atlantic, the "Spirit of St. Louis", to most major cities in the United States. When the city fathers in Millen heard that Lindberg's route would take him over the town, they immediately sent a message inviting him to set down briefly at our crude landing strip.

I was thrilled at the prospect of Lindberg landing in Millen. I knew that Millen was just about the greatest place on earth and surely Lindberg – clever man that he was – must have known it too. Virtually the whole of the town's population gathered at the air strip, waiting for the arrival of the famous aviator and his plane. Then, almost exactly at the estimated time he was due, the famous aircraft appeared. To our dismay, however, it made no effort to land, but instead flew low over the crowd.

Then Lindberg tossed out something that looked like a sheet of paper or a small piece of cardboard. It floated down to earth where city officials promptly took possession. As the plane flew away, we were told that Lindberg had dropped a brief message saying how much he regretted having to omit Millen from his landing schedule.

Lindberg's regret was nothing compared to mine, but how was I to know then that his travel plans concentrated on 75 of the largest American cities? I was never to set eyes on Lindberg, and it would be many years before I would again see the "Spirit of St. Louis", this time in its permanent setting at Washington's Smithsonian Museum.

Nor was I ever able to see his letter of regret. Had the town's mayor kept it as his own possession? Did it wind up in an archive somewhere? Or does some autograph collector today count it among his most prized possessions?

That massive disappointment remained with me for a long time. Nonetheless, I continued to worship Lindberg and was left shattered when his infant son was later kidnapped and killed. In the run-up to World War II he naively praised Germany for its advances in military aviation, later making ammends by joining the Army Air Force in the Pacific. I also came to admire the writings of his gifted wife, Anne.

But the regret lingers. Why, oh why, didn't he make an exception and land at Millen?

16
I kill a sparrow – and a rabbit

I was eleven and just beginning the sixth grade in Millen when the stock market crash of October 1929 set in motion a chain of events that would profoundly affect my family for most of the next decade – a period we later came to know as The Great Depression.

No one in our immediate family owned shares and at first we couldn't understand why the crash of the market in New York City should matter to us. But small town banks throughout the South and the rest of America soon found themselves in trouble. Grandpa Mays, a successful farmer up until 1929, lost his life's savings in the bank at nearby Sardis.

The only people in small towns of the Deep South to survive the decade of the Great Depression were the well off – usually not more than half a dozen families in a typical community of two to three thousand. Between them they controlled the local bank, cotton gin, cotton brokering, law firms, the leading stores, insurance agencies, and other normally prosperous local businesses. Most were sufficiently diversified to avoid being totally wiped out, unlike the more vulnerable farmers and small businessman.

Before the Great Depression, farmers in our county found it profitable to ship watermelons all the way to East Coast cities such as Philadelphia and New York. But the rates for shipping by rail in the southern states were disproportionately higher than in most other regions of the United States. The railway operators argued this was because the South was sparsely populated, with great distances between shipping points.

Whatever the merits of the argument, the depression put an end to the profitability of shipping watermelons (and other products of southern agriculture) to distant places. Because of low prices and high shipping costs farmers sometimes owed railroad companies more than they received for their produce. There was, however, one happy result of this catastrophe for my family, albeit short-lived.

When the bottom dropped out of the watermelon market, farmers sought to find out the market position before loading the melons. If the price was not good enough, they simply ordered their wagon drivers to return the watermelons to their farms to be thrown away. That way at least they would not be out of pocket.

Some of these wagons passed by our house in Millen. One day a driver stopped and asked if I would like a watermelon or two, free. I replied "Yes!" without asking why. In the days that followed the same thing happened, as it did also to young friends of mine who lived on other routes to nearby farms. Although the melons had little nutritional value, they were welcome to our palates on those hot summer days.

Farmers were not alone in feeling the pinch after the collapse of Wall Street. My father was also affected, for suddenly no one could afford to buy new cars. The value of second-hand cars dropped drastically and anyone who held a stock of these, as did my father, saw his assets plummet. With fewer cars on the road, there was less demand for spare parts and servicing. It was terribly painful for my father to discharge men who had been with him since their late teens. Some, with young wives and babies to feed, pleaded for their jobs, but there was no work for them.

Our county weekly newspaper, *The Millen News*, also suffered lost revenue from both subscribers and advertisers. To remedy the situation (in common with many other small town weeklies), it hired a professional firm to increase its circulation. The person who sold the most subscriptions to their friends and neighbours would get an expense-free trip to Cuba.

To visit Cuba in those days was like crossing the Atlantic today.

It was a foreign country where people spoke a different language – never mind that it was only a few miles south of the Florida Keys. After a close contest with the other subscription sellers, my cousin Gladys won. I was almost as excited as she, for Gladys was the first person I knew who would be visiting a foreign country. I asked her to bring me back a Cuban coin. This she did, and as well gave me a first hand account of her adventures. That five centavos piece was the beginning of my life long interest in numismatics and although the badly worn coin was worthless, I retained it for sentimental reasons.

With income reduced to a trickle, my parents had difficulty paying the mortgage on our house. I had never given a moment's thought to the possibility that we might have to leave the home where we were so happily installed. Here was the gracious living room with its curving staircase leading to the upper floor, the piano on which my mother often played, and – best of all – the spacious back yard with its several outbuildings which were another world for my brothers, sister and our friends. My mother tried bravely to supplement my father's income by taking in boarders. There were boarders enough, but they, too, either proved unreliable guests or soon lost their jobs so could not, or would not, pay their weekly bills.

In desperation, my father tried one enterprise after another to bring in more income. Some people, unable to afford new cars but needing them for their work, were prepared to rent them. My father took several cars from his second-hand stock, where sales were virtually non-existent, and set up a small car rental business. At first this prospered, but then one car was stolen and another was completely wrecked by an irresponsible driver. What small gains there were originally now turned into heavy losses so the enterprise was abandoned.

During these dark days and others that were to follow, Grandma Mays helped us to survive. She came in several times each week from the farm, bringing milk, bread, vegetables and sometimes, meat. Even so, the food had to be carefully rationed and we seldom had our appetites fully sated. I well remember my younger brother, Harold, saying sadly on one occasion after we had consumed the small quantity of food on our table, "I'm *so* hungry".

Eventually the mortgage was foreclosed. I said good-bye to my school friends of six years standing and we left the old house for a large residence, known locally as the Parker House, on a small rented farm several miles away. Soon I was enrolled in a nearby small rural school. As there were not enough school buses to transport all pupils at one time, the drivers solved the problem by taking the one batch of children half way to the school, and then departed to pick up children on another route. We walked the remaining two miles, whatever the weather. This stay was a brief one and over the next four years, I attended no less than five schools.

My father had no intention of doing any serious farming for he still carried on his automobile business. The attraction of the move was the two storey house that went with the few acres. Nonetheless, as the land was available, he planted a few acres of cotton and corn (maize).

It was here that I mastered the art of using a sling-shot. One day I took aim at a sparrow in the cotton field. It was perched on the top of a cotton plant several rows away but I managed to hit it squarely with a pebble from my sling-shot. Before I made the kill, I had considered hunting a great sport, but when I rushed to find the fallen sparrow and picked up its limp, still warm body with its eyes closed, I was overcome with remorse.

What right did I have, I asked myself, to take the life of an innocent sparrow – one who probably was ridding us of the detested boll weevil at the very moment I killed it?

My mother, however, had no such qualms. Once when she saw a rabbit helping himself to our corn, she aimed her rifle and hit it right between the eyes. Neighbours soon heard of her shooting prowess and this reputation may have helped to keep any would-be prowlers at bay.

I had an altogether different experience with a rabbit, one which was to strengthen my resolve not to kill wildlife. Rabbits abounded on the farm and I was determined to capture a young one and raise it as a pet. One day I spotted a very young one and, after a brief chase, it stood still, exhausted and terrified. I picked it up. I had no concept of its dependence on its mother and so concocted my own plan to raise it. There were no rabbit hutches on the farm, and no prospect of buying one because they cost money, which we didn't have. My parents cautioned me against the chances of success, given the long periods I would be away at school when neither of them would be at the house to help care for the little creature.

Undaunted, I acquired a large cardboard box from a grocer and, leaving the top open for air, stocked it with leaves of lettuce and several receptacles of water. The very next day, as it happened, the entire family was to be away until the middle of the afternoon when I returned from school. Despite the weather being extremely hot, I was sure the rabbit would have plenty of air, food and drink to enable it to prosper.

On arriving home, I dashed eagerly upstairs to see how my protégé was faring. To my horror, it was dead. My parents could have reproved me, but they didn't. The futility of trying to make wild creatures adapt to a life of captivity was thus indelibly engraved on my heart.

At about dusk every evening during the summer when we lived at the Parker House, there came across the nearby valley one of the most haunting sounds I have ever heard. It was the voice of a young girl, accompanied by rhythmic beating of a metal wash tub. It was as if this child was baring her soul to God in exaltation. No words were spoken, only trills that rose and fell with regular beats. The pattern was the same each night, the voice starting off in low key and eventually reaching superb heights, after which, as if exhausted, it stopped as suddenly as it had begun.

I knew that a black family lived in the area whence came the nightly phenomenon but up to then my parents had no occasion to visit. Then one day my father needed help with the small crop he was growing, and we all piled into the car to call on the family to see if they could lend a hand. While my parents were explaining the problem to the man and his wife, I noticed a slip of a girl about my age shyly standing to one side. I spoke to her quietly, asking if she was the one responsible for the evening performances.

She smiled and hung her head, saying "Yes", it seemed, almost reluctantly. I told her she had a lovely voice, that the effect was magical and I hoped she would continue.

She did not reply, but merely looked at the ground in embarrassment. "Don't give it up", I said, "it's very beautiful". That night I awaited her voice with more than usual anticipation, but it did not come. Nor the next night, nor ever again during our stay at the farm. I have often wondered if I made a terrible mistake by complimenting the girl and entreating her to continue. Did I, by well meant praise, deprive the world of another Marian Anderson or Jessye Norman?

Our home was called the "Parker House" after the prosperous farmer who had built it. A wooden structure, it had once been very handsome, having two floors with four large rooms on the upper storey and more than adequate space for our family possessions on the ground floor. As two of the upstairs rooms were vacant, I asked if I could have one for a 'map room' to feed my growing interest in geography.

My parents had no objection, so I wrote off to various addresses, both in the United States and abroad, and received a wonderful assortment of maps. I still have two of my favourites, both illuminated: one of Germany, published by the national tourist board and, the other, the Pan American highway, distributed by the Standard Oil Company.

It was at the point when my map room was at its best, with maps adorning all four walls, that we received the only visit I can remember from my maternal grandfather, James Lutes. He was almost seventy and nearing the end of his life.

I was very much in awe of him, for he had a reputation as a stern school master. For several years I had written him letters about one "adventure" or another, only to have him return my letters promptly with errors in spelling and grammar marked in red. No wonder I wrote to him less frequently as time went on.

Then one day I made the mistake of writing letters to him and Aunt Julia in Savannah at the same time, but putting them in the wrong envelopes. Aunt Julia made light of the error, but Grandpa Lutes sent me a terse one-paragraph note saying, in effect: "If you have to write more than one letter at the same sitting, seal the first one in its proper envelope before going on to the next". I must admit Grandpa's advice was not lost on me; I have followed this rule faithfully ever since.

Grandpa Lutes was also a great traveller. He told me he had visited every state in the Union, not out of curiosity, but because his German ancestry made him duty-bound to know every corner of his family's adopted land. When he acquired a new book in California or Utah, for example, he inscribed on its fly-leaf not only his name and the date, but also the place of purchase.

Because Grandpa knew so much about geography, I assumed he would be very pleased with my Map Room and so proudly led him upstairs to see it. Just inside the door he paused and looked round at the four walls. I expected him to go nearer and study these beautiful, instructive pieces of cartography. Instead, he looked sternly at me and said, "Overdone. Remember, everything in moderation". With that he turned on his heels and descended the stairs. I was shattered, and only in later life did I see the wisdom of his words.

17
Hoboes flock to our house

As the depression deepened our family was forced to leave the Parker House and move to Savannah where, for a time, prospects of financial security seemed better for my father. At first I was overjoyed to think we would be living in the city I cherished more than any other – mainly for its beauty and its history. But the uncertainty of the times, coupled with a coldness of neighbours, left me, my brothers and sister very unhappy.

My misery was compounded when I went to my new school, Chatham Junior High. The school was named for the county of which Savannah is the county seat. The county was created in 1777, a year after the American colonies declared independence. So strong was pro-British sentiment then that the founding fathers thought it appropriate to name the county for the Earl of Chatham (William Pitt) who earlier had been Secretary of State and leader of the House of Commons.

I was amazed to find the school occupied an entire city block. The greatest shock came when I found I would not have all my lessons in the same room. Instead my classes were scheduled in half-a-dozen rooms scattered throughout the school's sprawling premises. With only a few minutes between classes, this meant rushing down the corridors to a different room – sometimes located on the other side of the block.

It was at Chatham Junior High that I was introduced to the controversial testing system that was to remain with me for most of my formal education – examination answers that had to be marked either "True" or "False", or putting an "X" by one of a group of "multiple choice" possibilities. I still remember the first such test I took. It comprised only 10 statements, half multiple choice and half true-false.

I had no problem with the multiple choice, but two of the five true-false statements were worded in such a way that one clause was true and the second was false. I had no precedent to go by, and so marked these two with both a true and a false (T or F) mark. When my paper was returned, I was given a mark of 80 with both of the mixed T/F answers marked wrong.

I protested to the teacher. She looked at me as though I was an imbecile. Glancing at my paper, she thrust it back without comment. Stung by what I considered a gross injustice, I immediately went to the school head and pointed out why I had marked my paper T/F. He was understanding and looked up my school record. When he saw I had previously been enrolled in only small schools, he walked with me back to my classroom. Without blaming either me or the teacher, he explained that the two marking systems were the only way teachers could quickly grade large numbers of students. Moreover, he added, this "new" (to me) method of grading meant a statement was wrong if any part of it was incorrect.

I got the message and, indeed, when I later attended the University of Georgia, I found that similar marking systems were used for all large classes. Nonetheless, I vowed that should I ever teach I would – when there was a choice -- never set such papers for my students, but instead rely on the traditional "essay-type" questions.

One day my father and the young son of a prominent Millen businessman formed a partnership which would allow them to set up an extensive automobile dealership and servicing firm in the town of Cordele in south Georgia, not far from future president Jimmy Carter's county of residence. Premises were secured and the necessary equipment installed.

We then moved to Cordele, only to learn shortly afterwards that a mysterious illness had struck down my father's partner and he had died within hours. Because we had already signed a lease for a rented house, we were obliged to remain there for the best part of a year. My father struggled as best as he could to operate a business which originally had envisaged two partners.

Banks were still failing and one day my parents received a letter saying the Cordele bank in which they had their meagre savings, had gone under. Times may have been improving in some parts of the United States, but the South, with its agrarian-based economy, was slow to recover.

We just managed to eke out an existence, but even then my mother could not say "No" to those in greater need than ourselves. Cordele was a major railway junction in south Georgia with lines crossing at right angles at the station – the only place in the world where I have seen this occur. All trains were required to halt and sound their mesmerising whistle before continuing.

The Great Depression saw tens of thousands of men, of all ages, take to riding the rails. They were dubbed "hoboes", but not all were shiftless. Some were penniless and trying to find work for their wives and children in the Midwest or elsewhere. They had no hope of saving enough for the train or bus fare to some distant city where they might find employment.

Other men, considerably younger, were hoboeing for the thrill of it – trying to see what great distances they could cover without being caught by the railway police or other law enforcement officers. A few had guitars and they spawned many hobo songs.

Hoboes flock to our house

At major junctions these travellers established "jungles" (hideouts) where they could take a break, seek a temporary job or a free meal. These hideouts usually were near a derelict building which offered protection against the elements. Their walls also allowed the hoboes to scribble directions to those homes in the adjacent town where previous travellers had found soft touches.

Our house must have been prominently indicated on these walls, for hoboes visited us several times a week – occasionally, twice in the same day. A house such as ours also would have been marked in some secret way, perhaps a slight mark across the gate or nearby telephone pole. My mother was often alone when these men came; on other occasions my brothers and sister would be home from school when they arrived. My mother knew she was being "had", but also remembered how every one of us in the recent past had not known from one day to the next when a meal would be forthcoming.

She was never molested or threatened; on the contrary, we came to know a great deal about the hard lives of the men then roaming the country in search of work. True, not all cared to work and others may have exaggerated their plight, but the vast majority laid bare their souls as they shared the pittance of food placed before them. Perhaps more than one left thinking they were better off than we were.

Despite the hardships of the Great Depression, my family's stay in Cordele resulted in my being introduced to two new interests: public libraries and politics.

I had never heard of the Scottish-American, Andrew Carnegie before, but soon I placed him among my heroes. He had provided the means whereby Cordele and 2,800 other towns in America and Britain could have public libraries. Every summer the Cordele library conducted competitions for young people to introduce them to the joy of reading. I had no need of such inducement and probably became one of the library's most frequent users. Moreover, I considered it a great triumph when I convinced the librarian to let me take away more volumes than the stipulated maximum.

In adult life, my respect for Andrew Carnegie grew even more when I learned of his goal to dispose of his entire fortune (then one of the world's largest) before his death. I was astounded to learn that his generosity embraced not only libraries, but medical schools and foundations – some devoted to the cause of world peace. Here, it seemed to me, was a man who, although not an aristocrat, nonetheless became wealthy and was determined to exemplify the spirit of *noblesse oblige*.

It was in Cordele that I first set eyes on the foremost political figure of my generation of Georgians – a short, energetic man named Eugene Talmadge. For some years the Georgia Department of Agriculture had published a weekly *Market Bulletin* in which farmers could offer for sale or barter anything produced or made on their farms – plants, animals, chickens, fruit, preserves, crafts or whatever.

During the depression years this little paper enjoyed an

enormous circulation, for any extra income helped a farmer make ends meet, and anything bartered meant no money was required. The great majority of Georgia farmers at that time had small holdings and lived on or near the poverty line. Very few black families owned farms.

The *Market Bulletin* conseuqently went to the most powerful block of voters in Georgia, the farmers. 'Gene' Talmadge, as he came to be known, lost no time in using the journal to further his political aims. As State Commissioner of Agriculture, his column in the journal was supposed to be advisory only, but he subtly introduced two political themes guaranteed to make him popular – hatred of the 'rich big city dwellers', and latterly, hatred of blacks.

Both the inhabitants of cities and the blacks were largely disenfranchised by legal devices. Six 'electoral votes' were assigned Georgia's largest counties, four to a few middle-sized counties, and all the rest – including some with only 4,000 inhabitants – were assigned two. In this way three poorly populated rural counties with a combined population of only 12,000 could cancel out Fulton County in which Atlanta was located. Poorer blacks were unable to vote because they could not afford the infamous poll tax levied for the right to vote. If somehow they were able to raise the money, few dared to vote for fear of intimidation.

This system insured that a clever demagogue could inflame the emotions of white people and gain the inside track in any election in which a moderate candidate could appeal only to voters with high moral values. Talmadge, who made no secret of his aspirations to become Governor of Georgia, was to become a master of the art of appealing to base emotions and fear.

I was only 14 when I saw Talmadge in Cordele. It happened when I was passing the county courthouse just as he arrived to meet an influential group of local farmers. A car pulled up to the kerb and out stepped a man not much taller than I. He was hatless and wore a coat, which he fingered with both hands as he moved towards the group. The fingering was necessary to reveal his "emblem" – a bright red pair of braces supporting his trousers. The red braces proved a great attention-getting device and Talmadge retained them for most of his political career.

When he reached the group of men, Talmadge moved quickly to every one, shaking hands and gently pinching arms (a device guaranteed to make an impression on a voter) and in a few minutes had greeted them all. Then they went inside where he addressed them on their misery and his well known solutions for rectifying it.

I knew that Talmadge had two degrees (one in law) from the University of Georgia, and was amazed how farmers overlooked this when he spoke to them in their own, frequently ungrammatical language. I concluded he was cunning, intelligent and a master showman, as well as a demagogue, and that there would be no stopping him in his campaign to become Governor of Georgia.

I had no inkling at that time that Talmadge, after being elected Governor of Georgia, would threaten my higher education when he would use the “Nigger lover” issue to depose the dean of my college at the University of Georgia.

Near the end of our stay in Cordele the First Baptist Church hosted a well known missionary, the Reverend Scott Patterson. He had, as a young, enthusiastic missionary, gone out to West Africa where he caught a debilitating disease that almost took his life. He returned to the South, frail and crippled and looking like an old man. Yet, when he recounted his missionary efforts, he did so with a smile on his face and peace in his demeanour. As a teenager, I was deeply impressed by his sacrifice and for a time wondered if a missionary’s life was what I should strive for.

By 1932 the South (and much of the nation) had seen the worst of the Great Depression and the first signs of recovery appeared. The massive welfare and public works programs initiated by President Franklin D. Roosevelt began to make an impact on even the smallest rural communities. Public confidence in banks was restored overnight after the Federal Government’s guarantee to insure deposits up to a certain limit. With renewed hope of better times ahead, my father decided we should move from Cordele to Louisville – a pleasant town steeped in history, and not far from Millen.

18
Grandpa wins the chase

Although Louisville was, and is, considered one of the most attractive small towns in eastern Georgia, I was thrilled for another reason – a chance to live in the town where my Grandfather Lutes had once held sway as the local headmaster.

Grandpa Lutes’ stern manner and Teutonic thoroughness must have been useful characteristics when he was Headmaster of Louisville Academy during 1886-90. At that time he was in his early thirties.

Louisville Academy was one of several academies (high schools) founded in Georgia during the latter half of the 1700’s. All stressed a classical curriculum, including Latin and Greek, with Louisville Academy being among the last to give up the old standards.

It was a distinguished jurist, Judge John Robert Phillips, at one time chairman of Georgia’s highway board, who first told me about Grandpa Lutes’ stamina.

Judge Phillips recalled a local boy named Warren who was notorious for his disobedience. One day, after the boy deliberately set out to sabotage Grandpa’s instruction, he was warned that one more interruption would bring dire consequences. The boy laughed and continued his disruptive tactics. With that, Grandpa Lutes made for the boy who, young and agile, darted out of the classroom. Paying no heed to the riotous classroom laughter, Grandpa chased Warren through the corridors and then onto the school grounds.

By now young Warren had taken a somewhat more serious view of the situation and decided he should head for home, more than half a mile distant. On ran the culprit with my grandfather in hot pursuit. Down the main street sped the boy, causing puzzled shopkeepers and customers to stare in amazement.

Then, some way behind, they saw Grandpa, puffing heavily but nonetheless maintaining a steady pace. The boy soon disappeared from view, but my grandfather knew exactly where he was heading – home, where, no doubt, he hoped he could count on his mother's protection.

Into his bedroom and under the bed he went. A few minutes later Grandpa Lutes arrived and encountered a startled Mrs. Warren who was unaware of her son's arrival.

"Where is his bedroom?" demanded Grandpa. Mrs. Warren pointed it out, whereupon Grandpa dashed inside, pulled the crestfallen boy from beneath his bed, and administered a good dose of what today is frowned upon as corporal punishment.

Mrs. Warren looked on, first with amazement, and then with good humour. When Grandpa explained his mission, Mrs. Warren at once took his side, rebuked her son, and at once ordered him back to school and to be on his best behaviour. Thereafter, according to Judge Phillips, the boy became a model student.

It was one day in 1911 that Grandpa had learned that his parents, Jacob and Marcilla Lutes, who operated a grist mill, blacksmith shop and saw-mill near Steele, Alabama, had been murdered. Considered wealthy but kind by their neighbours, they frequently loaned money to struggling farmers until their crops could be harvested. It was generally assumed that they kept considerable sums of money on the premises. A local boy, noticing that the Lutes' cows had not been fed or milked, climbed up to look through a window after his shouts had gone unheeded. Peering inside, he saw the miller and his wife lying on the floor with their throats cut.

Then followed one of Alabama's most sensational murder trials which ended in three men being sent to prison for 12 years. Only when a fourth man confessed to the crime years later on his deathbed was it clear that three innocent men had been wrongfully convicted. My mother kept newspaper accounts of the murder, trial and deathbed confession. These made fascinating reading for my brothers, my sister and me and we frequently asked her to take them out of her trunk for us to peruse. We always ended with the same conclusion; how merciful the three men had not been hanged.

Both Grandfather Lutes and his father changed their names by deed poll, but for different reasons. Jacob Lutes, although born in Georgia, was a first generation German-American and in deference to his love of America, changed the spelling of the family name from Lutz to Lutes. The elder Jacob served with distinction in the Confederate Army, seeing action at several of the futile battles during Sherman's "March to the Sea". My grandfather, also christened Jacob at birth, took a dislike to the name and altered it to James while still a young man.

Visiting Grandpa Lutes at his humble home in rural Georgia was always an exciting experience for me because two walls of his bedroom were lined with books. My favourite was Arthur Mee's *Children's Encyclopaedia*, which I did not then know to be of British origin. Here I found many treasures of knowledge laid out in simple illustrated form. Those I liked most were the full page lessons in French, set in a shop, train station or a schoolroom, with French words to go with the objects pictured. I think I determined at that early age that I would one day learn French, although in my wildest dreams I never thought I would one day live in France with my family.

Grandpa's knowledge was not limited to what he had read in books. One year we happened to be visiting him on 22 September, the autumnal equinox.

When I said I had never heard of the term, he led me to the front porch and pointed out the position of the sun sitting precisely in the fork of two branches of a large tree in front of the house. He explained that the sun would be in exactly the same position six months later, 21 March. He concluded this basic lesson in natural science by giving me a few fundamental facts about the earth in relation to the sun. How easy it was for me to understand these principles with the visual example before my very eyes.

I never knew Grandpa Lutes to smile or laugh at a joke, but I always respected his wisdom, knowledge and determination to teach me a lesson on any subject that suddenly crossed his mind.

19
I almost drown the preacher

Our father's hope for better times was slow in coming, so we children understood we had to help our family save and buy a home of our own. For her part, my mother took up house-to-house selling and was moderately successful.

Charles Lindberg, who made the first solo flight across the Atlantic, was still very much in the public mind. Book publishers took advantage of his popularity to turn out many works on his exploit, some good and others indifferent. My mother signed up as the agent for one title in Louisville and over the ensuing months sold the book to many local families.

At other times she sold cosmetics for a well-known national firm. House-to-house selling took up more and more of my mother's time and she was reluctant to continue, even though she was by now saving useful sums for our future house. I persuaded her that I could do the family laundry and some of the cooking, two of the most time-consuming chores. Accordingly, I gathered our dirty clothing and scrubbed it in the bath once a week, afterwards drying it in the backyard. My mother did find time for the ironing, a craft I never mastered. She also taught me basic home cooking, an art which was to stand me in good stead in later life.

My brothers and sister, being younger, could contribute little to the family's home ownership goal save to accept gracefully the necessity of wearing hand-me-downs (in the case of my brothers) and never expecting more than the bare essentials of life. We were lucky to be living in the temperate climate of the rural South where most boys went barefooted for much of the year. Not until I was 14 did I wear shoes year round.

Not that we boys would have wanted it any other way. Even the sons of some well-off families went barefooted until they became adolescents. Like Tom Sawyer, we equated bare-footedness with being free spirited. Most of us resisted wearing shoes until the first frosts arrived and we could hardly wait until spring when we could discard them again.

The clothes I wore had been bought new and I took care not to be unduly rough with them, knowing that my two brothers eventually would inherit them. I took this procedure as a matter of course, not realising, in the eyes of my brothers, that I was seen as privileged. Many years later my brother Floyd told me how he dreaded wearing my hand-me-downs, knowing full well it would never be his lot to have anything new.

Our family's efforts at saving, combined with slowly improving times, eventually allowed us to buy a large two-storey house on the corner of the same street as our school, Louisville Academy. This we accomplished without inherited money or assistance from relatives or friends. Because we children had contributed in one way or another, we took great pride in the feat of home ownership and worked together to improve the house's amenities over the following years.

Louisville, I soon learned, was a friendly town whose origins lay deep in Colonial American history. It was noted by the explorer Desoto in April, 1540, during his trek from St. Augustine (now Florida) northwards. Its nearby settlement, known as "Old Town", was one of the earliest Indian trading posts in the South (1718).

Easily its best known landmark is a wooden market house, erected in 1758. Repaired many times, it still stands despite two close calls in its long history. When General Sherman's troops were burning the town centre to the ground, they spared the market from their nefarious torches. A century later the market was threatened when fire destroyed several adjacent shops. Yet it survives to this day as a reminder of the time when it served as the venue for selling all manner of goods.

In the late 1770s the market acquired a large bell, cast in France by François Gourvillon in 1772 for a convent in New Orleans. How the bell wound up in Louisville is a remarkable story in itself. The merchant ship bringing it and other goods to New Orleans was captured by pirates off the Georgia coast. When the booty was subsequently disposed of in

Savannah, the bell somehow found its way northward to the junction of the two Indian trails where Louisville eventually was founded. The bell was rung to assemble settlers when an Indian uprising was feared. It was also rung to celebrate the independence of the original 13 American colonies. Latterly the town's fire siren was sited there.

When Georgia was founded by General Edward Oglethorpe, Savannah became the capital of the new colony. As settlements expanded northward, the capital was moved to Augusta. In both places, the capitol buildings were adapted from existing edifices. When, in 1795 the capital was moved to Louisville, the state's first purpose-built Capitol was erected.

While the capital was Louisville, probably the most infamous incident in the state's history occurred – the "Yazoo Fraud". This was a land deal in which, ironically, a Senator from Louisville was a culprit. He and others conspired to sell land comprising huge areas of present day Alabama and Mississippi, for a pittance. The state of Georgia fought the deal all the way to the US Supreme Court, which held that the transaction was valid. Had Georgia retained its original territory, it would have been the fifth largest state today.

Louisville was one of many small towns to suffer the wrath of General Sherman's firebrands during their march from Atlanta to Savannah. One Union Army unit under General Slocum made Louisville its temporary headquarters and methodically burned the town's shops and other buildings, in the process destroying precious archives.

During my teenage years in Louisville the American South was known as the 'Bible belt'. There were few families, white or black, that did not attend church on Sunday. In my own family, all of us attended Sunday School as a matter of course. As an adolescent I was expected to stay on for the morning service as well.

At that time our Baptist preacher, known as 'Red' Marshall for his flaming red hair, was as much interested in politics as religion. If a controversial candidate or issue was in the news, Marshall found some way of working them into his sermons. He was fearless about taking sides, even if he knew the majority of the congregation was sometimes against him. Few dared to challenge his belief that politicians rule the world, and that it was the duty of clergymen to denounce leaders from the pulpit if he felt they did not measure up to accepted ideals of public service and morality.

It was as an adolescent that I, along with several other boys and girls of my age, were baptised at Louisville Baptist Church. The baptismal pit, adjacent to the altar, was several feet deep. None younger than teenagers were ever baptised.

Our minister at the time was the youthful Reverend Henry Stokes, fresh out of the United States Naval Academy where, as will be seen, his training to cope with maritime challenges was to stand him in good stead. I was not a good swimmer at the time and much afraid of deep water.

Thus, it was with some trepidation that I heard Reverend Stokes call my name. I slowly descended the steps into the pit and immediately found myself in about three feet of water with a lifebelt nowhere in sight. Before I could protest, the "triple-dip" began – one for the Father, one for the Son and one for the Holy Ghost. When Reverend Stokes was ready for the Holy Ghost, I was already spluttering and hardly able to get my breath. To put it mildly, I didn't want to be immersed a third time.

"Go down!" he ordered in a stern voice.

Fixing him with a crazed stare, I dropped like a stone, but although terrified, this time I was determined he should go down with me for protection. Unprepared for my sudden drop and tenacious grasp, he momentarily let his supporting arm slip. All the congregation could see were flailing arms and bobbing heads. Then, for a brief moment we both were lost to view. His Annapolis life-saving technique, however, saved the day and I was baptised for the first time and he the second.

In common with thousands of other American boys of our generation, my brother Floyd and I gloried in the mischief derived from the products of Johnson Smith and Company. This mail-order firm, based in Racine, Wisconsin, issued an annual catalogue of several hundred pages. Thousands of items were vividly illustrated and described.

The section on tricks and novelties was the largest, and it was there that many a boy let his imagination run wild as he attempted to emulate the mischief portrayed in the pages of the catalogue. There was a little leather disc that, when inserted in the roof of the mouth, was supposed to "throw" one's voice. No boy I knew ever managed the trick, but it wasn't for lack of trying.

Mothers and sisters were particularly vulnerable to Johnson and Smith's devices. There was a special crayon which marked a mirror as if it were cracked. When the naughty son dropped two pieces of metal which emitted a sound like breaking glass, the harassed mother rushed into the room to find her favourite mirror "cracked" from one side to another.

Sisters were terrified when their dinner plates, full of food, started moving up and down because of the inflatable rubber pad Junior had placed there before the meal. There were much naughtier tricks, like the small pile of fake dog faeces "deposited" on the living room carpet, and the gadget which let off unmentionable noises beneath the guest's cushion as he sat down for a meal. Floyd was more adept than I at choosing the most effective devices. Many of these he kept and used when his own children came along.

During my high school years (1932-36) it was impossible not to be aware of intense feelings generated by state politics. The central figure, as mentioned earlier, was the demagogue, "Gene" Talmadge. In appealing to the farmers who controlled elections in those days, he invoked the "devils" of Wall Street and wealthy Northerners (harking back to Civil War prejudices) to maintain his power. When the going became tougher, he added another – racial prejudice – to his stock of threats to the economic and cultural life of Georgians.

When Talmadge campaigned in Louisville, thousands of farmers from adjacent counties converged to hear him. Preceding his speech was a solo performance by the state's best known fiddle player, "Fiddlin' John" Carson. Carson was a cult figure in his own right, guaranteed to draw crowds of enormous size. When Talmadge advertised Carson's appearance, along with a free barbecue, crowds of 10,000 to 20,000 were common wherever he spoke. Although fascinated by Talmadge's cunning, I could never accept his emotional appeals to voters. Nonetheless, I freely availed myself of "Fiddlin' John's" lively music and the free barbecue and Brunswick stew served up on those occasions.

My interest in politics probably reached its height in my high school period. Apart from its rough and tumble aspects, state politics required a certain temperament and staying power that I lacked. The quieter realms of representing Georgians in Washington, however, much attracted me. I much admired our local representative in Congress, Carl Vinson. He had been elected time after time, usually with no opposition, and would continue to do so for many years to come.

Carl had been in office so long, as one friend told me, that he had "done a favour for everybody". Certainly my family knew of postmasters he had appointed, young men he had helped get into West Point or Annapolis, and numerous patronage jobs he had filled. In all these matters he seemed fair and just. He seldom missed a chance to become personally associated with his constituents and thus everyone had a good word for him.

An incident involving my family revealed his astuteness. One Christmas our family was returning from a visit to Atlanta when a drunken driver ran into our car, head-on, just outside Vinson's home town, Milledgeville. The driver was killed instantly and I suffered a broken wrist, but my little sister, Hope, seated between my parents on the front seat, was dashed against the gear lever – fracturing her skull.

For days she lingered between life and death, before recovering. During that time Carl Vinson visited my parents in hospital, having heard of the accident on the radio and realising that we were part of his constituent "family".

While still in high school I began corresponding with Vinson and in due course he provided me with a free subscription to the *Congressional Record* and, as well, complimentary copies of numerous other government publications of interest to me. I maintained my interest in becoming Congressman for our district until well after the end of the Second World War. But "Uncle Carl", as he was now known all over America, refused to retire or die, and went on to greater heights – becoming a friend of President Kennedy and having a giant aircraft carrier named after him. Friends who knew of my interest regarded Vinson as the most unbeatable member of the US Congress. There was no solution to my dilemma, for in US Congressional elections candidates must be residents of their respective constituencies. As Vinson obviously had no intention of resigning or dying and showed no sign of losing his vote-winning charm, I abandoned any thought of a future in politics. In retrospect I have never regretted that decision.

20
Snakes alive!

We were lucky to have an excellent weekly newspaper, *The News and Farmer*, in Louisville. It was edited by Virginia Polhill Price, whose "Blooming Beauties", was a widely read column of miscellaneous items gleaned from her many friends in the community. Frequently she wrote mini-essays on local events, bygone customs and humorous happenings. Some of these were reprinted in the prestigious Atlanta dailies. For many years Mrs. Price also was Georgia's committeewoman to the national conventions of the Democratic Party. In that capacity she came to meet President Franklin D. Roosevelt.

Virginia took a personal interest in my attempts at writing, and encouraged me to contribute little news items to *The News and Farmer* whenever I liked. When I told her I dreamed of being a country weekly newspaper editor myself one day, she smiled and said I should keep in touch.

I did not know it at the time, but my high school days were to be the last when radio would be king of the airwaves. There were many family-type shows whose principal characters were household names: Amos and Andy, Red Skelton, Lum and Abner, and Jack Benny, among them. Many a prominent entertainer was launched on Major Bowes's "Amateur Hour". And the concept behind the modern pop and country music charts goes back to Lucky Strike's weekly "Hit Parade" on which the top ten songs of the week were played.

My high school, Louisville Academy, was created by an act of the Georgia legislature in 1796. From its beginning the curriculum was oriented towards the classic subjects: Latin and Greek, advanced mathematics, English grammar and literature, science and history. Although some Georgia high schools had by then offered vocational courses in bookkeeping, agriculture, home economics, and basics of mechanics, these innovations had not been introduced at Louisville Academy during my time (1932-36).

The result was a massive dropout of gifted students who had no intention or hope of going to university. When I enrolled in high school there were just over 30 pupils. The fallout over the next four years was so great that only eight of us were graduated. Six of these went on to higher education, but it was tragic that the needs of the other students had not been addressed.

No black children then attended Louisville Academy or, as far as I know, ever had. This situation prevailed in virtually all of Georgia. Because there was a shortage of qualified black teachers, talented black pupils gained little from school attendance. Fortunately for black pupils in our area, a gifted educator, Charles C. McCollum, was named our county school superintendent. Although he did much to improve the quality of education in all of the county's schools, his special goal was to raise the qualifications of black teachers. He organised intensive summer school training for many, and others were sent to black colleges. By the end of his 15 years in office, some of the instructors in the county's black schools had university-level preparation for the first time.

Occasionally in our high school classes we touched upon the subject of racial inequality, but neither our teachers nor my fellow pupils had solutions. Our school principal, the Rev. Moffatt Plaxco (who was also the local Presbyterian minister), did confide to us that he was unhappy no black people attended his Sunday services (the only exception being the devout black church caretaker who sat by himself in the gallery).

In summer, when school was not in session, boys in my age group went to the school sports ground to play baseball. We divided ourselves into two teams and played many spirited games. Occasionally a few black boys turned up, ostensibly to watch, but clearly hoping for a chance to play.

I don't think we ever failed to ask them to join us but they were so apprehensive about their presence that they seldom remained for an entire game. Nonetheless they showed they were gifted athletes – so gifted that they could hit harder and run faster than most of my friends. They could not go on to higher sporting levels, however, for black athletes at that time were not allowed to play in baseball's big leagues.

One summer vacation I had what I thought a superb idea: making a boat trip down the Savannah River from Augusta to Savannah and back. There were times in the distant past when steamboats had operated on the river, taking both cargo and passengers. But the river was shallow in places and the cost of dredging expensive. What with competition from the railways and later from mammoth trucks, river transportation was considered uneconomic. Now, however (the early 1930s), the Pure Oil Company decided that it was viable to ship petroleum by barge from its Savannah terminal to Augusta.

Seeing myself as a modern-day Tom Sawyer, I wrote to the Pure Oil people and asked if they could allow me to make the return voyage, either as a paying passenger or a member of the crew. I added that I hoped to make notes and photographs which almost certainly would result in the company receiving favourable publicity in several Georgia newspapers. At first the company gave tentative approval, but when it later considered trade union objections and my personal safety, it turned down my request. I had built up such high hopes for this adventure that I was shattered when the letter of rejection arrived.

However pleasant were those carefree summers, autumn always brought us children down to earth with the start of the new school year. I knew I was nearing the time when I would seek admission to university. This meant I could no longer treat my studies casually, for admission depended in large part on the grades I earned. When my grandfather was headmaster of Louisville Academy, its curriculum included Greek. When I attended, Greek was gone and Latin and French had taken its place. We also had maths, English, history and science.

Although I found French easy, Latin was a nightmare. Had it not been for a senior student who took time to coach me, I would have failed it. Maths and science were also extremely difficult. Realisation of this made me aware that my future career did not lie in some technical field. I accepted that English grammar was necessary, even if boring, but English literature I enjoyed most of all because it introduced me to many American and British writers.

Two memories of those classroom days remain bright. In our French class we were told that the expletive "Mon Dieu!" was a mild one – no stronger than "Gosh" in English. One day when we were translating French, fellow student Mike Cox came across "Mon Dieu" for the first time. He had long since forgotten the expression was to be given little emphasis. As far as he was concerned, "My God!" meant a calamity of the direst sort.

Mike, always one to put vigour into his reading, hesitated only a moment when he came to "Mon Dieu". Then, drawing a deep breath, he shouted at the top of his voice: "My God!" Both those pupils who were attentive and those who had been dozing were startled out of their wits. But not for long, for soon they – together with our understanding teacher – cheered Mike for his literal translation.

In our English literature class Addison's and Steele's "Spectator" essays much impressed me and several of my classmates. The notion that two men could produce lively essays daily over several years, distribute them to London coffee houses and gain a national following, was an exciting concept. And how we felt for Sir Roger de Coverley as he suffered one mishap after another.

In the midst of our adulation for Addison and Steele, two of my friends and I decided to start up a school newspaper. As Addison and Steele had already used *The Spectator*, we employed the only other similar sounding word we could think of: *The Dictator*. After all, we were going to dictate to our fellow students what they should read!

Our journal contained little of literary value, but we did take care to present both sides of controversial issues. Whether or not the state of Georgia would allow beer to be legally sold was being widely debated at the time. On one page of *The Dictator* we editors decried the evil drink and the woe it might bring to affected families; on another we pointed out that the taxes received from beer sales would help schools (including our own) to be better financed. Was it our even-handed presentation, we wondered, that eventually led to such a close vote in our state?

Georgia was to remain 'dry' for several years more, but South Carolina (was it progressive or decadent?) voted to legalise the sale of beer. Our family, along with many another, wondered what that evil drink (it contained 3.2% alcohol!) was like.

There was only one way to satisfy our curiosity: drive to Augusta, whose Savannah River separated it from North Augusta, South Carolina, and taste the stuff. When my father's car crossed the river bridge, I was surprised to find South Carolina no different from Georgia. Except for a large sign saying "You are now entering South Carolina" we wouldn't have known it.

We soon found dozens of roadside shops with large signs: all said "BEER FOR SALE". My father pulled in at one, paid his money and we all waited our turn to sip the much-hyped liquid. My father pronounced it foul, my mother refused to put the bottle to her lips and I spat out the dreadful tasting beverage. My younger brothers and sister recoiled when offered the bottle. Eventually my father emptied the bottle through the car window. We drove home silently and thoughtfully, wondering what all the fuss had been about.

During our school holidays the place Floyd and I most cherished was the "good ol' swimmin' hole" in Rocky Comfort Creek on the western fringe of Louisville. The creek, which could reach terrifying heights during a flood, was then spanned by a steel bridge which, however frequent or violent the floods, remained proud and undamaged. When a car crossed over it there was an almighty metallic rumble which could be heard by people in their homes a mile away.

The path to our swimming hole lay to the right of the steel bridge along the bank of the creek. Although Floyd was four years younger, he already knew how the creek meandered until it eventually joined the nearby Ogeechee River. His knowledge of fishing and wildlife in the area was equally extensive, the latter being especially welcome to me for I knew the Rocky Comfort banks to be infested with rattlesnakes and "cotton-mouth" moccasins, both poisonous. En route from the steel bridge to the swimming hole, a distance of fifty yards or so, Floyd would constantly warn me to look carefully before stepping over logs.

"These are the favourite sunning places for snakes," he said "and while they seldom will attack you first, they will if you step too near them."

The swimming hole was just the right depth for us to dive without risking a broken neck. Even when the temperature was 100 degrees (Fahrenheit) or more, the old hole was refreshingly cool. Occasionally I would be basking on the surface of the slow-moving stream when Floyd would call out softly, "Better come back towards the bank – there's a moccasin swimming just behind you."

I never feared for my safety during these outings with Floyd. In the years that followed he added to his knowledge of our area, particularly his beloved Ogeechee River. There was not a bend or stretch of the stream for miles around that he did not know intimately. He studied the habits of reptiles, not from books but first-hand experience, so that he could unerringly tell where they were and how they would react when approached. Many times he captured large rattlesnakes and took them to my father's automotive premises where callers could view them in barrels.

Once Floyd acquired a toy snake, made of small pieces of wood, linked together loosely so when one gently swayed it, the "snake" wriggled and seemed lifelike. One day, after a quick visit to one of his Ogeechee River haunts, he returned with a small grass snake, almost the same colour and size of his wooden one.

On sunny days a few local men would take advantage of the shade in front of my father's business to sit for a while in one of the chairs there, swapping news and gossip and telling jokes. On one occasion Floyd nonchalantly wandered up and casually dropped the wooden snake into the lap of one of the locals. Pandemonium followed and chairs were knocked over as the men leapt to their feet to avoid what they believed to be a live snake. When they saw it was only a toy, great laughter and teasing followed after which all resumed their seats.

Floyd then disappeared to the rear of the premises and picked up the look-alike grass snake and made his way back to the idling men. Again he sauntered up to them, only this time – with knowing glints in their eyes – they told him they wouldn't be fooled a second time. Floyd said nothing, but produced the live snake and carefully dropped it onto the lap of one of the most self-assured men.

Having been taken in once, the man picked up what he was sure to be the same toy snake, intending to throw it back at my brother. As soon as he felt the body of the wriggling live snake and saw its unhappy spitting, he let out a tremendous yell and fell over backwards in his chair while his companions scattered in all directions. Floyd calmly chased the creature, picked it up with his bare hands and assured everyone it was harmless. He was to employ variations of this trick several times before the supply of innocent victims dried up.

Little did Floyd or I realise that those carefree days were soon to come to an end and that a world war would see us in uniform on opposite sides of the globe. Never again would we enjoy those visits to the old swimming hole.

Among my high school classmates at Louisville Academy was a lovely girl named Van. I asked her what Van stood for and she replied: "Savannah -- my parents named me for the river and city." So impressed was I with the beauty of Indian words of Georgia's rivers that I decided I would give all my children these lovely names. After all, hadn't Senator Bankhead from Alabama named his actress daughter Tallulah after the Gorge and Waterfalls of the same name?

That notion sent me rushing to a map of Georgia to see how extensive my possibilities would be. After all, Grandpa Mays had 12 children; I might do the same or better. How delightful it would be to have little ones running about the house with lovely names like Canoochie, Ohoopee, Toccoa, Chestatee, Chatooga and Suwanee!

Then, as I discovered more Indian names of rivers, I realised I had to be careful. My little girls might never forgive me if I named them Withlacoochee, Coosawather, Tallapoosa or Ochlockonee.

I need not have bothered about those lovely Indian names. My wife was to have ideas of her own.

21
George Washington Carver, the "Peanut Man"

As had happened at my elementary school in Millen, so, too, did Louisville Academy invite prominent speakers for our weekly school assemblies. The two most memorable were Jeannette Rankin and George Washington Carver.

Jeannette Rankin was the first woman to be elected to the US Congress. Her home state was Montana, but she quickly became a national figure through her vigorous promotion of women's voting rights. She later took up other causes, among them world peace, and was the only member of the House of Representatives to vote against the American declaration of war in 1941. She spoke to us on several of her causes, emphasising the need for women to take a more active role in American political life.

George Washington Carver was the son of Missouri slaves. His owner, Moses Carver, a German immigrant, gave the boy his name. George was a good student and eventually attended Iowa State College where he earned both bachelor's and master's degrees in agricultural science. At the age of 32 he was invited by the prominent black educator, Booker T. Washington, to direct Tuskeegee University's agricultural research programme. This field was to become his life's work. Among his research achievements were 118 products derived from the sweet potato and over 300 from the peanut.

When Carver spoke to us in his high-pitched voice, we students sat enthralled. We gaped with disbelief as he displayed product after product he had made from the lowly peanut. During his inspiring talk he urged farmers of the South (among whose sons and daughters there were many in our school) to drop their traditional dependency on cotton and diversify their output into peanuts and other crops. (In his wildest dreams he would not have imagined that one Georgia peanut farmer, Jimmy Carter, would one day become President of the United States.)

At the end of his presentation Carver invited us to come up to the stage and see the product samples he had brought along. We all rushed forward to see his soaps, oils and other products.

In my last year of high school I became an avid SWL (short-wave listener) and spent many hours at night tuning in to both amateur radio ('hams') and commercial radio stations all over the world. I posted my attractive SWL. card to each foreign station I 'captured' on the short-wave band of the family radio, and was thrilled to receive, in return, pictorial confirmation cards from many lands – among them one showing the BBC's bank of transmission towers at Daventry.

Those high-school years were wonderfully stimulating. It seemed there was no end of knowledge to be acquired and new horizons to be explored. It was only in the field of sports that I had to impose limitations on myself. I was tall enough and heavy enough to play on the Academy football team, but every time I decided to try for the team I was haunted by the words of the eye specialist: "If you injure your only good eye, you will effectively be blind for the rest of your life!"

Of all the sensory gifts, sight is the one people most dread to lose. In the end I decided to forego football and do my utmost in the school's only other competitive sport – track and field athletics. In my first three years of high school I mastered the basic techniques of throwing the discus. In the Spring term of my senior year my weight reached 140 pounds and at last my throws of the discus reached respectable distances. Moreover, our Academy team boasted enough good athletes in other events to give the school a fighting chance of winning our regional competition – winners of which would automatically qualify for the Georgia State Meet.

As our school had won the regional meet for the previous three years, hopes were high that we could do it again. Dr. Ramsey, our local pharmacist, offered to give every member of our team an ice cream sundae if we won. He was amazed, but pleased, when we all marched into the Louisville Drug Store to receive our treats after winning seven of the ten first places – my discus event being one of them.

Entering the State Meet in Athens would oblige us to stay overnight in a hotel in Athens, on whose University of Georgia track we would perform. As the school had no funds for this kind of outlay, we were faced with the possibility of not taking part until someone remembered the manager of Athens's largest hotel had once been the proprietor of Louisville's only hotel. A hurried phone call and – miracles of miracles – he would allow all seven of us to sleep in the same room if we were up to it! With wall to wall mattresses, plus twin beds, we slept like logs. Alas, we did not win the State Meet, but were placed a respectable fourth – I being the only first place winner with the discus. Although I was never to play a game of football for the Academy, I hoped my state medal in the discus would, in a small way, redeem my honour.

When the meet was over, Athens' "Put" Palmisano, kindly let us transmit our results back to Louisville (and throughout Georgia!) on his ham radio.

A dramatic incident in my last year of high school was to ensure that I would never again be superstitious. Like many another youngster in the rural South, I had accumulated an assortment of superstitions. The number 13 was the most common one. Walking under a ladder was another and so was a black cat crossing one's path. Inside the home, minor superstitions sometimes could be nullified by tossing salt over one's left shoulder.

One day during school 'recess' (the compulsory outdoor play period) one of my classmates spotted fire coming from the chimney of a house just opposite the school. All the boys immediately abandoned their games and raced to the house with the intention of rescuing the family and its belongings. When we reached the house the occupants were already aware of the fire and had telephoned the local fire department.

The family had been trying to remove the most valuable contents just before we arrived. They agreed we boys could remove the furniture, beginning on the upper floor where the fire was, and then continue downstairs. We calculated it would take the fire-fighting appliances at least ten minutes to arrive and in that time most of the upper floor would be consumed. Dividing into teams of two boys each, we set to clearing the rooms, starting with the room where the fire was erupting from the chimney. Luckily, the fire seemed confined to the chimney so we did not panic as we removed the furniture.

My schoolmates and I congratulated ourselves on how quickly a group of 20 boys could clear a room. We listened for the sound of the approaching fire engines, but they were not yet within earshot. Then my co-worker and I slowed our frantic pace to gingerly pick up a dressing table with a large mirror attached. It was all we could do, between us, to wriggle it around the bends of the staircase. Then, suddenly, we miscalculated a turn and the mirror crashed into the banisters.

With horror we saw the huge mirror had been cracked from top to bottom. The same thought passed through both our minds at the same moment: breaking a mirror was one superstition guaranteed to bring the offender appalling bad luck. As other boys were behind us waiting to descend with their pieces of furniture, we did not have time to commiserate with each other.

Once we had reached the garden and deposited the dressing table, we viewed the damage we had caused. At that moment the owner of the house arrived and saw our crest-fallen faces. With true magnanimity, he said breaking the mirror was of little consequence and that the important thing was that we boys were saving his possessions.

My friend and I smiled. Then we professed to each other that, henceforth, we would never be superstitious again. It was as if a great cloud had been lifted from our shoulders. Never again would I give even a passing thought to all those constraints that had previously marked my life. Our good deed on that memorable day had somehow exorcised all concern about superstition. The episode ended happily for the home owner, too, for the firemen managed to confine the fire to the chimney.

Increasingly during my high school years I had become imbued with a strong sense of duty, almost like that of a missionary, to serve my fellow citizens. Just how I might put my idealism into action was then unclear, but I felt the university years that lay ahead might point the way. Having been born on a farm and grown up in small towns, I felt a strong urge to identity with rural Georgia. On the other hand, my fondness for geography and the French language also drew my thoughts toward the international scene, albeit only vaguely.

Concluding that journalism was then exerting the greatest impact on my career aspirations, I decided to apply for admission to the University of Georgia's school of journalism. Acceptance turned out to be not a problem as my high school grades were of sufficient standard to guarantee entry.

The greatest worry was how my parents and I could find the money necessary to finance my freshman year. Between us we did not have anything like the $400 required for tuition, room and board. Fortunately all the money would not be needed at once, for the university year was divided into semesters and payments could be made in instalments.

We just managed to scrape up the means to cover costs for my first term. That would take me up to Christmas, but what would happen after that? My parents and I both knew that we had little prospect of finding money for my remaining time. Would my university education be short-lived, or would some miracle occur to allow me to continue? I could only hope and pray.

22
Free meals!

Enrolling in a university of 3,000 students, after 18 years spent in rural Georgia, was an overwhelming experience, to say the least.

Apart from the ever-present concern over where I would find the necessary money after my first semester, there were other – more immediate – worries when I arrived in Athens in early September, 1936.

For the first time in my life I felt grown up, alone and bewildered. There were many unanswered questions. I would be living in Candler Hall, but in which room? More important, who would be my roommates? I knew there would be three other students, for the cheapest rate applied only to those students who agreed to sleep four to the room.

While personal living arrangements loomed high on my list of concerns, there were more serious ones that were almost frightening. Which additional courses would I take other than those in journalism? In which buildings of the far-flung campus would they be taught? How many textbooks would I need, and what if I did not have enough money to buy them all? My "wardrobe" was virtually non-existent: a single suit with a few extra shirts and trousers. What if a certain standard of dress was required?

The tedious administrative processing completed, I made my way slowly towards the campus dining hall, known as "The Beanery" among students. I soon found myself abreast of another bewildered student who, I was sure, had to be a freshman like me. I introduced myself and to my surprise, learned he came from a small town, Vidette, in neighbouring Burke County, only 20 minutes drive from my hometown of Louisville.

He was Paul Rowland and like me, had signed up to live in Candler Hall. We quickly decided we would room together, if possible. This turned out to be the first psychological break-through for us, and thereafter we were better able to face up to the difficulties we later encountered. We agreed that when one of us learned the answer to a problem, he would pass it on to the other.

Paul and his two younger brothers made up 60% of Vidette's

high school basketball team which won several championships in our region of Georgia. In the ensuing years, Paul was to be joined by one brother and then the other – all of us living in room 12 at Candler Hall.

The Beanery sold meal vouchers which allowed students to choose what they wished. We quickly learned that meat could quickly consume one's entire budget in a short time, and so Paul and I, along with many other hard-up students, frequently selected vegetables or less expensive dishes such as macaroni and cheese. We all knew there was no more money forthcoming from our parents and if we wished to improve our quality of life, the means had to be found at the university – not from our families.

While eating our first meal we saw several students helping to clear and clean the tables. When the meal was over, we asked the manager if he needed other students to help in The Beanery. To our surprise and joy, he responded "Yes". Later, after referring to our class schedules, Paul and I were taken on to help with a certain number of meals each week. We received no money, but were allowed to eat our fill of anything and everything we could consume at our designated meals. We both proved to be reliable, willing workers and thus were able to earn many free meals during our university years.

Although Paul was enrolled in the College of Agriculture, we found that for the first two years – in common with other freshmen – we had to take basic courses in English and the social sciences. Once into the last two years of our study we would be allowed to take courses in our specialised fields.

An annoying feature of these "survey" courses, as they were officially called, was the large number of students in each class. Most had 60 to 70, and a few even exceeded one hundred. There were few opportunities for questions and almost all written examinations were the true-false and multiple-choice types I had been introduced to in Savannah. When we first sat these exams, Paul and I felt we had scored something like 80 to 90% correct answers, and so were inwardly pleased that our high school work had apparently prepared us well for these university courses.

My shock in finding that I had failed the first test, even with something like 85% correct answers, left me furious. Paul fared only slightly better. We then discovered that grading at that time was based on an infamous system known as "The Curve"', whereby a small, set percentage of students would receive grades of "A", slightly more "B" and a similar number, "C". The grade of "D" was just passable, and all the rest received an "F" for failure. What was the rationale behind a grading system, we wondered, whereby a student with 85% of his examination answers correct, could receive a failing grade?

Our moans and groans were heard by some of the older students in Candler Hall who promptly told us the only way to beat the system was to cheat. Cheating may have been practised in some of the state's large high schools, but among the small rural schools such as Paul and I attended, it was unknown.

The older students smiled understandingly, for most of them, too, had come from rural backgrounds and appreciated our dilemma.

"Look at it this way," explained one fourth-year student. "If the university will not arrange either smaller classes or essay-type questions on exams, then we have the right to resort to any means to obtain passing grades – especially when we know most of the correct answers and that is not good enough to merit a passing grade. What's more, if your instructor wasn't so lazy, he would develop original tests every semester. That way, you would never know what would be included in an exam. As it stands, we know most of these exams are unchanged, semester after semester."

Being freshmen, the last thing we wanted was to be sent home in disgrace after failing our very first courses. But neither did we want to be sent home for cheating! What to do?

Although both the grading system and our solution to beat it were immoral, we reluctantly agreed to go along with the cheating. This practice had gone on for some years and involved someone obtaining a copy of each upcoming examination and then passing it around to freshmen students to memorise.

There were several ways of getting copies of exams, the most common being for a student, sitting in a row of seats, to pocket his examination paper and immediately claim he had not received a copy. The instructor invariably gave him another. This trick did not help with the exam being given, but would be useful for the following term. Another device was to get the student assistant who printed the examinations in the administrative office to run off extra copies.

Thus the night before these exams, we would gather in a student's room where a "master copy" of the correct answers was available. A student would call out the answers to, say, the 50 true-false questions, shouting "Numbers 1, 4, 5, 9, 11, 12 etc., are false." We wrote down those numbers and later memorised them, knowing the numbers not memorised were true. Similarly, with the multiple-choice questions, all we had to memorise was the correct letter among the "a", "b" and "c" choices. Apprehensive at first, we soon mastered this art and had no difficulty in obtaining passable grades. Sadly, knowing we had to cheat to survive left us with little inclination to pay attention to the instructors' words.

Fortunately, the number of those crowded survey courses was small. Even so, a hard-working instructor could have prevented cheating in his class. One conscientious young professor from Wisconsin never gave true-false or multiple-choice exams.

Instead, he assigned us essays in which each of us was encouraged to write solutions to the many problems facing Georgia and the South at that time. Although his classes were very large, he always took pains to read our papers and make detailed comments about them. My own desire to contribute in some way toward improving the life of my fellow Georgians received a great impetus from this one young, idealistic professor.

23
The Kangaroo Court metes out "justice"

Whatever woes we encountered in our classrooms or elsewhere on the campus, my roommates and I could be sure of a warm reception when we returned to our "home" dormitory, Candler Hall. Apart from being united by a common degree of poverty, we freshmen banded together as we groped our way through academic life and that peculiarly American institution of "hazing" (initiation) known as a "Kangaroo Court".

In my day the custom of upperclassmen making life intolerable for freshmen was firmly rooted in much of American higher education. While administrators turned a blind eye to hazing of male students, most ensured women students were not put at risk. Indeed, in some small colleges and universities, hazing was entirely harmless. In some larger ones (especially the state universities), serious injuries and the occasional death occurred.

Hazing in Candler Hall (and in other similar dormitories) took several forms. One required us to respect our bottom-of-the-pecking-order position as freshmen by always wearing our red caps, not walking *through* but *around* the Georgia Arch – the main entrance to the campus – and always addressing and responding to upperclassmen with "Sir". These formalities were nothing compared to two other, sometimes dreaded initiation rituals: the annual "shirt-tail parade" and a mass hair-cutting, popularly known as "scalping".

The shirt-tail parade usually began at the Arch and continued through several streets in Athens' business and residential districts. We freshmen arrived at the Arch fully dressed, but were instantly required to remove our trousers. Holding these in one hand, we were made to march or jog through the streets – much to the amusement of spectators along the way. Upperclass "shepherds" closely guarded their flock just in case an errant freshman tried to break away down a side street. Most of us were not bothered by this parading of semi-nudity in public, but a few deeply introverted students were mortified.

The mass cutting of hair was quite another matter. This practice by upperclassmen had been dormant for several years, but was reinstituted with great vigour for our freshman class. All the first-year students from my dormitory and several others were herded together and marched to a dormitory on "Ag Hill", that part of the campus then occupied mainly by the College of Agriculture.

There, over a period of several hours, we freshmen had our hair shorn amid much good humour and the occasional unchecked tears. There was no intent to simply make us all look like skin-heads; that would have been dull, indeed. Instead our expert barbers outdid themselves by producing every permutation imaginable: right side shorn off, left side shorn off, front shorn off, back shorn off, zig-zag patterns, Apache cuts, knots in the middle or to one side, Friars' rings, and so on.

My roommates and I considered the shearing a great joke, but forsome students – vainer than us – the thought of losing their hair until

Christmas was more than they could bear. Some parents (but none whose sons lived in Candler Hall) made strong representations to the University administrators and the practice was prohibited thereafter.

The most colourful and frequent form of initiation was the Kangaroo Court, an institution that evoked both joy and fear in our freshmen hearts. It was called without warning, but seldom before 11p.m. when most students would be sure to be in their rooms. Assembled in the dormitory's reception room, it was usually presided over by the dormitory proctor, a senior student responsible to university authorities for student welfare. He could, if he wished, delegate his authority to other upperclassmen.

Court started with the roll-call, in which each freshman answered to his name with a resounding "Sir". Woe to any first-year student who did not appear. He would be sought out, routed from his hiding place, and dragged before the Court to receive his punishment. The punishment was uniform: so many licks from a ping-pong bat or blows from an upperclassman's belt. What mattered to us was *how many* blows we received, for we knew some "punishment" was inevitable.

The "judges", however, usually took into account the robustness of a student's body and the penalty meted out was accordingly adjusted. Indeed, some "judges" were law students who in later life were prominent in Georgia's judiciary.

The "trials" were fascinating psychological events in which justice was often seen to be done – however farcical the "charges". We all knew there would never be a question addressed to us that would allow us to escape a beating. Neither a "Yes" or a "No", nor an impressive reply made the slightest difference. The only way a freshman could be guaranteed to receive minimal treatment was to be good-natured and respectful of his superiors.

Physical resistance seldom occurred and, if it did, heavyweight upperclassmen were called on to administer "appropriate" punishment. Neither was arrogance tolerated. In all this mental sparring, the freshman before the court was aware that not only upperclassmen were judging him, but also his freshman peers. In short, impressions formed in these courts frequently revealed human strengths and foibles that were to be lifelong.

"Freshman," the judge begins, "tell us your name."

"Henry Peterson."

"Five licks!" roars the judge, to the disbelief of the student.

"Now, once more, freshman, what's your name?"

Again the same reply, and another five lashes with the belt. Then someone whispers to the dumbstruck freshman.

"For the third time, freshman, what's your name?"

The good-natured Peterson beams:

"Henry Peterson, *sir*!"

Everyone smiles except the stern judge.

"Correct, freshman, but wipe that smile off your face." Peterson quickly wipes his hand across his face, extinguishing his ready smile.

"And remember next time to say "Sir!" when an upperclassman addresses you. Now, next freshman, please."

The next freshman meekly steps forward, knowing whatever he is asked and whatever he replies, he will be lashed.

"Freshman," drones the judge in his deepest voice, "I have just one question to put to you and I want a simple, straightforward answer. Do you understand?"

"Yes, sir," replies the doomed freshman.

"Good. Then tell me why does a door knob?"

All except the student burst into laughter. His forehead wrinkles, but he cannot think of an appropriate answer – silly or otherwise. He starts to stammer something, but he is too late.

"Freshman," intones the judge in his sternest voice, "he who hesitates is lost. Give that man ten licks!"

The freshman grins broadly, knowing he cannot beat the system. The ten lashes are administered almost gently.

Our judges relished dealing with cases of excess vanity, and there were always some among our number. In many Southern families, sons were given the identical names of their fathers, grandfathers, and great-grandfathers. This was often confusing, for three generations bearing the same name were often alive and there could be problems in dealing with telephone calls and correspondence – not to speak of articles in the press.

Among our group was one such, who had best be remembered as John Milledge McIntosh IV. Not only did his name sound regal, but his bearing and manner let it be known to all that the *Mayflower* must have made an unscheduled stop at Savannah to allow his blue-blooded forebears to get off.

"Who's next?" demands the judge.

"I am," says the would-be aristocrat, standing proudly and forgetting the previous student's experience.

"My deah, deah fellow," mimicks the judge in measured tone, "you seem to come of a good family, but were you nevah, nevah taught to respect your superiors?"

The freshman is trapped. In reality his manners were usually impeccable, but he hardly considered the judge, or anyone else present, his equal. But he knew he couldn't say so.

"I – I wasn't thinking," he stammers, quickly adding the "Sir" at the end.

"Ah, my good man," says the judge, with a sorrowful look on his face, "but that's exactly why your deah, deah, deah parents sent you to this great, *great* u-ni-ver-si-tee – to teach you to think!"

Amid the laughter which follows there is a growing hope among us that humility will grow on this student who previously could be described only as "being stuck on himself". But our hopes were slightly premature.

"Well, now," says the judge, "what about trying hard to think what your name is."

"John Milledge McIntosh IV," replies the student, proudly.

"My God!" exclaims the judge, "the freshman thinks he is King!"

Another outburst of laughter during which the student manages a feeble grin.

"Well," says the judge solemnly, "the punishment has to meet the crime. Let's see, John Milledge McIntosh IV (he dwells deliberately on the IV), four times five makes 20 – yes, 20 licks for the Freshman King, please, and another five for not saying 'Sir!'."

The appointed "executioner" duly administers the penalty, but not with malice. At last the freshman arises, this time wearing an understanding smile. John Milledge McIntosh IV has passed his Kangaroo Court baptism with flying colours. He retires into the background, secretly elated that he seems to have been accepted.

Our dormitory, Candler Hall, was one of several whose residents entered the annual cross-country "Cake Race". In this race students had to run a course of about 3½ miles on the minor roads of the sprawling university campus. The first 20 students received layer cakes of assorted flavours, compliments of the university's athletics department. As most of us could not afford the luxury of cake with our meals, here was our chance to taste cake at least once during the year. Most able-bodied Candler Hall students entered the event and many of us managed to get into the top 20. We proudly returned to the dorm with our hard-earned prizes which we happily shared with the others.

Our only other culinary largesse came one autumn when a long refrigerator train, en route from Florida to New York laden with thousands of crates of oranges, was derailed just outside Athens. Word quickly spread among the students, and our professors wondered why their classrooms emptied so suddenly. Virtually the whole of Candler Hall turned out for the fruity expedition. Railway authorities made no effort to stop us, for it was uneconomic for them to save the spilled fruit. Never before or since have I eaten so many oranges in such a short time.

24
"Dean Will", our faithful friend

Apart from the Kangaroo Court and our occasional sports triumphs, the greatest boost to Candler Hall's *esprit de corps* came from a remarkable black man, "Dean Will" Thurmond, the dormitory janitor. Dubbed "Dean Will" many years before, he was universally loved. A short, thin man with an ageless face, he had many tasks. Foremost was cleaning students' rooms and lavatories, checking for broken furniture and windows, and insuring that we always had hot water daily and heating in winter.

Candler Hall's rooms had no carpets, making it difficult for Dean Will to clean between the cracks of the floorboards. One student who had punched holes in his writing paper to enable it to be bound, unthinkingly let fall onto the floor the dozens of punched-out paper discs. When Dean Will entered the room and saw the student not using the waste-paper basket, he stood erect with his broom and delivered a reprimand worthy of the sternest general. Remaining silent until the tirade was over, we stood up and cheered when he finished. The chastised student knelt down and picked up every one of the paper discs. Thereafter we took great care not to add unnecessarily to Will's many chores.

We looked upon Dean Will not only as someone who helped tidy our rooms, but as a friend, confidant and, occasionally, philosopher. If one of us had a broken love affair, was homesick or did badly in examinations, he listened sympathetically, then stood thoughtfully for a moment before uttering one of his famous one-liners. The one he is most remembered for and which covered almost any student problem was "It's a great life if you don't weaken."

Will closely followed Georgia's football team, whether playing at home or away. Freshmen were responsible for tolling the great bell behind the University Chapel the moment a Georgia victory was known. Home wins were quickly known by the tremendous roars erupting from Sanford Stadium, but news of away victories came only from listening to a sometimes weak signal over our radio sets. Dean Will, who had his own radio in the bowels of the dormitory, was always the first to reach the bell and start the joyous ringing. We freshmen never begrudged Will's early arrival; indeed, we would have thought some disaster had befallen him if he wasn't at the head of the line. But Will's love of football was not confined to Georgia's varsity team.

Candler Hall had a long-standing rivalry with its neighbouring dormitory, Old College. Both dorms were largely occupied by students from low-income families, but once a year we engaged in a bitterly fought football game. The university athletic department generously let us use helmets, padding, shoes and other football gear that had long since seen its best days. The game was played on a practice field where the only spectators were the non-playing residents of the two halls.

In all these games Dean Will rushed onto the field when there was a time-out for injury or much-needed rest. His pail of refreshing water was always welcome, but he would also lend a hand in reviving a player who had been knocked out of breath or hit in a vulnerable spot. He was to us not only water-boy but trainer, doctor and, most of all, inspirer in our moments of adversity.

Will never refused a sip of whiskey when we celebrated special occasions, such as a football victory or someone's birthday. He was an excellent 'buck dancer', but would not perform unless we ceased our homework and paid strict attention. Often we would sneak next door to invite neighbouring dorm mates. Once he was assured of a reasonable audience he would let fly with a dazzling display of dancing which belied his ageing legs. Tears would come into his eyes when we applauded loud and long.

25
Getting a lift in a cross-country race

Track and field athletics had always been my favourite sport and the year I entered the University of Georgia, 1936, was an auspicious one. That August in Berlin, the university's great 110-metre high hurdler, Forrest (Spec) Towns, set a new Olympic record in his event with a time of 14.1 seconds.

In the Berlin Olympics another University of Georgia athlete, sprinter Bobby Packard, did well in his preliminary heat, but later was eliminated. The star of the Berlin Games was America's Jesse Owens, who won four gold medals. Adolph Hitler, on hand mainly to applaud victories by German athletes, instead saw Owens take medal after medal. Ironically, the 1936 Games were the last before the Second World War and it was the host country, Germany, which would propel the world into the conflict.

Towns and Packard formed the nucleus of the university's outstanding track and field team the following year. As a freshman discus thrower I had the opportunity to meet the two Olympians and other members of the Georgia team. Towns continued to win his hurdles event in major championships and "relays" meetings. I had an interesting conversation with him that reveals how far the world of sport has moved from those days when an effort was made to retain the amateur status of winning athletes.

Although athletes at that time could have their travel expenses and accommodation paid for by meeting organisers, cash could not be paid. Instead the winners received expensive prizes, such as gold watches. I had heard that Towns had several watches and was thinking of selling one. He then explained to me that one good watch would last a lifetime, so what need had he for an extra one or two? The obvious answer was to sell them, yet the notion seemed somehow crude at the time.

I also became a member of the university's freshman cross-country team, coached that year by the Dean of Freshmen, William Tate. He had entered the University in 1920 and eventually joined the faculty of a well known boys' school, McCallie, in Chattanooga, from which he was recruited to return to his alma mater. He became a legendary character, in part because his encyclopaedic memory allowed him instantly to recognise and name every freshman in the university. Indeed, after four years he could identify every male student on campus.

During my second year of study, Dean Tate entered a class I was attending and asked the instructor if he could speak to me privately. I was shocked at this sudden arrival and assumed some catastrophe had befallen me, although what I could not remotely imagine. He then informed me that my mother had just come through an operation for breast cancer at Emory University Hospital and that she was now out of danger. As my parents had kept news of the illness from me, I at first was shocked to learn about the operation and, afterwards, elated that it had gone well.

Dean Tate, seeing my state, suggested I retrieve my notebook and leave with him. This I did and, as we walked back slowly towards his office, he explained that my parents clearly had my interest at heart by keeping the illness secret until the operation was over. He left by saying that surgeons worked marvels and that my mother might now live a normal life for many years to come. She, in fact, did live another 20 years before succumbing to the cancer.

Tate often practiced with the freshman cross-country team, no easy task, for he had put on considerable weight since his student days. Long distance running was not to be my forte, but there was one memorable race in Atlanta against the University of Georgia's arch rival, Georgia Tech, that almost earned me fame. The race took place along several streets adjacent to the campus of Georgia Tech, and ended near the football stadium, Grant Field.

As the slowest runner in the race, I soon lost contact with those in front and, to my dismay, realised I had no idea where the Tech campus was. At that stage of the race I was running on a street served by street cars and, as luck would have it, I saw one gaining on me from behind. I waved at the driver and he stopped and asked the problem. I told him I was lost, had to get to Tech campus, but had no money.

"Jump aboard," he said, grinning. I clambered up, to the mirth of elegantly dressed ladies on their way home after visiting shops in downtown Atlanta. After a few minutes, the driver pointed out the Tech football stadium. He stopped, I thanked him, and away I sped.

Now considerably refreshed, I saw I was quickly gaining on the rear runners now just ahead of me. With a great burst of speed – more like that in the 100-yard dash than cross-country – I managed to overtake several of the weary runners. Alas, my final burst was not enough to earn me or my team points, for the Georgia Tech squad was much superior to ours. One or two of my team-mates did ask how I managed that tremendous spurt at the end. I smiled and said, "Circumstance, pure circumstance."

26
The pimply, bow-legged bride

There were not many American universities with faculties for teaching journalism in 1936 when I enrolled at the University of Georgia. Ours was called the Henry W. Grady School of Journalism in honour of the legendary editor of *The Atlanta Constitution* who, when Georgia and the South were still reeling from the physical and economic effects of the Civil War, urged Southerners to put the conflict behind them and adopt progressive measures to bring about a "New South".

Our school was headed by Dean John Drewry who was regarded as the best book reviewer in the state of Georgia. Also an able lecturer and administrator, he was held in high regard by the newspaper and magazine fraternity nationally and by other leaders in journalism education.

A native Georgian, Drewry shocked some of our class when he announced – in his characteristic southern drawl – that if we had come to "Mr. Grady's School" to learn how to write, we were to be sorely disappointed. If we didn't already have that nose for a good story – news, feature or otherwise – and the ability to put it into words, it was too late. He went on to say the school could teach us techniques that would improve our standard of writing but that inner competence had to be already there. Naturally we all assumed we had it.

Some may question whether the study of journalism ("media studies") is worthy of inclusion in a university's academic programme. It is still viewed by some British and European universities as a "frill" but this overlooks the growth and importance of the printed page, radio and television in our age. There are tens of thousands of newspapers, magazines and local radio stations in the Western World and television networks that span the globe. Surely a case can be made that professional training of people in this field must be a good thing.

Some of my classmates and I at first viewed writing news stories and journalism as one and the same thing. It did not take us long to realise there were many kinds of writers: news, editorial, feature, advertising copy, radio and television, financial, society, travel, agricultural, book and theatre reviewers and sports – to name but a few. Of these, Dean Drewry added, sports writing provided the best training for advancement because it required the writer to deal with the vocabularies of many different sports to become successful. He then reeled off the names of several prominent American editors, our own Ralph McGill of the *Atlanta Constitution* among them, who started out as sports writers.

Dean Drewry stirred our egos when he asked if we dreamed of seeing our by-lines above newspaper articles one day. When we all readily said "Yes", he stopped us short by saying newspapers gave by-lines for two reasons. The first was because the article was well written and the journal was proud to display the writer's name above it. The other, he added, was for the opposite reason: if the paper had doubts about the quality or style of the article, a by-line was one way of disassociating itself from the writer.

Our courses ranged from the history of journalism in the United States to the latest techniques in radio broadcasting, including hints of the world of television that would erupt in the future. We learned about William Randolph Hearst and other press barons, but it was the rural newspaper editor who most interested me. Libel laws were also of great interest to those of us who one day might dare to enter the dangerous business of investigative journalism.

In news writing we were given the bare facts about such dramatic events as the sinking of the *Titanic*, the Great Fire of Chicago and the assassination of President Lincoln. The facts were jumbled up in no particular order; we had to rearrange them and come up with a story so vividly written as to suggest we had been present. Easily the most moving story was the Mary Phagan trial of 1913, in which a Brooklyn Jew, Leo Frank, brought to Atlanta to manage a pencil factory, was accused and found guilty of killing a teenage girl employee. The prosecutor, aspiring to higher office, fed the popular press with anti-Semitic innuendos about Frank while conveniently ignoring other suspects who might have committed the crime. Eventually a mob took Frank from his prison cell and lynched him.

Dean Drewry also had a sheaf of badly written news, feature articles and editorials. At first, we could not see the faults in some of these pieces, so imperfect was our own judgement at the time. One "how-*not*-to-write" story was this 1934 account of a wedding written with utmost frankness, which was supposed to have appeared in a rural weekly paper:

THE BRIDE HAD PIMPLES AND BOW LEGS

"Walter J. Evansby and Mary Louise Murphy were married in St. Charlie's Church last Friday evening at 5:30 o'clock. The church was filled with the usual crowd of curiosity seekers who wanted to avail themselves of the opportunity of criticising the dresses, flowers and everything connected with the ceremony.

"The ushers were Hiram Higginbottom, proprietor of Higginbottom's Grocery Store, and Alfred Jarvis, manager of the Aristocrat Filling Station, corner of Jones and O'Brien Streets. The bridesmaids were Martha Wippets, in charge of the perfume department at Woolworth's and Myrtle Sosonby of the Kute Little Beauty Shoppe. The dame of honour was Mrs. Euclid Simpson who was divorced from her husband three weeks ago. He got drunk one night and beat her up, so she sued him and was awarded a verdict.

"The bride entered with her father, Horace Murphy, of Murphy's Up-to-Date Plumbing Shop. The old man was grinning from ear to ear and he had a right to be. Mary Louise is 27 years old and he was beginning to think that he was going to have to keep her up for the rest of her natural life. He was dressed in a suit which he had borrowed from his brother, Jake. Jake used to clerk for the Bon Ton Department Store but he's been out of work for the last three weeks.

"The bride was making a determined effort to appear nervous, but she couldn't quite make the grade. Triumphant would express it better. To tell the truth, she didn't look so hot. Plenty of rouge and powder had been used but these and other cosmetics couldn't quite conceal her pimply expression. Her dress, of white crepe, was rather long, and it's a good thing it was because she is inclined to be rather bow-legged. Always has been, from a child. Her feet were shod in white satin slippers, size 7, although she told everybody before the wedding they were 5's, but really they weren't.

"The groom was attended by his best man, Gerald Jimson, who looked rather glum about the whole business. As a matter of fact Gerald had lent Walter $25 to help defray the expenses of the wedding and he realised that he stood a damn slim chance of ever getting his money back. However, he and Walter had been friends since their boyhood days, so there was nothing he could do about it.

"The ceremony was performed by the Reverend Stanley O'Brien, who wasn't in particularly good humour either. Walter had called on him in his study, just prior to the ceremony and had presented him with two dollars as a fee for performing the marriage. Two dollars! A week before, when he officiated at the Walter-Weeks wedding, he had been given a twenty-dollar gold piece. Just for that he'd seen to it that no special frills were included in this particular ceremony.

"The organ played while the vows were being spoken. The organist, Edmund Fardin, was half drunk as usual. He almost fell off the bench while reaching for some of the organ stops, but managed to get through in pretty good shape. The bride tried her darndest to blush, but it had been so long since she had done anything like that, that she failed rather dismally. Her mind was more interested in wondering whether her brassiere had slipped than it was in the words which the Rev. Stanley O'Brien was saying. The brassiere had been borrowed from her sister, Opal, who weighed about forty pounds more than Mary Louise did, so there really was something to worry about after all.

"After the wedding ceremony, the bridal party and a number of guests were entertained at supper at the Murphy home. Old Man Murphy, of course, proceeded to get tanked up. So did Gerald Jimson, the best man. And so, too, did Andrew W. Peabody of Peabody's Florist Shop, who had furnished the flowers for the wedding. To tell the truth Peabody was rather worried about whether his bill would be paid or not, so he decided he might as well get what he could – and he got drunk. And you ought to have seen the way he waded into the sandwiches!

"The bride's mother told the society reporter that the happy couple would leave on a bridal tour to points north. That sounds rather high falutin', but as a matter of fact they went up to Uncle Ben's farm in Northampton County. Still, Northampton County is north from here, so there's no lie after all.

"We are not in a position to say whether the bride will resign her position with Hodfelter's Jewelry Store or not... if she asks our advice, we'll tell her she'd better stick to it because with conditions the way they are now, there's no telling how long Walter is going to be driving a truck for the Coca Cola people."

27
The great newspapers of America and Britain

A common teaching technique employed by Grady School professors was to give us the bare facts about a news story, or the elements that were to go into an advertisement. It was up to us how we were to write the story or compose the ad. When we had finished our mentors read out the original story – often winner of a national award – or showed us the ideal advertisement.

For example, in tackling an ordinary news story we were first supplied with the necessary facts, then required to write a complete account of the event within our 50-minute class period (which could be less than that available in a real-life situation). We always had to be aware of the requisite "5 Ws and H" (Who, What, Where, When, Why and How). Writing leaders (editorials) was the most demanding, for the finished product had to appeal to the public's sense of morality or patriotism, but without being verbose or patronising. Of all the types of newspaper output, feature writing most appealed to me because of its inherent challenge to create a "mini-story" about one person or event.

In the advertising courses we were introduced to the techniques of writing and layout. We learned that a display ad on a right-hand page had more visual impact on the reader than one on the left, thereby permitting more to be charged for it. At first we thought that the more adjectives used and the more flamboyant they were, the stronger the message. To our amazement, we learned that simple layouts and simple words usually made the greatest impact. We also learned about the role of advertising agencies, the commissions they received and the cut-throat competition that prevailed.

In the journalism school laboratory we had fonts of the most popular type-faces. We composed headlines employing such old favourites as Baskerville, Bodoni, Caslon, Garamond, Helvetica, Optima and Roman. We also composed full-page "forms" and then ran off proofs on hand-operated presses. England's John Baskerville and Italy's Giambattista Bodoni gave their names to type-faces created by them in the 1700s. They became my favourites and later in life I was able to employ them in books I published. I think Baskerville type, used extensively in the works of Addison and Steele and other 18th century English writers, is as fresh and attractive today as it was two centuries ago.

We had a small radio broadcasting studio where students read scripts they had written about news events, features, sports, and, of course, advertising. Once his or her "masterpiece" had been delivered, the student would return to the adjacent classroom to be greeted with applause or criticism from fellow classmates and the instructor.

In another course we studied the great newspapers of the United States and the English-speaking world. To do this properly, Dean Drewry arranged for subscriptions to come to the school for one semester each year. We divided up into teams to read and analyse the papers, one student reporting on the news coverage, another the editorial presentation, another the typographical appearance and so on. In that way we quickly gained general impressions about the most prominent papers in the South (among them the *Atlanta Constitution*) and the rest of the country.

The three most highly regarded nationally were *The New York Times*, *The Christian Science Monitor*, and *The Washington Post*. Of this trio, *The Christian Science Monitor*, with its worldwide string of able correspondents and its frequent crusades for one cause or another, quickly became my favourite and I have read it regularly over the ensuing half-century. We also examined two English newspapers, *The Times* and *The* (then) *Manchester Guardian*. Two questions about the English papers bothered us at the time: how could *The Times* justify running only advertisements on its front page, and how could *The Manchester Guardian* achieve such a high standard of excellence when it was not printed in London? We need not have worried, for 50 years later, both questions became redundant.

Apart from course-work, journalism students often helped with two annual events sponsored by the school. One was the Georgia Press Institute, a gathering of editors and publishers from all over the state; the second was the counterpart from Georgia's high schools, the state scholastic newspaper group. The Press Institute was personally organised by Dean Drewry and always commanded national attention. Year after year he managed to bring to the university some of the nation's best known figures in journalism.

Drewry was a master at persuasion. I had a part time job in his outer office and sometimes heard him telephoning the editor of a leading New York or Washington newspaper, or a nationally respected radio broadcaster. He began by congratulating the man or woman on something they had written or broadcast recently, taking great pains to show he had read (or listened to) the item carefully. After three or four minutes when his congratulations had been sincerely and thoroughly communicated, he added – almost at the point of hanging up, something like this:

"By the way, we'll be having our annual Georgia Press Institute in a few months time and I wonder if you could spare a day to be with us. We would all be most honoured if you could".

Very few turned him down and then only because of earlier commitments. When the time neared for the Institute to be held, he started a series of weekly publicity campaigns. The first was about three weeks in advance and highlighted the third most important speaker; the next week's promotion featured the second most important guest. Finally, a week before the Institute was to begin its sessions, came the announcement of the top speaker – a "giant" whose remarks were guaranteed to make national headlines. This phased naming of speakers, revealed in ascending order of importance, always insured a dramatic, rising crescendo of interest in the Institute's programme and thereby, excellent attendance and media coverage.

Through his personal contacts with both large and small newspapers and the national broadcasting networks, Dean Drewry was able to establish an intern system whereby students, in the vacation between their third and fourth years, could work alongside some of the most able journalists in the country. Some students did so well that a year later, after graduation, they were taken on as full time employees. Years later some became editors of major newspapers and others attained high positions with the national broadcasting networks. Others became academics and wrote books.

28
"More intercourse among peoples"

I discovered university life was far more than course work. We students were ever mindful of the ancient "whole man" concept and so attempted to fill our free time with a variety of activities, ranging from sports to special interests. We also had constantly to be on the lookout for part-time work which could bring in a few dollars. Thanks to good luck and hard work, I was able to earn all the precious dollars needed to meet my first year's expenses.

Because a career in politics still vaguely appealed, I decided to take part in the annual oratorical audition of the University's prestigious all-male Demosthenian Literary Society. The most successful students would go on to be trained in the art of collegiate debating, with the honour of representing the university in competitive debating against other universities in the United States – and, occasionally, in England.

My longing to become involved in international affairs increased dramatically after I met several students from abroad. I thus decided my audition "speech", which was limited to only three minutes, should deal with the ideal of international goodwill. Confident that such a broad brush approach was a sure-fire winner, I began my speech with all the earnestness I could muster:

"What we need in this world is more intercourse among peoples....."

To my amazement, a tremendous roar erupted, accompanied by loud cries of "Amen!" and much stamping of feet. The more I attempted to go on, the louder was the laughter and, at length, the chairman asked me to step down. Those 11 words marked the beginning and end of my oratorical career.

The university's student newspaper, *The Red and Black*, was published weekly and edited entirely by students. In national competitions *The Red and Black* consistently came away with top awards. The paper received a university grant, but also earned some funds from the sale of advertising. The money in excess of printing costs allowed senior staff members to receive small salaries. For me and other hard-pressed students, this was manna from Heaven.

My efforts were concentrated on features and sports writing, but even so the time required was almost overwhelming. We worked through most of Wednesday night and then had to attend 8 o'clock classes; on Fridays we had to visit McGregor's printing plant to ensure no errors had been made in the composition or page makeup. We formed first-name friendships with the printers and compositors, who invariably took great pains to explain techniques to us students. This experience was to prove invaluable in years to come.

Apart from the small salary received from *The Red and Black*, I developed another journalistic source of income by becoming *The Augusta Chronicle*'s "stringer" for the university. *The Chronicle* was the daily newspaper most read in the vicinity of my hometown, Louisville, and in the Augusta metropolitan area.

The term "stringer" meant the representative designated by a newspaper to cover a specified town or geographic area, but he received no retainer and would be paid only according to what was actually printed. The newspaper's business manager clipped all the correspondents' stories printed each month and pasted them on long sheets of paper – sometimes pieces of newsprint whose lengths could be indeterminate. These were paper strings – hence the origin of "stringer".

At the end of each month, the paymaster took his yardstick and measured the column inches published by each correspondent. This was then multiplied by the going rate – 5 cents per column inch in my time – to arrive at the monthly pay check. *The Augusta Chronicle*'s readership area covered nearly a dozen counties and I had to memorise every village, town and city in them so that I instantly knew when a student from any of these had achieved something newsworthy – an academic honour, a sports record and so on.

Welcome as it was to my purse, the work in "The Beanery" and on *The Red and Black* and *The Chronicle* did not meet all my fees and living costs. Happily one of President Franklin D. Roosevelt's humanitarian brainchilds, an agency known as the NYA (National Youth Administration), came to the rescue. It was a many-faceted agency but its principal role at the University of Georgia (and other universities throughout the United States) was to provide part-time work for needy students. During the Great Depression, educators estimated over half of the nation's university students needed paying jobs to remain enrolled.

I was immediately accepted by the NYA administrator, Dorothy Whitehead, and performed a wide range of part-time jobs for most of my undergraduate days. I helped organise and maintain Dean Drewry's professional library as well as the journalism school's reading room where virtually every newspaper in Georgia (over 100) was received and individually "racked" on a wooden spindle. Also, long before the days of the photocopier, I typed out entire catalogues of medicinal herbs for use by the university's pharmacy school.

Undoubtedly the most demanding task I performed over the four-year period was transporting a paralysed student, sometimes in his wheelchair, sometimes in my arms. There were only ten minutes between classes and it was all I could do to race his wheelchair between buildings, then gather him in my arms and dash up two or three flights of stairs (no such things as lifts in university buildings in those days).

This brave young man was a journalism student like myself, and went on to join one of the large Georgia dailies after graduation. Handsome, popular and outwardly cheerful, he would constantly be greeted by fellow students as I wheeled him along the campus streets. Only once did he break down and tell me of the hopelessness of his physical condition. Sadly, he was indeed destined for an early death.

There was enormous camaraderie among the university's needy students helped by the NYA programme, but we had no effective way of communicating with each other. I suggested to Dorothy Whitehead that we print a monthly newspaper in which she could have a column outlining new NYA policy and administrative procedures but that most of the paper would be given over to news and features about NYA students.

She liked the idea, asked for and received permission at the state and national level, and asked me to edit the new journal which, by common consent, was called *The NYA Timesheet* (a reference to the official time-keeping form each student was required to complete monthly). The paper was an instant hit and many students volunteered their services.

Some startling but pleasant revelations emerged. Our NYA students, although carrying full course work and often working part time for up to four hours a day, achieved higher academic standards than did students in some of the university's social fraternities where their costs were paid entirely by their relatively well-off parents. Another valuable truth learned during my student days was that the busier a person is, the more likely he is to be reliable and efficient. Moreover, he or she is likely to accept even one more task when asked.

While seeking additional means to meet my university expenses, I met Kendall Weisiger of Atlanta. He, together with a handful of other members of the Atlanta Rotary Club, had founded the Rotary Educational Foundation of Georgia. For many years he was also Vice President of the telephone utility serving America's southern states.

Weisiger was an idealist who helped and inspired thousands of students. In time, he came to be the one person – apart from my immediate family members – who made the greatest impression on my early life.

Descendant of a German immigrant family from Augsburg, he was born in Virginia and graduated in engineering from Virginia Tech. In 1900 he chose Atlanta as his home, believing it to be the city in the South destined to enjoy a remarkable future. He predicted that its metropolitan area would one day exceed a million people and that it would become an internationally renowned commercial and cultural centre. Although he would not live long enough to see his dream come true, he was to contribute much to the ideal of a "Greater Atlanta" in his lifetime.

Beginning as a lineman with Southern Bell Telephone Company, he never shirked from shinnying up tall telephone poles to install new lines or repair old ones. His intelligence, administrative ability and charisma, however, soon caught the attention of Southern Bell executives and he rapidly went up the ladder to become head of the utility's personnel and public relations departments and assistant to the company president.

During the First World War, as a Lieutenant Colonel, he helped develop the US Army's classification system, a scheme that sought to identify and assess the skills of soldiers. As most young men then had only a high school education, he helped devise physical and mental tests to determine how young men could best contribute to the military effort. This basic concept of testing and classifying members of the armed forces, although since modified, is still used today.

He was a governor or trustee of several universities and colleges, white and black. He strongly disapproved of racial and religious discrimination and worked hard to foster a spirit of toleration among Atlanta's Christian, Jewish and black leaders.

His two great interests were assisting needy young people and staging youth projects in Rotary Clubs. The fact that he and Mrs. Weisiger had no children, plus an unsuccessful attempt at adoption, probably contributed to his wish to see the impoverished youth of rural Georgia obtain the best possible education or training.

It was in the depressed early 1920s, when young Georgians began dropping out of universities and colleges for lack of money, that Weisiger became aware that these gifted, potential leaders were without hope. By 1952 the Georgia Foundation had loaned nearly $400,000 to 1,278 needy students to enable them to earn degrees in medicine, agriculture, home economics and other fields. The assistance was not in the form of grants, but loans, which the young people would start repaying only when they obtained their first jobs. Although most Foundation loans were made during America's Great Depression, the dedicated students defaulted only on 3.5% of the total funds advanced.

Almost all the students went on to successful careers in business and professions and some became regional and national leaders in their respective careers. One became a Governor of Georgia; another, Dean Rusk, became a Rhodes Scholar, headed a national educational foundation and eventually became American Secretary of State. The great majority, however, returned to their home towns where they made use of their newly acquired skills to foster better standards of living in their respective communities.

While always mindful of the educational contribution Weisiger was making to an entire generation of youthful Georgians, I came to value him most for his philosophy of life and lost no occasion to visit him, and we were to correspond regularly until his death many years later.

He introduced me early to the concept of producing inexpensive and modest promotional literature, often employing the black-and-white photo-offset technique instead of the more expensive letterpress printing.

"Beware of appeals for money on glossy paper containing

coloured photographs," he said. "The person who receives them is likely to reason that the charity which sends that kind of material doesn't need a contribution."

He sometimes teased me about my strict Baptist upbringing. An Episcopalian himself, he shared my maternal grandfather's advice about "moderation in all things" and reminded me, on the subject of drinking, that our Lord drank wine. He was not a habitual drinker but enjoyed the occasional sip of whiskey.

A person should enjoy his job, he said, but if for a time he is obliged to accept any kind of work, he should move into something more appealing at the first opportunity. He considered work on an assembly line 'soul destroying'. He held similar views about the lower reaches of the civil service. To illustrate this point, he once took me to the Georgia's state Capitol. Stopping before an open door, we saw inside some 30 or 40 women typing away at their machines.

"Now, observe closely," he said, lowering his voice. "See that lady in the front row there? She may be a senior typist, but she must be 50 to 60 years old and probably has worked for the state most of her adult life. She types one dull document after another, with nothing to inspire her. For all practical purposes, her soul is dead. What motivates her is her steady job and the assurance she will get a good pension when she can no longer work."

Then, nodding toward the back of the room, he went on: "Now, look at that lovely young girl with the brown hair on the back row. You can tell instantly she has personality – see, she's smiling at her neighbour. Even though she's typing quickly, and no doubt efficiently, just give her a few years in this room and she'll be just like the lady in the front row. The moral is never to get into a rut in employment – no matter how reliable the job is."

Several times in the course of my university career Mr. and Mrs. Weisiger invited me to spend weekends at their home in Atlanta, not far from the Georgia Governor's mansion. Sometimes we would go out into the business district of Atlanta where, it seemed, he knew everyone of importance. Mostly, however, we would sit quietly at home, or take walks in the immediate area, where he never tired of responding to my questions – many of which must have seemed naïve to him.

One evening after a particularly enjoyable dinner, we got to talking about those ideal attributes, apart from a good education, a young person should have to succeed in life.

"First," he said, "you want your family solidly behind you. Here young people who come from broken homes are at a disadvantage and they must call upon their inner resources of character to cope. But you have a loving family who have given you a strength and confidence no one can take away."

"And after that?" I asked.

"Faith," he replied instantly, his eyes glowing with animation. "Not just religious faith, which is important, but faith to survive and achieve in a world that can never be stable. Religious faith you have already, but you must make it outgoing and tolerant. We Protestants can learn a great deal from other faiths – from Buddhists, for example. There is much good in other faiths; study the best teaching from these, all the while keeping to the tenets of your own faith and you'll become a wiser and better man."

"How," I asked, knowing of his Army classification work and his experience in personnel administration, "can you size up a person's potential based only on a single conversation or interview?"

"A great deal can be learned from one meeting with a prospective employee, especially if it also includes a meal," he said.

"Why should that be?" I asked.

"Apart from faith, which you must develop yourself," he said, "all other attributes must be learned, and these will become apparent in the course of conversation or eating. I first look for signs of cleanliness or orderliness, which is often the same thing. I am not necessarily impressed by a young man dressed in an expensive suit. Another young man may come from a poor family and not possess a suit; yet if his clothing, however old, is clean and pressed, and his hair and shoes are tidy, I know that he is likely to be an orderly person."

"And the importance of the meal?" I asked.

"A meal gives the young person a chance to relax," he explained. "At the same time he reveals his basic manners – politeness, care in eating his food and the ability to speak while partaking of the meal. Being a good conversationalist is important; with some people it comes naturally, but anyone can improve with practice."

Reading lists were a strong point with Mr. Weisiger. He was constantly compiling and revising them for the new immigrant to America, for the prospective university student and for the graduate just embarking on his or her first job.

"It's a simple rule of life," he said. "Great people, successful people in all walks of life have revealed their secrets in their autobiographies. They may have died long since, but we can nonetheless profit by their examples."

29
Cycling through Appalachia

One of Kendall Weisiger's admonitions to young people was that they should be adventurous and willing to take risks.

"Even if you don't succeed every time," he added, "you will gain by the experience and your confidence will grow."

The concept of a gap year between University and the first job didn't exist then, but I reasoned I could undertake a real challenge if I devoted the whole of my 1939 summer vacation – three months – to a single enterprise. But what?

Travel much attracted me and I eventually decided on making a bicycle trip through my favourite part of the United States – the Appalachian Mountains – and on to New England if time permitted. While I obviously would enjoy the scenic and historic features along the way, I inwardly hoped I would observe social achievements in North Carolina and Virginia that my native state of Georgia could aspire to. Of the 48 states then in the Union, Georgia ranked 47th in most fields – education, farming, industry and wealth. "Thank God for the Mississippi!" we students used to say when we saw Georgia near the bottom of comparative tables.

With my route and basic purpose determined, I turned to the practical problems of mounting my "expedition". First, I needed a bicycle, preferably a lightweight one – but none of my fellow students owned one. Reluctantly I realised I would have to settle for a heavy "town type", but even so, no one had one to sell or lend. One fellow student, however, appeared interested and asked what kind I wanted and how much I could afford to pay. I told him I needed a sturdy bike, in good condition, and that $8 (a hefty sum then) was as much as I could afford.

He said he would "look around" and sure enough, a week or two later, he wheeled a red bike into my dorm room for inspection. It was in excellent condition and the tyres almost new. I readily paid him the $8 with a certain sense of guilt, for I was sure I had the better of the bargain. To my chagrin, many months later, another student asked me if I realised the seller was a well known petty thief and that my bike probably had been "stolen to order".

As my route north would take me through the highest mountains in Eastern America, I planned to travel lightly. A lightweight sleeping bag, a raincoat, water bottle, eating and drinking utensils, first aid kit, tyre repair kit, lightweight cardigan and a single change of clothing made up the principal baggage. In addition I carried road maps, a couple of notebooks, spare pencils – and, of course, enough cash to buy simple food.

I had also allowed a small allowance for overnight accommodation but I earnestly hoped this expense would be minimal. My budget for food and overnight costs was only $50 because I banked on sleeping rough in the open countryside and staying with a few kind-hearted farm families who would consider me as a real guest rather than the paying kind. Whether this last hope was naïve or realistic I had no way of knowing. One small source of income arising from the trip would be payment by *The Augusta Chronicle*, our regional daily paper, for written accounts of my adventures which I would post to them each day. But I would be paid only after returning home.

I carried with me five documents which I hoped would make me acceptable to would-be hosts. One was a membership card of the American Youth Hostels, the American off-shoot founded by Monroe and Isabel Smith of the international youth hostel movement, started in Germany by Richard Schirmann. I knew there were a few youth hostels in the South – principally in North Carolina.

The other four were letters or, to be more precise, testimonials to my character. The first, and only local one, was written by Virginia Polhill Price, editor of our weekly newspaper, *The News and Farmer*. It was full of praise and cited my early journalistic writing as perhaps being indicative of things to come. Dean Drewry, my journalism school mentor, wrote another, very much in the same vein. I did not personally know Harmon Caldwell, president of the University of Georgia, but when Dean Drewry suggested he might also be willing to write a letter on my behalf, I welcomed the prospect.

When the letter arrived I realised for the first time that testimonials could tell as much about the writer as the person they were supposed to assist. It had four short sentences, grouped together in a disproportionately small space on a large sheet of paper. All four were factual although there was not one word about my character or ability. The first sentence merely introduced me by name and hometown, the second said I was a student in the school of journalism, the third announced I was about to make a bicycle trip and the last said any courtesies extended me would be appreciated by the University.

Something else did not appear right about this letter. On closer examination I saw that most of the capital letters were typed half a space higher than the small letters; in other words, on a faulty typewriter where some of the keys had been sprung out of their normal position by wear and tear.

Such typewriters, I learned later from Kendall Weisiger, were kept by institutions and business firms to write non-committal references for people they didn't know well.

If such had been the concern of President Caldwell, he would have been pleased to know I presented his letter only once. That occasion came in North Georgia when a philosophical farmer tersely commented: "Harmon Caldwell may be a good university president, but he ought to get himself a new typewriter."

The final letter was written by Georgia's governor, E.D. Rivers. It was provided through the intervention of a local politician who knew him well. This letter was the most flattering of all, but then I expected that from a politician. (Rivers went on to become one of the most progressive governors Georgia ever had, only to mar his record by accepting large bribes from dozens of convicts who were pardoned during the closing weeks of his office.)

Now fully equipped, I posed for a photograph in front of Louisville's old market place before setting off for what I hoped would be the greatest adventure of my life this far.

Although the first leg of my cycling venture was from my hometown to Athens (seat of the University of Georgia), I was acutely aware that once I had left Athens, a new world would unfold before me.

And so it did as I encountered steeper and steeper hills. Then I glanced in the distance at the thrilling sight – the first view of the Appalachian Mountains of Northeast Georgia! Being a lowlander by birth,

I was overwhelmed by the beauty of the blue-tinged peaks. It was to be only the beginning of my love affair with the Southern Appalachians.

It was already past five o'clock when I rolled up to the small Clarke County hamlet of Macedonia where, according to the handbook of the American Youth Hostels, I would find my first youth hostel. But I could see nothing that looked as if it could be a hostel. Apart from the handful of simple mountain cabins, there were no public buildings other than the obvious centre of the community – the Macedonia Baptist Church.

Dismounting, I knocked at the front door of the nearest cabin and was greeted by Lucille Roberts. She explained that she was a Turpin – one of four families which comprised the bulk of the community's population. Lucille said Macedonia was a "cooperative community" founded by Dr. Morris Mitchell, an idealist and one-time professor at Columbia University's prestigious Teachers College, but now on the faculty of an Alabama teachers college. Mitchell had purchased the surrounding acreage with the view of converting its rocky, non-productive soil into an area that would provide a decent standard of living for its impoverished inhabitants.

His first step was to create a cooperative business model in which every adult had a specific job and all financial business transactions were to be conducted on the cooperative (non-profit) principle. Macedonia was far from being the first idealistic rural community to be established in the United States, but it was the first I had visited. Based on the Bible's simple socialistic command that everyone should be his "brother's keeper", Mitchell's long-term aim was to make the community self-sufficient and eventually, to become so prosperous that its members could enjoy a standard of life superior to anything they had previously known. He supported the Macedonia Baptist Church, the adhesive which bound the families together, and further endeared himself to the community by ensuring that all crucial planning and financial decisions were made democratically and not by himself.

The community's most important project was to a dam a small stream that ran through the heart of the area. Although not a river, it could reach terrifying levels after a sudden mountain downpour. This corner of Northeast Georgia, after all, had the second highest annual rainfall in the United States. The dam, when completed, would create a lake of several acres to provide fish to supplement the inhabitants' meagre diet, and a recreation site to attract fisherman and holiday makers.

I asked Lucille where the Macedonia Youth Hostel was, as I had not yet spotted any building designated for it. She pointed in the distance and said it was an old mill straddling the stream that ran through the area.

She added that about 20 university students from several states were working in Macedonia that summer on various projects under the auspices of the American Friends Service Committee, the 'hands-on' branch of the American Quakers.

One student, a music teacher, was giving lessons to children of community families. "This teacher has set up her living quarters in the youth hostel", she explained, "so we'll give you a room in one of our cabins so as not to dislodge her."

I was appalled. Having cycled so far to be able to stay overnight in the first youth hostel to be opened in the state of Georgia, I wasn't about to be denied what I considered my right. Lucille, seeing my keen disappointment, readily agreed I should move into the old mill. The music teacher was not best pleased and insisted that another student, a likeable young man from Washington, should be my hostel companion. I think she was not so much concerned that I would steal anything as much as she feared I might threaten the decor which she had so sympathetically had added to the mill's austere interior. She need not have worried. The student proved to be an intelligent, helpful young man who very quickly gave me a picture of what the community was about. We talked long into the night and by the time I fell asleep I had decided to apply to join the community the following summer.

The next morning, after ensuring my hostel membership card reflected my overnight stay in Macedonia, I remounted my bike, this time in the direction of the North Carolina state line. This was to be my first visit to North Carolina – a state whose progressive agricultural and industrial measures I had come to admire in our university social science classes about the "developing South". The burning question was: would I see for myself evidence of North Carolina's progress during my travels?

It was not long before I discovered that restaurants and cafés were subjected to inspection and grading by the state, with certificates awarded according to pass rates. This had nothing to do with the menus, but all to do with clean premises, adequate toilet facilities and basic food preparation equipment and techniques. Georgia, at that time, had no such requirement and I subsequently was able to point to the North Carolina example during my journalistic career.

Easily the most moving experience of my odyssey came in the heart of the Appalachians when, with evening coming on fast, I had looked in vain for a farmhouse where I might spend the night. At last, with dusk at hand, I saw a simple, unpainted cabin to the left of the road in the shadow of majestic Humpback Mountain. It was my last chance for an evening's rest in a bed. If, for any reason, this family refused to take me in, I would be obliged to sleep at the edge of the forest or meadow in an area where rainfall could bucket down in torrents.

I made my way forward, crossing a small tributary of the Catawba River as I neared the cabin. The little house nestled among several arbours of Niagara grapes, green at that time of the year. Calling out "Hello", I saw that the family – father, mother and a boy several years my junior – were seated on the front porch talking together. I propped up my bike, mounted the steps and – as I had done many times before – pulled out the letter signed by Governor Rivers which, because of the embossed seal at the bottom, was easily the most impressive of my testimonials. I introduced myself in the usual manner: a University of Georgia student cycling to see the South and in need of overnight accommodation. I added, as always, that I was prepared to pay.

The farmer listened without saying anything. Slowly he passed his hand over the embossed seal. Then, in turn, the letter was passed to his wife and son; each – without looking at the text – also ran their fingers across the raised golden seal. The letter was returned to the father who made a gesture as if to fold it and put it into his pocket.

I immediately realised he thought the letter had been meant for him to keep – a letter especially for him from the Governor of Georgia! Embarrassed, I explained that I had carried the letter with me since I began my journey, and would be needing it – almost nightly – as I continued on my way. He nodded understandingly and handed the letter back, I felt, with slight reluctance.

There was a long pause and I wondered if I had given offence by taking back the letter. I need not have worried. Turning his kindly, weather-beaten face towards me, he said: "We can't offer you much, but what we have we'll gladly share with you." Deeply moved, I hastened to assure him that I would be grateful for his family's hospitality, adding that I had known days – not that long ago – when my parents did not know where the next mouthful of food would come from.

His wife, who had been silent up to then, apologetically explained that although they had raised seven children, only one, their youngest – the teenage son at her side – remained at home and that I would be obliged to share his bed. I smiled and replied I quite understood.

A few moments later, the farmer – whose name I now learned was Denny – led us to the simple dining room. His wife, without comment, brought our plates, the simplest of cutlery and several dishes of food. These included a few pieces of chicken, no doubt left from an earlier meal, several vegetables and three dishes made from apples – whose trees I had noted in the vicinity of the farmhouse.

For the last dish Mrs. Denny brought in a round pone (flat cake) of corn bread, hot from the oven. It was placed in front of her husband who, first catching our eyes, led us in a short, simple grace. Then, naturally and no doubt in the same way he had done thousands of times before, he took up the pone of bread and broke it into several pieces. His wife passed round the dish and we each took a portion of the broken bread. I could not avoid comparison with the Communion rite and wondered if this simple mountain custom had its origin there. Wine and other alcoholic beverages were virtually unknown in most rural southern homes at that time because of the prevailing regard for temperance. Instead we had rich, chilled whole milk from the dairy cow, unspoiled in taste or texture by pasteurisation or homogenisation.

We did not tarry after the meal. Knowing that hard-working farmers were "early to bed and early to rise", I nodded assent when my host asked if I were ready for sleep. He then led the way with his son, who had said not a word since my arrival, to a corner bedroom nearest the little stream I had crossed over not far from the house.

Pointing to a small rope dangling from a crude hole cut in the wall, he said:

"This rope, I am about to pull, closes a sluice gate of the little generating plant on the stream outside. There'll be just enough water in the sluice for the light to last a few seconds, so you'll have to undress and get into the bed in that time – or else you'll find yourself in the dark!"

His son, long used to the timing, was already undressing, well ahead of me. Grinning, I thanked Mr. Denny and stripping in record time, leapt into the bed beside the son. Mr. Denny then yanked the rope and after a second or two, the light began to fade and eventually went out. To my great surprise, the mattress was filled with "shucks" (husks) from ears of maize. The hard ends of these protruded everywhere and it was impossible to find a position to avoid them. The son, however, had no problem and was soon sound asleep. My weariness soon overcame me, and I, too, slept deeply in spite of the early discomfort.

We all awoke at dawn the next morning and, after a hasty breakfast, my host showed me the simple electric generating plant he had installed in his front yard over the tiny tributary of the Catawba Rover. Using a generator from an old Model T Ford, he had built a sluice on one side of the stream that turned a small wheel attached to the generator, thereby creating enough electric current to light the simple farmhouse. Attached to the sluice gate was the other end of the rope connected to his son's bedroom. Turning the electricity off and on meant only raising or lowering the gate by means of the rope and a spring. I could only marvel at this humble farmer's ingenuity at a time when President Franklin D. Roosevelt had not yet seen fulfilment of his dream to bring electricity to all of America's rural areas.

The other memorable experience came in the little town of Scottsville, situated on the James River in Virginia. When I knocked at the door of the modest home and asked if I could stay overnight as a paying guest, the husband and wife quickly sized me up, smiled and bade me welcome. They warmed to me immediately, almost – it seemed – as if we were old friends. They asked about, and then listened with rapt attention to my adventures.

Then, recalling his own boyhood, the man told me how his parents had planned a summer boat outing on the James River which flowed within sight of the family home. In honour of the occasion his parents had bought him a new pair of shoes and he was to christen them on the boat trip. The boy had never been on a boat before and leapt around with great joy, eventually losing his balance and falling overboard. An alert member of the crew quickly fished him out, none the worse except for being wet – and having his new shoes soaked.

My host stopped to laugh before continuing. "The funny part," he explained, "was that my father was not in the slightest worried about my drowning, but he chastised me severely for getting my new shoes wet."

The next day, when I prepared to depart, the couple took me to the front hallway where we halted beside a simple little chest with a single drawer. The chest was just large enough to hold a pot of flowers, and I did not at first understand its significance. The husband slowly, almost reverently, pulled the drawer out and handed me a set of school papers, now slightly yellow with age. They included superb drawings of bridges and buildings, all bearing top marks in an instructor's hand.

"These," said the man, "were done by our son, killed in World War I. He had a wonderful mind and would have made a great civil engineer had he lived." He stopped, unable to continue. For a few moments I continued to admire the immaculate drawings, then handed them back. Then as I turned towards the door to take my leave, the mother spoke.

"The moment we saw you," she said, "my husband and I thought you reminded us of our son. Thank you for staying the night with us."

I hoped my eyes would convey my thanks. What gentle people, what kind folk to thank *me*, their guest, for a visit I would never forget.

30
Selling expensive Bibles to poor farmers

September 1939, the start of the final year of my undergraduate study, was to be a momentous time in the history of the 20th century. Before the month was over, Germany would invade Poland and the stage would be set for another world war – an event that would profoundly affect my future.

Although heavy bombing raids on Britain soon followed, the war seemed far away and of no immediate concern for Americans. My friends and even our faculty members did not expect the war to last long. I wanted to study Denmark's folk high schools, believing they held some lessons for improving the lot of rural Georgians. When the Rosenwald Foundation offered scholarship assistance for study abroad such as I contemplated, I was encouraged to apply by Dean Walter Cocking of the university's college of education where I was undertaking my "minor" studies. I made the short list, but was not accepted.

Had I gained the scholarship, I might have left the university before receiving my diploma and thereby could have been interned by the Germans when they invaded Denmark in April 1940. But I had no way of predicting the future and so was greatly disappointed at coming so close to my goal and failing to achieve it.

Dean Cocking then suggested that I apply for a scholarship to enable me to take a master's degree in educational administration at his college. This I did and was readily accepted. Happily, the resulting stipend enabled me to meet almost all my expenses for the following year, thus putting to an end my parents' anxieties about funding.

As the final year of our bachelor degree program began, my three roommates and I marvelled at the good fortune – and hard work – that had enabled us to come so far on virtually non-existent family support. For three years we had survived and somehow we knew we would cope in the final year.

Although I undertook as much part-time work as I dared at the university, I still needed some summer income for clothing and other necessities. Thus it was that my father obtained for me a three-month lease of a small petrol station in Louisville. My income would mainly come from a few cents profit on each gallon of petrol sold. The brand of petrol, Sinclair, was not as well known as Texaco or Standard Oil (later Esso), but I hoped that the tourists travelling to and from Florida on US Route No. 1, which passed by the petrol station, would generate enough trade to bring in the additional dollars I needed.

But these were still dire economic times and there were far fewer tourists than I had imagined. Thus the small income from the station, while welcome, fell below my expectations.

Nonetheless two incidents helped me to become much wiser about human nature by the end of that summer. The first was the arrival of a well-dressed man who said he owned a trucking company. One of his large trucks, he said, was following him and would shortly be stopping at my station to fill up with petrol. Meanwhile, he needed to have his own tank filled. When I did so, he reached into his coat and pulled out a cheque-book, saying he paid all his transactions by cheque.

I was utterly confused, for this was my first venture in business and I did not want to offend the man and perhaps lose the chance to fill the tank of his truck, which would be arriving momentarily to receive many gallons of my petrol. I had already mentally calculated what those 40 or 50 gallons would bring me in profit. So I accepted the cheque. The "Following truck" never arrived.

A few days later my local bank informed me the cheque was worthless and that I had been conned. Nearly a year later the county sheriff suddenly appeared at our house with the same man who had given me the bogus cheque. The sheriff explained that the man had been caught in another part of Georgia and that altogether he had passed over 20 bad cheques. The penalty was several years' imprisonment for each one.

Unlike in Britain, there was no such thing as a bank overdraft and anyone passing a cheque without having funds to cover it was liable to a penalty. The sheriff went on to say that the sheriff where the man lived had vouched for the con-man's family situation (a wife and several children) and that if I – and all the other people who had been conned – would now accept payment in cash, the man would not be brought to trial and his family would not suffer for his misdeeds.

I was still angry at the man for causing me to be out-of-pocket and at first I welcomed the chance to help send him to prison for several years. Should justice or compassion rule? Our local sheriff, whom I much respected, pointed out that I was not obliged to "make a deal" with the man, although every other person the man had conned had done so. With some reluctance I agreed and, in the end, the man went free. Free, I sometimes wondered afterwards, to go straight or to resume his evil ways.

The second unusual experience of that memorable summer was equally enlightening but shocking because I was suddenly confronted with the prospect of abetting unlawful sex. On a quiet summer afternoon when the temperature was in the high 90s, a man and woman walked into the station from nowhere. I looked for their car but it was nowhere to be seen. Both were well dressed, but definitely strangers to Louisville. As they apparently did not have a car or had left it some distance away, I assumed they wanted to buy cold drinks or sweets – the only items I sold other than petrol and oil. Before I could ask how I could help them, the man demanded in an impatient but subdued voice:

"Where can a man take a woman here?"

I stared open-mouthed, first at the man and then at the attractive woman – probably in her 30s – standing behind him. She had a full figure and was neatly dressed. Seeing my hesitation, she gave me a warm smile. That only made my situation worse. It finally dawned on me that the woman had to be a prostitute, or at least a "loose woman" carrying on an affair with someone not her husband.

What was I to do? My rather puritanical upbringing meant I vaguely knew about prostitutes although I had never seen one. Although my petrol station had a small storeroom at its rear, it wasn't large enough to assist the couple in their quest for sex. I had heard about raids on bawdy houses where such things took place and the enormous fines and prison sentences subsequently meted out to owners of such places.

Composing myself, I told the couple I had no room for them and suggested they continue on down the road where there were other petrol stations. They spun on their heels and left angrily in the direction I had pointed without a word.

Like me, all my university friends had stories to tell about their summer fund-raising. I admired most my three roommates, Paul, Philip and Robert Rowland who, during successive summers, set out to sell enough Bibles to pay a substantial part of their university expenses. They were far from unique in this venture. For many years hard-up university students throughout the South had sold Bibles during their summer vacations. Some students, natural salesmen, did very well and financed the major part of their following year's costs; others, not so gifted, soon learned valuable lessons in self-confidence and basic principles of finance.

A Texas Bible publisher who concentrated his sales in the southern and southwestern areas of the United States devised an ingenious plan to train and send out university students each summer as salesmen to specified rural counties. The "target" of these young salesmen (only men students were accepted, as far as I know) was the white farmer, whether prosperous or poor.

A family Bible went to the heart of the rural white southern farmer's heritage. The crucial fact was that most of these families were deeply religious in their home life and within their communities. As such, they supported their rural churches, mainly Baptist and Methodist, scattered through farming communities from Virginia to Texas. The most devout of all resided in the so-called "Bible Belt", the two Carolinas, Georgia, Alabama, Mississippi, Tennessee, Kentucky and Arkansas. It was here that the greatest sales could be achieved.

Long before the summer vacation began, the publisher would advertise on southern university campuses – by word of mouth through salesmen who had worked the previous year and through notices placed in buildings most frequented by students. By the end of the academic year the publisher knew how many young men were prepared for the salesmanship adventure.

On a specified date the future salesmen reported to a central training site where, for several days, they were instructed in techniques of selling expensive Bibles to mainly poor farmers – most of whom had little ready cash.

The successful student salesman persuaded the farmer to part with the maximum down payment, the rest to be paid when his crop was harvested. The greater the down payment, the greater was the chance of the farmer completing the deal. The training session also included mock sales situations in which the students were taught to be relaxed rather than serious in their initial approach, to have a small stock of family-type funny stories, never to rush the farmer into a decision and, most important of all, how to deal with those who could not make their final payments and yet did not want to forfeit their down payments. The publisher warned students that they should expect up to half of their customers to default.

A car was essential to reach the hundreds of farms situated in the counties assigned to each student. In those days our impoverished students had no cars of their own, so the only solution was to buy the cheapest possible second-hand car, praying earnestly that it would survive the summer (some didn't), and then sell it for whatever it would bring afterwards.

Occasionally an honest second-hand car dealer would rent a usable car for a nominal charge. The car requirement was a tricky one, for a student could easily lose a good proportion of his summer's earnings by paying too much in the first instance. On the other hand, a few 'super-salesmen' managed to make small profits on their cars when it came time to sell.

The psychology of dealing with the farmer was crucial to making a sale. At all times he was to be treated with the deepest respect. If the student came from a deeply religious family (and most did), it was no good showing off his knowledge of the Bible. He might be amazed to find that the farmer, though possessing only a high school education, could be an avid student of the Bible and as knowledgeable as some clergymen. Better to dwell on the importance of owning, or giving a Bible to a son or daughter recently (or about to be) married. The student took great care to emphasise how the family Bible should be the centrepiece in every Christian home.

These massive Bibles were stoutly bound with the text printed in large, easily readable type. The centre-fold was the place referred to most often, for it contained the family tree. Here each family marriage, birth and death was recorded. Divorces were then virtually unknown in the Bible Belt, so there was no place set aside for entering these. Although wives were known to want family Bibles more than husbands, the students had to tread carefully in approaching them for it would be the husbands who would have to foot the bill.

Some students discovered salesmanship to be their forte and went on after completing university to lucrative positions in industry. Others (most, in fact) found it a struggle, but nonetheless were grateful for the experience.

Apart from the earnings, small but vital to remaining in university, they had learned humility and empathy – and a few fortunate ones came away with lovely farmers' daughters as their life partners. Year after year my three roommates returned to campus after their summer "ordeals" vastly underweight, faces worn and weary. It was impossible not to admire their courage and perseverance. All three went on to obtain degrees and made their marks in the real world as useful citizens.

As for that southwestern Bible publisher, I never learned if it received plaudits of any kind. Yet the fact remains that it enabled impoverished students during the Great Depression to obtain higher education which otherwise would have been denied them.

Throughout my undergraduate years my roommates and I kept abreast of local, national and world news by listening daily to our principal radio station, WSB (for "Welcome South, Brother!"), on the old set my parents had given me at the start of my freshman year.

Georgia politics much interested – and sometimes concerned – us. More worrying were the daily reports of the war raging in Europe. We sat in dazed silence as we learned how Britain was being blitzed and how ever larger numbers of ships were being sunk by German U-boats. We sensed, but dared not put into words, the inevitability of the United States' involvement.

Sometimes we gained solace from listening to folk songs and "mountain music" with their constantly recurring themes of love, betrayal and death. One such "Will the Circle be Unbroken", conveyed the heartbreak of a son over the death of his beloved mother. The "Circle", of course, was the closely knit family of those carefree and largely divorce-free days.

One day, out of the blue, the elder brother of my Rowland roommates arrived to say that their father had suffered a stroke and all three sons should return home with him at once. Stunned, they quickly packed a few belongings and departed. Not until they were gone was I told by a fellow student, who had managed a few words with the elder brother, that the father had, indeed, suffered a stroke while seated in his chair before the fireplace. What my three roommates were not told until their journey was well underway was that their father had died as he fell forward, his hair being singed by the fire.

Thereafter we all found it too painful to hear the "Circle" again and rushed to turn off the radio when the song's title was announced.

31
My first kiss!

Coincidental with my graduate study, a dozen or so friends and I formed 'GRYC' (Georgia Rural Youth Council). All of us were fired with zeal to serve rural Georgia and our rural Southland by using our God-given talents to maximum advantage. We were about 50:50, boys and girls.

For the young ladies the choice of careers was either teaching or becoming "home demonstration agents" - the term then used for those dedicated to improve the lot of the rural housewife. We young men had more diverse callings. Some also would teach, but others would farm, operate small businesses and one or two aspired to (and later reached) high political office. For myself, I remained committed to a journalistic career that would allow me to promote a better standard of living for our rural population.

At that time a substantial proportion of Americans still lived on farms and in small towns. Although the techniques of television had been perfected, it would be several years after the end of the war before sets were mass-produced. Hence the youth of rural America had only school and church activities to occupy their spare time.

The goal of our GRYC was to enrich the lives of young rural Georgians by encouraging more activities in their local communities. Using rural schools and churches, we taught basic parliamentary procedure so that young people could organise themselves into effective groups to help achieve their goals. These might range from organising recreational activities to starting up small industries or cooperatives to market their farm produce or crafts.

We GRYC members also learned some of the old singing ("play party") games that had been popular with our parents and grandparents. When we reintroduced them in rural communities, we were delighted to see how well they were received and how eager the young people were to continue them after we had departed. The older generation often turned up as well, thrilled to take part in such old favourites as "Jennie Crack Corn" and "A Bicycle Built for Two" which they had enjoyed in their youth. Many of these old singing games and folk songs were of English origin.

Our indispensable aid in leading these games was *The Handy Play Party Book*, a sturdy, pocket-sized manual containing nearly 100 games and 50 folk songs. This little volume cost one dollar, a respectable sum in those days, but worth every cent. Apart from being vital to our GRYC social evenings, it was to prove invaluable during the coming war when I used it when visiting youth clubs in the Southampton area. I had no inkling how prophetic one particular game would prove in my own life.

That game was "Brown Eyed Mary" which began with a circle of partners, facing ahead for marching with the boys on the inside and girls to their right. In the action that followed, the boy twirled the girl around, after which she moved forward as everyone took new partners. But it was the words of the first movement which were to perfectly describe my future wife:

"If perchance we should meet
On some wild prairie
In my arms will I embrace
My darling brown eyed Mary."

The Handy Play Party Book went into countless printings and still survives in the English-speaking world as a basic guide to English, European and Appalachian singing games.

If young people in a rural community wanted more advice for producing a new crop, starting a rural industry or forming a producer cooperative, we made no attempt to provide this specialised knowledge ourselves, but directed them to advisors in the state or national agricultural service. As part of our own training, we visited the Campbell Folk School at Brasstown, North Carolina. Founded by John C. Campbell and run for many years by his widow, Olive Dame Campbell, the school sought to preserve the old handicrafts (principally weaving and wood carving) of the Southern Appalachians. George Bidstrup, a charismatic Dane, joined the school and helped the mountain people to form cooperatives for marketing their produce and crafts.

When several rural communities in Virginia heard about the work of our GRYC, they invited us to spend a week with them discussing and demonstrating our activities and those they planned to undertake. While en route to Virginia, we stopped off at the Campbell Folk School where Mrs. Campbell again graciously received us, answered our many questions, and then arranged a tour of the school and its farms. Not until our visit to the school did we realise that the Campbells had assisted the English folk song collector, Cecil Sharp, in his successful quest for long-forgotten songs and ballads in the remote valleys of the Southern Appalachians.

Among our GRYC members was a lovely young lady who captured my fancy. Like most of the other young women in our group, she was enrolled in the school of home economics. She was a superb cook, made most of her clothes, was an effective speaker and organiser, and had a radiant personality. In short, she was every young man's dream.

While the most impoverished male university students lived in Candler Hall, where we could economise by sleeping up to four in a room, the equivalent for young ladies was the "4H Club House" which was run on a cooperative (actual cost) basis. It was here that I came to date this lovely, gifted girl. One day, as we were about to part on the veranda after a particularly enjoyable period of pleasantries, the young lady – still holding me – whispered softly "Would you like to kiss me?"

Kiss her! Why, that had been my dream ever since first meeting her. But I was startled – though for only a few seconds – to think she had the same urge! With surging passion, I embraced her more tightly while smothering her sweet, tender lips in a flood of kisses. Not until some minutes later, when an anxious look came across her face and she uttered "I think that's enough", did I relent.

"Wow!" I thought, "that's what real love is about!"

As I turned to wave goodbye, I noticed a slight movement behind the lace curtains at the veranda window. Peering more closely, I saw a group of my girl's friends giggling uncontrollably.

How, I wondered, had they happened to be at the window at the exact moment of our tender exchange?

32
Our degrees become worthless!

The graduation ceremony for my class of 1940 was held outdoors. My parents drove up to Athens for the event and I was acutely aware that my degree probably meant as much to them as to myself. Both had been enrolled briefly in university, but had been unable to continue their studies. I was, therefore, achieving what they had once dreamed of. When the ceremony was over and I joined them, they both shed unashamed tears of joy.

The ride home was the first time I had relaxed in four years. But the "honeymoon" was short. Although I would have no financial worries for the following year, I knew far greater demands would be made of me as a graduate student than before. Was I ready for the challenge? The thought of undertaking year-long serious research, culminating in a thesis, was both frightening and challenging.

Thankfully, I had signed up to spend most of the summer in the work camp run by the American Friends Service Committee (Quakers) at the Macedonia Cooperative Community to which I had been introduced the previous summer on my bicycle adventure. My return to this beautiful spot in north Georgia's mountains was even more inspiring than my previous visit. This time I had two months to work closely with men and women students from all over America and one young lady from England. Directing the camp was a small staff from Guildford College, a North Carolina Quaker institution whose academic standing and community service programmes had long commanded national respect.

By that summer of 1940 war was raging in Western Europe and most of the discussions at our work camp centred on what the United States should, or should not, do. Some, mostly Quakers, already knew they would become conscientious objectors if the United States joined the fighting. Another group said it would support the war effort, but only as non-combatants. Two university students from Alabama and I were among the few who thought that Hitler and his ideology were too great a threat to ignore and American entry into the war was inevitable.

A brilliant 17 year-old high school student from New York City posed us a theoretical question which went to the core of the dilemma. "Let us suppose," he said, "the United States decides not to increase its military strength to resist a German invasion of America's shores, but instead relies on its civil force (i.e. the police) to repel the invaders. Let us say this engagement is delicately poised with the Germans having an even chance of overrunning the United States. Would you, under such circumstances, surrender to the Germans, or raise the necessary military forces to throw them back into the sea?"

Some of the more devout Quakers among us, citing William Penn's passive life among hostile Indians, said they would accept German domination if the civil forces failed to halt the enemy. Others, among them the two southern girls and I, disagreed. We felt it was not in the American tradition to accept domination by force. On this point of self-defence, we could not agree with our Quaker friends.

In the years to come I was to admire greatly the Quaker record of service to underprivileged areas of the United States and elsewhere, their superb system of schools in which service to others is the paramount principle, and their relief projects in areas hit by disasters, natural and economic. It thus came as no surprise, years later, when the organisers of our work camp, the American Friends Service Committee (together with the British Friends Service Council) were awarded the Nobel Peace Prize.

It was with a mixture of excitement and apprehension that I began my graduate study in September 1940. Friends cautioned me that my brain would be stretched as never before and that I should expect periods of both elation and depression. They were to be proved correct, but having been forewarned I was at least prepared for the ups and downs that were to follow.

I had elected to specialise in educational administration, a field whose students usually become school and university administrators. There were about a dozen of us, but I was the only one who did not anticipate immediately using this specialised knowledge. I was still convinced my life was to be in journalism. With so much of Georgia's future linked to the quality of education offered its young people, however, I thought an understanding of the problems of school administration would serve me well as a journalist.

In our group were a few students newly graduated with bachelor degrees, but the majority had already been teaching – some for several years. Most were in their thirties and I, at 22, was among the youngest – a fact which was somewhat terrifying as I looked round the classroom on my first day.

We were soon greeted by our college dean, Walter D. Cocking, a genial Iowan with great charisma. He was among a number of educators from other parts of the United States who had been brought in by the university to generate new ideas and inspire students at a time when the state's schools were among the worst in the nation.

Cocking surprised us with his opening statement.

"Since research is to be a major part of your graduate study," he began, "the least you can do is to pronounce the word correctly. It is never *ree*-search," he said, emphasising the first syllable, "but always research – stressing the "search" which is what it is all about. You will hear the word mispronounced by people who should know better – public speakers, radio broadcasters and even some educators but you, I trust, from now on will not be among them."

Cocking turned out to be a no-nonsense man, one who would rather deal bluntly with problems than dish out meaningless praise – although he did not hesitate to praise when it was deserved. We weren't long into our graduate year when our college was asked by officials of a north Georgia county to conduct a study of the county's educational system and come up with concrete proposals for improvements, without regard to personalities or deeply entrenched traditions. The county offered to pay for a substantial part of the survey costs.

Here was an opportunity for a class of future education administrators to become involved in a real situation that would test all the principles we were learning in the classroom. When Dean Cocking laid the proposal before us, he said the university was prepared to meet the remaining expenses but the decision to accept the challenge was ours. We were promised academic credit for the time we would lose, but he warned we had to work long days, be extremely efficient in our field work and, finally, to put in many more hours when we returned to the campus to formalise our findings.

There was no need to take a vote on the proposal; we were unanimously in favour of undertaking the study and the sooner the better. Shortly thereafter Dean Cocking called us together again.

"It is my view," he said, "that the planning stage of any study or enquiry is crucial to the project's success. It follows that the people who are to conduct the study must have privacy so that they cannot be interrupted by the demands of everyday life. The only way to achieve this is to remove the participants from their normal setting to some place sufficiently distant to guarantee total concentration. If the venue is also congenial, that will be an added bonus."

All very well, we murmured, but where was there such a place as he described?

"Accordingly," he went on, "I have reserved rooms for you in a small hotel in Highlands, North Carolina, where there are also committee rooms for our several study groups to meet. We will be there only one long week-end, but with morning, afternoon and evening sessions, we should be able to complete most of our planning."

Highlands, a small, quiet town in the Southern Appalachians which I had passed through on my bicycle trip in the summer of 1939, is only a few miles north of the point where the states of Georgia, South

Carolina and North Carolina meet. The little hotel was just right for our small group; during the weekend we had it all to ourselves and so accomplished a great deal.

In this retreat-like atmosphere, we drew up questionnaires and check lists for all aspects of our study: age and condition of school plant, a class-by-class count of teachers and children, an assessment of teacher qualifications (including recent refresher courses), testing procedures, recreational facilities, adequacy of the school libraries and laboratories, salaries as compared to local cost of living, financing and budgeting procedures, fire and general safety measures, quality and quantity of textbooks, composition and policies of the local board of education, percentages of graduates going on to higher education or directly into industry, the schools' image with the general public, prospective employers of graduates, and so on.

It was an exhilarating experience for our graduate group. Aided by Dean Cocking and other faculty members, we prepared the many forms, charts and questionnaires that we would use in visits to the schools. We were cautioned to regard our study as a fact-finding exercise only; it would be left up to the county board of education to make any decisions based on our conclusions.

In due course our task force visited the schools, gathered reams of facts and returned to the University to organise, digest and evaluate the data. True to its announced intention, the county's board of education moved quickly to improve its schools, its actions largely motivated by our conclusions. We were thrilled that we had been able to make a real contribution in the realm of education so quickly.

Our inspired graduate study in no way, however, prepared us for the next event, one that would bring great shame to the University and profoundly affect us and Dean Cocking.

The Governor of Georgia, Eugene Talmadge, was then the idol of Georgia farmers who represented his power base. Before 1941 Talmadge had gained their sympathy by criticising the state's big cities, Northern industrialists and Wall Street. Now, for the first time, he was to incorporate racial hatred into his political programme.

Dean Cocking was immediately vulnerable, for one of the first tasks after joining the University in 1937 was to assess the quality of black education in Georgia. The Rosenwald Foundation, based in New York, financed the study, which revealed appalling conditions in the state's black schools. Cocking, thus identified as being sympathetic to blacks and having undertaken a study paid for by a northern foundation founded by a Jew, soon became Talmadge's target. The governor had thus cleverly managed to link Cocking with several of the basest prejudices in the minds of many white Georgians – North versus South, hatred of blacks and anti-Semitism.

As our academic year drew near its end, matters went from bad to worse. A few disloyal members of the college of education secretly fed Talmadge any scrap of information, or quotation that might link Dean Cocking with so called "progressive education", particularly any plan that sought to improve the lot of blacks. One proposal by Cocking's faculty advocated a teacher training school to which both white and black teachers would be admitted. Writing about this suggestion in his private weekly newspaper, Talmadge said: "We don't need no niggers and white people taught together."

Cocking was not alone in feeling the weight of Talmadge's ire. Another prominent educator, Dr. Marvin Pittman, president of a teachers' college which today is Georgia Southern University, was also targeted for his "liberal" views on educating blacks. In a move that was a prelude to the era of McCarthyism two decades later, Talmadge ordered the library at Pittman's college to be searched for books that advocated 'Communism or anything else except Americanism.'

Within the college of education there was an eerie feeling that knives were out for Dean Cocking, some secretly wielded by a few members of his own faculty. We graduate students felt something sinister was building up, but never dreamed that our graduate degrees might soon be considered worthless. Dean Cocking never spoke to us about any views he may have held, or the campaign of hate being mounted against him and Dr. Pittman by Talmadge.

For most students the culmination of graduate study comes when they complete book-length theses and then submit themselves to a gruelling oral examination. For our master's degree students these formidable barriers were an anti-climax, given the all-pervasive atmosphere of evil that had preoccupied our minds since we first got wind of Governor Talmadge's intentions. Whether our examiners took this into account I never knew, but we all cleared the final two hurdles without much difficulty.

My thesis suggested that youth hostels would, in future, become a useful tool in assisting teachers to acquaint their students with rural life and natural history. My introduction went back to the creation of the hostel movement by Germany's Richard Schirmann and the pioneer work in the United States by Monroe and Isabel Smith. When my oral examination was over, the chairman of the examining panel turned to me and said, smiling: "There was no way we could fault you; the subject you chose for your thesis is one that none of us knows anything about."

As the day neared when members of our graduate class would receive diplomas, our thoughts were still very much overshadowed by the crisis brought on by Governor Talmadge. Georgia's system of higher education was controlled by a board of regents – in theory above party politics. But regents are appointed by governors and Talmadge, anxious to incorporate racism into his increasingly unpopular administration, knew that he could demand the resignation of those regents whom he had appointed in the first place.

When members of our class received their degrees in the summer of 1941, few of us believed Talmadge would stoop to firing those regents who opposed his thinking and replace them with his "yes-men". Neither did some of his closest friends, who warned him that tinkering with the state's institutions of higher education could be a political disaster. Talmadge, however, was unrepentant.

A "show trial" was staged by Talmadge a month after our class was graduated. It was held in the general assembly chambers of the State Capitol in Atlanta before galleries packed by his supporters. Here a Talmadge backer read excerpts from a book (*Brown America*) by a Rosenwald Foundation official; the supporter claimed the purpose of the book was to "erase the feeling of superiority of the white man".

In a description of the Rosenwald Fund which instantly reminded many Georgians of the emotions aroused in the Mary Phagan trial of 1913, Talmadge claimed the foundation's aim was to provide "Jew money for niggers". In the Mary Phagan trial the state's goal was to have Leo Frank (a Jew) hanged; Talmadge's aim was only somewhat less sinister: character assassination of Dean Cocking and Dr. Pittman.

Talmadge knew about the Rosenwald Fund's broad philanthropic programme, but deliberately attributed mainly racist motives to it. An early backer of the giant retail chain, Sears Roebuck, Julius Rosenwald saw his investment in the firm grow from $35,000 to $150,000,000 in 30 years. Unlike many wealthy donors whose funds often were narrowly distributed, Rosenwald established a foundation which gave freely to every creed and cause imaginable: libraries, schools, hospitals, universities, museums, welfare projects, individual study projects and even the non-Jewish YMCA. It was to this foundation that I had applied for study in Denmark.

Smoking a cigar and wearing a ten-gallon hat throughout the "hearing", Talmadge hoped to link Cocking and Pittman to the Rosenwald Foundation and, by implication, to the fund's many efforts to assist disadvantaged Americans – among them Georgia's blacks. Cocking watched incredulously as the farce continued. At length he rose and said:

"That such tactics could be employed in any country on earth is hard to believe; that they are employed in Georgia has all the earmarks of a terrific nightmare."

As members of our class set out on their respective careers we did not know if the degrees we had just earned would be acceptable to our prospective employers. American universities are accredited by regional agencies which regularly check on institutions' funding, personnel, teaching standards and, above all, freedom from political interference. Our worst fears were realised when the Southern University Conference dropped the University of Georgia from its membership, thereby temporarily rendering our degrees worthless.

Suddenly the wrath of Georgia rural voters erupted against Talmadge. Despite his unrelenting racist remarks, many of the farmers and small town residents who previously supported him, now left in droves when they realised the degrees earned by their sons and daughters could be of no use in their chosen professions and trades. Paying no heed to advisors who warned he could lose the next election for interfering with the state's higher education system, Talmadge pulled out all the stops in his subsequent campaign for re-election.

Huge crowds were assured by the prospect of several tons of

barbecue or fish, and hundreds of gallons of iced tea to wash it down. “Fiddlin’ John” Carson, a folk figure in mountain music, again and again entertained followers before Talmadge arrived. Predictably, many who came to eat did not share Talmadge’s views and he lost decisively to his opponent.

The nightmare that Dean Cocking dreaded was now over, but it would be several years before Georgia’s universities would command the respect they once enjoyed. In the process many gifted instructors and some students, dismayed by the unbelievable depths to which Talmadge had gone, left the state. Others were more patient, hoping the experience was a watershed that would never again allow a politician to interfere with the state’s educational system.

The four years of undergraduate study had opened innumerable vistas of growth for me, but they could not compare with the single year of graduate work under Dean Cocking. It was as if I had aged greatly in one year. If I had once been impatient to get out into the real world, in the words of an old Baptist hymn, to “Brighten the corner where you are”, I was even more restive now. But with a war raging in Europe, who could say if and when the United States might be involved?

As I made my way homewards from Athens for the last time on the Athens - Augusta bus, I realised I would miss this little journey which occasionally produced unpredictable pleasure. Several times annually, during the five years of my study, I had taken the bus along with dozens of other University students. My point of leaving the bus was at Thomson, where my parents met me with the family car. On these trips virtually all the passengers were students. The bus drivers sought to squeeze in as many as possible to avoid having to call for an additional bus or hire expensive taxis.

Consequently, there was always a delay while the drivers tried to fill every seat. Unfortunately for the bus company, sometimes there were several men students left standing. The dilemma was resolved only when one young lady, then another, suggested the problem could be overcome if they sat on the young men’s laps. Once the ice was broken, we men paired off with young ladies willing to sit on our laps for the better part of the next hour.

Usually my lap companion and I were sufficiently relaxed to endure the journey by discussing classes and professors, people we knew in common and our special interests. On this last ride, I was lucky to have by far the most lovely young lady sitting on my lap.

It was as if I had hit the jackpot. Not only was she beautiful and vivacious but she had a perfect figure which caused her upper regions to vibrate wildly when she had a fit of laughter or when the bus turned sharply or hit a bumpy patch of road. By the time we reached our destination I was utterly exhausted and drained.

Other students rushed to embrace their parents with hugs and kisses, but mine were hurt as I ignored them and made a wild dash to the men’s room.

33
I learn to produce a weekly paper but not how to impress the opposite sex

The year 1941 was to be a momentous one for me – and many other Americans.

By the end of that year the United States would have declared war on Japan and Germany – a war that would dramatically affect the lives of millions of my fellow countrymen – and myself. But in the summer of 1941, unaware of what lay ahead, I accepted my first full-time job in my chosen career of rural journalism.

A letter had arrived offering me the post of City Editor with the *Cobb County Times*, a highly respected weekly in Marietta. Its owner, Otis Brumby, wanted a quick reply. The previous editor, Chet Abernathy, had brought *The Times* a national typography (make-up) award and that recognition had allowed him to move on to greener pastures. Brumby was stuck with a monster newspaper without a head for, as he explained to me, I would virtually run the paper. Writing the news, features, leaders (editorials) and even coping with the photography, would be my responsibility.

The pay was not great, but I calculated work experience on *The Times* would be in my favour when I sought my next job. So I accepted his offer and a few days later found myself in Marietta for the first time in my life. It was a prosperous, growing town, not yet dominated by Atlanta, but connected to it by road and rail.

I was apprehensive as I neared *The Times* plant to meet my future boss. Among Georgia's publishers Brumby had a reputation for bluntness and being reluctant to compromise.

A man of average height, his weight suggested he was fond of eating. He shook hands, waved me to a chair and said: "I am not an editor but a publisher. We print trade journals for the automotive industry and several trade directories. They are our money spinners, but the *Cobb County Times* is our flagship. I am proud of the newspaper. We have had some great editors in the past. Chet Abernathy, our most recent, won us a national award for typography."

He paused and looked at me. Page make-up was never my strong point, and here my first boss was perhaps suggesting I could follow Abernathy's act. I knew I couldn't and told him so. He smiled and went on.

"Don't let it bother you," he said. "We all have our strong and our weak points." Then he leaned forward and added: "I'm not a writer myself, but I do put together a weekly column of odds and ends – a kind of lively *pot pourri* – which I call "Jambalaya". I came across the word when I was in Mexico and was once served a fabulous stew. When I asked the chef what was in it, he said "Everything". Well, my grammar and spelling are not perfect and one of your jobs is to edit my column and make sure it is correct."

He went on to say that I had total responsibility for the newspaper, other than his column and the advertising, for which a manager was employed. He pointed out that on the *Times* we had formidable competition from a respected daily paper, *The Marietta Journal*. Were there any questions? Well, I had so many I didn't know where to begin. I was overwhelmed by the tremendous responsibility I had taken on. At length, I said I was sure there would be many questions, and I hoped he would allow me to barge into his office when they arose. He nodded amiably, stood up to dismiss me, and that was that. I was on my own!

In the next few hours I met most of the *Times* "family" with whom my immediate future would be linked. The advertising manager proved to hold the key to how many pages we would print each week. "We operate on a two-to-one ratio", he said sternly, "For every two pages of ads I sell, you will have one page to fill with news. I will be selling ads right up to press time, so you must be prepared to revise the number of news pages on no notice at all."

I had encountered a mild form of this economic constraint on the number of pages of editorial content while working on the University of Georgia's *Red and Black*; on that paper we could ignore the constraint up to a point, because we received a generous subsidy from the university. With the *Cobb County Times* it was clear that the constraint would be absolute; i.e. if advertising revenue fell, so must the number of pages in that week's paper.

I next met a shy lady who was in charge of "country correspondents". American weekly papers serving predominantly rural areas appointed in each community one person, usually a woman, to report weekly social and personal news. Cobb County, although soon to be overshadowed by Atlanta, still had about a dozen small towns and hamlets. Sometimes the name and telephone number of the local reporter were printed at the head of each town's weekly column. Some papers carried small photographs of their correspondents, but the *Times* did not.

Residents in these rural communities were most pleased to see their names in print and so correspondents were seldom short of news. Metropolitan daily editors might turn up their noses at what constituted "news" in rural areas, but country weeklies could not hope to succeed without a plethora of local names in print.

And what kind of news would be reported? Here are a few examples, whose counterparts could be found in hundreds of American weeklies at that time:

"Friends of Mrs. William Jones will be sorry to learn she is in the County Hospital with a recurrence of her old back problem." (Comment: Those in the community who didn't know of the illness will now either visit Mrs. Jones or send her a get-well card. When Mrs. Jones returns home, the correspondent will duly report she has "recovered".)

"Mrs. Harold Evans of New Orleans, mother of Robert Evans, is vacationing with her son and his family. Before her marriage she was Betty Smith, and grew up in our community. Her husband was killed in the war and since his death she has been employed by the New Orleans jazz festival committee." (Comment: The older generation will remember Betty Smith and her husband; the young generation will want to ask her about the state of jazz in New Orleans. The alert editor will go to this rural community and interview and perhaps photograph Mrs. Evans for the next issue.)

"Fred Barrows will celebrate his 90th birthday next Thursday. Family and friends have arranged a birthday party in the Baptist church hall at 3 p.m. where a large cake and plenty of iced tea will be available for all." (Comment: This party, in effect, will be of general community interest and will be attended by most of the adult population. Naturally it will be a "must" for the paper's photographer.)

The lady in charge of the *Times*' dozen or so rural correspondents showed me their weekly input. All except one or two were written in longhand on notebook paper. Some were illegible to me, but she had long since come to recognise each correspondent's writing. Some were filled with errors of spelling and grammar, which she duly corrected. Her final task was to provide me with the total weekly output, neatly typed, double-spaced. This she did, week after week, never complaining and always on time. Small wonder that some of the *Times*' most loyal subscribers resided in those rural communities.

Most of the "hard news" came from expected sources: the police, law courts, firemen, churches, schools, sports organisations and reporters from clubs and societies. There was also a sheaf of press releases from agricultural and other government agencies; some newsworthy and others "puffs" of self-praise.

Our journalism school had urged its students not to be only reporters, but "photo-journalists" and the training I had received towards this end was to serve me well. I soon learned the truth behind the adage: "A picture is worth a thousand words" and managed to have at least one local photograph on the front page of each issue, a formula many rural publishers relied on to maintain circulation.

There was never a week when there wasn't some "over-setting" of type. It had to be that way, for I never knew when I would have to fill an extra page or two with news if more advertisements were sold at the last minute. Fortunately much of the over-set material could be used the following week. The great trick was to get into print anything that was of time value.

Occasionally this meant that a long feature written by a contributor had to be omitted. When this happened, he or she inevitably complained – not to me but to my boss. When the offended contributor had departed, Mr. Brumby would call me in and report the complaint. Then, without waiting for my reply, he would smile and say: "I know how it is. I have the same problem sometimes with people who contribute to my weekly column. Just do your best."

Who, among our *Times* 'family' derived the greatest satisfaction when each issue was at last put to bed and the presses started rolling? Was it Mr. Brumby himself, the lady in charge of the rural correspondents, the sports contributors, the advertising manager or those technicians – the typesetters, compositors and pressmen - without whom there would be no paper? I quickly concluded we all shared the enthusiasm and pride of producing our weekly "baby". At 23, I had to admit to the greatest thrill of achievement I had yet known.

The Times shop was enormous, with a virtual battery of linotype machines arranged in one long row. There were several small presses and one gigantic one operated by the genial Harold Derby. The centre-piece of the large working area was a group of granite-topped tables where the page "forms" were put together under powerful lights. A small, wizened man with a gentle sense of humour, Grover Fennell, presided over this team. His son, an American Marine, happened to be on the island of Midway when the Japanese attempted to take it during the early stages of the Second World War. The Battle of Midway was to become an epic struggle of the Pacific theatre and Grover was first fearful, then thrilled as the island's garrison (including his son) held off the Japanese.

Grover was quick to tell me that my front-page make-up didn't hold a candle to the previous editor's workmanship. "What you want to do," he said, "is to complete *most* of your news stories on the front page and not carry them over inside the paper. Otherwise, you will have the readers jumping backwards and forwards the whole time." How right he was, and how lucky I was to have him teach me a basic truth about make-up not covered in journalism school.

The most daunting characters in the print shop were the linotype operators. A popularly held myth was that they were heavy drinkers and semi-literate. Nothing could have been further from the truth. If they drank, they must have done so off duty for their output was never affected.

As for literacy, I had them to thank for catching my all too frequent mistakes in spelling and grammar. More than once the most outspoken of the operators, a man with whom I never argued, came storming into the office with my copy in hand. "What do you mean by this?" he would ask. "It's as clear as mud." Or, he would spot a split infinitive, an error in history or geography.

Typesetters were under orders not to correct supposed facts in stories they were setting up, but my outspoken friend did not hesitate to march into my "sanctuary" demanding that a sentence or a phrase be rewritten before he dignified it by putting it into hot metal. I soon learned that if I had a query about style or a question of fact, he was the walking encyclopaedia I needed.

Gradually I came to know all the editorial and pressroom people vital to the paper's weekly appearance. I worked hard to get most of the pages set up on Mondays and Tuesdays to avoid the panic of the weekend when the paper appeared. However much I prepared in advance, there were always last minute stories to insert with a corresponding amount to be deleted. The pressure was enormous and I was drained when the paper finally went to press. Only then was I off the hook until the following Monday morning.

I learn to produce a weekly paper but not how to impress the opposite sex

Once a month there was a particularly bright moment when a gorgeous teenager, editor of the Marietta high school paper, came to the *Times* to organise the paper's layout and printing. She was shy and embarrassed by the attention caused by her stunning looks. Despite a five-year age difference, I was attracted to her and tried to convey my interest by passing sincere compliments about the excellent quality of her school paper. To my dismay, she parried my words with polite but indifferent responses while continuing the serious work of editing. It seemed I had not yet mastered the art of dealing with the opposite sex.

PART II

The Allies win a war and I win a bride

1942-1946

34
Pearl Harbour puts me in uniform

Apart from the satisfaction of turning out a readable newspaper every week, there were other benefits accruing from my work. New friendships were forged as I became known as the person to contact to get a story into print. As I was offered more free tickets to community events than I could attend, I had the luxury of accepting only those that were either truly newsworthy or held a special interest for me.

Thus it was that I was introduced to an aspect of southern folk culture previously unknown to me: the fasola and shaped note singing held regularly in the Cobb County courthouse. The story of fasola singing is too long to be told here, but its original songbook, *Sacred Harp*, was a necessary companion to the Bible itself in the rural South from its appearance in 1844 to relatively recent times. Not all lovers of music appreciated fasola singing. Some critics said it all sounded the same, others claimed it was "minor music", and still others maintained there was no tune to it. Some devotees, on the other hand, say the music is best appreciated by the singer, not the listener.

Fasola enthusiasts use only four syllables in singing the notes of the scale: *fa-sol-la-mi*. They are Old English in origin and may be found in several of Shakespeare's works. The system was brought to the United States by the first colonists and remained in popular use until a century and a half ago when the Continental European *do-re-mi* scale largely supplanted it. With fasola singing virtually extinct in Britain today, the rural American South may be the only place where it survives – and even there, only just.

Through my articles in *The Times* I sought to keep alive these annual singing "conventions", for like the native fiddlers of the Southern Appalachians, the fasola singers were rapidly becoming an endangered species.

Marietta's Kennesaw Mountain was the site of one of the epic battles of the American Civil War. It was now a National Monument and its curator, Leo Aikman, was a likable man with a keen sense of humour. He wrote regular features about the monument and the Civil War battles that had raged in the area. He held the view that Sherman's by-passing of Confederate positions on Kennesaw Mountain was one of the finest examples of the flanking technique to be employed in the war.

We southerners reluctantly put up with the premise that the Confederate forces were out-smarted; this was especially painful to hear from Aikman – not a native southerner. He was, however, such a genial and persuasive writer and speaker that we never doubted his analysis. Aikman went on to become a popular columnist with *The Atlanta Constitution* and one of the finest after-dinner speakers in the state.

Kennesaw Mountain became associated in my mind with another great event in American history. On Sunday, December 7th, 1941, several friends and I decided to walk the trail to the mountain's peak. Although the mountain is not high by Appalachian standards, it does afford wonderful views in all directions. The superb trail and gradual slope make the walk popular with all ages. My friends and I savoured the leisurely descent in crisp but sunny weather and prepared to go our separate ways as we reached the bottom. There waiting for us was another friend with a serious look spread over his usual genial features.

"Have you heard the terrible news?" he asked.

We hadn't.

"Pearl Harbour has been bombed by the Japanese and there are hundreds, if not thousands, of casualties", he said. "It is almost certain Congress will now declare war on the Japanese, as well as the Germans."

We were numbed. My first reaction was to wonder what effect war would have on my work. Would Marietta become involved in some part of the war effort? Then it dawned on me that I might not be around to see what happened to Marietta and Cobb County during the war. I was only 23, single and – except for having only one good eye – in excellent health.

American entry into the war, a conflict that seemed only a distant possibility when I was in university, had immediate and profound effects on my life. Otis Brumby, my publisher, called me in and said that *The Times* must support the American war effort in every possible way, starting immediately. There were editorials to be written backing the American entry, features to be developed explaining the necessity for rationing and conservation of resources and articles predicting that a national military service requirement was a certainty.

Then out of the blue came a thunderbolt announcement from Washington: Marietta had been selected for the site of a huge aircraft plant to be built by the Bell Aviation Company. The plant was to manufacture some of the aircraft which, it was hoped, would bring a speedy end to the war. Suddenly Marietta was filled with land and housing speculators from all over the United States. As thousands of workers would be employed in the building of the plant and making bombers, land was at a premium for new houses, shops and service industries. *The Times* reaped great advertising revenue from these new enterprises, for all planning applications had to appear in print before they could be considered legal.

By the spring of 1942 the American war effort was rapidly gaining momentum. Military camps were being created or enlarged all over the country and I knew it was only a matter of time before I would be called up. But with only one good eye and a susceptibility to hay fever, I knew that I was eligible only for "limited service". That could be a desk job, a depot position or some other assignment far removed from combat.

But I was anxious to go abroad – not to sit out the war in the United States. At that time there was concern that the Japanese would attack the American west coast, anywhere from Alaska to California. To counter this threat, the United States and Canada hastily agreed that an all-weather highway should be built through Canada, linking continental US with Alaska. Advertisements appeared in newspapers for construction workers and others needed for this tremendous undertaking, by then called the "Alcan Highway".

I wrote to the administrative headquarters of the highway, offering my services as an information officer, knowing that such a massive project required a great deal of goodwill and public support both in Canada and the United States. So as not to mislead, I pointed out my disabilities. I received a prompt reply saying my disabilities (especially the hay fever) ruled out my eligibility. Disappointed, I could only await the establishment of the selective (national) service board in my hometown of Louisville. Once this was created, I wrote to ask that I be included in an early contingent of men called up in my county.

In due course I was given a date for reporting to the board in my hometown, Louisville. My publisher knew of my desire to become involved in the war and accepted my departure with grace. In Louisville I learned that eight men had been selected for a contingent to report to Fort McPherson in Atlanta. Because I was the only one among them with a university degree, I was given "command" with the obligation to see that nobody went absent en route to Atlanta. We duly set off by bus to Macon where we had almost two hours to wait before connecting with a bus to Atlanta.

There was no problem en route to Macon, but the two-hour layover was to prove a nightmare. One of the men, a farmer's son who had never been away from home before, promptly set about drinking heavily in the bus station, despite my earnest pleas. When the time came to board the Atlanta bus, he had literally drunk himself under the table.

I did not know what to do and visions of starting my Army career with a court-martial loomed ominously. Then a kind policeman arrived. Quickly sizing up the situation, he told me he would take the young man and his suitcase in tow, sober him up overnight and put him on the first bus to Atlanta the next morning.

With great trepidation, I told the adjutant at Fort McPherson that our missing man had become "ill" in Macon, but hoped to join us the next day. To my great relief, he asked no questions and, sure enough, the young man arrived safely just as the Macon policeman said he would. Six months later, while scanning the front page of my hometown weekly, the *News and Farmer*, I was amused to read that this young man was the first in our group to receive the Good Conduct Medal.

Fort McPherson was the induction centre for a large part of Georgia and neighbouring states. Here we were to receive medical examinations, uniforms and learn "close order drill" (marching in small groups). We would also have talks and indoctrination films covering basic aspects of military life (discipline, security, loyalty, venereal diseases etc.).

We quickly learned to accept with good grace our rightful share of menial duties, including KP (kitchen police), latrine orderly and "policing the area" (cleaning up). KP duty was every bit as tedious, and humorous, as the many cartoons that showed the poor private faced with peeling a small mountain of potatoes. At that time some labour-saving devices for the kitchen had been invented, but the Army didn't want to hear about them, for it was always a challenge to find useful employment for all the men passing through induction centres.

Latrine duty was not so onerous. Here all the essential mops, brushes and cleansing materials were provided in profusion. Of the many humorous aspects of latrine duty spawned during the war, that portrayed in film, "No Time for Sergeants", must be tops. In it there is a scene where an ingenious GI, given the job of latrine orderly, connects all the toilet seats with a wire terminating at a board which, when stepped on, causes the toilet seats to rise or fall. When the commanding officer enters to inspect the orderly's work, the GI shouts "Attention!" and simultaneously stamps on the board connected to the wire. Instantly all the toilet seats fly up to salute the flabbergasted inspector.

In truth, our sergeants were hard pressed to find work to keep us occupied. Sometimes the same grassy area was "policed" again after only an hour or two. Sometimes several men were put on a chore that required only one. Accordingly, we learned to perform these "pretend-chores" slowly and deliberately. All too often, we had discovered, hurrying anywhere only meant waiting when we got there.

"How many of you know how to drive?" asked our sergeant one day.

Every hand shot up. My trainee friends and I would have liked nothing better than driving a jeep or a small truck somewhere. Here at last was a sergeant, we thought, who would give us interesting work.

"Great!" shouted the sergeant. "There are 24 wheelbarrows round the corner of the shed waiting to be driven by you. All you have to do is move that pile of dirt to the other end of the parade ground so it can be used to fill in some ditches."

From this point on, we learned never to volunteer for anything.

35
We cure the Sergeant of his egotism

Life in American induction camps seemed pointless and frustrating at times, but it must have been far more difficult for the planning staff who had to decide what each of us was best qualified to do in a war that might last for years. They had little to go on except our medical and education records, aptitude and IQ test results.

I did not know at the time that the IQ test we took was the same as that given nationally at educational institutions. Graduate schools, in particular, had employed them before developing their own specialised tests. The day after taking the tests we were called in and given our results. Mine was in the 140-150 bracket which, the administrative clerk told me, put me in the upper 10% of those tested. When I asked what that meant insofar as my future work in the Army was concerned, he shrugged his shoulders and said, “Who knows? You can never tell what the Army is going to do next.” He was right, of course.

Eventually the planners decided that a battalion of us should go to California to become military police specialising in protecting ships and piers in San Francisco’s sprawling dockland area. Our officers hinted at a certain urgency in our assignment, for Japanese submarines were known to be active off the California coast.

The only MPs I knew about were those burly characters who roamed American cities in jeeps, looking for errant servicemen. At first we were deeply disappointed to think we would become MPs, but on reflection we imagined guard duty on the San Francisco waterfront could prove more exciting than we had bargained for. As we chatted with one another discussing our assignment, we made an interesting discovery: every one of us was on “limited service”, that is, each had a physical disability. About 90% of us had eye defects, a fact which promptly caused us to dub ourselves “One-Eyed Wonders”.

After packing our possessions into newly issued duffel bags we boarded a troop train at the fort on August 28th, 1942 – resigning our fate to Uncle Sam. Most of us had never been out of the South, and an all-expense paid trip to California was not to be sneezed at – even if we were in uniform. For the next five days our train snaked its way north through Chattanooga and Louisville, then westwards through St. Louis and through the Rockies and then on to Utah, Nevada and finally, California. There was no guide to point out sights, but we country boys didn’t need one, for everything along the way was a revelation to us. I used my simple “Brownie” camera to record some of the sights glimpsed from the window of our train. Two spectacular ones were the long causeway across the Great Salt Lake in Utah, and the massive Feather River Canyon in eastern California. At last our train rolled into San Francisco where a convoy of trucks waited to carry us to our first Army “home”,

Home, we discovered, was to be Funston Park, then a part of Fort Mason. Here a “tent city” had been erected. Because the land was flat and rainfall heavy, the tents had wooden floors. Likewise, wooden cat-walks linked the tents to latrines, mess-halls and company headquarters. “Tent City” seemed dour and depressing when we arrived that fine day, but worse was to come. We soon learned the park was prone to flooding after a heavy shower. On such occasions we were grateful for the wooden floors and cat-walks.

After a short period of small weapons training, instructions about guarding port facilities and more close order drill, we were taken to the waterfront for our first guard duty. There was a small team of MPs for each vessel, the number being determined by how many holds of the ship were being worked. If a four-hold ship was being loaded, there would be a guard for each hold, one fore, one aft, and one at the gangway – seven altogether. Having a good man at the gangway was crucial, for letting an enemy agent on a suicide mission aboard a vessel laden with explosives would be disastrous.

We also placed guards at pier ends and on the quayside, for there was always the possibility of Japanese raids by midget submarines. No one seriously thought the Japanese were capable of invading and holding any part of the California coast, but small submarine attacks could not be ruled out. There was also concern about the loyalty of Japanese-Americans ("Nisei"), many of whom had lived in California for generations. Theoretically all could be potential enemy agents, but the forced removal of Nisei to detention camps away from the Pacific Coast became one of the most controversial acts of the war.

The landing of a few men, skilled in the techniques of sabotage, was thus a real threat. The pier end and quayside assignments were both lonely and subject to extreme cold and dampness, especially at night, being right at the water's edge. Although clad in five layers of clothing, three of them heavy wool, I suffered greatly from the cold fog rolling in across San Francisco Bay from the Pacific. Stamping my feet, flailing my arms against my chest, walking briskly – none of these kept the cold from penetrating right through my bones.

Daytime guard duty on the pier end, however, could be rewarding. From our vantage point we could see the Golden Gate Bridge and scores of great cargo liners coming and going – most engaged in the war effort. At some pier ends, mammoth sewers discharged their raw contents into the bay. My fellow guards and I never ceased to wonder at the tens of thousands of condoms constantly flowing from these sewers, no matter the time of day. We might have expected to see them on the morning shift, but there they were, in their teeming thousands, at midday, mid-afternoon and early evening. Were we the only ones in San Francisco, we wondered, contributing to the war effort?

Guard duty aboard ships was always exciting. Our primary concern was to prevent smoking, for most vessels carried explosives and some had only explosives. We were not supposed to talk with crew members and stevedores, but there was nothing we could do to keep them from talking to us.

There were some colourful characters among them, such as one gnarled old seaman who each evening sat alone in the bow of his vessel eating cloves of garlic. Decades ahead of today's healthy eating advice, he told me garlic was keeping him fit and would guarantee him long life. I made the mistake of getting too near the first time I saw him. Whether the garlic kept away illness I did not know, but it kept me away from him thereafter. Delicious coffee, on the other hand, was always available in a vessel's galley; likewise plates of chocolate brownies deliberately left out for us on our lonely night shifts.

We also guarded pier sheds and their adjacent outdoor storage areas. Here fires, started either by a careless smoker or an enemy incendiary device, were our greatest worry. Guard duty lasted 24 hours a day, whether or not there was shipping activity at every pier. We manned three eight-hour shifts, of which the "graveyard" period from midnight to eight in the morning was the most dreaded. It was usually the coldest, wettest and loneliest. For these, shifts were arranged strictly by rotation, so that no man felt he had been taken advantage of.

Apart from the San Francisco dockland area, our military police unit also maintained a small detachment at the Bayside railway marshalling yards near San Bruno, a few miles south of San Francisco. Our tents at San Bruno were only ten or fifteen yards from the main San Francisco-Los Angeles line. Every few minutes freight trains loaded with war materiel roared by, going in one direction or the other. When a train passed, our Army cots shook violently and at times left the tent floor. The first few nights I was terrified and slept little, but I soon discovered the human body and mind can accommodate themselves to any discomfort, however unusual it may be.

We had two principal tasks at San Bruno. The first was to be on the alert for smoke or fire, for our area of the marshalling yards handled only freight cars laden with explosives. Our second task was to prevent locomotive engineers from "humping" (joining together units of a train with unnecessary speed or force). This, from the start, proved to be only an academic exercise for, when I and my fellow guards approached burly engineers whose cars loaded with TNT had been joined together with almighty smacks, they bemusedly looked down at us from their cabs as much as to say "So what?". One veteran engineer eventually told me that all explosives were carefully packed and that, to his knowledge, no consignment had ever been lost due to humping. That may or may not have been so, but I was much relieved when my brief tour of duty in the marshalling yards came to an end.

I then returned to the spartan life in Funston Park's tent city. My best friend, Earl Webster from Alabama, and I shared a tent with two other men, one an inductee like ourselves, and the other a Regular Army man with many years' service. He was still a private and resented the intrusion of the new "civilian army" which he considered a threat to his advancement. There was a considerable age gap between him and us and he declined to join in our jokes or conversation. What annoyed us most was his practice, in the middle of the night when it was particularly wet or cold, of not going outside to use the latrine but using a knot hole in the wooden floor near which he had conveniently sited his cot. He may have been a sharpshooter with Army weapons, but his aim in other respects was not always accurate.

My new-found friend, Earl Webster, confided to me that he had a rare ailment that affected his sense of balance and speech when he became cold and damp. Our Funston Park tents afforded him no protection against these elements. One damp night he awoke mumbling nonsense and rubbing the back of his neck. I helped him get dressed and together we went to the company headquarters where a sleepy young lieutenant promptly pronounced him drunk. He did not believe my account of Earl's medical history and, only after my strong insistence, agreed to send Earl to the hospital rather than turn him over to the military police.

I accompanied Earl to the hospital where the doctors readily accepted my explanation and placed him in intensive care. That was the last time I saw or heard from Earl. His condition worsened and he was moved to an army medical centre in a warmer climate where his health continued to deteriorate, and he eventually died. Earl's illness, and subsequent death, shocked me into the realisation that not all Army deaths came on the battlefield or even as the result of horrific accidents.

In a move calculated to improve our living conditions, the army requisitioned an old warehouse, the Fontana Building, adjacent to the Ghirardelli chocolate factory in San Francisco. We southerners had never heard of Ghirardelli chocolate, but we learned it had long been a popular brand name on the Pacific coast. East of the Mississippi we ate only Hershey bars.

In the converted warehouse our cots were laid out in row upon row on floors that had once held commodities of various kinds. The daily effort to remove the dust, accumulated through the years and firmly entrenched between the great planks, proved futile. This "sweeping" only served to create a fog of dust in the giant sleeping area. Linoleum was ruled out as being both expensive and unmilitary. The result was constant turmoil among the three eight-hour shifts. One was away at guard duty, another was getting dressed or idly passing the time of day and the third was trying to sleep. No one ever thought of erecting partitions for the various shifts.

My fellow hay-fever sufferers and I had a miserable time, for there were no such remedies as anti-histamines then. We slept between woollen blankets and my skin, already affected by the dust, soon developed a rash. Sheets were neither issued nor permitted, but I went out and bought them for my own use – taking care not to leave them exposed during inspections.

A touch of comic relief came one day when small groups of us went to a nearby public park to practise close-order drill. Our drill sergeant was a vain young man in love with his voice and the cadence routine he had developed. As the park was convenient for young secretaries and other office workers taking their lunch breaks, our sergeant liked nothing better than to parade his minions in front of these young female admirers.

For the sergeant there was only one problem: at times, especially when a wind was blowing, his voice was difficult to hear and we sometimes missed his commands. A few friends and I decided one day to "cure" the sergeant of his egotism. We planned, after he had given us the order "To the rear, march", to pretend we hadn't heard the order and to continue marching in the original direction. This we could easily do as we were the leading four men and he was at the back of the column.

Sure enough, the expected command came, barely audible, but we pretended not to hear and carried on. We knew the sergeant had assumed the entire column had reversed itself, for his voice, intoning "one, two, three, four," was fading in the distance. We four kept straight faces, quietly counting "one, two, three, four" among ourselves to keep in step. The sergeant's bevy of admirers broke into hilarious laughter and shouted in a chorus "Your lost sheep!"

Meanwhile, we were getting dangerously near the main road and its traffic. Our trick would be blown unless something happened quickly. Suddenly, there rang out a raucous, high pitched scream: "Squad, HALT!" The on-lookers roared with laughter as we stopped at the park's very edge. Then the sergeant shouted "About face!" and marched us back to join the main part of the column. Some of our fellow soldiers could not avoid smiling but we four kept straight faces and said not a word. From that day onward we had no problem hearing the sergeant's commands.

36
I am asked "Can a murderer go to Heaven?"

Although our guard duty was exciting at times, it was arduous. Consequently, we applied for three-day passes as often as was permitted. Being so close to Hollywood (as it seemed to me), I applied for a pass to go there one weekend. I had not saved enough from my private's pay to buy a bus ticket to Los Angeles, and so had to hitch-hike. Servicemen had little trouble in obtaining rides during the war and soon a kind man came along and agreed to take me all the way to Los Angeles – provided I shared the driving with him. I had driven only in Georgia, but thought driving along the Pacific coast road to Los Angeles would be no problem.

To my consternation I learned the distance from San Francisco to Los Angeles was over 400 miles and that we would be driving right through the night. When dusk approached I noticed my companion did not turn his headlights on.

"Against the law," he explained, "in case a Japanese sub spots us lighting up a potential target."

"But," I protested, "how are you going to see all the twists and turns on this road without lights?"

"No problem," he said, "just watch and you will see."

He slowed the car deliberately and soon a giant "semi" truck overtook us. My friend then accelerated and began to "tailgate" the truck. Its broad aluminium rear was easy to keep in view, but keeping the right distance behind – never knowing when the truck would brake to take a sharp bend – was hair-raising. About midnight my friend became exhausted and asked if I could take the wheel for a few hours. He pulled in at a lay-by and I wondered if I would ever catch our "pilot" truck.

I need not have worried for the highway was full of semis with their crucial war materiel. One passed our lay-by and I quickly sped up to its tail. The semi drivers seldom expected cars to overtake them at night, knowing how useful their large vehicles were as guides to cars travelling behind them. My friend had hoped I would stay at the wheel until dawn, but after a few hours the strain was more than I could take and I was obliged to awaken him. Fortunately the rest had completely revived him; he took over the wheel again and drove the rest of the way to Los Angeles without stopping.

Hollywood made a great effort to welcome servicemen to the sets where movies were being made and stars willingly posed for photographs with us. I encountered Joan Leslie, only 20 at the time, who was the sweetheart of Sergeant York in the film about America's Congressional Medal of Honour winner in the First World War. She flashed her famous smile and gave me an autograph and a snapshot. It was easy to see why she was such a favourite with servicemen.

Two war-time classics were being filmed the day of my visit. One, "The Edge of Darkness", portrayed Norway's resistance to the Germans and starred the veteran actor, Monty Woolley. The other was "Mission to Moscow", in which a Moscow railway station had been authentically reproduced inside a great hangar-like building. I marvelled at how this could be done, until someone at my elbow remarked that Hollywood employed as advisers people from every corner of the globe and that any scene, anywhere, could be reproduced with little difficulty.

Other highlights of the Hollywood visit were seeing Rudy Valee, the entertainer, broadcast, and watching artists create images for cartoons. We also toured Warner Brothers' vast premises – including a complete Wild West town. How I managed to fit all these adventures into a three-day pass (including the two long trips) I can't imagine. I do recall getting almost no sleep and going round like a "zombie" much of the time.

The attractions of the San Francisco area were so numerous that we managed to sample only a fraction during our brief stay there. We knew we could be transferred at any time and so made good use of every free moment. In downtown San Francisco there was a large USO (United Servicemen's Organisation) centre where we could be assured of coffee and doughnuts at any time. Like the jeep and the Dakota aircraft, the USO centres were among the great successes of the war.

Set up in built-up areas and railway stations in cities and towns near military installations, their number soared to over 1,000 by the end of the war. Conceived as inter-faith projects, they enjoyed the support of Protestants, Catholics, Jews, the Salvation Army and the YMCA. and YWCA. The Federal Government also made buildings available. Apart from providing ready refreshments, the USO's offered rest facilities for weary servicemen en route to distant locations. At some of the larger centres, many nationally renowned entertainers provided free shows. Suffice it to say, the American serviceman was assured a warm reception almost anywhere he went in the country.

Just how universal was that kindness was demonstrated one day when a friend and I had an afternoon free of guard duty. We were in the centre of San Francisco's downtown area when we spotted a gorgeous young woman, probably in her thirties, near one of the city's largest hotels. She was dressed in a magnificent fur coat and seemed not in a hurry. We surmised she probably was a high class prostitute, although she possessed the beauty and poise of a lady. Having my camera with me, I dared my friend to join me in asking the young woman to pose with us for a photograph. He agreed.

"Excuse me," I said, "we're stationed here in San Francisco and would like to send our folks a snapshot of us with a pretty girl, but we don't know one. Would you mind posing with us?"

To our great joy the young woman instantly agreed. Placing her between us, we persuaded a passer-by to snap the picture. As he did so, all three of us produced broad grins. We thanked the young woman profusely and continued on our way. Later when I handed in the film to be developed, I indicated that one print should show my friend with the young lady with myself omitted, and the other should show me beside the gorgeous creature with my friend cropped out. The resulting prints, which we promptly sent home, generated envious remarks about "those lovely San Francisco girls."

Hollywood wholeheartedly joined in the American war effort by producing many films emphasising patriotism and heroic actions. Apart from mainstream films, it also made propaganda films depicting the Axis power bent on destroying our American way of life. In San Francisco an Army friend and I were able to see several movies with war-time themes, thanks to the generous ticket discounts offered men in service.

One evening, my friend and I viewed an excellent film in which gallant soldiers had carried the day. We emerged from the theatre behind two lovely teenage girls – obviously high school friends. They also had been captivated by the film, for one of them turned to us and said:

"Soldiers are our heroes, and we think the most patriotic thing we can do is have a baby by one." With an imploring look she added: "Will you help us?"

My friend and I were speechless. Coming from puritanical families in the Deep South, we were astonished to find such naiveté in two lovely, vulnerable girls. These were not "street-wise" creatures, but well-spoken girls no doubt from happy family backgrounds not dissimilar from our own. My friend and I had sisters of similar age.

At length I recovered sufficiently to stammer that we were probably in for a long war, and that they would have plenty of time to complete their education, after which – if they still liked soldiers, they might consider marriage. Happily, they were not offended by our rejection and instead thanked us warmly as we parted.

A favourite haunt of soldiers in San Francisco was a large indoor skating rink known as the "Ice Palace". Here we could skate free of charge for as long as we liked, tutored by a bevy of beautiful, stalwart young ladies. It was here that I first heard Alven's "Swedish Rhapsody", often played as skaters glided round the rink. Somehow it seemed the perfect accompaniment to ice skating and I never hear it without thinking of those San Francisco efforts to keep my balance.

As far as I know, there were no ice skating rinks in the South before and during the war. Hence, for most southerners in uniform, this was both a novel and challenging experience. How the gorgeous instructors coped with so many flailing servicemen night after night I can't imagine, but their patience and skill were always appreciated. It was the height of comedy to see a young woman take a uniformed beginner in tow, determined, at least, not to allow herself to fall. In this goal she was usually, but not always, successful. The greenhorn usually began by splaying his feet in opposite directions, with the girl just managing to keep him from falling prostrate on the ice. Then having learned to keep his feet together, he miraculously managed to shoot both feet forward at the same time.

The permutations were endless: grasping the instructor tightly round the waist and lunging forward, letting his grip slip lower and lower as his splaying became more frantic, or, with a last desperate effort to restore his balance, he grabs the young lady's ankle as his body shoots through her legs and brings her down solidly on his stomach. She has lost the battle, and they remain inert for a moment, amid a crescendo of laughter from onlookers. Then the gallant young lady gets to her feet, pulls the soldier onto his, and the ordeal starts all over again.

San Francisco's cable cars were also a never-ending fascination. Operator and passenger treated each other as family. Conversation flowed as if we had known each other for a lifetime. The incredibly steep hills afforded panoramic views for miles around. Some people used the cable cars to get to and from work; others, including those of us in uniform, were just content to be riding anywhere.

On one cable car ride, I experienced an unpleasant surprise. A middle-aged man, crippled and using a crutch, was having difficulty in mounting the car. I was aware that people with crutches could easily be thrown off balance by well-meaning bystanders and so approached the man cautiously, and asked if I could be of assistance. He scowled at me, gave me a sharp crack on the shin with his crutch and replied that he was perfectly capable of looking after himself. The other passengers were as shocked as I but we said nothing as the man awkwardly mounted the steps. Then I realised that he, like a man condemned to terminal illness, was probably embittered by his infirmity. I could only rejoice that I was of sound body and mind.

Having been a church-goer all my life, I was determined to seek out San Francisco's Baptist churches. There were bound to be more than one, so where to start?

I had not yet visited the city's Chinatown -- an attraction in its own right -- but surely it did not have enough Baptists to warrant a church of its own. Chinatown, indeed, lived up to its reputation of reflecting the old country, for everywhere I turned I saw shops selling traditional food, herbs and medicines. Moreover, many buildings bore roofs and other features modelled on Chinese architecture. There were no festivals during my stay in San Francisco, but I was told that on these occasions the "real Chinatown" was on display.

As I continued to wander through the narrow streets, I suddenly came upon a Chinese Baptist Church! I did a double-take, but sure enough, there it was in the heart of the area. I rushed inside only to find it empty, but then noticed a Church House adjacent. There I was greeted by several staff members who invited me to return the following week when the young people of the church would be celebrating American Thanksgiving Day. I duly returned and was warmly welcomed. Apart from the children, there was a servicemen's Sunday School class. They, like myself, were in uniform. Several were in the Army Air Corps training to be pilots. We exchanged addresses and on my departure, they gave me a copy of the Lord's Prayer in Chinese. I carried it in my wallet throughout the war. I corresponded with several young Chinese-Americans until our sudden, frequent change of military postings caused us to lose contact.

Not long before being shipped out of San Francisco I located the city's First Baptist Church. Here, as with the Chinese Baptist Church, I was given a warm welcome by the servicemen's Sunday School class. The church used the Southern Baptist hymnal and the preacher delivered the same direct, simple sermons I had known in Georgia.

One Sunday I was approached by a frail but beautiful girl about my own age. She was blonde, simply dressed and wore no make-up or jewellery. Smiling nervously, she peered questioningly into my eyes. I sensed she wanted to ask me something that was very much on her mind. We chatted casually for a while about the war and the upheaval it was bringing into our lives. Suddenly she stopped and again gave me that mysterious, pleading look.

"Do you believe in the Ten Commandments?" she asked.

Taken aback by her abrupt question, I hesitated for a moment and then replied that I did, adding that those ancient laws make an excellent guide for daily living. My reply, though well intended, evidently did not satisfy her, for an expression resembling panic spread across her face.

"Does that mean," she asked, "that a person who has broken one of the Commandments cannot go to Heaven?"

I felt my answer to that question would mean a great deal to her – and even might lead her to the revelation of the secret behind her approach to me.

"Many people break the Commandments," I said, "but I believe all violators can be forgiven if they truly repent."

Instantly her expression changed. In place of the drawn, lined face there was now a magnificent radiance. Tears came into her eyes as she grasped my hand.

"I want you to have this," she said, letting go and opening her Bible. She handed me a small sheet of paper which seemed to be a religious poem. I placed it carefully in my Bible, thanked her, and we parted.

Back in my warehouse quarters I opened my Bible and took out the little sheet of paper. Turning it over, I saw glue stains on the four corners, indicating it had once been in someone's scrapbook. But there was something odd about the sheet. It had not come from a newspaper or magazine for there was no printing on the reverse. But, I realised, it could have been a "proof copy" – such as is produced by the printer before a page goes to press.

Turning the sheet over, I saw inscribed beneath the verse:

"This poem was presented to Chaplain Bass by a prisoner (who is supposed to have written it) in King's Penitentiary, Brooklyn, New York."

The following week my unit was ordered to New York for embarkation to Europe. I never saw the girl again, nor had we exchanged addresses.

I long pondered about the meaning of the poem, the girl who had given it to me and her emotional response to my words. Of the several possible explanations for her action, I concluded the verse probably was written by someone very close to her – most likely her father or brother, and that he was in prison – perhaps the very one indicated at the bottom of the poem. Perhaps, also, serving a life term for murder. She would have treasured the poem, seeing in it a glimmer of hope for her father's or brother's salvation.

Nonetheless, on her own she had been unable to answer the crucial question: "Can my someone (father or brother?) enter the Kingdom of Heaven if he is a convicted murderer?" Had I given her the assurance she wanted?

37
"Never criticise the King or Queen"

A train of events put a quick end to my duty in San Francisco's dockland and the adventures I enjoyed during off-duty hours. The Army, in its wisdom, encouraged some of us to apply for OCS (Officer Candidate School); in our case, that meant the Transportation Corps OCS, for our newly acquired knowledge of ports and ships theoretically made us ideal candidates.

One day in February, 1943 I was told I had been promoted to Corporal (necessary to enter an OCS) and that I would be off the next week to Starkville, Mississippi, where the Army's Transportation Corps OCS was located. It transpired that the school occupied a huge dormitory (reputedly the world's largest at the time), classrooms and other facilities at Mississippi State College – a long-time football rival of my alma mater, the University of Georgia. I welcomed this chance to return to the South and particularly to Mississippi, which I knew to share with Georgia the unenviable positions at the bottom of the America performance tables in education, per capita income, and just about everything else.

Like most of the other crash officer candidate schools operating in war-time, our OCS sought to turn non-commissioned officers into commissioned ones in three months. This caused the graduates of these schools to be called "Ninety-day Wonders". Our course work was intensive. We were "introduced" to all aspects of a military organisation: administration, the legal system, signals, quartermaster, etc., but very little about fighting in combat. This omission seemed to confirm our role as support troops. The Transportation Corps had been created only since America's entry into the Second World War, but already its mission was well defined. It would operate all support vehicles, fly helicopters and small Army aircraft, run railways and operate mobile ports abroad.

In a departure from usual Army procedure, the head of the Army Transportation Corps was drafted from the American railroad industry. He was not a striking military figure, but he knew the railway business inside out, detested bureaucracy and proved a great success.

What most fascinated me was the marine element of the Corps, especially the newly created Army port organisations that could be sent to any part of the world to operate port facilities, tug boats and other small vessels. Little did I realise the next stage of my Army career was to lie in this field.

We soon embarked on a rigorous training programme that far exceeded the modest exercises we had known in San Francisco. Apart from fearing we might trip up on the drill field or in a written examination, we were always under great stress from the school's "demerit" system. The tidiness of our rooms, especially our wardrobe, was subject to demerits if we slipped up in the smallest way. We were allowed only three demerits for the entire three months; four and you were expelled.

One day, in my very first week, I returned to my room to find I had been given *two* demerits! Hanging on the light fixture in the middle of the room were two of my shirts, both neatly pressed just as I had left them that morning. On close examination I saw that one had a button not fastened (as required) and another had a button not quite through the button-hole. For these sins I was now two-thirds of the way out of officers' school! I wondered if I really had been so careless, or if the inspecting sergeant was just trying to instil more discipline. If it was the latter, he succeeded, for I earned no more of the infamous awards.

Apart from a great deal of practical knowledge about the operation of a port, I came away with a useful technique for remembering a large number of points when no pen or pencil is at hand. The system involves pairing each letter of the alphabet with an easily remembered object, which can be recalled in a flash, and recalled for several hours or even days afterwards. For example, I paired the letter "A" with an apple, the letter "B" with an open cardboard box, the letter "C" with a car, "D" with a dog and so on to "Z". Then, if I were listening to a talk or receiving instructions with no chance to make notes, I would "place" the first point in the context of an apple, the second inside the cardboard box and so on.

Thus, if I were receiving directions that involved going west, I would picture an apple pierced by a weather-vane arrow pointing west. If the next part of the instruction required taking along only a package of rations, I placed the package inside the cardboard box and so on. The instructor, daring us to foil him in this technique, asked several of us to come up with random points on *any* subject. This we did, and the variety was so great (sports, politics, sex etc.) that we were sure he would be caught out. To our amazement, he repeated all the points in the same order we had given, and with only slight hesitation, as he extrapolated them from the objects they had been paired with.

The three months passed swiftly. We ended our OCS training with a week of familiarisation with small weapons in New Orleans. To our surprise and joy, we discovered that some of us with only one good eye could chalk up reasonable sharp-shooting scores.

We were now ready for the great day when we would become commissioned officers. The moment the ceremony was over, groups of candidates from future graduating classes traditionally clustered round the entrance to the auditorium to receive the customary largesse of one dollar from each new officer whom he was the first to salute. A fast operator could pick up ten or fifteen dollars after these graduation exercises.

Then it was back into a troop train, again headed for California but this time following a southerly route through Louisiana, Texas, New Mexico and Arizona. We all knew Texas to be America's largest state, but we didn't expect to pass two nights and still be in Texas. At El Paso we hoped for an hour or two of free time to cross the border into Mexico but, sadly, the Army was not remotely interested in our wish to be tourists. The route through southern New Mexico and Arizona was sometimes desolate, sometimes spectacular but our route took us nowhere near the Grand Canyon.

Then came a brief stay at Camp Stoneman, California, where we continued basic training while our numbers were being increased. At the same time any unsuitable men were discharged. Some had more serious physical deficiencies than had been first apparent. Others just could not make the adjustment to military life.

One soldier in the latter category, a small man in his early thirties, was from Washington County in my home state of Georgia. His people were cotton farmers and were proud that he, David, was in uniform and ready to serve his country. When the company commander crudely told David he was unfit to remain in the service, he was crestfallen. Unable to comprehend that he was not up to the Army's minimum requirement, he instead believed his patriotism was in question. He was about to be shunted aboard a train for the long, lonely ride back to Georgia where, no doubt, he would face difficult questioning by family and friends.

I obtained permission to accompany David to the station. On the way I explained that the Army needed tank drivers, aircraft pilots and others with technical skills that neither he nor I possessed. But, I added, the country also needed farmers to produce more food, cotton and other crops for the United States was now obliged not only to take care of itself but also our allies abroad. In short, I said, he and his family had an important contribution to make to the war effort. David's expression changed. For the first time a smile lit up his face. Where there had been despair, now a degree of purpose was reflected. As he leapt aboard his train, he waved a cheery good-bye. He had made my day.

At length word came that we were soon to go overseas. As the Pacific theatre of operations was not yet ready to receive our type of unit, our destination had to be Europe and Europe had to mean Great Britain and, most likely, England.

We had just one "orientation talk" on Britain before leaving California. It was given by one of our older reserve officers who had visited Britain before the war. All of us were anxious to pick his brains and learn all we could about living in a foreign country – even one where everyone spoke English.

"In a way," he said, much to our surprise, "you will find it more difficult adjusting to the British way of life than if you were going to France, Germany or Italy. In those countries you expect the language and customs to be different, so you make allowances. In England, where you are going, you will expect life to be much the same as in the United States because we speak roughly the same language. But much is not the same."

He then passed round a shilling coin which he had saved from his time in Britain.

"Take this shilling coin, for example," he said. "It's worth about 20 American cents, but it's made up of only 12 British pennies. Twenty of these shillings are worth a British pound, which in turn is worth about $2. Don't ask me why they don't organise their money into 10s and 100s. They might one day but for the time being you'll have to get used to their way of doing it."

He went on to say that although both countries spoke English, words didn't always mean the same thing in both countries.

"An Englishman visiting us would have as much of a problem understanding differences in our language as we will when we get over there. The best way to get along is to think of Britain as an ally but nonetheless a foreign country which happens to use the original form of the English language – one that is now slightly different from our own. You must also get used to some cultural differences."

The War Department issued a little guide about Britain that fitted neatly into our pockets. It covered most of the sensitive situations we were likely to get into. The overall impression we got was that the British were more reserved than us – meaning we were likely to be considered loud-mouthed and boastful.

We were also told our pay was several times more than that of our British comrades in arms. While this might be an advantage in competing for girls, it obviously could create bad feelings. Instructions then went out to encourage our men to allocate a substantial part of their pay to relatives back home so there would be less to spend in Britain.

While training in the United States we had seen many American propaganda films portraying Hitler the villain he was. Now, in this little guide to Britain, the introduction - with three sharp references - made it clear he was still the Number One Enemy.

First, we were going to Europe, it said, to "meet … and beat him".

The second said Hitler feared Britain and America together would defeat him. But it was the third which, the little book said, each American serviceman had to be aware of at all times: Hitler's continuing effort "to separate Britain and America" and cause us to distrust one another.

Thus forewarned, we were advised never to bring up the American Revolutionary war which led to our independence. (Oddly, however, I was to find later that my British friends liked to joke about the war and adding, if it had never occurred, we would all be one country today – and perhaps "drinking from the same teapot".)

Americans never use the word "bloody" except to describe something or someone covered in blood. Nonetheless, the guide told us not to use this in public as it was a swear word in Britain.

Many of my American compatriots had forgotten that Britain had been at war since 1939 and that many of its cities had been severely bombed and 60,000 of its citizens killed. Although we would see a shabby country, the British people, the guide explained, hoped we would understand that 'in normal times, Britain looks prettier, cleaner and neater'.

The British monarchy was a delicate subject for the guide to deal with. Given the origins of the American republic and a Constitution that forbids Americans to receive 'any present, emolument, office or title, of any kind whatever from any king, prince or foreign state', the guide emphasised treading carefully.

"NEVER," it stipulated, "criticise the King or Queen."

Although the little book frequently referred to contributions by British "workers", it was reluctant to describe Britain as a country made up of different classes. Instead, it pointed out that the "upper crust" speaks pretty much alike. For example, it said the BBC broadcaster "has been trained to speak with a cultured" accent. That announcer, the guide went on, will say "hyah" instead of "here". Work hard at understanding the pronunciation difference, the little book said, and "you will get over thinking it is funny."

One of the best lines in the guide dealt with our respective national drinks:

"The British don't know how to make a good cup of coffee. You don't know how to make a good cup of tea. It's an even swap."

In May 1943 we entrained for another trans-continental ride, this time just south of the Canadian border. At Detroit we crossed into Canada and re-emerged at Niagara Falls. I had timed my night's sleep so as to rise just before we reached the falls, but when I awoke I found the train had travelled at such speed that we had left them behind. I was never to see them. At Buffalo we went southwards along the Hudson River, eventually disembarking at Camp Shanks – a holding area for troops due to sail out of New York City. Again we marked time by hiking, drilling and seeing orientation films. It was here that I first met "Herby" Niederberger, a native of Pittsburg, who was to become a good friend.

We all knew our next move would take us to Europe, across an ocean where German U-boats were inflicting heavy losses on American convoys. It was general knowledge that our troops, however, were mainly transported in fast British passenger liners, converted to hold thousands instead of hundreds. This gave us a degree of confidence when we were suddenly ordered to a New York pier where the 45,600-ton *Aquitania* awaited us. For the next five days we zig-zagged across the Atlantic, changing course abruptly at irregular intervals to thwart the ubiquitous German submarines. Eventually the ship reduced speed and we found ourselves entering the mouth of the River Clyde. Just off Gourock we disembarked onto a flotilla of lighters and made our way towards the shore.

Suddenly I remembered a story Kendall Weisiger had told me about his arrival in the same area several years earlier. Then he, along with many other American delegates to a Rotary International Convention, had disembarked aboard a lighter in the Clyde. They soon discovered that fellow passenger, Sir Harry Lauder, then the most popular singer of Scottish songs, was returning home after a successful tour in the United States. After some persuading, Sir Harry agreed to sing one of the better known pieces from his vast repertoire. This brought applause and requests for "More, more!" But this time Sir Harry was not to be swayed.

"If you want any more," he said, "You must sing it yourself."

The lighters quickly reached shore and we immediately headed for waiting troop trains. "England!", shouted some of our group excitedly. "No", an officer from the First World War reminded us, "you are *not* in England – this is Scotland."

Well, at least we were in the United Kingdom. Where the train would take us, no one seemed to know; or, if they knew, they weren't telling.

38
Ben Nevis almost defeats me

For once, the Army did not keep us waiting; the troop trains stood ready to receive us. Although we were in Gourock, we did not know it at the time. "Somewhere in Scotland" was the most we could get from anyone. We filed on quickly and immediately the train got under way.

We presently saw from the train windows street after street where houses were joined together in long, dreary rows. Coming from the wide open spaces of the American South, my fellow southerners and I were horrified at the thought of so many families living in such cramped conditions with small gardens, only the tiniest open space at the rear, and no garages. The roads were jammed with bicycles pedalled both by men and women. Once or twice we passed near factories where shifts of workers were changing. Here we saw armies of cyclists leaving and entering the work premises. Now we understood why there were no garages in those endless rows of houses: none of the families there owned a car. Car or not, these workers seemed determined to fulfil their wartime duties. Here was our first glimpse of Britain's "bulldog spirit".

From the names above shops and other signs we soon gathered we were somewhere in the Glasgow area but if our senior officers knew more they weren't telling us. On sped our train, seldom stopping or slowing – even when passing through large stations. Our direction was generally southwards, which indicated little except that our Army unit definitely was not destined for Scotland. As we were an Army port unit, we assumed our destination would be an English port, but which one? We had vaguely heard about the bustling ports of Liverpool, London and Southampton. Would one of these become our wartime 'home', or were we destined for another that we had never heard of?

We imagined London would be pleasant duty with its many historic and cultural attractions. As for other ports, we knew so little about them we had no opinions. A friend said we were wasting our time at a pointless guessing game. "Army postings are a lottery, like life itself," he said. "Don't even think about it."

Sometimes we amused ourselves by poring over the little booklet intended to introduce us to Britain and its people. The money may have been difficult to learn but the customs were much more intriguing.

"If Britons sit in trains and buses without striking up conversations with you", the guide said, "it doesn't mean they are being haughty or unfriendly. Probably they are paying more attention to you than you think. ... if they don't speak ... it is because they don't want to appear intrusive or rude." The guide gave several examples of language to be avoided. One likely to trap us was "bum" – a word celebrated in the well known American song, "Hallelujah, I'm a bum!". The booklet said: "To say 'I look like a bum' is offensive to their ears; for the British this means you look like your own backside."

Dawn came early and we peered intently through our grimy windows to get glimpses of our temporary homeland. We had to be somewhere in the middle of the country, for here were numerous factories, belching great clouds of black smoke which sometimes seeped into our carriages. Even worse were the tunnels, often unnecessarily constructed – so it seemed to us – at ground level. In these tunnels our carriages were instantly filled with putrid fumes that left us gasping for breath. We quickly learned to close our compartment windows, but often not in time to keep out the engine's smoke.

We could not tell what the factories were producing. If once they had borne signs proclaiming their products, they did not do so now. It soon dawned on us the reason for the anonymity: security against spies and potential German paratroop drops. That, we surmised, also accounted for the lack of direction signs in the cities and countryside.

We saw no idle factories. Some were quite small, but

nonetheless producing. Others were huge, sometimes extending for a hundred yards or more alongside our railway track. Once or twice we got a clue as to what was being produced: huge stocks of metal bars pointed to some kind of war materiel. The more we saw, the more we realised we were probably in the heart of Britain's manufacturing area – a region that somehow had survived the Battle of Britain and now was producing the equipment that would enable British forces to be re-supplied and join with Americans in a united assault on Hitler's armies on the Continent.

Britain, and in particular England, seemed much larger than the impression we had gained from our few geography lessons – or at least the distance from north to south seemed surprisingly great. Suddenly we left factory land behind and, to our amazement, entered the most beautiful countryside I had ever seen. Green, undulating fields spread out on each side of the train as far as the eye could see. Sometimes we caught sight of farmers working with farm animals, but we saw few tractors. Had tractor production ceased in favour of tanks and trucks for the British Army, I wondered? Occasionally we saw tiny villages, some with ancient thatched-roof houses but all boasting a parish church.

Then, without any warning, our train slowed to a stop in what appeared to be the industrial area of some city. We were ordered to detrain. Someone passed along the word that we were in Southampton, and that the station where our train had halted was Southampton Southwestern. Army vehicles were waiting to take us to billets scattered around the town. The enlisted men went to Ascupart Road School, my fellow officers and I to rooms in the Polygon Hotel.

Our unit, a cadre of less than a hundred men, was now officially designated the "14th Major Port". Within a few months, our strength grew to several thousand. The largest augmentation was composed of black soldiers, quartered largely in the former Ordnance Survey buildings. At that time the American armed forces segregated its white and black servicemen; it would not be until after the war that colour discrimination became illegal. Most of the black troops were destined to become stevedores and truck drivers. Given their scant formal education, they were to adapt well to their new environment.

Several of our stevedore companies, commanded by young Jewish officers, were to establish record after record in tonnage handled. I wondered at the success of this combination; could it be that the Jewish officers, some of whose families had known pogroms and persecution, were somehow able to communicate a sense of *chutzpah* to their black comrades-in-arms?

Before our unit arrived in Britain we knew in a general way that its mission would be to load and unload men and war materiel. Now, based at one of the world's great ports, we saw the reality of supporting the war before our very eyes. Here were the docks and sheds where we would be working. All round us were some of the world's largest passenger, cargo and naval vessels and, yes, we were even to experience a few raids by German aircraft to remind us the enemy attached great importance to our work.

Most of all we wondered how our planners could possibly cope with the mammoth logistical nightmare of suddenly despatching vast quantities of men and materiel across the Channel. Men could not be moved to the vicinity of Southampton until there were places for them to sleep and be fed. Ships could not accept heavy weapons if the necessary cranes and storage areas were not available. Movement of men and materiel by train or road required meticulous coordination to avoid jams at bottleneck points – of which there were many. At first we did not always achieve these goals but with experience and the patience of our British dock, road, rail and police comrades, we gradually managed to get things right.

At first we received large American shipments of weapons, tanks, vehicles, food, clothing and ammunition at Southampton's two dock areas, the "Old" and the "New". Our first operational headquarters was in the Maritime Chambers of the Old Docks complex. Southampton was fortunate in having two dock areas which could operate independently. The Old Docks – home to the famous Ocean Terminal where the great pre-war liners tied up – was especially vulnerable to enemy action because a single bomb at its narrowest point could have put virtually the whole of the complex out of action.

When it sunk in that I was likely to be stationed in Britain for an indefinite period, I could not believe my luck. I immediately made two resolutions: first, to visit as much as possible of "the old country" (as we sometimes referred to it in the American South) and second, to marry the "right girl" if I should stumble across her.

Apart from strong historical ties dating back to colonial times, Southerners admired much about Britain and its people. For example, there was the folk lore and music of settlers in the Appalachians, the architecture and other cultural influences in Charleston and Savannah and historic educational institutions like the College of William and Mary in Virginia.

I did not have long to wait for my first venture away from military duties. There came a brief interlude in our D-Day planning (later formalised as Operation Overlord) in the winter of 1943-44 when the Army announced a week-long educational tour in Devonshire for officers with backgrounds in agriculture. Lucky officers would visit model farms and farm industries in Devonshire, and hear lectures by the Devon county organiser and staff of the Seale-Hayne agricultural college. I applied, was accepted and shortly received orders to report to Exeter whose townspeople had volunteered to give us bed and breakfast for the week.

I made my way to a large home in one of the city's residential areas where I was greeted at the door by a white-haired lady in her sixties. She took me to my room, and then asked me to leave my suitcase and join her for tea. It turned out that she was a widow who knew little about farming, but had gladly volunteered to play host to a visiting American serviceman for the week. She wanted to know my "background" which I quickly related.

When I finished, she startled me by asking: "Are you a Catholic?"

I replied that I was a Baptist and thought of adding the old cliché "...but some of my best friends are Catholics" (most notably, my roommate, Herby Niederberger). She beat me to the draw by interrupting: "Well, I ordered a Catholic and they have sent you – a Baptist!"

Silently I wondered about the religious faith of the other officers in our group. It dawned on me that there were several other southerners – no doubt Baptists or Methodists – and some men from the Midwest, perhaps Lutherans of Scandinavian descent. It was just possible, I explained to the lady, that there were no Catholics in our group, or so few that there were not enough to go round for the Catholic families who might have requested them.

It soon became apparent that the United States was far more heathen than the dear lady had ever imagined and nothing I could say would assuage her disappointment. Each day I came "home" to this atmosphere; no amount of explanation or enthusiasm about my rural adventures had the slightest effect. Fortunately, the programme for the week was both busy and exciting. We toured a leading cider factory, were introduced to the hardy Devon cattle, saw some lovely Land Army girls at work and met several farmers and agricultural leaders who gave us a vivid picture of how, in spite of the war, Britain was providing 70% of its food needs.

Alas, we got only a passing glance at the lovely Land Army girls but the fire had been lit inside me to be on the lookout for more of the same. The time came to say farewell to my Exeter hostess, but the disappointment she had shown at our first meeting was still there. I shook her hand warmly and expressed my gratitude again, but to no avail. A heathen I arrived and a heathen I departed.

During that winter my friend, Bill Ehlert, and I decided we wanted to see more of Scotland than our non-stop journey from Gourock had afforded. We managed to obtain a few days' leave which, combined with a weekend, allowed us to make the long trip north. Bill had some knowledge of Scotland so I left the itinerary to him. At Aberdeen we went to the local theatre and saw a lively programme of Scottish music, song and dance. It was the first and only time I heard "My Highland Mary" and its lilting tune was to haunt me for a long time. The weather was very cold and occasionally, as at Inverness, we were grateful for hot porridge to warm our "innards".

When we arrived at Fort William, Bill and I had our only disagreement about what to see and do. He had heard much about the crofters and wildness of the Isle of Mull and was determined to go there. I knew that Britain's highest mountain, Ben Nevis, was near Fort William and could easily be climbed in good weather. We decided to go our separate ways and meet later at our Fort William hotel.

Bill set off for Mull via Oban and I dug out my paratrooper boots and warm hiking gear. To my consternation, I saw in the distance that clouds had suddenly descended over part of Ben Nevis; I just hoped the entire summit would not be covered – at least not until I could complete my hike up and back. The hotel receptionist looked at me in alarm as I prepared to leave. When I told him of my intention, he became grave and told me two climbers had been killed only a few days earlier while attempting to negotiate a narrow causeway which had become frozen with ice. I thanked him, but said I was determined to continue, but would be careful.

The paratrooper boots had thick soles, sturdy ankle supports and came halfway up my legs, giving me great confidence. There were no other hikers to be seen, so I set off on my own and made rapid progress until I came to the crevice which undoubtedly had been the scene of the tragedy two days before. I went slowly, testing the surface before putting my full weight on each foot, and at length scrambled across.

After that, the climb went well and the summit loomed nearer. Just as I reached a wooden hut near the crest, the weather deteriorated further. The wind picked up and snow started falling in a mini-blizzard. I had no clear view from the summit and realised further lingering was unwise. Likewise I stood a good chance of becoming disoriented. Moreover, it would be highly embarrassing to have a rescue party launched on my behalf. I could imagine the headlines and what my commanding officer might have to say about it.

As I turned to retrace my steps, I saw a thick snow cloud enveloping that part of the track I had used in climbing. To attempt to find it, with new snow falling, might spell disaster. The only way to outrun the fast-descending cloud and snow was to strike out down the slope in the general direction of Fort William, which I believed I remembered. The slope was sometimes steep and rarely gradual, but by taking long running leaps I descended at an amazing rate.

Providence was with me, for not once did I lose my footing or twist an ankle. At length I was in clear light again and, to my surprise, the treacherous causeway loomed just to my right. This time I decided to by-pass it, lest the swirling weather overtake me. I slowed my rate of descent and picked my way carefully down the remainder of the slope and eventually rejoined the track on which I had originally set out a few hours before, but which now seemed an eternity ago.

The receptionist stared, half in disbelief and half in annoyance, as I entered the hotel. That evening over dinner Bill and I shared impressions of our respective adventures. He enthused over his visit to Mull, saying every minute had been exciting. Could I say the same for my climb? “Yes”, I replied, with slight hesitation as I explained my close call.

39
How to eat a soft-boiled egg

Our preparation and planning to support the invasion continued round the clock. At times it seemed to us junior officers that there was an uncontrollable mass of men and materiel being squeezed into southern England. Could we ever bring about the coordination necessary to move them across the Channel?

Even though the US Army had specially trained military police to direct movement into the port area, we very quickly realised how indebted we were to Southampton's port authorities whose knowledge and know-how were indispensable to our joint goal. Assisting them were the Dock Police who knew every nook and cranny of the port complex.

We also formed close ties with the town's police, for there were convoys to be coordinated, vehicle accidents to be investigated and, yes, crimes to be solved. Although we came to know many by name, we were hard pressed to find ways of thanking them for their help. Even when we tried, our efforts sometimes backfired.

For example, one day a fellow officer and I saw a constable, well known to us, cycling with great effort against the cold wind and rain. We stopped and invited him to climb aboard our personnel carrier to ease his pain. He did so gladly and presently we arrived at his destination. On removing his bicycle he discovered, to his horror, that he had lost one of the rubber grips for his handlebars. Instead of thanking us for the lift, he explained that no more bicycle grips were being made during the war and he was now condemned to cycle with one hand thoroughly frozen for the duration. Then he smiled and said: "Better you had not spotted me today!"

A fair-sized contingent of American Red Cross "girls" arrived to help with troop morale, especially when long convoys of vehicles were delayed on roads and streets. Their standard "menu" was hot coffee and doughnuts, both prepared to suit American palates. More than these goodies, however, the homesick men leaped at the chance to chat with attractive young ladies who just might be from their hometowns.

Most Saturday evenings, if no training exercise was scheduled, the girls met informally with us over coffee. For two or three hours we would sing songs and tell stories – some on the bawdy side. The star story teller was a former Master Sergeant, Frank ('Red') Bardella, who had been promoted to major at the outbreak of war. He had the rare knack of telling a funny story while keeping a straight face. He endeared himself to the Red Cross ladies, and the rest of us, by relating many of his off-duty Army adventures. He had served all over the world – including China, which was the scene of some of his more colourful exploits. "Did you ever hear that women in China only make love sideways?" he once asked the startled Red Cross workers. They nodded, embarrassed, not wishing to appear naïve. "Well," he replied, "it ain't so. I know – I've tried it."

As the invasion date inexorably neared, our preparations continued at a frantic pace. Concrete ramps ("hards") were erected in the dock area as well as at the Royal Pier. These were to accommodate landing craft of several types, of which the most common were LCT (tanks), LCM (mechanised), LCI (infantry), LCVP (vehicle and personnel) and the larger LSTs (landing ships, tank) which were also to be used for railway rolling stock.

Virtually all our officers and senior non-commissioned officers, regardless of their normal duties, were obliged to take part in simulated training exercises to allow us to have an "in depth" ability to operate in the event of heavy casualties once the invasion started. Holding (or staging) areas (Southampton was the hub for Area "C") were established to facilitate an orderly flow of men and materiel from distant camps and depots to our area.

Each landing craft was assigned a serial number together with the number of vehicles and men it could accommodate. This was passed 'up the line' to the appropriate headquarters, which decided the type of troops (engineers, signal corps, etc.) that were most needed at the moment. The units were then despatched to a staging area camp to await the call to proceed to the dock area.

Farther west on the Channel coast, exercises were held in which American troops were actually loaded onto landing craft which then put out to sea. In the largest, Operation Tiger, some 800 men were lost when two German E-boat flotillas, comprising nine boats, attacked and sank two LSTs and damaged a third off Slapton Sands, southwest of Dartmouth.

Despite the heavy loss of life and almost the whole of the reserve LST fleet, the exercise was valuable for the many lessons it provided. The Germans correctly guessed that what they had come upon was only an exercise; had they realised the invasion would take place within weeks and gone on to raid the many south coast bays and harbours then saturated with landing craft, Operation Overlord undoubtedly would have been placed in jeopardy.

As more combat troops and war materiel reached Britain, additional support units arrived in the Southampton area to assist with the invasion preparations. Several harbour craft companies, equipped with American-built craft, made plans for towing barges, cranes and specialised vessels to the French coasts. US Navy and US Army Hospital units went to Netley and other sites in southern England to establish facilities for the wounded who inevitably would arrive in large numbers following the initial landings. Military police and signal corps specialists joined ranks to ensure security and coordinate the flow of men and supplies in our busy area of operations. Sometimes the scene seemed confusing and without purpose, yet the master plan moved inexorably forward.

A month before D-Day our administrative headquarters was moved from the dock area to the Southampton Civic Centre. Here we occupied space which today is the city's Art Gallery. (I later had the honour of composing the text of a plaque recording our war-time tenancy there; it remains above a door in one of the gallery rooms.) The move from the docks to the more spacious Civic Centre was made possible by the Mayor, Rex Stranger, and the town council. This thoughtful act was typical of the cooperation and kindness shown by Southampton officials during the whole of our unit's stay in the town.

While Mayor Stranger daily pondered the help he could render from his Civic Centre office, the Almighty provided His assistance every four hours through the pealing of Isaac Watts' "O God Our Help in Ages Past" from the centre's clock tower. Whether at our quarters across the park from the Civic Centre or at our desks beneath the clock tower, our staff considered it a miracle of serendipity that this inspirational hymn had been selected by the 'city fathers' years before our arrival. As my roommate and I were "fresh air fiends", we slept with our window opened at the top, whatever the weather. Although awakened many times during the night by the hymn, I never regarded it as other than a prayer that we (the Allies) would emerge from the war as moral and military victors.

Watts, I discovered, was a native of Southampton. According to local legend, he undertook to compose a lively tune for one hymn each week, so unhappy was he over the solemn music originally composed for it. Sadly, his church near the ancient Bargate was destroyed in a German air raid, but a monument to his memory stands in a nearby park.

Apart from being on call for loading or unloading ships whenever needed, most of our officers had regular duties. I was the port's public relations officer, historian, passive (civil) defence officer and a permanent member of three courts-martial. At other times I was the port mess officer (promptly relieved of duty when I banned smoking during meals) and exchange ("PX") officer.

At one time I had seven jobs and it seemed the end was not in sight. No one seemed to know, or care, that I was stretched to the limit. Some drastic remedy was necessary or I would collapse from exhaustion. Then I had an idea: I placed an order with our engineers to make seven small boards, suspended by tiny chains from the ceiling. From top to bottom the signs indicated my office was inhabited: Public Relations Officer, Port Historian, Passive Defence Officer and so on. From top to bottom the signs took up just over two feet – the lowest sign being just high enough to hit the head of any unsuspecting person passing my office door.

Two or three fellow officers *did* hit the bottom sign and angrily poked their heads into my office to say I should do something about it. I mumbled that I would get around to it when I had time, but I hoped the right person would come along first. He did – our Commanding Officer. I heard a solid clunk as he whacked his head. Colonel Sherman Kiser was not named Sherman for nothing; he was cool, efficient and confident. I knew, too, that he had a sense of humour and hoped it would now save the day. It did.

"Lieutenant", he said, rubbing his head, "better drop by my office so I can relieve you of one or two of your duties." He did so and life thereafter became more bearable.

The courts-martial were fascinating, for they reflected the behaviour of our troops – whether within our own units, or with the British public. With around 14,000 troops in our port organisation, we were a "city within a city". If the number of assaults, accidents, brawls, rapes and other incidents was unduly high for our troop strength, the public might perceive that we Americans were ill-disciplined and, at times, violent. In short, there might be some truth to the cliché which I often heard from some British acquaintances, that we Americans were "Overpaid, over sexed and over here".

As public relations officer, I was acutely aware of the impact each negative incident had on the people of Southampton – most of whom read the *Evening Echo* daily. In spite of stern lectures to our men, unpleasant incidents still occurred.

Among the courts-martial cases in which I either prosecuted or defended the accused, one poignant one stands out in my memory. A black soldier from the South was driving a truck which collided with a Southampton city bus, resulting in injury to an elderly lady who later died. It was important that the court make the point that American servicemen should drive with utmost care, for a death had resulted from this accident.

On the other hand, an unduly severe sentence by an all-white court could be interpreted by the British as being racially motivated. In the end the court took a decision which was considered to be "middle-of-the-road": the driver was sentenced to a long term of imprisonment. Some British observers nonetheless thought the sentence too severe for a traffic accident.

The assistance which the 14th Port received from Southampton civic officials and the dock board of Southern Railways was matched by the kindness and hospitality of the town's citizens. My staff received hundreds of invitations from families anxious to have servicemen for a meal or tea, or to join them in some sporting or cultural event. Many more were issued spontaneously by townspeople when they came across Americans on streets, in shops, on buses or trains, in churches and elsewhere. In short, few Americans were lonely, unless they wanted to be.

I shall never forget my first invitation to a British home. It was for Sunday tea – something unknown to me – so I wondered what was in store as I knocked at the door of a modest semi-detached home. My hosts warmly greeted me, assessed the weather (which I came to learn was standard procedure for any social gathering) and shortly adjourned to the dining room.

Before me was a plate holding a slice of bread and a pat of butter. Tea cups all round the table indicated tea was coming soon. I put the butter on my bread, made short work of eating it and asked for another slice of bread and more butter. A plate of bread was passed but my male host embarrassingly explained there was no more butter – we had already consumed the family ration. It was my turn to be embarrassed but worse was to come.

The man's wife and daughter retired to the kitchen and soon returned with the tea and small plates, each bearing an egg standing on one end in a kind of cup. I had eaten many hard boiled eggs at picnics and parties, but had never seen one standing alone – on one end – before. What was I to do about it – or with it?

I stalled for a moment, hoping my hosts would pave the way for me. They did, but in a strange, delicate way. Gently they chipped into the tops of their egg and with their knives. I wondered why all the fuss when all they had to do was to put the egg into the plate, bash it with the knife and, hey presto, the shell would fall away.

Politeness, however, dictated I should prepare my egg the British way, so I gently started tapping it with my knife. When the shell seemed reluctant to come away, I bashed harder and suddenly, the yellowish liquid egg started squirting onto my plate. Horrors! My poor hostess hadn't let it boil enough. But what could I do?

I raised my eyes slightly and saw to my surprise that everyone else at the table had not only finished opening their eggs but had spread out the bright yellow goo on their plates. By now I could smell the rawness of my undercooked egg. I thought I was going to be sick, but dared not for I was a guest.

They were doing something incredible – eating their raw eggs with bread. Only once before had I faced – and failed – in a similar situation. That was when I was about to be initiated into a club at university. Those who failed to consume a raw egg on the spot were not accepted.

My hosts were calmly eating away, no doubt putting on an air of nonchalance to mask the error of under-cooking the eggs. I gingerly smeared a bit of the yellow stuff on my bread but gagged as it neared my mouth. Hastily I asked for the salt and pepper which I then sprinkled generously over the mess. The salt only seemed to accentuate the raw taste.

"Ketchup." I shouted. "Mustard!" I cried, as the wife and daughter rushed into the kitchen. They emerged with both and a bottle of HP sauce. I poured on bounteous amounts of everything, stirring vigorously all the time. My concoction turned first red and then a dirty brown. Never mind, most of the raw egg taste had disappeared. With the aid of several more slices of bread, I managed to clear my plate. Later there was jam but, by now, no butter to go with it.

Tea over, we chatted amicably about Britain and America and when we thought the war would end. When I took my leave and my new found friends had closed their front door, I heard the unmistakable sound of laughter – I was relieved. They had enjoyed my visit despite my goofs.

40
D-Day tears and prayers

As our unit gradually built up to full strength, we received our first intake of WAC's (Women's Army Corps). One day while I was waiting for a friend in the lobby of our hotel, a WAC captain entered with orders entitling her to a room in our billets. She duly reported to the British receptionist, a dignified man in his 60s revered by us all for solving many of our problems.

After writing down the lady's name, rank and serial number, he assigned her a room and handed over the key.

"And when does the Captain wish to be knocked up?" he asked in his usual friendly manner.

The startled WAC captain turned red with rage and retorted loudly: "I beg your pardon!"

I jumped from my chair, rushed to the reception desk and explained to the shattered man that the expression he had just used referred to the process of a woman being made pregnant, usually against her wish. This time he was the one whose complexion coloured, except he turned white. I then explained to the WAC officer that the receptionist maintained a "call" list so that officers could be awakened at their required times each morning. The two embarrassed parties then had a hearty laugh as I beat a hasty retreat.

In the midst of this tense period of waiting and wondering there occurred an event which was to have a profound effect on my life. One noon in May I was standing in the queue for lunch at the improvised officers' mess near the Bargate when I was joined by a friend, Lieutenant Grey. He remarked on the pleasant weather we were then enjoying and I replied:

"I'd give anything to visit an English farm right now."

I then briefly related how I was born on a farm and spent my early years there.

Lieutenant Grey placed his hand on my arm –

"I just may be able to help you." he said, with the hint of a twinkle in his eyes.

Taking out his wallet, he extracted a piece of paper on which was written "Mary Roberts, Wickham 3175."

He went on to say he had just left his billet near the Toogoods Seed building, when he spotted a girl in Land Army uniform fiddling with the engine of her car. As she seemed in some distress, he asked if he could be of some assistance.

She replied that she had been sent to pick up seed from Toogoods and, as was advised to motorists in the Southampton area at that time, had removed the engine's carburettor cap. This was standard advice to prevent German paratroops seizing vehicles once they had hit ground.

Unfortunately, the girl had not remembered how she was to replace the cap. My friend quickly refitted it, but did not let the comely lass escape before obtaining her name and address.

"You may have it," he said to me, "for I will be leaving for France once the invasion begins."

I pocketed the piece of paper without further thought. D-Day, indeed, came quickly and I was never to see or hear of Lieutenant Grey again. I later learned Toogood's slogan was "The King's Seedman"; with ample justification, as will be seen later, I decided it should be changed to "The Lord's Match-Maker"!

By the end of May, 1944 we knew the invasion of France was imminent. Heavy bombers of the American and British air arms increased their raids on targets in Normandy. Tactical aircraft based in East Anglia and elsewhere were readied to support landing operations. Southern England was utterly saturated with airborne troops and gliders, infantry and armoured divisions, and support units of all types. A brief secondment to Dorchester and Weymouth brought me in contact with units designated to take part in the initial onslaught on the Normandy beaches. On one of my visits to the area, I was waved down by a general wanting a ride to another part of the deployment area. As he stepped into my jeep I discovered he was James Gavin, later to become American ambassador to France.

The entire coast was dotted with enclaves of assault forces designated to embark on landing craft positioned in selected harbours. This was as true of British and Canadian forces to the east of Southampton, as it was for American units to the west of the town. Ships of the American and British navies stood by for the signal to sail. All that was required to trigger the long-awaited Allied assault was good weather, but when would it come?

At the last minute came a flood of war correspondents attired in para-military uniforms. They represented well known American newspapers and radio networks. Certainly, they would not be converging on Southampton if D-Day was not imminent.

Foremost among these was a woman politician and writer from New York state, a personal friend of President Franklin D. Roosevelt, who arrived bearing orders saying she was to see Major General Walter Bedell Smith, General Eisenhower's chief of staff, immediately. By this time, access to the top military commanders by the press was all but prohibited, except for a handful of trusted senior war correspondents.

I escorted the lady to Southwick House, near Southwick village just north of Portsmouth, where General Eisenhower's SHAEF (Supreme Headquarters Allied Expeditionary Force) was located. General Smith was waiting for his guest, who shouted out "Bedell!" as she spotted him. As I took my leave, they were already engaged in earnest conversation which I knew was about the forthcoming assault.

Although the German Luftwaffe by this time had been roundly defeated by the RAF, it was still capable of mounting the occasional sortie and reconnaissance run. One Saturday morning my roommate Herby Niederberger and I were standing near the window of our third-floor room in the Polygon Hotel when he spotted an aircraft coming straight towards us at an elevation of only a few hundred feet. It was not propeller driven, but (as we later learned) a twin–engined jet, a Messerschmitt Me 262.

"It's German!" shouted Herby, as the plane neared the hotel. We each had the same thought: had Luftwaffe intelligence identified the Polygon as housing most of the 14th Port's officers? We were mesmerised by the fast approaching plane, with no RAF fighters in sight. It was flying too low for anti-aircraft fire to be effective. At any moment we expected to see bombs unleashed towards us. As the plane passed directly overhead no bombs fell, and we clearly saw the aircraft's insignia. The plane presumably continued on its path, which would lead it directly over the New Docks area.

We listened for bomb explosions, but none came. We concluded the plane was either on a reconnaissance mission or, while being chased by RAF fighters, was totally concerned with evading them. We asked each other: "Would the Allied invasion effort be threatened by the photographs this intruder had taken?" Only time would tell.

Another omen of the impending departure of Allied convoys came one morning a few days before D-Day. An agitated American civilian of about 45 was brought to my office by a military policeman. He started asking, almost incoherently, if I could take him on my staff as a writer. I asked him to sit down and explain what he had in mind.

He said that he was a crew member of a small American vessel destined to take part in the initial assault. He frankly admitted his chances of surviving were small, for his slow boat would be moving through the waters known to be alive with German E boats. He painted a graphic picture of how vulnerable his small craft would be. "I can write – write well!" he exclaimed. "I'll take any job you have – even typing."

I explained that my small staff was complete and there was not the slightest possibility of its being increased. Even if additional people were authorised in the future, I added, they would have to be either men in uniform or British civilians. The man became tearful, and then almost hysterical. "I'll tell you what I'll do," I said at length. "I'll give you a letter stating *if* you can get yourself released from your present assignment, and *if* I am allowed to take on another person, I'll give your application every consideration." I typed the letter, added my signature and handed it to the man who, only slightly mollified, thanked me and left.

As the world now knows, terrible weather conditions caused postponement of the invasion. Most of our 14th Port staff knew the assault units were already in their landing craft, and that back-up forces would sail once the invasion convoys were under way. For several days we waited for the tell-tale sign, passage of Allied aircraft overhead, that the battle to liberate the Continent from the "forces of evil" had begun.

Early on the morning of Tuesday, 6 June, Herby and I were awakened by the drone of hundreds of planes flying overhead. We rushed to the window and saw the morning's dim light was almost blotted out by a seemingly endless procession of aircraft, most of which were towing gliders. The droning went on, and on, and on – proof that this was the real thing.

We knew these included troops of our 82nd and 101st Airborne Divisions and hoped that they would reach their objectives safely. Then it dawned on us that simultaneously the entire Allied landing force would be storming the beaches of Normandy. Here we knew there had to be enormous casualties.

But could enough support be given these brave men to enable them to stand up to, and eventually overcome, the German forces so firmly entrenched there? Without a word being spoken, we each in our own way uttered silent prayers for the success of the crusade which had been so long in preparation, and which now was at last under way. In the first newscast of the morning, a solemn BBC announcer confirmed that the invasion was in progress.

41
We almost capsize

From D-Day onwards members of our unit laboured day and night to supplement the invading force with more men, weapons and other necessities of war. The streets of Southampton and the roads leading to the port from the north were jammed with vehicles and the precious cargoes, human and materiel.

The good people of the town, sharing with us the fervent hope that the invasion would be successful, warmly greeted the troops whenever their vehicles came to a halt. Sometimes, when the loading at dockside was delayed, they brought cups of tea or coffee to men temporarily held up in the streets outside their homes.

American Red Cross workers did their best to serve American-style coffee at strategic points along the military routes, but they could not be everywhere. Thus the GIs, weary with waiting and uncertainty, welcomed a hot drink of any kind. More important to their morale was the unspoken gratitude of the British people for the willingness of ordinary Americans to join the battle for the liberation of Europe.

Until a firm beachhead was established, the seriously wounded were brought back to England for treatment. At first they came on the same landing craft which had taken assault troops over. As soon as they could be deployed, hospital ships entered service. Long columns of Army ambulances met each vessel bearing the wounded. Some men, barely alive when placed aboard the vessels on the Normandy beachheads, expired during the crossing to Southampton. Some were so badly burned by German flame-throwers that they had little prospect of recovery.

Surgeons, doctors and nurses at hospitals throughout the south of England worked round the clock to perform medical miracles. When field hospitals were eventually established in Normandy, the survival rate improved dramatically; nonetheless, men with serious wounds continued to be evacuated to Britain where complicated surgery and convalescence could be provided.

In the midst of these hectic activities I received an envelope from the Army war graves and registration unit. It must have arrived about a fortnight after D-Day and at first I could not understand why I – having nothing to do with the identification of war dead – should be hearing from them. The covering note stated that the attached document had been found on the person of a casualty of the invasion, and any information I could provide would help to make a positive identification.

I looked at the attachment and found it to be the letter I had written to the American civilian who had come to my office a few days before D-Day, pleading that I take him on as a writer. His boat presumably had hit a mine as it made its way from Southampton to Normandy. There was no mention of any other papers or possessions. I was to provide everything I knew for the only clue to his identity was my letter.

I dutifully sat down with pen and paper and recalled the day the man came in and our conversation. Through records of our Transportation Corps vessel crews, there would have been no difficulty confirming his name and address so that his next of kin could be notified. Soon after this chilling incident, in a gesture to recognise the heroic duty of the civilians who manned these harbour craft vessels, the Army renamed many of its small craft after crew members who had given their lives in the invasion. Appropriate photographs of the renaming ceremonies were then sent to the next of kin, affording them a measure of posthumous solace.

In July I volunteered for several "courier runs" to Omaha beach. Whenever a convoy of cargo vessels left Southampton for the beach, a copy of the manifest for the entire convoy had to be rushed to our Transportation Corps unit there. This enabled battlefield commanders to know which ships held ammunition, replacement weapons, medicines and so on. The convoys moved slowly, enabling the fast courier boat to arrive several hours, or even a day, in advance.

On the "far shore" (our term for the two beaches, "Omaha" and "Utah") I was amazed to see that most of the artificial harbours, so meticulously planned, had been wrecked by storms. The British beaches, better protected from the elements, did not suffer so badly.

On embarking from my courier boat, I saw that much of the beach area had not yet been cleared of mines, for the objective of the advancing troops was to push inland as quickly as possible. Paths had been cleared of sufficient width to permit two-way traffic between the beaches and the front lines. As I was driven inland, I saw that the beachhead area, as far as the eye could see, was covered with war materiel. It was as if the entire area was one vast, outdoor depot.

Some delicate equipment was covered with tarpaulins, but most items stood open to the elements. Attempts had been made at isolating ammunition and POL (petroleum, oil and lubricants) dumps, but the beachhead was not then large enough to provide the generous space usually accorded such volatile storage areas. At no time during my brief stay (less than 24 hours) did the thundering of heavy guns cease.

As I departed for Southampton aboard the returning courier vessel, I marvelled at how our forces had been able to progress anywhere at all, given the enormous advantage the German defenders held. Only later did I learn that Hitler's orders had prevented reinforcements from being sent from the Calais area which, he mistakenly believed, was to be our real objective. Time was on our side for the moment, but it was still of the utmost urgency to keep pouring war materiel into Normandy for the time when a breakout from the beachhead could be attempted.

On my second courier run the circumstances were much the same, except this time a dozen other officers and I – among them tactical pilots of the Army Air Corps – were billeted for the night in an abandoned French farmhouse. It contained Army cots and blankets – nothing more. Some of the pilots had spent the previous night there and told the rest of us we would be in for a show. They were right. As soon as darkness fell, a German pilot flew his plane high over the beachhead area, attempting to disgorge his load of bombs and take evasive action at the same time.

We gathered at a window to see the action. "He is a very brave man, but he won't make it," said one young pilot, "for this is probably the most heavily fortified area in the world." His prediction proved true: seconds later, the plane – never free of myriad searchlight rays – was hit and immediately burst into flames as it plunged earthwards.

Another pilot asked if anyone present had flown near Tours. None had. "Give it a miss if you have a choice," he advised, "the German gunners there are so accurate they can pick out a single plane at a height of five miles." The others listened silently. I admired the calm way these young pilots, all in their early twenties, respected both the courage and ability of their German foes.

A few days later I volunteered for another courier run. In due course I set out in one of our sturdy tug boats.

"The weather's foul," the captain told me, "but we should make it all right."

He saw me turn pale.

"Do you get sea sick easily?" he asked.

I replied that I usually coped with normal sea conditions, although I didn't relish the thought.

As we set off from Southampton the wind and waves mounted by the minute. It was impossible to lie on my bunk so I tried standing in the doorway where I could grip the doorframe with both hands. The little vessel tossed and turned, sometimes taking what seemed ages to right itself. I was not so much seasick as exhausted from trying to avoid being thrown against the wall or the ceiling.

Suddenly a massive wave hit us and the entire boat was engulfed. Was that the end, I wondered. Then the captain loomed through the spray and said:

"We're turning back. There's a raging storm between us and the Normandy shore. We'll surely capsize if we continue."

I nodded, in agreement. but it would be some time before the storm abated. On disembarking at Southampton, I was met by one of our Port dispatchers.

"You were very lucky," he said grimly, "the beach installations on the other side have been severely damaged."

A few weeks later I made another courier run, this time to the port of Cherbourg. The American Army badly needed Cherbourg's port installations for unloading supplies crucial to breaking out of the Cotentin Peninsula and the expanded beachhead area. Although the airport hangar was intact, as was also much of the city and its rail network, the Germans had thoroughly wrecked the harbour installations. In addition, they sank several ships at crucial points and littered the harbour with mines. Any hope for early use of the port seemed remote. Nonetheless the mines were soon cleared so that DUKWs (amphibious cargo carriers) could discharge their cargo.

Already elements of a Port Construction and Repair Group were hard at work. They proved to be as efficient in reopening the port as the Germans had been in demolishing it. If it was impossible to repair a pier, a ship was simply scuttled at the water's edge, the superstructure removed, and metal causeways erected on which vehicles and cargo could be unloaded from anchored vessels. Day by day the amount of tonnage unloaded increased; by November Cherbourg would receive more than half of all tonnage discharged in France. The emphasis placed by Overlord planners on early capture of Cherbourg had been justified. Some even said the fall of Cherbourg to the Americans would be the preamble to the defeat of the German army.

One of my courier runs was on July 4th when the beachhead was so greatly expanded that I could travel inwards for a few miles. The glimpse I got that day I described in the letter below to my hometown newspaper, the Louisville *News and Farmer*:

A LETTER FROM NORMANDY
July, 1944

By a stroke of good luck I happened to have visited the Normandy beachhead on the Fourth of July, our own national day of independence and one in which the French joined in with us.

Many of the houses in the liberated area were adorned with tiny French and American flags. As if by magic, the French inhabitants produced the flags the minute their towns were freed. In some cases, improvised flags torn from windshields of American vehicles or ripped from the field jackets of obliging "Yanks" served the purpose.

All along the crowded French roads, people stood and waved at the never-ending streams of tanks, trucks and other American vehicles of war. Whenever the traffic halted, French children rushed to the vehicles and asked in a cheerful voice, "Bonbons, M'sieur?" That was their version of the British "Any gum, chum?"

In one of the larger towns recently liberated, a little French girl approached our jeep and asked, "Souvenir Americain?", but alas, I had nothing to give and, in my best Louisville Academy French, replied "Non". Seeing that my French apparently was being understood, I decided to venture further. To my question of "Quel age avez-vous", she replied "Dix ans". I then asked if she enjoyed school and, dashing her brilliant red hair back across the top of her head, she answered, "Mais oui, M'sieur".

"Where is the school?" I asked. With a look of despair she replied: "Oh, the school – it isn't any more". Later I discovered what she told me was true. A large part of the village, including the school, had been demolished by the combined blasting of American weapons and retreating German demolition units.

Yet, in spite of the widespread chaos, the inhabitants went about cheerfully. Perhaps it was because the American engineering and signal units had started the job of reconstruction quickly. Already bulldozers were clearing away rubble and repairing such buildings as were still usable. Telephone lines were being re-strung and, in a few places, water mains re-laid. In short, insofar as combat operations permitted, American civil affairs units were bringing back a semblance of normality to the French village.

In striking contrast to the much-shelled towns was the peaceful setting of the Normandy countryside. Herds of dairy cattle abounded, and I wondered how they had survived the destruction caused by the invasion. At one farm I even saw a pair of beautifully groomed horses.

Near one of the beachhead towns I saw a cooperative dairy, working normally. Farmers could be seen converging with their churns of milk drawn on little carts. The situation may have been different near large cities, but here there seemed to be no shortage of milk and dairy products. In shops at the next village I saw familiar mini-cubes of cheese, packed in traditional wooden boxes. One of these little boxes, I learned, cost only 15 francs – or about 30 cents in American money and not far off the pre-war price.

What few French civilians remained were repairing and widening roads, working on damaged buildings, or employed at American Army camps and depots. Everywhere were German signs, "Achtung: Minen!" ("Warning: Mines!"). Only two days before I arrived, a captain whom I had known in England, but who had since joined the beachhead support forces, was obliged to turn his jeep around in the middle of the French countryside. Spotting a small space before a farm gate – just big enough to reverse his jeep into – he backed the vehicle. Instantly a mine erupted, blowing the jeep apart and seriously injuring the officer. This instance was typical of the cunning the Germans used in laying their death-traps.

Only from the air could one gain a real notion of the tremendous operations of the beachhead. From a plane it was also possible tovisualise the fierce struggle which took place before the Americans could gain the beachhead. I could also see the results of a more recent disaster – the destruction of many small ships by a storm which raged for four days. So great was the force that unloading was stopped for the entire period. Although few lives were lost in the storm, the effect on the American build-up of supplies could have been disastrous had the storm lasted longer.

So, on this Fourth of July, 1944, when enemy lines are so close that the rumble of artillery reaches deafening proportions, the Americans – together with their British and Canadian Allies – are pressing forward to insure the independence of a nation which itself gave America its cherished symbol of independence, the Statue of Liberty. Interestingly, the editor of Southampton's daily newspaper has proposed that the United States and Britain inaugurate a fund to provide France with a Statue of Liberty when the last battles have been fought.

42
Embarrassing British generosity

Occasionally my duties required me to go to London. These visits, although brief, revealed the austere conditions under which the city's inhabitants lived. As the months went by I saw areas that were hit, first by conventional bombs, then the V1 ("Doodlebug") flying bomb and finally the V2 rocket.

The V1s were no strangers to the Southampton area. Many times, after the cut-off of the plane's engine, I had waited – along with many others – for the sound of the bomb's impact. One of the Southampton area V1s made a direct hit on an anti-aircraft battery manned by women gunners, inflicting several casualties. In London I was to see more widespread evidence of the V1s' damage.

One day when I was walking near the American Embassy I heard a tremendous explosion. I darted into the nearest doorway, only to realise that what I had heard was a V2 rocket and that my instinctive reaction would have been too late had the bomb been nearby. There was no warning or defence against these rockets; ironically, they signalled the advent of space exploration.

Being assigned to wartime London was by no means an exciting post for all young Americans in uniform. A few, I learned, found the capital unpleasant. One day, as I approached four WACs walking abreast towards me near the Marble Arch, one fixed me with a stare and shouted, just as we met:

"Lieutenant, I don't like this weather and I want to go home. The only way I can be sent home is to become pregnant. Will you make me pregnant, sir?"

Too taken aback to reply, I passed the young ladies by and beat a hasty retreat.

The weeks following D-Day were hectic, for southern England had been filled almost to the bursting point with combat and support troops awaiting movement to Normandy. Our Southern Command headquarters at Wilton, just outside Salisbury, was severely stretched as more and more of its staff were transferred to the combat zone. When the call went out from the Command for temporary help with its public relations work, I offered to leave Southampton and lend a hand.

It wasn't until I reached Wilton that I realised how many war correspondents were in Europe and how difficult supporting them could be. Some, whose names were by-words with the American public, attempted to throw their weight around and demanded facilities and privileges impossible for the Army to provide. Others, equally famous, were grateful for whatever housing and transportation we could provide and cheerfully accepted the same austere facilities available to those of us in uniform.

Meanwhile, the British appetite for more information about the United States and its people was as insatiable as ever. In Southampton hardly a day had passed without some club or society asking for an American speaker. Happily, I had a small band of competent officers and sergeants who cheerfully gave up many hours of their free time to speak to these groups. By the war's end I had given nearly 200 talks myself.

During my brief secondment to Southern Command in Wilton we received a request to provide a panel of officers to talk to the inhabitants of three adjacent Wiltshire villages known as "The Wallops" – Over Wallop, Middle Wallop and Nether Wallop. Three other officers and I agreed to visit the villagers, but we never dreamed this experience would be one of the most humbling of our stay in Britain.

We were greeted warmly as we arrived at the village hall. By this time it was already packed and many people were standing. I had chosen panellists to represent both urban and rural America and who also were knowledgeable about a wide range of subjects. The evening went well and, as so often happened on these occasions, the organisers had to call time to allow us to get back to our quarters at a decent hour. Then, after we and our hosts had exchanged thanks for a mutually enjoyable evening, a man stood up and proposed that all present should make a contribution to the American Red Cross.

My fellow panellists and I were both startled and embarrassed for we knew the American Red Cross was not short of funds. We also knew that the wage of the average British worker was only a fraction of our military pay. We protested strongly, but not wishing to offend our hosts, in the end we gave in to their wishes.

As we four sat on the platform, collectors passed among the audience and gathered a large sum and presented it to me. We thanked members of the audience warmly and said we would provide them with an official receipt in due course. When we returned to Wilton the Red Cross officials were amazed to learn of this spontaneous act of generosity.

My most harrowing public speaking engagements were a series of talks at schools in the Isle of Wight. The county's Education Officer, Leslie Hutchinson, had suggested short, fact-filled talks would be ideal.

To my horror, however, I learned that the island's schools had been visited previously by a salty old American sea captain who had regaled the children with his eye-popping adventures. After my initial dismal performance I was forced into developing light hearted comments that were short on facts and heavy in humour. Even so, the children were clearly disappointed that all American visitors were not lovable sea captains.

43
My brother's close call

The second half of 1944 was almost surreal. It seemed as if I had several beings. My Army duties, of course, were paramount, although the pressure on us was now not so great and we were given weekend leave almost routinely.

Always hovering in the background was my quest for a wife. From the day our troop ship disgorged us in Britain I never lost sight of my goal – but just how I would find the girl of my dreams I hadn't a clue.

Finally there was nagging concern for my two brothers, Floyd and Harold. Would they come through the war safely? News of my brothers, however, arrived only spasmodically through the long arm of the military postal service.

Floyd, after giving up his agricultural engineering studies at the University of Georgia, worked briefly in the shipyards at Brunswick, Georgia, helping to build Liberty ships. Unhappy with this "tame" aspect of war work, he became a member of a US Navy Seabees' UDT (Underwater Demolition Team) – arguably the most hazardous of military duties.

My younger brother, Harold, joined the Navy's pre-flight training scheme, but the end of hostilities came before his instruction was completed. Thus, of my parents' four children, only my sister Hope remained at home.

Floyd, married and with two children, was to see some of the toughest action in the Pacific Theatre. Out of the blue I received a letter in which he nonchalantly wrote:

"Today I got me a Japanese Major – right between the eyes."

I knew, for this to be the case, that he must have been engaged in close combat, but months went by before I learned the full story.

UDT's often undertook the reconnaissance of, and the initial assault on islands held by the Japanese in the Pacific. Like the first wave of troops landing on the beaches of Normandy, these men suffered heavy casualties. Even when American forces succeeded in dislodging the Japanese from a particular beach, they often continued resistance by sniper fire from concealed inland positions.

It was in a situation similar to this, when the Americans thought they had firmly secured a bay off an island in the Philippines, that a handful of Japanese began slipping into the harbour and causing considerable damage. Despite keen vigilance, the Americans could never spot the marauding Japs.

When the sabotage continued unabated, Floyd's UDT, led by Ensign Gordon Basler, was given the task of detecting and eliminating the "invisible" enemy. Basler and Floyd waded along the shore, prodding the waters for anything that might reveal a Japanese presence. Suddenly they saw a large, upturned pail floating nearby. Motioning silently to each other, they approached it carefully.

When they were almost within arm's reach, the pail was suddenly flung aside by a Japanese officer aiming his pistol at Ensign Basler. He pulled the trigger but the gun misfired. Before he could squeeze a second time, Floyd drew his own weapon and shot the Major squarely between the eyes. The Japanese underwater raids into the bay ceased at once. Ensign Basler later remarked that Floyd failed to receive a high decoration for valour only because a senior officer had not been present to witness his courage.

Almost simultaneously with the receipt of Floyd's letter came news from the Secretary of the Navy that Floyd had been awarded the Bronze Star while serving as a machine-gunner on a landing craft making a daylight reconnaissance of enemy beaches and defences at Leyte in the Philippines. Despite heavy enemy fire on the landing craft, Floyd had emerged unscathed. I knew the island-hopping of American forces in the Pacific still had a long way to go, and that many lives would be lost before the Philippines and other areas could be liberated.

Would Floyd's luck continue to hold? I prayed that it would, but it would be several months before I heard more news of him.

44
I meet Mary

Eventually real summer weather arrived and I was determined, on weekends when I had more free time, to see something of the Hampshire countryside. Then suddenly I remembered the piece of paper Lieutenant Grey had given me with the name and telephone number of Mary Roberts on it.

As luck would have it, there loomed on my calendar of courts-martial a case that required contacting the police in Bishops Waltham – only a few miles from Wickham where Mary lived. Here, I thought, was a chance to kill two birds with one stone: I would go first to Bishops Waltham, complete my investigation there and then drive to Wickham.

The night before my planned trip, I telephoned the number written on the slip of paper and, to my surprise, Mary answered the call herself. I quickly explained how I had come by her name and telephone number, said I would be in the Wickham area in the afternoon of the next day and could I drop in to meet her. A little flustered at first, she eventually said "Yes". She then gave me directions for finding her home, Frith Farm, after which I thanked her and hung up.

Wickham was a charming village with a huge open area in its centre, the square having been used for many years for an annual fair. I later learned it was also the birthplace of William of Wykeham, one time Lord Chancellor of England and founder of Winchester College and Oxford's New College.

As I proceeded out of Wickham along Frith Lane, I came upon a farm on my left whose name, "Frith Farm", adorned the farmhouse gate. When I knocked on the front door and got no results, I walked round to the back. There I found the kitchen door open with a woman inside busily bottling plums. She was probably in her sixties, had greying hair and a ruddy "country" colouring. I quickly introduced myself and added: "You are doing exactly what my mother would be doing at this time of year – preserving fruit".

She smiled broadly and told me she was Mary's mother. She suspected I wanted to see Mary, for she had told her parents I would be coming that afternoon. I said "Yes" and looked around to see if Mary was in sight.

"She's not here," said Mrs. Roberts, "but if you carry on up Frith Lane, you'll see a bunch of Land Army girls making hayricks. She'll be with them."

I thanked her, took my leave and continued up the lane. Soon I saw a group of lively Land Girls with pitchforks busily erecting a hayrick. I stopped the jeep and approached the group – half a dozen or so. Although they all wore shorts, they were sweating profusely from the heat and pieces of straw were stuck in their hair. When no one came forth to greet me, I called out:

"I've come to see Mary Roberts. Is she here?"

With that a pretty red-faced girl with gorgeous brown hair and dancing eyes came forward. I introduced myself as the American who had telephoned her the night before and asked if I could visit her that weekend. She shyly admitted she was Mary, looking down at the ground rather than at my face. The other girls were much enjoying what they saw and at intervals uttered appropriate "oohs" and "ahs".

"And about this weekend?" I persisted, "Is it all right?"

Before she could reply, a chorus rang out behind her: "Say yes!"

Despite the teasing, Mary managed to explain that a bus ran from Southampton to Wickham every two hours and suggested I should come on an early one so we could have tea with her family. The arrangement made, I apologised to the girls for my interruption and took my leave. As I returned to my jeep, I could hear the teasing still going on. My first impressions were of a beautiful girl full of vigour and full of figure, but was there even more to come?

I didn't know it at the time but the following weekend was the beginning of a romance made in Heaven. Mary explained that her father,

A.E. Roberts, was a fruit grower and nurseryman who had been supplying Woolworth stores all over Britain with plants and seedlings for three decades. He had been a prisoner of war in the First World War but on returning to civilian life had made horticulture his life's calling. He had married Rose, a pretty nurse from nearby, and they had two older daughters, Joan and Betty. Joan was a nurse in Bristol and Betty also worked on her father's farm as a Land Army girl.

We spent several hours walking round the farm. The principal outbuilding was the "Woolworth shed" where all of the packing for the national retail chain was done. Together we inspected the dairy where Mary pointed out the names of the cows, explaining that this one was a good producer of milk and that one was not. I had my Brownie camera with me and despite her protestations, persuaded Mary to pose with one of the cows. It was the first of many photos to follow.

During tea I cast my eyes round the dining room and saw that the family had a collection of Colliers "classics", a set of books which contained many of the world's best known writings. Issued by one of America's major publishing houses, the collection was a great hit with the reading public. I could hardly believe my eyes, for my parents had the same set in our home in Georgia!

After returning to Southampton, I wondered if at last I had met the girl of my dreams. Was there some magic omen wrapped in the coincidence of our two families possessing the same set of books – albeit our homes were 3,000 miles apart? Did that mean our families possessed similar values? And if so, could it be that Mary and I also could have a great deal in common?

The idea seemed too good to be true. It was enough to send me off to the soundest sleep I had known for a long time.

45
The Mayor keeps his word

"There were so many depots laden with American war materiel in Britain that the island would have sunk had it not been held up by all the barrage balloons above."

This popular saying of the time had some relevance for Army mobile ports, our own 14th at Southampton and the 13th at Plymouth, for between us we emptied the bulk of fighting equipment and other military stores from hundreds of depots and dumps scattered throughout Britain. The same was true of combat and support troops who at their peak exceeded 1,500,000 men and women.

Impressive though these statistics were, they did not always reveal the human side of our efforts. One particularly poignant event was the One Millionth Yank to be processed by our unit. We knew well ahead of the day that the 1,000,000th man would be destined for service in the critical "Battle of the Bulge". This was the Germans' all-out push to capture Antwerp, a key port for supporting US Forces, by breaking through Allied defences in northwest Europe.

Many American support troops then serving in England were hastily trained in basic combat techniques and shipped across the Channel and almost immediately saw action. Private First Class Paul Shimmer from Chambersburg, Pennsylvania, who had been identified as our "one millionth man", was one of those being rushed to Belgium to stem the tide of the German onslaught.

The date of Shimmer's departure was October 24th, 1944. He was awed by all the attention being showered upon him. Our top brass was there, as well as dock board officials and Red Cross workers. So was Southampton's Mayor, Rex Stranger, who had been briefed about the occasion. Private Shimmer was stopped at the foot of the gangway, adorned with a large white placard proclaiming him to be a numerical milestone, and given a handshake by the Mayor. Had the event ended there, it would have been no different from others held under similar circumstances.

Mayor Stranger, however, took more than a passing interest in the ceremony. He asked Shimmer how old he was, if he was married, and had any children. Shimmer replied that he was 26, married and father of a little girl, Patricia Ann. Stranger asked what the little girl looked like. "She's kind of pretty," said Shimmer, proudly pulling out her photo. The young soldier warmed to the Mayor and told him he was happily married to his childhood sweetheart, Marion.

"Both my father and Marion's father are barbers," Shimmer volunteered. "Strange coincidence, isn't it?"

The two continued chatting, but just before Shimmer turned to join his comrades-in-arms aboard the ship, Stranger said it would be nice if they could meet again after the war. Shimer warmly agreed, but with a hint of premonition in his voice, added: "But I may not be around then." Stranger smiled and said, "Of course you will, but just in case you aren't I'll make sure your little girl has a start in life." The Mayor later recounted how tears came to Shimer's eyes, as he grasped the young man's hand. Shimer turned, mounted the gangway and was soon lost to view.

When 1945 dawned we hoped, but could not foresee, that it would be the year when the Second World War would end and that we might again focus on our personal lives.

I was jolted out of my concentration on routine Army duties by a letter from my parents announcing that my brother Floyd had been seriously wounded in the Pacific. The Navy's two-page telegram said only that he had been wounded in the right knee and leg and that the injuries were serious. Then a graphic letter, delayed until after my parents could receive the Navy's official notification, arrived from Floyd's UDT commander, Ensign Basler. He wasted no time in acquainting my parents with the facts:

"He was wounded in action on January 12th. He manned his gun as long as he was physically able, and even after he was handicapped by knee and leg injuries attempted to render first aid to a dying comrade at his station. Floyd has since been transferred to a hospital ship and is now receiving the best care the Navy has to offer."

My family later learned that Floyd's ship had been hit by a Japanese *kamikaze* plane, starting fires and severely damaging the superstructure. This, however, was to be only the first of two Japanese suicide attacks on ships with Floyd aboard. No sooner was he taken aboard another Navy vessel than it, too, was also hit by a *kamikaze* plane. Floyd sustained minor new injuries, but 40 of his Navy comrades were killed in the attack.

For Floyd, the war was over. I did not know until later that Navy surgeons wanted to amputate his badly mangled leg. Floyd pleaded with them not to, for the thought of returning to his little family as an amputee, and of giving up cherished expeditions on his beloved Ogeechee River, was more than he could accept. In the end, the surgeons granted his wish, but warned that he would be severely disabled for the rest of his life.

In Southampton we also had a shock a short time after news arrived of Floyd's fate. Paul Shimer, the shy Pennsylvania Private whom we had processed as "The Millionth Yank" through the port, was killed in action while fighting in Germany with the 15th Infantry, Third Division, Seventh Army. Promoted to Staff Sergeant during his six months in Europe, he was one of those unlucky men to die when the war's end was so near.

Former Mayor Rex Stranger was shattered by the news but determined to make good his vow that he and Shimer would "keep in touch" after the war.

He kept his word. Restrictions on exporting British currency and other bureaucratic delays did not allow him to visit Chambersburg until 1947. He was given a warm welcome by Shimer's family and local citizens, and later set up a trust fund of approximately $4,000 (a sizeable sum in those days) for little Patricia Ann, to be used for her education or other worthy purposes.

When the people of Chambersburg heard about the generosity of Southampton's former Mayor, they responded by collecting $3,000 for needy residents of the much-bombed port, and by sending a car-load of apples, donated by fruit growers in the surrounding area, for the children of Southampton. In subsequent years both Stranger and his wife made additional visits to the Chambersburg area. Stranger lived long enough to see his dream come true when Patricia Ann enrolled as a first year student in a South Carolina university in 1959. "Watching her progress," he told an American newspaper at the time, "has indeed been a rewarding experience".

46
We send Russian POWs to certain death

Amidst all the progress of the Allies in Normandy and the pride with which our logistical unit shared the American advances, there suddenly arrived in Southampton several hundred men who broke the hearts of all those involved in their processing.

When the massive German fortifications in Normandy were overrun, many non-combatant prisoners were taken. These turned out to be Soviet civilians who had been captured by the Germans in Russia, brought to Normandy and forced into labour battalions to help construct and maintain the German fortifications.

During the intense fighting in Russia, hundreds of thousands of these men were captured by, or defected to, the Germans. As the Allies advanced through Western Europe, many fell into British and American hands. After the Yalta Agreement the vast majority, some three million, were forcibly repatriated.

Those captured in Normandy, however, were brought to Britain for purposes of expediency. I was present when the first contingent arrived at Southampton aboard US Navy LSTs. The military attaché, together with his aides, came down from the Soviet Embassy in London to oversee the disembarkation. In my naivety I could not at first understand why the Soviets insisted that armed American military police guard the prisoners from the moment of their arrival to their transfer by train to temporary camps. Were they not all Soviet nationals?

As the men emerged from the landing craft they first spotted American military police stationed strategically along the whole of their route to waiting lorries. This clearly caused some concern among them. When, however, they saw the stern faces of high-ranking Red Army officers from the Soviet Embassy, their demeanour seemed to hit rock bottom.

As I saw these bewildered and dejected men walking with crude placards and hastily-made flags, the awful truth dawned on me. Their faces indicated they were not from Russia but came from other parts of the Soviet empire. It seemed they now hoped that "kind" Britain would offer them asylum, even if, strictly speaking, they were traitors in Soviet eyes.

To impress the British, American and Soviet officials who "greeted" them on landing at Southampton, they attempted to show loyalty to the Allied cause by displaying hastily made placards bearing the portraits of Stalin, Churchill and Roosevelt. The men silently boarded the waiting lorries which took them to Southampton Central Station. From here they travelled to POW camps. After alighting from their lorries, they were formed into double ranks to await the moment their special train arrived.

Suddenly, without notice, their voices burst into "Moscow My Beloved" and other Russian patriotic airs. When the train arrived, the singing stopped abruptly. The men then walked silently to their coaches, taking their seats without a word. As an Army photographer took their picture, some turned towards the camera – revealing the same expression of utter dejection.

All this manifestation of loyalty to the Allied cause was to avail these unfortunate men nothing. Knowing that repatriation to the Soviet Union would result either in exile to harsh labour camps in Siberia or instant execution, some committed suicide in their British camps. Many had banked on being saved by "British kindness", but this was not to be.

Concerned that the Soviets might make hostages of Allied servicemen taken by the Red Army after overrunning the German POW camps, British and American leaders did not want to risk anything that would upset the delicate support of the Kremlin for the Allied cause. To their credit, Field Marshal Alexander and a few other high-ranking officers "closed their eyes" to allow a few of the unfortunates to escape the Soviet net.

A month after D-Day there were 1,200 Russian prisoners in Britain. This figure would eventually swell to 20,000. Looking closely at the faces of the men in the first group to arrive in Southampton, I saw none who resembled the typical Slavic Russian. Instead their features indicated a great diversity of origins – some totally unknown to me at the time. I later learned they comprised Georgians, Tartars, Turkistani, Tajiks and others I had never heard of.

Some went briefly to Devizes, others to Surrey, but eventually most wound up in Yorkshire. Here they were visited and interviewed by British and Soviet authorities. Gradually it dawned on the men that they would not be allowed to remain in Britain, but would be forcibly repatriated to Russia. This led to strikes and a small number of suicides.

Eventually the 20,000 were shipped to Odessa. Some may have been executed there. When one convoy arrived, two Soviet bombers circled the dock area for a quarter of an hour or more. At the same time a mobile sawmill, earlier brought to the dock area, began its deafening screeches. More than one seasoned observer recognised this scenario as a familiar Soviet tactic for covering up the sounds of shooting and shrieks. Those not massacred were shipped off to gulags.

The terrible dilemma which faced the Allies was best expressed by the British Secretary of State for War (P.J. Grigg) at the time:

"Obviously our public opinion would bitterly and rightly resent any delay in getting our men home ... and if the choice is hardship to our men and death to Russians, the choice is plain..."

Just how many non-Russian Soviet 'citizens' were executed or sent to labour camps may never be known. Nicholas Bethell's book, *The Last Secret* (1974) and Nikolai Tolstoy's *Victims of Yalta* (1977) go a long way in portraying this poignant and tragic aftermath of the Allied invasion.

For me, it was enough to witness a small glimpse of that tragedy – one so vividly reflected by the faces of those doomed men.

47
A man and his dog sail together

Late in 1945 our unit was faced with a distressing problem, one that must have concerned commanders in previous wars. A small number of men had adopted stray dogs during the fighting on the Continent. Most were determined to take their dogs back to the United States, even if regulations strictly forbade it. Some took to doping their pets just before boarding their ships home, hoping to conceal the animals after they had been revived at sea. Eventually reports of pets being separated from their devoted owners reached our highest echelon of the US Army. It decreed dogs should now be transported to the United States.

The result: the 14th Port found itself in the kennel and pet-shipment business overnight. Hastily, we came up with a procedure to deal with the mini-crisis. Men who owned pets had to declare them openly, and agree they could be escorted back to the United States by one or two other pet lovers, who would be responsible for their care and feeding. There was no shortage of volunteers for the escort duty, for every man wanted to accompany his dog. This, of course, was impossible, but dog lovers trusted other dog lovers, so there was no problem in the end.

The story of one man and his dog is illustrative of this special relationship. Private Raymond "Rocky" Doolittle of Detroit had acquired his Alsatian, "Buck", two years earlier in Sicily. When his unit embarked from Weymouth to storm the Normandy beaches on D-Day, Buck was right beside him. In the mêlée and confusion of the landing, Buck became separated from his master. Rocky feared the dog was lost forever.

"Two days later", he recounted, "I saw Buck run out of a side street in a beachhead village which was our ammunition storage point. I quickly gave a whistle and he heard me. Since then we have been together through thick and thin."

Buck became an ever-alert sentry for Rocky's machine-gun platoon. Each night he stood guard over the foxhole manned by Rocky and his 1st Division comrades, several times detecting Germans about to infiltrate the American lines. His fierce barking alerted all around him to the impending danger.

During the long, difficult battle to capture St. Lo, General Eisenhower visited units of the 1st Division and was told about Buck's crucial sentry work. The general insisted on meeting Rocky and, after hearing his account of Buck, said: "If you have any trouble getting your dog home, just let us know at SHAEF Headquarters."

At Aachen Rocky was ambushed while running to aid a wounded man whose cries he had heard while passing by in an Army half-track. Hit in the stomach by machine gun fire, Rocky was unable to move. With no help in sight, he realised his only chance of survival lay in calling Buck. From his prone position on the ground, he whistled for Buck. At length he saw the dog approaching through the ruins of the town.

As Buck neared his fallen master, he was bounced off a nearby wall by a heavy burst of mortar fire. His rear right leg was severely injured by the blast. When aidmen arrived they at first refused to take the dog. Only after Rocky's fervent plea that Buck should accompany him did they agree that the dog might also be treated as a casualty. They then were taken to an aid station on the same stretcher; for the next five months they were moved from one hospital to another – always together.

Rocky recovered sufficiently to become ambulatory, but was judged unfit to return to duty with his unit. When his turn for embarkation to the United States came, he went to the port of Le Havre to board his ship. To his dismay he was told "No dogs." Rocky responded: "If Buck can't go, I won't go." He was offered a place on two subsequent ships, but again refused when told there was no authority for bringing along a dog.

On each occasion he spoke by telephone to his mother who did not at first understand why Rocky would forego offers to return home after so long an absence. Eventually she came up with a standard response to his announcements of further delays: "What? That dog again!"

It was at this point that General Eisenhower's headquarters, moved by Rocky's plight and that of other dog owners, gave the order that our unit in Southampton should arrange to ship servicemen's pets to the United States at government expense. Rocky and Buck were sent to Southampton where, after a minimum of ten dogs had been collected and quarantined, a ship with a team of carers was allocated. The happy end to this true story was that Rocky, after Buck had been in quarantine for the required time, sailed with his friend from Southampton to New York aboard the troop transport.

In the great rush to redeploy American troops to the United States "ship spotters" must have thought they were in paradise as ship after famous ship sailed from Southampton. Although Southampton was her home port, the Queen Elizabeth had never been there during the war because she would have been a prime target for the Germans. Now, however, she carried nearly 15,000 men and women – among them actor-airman, Colonel Jimmy Stewart – on her first voyage as an American troopship. The Queen Mary could transport almost the same number. Other famous vessels taking part in the redeployment were the aging Aquitania (which originally brought me to Britain), the former German liner Europa, and even large US Navy vessels like the aircraft carriers Lake Champlain and Enterprise. In the first 30 days of the operation more than 75,000 troops were shipped from Southampton to New York.

Meanwhile the Nuremberg Trials, one of the century's great judicial events, were taking place in southern Germany. It had begun in November, 1945 and was to continue for almost a year. On my last visit to the Continent before returning to the United States, I spent several days observing the trials. Except for Hitler and those who died with him in Berlin, here sitting in front of me were the architects of Nazi crimes against humanity that had claimed millions of lives.

There was no problem following the trial, whatever the language being spoken, for the marvel of simultaneous translation made the task easy. The accused sat impassively, listening to the German version over their headphones. During my few days at the trials, none of the major defendants showed any sign of remorse or guilt. Had they pinned their hopes on the premises, put forward by their counsel, that victors could not try losers in court, and that the accused had only followed orders given by their superiors?

I sensed there was a spirit of defiance among some of these men. Thus I was not surprised when I later heard that Hermann Goering managed to commit suicide only hours before he was due to be hanged.

48
An uncooperative father

Had I known in advance that my future father-in-law, Alfred Edward Roberts, was a renowned "character", I might have thought twice about wooing his lovely daughter.

Born in Wimbledon in 1889, he early developed a love of singing – possibly inspired by the lively morning services of his parents' church (Emanuel) and, later, by London music halls. While still in his teens, he was apprenticed to a nearby nursery where he soon picked up basic principles of horticulture. When his parents read of the forthcoming sale of a 10-acre plot of farmland in Hampshire's highly regarded fruit-growing area, they bought it for him as a challenge.

Living at one time in a bell tent and later in a crude shack, he was soon producing large quantities of strawberries for the London market. Thus encouraged, he acquired more land, expanded the range of his fruit and soon established himself as one of the leading horticulturists in Hampshire. In his spare moments he oversaw the construction of a house that later was to be home for his parents.

His view of life was that a successful businessman at all times should lead a parallel life of leadership in his local community. Thus he formed and led the local Scout group and also stood for his Parish Council. By now his reputation was well established and he came top of the poll in the Council election. On the day he was to assume his duties, however, the Council Chairman announced he had sent off to London for a copy of the newly elected Councillor's birth certificate, only to discover he was not yet 21: therefore ineligible for public office. The "child" was promptly dismissed from the meeting.

Although his soft fruit business prospered, the First World War intervened and he joined up in August 1914, at the age of 25. By this time he had become thoroughly besotted with a pretty nurse/midwife, Rose Houghton, from nearby Wickham. It was to be another five months before he could obtain enough leave from the Army to marry her. By the end of 1915 their first daughter, Joan, was born. The adjutant of his unit duly incorporated a notice of her birth in the battalion orders.

During the Battle of Ypres his unit overran a German position and took several prisoners. On that memorable occasion a teenage boy surrendered to him, calling out "Mercy, Kamerad, Mercy!" Corporal Roberts, as he was then, accepted the surrender and passed the prisoner to the rear for processing. Almost immediately he heard a shot. Turning, he saw that a fellow soldier - one well known to him - had shot the German boy in cold blood, apparently for no other reason than to boast he had killed one of the enemy. Roberts levelled his own weapon at his compatriot but could not bring himself to pull the trigger - suddenly realising that would not be the end of the matter. He was to be haunted by the memory of the pleading German youth for the rest of his days.

Eventually his unit, in turn, was overrun and many - including himself - were taken prisoner. He was destined to spend the next 18 months in a German POW camp in the village of Bohmte near Osnabruck. Working in a nearby forest, he made contact with a sympathetic German family who promised to furnish him and a fellow soldier with civilian attire so they might escape. The father of the family had been befriended by a British soldier while stationed in South Africa and now he sought to repay that kindness. Unfortunately, the sympathetic German was spotted one day by guards. He was carrying the clothing intended for the two British soldiers, one kit for Corporal Roberts and the other for his comrade who was six feet three inches tall. The tall soldier was quickly identified and removed from the camp, but Roberts' identity was never established.

His POW confinement left the young corporal with several vivid impressions. One was the German obsession for cleanliness, manifested by placing guards over prisoners to make sure they washed themselves thoroughly before meals. Another was the emphasis placed by the Germans on the work ethic, as evidenced by inscriptions on village memorials.

But it was an Englishman, Sergeant Sam Kilburn, who was to make the greatest impression during these months of confinement. Born in England, Kilburn had gone to live in America as a young man but - moved by patriotism - returned to sign up for military service when Britain entered the war. A man of great charisma, Kilburn told Roberts how he arrived one day in a small California town where he saw a remarkable inscription across the clock face of the local church. It read:

"Count that day lost, whose low descending sun, views from thy hand, no worthy action done."

When he resumed his horticultural career after the war, Roberts adopted this precept as his own, placing it at the bottom of the page of his correspondence. Thereafter, on retiring each night, he assessed his day's work by this yardstick. As it happened, Kilburn's gem was a perfect complement to Roberts' other great love, scouting, whose aim was "A good turn every day."

Eventually A.E. Roberts Ltd. became suppliers of fruit and flower seedlings to Woolworth stores throughout Britain. Attached to each plant was his label giving instructions for growing. When novice gardeners subsequently wrote to him after encountering problems, he replied to each one individually. His strawberries were originally planted adjacent to the main road, a convenience that allowed pilferers to come in the evening and eat vast quantities undetected. He smiled at the account related by two soldiers from nearby towns who met in France during the Second World War and found they had daring exploits in common – stealing strawberries from his fields.

As a young man he became friends with Richard St. Barbe Baker, founder of Men of the Trees. The movement encouraged planting of trees all over the world, the benefits of which are now widely appreciated as helping to preserve the natural environment. Later, when he became chairman of his local Council's housing committee, he saw to it that newly developed housing estates were supplied with young trees from the outset. Mr. Roberts received many honours for his public service as well as the cherished Silver Acorn Scouting award.

He was respected by his employees for his optimism, sense of fun and patriotism. Long before the British government encouraged factory owners to broadcast music to ease the monotony of mass production, he placed radio sets in his packing sheds for the benefit of his workers. At the end of each growing season, he organised outings to Portsmouth's music hall. On patriotic occasions, such as birthdays of famous military and naval heroes, he conducted impromptu ceremonies beneath the farm's flagpole.

Impressed by this background and the respect accorded my future father-in-law as he took me round the farm and the village of Wickham, I quickly learned he was also the dominant personality of his family. If there was any problem, he immediately called a "family conference" to resolve the matter. A family event of any significance whatsoever required a ceremony of some kind. I was present once when the family cat gave birth to a litter of kittens. He ordered all activity to cease while he — attired in his dressing gown – solemnly christened the tiny creatures one by one.

At meal times he insisted on sung grace. When he came across an inspirational text he immediately had it typed and distributed to all family members. Gradually it dawned on me that his daughter Mary was possessed of the same zest for life as her father. Their personalities and traits were so alike they could be taken for identical twins rather than father and daughter. Most of all, she oozed with enthusiasm, optimism and charm — characteristics I came to cherish.

Early in our courtship Mr. Roberts made it plain to me that he had no problem about Mary and me becoming good friends, but anything more than that - meaning marriage - was out of the question. On one occasion he was quite happy to "show me off" as a "family friend" by taking me to a meeting of the Wickham Parish Council. The problem was that Mary was only 19 when we first met and she had to be 21 before she could wed me in her own right. Until then, Mr. Roberts made it clear to me many times, that he would not give permission to marry. It was this obstinacy that was to cause great pain to Mary and myself.

I fared much better in my relations with Mary's mother. Mrs. Roberts explained to me that her husband had always wanted a son and heir, but when Mary was born (their third daughter in succession) he locked himself up in his bedroom for two days without speaking to anyone. As the little girl grew up, he came to realise she was much like himself and so became very protective of her. That she might marry a foreigner and go abroad was his worst nightmare. At times I despaired so much that I wondered if I should abandon my quest to marry.

Fortunately our love for each other prevailed, and we determined - whenever we were together - to marry regardless. Yet I saw Mary was cruelly being torn by her devotion for the family - her father in particular. Clearly, we had embarked on a long and rocky courtship, but where it would lead to neither of us could foretell.

49
The wedding date is set!

As an Allied victory loomed ever nearer, our unit in Southampton reflected quietly over the role modern logistical equipment was having in the war effort. Much praise has been lavished upon the well known "work horses" of the American military: the jeep, the Dakota (C-47) aircraft, the landing craft (LSTs and others) and the Liberty ships. All deserve their niches in military history for their contributions to the Allied effort.

Not so much noted, however, were two other logistical marvels – the Y class tankers and American-built railway stock. At Southampton we were able to see how these two elements also played a role in gaining supremacy of movements in Normandy.

A fleet of 20 Y-boats, none more than 183 feet long and capable of carrying from 600 to 800 tons of petroleum, ferried more than 130,000 tons of POL (petroleum, oil and lubricant) supplies from Southampton Water to Continental ports under extremely hazardous conditions. Their small size enabled them to penetrate small harbours and rivers where their urgently needed cargoes quickly reached combat units. Mines were a constant peril; Y-17, for example, hit by an underwater mine while crossing the Channel, instantly went to the bottom with no survivors from its 18-man crew.

Correctly anticipating that French railway rolling stock would be largely destroyed during the fighting before and after D-Day, American Transportation Corps planners ordered construction of many thousands of units – locomotives, wagons, petroleum carriers, etc., to Continental rail specifications. These were shipped to Britain, reassembled and stored until needed in France. Fifteen LSTs were installed with rails so that stock could be "rolled on, rolled off" in the same way as military vehicles. Much of the railway stock was loaded from embarkation 'hards' near Southampton's Town Quay. By the time the operation ceased we had shipped 21,500 units to France, including 665 locomotives.

(In the later stages of the war and in the months immediately following VE-(Victory-in-Europe) Day, some stock was routed to the Soviet front on the understanding that, once unloaded, the empty wagons would be returned to American control. Increasingly, our Soviet-bound stock was destined to remain in the east. Years after the war's end, travellers in the Eastern Bloc reported sightings of the Transportation Corps wagons – some still bearing the TC insignia.)

VE-Day was an occasion for much celebrating in Southampton, as it was in every community in the Allied world. The evening of 17th May found many thousands of townspeople celebrating in every part of the town. There were many events – some spontaneous and some planned – including parades, bonfires, dances and, of course, services of thanksgiving.

After the fall of Paris and central France, our commands were transferred from the United Kingdom to the Continent. I was invited to spend several days at our Transportation Corps headquarters in Paris to assess first hand the continuing build-up of American supplies as the Allied armies pressed on to the east. There was great elation as our field commanders now chalked up victory after victory against the Germans.

One day I was taken to a large building on the Champs Elysee where a massive propaganda leaflet centre had been operated by the Germans with the help of French artists and writers. When Paris fell the staff fled, leaving behind tens of thousands of leaflets of every description imaginable.

As a journalist who had been trained in the power of words and art in advertising, I was fascinated by the techniques employed by the German and French propagandists. I was not surprised to find one leaflet, aimed at American troops, depicting President Roosevelt as the friend of wealthy American Jews who profited from the war while caring nothing for the lives of our men in uniform. Other leaflets sought to demoralise American troops by asking why they were willing to risk their lives on foreign soil.

Most insidious were leaflets intended for British troops; they invariably showed American soldiers making sexual advances to their girl-friends back in England. Half of the design was printed on each side of the leaflet, making it impossible to take in the whole picture without holding it up to the light. This had the added advantage of making the soldier a perfect sniper's target.

Meanwhile I managed to visit Mary almost every weekend after our port activities became less hectic. I could not be sure however, that I was getting any closer to winning her heart.

It seemed there was no doubt of her devotion to me when we were together, or when she penned her thoughts to me in the letters that arrived in midweek. Yet, as long as she remained under the spell of her father, she could not bring herself to say "Yes".

The wedding date is set!

The closest I had come to making a proposal was when we cycled to Hambledon, the lovely village where the game of cricket was born. Overlooking the village is Speltham Down, a hill not too difficult to climb but yet high enough to enjoy a view of the village and fields beyond. It was while picnicking there, gnawing on a chicken drumstick, that I casually asked Mary if she would consider becoming the wife of a Georgia newspaper editor one day. Apparently without taking in the full implication of what I had said, she mumbled, "I suppose so."

But that tentative agreement brought us no nearer to a firm decision and, crucially, setting a date. So I picked December 1st (1945) as our wedding day and told Mary we had to stick to it – or risk our marriage not taking place. It was difficult enough for me to calm my roommate, "Herby" Niederberger, with whom I shared my hopes. For Mary, however, it was daily torture as her father adamantly refused to give his consent, causing her to become deeply depressed until we next met or exchanged letters. Would our torment ever end?

Once I suggested she read the Old Testament story of Ruth. She did and replied:

"(You must) be thinking of me, away from my parents and friends, going to a strange new land, settling down and making a success of the new life. Somehow, I really believe I could – in fact *I know* I could."

In her next letter she referred to our Hambledon adventure; I was overjoyed to learn she had, after all, taken in my clumsy proposal.

"Since our visit to Hambledon," she said, "my brain seems to have stopped functioning. You seem to have a strange effect on me. Little things happen which haven't done so before. Like not sleeping at night when I'm terribly tired after a long day's work. Staring into space at the dinner table, so that the family suddenly comes down on me like a ton of bricks. Forgetting things."

So she was going through the same pangs I felt – and more, as her letter continued.

"So I've come to the conclusion a very important change has come over me ... Goodnight, happy dreams. Loads of love, Mary."

In August Mary took up my suggestion to visit Wales, taking along her Land Army friend, Monica. Their stay with my new friends, Farmer Jones and his wife, coincided with VJ-Day, as she was to chronicle in her letters.

"Isn't this simply wonderful! News from the kitchen has just confirmed this is the final victory. To me this means so much. Our friends abroad will no longer be in danger. Those in Japanese prison camps will be able to return home."

Then, in a poignant personal reference, she added:

"To us – you and me, this will also mean a lot. I wonder where either of us will be next year at this time. Will we be together?

"I can't imagine why, but I seem to think of you a terrific amount on this holiday. One comes upon a beautiful scene and instinctively one thought comes uppermost – you should be here to share it."

Mary's 21st birthday was August 11th. She planned an evening campfire with friends (but not her parents) where we would enjoy a sing-song and snacks. From the sly looks and whispering we knew those present expected to hear news of our engagement and date of the marriage.

Because of Mr. Roberts' refusal to approve of our union, everyone assumed Mary would now make an announcement in her own right. But she desperately wanted to win her father round and, clinging to that hope, she begged me not to force her hand.

Of course I did not. But I decided to go ahead and invite all of my Army colleagues for the December 1st date and not bother to tell them of the difficulties. I filed the official request for the marriage and the same day booked an Army bus to carry them from Southampton to Wickham.

That is, all except my roommate Herby. I told him there was every chance Mary's father might kidnap her and disappear. It would be his task, I said solemnly, to tail Mr. Roberts and Mary all the way from the farmhouse to the church.

As my future best man, he had no choice but to accept.

50
Will my bride be kidnapped?

The fact that Mary had reached her majority on August 11th meant her father's refusal to approve our marriage no longer carried any legal weight, but it did not dent his determination to stop us from marrying.

He now embarked on a campaign to rip apart our emotions. I detected this change in strategy immediately in Mary's letters and in our discussions whenever we met. My letters to her have not survived, but they reflected the same pangs of misery she described in hers.

Meanwhile, I gave her books and other material which I hoped would go some way to introducing her to life in the American Deep South. One of the books was Lillian Smith's *Strange Fruit*, a best seller in its time. She was not prepared for the work's description of emotional funerals or use of capital punishment.

"In the book," she wrote, "a funeral service is described in great detail. Is that the usual way one's relations are buried? Also, do the natives (her word for Americans) actually kill off their brethren if they commit a crime?"

In the first week of October (less than 60 days before the date set for our wedding) a letter arrived from her father in reply to one from me asking him to bless our marriage. I knew this would mean a great deal to Mary.

He ignored my plea and went directly to this new strategy, which he hoped would drive Mary and me apart.

"'I want to make it quite clear we have nothing whatsoever

against you personally," he began. "On the contrary we very much admire your ideals and plans for the future.

"What I wish to make equally clear is that in view of the seriousness of the step you suggest, it is absolutely imperative that Grace Mary should not be rushed, but should have time to know her own heart and mind. The same applies to you. The length of time Mrs. Roberts and I desire is one year from the time you leave England. I am quite sure no reasonable individual would think this *unreasonable*.

"Finally, you will know that any playing for time is for the sole purpose of making sure what is the RIGHT path for our daughter and, incidentally, for you."

A week later Mary's letter described the turmoil she had been going through.

"As you know," she said, "I have been feeling very worried about 'our problem.' Everyone and everything seems to be against us. How on earth you have put up with me for the past three or four weeks I cannot imagine. I have been moody, disagreeable and a thoroughly miserable person.

"Tuesday night I realised this, so when I awoke on Wednesday morning I was a different person – leaping out of bed, thinking what a wonderful day it was! My troubles seemed to leave me in a flash and I realised whatever problems we had could be overcome. So, you see, from now on we will be new people moving forward – fighting together for our ideals which we know to be right!

If I had been smarting from her father's earlier letter, I now took heart from her closing words:

"I love you with a real love now – more than ever before."

It was signed; "From your own Mary.

When she had a spare moment Mary worked on a cardigan she was knitting for me. With the housekeeper, Aunty May, always on hand for such family chores, Mary had little experience at knitting and so struggled for weeks to come up with something that vaguely resembled a sweater.

Towards the end of October she wrote that she was mailing me the long-awaited garment.

"But before you look at it," she cautioned, "let me give you a warning. Remember I told you about the pattern? Well, it was one of those offered free in the papers and there must have been something wrong with it for there are literally yards of it. Personally I like it that way - it will keep your behind warm!

"If you do find it far too big in various directions, just do one of the following: (a) get yourself a bit bigger so it will fit or (b) send it back and I'll unpick and start all over again. You'll see it's a different colour round the neck. That's because there wasn't enough of the original wool and I had to use some of my own. As you will see, it hasn't matched very well but I hope it will improve after a few washings."

Then came a bombshell that sent both me and my roommate, Herby, into despair.

"O'Donald, it has been decided that the moment I leave the farm with you, it will be put up for sale. I can't marry you!

"I can't go to America! I must have been a fool ever to think I could.

"I have prayed for a long time," she said, "to be shown what to do. God must mean for me to stay here. We are placed in this world to face battles and problems and to make decisions. I must make up my mind whether I do as I want, that is, have my own way, or let down my whole family.

"My father and mother have worked all their lives for this business. I just don't think I can leave them! I'd be haunted by that for the rest of my life and I would also make a misery of yours, too."

She signed the letter: "A deeply saddened Mary."

What to do? With the wedding date barely a month away, it seemed that Mary was withering under her father's constant assaults about her "loyalty" to him and her family.

I decided to tell no one of my dilemma except Herby and pledged him not to tell others. Somehow I hoped a miracle could be wrought out of this highly charged situation which was leaving Mary a nervous wreck and me on tenterhooks.

Then I remembered Mary's older sister, Joan, a nurse in Bristol, had said I could approach her about any delicate aspects of my relationship with her father. Joan had already told me she approved of our marriage, but added her father was bound to make an awful fuss because Mary was the apple of his eye. So I told Joan about Mary's last letter, saying she felt she couldn't bring herself to break with the family.

Joan wrote back promptly, giving me renewed hope that the marriage could still go ahead as planned

"Mary is such a sensitive girl," she began, "and with such a wonderful and unusual sense of dutifulness that I'm afraid she takes things too much to heart. In the past when some delicate family matter has arisen, my father has threatened to sell Frith Farm. It has happened time and time again and Mary knows that. Take my advice, Donald, and don't let the fear of the farm being sold make a bit of difference to you and Mary. It would be such a tragedy!"

Then, touchingly, she signed her letter: "Little Sister."

But the battle was not yet won. When next I visited the farm, Mr. Roberts insisted the marriage should be discussed in a "definitive" family conference. Mrs. Roberts and Mary were present but given little chance of saying anything. In fact, Mr. Roberts spoke mostly and said nothing new: only the same demand that we wait a year before making our decision.

The very next day he followed up the discussion with a blunt letter appealing to, as he thought, my religious convictions.

"In most branches of the Christian church," he said, "it is laid down that there must be a year for preparation of marriage, with the result that there are very few failures."

Then, in a dig about the increased rate of divorces in the United

States, he added: "In your country apparently this time for preparation is not considered necessary and the result, alas, we all know so well."

His final paragraph sought to introduce my mother's concern, as he imagined, about my marrying a girl she had never met.

"Grace Mary is but twenty-one," he pointed out, "and she has been asked to give up her country and all those near and dear to her. We merely ask for this time of one year. We are confident you will put your own feelings aside and allow our child this time of preparation. This is our wish and Grace Mary's wish (when not with you) and I believe also the wish of your dear Mother. We shall judge you on your deeds and not words."

The letter was signed both by Mr. and Mrs. Roberts, but not Mary.

This turned out to be our final skirmish, although I never knew when or if the battle lines would be drawn again. With very little time remaining, I instructed Herby to have his own Jeep handy so as to prevent the kidnapping of Mary by her father. Then Mary and I agreed we should stick to the wedding arrangements and confirm the details with our respective ministers, the Reverend W.H. Compton of Southampton's Polygon Baptist Church, which I had attended regularly, and the Reverend C.H. Clarke of the Wickham Methodist Chapel. We decided against issuing printed invitations, however, so tentative was our situation.

As December 1st approached, neither Mary nor I could say with assurance that we would be man and wife by the end of that day.

Throughout the bitter confrontation with Mary's father, I felt her mother approved of me – even if our marriage meant she would leave England. Yet she was loyal to her husband in agreeing with his plea that the wedding be delayed until I had returned to the United States.

Over time I learned that Rose Roberts had a rural background not that much different from my own. Her family, the Houghtons, came from a long line of Hampshire farmers and timber merchants.

Apart from their connection with the land and forestry, they were best known as devout Methodists. When the Methodist Church decided in 1898 to raise one million guineas from its one million members, the Houghtons of south Hampshire responded enthusiastically. Once when I was invited to explore the attic of the farmhouse I discovered illuminated certificates documenting donations to the "Wesleyan Methodist Century Fund" by half a dozen members of the Houghton family.

These handsome documents bear portraits of Charles and John Wesley together with scenes of early evangelical services. Rose Houghton, Mary's mother, and the family housekeeper, Mabel Duffin, were loyal members of Wickham's Methodist congregation. Mabel loved the old Wesley hymns, played the organ and years later, attended Billy Graham's services in London.

Rose was acutely aware of Mary's dilemma as she was buffeted one way, then another, as I and her father vied for her loyalty. When Mary became dispirited by the continuing ordeal, Rose took me aside one day to say that all would be well.

"She is like her father", she confided. "When things go wrong, she is crushed – but when things go well, she'll take you to the very gates of Heaven."

Although her husband belonged to the Church of England, Rose was a devout Methodist. This schism in no way affected their marriage, so they went their separate ways. When it came time to choose our wedding service, Mary agreed with me (a Baptist) that the Wickham Methodist chapel was the most appropriate venue.

Rose's 'nursing instincts' were appreciated by many whose lives had been restored to normality. Through the years she had acquired several caravans and converted them into temporary living quarters. Although planning permission would not be granted for these today, there was no problem in her time. When she heard of a woman who was devastated by bereavement, divorce or some other personal calamity, she would invite her to stay in one of the caravans until she had recovered. The combination of simple living in the beautiful Meon valley while being attended by Rose, always did the trick. Mr. Roberts was not best pleased as one caravan after another appeared on the landscape, but eventually he joined Rose in helping to fill them with some of life's unfortunates.

When it came time to furnish the caravans with beds, chairs and other essentials, Rose liked nothing better than trundling off to the sales rooms at Southsea which could always be counted on for furnishings from bankrupt hotels and boarding houses. A tour of the caravans would always guarantee the sight of a Royal Doulton chamber pot with the name of the now defunct hotel emblazoned on its side. Nothing like relieving oneself in style, I thought.

At times Rose had a virtual colony of disadvantaged people living in the caravans. When one departed – usually in robust health and high spirits – a new one arrived.

Only a few miles away was a large lunatic asylum. The inmates ranged from those with serious cases to some with modest mental disorders. Rose regularly "employed" some of the latter to do odd chores in the farmyard. Ostensibly they were supposed to help with tidying up or feeding the chickens, but frequently they forgot where they were – and who they were – so engrossed were they by the sight of fledgling birds or a rose in bud.

Somehow I instinctively felt this Good Samaritan was on my side and that I would eventually win the hand of her daughter – whatever obstacles her husband put in my path.

51
The knot is tied!

A week before our wedding date Mrs. Roberts took Mary away from the farm to an apartment at Southsea. I was later to learn that Mary had been in such a distressed state -- pushed by me to marry her and her father not to -- that her mother decided some quiet, neutral ground was necessary for her daughter to compose herself for the biggest event of her life.

Although the Women's Land Army headquarters had graciously supplied a wedding gown, there remained several other articles of clothing to complete Mary's trousseau. For these she and her mother made a trip to London the day before the wedding. Family and friends knew we had planned the wedding for December 1st, but not until Mary returned from London late on the previous day was she able to confirm by telephone that the wedding was still on.

Mary's diary recorded what happened when she awoke on the morning of the eventful day:

"I had been thoroughly exhausted by the trip to London and all the telephone calls made after we returned. I sank into a deep, restful sleep and awoke to the sound of women's voices downstairs. Only then did I realise this was to be my wedding day and those voices came from my mother's friends who had promised to turn up at 6 am to begin making sandwiches! I hurriedly joined them in preparing the food, but before I knew it, the time came for me to have a bath and get dressed. I had one recurring thought: would my father turn up to give me away?"

Half an hour before the scheduled time for the ceremony the Army bus arrived, bringing me and half dozen of my best friends, the Rev. Compton, Ron Perrin (the British manager of the "New Dock" area where I had put in many hours) and Bill Patience (friend and photographer of the *Southern Daily Echo*). As we got off the bus, I saw guests arriving at the chapel with not an usher in sight.

With the cloud of uncertainty hanging over the wedding, I suddenly realised we had not arranged for ushers. Hurriedly I applied myself to the task, As the chapel was small I just about managed to get one guest seated before having to dash back up the aisle to take another in tow. One elderly spinster, overcome by the sight of several uniformed Americans, whispered in my ear:

"Which one of those Yanks is Miss Roberts' man?"

"None of 'em," I replied. "I'm him."

Her jaw dropped as I led her to an empty seat.

Meanwhile, matters were not going so well a mile away at the farm. Mr. Roberts had twice gone out to the road and tried to persuade Herby, my best man, to leave.

"Not on your life!" was his reply both times.

Eventually Mary was ready and her father led her to his waiting car. Herby, watching intently, saw Mr. Roberts rev up his engine and begin moving away. Mary later recounted how Herby had tail-gated her father's car to the very entrance of the chapel.

With only a minute or two to go, I heard the start of the familiar wedding march and knew that Herby had faithfully performed his mission. The service went like clockwork with the two ministers alternately taking charge. When the time came for me to place the ring on Mary's finger I took my time as this was an important part of the ceremony and the one thing I feared was dropping the ring. Mr. Roberts, impatient with my slowness, grabbed my hand and manoeuvred the ring onto Mary's finger.

After the ceremony we adjourned to the vestry where all the principal parties had to sign the register. Soon the room was filled with family and friends who wanted to sign the certificate as witnesses. By the time the signing was over, the document looked more like a petition than a certificate. As Mary and I emerged slowly from the chapel, we passed beneath an arch formed by Land Army girls holding farm tools and my Army friends saluting. Then everyone made a mad dash to the farm for the reception.

Because none of the rooms in the farmhouse was large enough to hold the 70 people invited, guests were divided into two groups, one in the living room and the other in the dining room. This meant that food and drink had to be offered in both rooms. It also meant Mary and I were constantly moving back and forth so that we could receive the congratulations of everyone present.

Ron Perrin, who possessed a wonderful baritone voice, had offered to sing one or two songs appropriate to the occasion. Unfortunately, some of the Land Girls thought it their duty to accompany him. This they did with such varying degrees of competence that Ron burst out laughing and gave up.

That was not the only mischief to come from Mary's Land Army colleagues. Unbeknown to us, one of them had brought along a bottle of gin and emptied it into one of the punch bowls. As far as the rest of us knew, the punch bowls contained only blackcurrant juice from the farm, supplemented by juices from other fruit. It was not until Mary and I noticed that the two ministers, by now quite talkative, kept returning to the doctored punch bowl. We wandered over and asked if they were enjoying themselves.

"Best punch I've ever tasted," said the Reverend Clarke, grinning broadly. The Reverend Compton smiled in agreement.

Time flew and soon so did we. The Army bus returned its passengers to Southampton, but most of the other guests accompanied us to Fareham station where we were to catch the next train to Salisbury before changing for the London-West Country express. The wedding party took over the entire platform, dancing jigs and singing merry songs. When the stationmaster complained, they roped him into the procession and he had no choice but to smile and join in. Out of the corner of my eye I saw Mary and her mother in deep conversation. I knew there could be only one subject: our wedding night. Mr. Roberts throughout was close to tears and did not join in the jollity.

Suddenly the train arrived and in a flash two of the guests

daubed our compartment door JUST MARRIED! Others took our suitcases and placed them in the overhead racks. In another moment the stationmaster blew his whistle and the train moved off.

I turned to Mary. It was the first time the two of us had been together during the tumultuous day. Taking her hand in mine, I kissed her tenderly and asked: "How does it feel to be a married woman?"

"Exhausting!" she replied, grinning mischievously.

"Ah," I replied, "you ain't seen nothing yet!"

As the train roared on into the night, we kept looking at each other and marvelling – "We're married!"

I now confessed a slight concern to Mary. After flipping through the pages of the AA (Automobile Association) handbook, I had picked Totnes as our honeymoon base and the town's Royal Seven Stars as our hotel. I explained to Mary I hoped we could do excursions all during the week of leave the Army had granted me. How pleasant it would be, I added, to return to an ancient hostelry (the guide said the Royal Seven Stars had been a famous 17th century coaching inn) at the end of each day's expedition.

Mary liked the sound of it and asked what I was concerned about.

"When I telephoned the hotel to reserve our room," I replied, "I didn't have the nerve to say we would be newlyweds."

"But you did ask for a double room?" she asked.

"Yes", I said, "and the clerk did confirm it had a double bed instead of two singles. In fact, he said all the hotel's double rooms had double beds."

"Oh, well", said Mary, laughing. "He would know instantly we are newlyweds. Who knows – we might even get the bridal suite!"

It seemed an age before the train reached Newton Abbot, which was as close as we could get to Totnes by rail. I had asked the hotel to order a taxi to meet us at the station, but on emerging with our bags there was not a vehicle in sight. I quickly telephoned the Royal Seven Stars and the clerk confirmed the taxi had been booked. He said it should arrive any minute.

There was nothing we could do but cool our heels in the waiting room. And cool them we did, for there was no fire in the tiny fireplace. An hour went by and I again telephoned the hotel and got the same reply. After nearly another hour, the taxi at last turned up. I was much annoyed by the delay, but held my tongue.

"I'm very sorry", the driver explained as we got underway, "but the car suffered a broken axle just as I started out and it has taken me until now to find a garage open that had a new axle. You see, it's late Saturday night and almost everything is closed."

Minutes later we arrived at the hotel where a sleepy-eyed clerk unlocked the front door to let us in. I hastily paid the taxi driver, giving him more than the usual tip because of his extraordinary bad luck.

The clerk grabbed the largest bag but did a double take when it failed to come off the ground. What he didn't know was that it contained 14 large tins of orange juice – two per day for Mary and me for the duration of our honeymoon. Orange juice was supposed to be full of vitamins and I had reckoned we both would need plenty if we were to carry out the daily expeditions as well as our nuptial obligations.

Now fully awake, the clerk tried again, this time managing to just raise the bag off the ground. He limped into the hotel where I quickly signed the register. Then, taking another forlorn look at the bag, he led us upstairs to our room. Rubbing his sore arm, he managed a weak grin as I tipped him generously.

Mary and I rushed to embrace each other. Here we were, man and wife – both virgins – and about to fulfil our vow of honouring each other with our bodies. After an 18-month courtship and what seemed like an endless battle to gain her father's approval, we had arrived at the crucial magic moment of starting our adult life as husband and wife. We clung together briefly with emotions rising, each looking at the inviting bed out of the corner of our eyes.

We were not to know it, but this was but the beginning of a week that was to be extremely cold and with rain off and on almost every day. It was clear that only in bed could we escape the permeating chill and dampness.

I quickly stripped off my clothing and dived between the covers as Mary struggled to come to terms with undressing in my company for the first time in her life. With her back towards me, she at last managed to get everything off.

"Come on just as you are!" I called, "I've got the bed warm for you!"

But she would not have it. Having bought a lovely nightgown for the occasion, she was not about to come to bed without it. Eventually she managed to put it on with her back still turned to me, all the while murmuring, "Oh dear, this is so awkward!" Moments later she joined me for a night of heavenly bliss the like of which the world had never known before. (Except, of course, for all those other newlyweds who have thought the same.) Over and over we pledged our devotion for each other as we joined in the magical blend of spiritual and physical love.

We woke late Sunday morning and were grateful that the hotel had allowed us to have breakfast whenever we descended. We were digging into welcome bowls of hot porridge and plates of poached eggs on toast when the hotel clerk arrived at Mary's shoulder and handed her a telegram. A mild shudder came over her features; was there bad news from home? I placed my hand on her arm as she opened the envelope. Then she beamed her glorious smile – the one that would always lift me to "the gates of Heaven" as her mother had put it. Her smile was like no other I had ever known: a beam that took in her eyes, lips, cheeks and the whole of her face.

"Daddy has blessed our marriage!" she exclaimed, leaning over and giving me a kiss.

There were already tears in her eyes as she passed the telegram for me to read. I'm afraid I, too, shed one as I realised what the message meant to her. Then I knew the hostility which Mr. Roberts had shown me up to now had to be a thing of the past. It was my turn to give thanks for the blessing.

We finished breakfast just in time to hear church bells ringing in the town. Why not, we asked ourselves, begin our honeymoon adventure with a church service! The first one we found was Methodist and, glad to escape the pelting rain, we rushed inside. We held hands throughout. By the time the service was over, I'm not sure either of us remembered a word of the sermon. We had spent the time giving so many amorous glances at each other that members of the congregation behind us would have had no doubt of our newlywed status.

Although the rain poured incessantly, we trundled through the narrow streets of Totnes trying to get a feel for the ancient town. At last, cold and hungry, we returned to the hotel. We were happy just to flop into the comfortable leather-backed chairs and enjoy hot tea with scones in the atmosphere of the old-world panelled lounge.

Our first expedition out of Totnes, the next day, was to Dartington Hall, a few miles northwest of the town. The Hall itself was built in the latter part of the 14th century and must have been a magnificent medieval building in its time. Unfortunately it was not well maintained in successive centuries and when Mary and I saw it, extensive repairs were underway. The cost of the renovation and the acquisition of the surrounding estate was largely borne by an American, Mrs. Leonard K. Elmhirst, who - together with her English husband – developed the concept of restoring the ancient hall and its lands. Mrs. Elmhirst was alive at the time of our honeymoon visit and she said it was her husband's and her dream that Dartington Hall should not only be a viable enterprise but also a centre for local crafts and a college of arts.

To accomplish this ambitious programme the Elmhirsts created a trust: since then the enterprise has gone from strength to strength. The estate's original 800 acres has grown to 4,000, Dartington glass enjoys a global reputation and the centre's musical and educational programmes attract many gifted students and tutors. At the time of our visit some of these endeavours were only in the planning stage, but Mrs. Elmhirst had every confidence in their eventual realisation.

We enjoyed a hot meal in the kitchen as the great hall had not yet been adapted to its original purpose. Already, however, it was impressive with its minstrel's gallery and large fireplace. High above were coats of arms and flags associated with the history of Dartington Hall.

Fortified by the meal, we ventured out into the driving rain to see some of the enterprises then underway on the estate. Immediately surrounding the Hall were spacious gardens which, due to the pouring rain and season of the year, we could not appreciate. Our first stop was to the model dairy which seemed to have every device required to produce milk in quantity and under the most hygienic conditions.

Another nearby industry was a combination sawmill-furniture enterprise. The estate had many mature trees and some of these were being sawn and made into "utility" furniture compliant with British wartime regulations. There were no elaborate pieces on which a craftsman could display his talent. Instead, here were simple, practical items that would serve usefully in the homes of a nation that had known wartime for more than seven years.

Being an ardent supporter of fruit juices, I was much interested in the last enterprise we visited – an apple juice plant. Devon and southwest England in general had long been the centre of Britain's cider making. It was natural, therefore, that a centre for producing apple juice should be attempted here. We toured the plant and saw the process from beginning to end. The juice was sharp and delicious.

My only concern was whether it would be viable for, at that time, Britain had not yet taken to apple juice in the way that Americans had. Nonetheless, the apple juice venture typified Dartington Hall's approach to all its enterprises, whether industries, crafts or its educational programmes. Here was being tested a positive spirit of experimentation – trying a variety of new approaches while retaining those that worked.

52
Lady Astor advises Mary: "Immerse yourself in American life"

On another day we set out from Totnes with the hope of walking to the nearest village on the River Dart in the direction of the Royal Naval College at Dartmouth. There was no problem making our way through the outskirts of Totnes itself, but thereafter the heavy rains had so inundated the footpaths that we soon were forced to abandon our plan. In summer it would have been possible to take a boat trip to Dartmouth from Totnes, but that service did not operate in winter. Thus our dream of seeing this idyllic stretch of waterway was thwarted. Meanwhile, the heavens opened again and we were grateful when a country bus came along and took us back to the warm glow of the friendly hotel.

Brixham, a sprawling fishing port on the southern tip of Tor Bay, was our destination another day. Our bus arrived just before the fishing fleet returned to port and from our vantage point on the dock we could see the vessels swarming into the bay. Clouds of seagulls were following the boats for handouts during the gutting which was already underway. One by one the little boats tied up and then we saw the gutting had not been completed. We marvelled at the dexterity of the crew who, it seemed with a single movement of their knives, slit open and gutted the fish. Waiting packers with ice chips quickly filled barrels which were immediately sent on their way to London.

The next day we ventured to Torquay, the famous south coast resort. D-Day saw Tor Bay as one of the American embarkation points. This bay, normally not used for passenger or cargo traffic, was jammed with landing craft prior to the Normandy invasion. Indeed, this part of

Devonshire – like most of southern England – was saturated with American Army and Navy units during the months preceding D-Day. Little remained of this grim period except for the occasional loading ramps, or "hards".

In nearby Cockington we found an old blacksmith shop where, in the days gone by, the faithful village smithy had laboured to supply "equine footwear". Now, however, the old shop had a commercial tinge that we did not fully appreciate. The smithies were still there, but making miniature horseshoes which they sold as souvenirs. Hundreds of these little horseshoes adorned the doors and walls of the old shop, giving it the appearance of a souvenir-manufacturing plant rather than a blacksmith forge.

Many times I had heard "Widdecombe Fair" in family sing-songs at the Roberts farm. With the village only a few miles away from our Totnes base, it was a "must" for our honeymoon agenda. What Englishman has not revelled in singing the familiar words describing how so many villagers managed to get astride of Tom Pearce's animal!

"Tom Pearce, Tom Pearce, lend me your grey mare,
All along, down along, out along lee;
For I want to go to Widdecombe Fair,
with Bill Brewer, Jan Strewer, Peter Gurney,
Peter Davy, Dan'l Whidder, Harry Hawke,
Old Uncle Tom Cobleigh and all
Old Uncle Tom Cobleigh and all."

As we set out for Newton Abbot by bus, the rain began to fall. After leaving the bus, it started pelting down. But we were on our honeymoon and nothing, we said, would deter us. On we plodded through the country lanes, becoming colder, wetter and hungrier by the minute. We passed through one hamlet after another but there was not a pub in sight. Desperate for food, we decided to eat the biscuits and fruit we had brought along. Suddenly a small church appeared on our right and we rushed inside to escape the rain and cold, and to eat. But it was colder inside the church than outside and so we made quick work of our food and resumed walking.

At last we arrived – damp and very cold – at Widdecombe. A man greeted us in the outskirts of the village and gave us some background to the famous fair which had been held there. According to him, the fair was an ordinary English country village affair but had been glorified by the song. He went on to say that, before World War II, local people capitalised on the fame of the village by staging Widdecombe Fair annually.

"Why, there'd be cars stretched along this 'ere road for miles in every direction," he exclaimed waving his hand toward the village proper.

"There was one fellow," he continued, "who used to claim that he was the original Uncle Tom Cobleigh mentioned in the song. Everybody around here knew better, but the tourists didn't. They went for that sort of thing and used to take his picture by the hundred!"

After asking where we might get tea, we bade adieu to our newfound friend and made our way into the village – a mere handful of houses. We inquired at the village inn and found - though our arrival was ill-timed for tea - that the lady would serve us. Inside we found a small stove and lost no time warming our numb limbs. When the tea and biscuits were brought, we quickly devoured them. Our hostess was slightly amazed when we asked if we could have the same thing again.

Our sole souvenirs of our visit to Widdecombe were the postcards we bought at the inn. The atrocious weather ruled out snapshots. These cards we treasured, for they not only portrayed the Uncle Tom Cobleigh and All on one side, but gave all the verses of the song on the reverse.

Our return trip to Newton Abbot by bus was one of the most fascinating short journeys we have ever made. First, the rain changed to snow just as we left. But it was the bus driver who kept us on edge for the whole of the journey to Newton Abbot. The man was hardly five feet tall and it was all he could do to handle the bus. Although the vehicle was not a double-decker type, it was long and wide and the roads over which we were riding were narrow and winding.

Every time we came to a curve, or stopped to pick up a passenger, the little man stood erect in his seat to put the necessary pressure on the brakes. He sped along the narrow lanes and if he had happened upon another car, I know not what would have happened.

Driving the vehicle apparently was only secondary to the man's other responsibility. At one house he stopped, grabbed a dead rabbit from the bus and rushed into the front door where we could hear a lady thanking him. Back in the driver's seat, he drove on another mile or so and then stopped again. This time, he picked up a large market basket of assorted items and carried it into a house. And so on, down the road – it was drive a mile, deliver something, drive another mile, deliver something else.

We were marvelling at the man's memory when suddenly his luck ran out. An old fellow with a six-inch beard waved the bus to a stop, came up to the driver's window and asked where his newspaper was. The driver had forgotten it and he was very sorry. In fact, this one omission was about to ruin his day. As we continued down the road, he kept remarking aloud: "I knew I had forgotten something. Just couldn't think what it was. I won't do it again. Guess that chap thinks I've let him down." And so he went on until we reached Newton Abbot. The driver's (and our) eventful day was over.

When we set out another day for Buckfast Abbey, the rain held off but it was still bitterly cold. Yet, as we made our way over country roads, we noticed wild strawberries growing on the verges. Eventually we reached Buckfastleigh where I asked the first person we saw where we could get tea. He suggested the guest house of the Abbey – something we didn't know existed. I wondered if we might do better than tea. Timidly we approached the house, hoping for the best. A charming lady greeted us at the door and said we could not only have tea, but a full meal if we so desired! What a welcome! Of course we would.

Given the icy weather, that meal was one of the most invigorating we ever ate. Starting with hot soup, it followed with roast beef, potatoes and cabbage. A steamed pudding was trotted out for our dessert. Then the lady invited us into the lounge where she served us with multiple cups of coffee.

The Abbey itself was not yet completely finished. It had been under construction for several years, the monks themselves having done most of the work. We were barely able to look around the chapel before services began and all movement in the Abbey ceased. A guide told us the gift shop would be open immediately after the service. While waiting, other visitors arrived and the monk told them the same thing. By the time the services began, there was quite a number of would-be gift buyers waiting – all captive worshippers!

Easily the most exciting expedition of our honeymoon holiday was our visit to Plymouth. On a previous stay I had met Lady Astor who had invited me and accompanying friends into her home on Plymouth Hoe. She had been very popular with American troops stationed in South Devon. Hundreds called on her – especially those from Virginia and other southern states. Lady Astor never forgot her American South roots and frequently referred to herself as a 'rebel'.

She had been born Nancy Langhorne, member of an old Virginia family whose women were noted for their beauty and vivacity. After divorcing her first husband, she married Waldorf Astor who became a Viscount in 1919. When he entered the House of Lords, Nancy was elected to fill his Plymouth seat in the House of Commons. She thus became the first woman to sit in Parliament.

She made no attempt to play down her American birth; her book, *My Two Countries*, was published in 1923. I was only vaguely aware that she and her husband had been leaders of the "Cliveden Set" – a group of British notables who sought appeasement with Germany. Once the conflict had begun and especially after the American entry after Pearl Harbour, she was solidly behind the British war effort.

Her hospitality towards nearby American troops was widely known. On my previous visit to her home on Plymouth Hoe, she repeated her invitation to drop in when I was next in the town. This time, the maid answered the door and clearly was hesitant about our seeing "My Lady" as she was "just going out." I asked her to tell Lady Astor there was a "rebel at the door" and waited to see what happened. But before the maid could relay the message, a shrill voice came from upstairs.

"Did you say a rebel? Come on up – what are you waiting for?"

We climbed the stairs quickly with some degree of trepidation.

"Oh, you poor children!" Nancy (as she preferred to be called) exclaimed. "Do come to the fire, won't you?"

We gladly walked over to the open fireplace and proceeded to take off our coats.

"I am just on my way to talk to a Rotary Club," she said, "but do sit down for a few minutes."

We did, and then she wanted to know who we were and what we were up to. Hastily we explained that we were on our honeymoon and that shortly we both would be sailing to the United States. Thereupon she asked which state. When she heard it was Georgia, she shouted to Mary "You lucky woman!" "Of course," she winked, "Georgia isn't Virginia, but then, there's only one Virginia."

She went on to ask Mary if she was looking forward to life in America. When Mary told her she feared she would be home-sick for Frith Farm and her family, she kissed her on the cheek and said:

"My child, have no fear. I know a person never forgets where they're from. I shall never forget my roots in Virginia. But you can make yourself useful wherever you go if only you occupy your time with worthwhile activities. Remember that!"

We both thanked her for inspirational challenge. Then I asked if she would show Mary the painting I had seen on my earlier visit. We went to the adjacent room and there, on canvas, Mary saw Lady Astor being presented as Britain's first woman Member of Parliament. We stood admiring the painting for several seconds and would have remained longer, had not we remembered the Rotary Club talk our host was due to give.

As we were about to leave, Lady Astor took Mary by the arm and led her over to a side table on which were standing several figurines. Sweeping up two, a Dutch flower girl and her boy friend, she handed them to Mary. We were so overcome by this generous gesture we could hardly express our thanks.

On the way out I mentioned to Lady Astor that I had eaten meals previously in the George Club, a dormitory-dining room accommodation for Allied servicemen not too far from Plymouth Hoe. Since we had not eaten our noonday meal, I asked her if the club was still in operation and if she knew if meals were available at that hour. (Lord and Lady Astor's generosity played a part in the establishment of the club, frequented by hundreds of Americans during World War II.)

Instead of giving us directions, she insisted on accompanying us to the club. But, even that wasn't enough; she told the steward we were her guests but that she was out of food and wanted us well taken care of! With that, she bade us farewell again and went out into the rain to her taxi. As we said our goodbyes, I expressed my concern that she might have missed her meal at the Rotary Club.

"Don't worry a bit!" she said, taking her seat in the taxi, "I can never eat when I'm supposed to give a talk. Besides," she added, "you two have made my day!"

53
Your sins will find you out

"Have you two given any thought as to where you will live after the wedding?" Mrs. Roberts had asked just before Mary and I departed for our honeymoon.

"Well", I replied, "I assumed we can continue being together on weekends at the farm unless you are too crowded." I thought she had in mind offering us the guest room, although that would mean the family no longer could receive guests.

"Would you like to have a place of your own right here on the farm if it can be arranged?" she continued.

What a question for newlyweds! Of course, we would – but how could that be possible?

"I think you ought to set up home in Rosemary," she said calmly.

"Wonderful!" exclaimed Mary, before I could respond.

I hadn't a clue what Rosemary was, but Mary went on to explain its history. It was a caravan or more precisely, two caravans connected together. They came from Hayling Island, a popular seaside resort area south of Portsmouth. When the war broke out, all Britain's beaches had to be cleared because it was assumed there would be a German invasion. Owners of most caravans, beach huts and other seaside buildings had to vacate or remove them.

Mrs. Roberts had acquired several and two had been sited on Prickett's Hill, the highest point on Frith Farm. Other caravans stood nearby. Rosemary consisted of two caravans sited at right angles, one serving as living quarters with the other as kitchen-cum-dining area. The third unit was a privy set off to one side. I had never noticed Rosemary, but Mary assured me it would be a pleasant place to start our married life together – however short that might be. I thanked Mary's mother profusely for her forethought and promptly forgot about her offer as we set out for our honeymoon.

A week later we returned from Devon, our heads full of adventures. It was well after dark when we reached the farm. Mrs. Roberts greeted us with her standard refreshment welcome – cups of hot blackcurrant juice. Then, after Mary had related some of our honeymoon highlights, Mrs. Roberts noticed me yawning. With a mischievous glint in her eyes, she turned to me.

"It's cold and wet outside," she said. "Instead of tramping through the mud up to Pickett's Hill, would you prefer to sleep in the guest room tonight?"

"What?" I cried. "Stay in the guest room when we have a home of our own! We wouldn't think of it."

She laughed, for she knew exactly what I would say.

As we plodded through the mud and puddles to the top of the hill, we glimpsed a faint glow through one of the caravan windows. Guest room, indeed! Mary's mother had been so sure we would opt for Rosemary that she had made a fire in the tiny fireplace.

I hesitated before entering.

"What are you waiting for?" Mary asked.

"Too bad," I murmured, "can't carry you across the threshold – the door isn't wide enough."

Mary, cross at the inference that *she* was too wide, snatched the keys from me and opened the door. Pure serenity awaited us: the warm glow of the fire, flowers on a bedside table and the covers of the bed turned back. The place exuded cheerfulness. Later we found hot water bottles beneath the covers.

"Now!" shouted Mary, "to the other one!"

This time I did not hesitate before unlocking the door. Mary went ahead and once inside, stopped in her tracks and embraced me. We stared in disbelief. Directly in front was a new paraffin stove with an oven large enough to hold a roast – a gift from her mother. A quick glance round revealed all the necessities for simple housekeeping – dishes, pots and pans, cutlery and silverware. At the same instant we spotted something in a corner nook we had almost overlooked: a small table with a linen tablecloth laid for two.

The only impracticable feature of the bedroom caravan was the arrangement of beds. Two single beds, positioned one above the other in barrack style, measured less than six feet in length – too short for my height. It was our first order of business the next day to place them lengthwise, side by side, with a small box at the end. Together they made a double bed over seven feet long.

In the halcyon days that followed we developed routines that would allow Mary to have the evening meal ready by the time I arrived from Southampton. This daily commuting was made possible when my friend Herby allowed me to use his jeep outside his working hours. My duties were to provide the daily supply of fresh water and look after the privy. The washing up we joyfully did together.

While I was stationed in England, I subscribed to *The Atlanta Constitution*, one of the great American regional daily newspapers. At one time its editor had been Henry Grady, the optimist who predicted that one day the poverty-stricken rural South would become as prosperous as any other part of the United States. Its current editor was Ralph McGill, also an optimist. It was his vigorous writings that had spurred opposition to Eugene Talmadge, the despotic Governor of Georgia during my collegiate days.

I took to Frith Farm copies of *The Constitution* as they arrived and attempted to acquaint Mary with a few aspects of the American way of life. Using American coins and notes, she was able to "shop" for food by perusing the full page advertisements of Atlanta's supermarkets. To my surprise, she had as much trouble dealing with the American decimal system as I had with the British one.

On our first Sunday in Rosemary, we decided to attend the nearest church. This happened to be the Methodist chapel in Shirrel Heath, a church well known in the district for its hand-bell ringers. I had persuaded my Army mess officer in Southampton to give me a joint of beef, pointing out I was never in the mess on Sundays anyway. Before going to Shirrel Heath, we put the joint into the shiny new oven, turned it on the lowest setting and set off on our bicycles. We calculated it would be beautifully roasted in the hour-plus it would take us to attend the service and return.

One could always count on a lively service at Shirrel Heath Methodist Church. Its choir was large and everyone sang with vigour. Its band of bell ringers played frequently at services, as well as in nearby villages. If the regular minister was not available, lay preachers delivered the sermons.

Although on this occasion the church was nearly full, Mary and I managed to get seats together. It was not long before we heard loud hiccoughs from a baby in the adjacent pew. We paid no attention at first, assuming it would stop as the service progressed. To our consternation, the hiccoughs continued when the lay preacher rose to deliver the prayer. Mary and I asked ourselves by exchanging anxious glances, if we could contain ourselves if the baby continued its affliction.

During the prayer we heard efforts, some not too successful, by others at suppressing laughter. The baby had an uncanny sense of timing, often emitting a loud "hic" at the end of a particularly vigorous exhortation in the prayer. Had the sound been an "Amen" it would, of course, have gone unnoticed. By this time Mary and I were grateful to be kneeling and to be unseen by the preacher. Both of us were inexorably trapped in one of those peculiar physical phenomena where explosive laughter is preordained and any effort at sane behaviour is impossible. We knew we were doomed to bring disgrace upon ourselves; the only question was when.

At length the prayer came to an end, followed by another hymn and then the preacher began his sermon. The baby continued in full throat and I began to wonder if the child was destined to become one of these medical cases in which fits of hiccoughs extend into adulthood. Mary and I fought to appear serious, determined to put those uncontrollable giggles behind us, as the minister launched into his simple theme.

"Let us remember (hic) the things going on around us (hic)," he began. "They can have a dramatic effect on our lives (hic)." With those introductory words, Mary and I exchanged sidelong glances which conceded our hopeless situation. We gained little comfort when some of our immediate neighbours began tittering, making the connection between the minister's words and the baby's emphatic hiccoughs.

"There was once a man who decided to take a nap beneath an oak tree," continued the minister, with the baby echoing a resounding 'hic'. "While dozing, an acorn fell (hic) and hit the man squarely on the forehead (hic). The man awakened, jumped to his feet and looked around (hic). There, where he had lain was the acorn (hic); up in the tree he saw many other acorns (hic)."

The preacher continued: " 'How fortunate I am (hic),' the man said to himself, 'that mangolds do not grow on trees – otherwise I would be a dead man (hic).' " At this point the minister smiled to let his point sink in. There was no need for him to pause; Mary and I, and all the people around us erupted into hilarious laughter. The rest of the congregation turned and stared, as if to say it wasn't all that funny. The minister was at first baffled by our spontaneous show of jollity, then pleased that his story had gone down so well. He continued:

"The man reckoned he had sufficient cause (hic) to thank the Almighty, which he promptly did by kneeling and giving thanks on the spot (hic). Then and there he became a Christian (hic)."

By affording us that single opportunity to disgorge the long suppressed laughter, we managed to survive the remainder of the service. When the last word of the closing prayer was uttered, Mary and I made a bee-line for the door, quickly mounted our bikes and sped away before some church official could reprimand us for our behaviour.

Our thoughts, meanwhile, turned to the joint of beef which we hoped had been cooking to perfection in our absence. As we dismounted at Rosemary we were greeted by ribbons of heavy black smoke emerging from the door and window crevices of the kitchen caravan. We dashed to the door, flung it open and were met by a wall of swirling smoke. After a few seconds it abated somewhat, allowing me to enter. I quickly turned off the stove, and retreated outside.

After a few minutes the smoke subsided and we entered gingerly, expecting the worst. We counted our blessings that the stove had not exploded and burned down the caravan. The havoc created was bad enough. The beef joint was a mass of charcoal, except the very centre. The Yorkshire pudding and vegetables we had so carefully prepared were impregnated with carbon. The once white tablecloth was now, no doubt, permanently black. The dainty curtains which Mrs. Roberts had so lovingly installed were now saturated with black smoke as was also the ceiling, walls and floor.

As Mary and I salvaged a few mouthfuls from the joint and managed to supplement our Sunday meal with tinned food, we pondered on the day's events. One certain lesson was never to leave unattended a new paraffin stove with its unpredictable virgin wick. The other was more of a moral: those who laugh in church may end up crying in the kitchen.

Our stay in Rosemary was short but "sweet". Already the American Army had developed a points system – based on how long servicemen had been abroad – to determine when troops would sail for the United States. I would leave sometime in the second quarter of the year, and Mary would follow a few weeks later.

When I was offered the prospect of joining an operations team to embark Norwegian brides of Americans from Oslo, I declined. With my wonderful wife in tow, I was not about to be delayed returning to America by a single minute.

During our short sojourn in Rosemary, there was one other hilarious moment before our stay came to an end.

The nearest caravan to us was occupied by an elderly widow who had been evacuated because of the intense bombing where she lived. Unknown to us, she had taken upon herself the duty of informing Mrs. Roberts if she thought I at any time might abuse Mary.

Coincidentally I had discovered that tickling the bottom of Mary's feet sent her into fits of laughter. One evening after we had gone to bed, I indulged in this playfulness as Mary laughed and shouted "Help! Help! Mercy! Mercy!" Suddenly there was a great metallic thump on the caravan steps. We rushed to the door and found the concerned neighbour had "returned" two huge cooking pots that had never been borrowed. Mary was relieved to know there would be no more tickling.

54
Brides sail with heartache and sadness

As the end of 1945 neared most troop movements had been completed, but there remained the mammoth task of locating, processing and embarking thousands of British wives (many with babies) who had married Americans. There had been no need to know the exact number until now and we were surprised to be told the total could be in excess of 50,000. In fact, it proved to be much greater.

To transport this number obviously would require a small fleet of ships, all of which would have to be specially adapted to cater for the needs of young mothers and babies. There was no question of packing them into every nook and cranny as had been done with men who were anxious to get home quickly. Fortuitously with the release of some hospital ships, additional doctors and nurses became available to staff both the staging areas and the brides' vessels.

Huge staging area camps with their austere living conditions were obviously unsuitable for wives and babies. Perham Downs Camp at Tidworth, a permanent British military installation near to Southampton, was offered for our use and gratefully accepted. In addition, the Carlton Hotel in Bournemouth (used earlier as an American Red Cross Club) was adapted as a supplementary staging facility.

One snag not fully appreciated at first was the lack of sufficient cots for the infants. Lt. Col. Tom Houston, who commanded the Tidworth reception area, solved the problem by sending teams to Army depots looking for wooden "foot lockers", familiar to every non-combat soldier as his portable wardrobe. The lids of these were ripped off, insides repainted and then lined with soft material suitable for babies. These devices, which admirably overcame the emergency, promptly became known as "Houston cribs".

Press interest in the embarkation of brides and babies was enormous. Deprived of reporting so much of the war's dramatic events because of censorship, newspapers, magazines and radio reporters were to have a field day. Stories about children command great human interest at any time; when these were combined with war-time romances and parting with families for unknown futures in the New World, the accounts were bound to be both heart-rending and entertaining.

Some journalists went to the homes of wives preparing to embark, photographing them packing their bags and saying farewell to family and friends. Others went to accompany the brides by train to Tidworth. Kathleen Lyon of the *Daily Mail* was one of those to follow the 'trail' of a departing bride all the way from her home (Dorking) to Tidworth.

Photographers, given free reign at Tidworth when the first contingent of brides arrived, filled their papers with pictures of young mothers with babies, Red Cross workers with babies and even officers trying to tease smiles out of young infants.

Feature articles covered every conceivable aspect of the processing: medical examinations, vaccinations, orientation talks and especially the American consumer items available to them in the reception area's PX (post exchange). Describing one bride's first Army meal the *Daily Herald* reporter wrote:

"There was a real American lunch – braised beef stew with buttered peas and mashed potatoes, brown gravy and pickled beets. Then rosy-cheeked apples and peaches. Coffee? Yes, with cream. Yes, they were almost in America."

Some reporters were interested in the 40 German prisoners of war employed in menial tasks at the reception centre. One writer listed their chores:

"They serve the wives' meals, prepare the babies food, pour out the tea, push the prams, carry each bride's 200 pounds of luggage, stoke fires and generally help to make the guests comfortable."

Many wives were sobered when the *Daily Express* carried a provocative feature from New York under the banner headline, "If a GI bride wants to be happy ...." It introduced, for the first time to many wives, the sobering thought that not all of them would be welcome in the United States:

"The women here are hurt over losing so many eligible men to overseas competition. ... most American women are still convinced that British women are cold, stand-offish and uppish."

When the first bride ship, the *Argentina*, arrived in Southampton on January 24th, reporters quickly descended on Captain Thomas Simmons to ask if he was ready for the 600 women and babies about whom so much publicity had been given. Was his staffing adequate? Did he have everything on board to cater for the special needs of the brides and their offspring?

"We are indeed all ready for them," Captain Simmons assured the press, pointing out that the crew had been augmented by two doctors, eight Army nurses, eight stewardesses and 18 WACs. In addition, special diet kitchens had been installed and large quantities of baby food, milk and bottles brought on board.

"We have cribs for all the youngsters," he added, "and, in the dining room, little seats so they can sit down with their mothers."

The first batch of wives and babies left Tidworth early in the morning, arriving at the ship's side at 10:30. She duly sailed that afternoon, but not before one bride had her baby "kidnapped" by her devoted grandmother. The bride asked that she and her child be deleted from the first sailing so that the domestic problem could be solved in time for a future embarkation. This incident was only one of many which saw fond parents unable to cope with the departure of their daughters and grandchildren to the United States. To lessen the emotional stress, we discouraged parents of wives from coming either to the staging areas or to the docks, but there were always some who managed to foil security and get through – causing great distress to the entire family and, at times, interrupting the embarkation procedure.

Music and song were to play a role in the human drama. The ship's radio, for its part, contributed the "Wedding March" and Dvorak's "New World Symphony" as the wives mounted the long gangway. The brides needed no orchestral accompaniment as they came on deck for the sailing, singing alternately, "There'll Always Be An England" and "God Bless America".

The Sunday Express captured a group of brides waving to their photographer as they mounted the gangway. This photograph later appeared on the dust jacket of the highly regarded study, *War Brides of World War II*, by Elfrieda Shukert and Barbara Scibetta (Presidio: 1988).

With the possibility of rough weather during the seven and a half days' crossing, the order was given that the *Argentina* should sail two hours before the scheduled departure time. Word of the earlier sailing was quickly passed to the Mayor, who had planned to be on hand for the departure. He and his wife arrived, however, after the gangway had been removed. They nonetheless stood in the pouring rain and shouted "Good luck!" to the departing wives. Despite this slight hitch in protocol, the processing and embarkation had gone well and the *Argentina* was soon on her way down Southampton Water.

The *Daily Mail* arranged for one wife to send a message after the first day at sea. The cable, printed in six columns across the top of a page, said in part:

"I am sitting on a deck. We are 300 miles out at sea. The weather is fine and the sea is very calm. I have been aboard the ship for 20 hours. I have not been ill so far this morning. For breakfast I had orange juice, cereal, eggs, roll and butter. I sleep in a converted hospital ward with 24 others. It is quite comfortable. There is a spacious lounge where church services are held and films shown. I was happy to leave England for my new home but I shall miss England, especially the country villages. To my relatives in England I would say everything is fine and I have no doubts or regrets."

It was well that this message was sent on the *Argentina*'s first day at sea, for fierce gales were to delay the ship by more than 20 hours before she arrived in New York. Although there were no serious injuries, the doctors, nurses and supporting staff were stretched to the limit helping distressed passengers.

The subsequent sailings of bride vessels, except for their variation in size, followed patterns similar to those we used with the *Argentina*. The *Queen Mary*, which embarked in early February with four times as many wives and babies, naturally came in for massive media interest. *Picture Post*, that wonderful pictorial journal of yesteryear, published a five-page spread of candid shots, made by its photographer on the *Queen Mary*'s first crossing.

Cartoonists from national papers found the movement of brides and babies ideally suited as subjects for their daily output. Giles of the *Daily Express* obliged with two gems. One showed the *Queen Mary*'s disgruntled British seamen handling rocking horses and other children's toys, cribs, cartons of talcum powder and other essentials for the transatlantic voyage. To this infantile activity the Captain retorted: "Possibly you don't approve, but you will, nevertheless, keep your opinion to yourself, Smithers!" Giles' other cartoon evoked a sociological concern for those wives headed for homes in America more modest than those they had known in Britain. It depicted a bride arriving at a crude shack, possibly in the Southern Appalachians, where the serviceman's parents had erected a sign reading "Welcum home Wally and his Bride."

55
A dead rabbit in a heated train

During the busy bridal shipment period, I enjoyed one delightful episode of comic relief. Mary had frequently mentioned one of her favourite relations, Aunt Annie in Liverpool and hoped, before I was sent back to the United States, that we could visit her. Aunt Annie had, for several years, taken a keen interest in Mary. Perceiving she had an ear for music she had bought her a violin on condition that she took lessons. She had, and by the time of our courtship Mary had mastered a small number of beginners' pieces.

Most were short, simple and sometimes poignant works intended to appeal to young violinists. When Mary played these lovely airs, competently it seemed to my unpractised ear, I was well nigh brought to tears at the realisation of yet another talent of my lovely bride.

I readily agreed that we should visit Aunt Annie as soon as I could obtain weekend leave. When the time came, Mrs. Roberts, ever mindful of the food shortages among urban dwellers, hurriedly brought eggs and other home produce to go into our suitcases. Just as we managed to squeeze in the last, she returned with a rabbit, dressed and ready to be cooked.

"Annie," she explained, "just loves rabbit and the least I can do is send her one."

Mary pointed out that our bags were full and, in any case, the smell of a rabbit inside a suitcase would hardly do our clothing any good.

The train journey to Liverpool would be five hours.

"Never mind", she said calmly, "I'll tie it on the outside."

Before we could protest she put the rabbit in a paper bag and tied it to the outside of my suitcase. Soon afterwards we boarded the Southampton train to Liverpool, rabbit and all. It was the dead of winter and we would normally have been grateful for a well-heated carriage.

As the hours went by, however, we began to detect a "high" smell from the over-head rack where my suitcase-cum-rabbit was stored. So, too, did the fellow passengers opposite us. Mary found it hard to refrain from laughing but I was more concerned that the guard might come along and throw us off the train. I thought I would die when the lady opposite twitched her nose and asked, "Do you smell something awful?"

It was fruitless of her to ask me, for I wasn't going to admit to anything. Mary covered her face to conceal her suppressed laughter as I lied, quite calmly: "No, can't smell a thing."

Eventually we reached Liverpool and made our way by bus to the outskirts where Aunt Annie lived. We had to walk half a mile through residential streets before reaching Aunt Annie's house. We had not progressed far before one family dog, and then another, sniffed the decomposing rabbit and joined us.

They paid no attention to my shouts and threats. By the time we reached Aunt Annie's there were half a dozen, fighting and barking to get near the carcass. It was all I could do to prevent them from tearing the rabbit from my suitcase. At last we gained the refuge of the front garden and quickly slammed the gate shut.

We told Aunt Annie that the rabbit seemed a little "high" and we hoped it hadn't been spoiled by the hot train journey north.

"Don't give it a thought", she said with a smile. "As with a pheasant, a rabbit tastes best when it is a little high."

Mary and I thought no more of the dogs until we retired for the evening in our bedroom overlooking the front garden. There, to our dismay, the pack of dogs was still baying at the house. Aunt Annie wondered at this curious circumstance but neither Mary nor I could enlighten her. The last sound I heard that evening before dropping off to sleep was the irresolute barking of the rabbit-hungry animals.

That should have been the end of the ordeal but it wasn't. Next day for lunch we had rabbit. Mary and Aunt Annie remarked on its wonderful flavour and texture but somehow I hadn't the stomach for it.

Scenes of the Georgia farmhouse where I was born

This house, where I was born in 1918, had everything a small boy could wish for – a large playing area beneath and acres of forest and fields just a few steps away. There was also a syrup-making shed, a building full of cotton and most exciting of all, an attic. Here my brother and I made a burglar alarm that almost crippled Grandpa. Eventually he ordered us not to take our vacations together.

Below (*left*) is the bell that was rung to summon workers for lunch. It was also rung to sound the alarm in case of fire. The front porch (*below right*) with its swing and rocking chair, was the favoured gathering place in the summer. Off to the right was an ancient sycamore tree carved with the initials of my many aunts and uncles – and their respective courting friends.

My grandparents produce twelve children

Right: Grandpa Mays with Grandma (in white) with several of their 12 children.

With his hand on the steering wheel, Grandpa Mays proudly stands beside his 1920s car.

My father Floyd was a natty figure astride his Harley-Davidson motorcycle. He developed an early and deep love for vehicles of all types.

One grandfather was of German descent, the other Scots-Irish – a typical mixture

My mother's father, J.M. Lutes, reflected his German ancestry by imposing strict discipline on his pupils at Louisville Academy where he was headmaster. Once he famously chased a disobedient boy all the way to his home and administered a beating in front of the boy's mother. She heartily agreed.

Of Scots-Irish descent, Grandpa Mays was an efficient farmer and also chairman of the County Commissioners whose main task was to keep the county's roads passable. His middle name was O'Donald. When my parents came to name me, they called me James after my mother's father and O'Donald after my father's father. Years later, the American military ordained that servicemen should be known only by their first and middle initials. This created havoc among those like myself who had never used their first names.

DIXIE appears at the bottom of our photographs

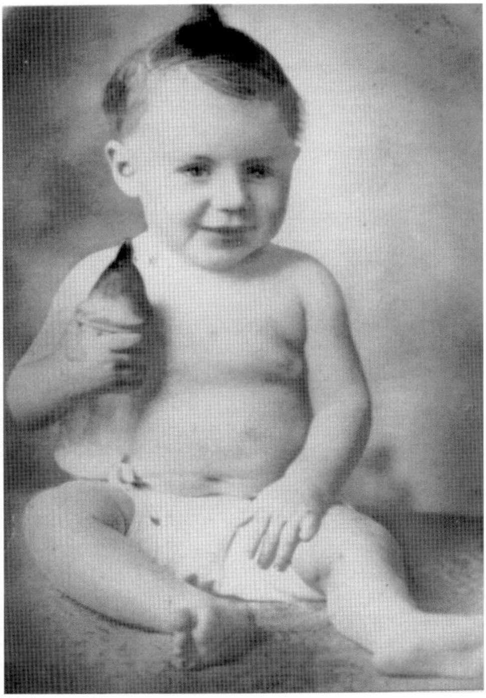

My liking for freshly produced dairy milk probably dates from the age of one when this picture was taken. As a child on the farm I came to know and like that delectable elixir of the American Deep South, “grandoldbuttermilk”. A bottle of it was once used to christen a new bridge across the Savannah River.

When I was six and in my first year of primary school, an itinerant photographer took this picture. When we children later received our prints, we found the word DIXIE at the bottom – a reminder of the days of the Confederacy.   It was about this time that I learned I had no vision in my left eye, a deficiency that later was to restrict my choice of sports and limit me to non-combat duty with the US Army.

My mother with her first two boys

My brother Floyd, pictured above with my mother, was born when I was four. Our looks of innocence betray the mischief we were shortly to rain down on Grandpa Mays. Although we always looked forward to our summer vacations on his farm, he came to dread our visits. Grandma, happily, did not share his trepidation.

Birdsville sparks an interest in history

My best friend, George Franklin, lived at Birdsville (*pictured above*), a plantation near my home in Millen. Its association with Colonial America and later, the Confederate States, fed my budding interest in events of the past.

The joy of sleeping in a four-poster bed

Birdsville's elegant wrought iron porch *(right)* was an attractive feature of the house's rear.

On my visits to the plantation, I slept in this magnificent four-poster bed (*below, left*).

My sister Hope *(below, right)* examines a spinning wheel dating from the Colonial period. Near the house was an ancient tree whose scars, according to family legend, were caused by cannonballs from Sherman's Army.

Louisville Academy, a school dating from the 1700s

The entrance to Louisville Academy, my secondary school, as it appeared in 1936. Reverend Plaxco, the principal, is standing with two of his pupils beneath the arch that denotes the school's 1796 founding. Below: the main building, long since demolished.

Vanishing sights of the Old South

Little did I know when I took this photograph just before the Second World War, that it would symbolise dramatic changes in America's Deep South. Cotton – shown here en route to the local gin – was to lose its "single crop" status. The horse and wagon also were to give way to tractors and other mechanised implements. Lastly, a mass exodus of blacks from farms would cause many to move to towns and cities of the South, and to industrial centres like Detroit.

Criss-crossing Appalachia on a bicycle

In 1939 I undertook a 1500-mile bicycle trip through four southern states. Here, in front of Louisville's Old Market, I am holding a copy of *The Augusta Chronicle*, which agreed to publish daily accounts of my adventures.

Farmer Galloway, with ox and plough. His Appalachian farm near Brevard, North Carolina, was my first overnight stay on leaving Georgia. The ox, he pointed out, was ideally adapted for working on mountainous slopes.

"I'm in the Army now"—and meet Joan Leslie

On a three-day weekend pass, I visited Hollywood and met lovely Joan Leslie who not long before had won acclaim as the sweetheart of Sergeant York. She briefly chatted with us servicemen and gave each of us a photo.

To celebrate my promotion from Private to Private First Class I had this picture taken for the folks back home.

A picture to fool the folks back home

One day when a friend and I were taking in the sights of San Francisco, we came across this lovely blonde leaving a famous hotel. We persuaded her to pose, a soldier on each side of her. When we had the picture printed, we each cropped out the other so we could boast about "our latest San Francisco girlfriend."

Sharing Thanksgiving Day with the Chinese

Chinatown has long been an attraction of San Francisco. I attended a children's party (*above*) at the Chinese Baptist church on Thanksgiving Day and was warmly welcomed.

There I met Chinese-American servicemen who gave me a copy of The Lord's Prayer in Chinese (*right*) which I carried in my wallet throughout the war.

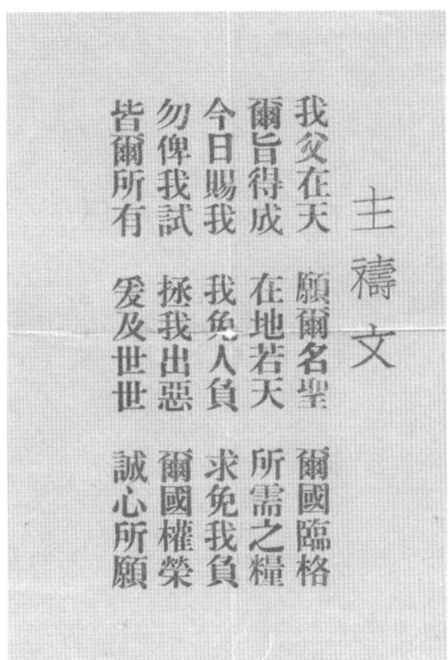

主禱文

我父在天　願爾名聖　爾國臨格
爾旨得成　在地若天　所需之糧
今日賜我　我免人負　求免我負
勿俾我試　拯我出惡　爾國權榮
皆爾所有　爰及世世　誠心所願

"O God our help in ages past …"

Our temporary Army Port headquarters was housed in Southampton's Civic Centre whose chimes appropriately played "O God our help in ages past" every four hours. Below, Mayor Rex Stranger with Colonel Kiser (*right*). (US Department of Defense photos)

D-Day inevitably brings heavy casualties but the machines of war roll relentlessly on

Before field hospitals could be established on Omaha and Utah beaches, serious casualties were returned to England. Above: wounded Americans are transferred from a hospital ship to a waiting ambulance (Southampton *Daily Echo*). Below: heavy vehicles head for Southampton Docks. (US Department of Defense).

A sixty-ton locomotive is loaded for Cherbourg

U.S. military planners correctly assumed most French rail stock would be destroyed by Allied aircraft or the Germans. Complete railway systems, numbering 21,545 locomotives and wagons, were shipped by our Army Port unit to Cherbourg. Shown here is a 65-ton diesel electric locomotive. (US Department of Defense)

Mayor Stranger remembers the orphaned daughter

Pfc Paul Shimer, the 1,000,000th soldier to be processed by our Port unit, chats with Southampton's Mayor Rex Stranger. Shimer told the Mayor he had a wife and baby daughter, Patricia Ann. When Shimer was later killed, the Mayor set up a fund to provide higher education for Patricia Ann. (Southampton City Heritage Services). Below: Entrance to the 14th Port Headquarters. (US Department of Defense)

An Army artist captures Southampton's hectic wartime scenes

To supplement photographic coverage, the Army sent one of its top artists, Technical Sergeant Harry Dix, to document our Port activities. Two of his "Southampton Album" views are shown here. Above: the busy Town Quay "hard" where LSTs (landing ships, tank) operated. Below: a hospital ship and an Army tugboat with the familiar barrage balloons floating above. (US Department of Defense)

A US Army unit marches past Southampton's ancient city wall

During the build up of forces on the beaches of Normandy, some US Army units arrived at Southampton Central station where they marched directly to the dock area, passing by the ancient city wall en route. (Both pictures: US Department of Defense)

Colonel Kiser, our Port Commander, presents a plaque to Lady Astor (with Lord Astor looking on) in appreciation of her services to US Forces. Standing behind Colonel Kiser, I witnessed the simple ceremony. Lady Astor, a Virginia native, later offered Mary advice for adapting to life in America.

How an errand to buy seeds from Toogoods led to my meeting a lovely Land Army girl

My first picture of Mary, posing with Cora No. 2, a cow renowned for yielding little milk. She assigned me to milk Cora, and I produced a record quantity. Had I made a favourable first impression?

I obtained Mary's name and phone number when she inadvertently disabled her car while purchasing seed from Toogoods, Southampton's prominent seedsmen. Below: one of their famous catalogues.

Is she to become the girl of my dreams?

John Bull's daughters

Diana
drives the tractor
Phyllis
milks the cows
Mary hoes the turnips—
John Bull stands
amazed !
Bless my soul !
Maidens in breeches !
'Tis too heavy work
for the pretty dears.
But the pretty dears
can't stop to explain.
They're busy.
The green fields of
England
must be ploughed ;
the seed must be sown.
From dawn to dusk
in byre and dairy
and on the far
ten acre field,
the land girls,
suntanned, and blown
by the free winds,
tend and husband
the generous acres
of this free land . . .
The red heavy corn
rustles in the light,
the stooks multiply . . .
Food for the workers,
food for the fighters,
munitions for the table
victuals for Victory !
John Bull,
all doubts forgot,
straightens his back.
Well I'm blest
he says.
And he is.
So are we all.

* * * *

These girls are saving shipping and saving lives. It is our duty to help them by spending less and saving more.

Above and below: two informal pictures of Mary during the early days of our courtship.

Left: a 1943 recruiting ad for the Land Army. If a farmer had daughters in the Land Army, they were allowed to do their war service on their father's farm.

Parents devoting their lives to serving the community

A.E. Roberts, a physical fitness fanatic in his youth, was a disciple of Bernard McFadden.

After meeting Nurse Rose Houghton, a whirlwind courtship and marriage followed.

The first quarter of the 20th century saw an enormous growth of the Scouting movement in Britain, thanks largely to the inspiration of Baden Powell. A.E. Roberts was among thousands of young leaders who introduced Scouting to boys. He and a friend founded the Sarisbury Scouts, shown here laughing. Roberts is in the centre of the front row, his hat off.

When Roberts' seedlings covered the English countryside

When Roberts took over Frith Farm in 1926, it was in poor condition. He soon put it in order and at one time had a 90-acre holding of black currants – one of the largest in Britain. At his wife's suggestion he approached Woolworths about supplying plants and shrubs for their nationwide chain . They readily agreed and he retained a contract with them for over 40 years. An array of his horticultural labels is shown here.

A goal for plants and family: Be fruitful and multiply

This 1925 photograph shows A.E. and Rose in a field of black currants surrounded by their three young. daughters, Joan, Betty and baby Mary – she in her mother's arms.

This "can do" leaflet is typical of many produced by Roberts to promote his horticulture plants.

Mary at five. Her classmates named her the girl with the sweetest disposition.

An 1898 certificate marking the time when British Methodists counted more than 1,000,000 members on their rolls

William Houghton, Mary's uncle, was one of a million who subscribed to the Wesleyan Methodist Church's Twentieth Century Fund in 1898. Each contributed a guinea. The certificate features leaders and historic events of the church.

The question is popped on Speltham Down

THE HAMBLEDONIAN

For the Parish and People of Hambledon

Hambledon from Speltham Down John Mellow

August and September, 1995

I popped the question to Mary when we picnicked atop Speltham Down, overlooking Hambledon – cherished by cricket lovers. To celebrate the momentous event, I took this photograph.

Half a century later the cover of Hambledon's parish magazine featured a sketch of an identical view by the artist, John Mellow. To the credit of local planning authorities there had been no development in the fields beyond the village.

The bride and groom emerge to be saluted

Mary and I pause before entering the bridal arch formed by her fellow Land Army Girls and members of my Army unit. Behind me is my faithful best man, Herbert Niederberger, who was charged with tailing Mr. Roberts all the way from the farmhouse to the church – just in case he decided to kidnap his own daughter.

Russian POWs: was their fate already sealed?

Above: Several hundred Soviet POWs embark from American LSTs at Southampton after being liberated as forced labourers of the Germans.

Left: The POWs hope to enhance their chances of survival by performing "Moscow my beloved" but grim-faced officers from the Soviet Embassy showed little interest.

Waiting to depart by train to prison camps, they display their anxiety. Some later committed suicide; others were either exiled to Soviet labour camps or executed – fates to which the Allies had agreed. (US Department of Defense)

We win an athletics championship

Above: In September, 1945, with our military duties much reduced, I formed and trained an athletics team which won the Hampshire County title. Two thirds of our team were black, an omen of the importance these athletes were to prove in post-war Olympic Games. (US Department of Defense)

Left: With more free weekends available, Mary and I were able to cycle to nearby Lee-on-Solent for brief swims.

Despicable German wartime propaganda

ROOSEVELT, THE FALSE PROPHET!

"I assure you again and again and again that no American boys will be sacrificed on foreign battlefields."

Franklin D. Roosevelt, Oct. 31, 1940

But you did go to war!

And what about the other promises in his campaign speeches?

The New Deal collapsed, the number of unemployed rose from one year to the other finally reaching 13 million. With their dependents, over 45 million people or one third of the population of the USA were living in misery. Billions had been spent for nothing.

Roosevelt was through - and he knew it.
Something had to be done.

He and his "brain-busters" invented the fairy-tale that the Axis Powers were to blame for this calamity.

He took those steps short of war, made them shorter and shorter until he had HIS war!

He wanted to kill two birds with one stone by plunging his country into a war:

First, he got rid of the unemployed by shipping most of them to the battlefields of Europe as cannon fodder. The rest were absorbed by the armament industry in temporary wartime jobs.

Second, he passed fat government contracts on to his rich sponsors, the Baruchs, Lehmans, Morgenthaus, Warburgs, Ginsbergs and the like, thus rewarding them for their cash donations during election time. This moneyed gang is reaping colossal profits as usual.

So you see that Mr. Roosevelt had good reasons for running after the war.

One of his spokesmen, James H. McGraw Jr., president of the McGraw-Hill-Publishing Company, Inc., put it bluntly by writing in the March 1942 issue of the magazine "Aviation,"

"And this, very definitely, is OUR war."

The American people, however, in their unimpeachable judgement set him right by saying:

This is the RICH man's war and the POOR man's fight!

A I - 040-2-44

This blatantly anti-Semitic propaganda leaflet (both sides reproduced here) was intended to destroy the morale of young servicemen whose education had been cut short by conscription. It was produced by the Paris unit of the German propaganda mission.

The text on the reverse of the leaflet names several prominent American Jews. The creator of the text knows the typical American soldier comes from a home of modest means, hence "the POOR man's fight."
(US Department of Defense)

Leaflets intended to divide the Allies

AMERICAN SOLDIERS!

Remember those happy days when you stepped out with your best girl "going places and doing things"?

No matter

whether you two were enjoying a nice juicy steak at some tony restaurant or watching a thrilling movie with your favourite stars performing, or dancing to the lilt of a swing band

you were happy.

WHAT IS LEFT OF ALL THIS?

Nothing! Nothing but days and nights of he heaviest fighting and for many of you

NOTHING BUT A PLAIN WOODEN CROSS IN FOREIGN SOIL!

A1-035-2-44

Above left and right: Another leaflet picked up when I visited the former German propaganda mission in Paris when the fighting ended. This one would not have fooled the American soldier because of the British spelling, "favourite."

On the right is a leaflet for British servicemen. It shows an American soldier molesting a British (his?) girl. The complete image can be seen only by holding it up to the light, thus exposing the viewer to sniper fire.

With the fighting over, the mission changes

When the war ended our Port had to deploy all remaining units to the United States. Among the several uniformed Hollywood stars was Jimmy Stewart (*top left*), who reached the rank of Colonel. When the 30th Infantry Division prepared to sail (*top right*), they draped an enormous 30 on the ship. (U S Department of Defense)

COUNTY BOROUGH OF SOUTHAMPTON

PRESENTATION

to the

14th Major Port (Transportation Corps)

U.S. Army

in

THE FORECOURT OF THE CIVIC CENTRE SOUTHAMPTON

on

THURSDAY, 14th MARCH, 1946

of the

SCROLL RECORDING THE GRANTING TO THEM BY THE SOUTHAMPTON TOWN COUNCIL OF THE RIGHT TO MARCH

THROUGH THE TOWN AND COUNTY OF THE TOWN OF SOUTHAMPTON WITH BAYONETS FIXED, DRUMS BEATING AND COLOURS FLYING

H. VINCENT
Mayor

COLONEL SHERMAN L. KISER
Port Commander

Left: Cover of the programme for the ceremony according the 14th Port Freedom of the Town of Southampton.

Mary says farewell to family and familiar surroundings

Not long before I was deployed back to the United States I took this picture of Mary holding one of her mother's rabbits. It was to give me great comfort during the hiatus before she could join me.

It had been Mr. Roberts' constant fear that he would never see Mary again or, at best, only rarely. In fact, it was the opposite. There was hardly a year when we did not visit Frith Farm at least once.

Mary's Certificate of Release by the Women's Land Army. It testifies to her wartime service of four years and four days.

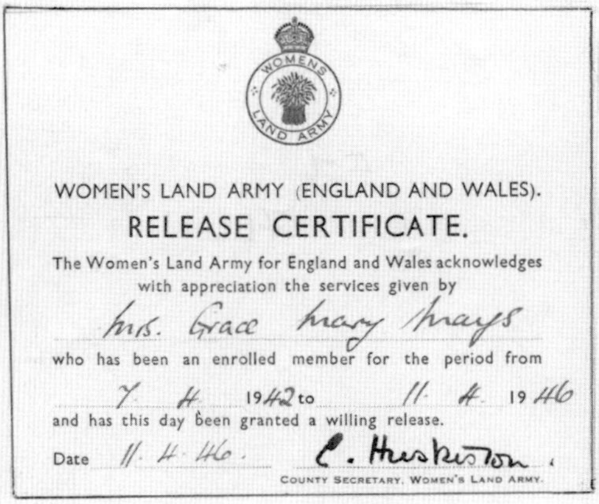

WOMEN'S LAND ARMY

WOMEN'S LAND ARMY (ENGLAND AND WALES).

RELEASE CERTIFICATE.

The Women's Land Army for England and Wales acknowledges with appreciation the services given by

Mrs. Grace Mary Mays

who has been an enrolled member for the period from

7. 4. 1942 to 11. 4. 1946

and has this day been granted a willing release.

Date 11. 4. 46. C. Huskisson

COUNTY SECRETARY, WOMEN'S LAND ARMY.

Giles' magic pen captures GI Bride drama

Copyright cartoon by Giles. Reprinted by courtesy of the Daily Express

"Possibly you *don't* approve, but you will, nevertheless, keep your opinion to yourself, Smithers!"

"But honey—where did you get the idea that all Americans live in skyscrapers?"

Copyright cartoon by Giles. Reprinted by courtesy of the Sunday Express.

Cunard's gracious welcome to the brides

"QUEEN MARY"

I send you my best wishes for your happiness and good fortune in your new life in the great country of your adoption.

C. M. Ford
Captain

Cunard Building,
Pier Head, Liverpool

May, 1946

25, Broadway,
New York

Cunard was counting on many more years of trans-Atlantic passenger travel when it issued its poignant welcome greetings to brides boarding at Southampton. Sadly for some (and no doubt happily for others) the era of multiple daily flights between Britain and America was about to begin.

Cunard White Star *Queen Mary*

Mary and I face our post-war problems

My parents' home in Louisville (*left*) was to give Mary her first taste of living in the American South where temperatures often ranged from 90 to 100 degrees throughout the summer. My mother and sister Hope *(above)* immediately set about buying her cooler clothing.

I was shocked to see how crippled and haggard my brother Floyd was. Here he is being supported by my younger brother, Harold. Floyd's crutches lie at his feet.

Shortly after shooting dead a Japanese harbour saboteur, Floyd posed for this picture.

Kendall Weisiger, cherished friend and Rotary Educationalist

Mary much looked forward to meeting Kendall Weisiger, my "guru" since university days. She promptly dubbed him "Daddy Whiz," a name she used to his death.

A crash course in American housekeeping

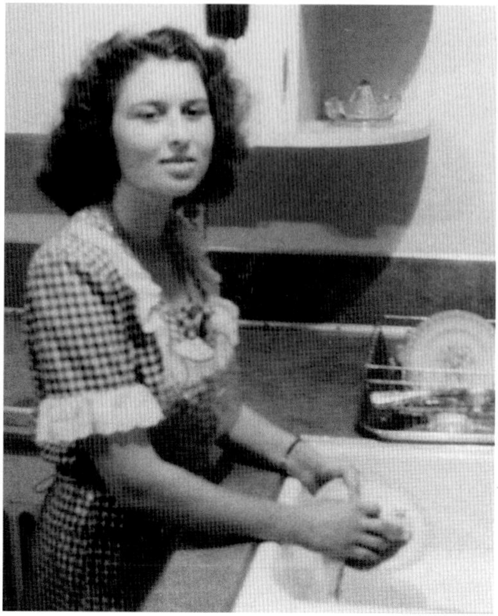

At the war's end, many American universities offered free tuition to wives of newly-wed servicemen. My alma mater, the University of Georgia, allowed Mary to take the "finishing off" summer course for seniors in home economics; she and they were the same age, 21. Although there was much laughter and a few disasters, she considered the course one of the most useful experiences of her life. Here *(left)* she is working as Maid in her Home Management house. Meanwhile I enrolled in a German course, hoping it would count toward a Ph.D. one day.

There were several "jobs" in the House, each task lasting nine days. Bottom right: Mary arranges flowers as part of her duties. Her house, "A," (*below*) was one of four devoted to the finishing-off course.

“Know Georgia, Go Georgia” winner

In the midst of her Home Management course Mary won a “Know Georgia, Go Georgia” essay contest sponsored by *The Atlanta Constitution*. Top: about to embark on her prize-winning trip which included visits to the Okefeenokee Swamp (*above left*) and (*above right*) Franklin D. Roosevelt’s Little White House.

A brief sojourn in Georgia's beautiful highlands

I briefly edited a weekly paper in Georgia's Appalachian region, allowing me to write feature articles about the local blacksmith *(above)*, butter-making at home (*above right*) and spinning (*below left*).

Trials involving illicit whiskey-making were held in the Union County courthouse (below).

Trekking over part of the Appalachian Trail

Mary and I spent one week walking on the southernmost section of the Appalachian Trail whose plaque is shown above. Top right: Mary examines one of the trail markers so useful for negotiating the mountain wilderness.

When I spotted this sign (*below*) pointing to a nearby spring, I could not resist ordering Mary to lie prostrate with her tongue hanging out for my camera.

We start our family with two in quick succession

While I wait anxiously outside the McGeary Hospital for Mary to deliver her first child, this group of locals enjoy a game of checkers in the shade of friendly trees. Alas, the baby didn't come. I returned home, only to learn Angela had arrived after all.

In 1949 Mary and I made the children the theme of our Christmas card (*left*). For several years I edited *Rural Georgia*, a journal devoted to improving the living conditions of farm families through the benefits of rural electrification.

Following in the steps of Robert Louis Stevenson

In the summer of 1955 I realized my childhood ambition of repeating Robert Louis Stevenson's trek through the Cevennes, described in his *Travels with a Donkey*. I began, as did he, in the ancient village of Le Monastier, whose rural tranquillity is reflected above. Below: Mayor Eugene Mazet traces the route I will follow.

Encounters along the road to St. Jean du Gard

Above left: Emile Senac, grandson of Goudet's inn proprietor in Stevenson's time, shows me the engraving of the family's fencing champion cited by Stevenson. Right: a Protestant girl displays the *coulombe,* indicative of her faith. Journey's end came at St. Jean du Gard (*below*) where I show my copy of Stevenson's work to a local scholar.

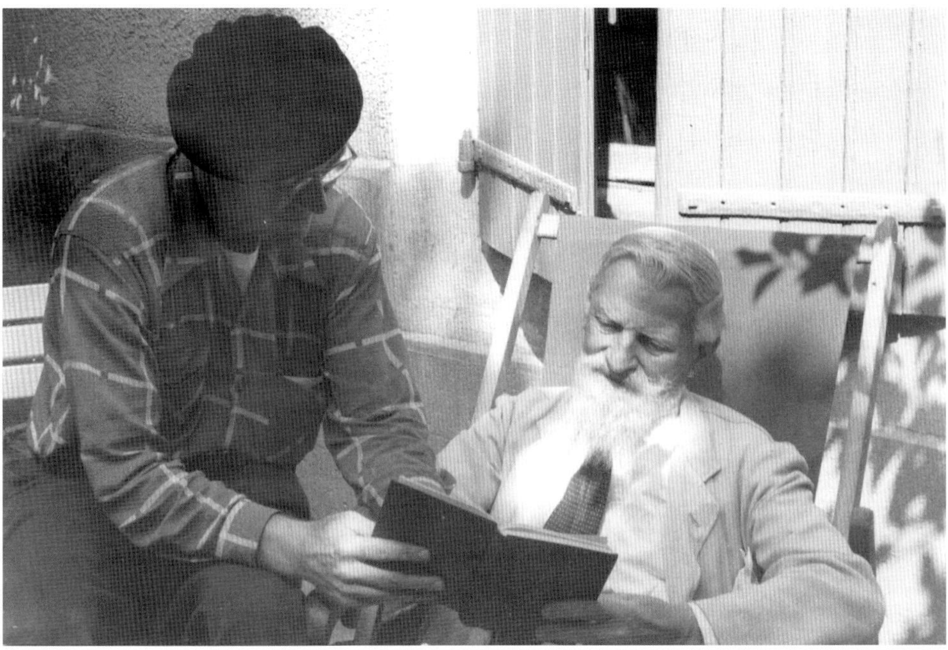

Pont de Montvert: peaceful today but once the scene of bitter fighting between Catholics and Protestants

Scrambling over several boulders, I was able to capture this peaceful scene of Pont de Montvert (note man fishing at top left). It was in marked contrast to the violence that erupted here between Catholics and Protestants in 1702, vividly related by Stevenson.

How faces of early immigrants to Israel resembled

In Israel, my first diplomatic assignment, I noticed the Embassy was staffed by people who had emigrated from all over the world. Despite being Jewish, many had facial resemblances associated with countries of their origin. The staff gleefully joined in my scheme to illustrate this phenomenon with pictures of them looking at newspapers published in their native tongues. Above: Israelis from England and Germany; below: others from Russia and Hungary.

those of people in countries where they were born

Above left: a Polish immigrant; on the right, one from Iraq. Below are two young ladies born in France (*left*) and Spain (*right*). Now, half a century later with intermarriages occurring, these facial indications of places of birth probably would not be so marked.

Israel: a land of contrasts and conflicts

The British, assigned the task of administering the mandated territory of Palestine, faced the wrath of both Jews and Arabs as they tried to perform their duties fairly. The existing anti-British sentiment caused this statue (left), portraying the Lion of Judah besting the British Lion, to be erected in a Tel Aviv suburb.

Israelis, who rely strongly on financial support from both the American government and the American Jewish community, always follow American presidential elections closely. As the Embassy's press officer, it was my task to prepare a booklet (*below*) about the 1956 election.

Below: Angela and Stuart being welcomed by Schlomo, driver of their school bus.

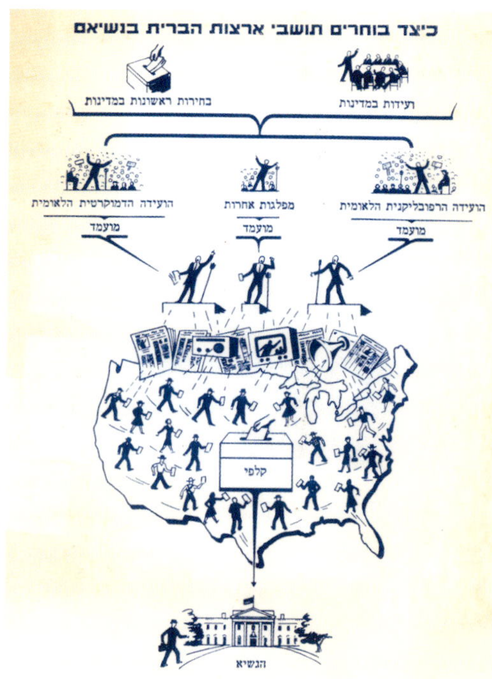

De Gaulle dislikes NATO's presence in France

Above: NASA's coordinator and I show a French starlet the program for the "Freedom 7" capsule exhibit at the 1961 Paris Air Show. (NASA)

When de Gaulle visited the NASA's exhibit he congratulated me and my secretary but pointedly ignored USAF officers nearby. (Peter Newark's Pictures)

To help inform the French public about NATO I organized several press tours to NATO installations in Europe. Shown above is the first of the groups before being briefed at SHAPE Headquarters near Paris. All the journalists, except one, filed stories daily. My secretary was unable to discover if the non-writer was a plant by some French ministry or a "free-loader" put forward by one paper. (SHAPE photo)

At work the VIPs are sometimes awe-inspiring ....

When none of my colleagues dared initiate conversation with Eleanor Roosevelt, Mary and I stepped in and found her to be charming -- not the formidable UN debator pictured above. (Peter Newark pictures)

As I helped former President Eisenhower to his car in the pouring rain, he grabbed the umbrella (someone else's) and sped away. The poor owner never even knew he had made a "gift" to the President. (Peter Newark pictures)

I come home – only to find more "VIPs"

Receptions, dinners and other social obligations frequently mean diplomats have little time to be with their children. Mary and I tried to keep our weekends free and on occasion pretended to be "booked up" to have a free week-day evening with them. Below, left: a family chess game and, right, our garden's "Renoir Corner."

High adventure: enrolling in a French school at the age of five

Boarding schools for very young children can be traumatic. We couldn't bear to part with Pipkin, our youngest, so enrolled her at the nearby Le Vesinet primary school. She felt at home from day one and soon spoke impeccable French. The photo above shows her at her desk, surrounded by classmates. Below is her "Billet de Satisfaction," awarded in 1962.

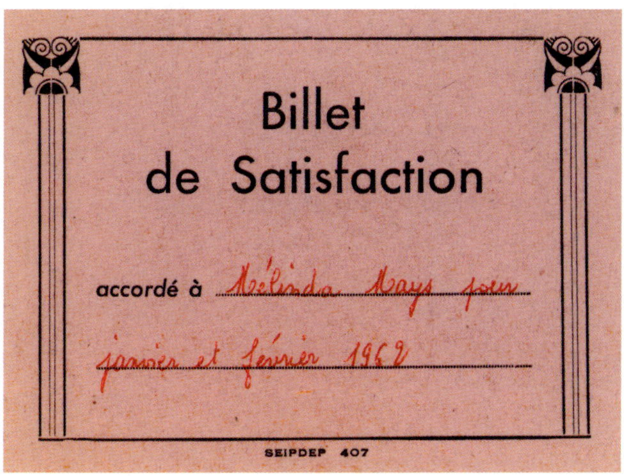

Billet
de Satisfaction

accordé à Mélinda Mays pour
janvier et février 1962

SEIPDEP 407

The Finns take John Glenn to their hearts

After I introduced John Glenn at our press conference he described how the American moon-landing project would be conducted. Later he gave several illustrated lectures. The Finns, renowned for their technical prowess, relished Glenn's skill of presenting complex space projects in simple terms. (USIA photo). When he, his wife and daughter prepared to leave Helsinki, Mary and I escorted them to their plane. (Lehtikuva)

An astronaut generously inscribes his photograph to the children

At the country's leading technical institute Glenn held young scientists spellbound when, using models brought with him, he "took them with him" on the lunar flight. As he was about to leave Helsinki, Glenn kindly inscribed his official photograph (*above*) to our three children. (NASA photo). Many Americans thought Glenn would make an excellent president, but his backers lacked the necessary finance for him to become a serious contender.

Dean Rusk says "I am a son of Appalachia"

Dean Rusk, U.S. Secretary of State, greets Finns after his arrival to promote President Johnson's Appalachia's awareness program. Ambassador Tyler Thompson *(right)* looks on with interpreter Chris Helstrom and me in the centre. (U.A. Saarinen photo)

When roving Ambassador Averell Harriman came to Finland, Ambassador Thompson asked Pipkin to greet him with a miniature American flag.

Above: Mary and I at the picture window of our apartment where we once famously failed to entertain Ambassador Timberlake. Below: stamps featuring Sibelius and his wife. I escorted the Cleveland Orchestra conductor to Sibelius' home from which we later "escaped" to see renowned Tapiola.

Sporting humour – and sporting pathos

Above: Paavo Nurmi (*centre*) – the legendary Finnish Olympian -- smiles broadly as US Ambassador George McGee relates how Nurmi was first and he was last in a Texas long-distance race when McGee was a university student. Faithful interpreter Chris Helstom (*second from left*) also grins while I (*left*) and Ambassador Tyler Thompson (*right*) look on. (USIA photo)

Finland's President Urho Kekkonen (*fifth from left*), former national high jump champion, movingly conveys his feelings to Brian Sternberg (*to his right*) just after the paralysed American pole- vaulter described how his injury occurred while exercising on the trampoline. Sternberg later received a blue and white Finnish track suit from Pentti Nikula, the then reigning pole-vault champion. I look on from the left.

Another country deposits its instrument of ratification for the nuclear non-proliferation treaty

In Washington for my last USIA assignment, I was seconded to the U.S. Arms Control Agency. Here I congratulate Ahamed Nasseem, the Maldives Charge d'Affaires, after he deposited his country's ratification instrument to the Nuclear Non-Proliferation Treaty. (US Department of State photo)

Miss Applebee celebrates her 104th birthday

Above: Miss Constance Applebee being escorted by Mary and me to her 104th birthday party in the garden of her Burley home, The Withies. She introduced women's hockey to the United States. The three F's on her famous badge (*right*) are for Fun, Friendship and Fitness.

The Bern Schwartz portrait of Miss Applebee

This portrait of Miss Applebee by the renowned American photographer, Bern Schwartz, appeared in his collection, *Contemporaries*, published in 1978. When told the volume contained portraits of many famous people, she quipped "What are they doing in my book!" In 2008 140 of these portraits, valued at £250,000, were donated to the National Gallery by Michael Schwartz, Bern's son. They joined the Gallery's Primary Collection alongside works by Richard Avedon, Irving Penn and Lord Snowdon. (National Portrait Gallery, London)

Mary's father concludes a lifetime of public service

Mary's father, A.E. Roberts, remained active in civic affairs despite his advanced years. Left above: he plants a tree with Richard St. Barbe Baker, founder of Men of the Trees. He and Baker had been close friends since their early twenties. Above right: Mary poses with her father by a sign commemorating her father's contribution to the construction of homes on Wickham's council estate.

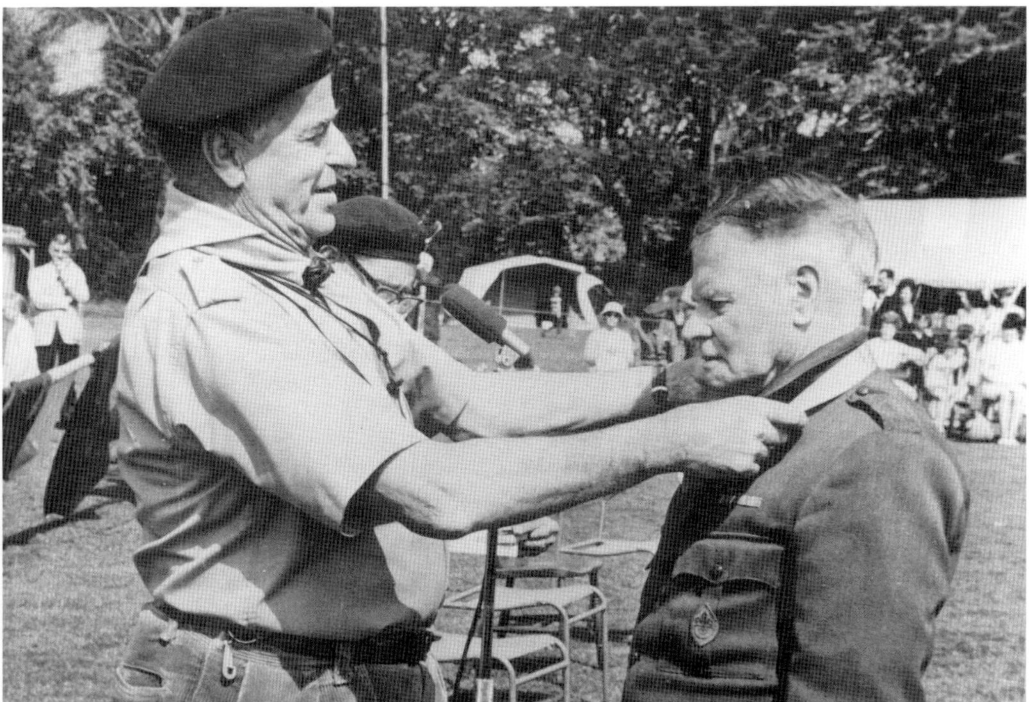

Above: In recognition of nearly three quarters of a century of service to the Scouting movement, Roberts was presented with the prestigious Silver Acorn award. (Portsmouth Evening News)

Being a small publisher can be great fun

Above: Our titles included three works on the Forest and two on numismatics. Our logo (*right*) features three popular New Forest trees: oak, beech and holly.

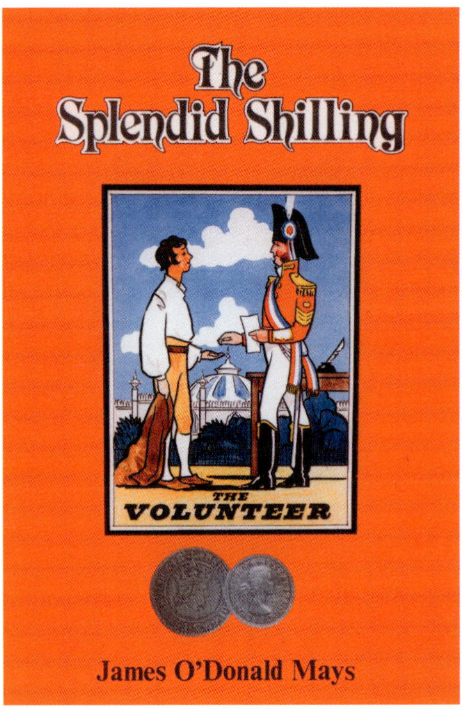

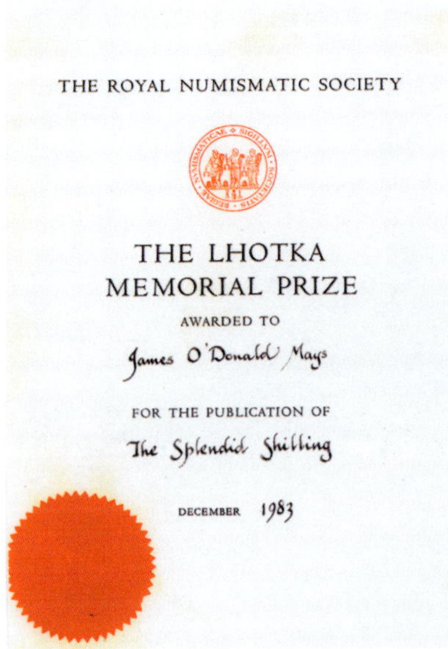

THE ROYAL NUMISMATIC SOCIETY

THE LHOTKA MEMORIAL PRIZE

AWARDED TO

James O'Donald Mays

FOR THE PUBLICATION OF

The Splendid Shilling

DECEMBER 1983

Left*: The Splendid Shilling's* cover taken from a Brighton pub sign. Above: the Lotka Memorial Award.

Everyone should be a village show secretary -- at least once

Above: The park of the manor (now Burley Manor Hotel) where the annual Village Show is now held to accommodate a growing number of visitors. For many years Burley School was the venue. I served as Secretary for seven years and once was blamed for giving a proud wine-maker only 3rd place for his bottle. Below: One year Mary presented the prizes as show officials look on.

The New Forest, where Nature and History meet

The New Forest is blessed with a number of streams that meander gracefully through sylvan settings, affording striking contrasts of water and trees. One of the most popular is Queen's Bower (*above*) north of Brockenhurst. Several tributaries merge near this point to form the Lymington River.

The Rufus Stone (*below left*), the best known New Forest monument. Centre: Arthur Conan Doyle's grave at Minstead. Right: Brusher Mills' grave at Brockenhurst.

The glory of the newly born – whether animal or human

Above: a foal near Wooton Bridge. Left: A foal asks if anyone has seen its mother. Below left: Badgers feasting on bread scraps in Burley.

Above: Anna, our first grandchild, enjoys a new book on her initial visit to Grandpa.

Words of wisdom from a Sanskrit poet

Not long before Mary developed Alzheimer's we sometimes relaxed beneath our century-old apple tree. Here we would caress our blind ginger cat and her kitten, as we contemplated the many blessings that had come our way. Mary found her philosophy of life (which I came to share) best summed up in these lines by the Sanskrit poet, Kalidasa:

> Look to this day!
> For it is life, the very life of life.
> In its brief course lie all the verities,
> all the realities of existence;
> the bliss of growth,
> the glory of action.
> the splendour of beauty.
>
> For yesterday is always a dream
> and tomorrow is only a vision.
> But today – well lived
> makes every yesterday a dream of happiness
> and every tomorrow a dream of hope
> Look well, therefore, to this day!

56
"When Irish eyes are smiling..."

During January and February of 1946 many vessels sailed from Southampton with wives. When the announcement came that the *Henry Gibbins* would sail from Belfast on March 4th, it evoked such media interest in both Northern Ireland and Eire that Colonel Kiser decided we should give every assistance to the Irish press and radio. I was delighted with the challenge of staging a press conference and arranging for photographic coverage, as well as the chance to visit for the first time the land from which my paternal forebears had come. I was even happier when Colonel Kiser saw no objection to Mary accompanying me, although if either of us had foreseen the political risk arising from Mary's presence, we might have had second thoughts.

The *Henry Gibbins* by now was a famous ship in its own right. Having been launched as the *Biloxi* in 1942, it was transferred to the Army Transportation Corps a year later and renamed the *Henry Gibbins*. It made history in 1944 when it carried 1000 Jewish refugees from Italy to the United States under an executive order signed by President Franklin D. Roosevelt, a voyage recounted in the book, *Haven.* For the several hundred Irish war brides, it was also to provide a memorable voyage to the New World.

Mary and I arrived well in advance to make contact with the media, and to get a feel for their questions. Would there be separate areas for brides from Eire and those from Northern Ireland or would they be together? (Answer: they would be together). Might there be other bridal ships? (Answer: too early to tell, as precise information on the number of wives and babies was still being compiled.) How many would sail on the *Henry Gibbins*? (Answer: approximately 314 wives and 140 babies.) How many originated from Belfast? How many from Eire? (Answer: more than half were from Belfast; 35 came from Eire.)

At the press conference some of the same questions were asked, as well as others about the size of the Gibbins (12,000 tons), how the ship was staffed and how it was equipped to deal with its precious human cargo.

Because of my Scots-Irish ancestry I had long ago heard from my Grandfather Mays and others about the vast body of Irish folklore and folksongs. Wouldn't it be wonderful, I asked Mary, if before we left Belfast, we could attend a Kerry dance? Surely there must be a club, a church or a folk dance group where we could see and perhaps join in one. At first all enquiries met with negative responses; everyone said we needed more time. On the point of giving up, I went in desperation to a large department store and asked every young lady not serving customers if she could suggest something. At last, a pretty red-haired girl said she knew of a place where there 'might' be a dance that very evening.

She wrote the address on a piece of paper and Mary and I immediately went there. We found a young man at the entrance who confirmed there was to be Kerry dancing that evening. I explained my reasons for being in Belfast, mentioned my Irish ancestry and asked if Mary and I could come along. He smiled, then hesitated slightly and said we might.

We grabbed an early snack and set off for the place where we had found the young man. From its appearance the building was a club of some sort, similar to many in England where young people gathered daily. As we neared the entrance we saw the same young man was there, this time seated at a table as if checking identities and collecting admission fees. He readily recognised us, but this time his smile was gone, replaced by what seemed an apprehensive frown.

"Just wait here a moment," he said, "and I'll see what I can do."

Mary and I glanced at each other. Neither the young man's tone nor his words reflected the assurance he had given us only a few hours before. Meanwhile, inside there started up a lively Irish tune, accompanied by the sound of dancing feet. I squeezed Mary's hand; at last we were to see real Kerry dancing!

The young man was away a long time – too long, I realised, to obtain a simple "Yes" or "No" to our admission. Could it be a question of payment? Was the club so strapped for funds that its leaders were too embarrassed to ask a visiting American and his wife for an admission fee? I realised I had not offered to pay, but then the question of buying tickets had not arisen.

The music continued. Presently the young man came back, not looking at us but the ground. "The boss says you can come in and he *thinks* it will be all right" he said, carefully emphasising his words, "but to be on the safe side, he suggests you slide along the wall behind the onlookers and perhaps you won't be seen."

Mary and I again exchanged quick glances – this time of concern, for it seemed incredible that we should have to slip in unnoticed. Nevertheless we slowly followed the young man who motioned to us that we should stand against the wall where, at the next level up, I saw a projection booth occupied by several men. Although we entered smilingly and silently, we saw that the heads of many were now turned to see us – among them that of the leader of the folk dance band.

I quickly glanced round the small hall and saw the walls were covered with posters. Some recalled events in the Irish uprising against the British, others urged that only the Gaelic language should be spoken. I suddenly knew this had to be the meeting place of young people dedicated to extending Irish rule to the whole of the island, in effect, a kind of youth club operated by the IRA (Irish Republican Army) or its political-cultural wing.

Before I could convey my conclusion to Mary, the musicians stopped dead in the middle of a movement with the dancers frozen in their tracks, staring sternly ahead. Now no one looked at us. I instinctively knew our presence was the reason for the dance being abruptly halted. Seconds later my guess was confirmed, as the young man who had admitted us, approached and whispered: "I'm terribly sorry," he said, "but the band refuses to play until you leave. You see, the British crown on your wife's Land Army uniform is offensive to them."

Mary was aghast and angry, but I knew the young man was serious. Apart from anything else, this was a private club, and private clubs are entitled to admit – or refuse – anyone. I led her quietly out of the hall, not looking back. As we walked away we heard the music and dancing resume. Mary was furious until I explained the probable IRA connection.

"But why the delay at the door before allowing us in?" she asked, "If they had decided it was all right for us to enter, why the change of heart after we had come in?"

I, too, had wondered at the sudden volte-face. I could only guess at the reason. "They probably saw us not as individuals, but as representing two countries, because we both wore uniforms," I theorised to her, "and when they had to choose between a friendly America and a hostile Britain – as they perceived the situation to be – they felt obliged to risk hurting America for the sake of showing their opposition to Britain." Mary considered the event too complex to comprehend. Thus ended our dream of joining in a Kerry dance, one that we were never to realise.

The social highlight of our Belfast stay was a dinner given by the American Consul, Quincy Roberts, and his wife, Margaret. Quincy was one of the "old school" consuls, whose service had begun in 1915 before the American consular and diplomatic corps were merged. He had exciting tales to tell of adventures in Venice, Genoa, Salonika, Apia, Suva, Saigon and Chefoo. He was extremely knowledgeable about the politics of Ulster and not at all surprised by our youth club incident.

Although the arrival of the *Henry Gibbins* was delayed by two days, media interest grew. Reporters wanted copies of the ship's menu. These later appeared in several papers, down to the last detail, so great was the public interest in food in a land where rationing had been in effect for seven years. One reporter managed to collar a ship's officer who candidly said: "There is no rationing aboard this ship. The brides can have four eggs for breakfast, if they like, and I mean shell eggs (this was an oblique reference to the familiar powdered egg prevalent in Britain). Back in the States nobody eats powdered eggs."

This somewhat embarrassing interview was supplemented by the news that each Irish wife (as was the case for all brides) was to receive a gift of $15 to spend in the ship's store during the voyage to New York. Fifteen dollars was a large sum at the time, especially when goods in the ship's store were on sale at cost price. Some of the officers on our loading team were uneasy over this emphasis on material aspects of the embarkation, but there was nothing we could do about it.

The media in Northern Ireland and Eire seemed more knowledgeable about American geography and wanted to know exactly how many wives were going to each state. It dawned on me that there must be few families in Ireland, given generations of emigration, that did not have at least one relation living in the United States. Accordingly, our staff quickly computed the totals by state, this inevitably reflecting the population ratios (New York, the largest state, had 45; Pennsylvania, the next most populous, had 42; and so on).

To avoid having young mothers standing and waiting about with babies in their arms, we spread the embarkation over two days. When the first group had been safely ensconced in their cabins and all the reporters and photographers had departed, Mary and I went to one of the principal streets to find a restaurant and to buy a few post cards. As I was browsing in a newsagent's shop, I felt a gentle tap on one shoulder. Turning round, I saw a young man, neatly dressed, but obviously in a state of some anxiety. Although there was an unmistakable smell of whisky on his breath, he was sober.

Looking at me earnestly, he explained that his "little sister" would be boarding the *Henry Gibbins* on the morrow for a new life in Pennsylvania. "Will she be looked after well?" he implored, his eyes filling with tears. "Will – will she be all right?"

Taking both of his hands in mine, I looked him in the eye and said not only would his sister be all right but she would also be much loved. I pointed out that there were probably over a million Irish in New York City – many more than in either Belfast or Dublin, that St. Patrick's Day was celebrated there with more enthusiasm than in Ireland, and that, in short, his sister would feel at home from the moment she set foot in New York. I then added there were tens of thousands of Irish Americans in Boston, Chicago and, yes, in Philadelphia.

The young man's apprehension disappeared, replaced by a glorious smile that spread from ear to ear. He grasped my hand tightly, tried to speak but choked up. Embarrassed, he turned quickly and disappeared into the crowd. That evening I did a brief commentary on the embarkation for the BBC's Northern Ireland service, immediately following the news. After relating some of the basic information, I concluded my comments by referring to my encounter with the young man – emphasising that every Irish bride was assured of a warm welcome in the United States. (The text of my brief remarks follows at the end of this chapter.)

Embarkation of the last group of wives the following day went off with no operational hitches, but the tug on the heart strings of those present was awesome. Several fond mothers attempted to restrain their daughters from mounting the gangway and only after intervention by other family members could they be persuaded to let the loading continue. The embarkation began with only a dozen or two relatives present, but by the time it was completed a crowd of nearly 300 had gathered, joined by many of the dock workers.

Thereafter, until the gangway was lifted, a "songfest" ensued with first the wives, then the shore party, trying to out-do each other. When the relatives sang "Land of Hope and Glory", the brides on the ship's deck responded with "When Irish Eyes Are Smiling". Not to be outdone, the families and dock workers started up "Come Back to Erin", by which time there was not a dry eye to be seen. Then with the gangway removed and the *Henry Gibbins* slowly edging away from the dock, everyone joined in "Auld Lang Syne".

The occasion was captured by a *Belfast Telegraph* writer who reported a voice from the shore crowd:

"Don't worry, Mary, I've posted on your shamrock."

Another cried out to her daughter on the deck:

"Keep up your heart. Perhaps we'll join you one day."

Our loading party, reflecting on the operation after the *Gibbins* was out of sight, agreed that none of the send-offs in Southampton had been as emotional as this.

TOPICAL TALK
N.I.H.S. 6.25 – 6.30 p.m. Wednesday, 6th March 1946
"BRIDES WHO CROSS THE ATLANTIC"
by
First Lieutenant O'Donald Mays, United States Army

We hear much nowadays about British exports – especially as they are related to the United States. But the finest exports of all are the wives and children of American servicemen such as sailed from Belfast harbour this morning aboard the United States Army Transport vessel, HENRY GIBBINS.

The four hundred and fifty four brides and children, who said good-bye to Ireland this morning, are part of one of the most interesting movements of civilian population the world has ever known.

The GIBBINS, Belfast's first bride ship, is one of nineteen such vessels being employed in Europe. It is likely that the GIBBINS (or a similar ship) will make two more voyages from Belfast before the estimated one thousand two hundred dependants in Northern Ireland and Eire can be embarked. Incidentally, the travelling expenses of the brides will be provided all the way from their family in Ireland to their new home in the United States. This fact means that those wives fortunate enough to have husbands living in California, Oregon or the State of Washington will travel another three thousand miles across America after disembarking in New York. This is indeed a wonderful journey that not many Americans have made.

Vessels used for transporting dependants have been specially converted. The GIBBINS is an excellent example: when the GIBBINS was a troop ship, she accommodated some two thousand eight hundred men. When she left Belfast this morning, there were only four hundred and fifty four dependants aboard – less than one fifth the number of troops. This ship is equipped with three play-rooms, two dining halls, a library, a lounge which can be used as a cinema theatre, an Army sales shop where brides can buy such items as facial creams, powders, hair pins, sweets of many varieties, biscuits, disposable hankies and many other useful articles. Aboard the GIBBINS are eleven American films which will be shown at various times during the eight day crossing. One of the Army officers will give a series of talks designed to acquaint the brides with life in America. The discussion, which Belfast wives have had in their own club here, will, no doubt, prove of vast benefit to them upon arrival in New York.

Specially assigned personnel will be available to administer to the personal needs of the dependants aboard the GIBBINS. A team of Army surgeons will be assisted in their work by eight Army nurses and six American WACs. Supplementing these will be a number of stewardesses supplied by the American Red Cross. An Army chaplain will be aboard to direct or help organise religious services.

One of the Army surgeons, who checked the children for signs of illness, told me that the youngsters that went aboard the GIBBINS were among the finest he had ever examined. "They are a truly magnificent lot", he exclaimed.

Embarkation of the GIBBINS was not without its human side. One of the brides, for example, was designated by the American Wives Club of Belfast to present the ship's master, Captain Nelson, with a real Irish shillelagh.

But the dependants aboard the GIBBINS will not need shillelaghs, or shamrocks, or anything else material, to sell themselves to the American people. Their warm smiles and charming Irish dialects will make them loved everywhere. Besides, they will find many other Irish already in America.

May I conclude with this little story. On Monday last a young man, of perhaps twenty-five, stopped me and inquired if I was on the loading staff of the GIBBINS. When I told him that I was, he said – in a voice tinged with emotion – "My little sister went aboard this morning."

"Fine", I replied, "and to which state is she going?"

"Pennsylvania", he responded.

"Oh, that's a fine state", I continued. At this point the young man clasped my hand so tightly that his own were trembling.

"Your little sister will like it in Pennsylvania", I added, "and the people there will like her, too".

The man uttered a difficult "Thank you", and turned his head quickly to the side and quickly walked away.

57
Remembering those who have fallen

When a war is over, the victors usually wish their legacy to be remembered.

On the plus side there are memorials to be built and plaques to be placed to mark significant aspects of the military effort. Sadly, the downside is the medals to be awarded to the survivors – usually wives – of the fallen heroes.

Our 14th Port officers were caught up in both aspects in the months immediately following the Allied victory in Europe. Plaques were placed on several of the buildings from which our operations were directed and where the men and women were billeted. These included schools, hotels, maritime offices in the dock area and, of course, Southampton's Civic Centre – site of our first headquarters.

The 14th Port conducted operations at other nearby south coast ports, among them Portland, from which large numbers of combat troops embarked in the crucial early stage of the Normandy invasion. When it came time to commemorate the role Portland played in the American assault, the American Ambassador, John G. Winant, flew down from London to unveil a plaque. The date was Wednesday, August 22nd, 1945, one which the Ambassador would remember well.

He obviously was deeply moved and honoured to be the central figure of the plaque ceremony, as his subsequent comments showed. But en route to Portland he had to endure a storm-force gale in a Flying Fortress which had flown him to the south coast. When he climbed out of the official car in Portland's Victoria Gardens, officials noticed how shaken he was. No doubt he was grateful for the serenity of Portland when everyone sang the third line of "O God our help in ages past": -- "our shelter from the stormy blast."

After unveiling the plaque (noting that 418,000 troops and 144,000 vehicles had been launched from Portland), Winant said:

"Today and forever our world lives with the sword of Damocles. We have at last learned how to destroy all life on this planet. We have uncovered the last secret of nature, but we must learn one more secret, a moral secret, before we can use this dynamic power for good. We must learn to live together in friendship."

Winant, a scholar and a sensitive man with high moral principles, was anxious that America and Britain understand each other. He was later to write in his *A Letter from Grosvenor Square*, that he observed a "growing disillusionment of today, which not only dims and obscures the present, but is trying to cloud the past." He added "Nor do I think it is sufficiently appreciated (by Americans) how much the British gave us in return for what we gave them, not only in loyalty, but in practical contributions."

Winant wrote "common courtesy requires mutual understanding" and illustrated his point by relating how an indignant American colonel rushed into the Embassy in London because he had just seen an American flag hanging upside down in a nearby residential street.

"I took the trouble to find out the reason," Winant said. "Two elderly people had bought an American flag out of hard-earned savings to show their appreciation to American soldiers who had just arrived in Great Britain. Even the best of goodwill sometimes leads to misunderstandings if we are not aware of the practices and customs of other countries."

In his book Winant paid tribute to the British women serving in the armed forces – the ATS, WAAF and WRNS – and then added:

"As for the Women's Land Army, which numbered over 80,000, there was no type of agricultural work some member did not do –

threshing, thatching, tractor ploughing, ditching, caring for stock – everything. In southern England this was not always the peaceful occupation that agriculture suggests. The Battle of Britain was fought above their heads; there were constant hit-and-run raids from the French coast and later the droning flying bomb. The most familiar harvesting hymn became, as one of the Land Girls said, also the most appropriate, for the first line runs:

"We plough the fields and scatter ."

Just over two years after unveiling the Portland plaque Winant took his own life. On the very day of his death his publishers had planned to present him with the first copy of his *Letter from Grosvenor Square* – the only book he ever wrote – but they arrived too late.

It was especially distressing for our 14th Port staff when news arrived of the deaths of American soldiers who had been newly wed to British women. These men had paid for the Allied victory with their lives and we were under obligation to recognise their bravery as quickly as possible.

If the widow was unable to come to Southampton, it was our policy that an officer should call upon her at her family's home and present the medal. In a brief ceremony, held in the living room, the officer would read out the tribute to the solider, after which our Army photographer would take a picture of the medal presentation.

I took part in two such ceremonies, both extremely moving. The first, at our Southampton headquarters, saw Mrs. William McClellan (nee Merry) of Broadstone, Dorset, come to Southampton to accept the Silver Star awarded her husband, a captain in the 9th Infantry Division who had been killed in the brief but ferocious Remagen Bridge capture. We chatted briefly and I learned that Captain McClellan was a close friend of another officer whom I had known at the University of Georgia. As the photographer was preparing his camera for the photograph, Mrs. McClellan asked if I would hold the baby while she wiped her tears away. I did so only to see her sob anew. She quickly apologised, saying that the sight of seeing me holding the child was all too reminiscent of the last time her husband had held little Baird. Shortly after, Colonel Kiser, our Port Commander – also deeply touched by the event – pinned the medal on the little boy's chest.

My second experience took me to a Dorset town where the teenage bride of a young American soldier lived with her parents. Their romance was typical of so many others: two young people meeting by chance, marrying and then being almost immediately separated. The young wife was an usher in the local cinema when the soldier first spotted her. She was a shy, beautiful slip of a girl whose charms, I could see, the young American lad had been unable to resist. They found their two families amazingly similar – both of modest means and no grandiose pretensions. Their courtship had been short and sweet, the wedding a gloriously happy moment and then – the sudden despatch across the Channel. They had dreamed of the time when they would return to his folks in the United States and start their family. But it was not to be.

There is an untold, enormously poignant story of these young brides – the hundreds who were widowed even before they could set foot in the United States. Some who were childless went over to meet their late husbands' families and usually did not remain. If they had children, as many did, they almost always visited their American in-laws who were desperately keen to see their grandchildren. Some remained in the United States, but many could not face up to young widowhood in a strange land, and so did not.

Awards were made also to military units for the roles they played in the war effort. Our own 14th Port – together with our sister unit, the 13th Port in Plymouth – received the Meritorious Unit Award. This permitted all our servicemen to wear a golden wreath on the sleeve cuffs of our uniforms. Our commanding officer, Col. Sherman Kiser, was awarded the Bronze Star for his leadership.

But our unit's most prestigious award came on March 14th when the civic leaders of Southampton accorded us the privilege to march through the ancient Bargate.

Traditionally robed and wigged, Town Clerk R.H. Meggeson faced the soldiers, and read in a loud voice:

"*Know all men by these presents* that *we, the Mayor Alderman and Burgesses of the Borough of Southampton,* by resolution of the *Southampton Town Council* conferred upon the 14th Major Port of the Transportation Corps of the United States Army, in recognition of the outstanding achievement of all ranks of that formation in embarking from the Port of Southampton between D-Day and VE-Day nearly 2,000,000 men of the United States Forces for the liberation of Europe, and in appreciation of the cordial relations, friendships, and cooperation they established with the citizens of Southampton, the privilege, honour and distinction of marching through the streets of the Town and County of the Town of Southampton with bayonets fixed, drums beating, and colours flying. *In Witness* whereof the Corporate Seal has been hereunder affixed in the presence of *H. Vincent,* Mayor, *R.J. Stranger,* Deputy-Mayor, *Ronald H. Meggeson,* Town Clerk."

Then the Mayor formally presented the scroll to Col. Sherman L. Kiser, the 14th's commander. In accepting it, Col. Kiser declared that the honour belonged not only to his organisation, but also to the people of Southampton, and to the 23,000 men who had been attached for duty to the 14th at one time or another.

Presentation and acceptance of the scroll was the highpoint in the ceremony, but it was only part of the day's events. Before actual "freedom" of the city could be given, the troops were privileged to march through Bargate – one of the famed walled city gates of England.

After the parade, officers and men were feted in the Southampton Guildhall. Toasts were exchanged. Later, the ceremony over, men of the 14th returned to headquarters with the unique distinction of being not only the first Transportation Corps unit to be so honoured but also the first military organization to be cited in such a fashion by Southampton.

Many noble words were spoken on that day, but the greatest applause came when Colonel Kiser unexpectedly paid tribute to the English weather.

"Weather permitting, I make a point of walking the three quarters of a mile from my quarters to the headquarters camp," he explained, "and on only three occasions this year has the rainfall been so heavy I have been obliged to use a car."

What Colonel Kiser didn't say was that most of the time he carried his raincoat by way of "insurance" and that many days he arrived at the camp almost drenched. Nonetheless, his comment – for an officer who eventually was to choose Florida as his retirement home – was warmly welcomed.

PART III

In search of my destiny:
My South or my world?

1946-1956

58
Whither shall I turn?

The return of American troops to the United States was proceeding in so orderly a manner that the Army's prediction that I might leave Southampton in April proved true. After farewells to my staff and other Army comrades, I said goodbye to Mary and her family – with a real prospect that Mary would join me in Georgia within the next four to six weeks. She had one last difficult task – one she was putting off to the last minute – resigning her leadership of Wickham's GTC (Girls Training Corps). She had worked hard to train this small group of teenage girls into "future citizens" – using their talents for the betterment of the community. Now she was obliged to leave them with no successor in sight. There was nothing I could say to comfort her as I prepared to sail. But this would be a minor heartbreak compared to leaving her parents.

My troop transport was a converted Victory ship, the *Tuscaloosa Victory*, named after the town in which the University of Alabama is situated. I was delighted that my voyage home was to be aboard one of the "work horses" of the United States Merchant Marine. The construction of Liberty and Victory ships had been one of the great technological achievements of American wartime industry and here I was, about to cross the Atlantic aboard one.

The basic Liberty ship was a 10,000 ton vessel capable of about 11 knots; its later derivative, the Victory ship, was slightly larger and faster. When they entered service in the early days of the war, they were being sunk by German submarines faster than they could be replaced. Thanks to the enterprise of Henry Kaiser and others of similar talents, the race to increase the American fleet took off. By the war's end, over 2,700 Liberty ships and 530 Victory vessels had been built. With a "cost-plus" contract assured for anyone able to set up a shipyard, these ships were constructed in some unlikely places – including the relatively small port of Brunswick in my home state of Georgia where my brother Floyd worked before joining the Navy Seabees.

Just as I was preparing to board the troop transport in Southampton's New Docks, I was given a warm send off by Ron Perrin, the dock superintendent who had provided the singing at our wedding. Ron was to remain a faithful friend until the end of his days.

The voyage aboard the*Tuscaloosa Victory* was uneventful except for two minor incidents. I had long since observed that when a group of men are thrown together by chance, there will almost certainly emerge from their numbers a "spiv" out to make a fast buck. On this occasion the entrepreneur organised a "daily mileage" lottery in which we each paid a dollar into the pot, which, minus certain "administrative costs" went to the person who came closest to guessing the mileage of each 24-hour period. The lottery was popular until someone accidentally came upon the organiser dividing his spoils with the first mate and a third person who, magically, happened to guess the precise mileage two days in a row.

In mid-Atlantic our ship suddenly slowed to a crawl, a mystery the Captain could not at first understand. He ordered the ship to stop, then reverse. Meanwhile, we all rushed to the bow to see if there was some clue to our abrupt halt. There, straddling the sharp point of the ship's prow, was a large whale. Its back had been broken on impact, and gentle attempts at reversing would not dislodge it. Finally, the Captain ordered full speed reversals combined with sharp turns, a manoeuvre which eventually freed the mammal. It floated away slowly, but whether it survived the horrific ordeal we were never to know.

On arrival in New York we were promptly despatched to nearby Fort Dix in New Jersey. Immediately we heard a rumour that we, as servicemen about to re-enter civilian life, would be entitled to one – and only one, thick American beef steak. Was it so, or merely one more Army rumour? Within minutes we were issued with a coupon entitling us to such a treat. When we lined up in the mess, we could hardly believe our eyes. There, in front of us, were giant serving trays, each bulging with enormous steaks. With them we could have all the mashed potatoes, gravy and vegetables we wanted. For dessert there was the complete range of American favourites, including apple pie topped by vanilla ice cream. Some of us believed that food aboard US Navy vessels was like this every day but for those of us who had lived on more austere Army food, this was truly manna from Heaven.

We were given small amounts of money and promptly spent most of it telephoning our families. My mother answered the phone in the richest Southern accent I thought I had ever heard. At first I had difficulty in understanding her. Then I discovered she had the same problem with me. During my three years' stay in England apparently much of my original accent had disappeared and I was even pronouncing the "g" at the end of words ending in "ing" – something many Southerners never managed. Eventually we made ourselves understood, and she was overjoyed to know I was now on the near side of the Atlantic and would be arriving home within days.

We remained at Fort Dix no longer than was required to separate us into "shipping groups" to travel to the several regions of the United States. My fellow Southerners and I were glad not to face another four days and nights of train travel to the West Coast like some of our friends.

The point of discharge for my group was Fort Bragg, North Carolina. There the processing went smoothly until the very last debriefing session. When the officer in charge rose to say that this was the last time any of us could give official notification of any medical condition we had contracted during the war, a "barrack-room lawyer" stood up and said we would be fools not to list any complaint, however slight, for once we returned to civilian life, the Army wouldn't be interested. If any of us was ill or had a complaint, we weren't going to tell. Not one person raised a hand, so anxious were we to start on that last travel leg towards home. Our erstwhile "advisor", seeing no response to his words, muttered "Don't say I didn't warn you" and sat down.

Within 24 hours I was in Louisville again. It was like a dream world at first with no responsibilities and no cares. I had outgrown my old civilian clothing, but everyone turned a blind eye to mixed dress until I could go shopping. For the first time I appreciated just how severe were the injuries to my brother Floyd, and that he would never enjoy normal health again. Only then, too, did I learn how many of my contemporaries had lost their lives in the war. My younger brother, Harold, had grown up to be as tall as me during his Navy service. Like my father, his enthusiasm lay in things mechanical – including aircraft, to which he had been introduced during the war, and he was anxious to start his own business.

I found my home town, no doubt like many another scattered throughout the land, had also changed during the war. The same orderly grid pattern of streets remained, but there were many new houses and more planned. There were several new small industries, some created as part of the war effort, which assured virtually 100% employment. As I walked along the old familiar streets I tried to reassure myself that life would be much the same as it was before I had left. Inwardly, I knew it could not.

Now that I was home and Mary would soon be joining me, it was imperative that I find work. Recalling the prospect Mrs. Price, editor of our local weekly had expressed not long before I entered the Army, I made my way to her *News and Farmer* offices. She had earlier said that if I decided I wanted to live in Louisville when the war was over, she would do her best to find a place for me on her paper. Beyond that, she added, she could promise nothing. The hope that I might join the paper and perhaps one day succeed her, was my dream throughout the war. As I entered her office she greeted me warmly, asked when Mary would be joining me, and then answered my burning question before I could pose it.

"I realise you are anxious to know if there is a place for you here on the *News and Farmer*, as I had hoped there would be when you went into the Army."

I nodded.

"We are still a small paper," she continued, "with so little prospect of growth that I cannot see us taking on another full time employee. In addition, my son has recently said he wants to join us and naturally I must give him that opportunity. Under the circumstances, it will be impossible for me to take you on. I do hope you understand."

I did understand. Placed in the same position, I would have done the same thing. Nonetheless my dream of life as a country editor in my home town was over. I reeled from the blow. The days ticked by relentlessly, with the date of Mary's arrival becoming ever nearer. I now was forced to re-think my future. Whereas I had originally assumed life would proceed smoothly in my hometown, I was now in turmoil with no job prospect and by bride due to arrive shortly.

My parents suggested I try television, the new medium that was taking America by storm. But I lacked the technical know-how and did not relish becoming a student again at the age of almost 28. Besides, I still held firm my dream of working in a rural area, or at least in a role where I could make a useful contribution to improving the lot of rural Georgians. Little did I realise I had been catapulted headlong into a "wilderness" – one that would take me several years to emerge from.

59
Diary of a bridal voyage

Despite my qualms about the unknown, I had to put aside my concerns and concentrate on Mary's imminent arrival. I knew she was due to sail sometime in the first week of May aboard the Queen Mary. Her superb powers of observation and ability to translate what she saw into pithy prose struck me for the first time. These excerpts from her diary enabled me to share the highlights of her embarkation and voyage:

"**Saturday, 4 May.** We boarded yesterday and sail today. Rise at 7:15 and have bath in salt water. Had to use special type of soap, but could get no lather. Second sitting at breakfast; super fare. Sun really warm. Standing by railing I see two huge white gangways with several hundred people scattered over dock area. Dockhands, families of brides, police, Army officers and men. Dash to cabin and collect flags and bump into O'Donald's friend, Major Bob Hitchman, who wishes me "Bon Voyage". Get back in place by rail. Band now playing familiar songs, British and American – "I'm 21 Today", "Dixie", "Old Black Joe" and "Tipperary". See Major Hitchman on dockside and wave. Then spot Mummy and Daddy. They see me, wave – but Mummy is crying. I frantically chew gum; it helps enormously. One gangway is removed, then the other. Hooters sound and band strikes up the two national anthems. Unroll my two small flags. Daddy sees me and unrolls his so we can see each other to the last. Tugs now push the ship right around and we dash to opposite side to get last look. Then, ironically, large white ship bringing demobbed British soldiers back to Southampton blocks our view. They wave and shout, we respond, but what are they thinking? Then we pass many familiar landmarks – the great hospital at Netley, the oil refinery at Fawley, Lee-on-Solent, Ryde on the Isle of Wight and Portsmouth with the ferries running between them. I volunteer to help in nursery starting tomorrow. American Red Cross girl gives me huge white apron and measures me for pair of slacks. Spend several hours trying to cheer up crying babies and wiping dirty noses. Din is terrific. Meet some nice Canadian brides who tell me of feud between some American and Canadian wives. Seems so silly when we all come from Britain. Rumour goes round that ship's shops will shortly be open. Witness terrible queues. Poor girls are buying up everything! Glad O'Donald warned me to buy nothing except the odd sweet and toilet article. Some girls go crazy and buy huge quantities of chocolates and other sweets and miss dinner altogether. Go on duty at library at 8 p.m., but as five other girls also volunteered not enough to do for us all. We learn to check books out and in, then are told to come back tomorrow. Ship begins to toss. There are five of us in cabin. Decide to retire early.

Sunday, 5 May. Just manage to get to breakfast in time. Choose hot tea instead of coffee. Quite a few girls are seasick. Ship now rolling continuously. Someone suggests walking round promenade deck four times – this equal to one mile. Do so and feel a different person. Attend religious service in lounge. First hymn is old favourite, "Stand Up, Stand Up for Jesus". Chaplain warns all mothers to hold tightly to children to prevent their falling overboard. Ship's speed is so great we could never stop in time to save them. His message: we are all ambassadors to United States and Canada and wherever we went, whatever we did or said, would reflect on Britain. End with another grand old hymn, "Eternal Father Strong to Save". Go to stern and sea looks marvellous, as if one is looking at a picture, water everywhere, bluish grey and calm. The ship leaves a long straight line of foam behind it with waves of lighter blue with white tips. Someone says if we aren't seasick by tomorrow morning we won't get sick on the crossing. Wonder if I'll need medicine bottle of brandy Mummy packed for me.

At 3 p.m. on nursery duty again. Babies roaming out of control, screams worse than ever. On return to cabin, babies' yells still ringing in my ears, find brides' newspaper, *Wives Aweigh*, has been delivered by small boy. Apparently small boys of wives, equipped with impressive arm bands, used for delivering paper. The paper is duplicated, two pages printed on both sides. There are several drawings. One shows a mother and child gaily springing up the gangway in Southampton and later debarking exhausted at New York. Our route from Southampton to Halifax and New York is sketched across the bottom of one page. An arrow marks our present position; this is updated daily. Most items are for information of wives, but we also have snippets of world news. Several humorous contributions including this one: "Staff Nightmare: Blondes and brunettes, and babies booing and bawling all over the blinking, blooming, bouncing, bumping boat".

"Continue to be fascinated by the sea. As the waves rise up on the ship's sides, they break up into smaller ones. The colour of the sea is like washing a pen out in clean water after it has been filled with both green and blue ink in it. Wash and change for dinner, which turns out to be one of the tastiest. Chicken casserole, buttered squash, cauliflower, Hollandaise and roast potatoes. Write quick note to Mummy before the "Chaplain's Hour". Chaplain arrives, we sing several old hymns and learn lovely new American one: "The Little Brown Church in the Vale". After service we continue with singsong: "A Lassie from Lancashire", "I Belong to Scotland" and "The Lambeth Walk", among others.

"Now the lights are extinguished and the film "All Eternity" is thrown upon the screen. It shows England, just as I know and love so well – the old cathedral cities of Canterbury, Durham, Salisbury and Winchester among others. And Buckfast, and I think of our honeymoon.

And the English countryside with labourers tilling the rich soil, gathering the harvest and picking the fruit. But now it is 9:30 p.m., so walk a mile around the deck. The wind goes right through one, but I feel fitter than ever before … so to a salt bath and bed.

Monday, 6 May. Ship seems to be going faster and pitching more violently than before. Glad to get up on deck again after breakfast. Meet a "private passenger", businessman who was born in Switzerland and now lives in New York. We agree to walk round deck six times. He came often to England before the war. Tells me the *Queen Mary* carried 14,000 troops at the time during war without a convoy; was so fast it could out-manoeuvre anything. He gives me advice on Southern customs and traditions, including how to make a mint julep. Afterwards go to main lounge where see film on state of Washington. Red Cross girls divide us into groups according to states where we are going and then tell us about the states and invite questions.

"Retire to sun deck with book but it is too cold and spray is rushing overboard from all directions. At noon daily newspaper comes out; seems we are roughly halfway to Halifax. Spend entire afternoon in a different nursery, one with only very young babies who sleep in cots – or are supposed to. Unfortunately, about five out of the 15 cry constantly. Learn from the only other person there that one has to nurse them until they become quiet, then put them back in cot and pick up another. Eventually you get so good at it you can nurse two at a time. Afterwards visit cinema. For first time feel very sick.

Tuesday, 7 May. Awaken very early. Sea looks really lovely in early morning haze from two portholes by my bunk. Not many people turn up for breakfast. Attend morning service. We assemble again in groups to learn more about our respective states. Receive cable from O'Donald saying I should proceed to Atlanta, as he is unable to drive up to New York as originally planned. Wives discuss our Chaplain. Most like him, but some feel he is not circumspect enough. I think he is marvellous, having to deal with such a mixed lot. Now the Canadian brides are getting very excited for we will reach Halifax about noon tomorrow. Before going to nursery in afternoon, help blow up hundreds of gaily coloured balloons for children's party. Lounge looking very gay with streamers everywhere and tables set for wee folk, with jelly and milk set in cardboard containers. Masses of toys everywhere: hooters, bells, drums. Library duty for two hours; all books have to be returned by tonight. Then to nursery. Am beginning to get quite fond of some of the squalling infants. Dining hall decorated with paper chains and flags as this is last dinner aboard for Canadian wives. Celebration food too: turkey and cranberry sauce, the first we had since before the war. Everyone getting excited about sighting land tomorrow.

Wednesday, 8 May. Rise early and to celebrate arrival in New World, get my hair washed and set, after much waiting. Loads of slimy liquid thrown over head, presumably to combat salty water. Pay 7/6 for these labours. Attend devotion where three small babies are christened. Read for remainder of morning on deck so that I can see land as soon as it is in sight. Can't see anything for pea soup fog. Same at 11:30, and at 1 p.m. fed up, go to lunch only to find on return to deck that we are in outer harbour. Pouring rain and very cold. On land can see only masses of trees and green grass. As we near dock area, see huge signs reading "Welcome to your new home" and "Welcome to the port of Halifax". Many people standing on dockside, most probably husbands and parents-in-law of Canadian wives. A band strikes up "Here Comes the Bride". Debarkation not planned until 4 or 5 p.m. Go to nursery, find very few volunteers present, but number of babies greatly increased. Here meet a German Jewess married to a Canadian Indian who lives on an island off Canadian cost. She will be only white girl there. Her mother and father were killed by the Nazis.

"One of "my" babies was born 10 weeks premature, but amazingly had two teeth. Poor little soul; it is so very tiny. When nursing it, the head has to be held in a certain position. Nursery so hectic we few helpers are brought cup of tea and cake. Rush up to deck in time to see some of Canadian brides depart. Hardly anyone in sight now, it is so cold and still drizzling. Was hoping to see some of the girls fly into their husbands' arms, but no such luck. Some wives late in getting off, loud speaker calls name after name to report to orderly room. Bustle everywhere. After seeing film, walk to sun deck and top deck to see lights looking cheery all round harbour. Reminds me of lights of Portsmouth harbour from Gosport ferry.

Thursday, 9 May. Awake to find sun streaming in on me as I lie in my bunk. The many lights of Halifax, seen last night, leave little trace of civilisation by day. Tiny island opposite dock sheds has house built at its top. On it also there is the lighthouse which last night gave out a bright green light in all directions. Remainder of island covered in bright green grass. The entire bay looks very beautiful in the morning sunlight. There are few houses; all seem built of wood and painted white and red. Quite a number of people are watching from dockside, as a few Canadian wives disembark. The women look quite British, wear the same fashions, little make-up. The men look different, large hats and sloppy coats. As sailing not until 10 a.m., rush down to laundry which is ship's former swimming pool. Very efficient: plenty of hot water, wringers, heated dryers, ironing boards and irons. Back on deck in time to see gangway raised.

"Great commotion as several Royal Canadian Air Force officers are not yet off ship. Gangway heaved back in position, they leave and at last we are underway. Six tug boats push us round. Red Cross girl who went ashore says Halifax climate much behind England's, much colder, wetter here, flowers not in bloom, no leaves on trees. Do very little rest of day except read and nurse babies. After lunch have medical inspection. I find wonderful statement by Lt. Col. W.E. Sutherland, OBE, the Canadian officer commanding the Queen Mary's military personnel, in last issue of *Wives Aweigh*. "May I say to the wives proceeding to the United States," he said, "you are going to a wonderful country and a wonderful people. Carry high the ideals and qualities of citizenship that will always bring credit to the Motherland which raised you, and to America, the country of your adoption. Yours is a wonderful opportunity." Much hustling and bustling as we are due in New York at 2 p.m. tomorrow. All shops are closed, library closed, reminders everywhere that deck rugs have to be returned to stewards.

"Assemble in main lounge at 4:15 p.m. where an Army captain gives plan of action. Wives living in New York area, plus those who will be meeting husbands from elsewhere, will disembark tomorrow. Others (including myself) will remain aboard until Saturday. At 8.30 there is a "guest night" programme put on by some of the more talented wives. Begins with community singing, then different girls sing and dance. A girl from Manchester impersonates the well-known "Sam, Sam, Pick up thy Musket". The star turn is French bride who sings in both French and English while playing the accordion. She has to be a professional. Farewell parties everywhere aboard ship, for this is to be the last voyage of the *Queen Mary* as a bridal vessel.

Friday, 10 May. The day dawns fine, blue sky and sea calm. Seem to be gliding slowly through water. Spend entire morning on deck determined to get good view of land. Someone shouts "Land!" We seem to go into a large bay with huge tracts of land on either side. Am told that on left is New Jersey, that on right Long Island. Ship stops and pilot gets on. Move slowly on. Skyscrapers in the distance. Huge white letters on Coney Island for returning servicemen: "Welcome Home, Well Done". Above a plane circles, writing "Pepsi Cola" in the sky. Every ship we meet gives three short blasts. We return them, at intervals.

"Pass Statue of Liberty which once may have been grey, but has greenish look now. Looks smaller than I expected, or is it because of huge buildings opposite on Manhattan Island? The Empire State Building looks colossal with its silver top gleaming in the sunlight. Meanwhile everyone moving about on ship, orders come non-stop over loud-speaker. Am so thrilled with this beautiful harbour I forget lunch and ignore all that is taking place on board. Ship stops again and immigration officers climb aboard. Pass numerous piers on either side owned by various companies, including Cunard, White Star and many foreign ones. Many decorated with Stars and Stripes and welcoming signs. See huge cars going up and down roadways clearly, also coloured taxis. At certain points cars disappear into underground roadways.

"A fellow passenger points out the George Washington Bridge, then where we will dock. New Jersey side still looks very fresh and rural with its hills and trees. People waiting for ship on dockside, most are Army personnel. One man spots his sister in crowd and they converse in loud yells all time ship is manoeuvring into position. Women waiting at dockside are very neatly dressed. Just like film stars with feathers, flowers and other things sticking out of their hats in all directions. As we dock a band strikes up, surprisingly playing all jazz. Loads of soldiers and nurses come aboard while private passengers get off.

"After a while, wives disembark. Am surprised how smart they look, all have been saving special clothing for this stage of their arrival.

They really put up a great show, despite being severely rationed for many years. Had hoped to see them meet their husbands at end of gangway, but evidently they meet somewhere else. Wave farewell to all those I have come to know at Tidworth and on the voyage. They are so very excited, some have not seen their husbands for years. Some husbands were transferred only a few days after their marriage. In no time it is 4 p.m. and all who are to leave have departed.

"Photograph taken of wife whose name appears last on passenger list. She is very worried lest her husband sees photograph of her standing beside Army officer! Show passport to immigration officer, then return to deck. Sit in warm sun and look out over Hudson River at New Jersey. Ship seems so quiet and deserted, yet 78 wives remain on board. Dinner one hour earlier, after which told to go to writing room to get labels for disembarkation tomorrow. Go there at 7:40 a.m., catch train at 10 and will arrive in Atlanta Sunday morning. Worn out by queuing, go to sun deck for few minutes before retiring. Three great funnels of ship lit up by spotlights. Not so many lights visible on shore now. Even skyscrapers have only few lights here and there. After packing bag, get to bed at 11:30 p.m.

Saturday, 11 May. Arise at 5 a.m., dash down early to breaka. Awkward business of tipping stewards. Manage to get rid of surplus English money this way. Decide to give little man who looked after our cabin so well Mummy's bottle of brandy which was never needed. At 9 a.m. call comes for all "Blue Ticket" wives (my category) to assemble in main lounge. Rush there, am assigned to Group 6. A guide leads us to A Deck, then down gangway to dock where await line of men wearing strange cotton caps and look as if they are of many nationalities. One man assigns himself to each woman and with her help collects baggage and carries it to large waiting room. There we sit while popular music is played. Soon we are up again, taken to a large lift and then to a waiting bus which is similar to an English one, except that the front is a little more streamlined. The driver seems a little crazy, talks the whole time but to no one in particular. Says he has just come back from the southern states (wonder if they all are like this down there).

"Dash along at such a rate we hardly have a chance to see where we are going. Pass 7th Avenue and 9th Avenue and many others. All roads seem to be laid out in blocks. Pass some very poor areas with miles of shops burning bright neon lights, even early in morning. Girls look smartly dressed but don't consider them smarter than those in London. Some shops literally loaded down with fruit: bananas hanging in huge stalks, apples, oranges, grapefruit – oh everything one could wish for! Also shops with clothing, some exclusively for men, and so many selling jewellery.

"Everything glistening under bright lights. Then restaurants selling only steaks or only seafood. Cinemas open with people going in at 10 a.m.! Bus pulls into side street at entrance to a station. On sidewalk see many black men and women, mostly well dressed. Army officer boards bus, checks tickets, says all of us are bound for Georgia.

We must wait for quite a while until our train comes in.

"Just then there is a rap on the window. There is O'Donald's good friend, Captain Bill Ehlert, with whom we would have stayed the night had O'Donald been able to meet me in New York. Fall upon the man with great glee. Says he met *Queen Mary* yesterday hoping to get me off to see sights of New York and stay the night with his parents in New Jersey, but authorities would not agree. Chat with him until our train arrives, then we all file out into Grand Central Station. Reminds me of Waterloo Station in London, except seems newer and cleaner.

"Go somewhere underground, train rolls in and in we jump. Go to No. 4 Upper Berth and find myself seated opposite slightly older wife with most beautiful baby I have ever seen. Our coach holds about 20 people and we fellow Georgians keep together. The carriage has a corridor running down the centre. When berths not in use, seats are very wide and comfortable with just one person sitting opposite the other. Much like dining cars on British trains, except here no table in between. For our exclusive use is cloak room and large dressing room, latter extremely nice. Loads of things I have never seen before. Hot and cold water. Iced drinking water with paper cups which, when used, are thrown away. Paper napkins to dry face and hands with, large mirrors everywhere.

"Soon our Pullman car is off. We pass old car dumps and large ugly advertising signs, which I suppose are always on edge of cities. Then we come to countryside with many trees, lush pastures. We rush through huge stations and cities, then more countryside. Train going so fast we have to read or talk instead of staring outside. Many farm buildings have red and white colour schemes. Many of houses near our track have verandahs where people sit in rocking chairs, rocking to and fro."

Thus did Mary record her transatlantic voyage and her initial impressions of the United States. My brothers Floyd and Harold and I duly met her in Atlanta the next morning and drove the remaining 200 miles to Louisville, stopping briefly in Milledgeville for lunch. With her healthy complexion and lack of make-up, she looked the lovely English rose she was in the sunshine of that May morning. Despite a somewhat restless night on the train, she was full of life and expertly fielded the jokes and teasing my brothers tossed her way.

60
Mary passes muster

The crucial question for me was how my parents and friends in Louisville would accept Mary. My mother naturally had hoped I would return home a single man and choose a Georgia wife. I had not, and thus awaited her reaction ; Mary even more so, After some initial language trouble (it is not easy at the outset for people from the Deep South and southern England to understand each other), they soon were swapping experiences and planning adventures together.

A reminder of Mary's tearful parting from England came a day or two later when a letter arrived from her mother. It read, in part:

"We were terribly pleased to see you just at the last, sailing away to meet your dear Donald. We should have felt very bad had we not come to know him so well. We only felt badly because of our own loss of you. It will be very largely in your own hands to prove what the future will be. I am sure Donald will be a great help and comfort when you need him, and you must be ready to help him when he needs you, for we all have times when we want just a little extra touch of comfort from those we love. ... I would like to give you both a good hug. Mummy."

While awaiting developments in my job prospects, I had already taken a temporary job with a US public health programme to eradicate flies, mosquitoes and other insects from rural homes in our county. This involved visiting families and warning them that sprayers armed with DDT would be calling within the next few days. To prepare for this it was necessary to move all furniture and belongings to the centre of each room and cover them over with a sheet. After the spraying no one should go into the house until it had been thoroughly aired. There was no charge for the spraying. At that time no one knew the adverse effects of DDT but, that apart, even by the second year of the spraying programme some insects had become immune to the chemicals and continued to reproduce.

As Mary had seen so little of her adopted land since arriving in New York, I thought it would be an educational experience for her to accompany me occasionally and see the conditions under which rural Georgians lived. To my surprise, I found that during the war many white families had given up farming and moved into small towns. Likewise, black families who had sons in the armed forces discovered these young men no longer wanted to work on the land. Some migrated to the county towns like Louisville, some to the larger cities of the south such as Atlanta, and many to the populous cities of the north. When Mary and I made our DDT rounds, there were virtually no young black men to be seen.

Cotton, after the perfection of the picking machine, was no longer a labour-intensive form of agriculture. Consequently, job prospects for young black men were bleak. After their wartime travels, many now wanted higher education and opportunities for personal advancement. Their World War II experiences, albeit segregated, had also opened their eyes to new horizons in sports and the arts, as well as to future careers in the military services, industry and the professions.

So it was that Mary and I came across one black couple after another, devoid of their children and with little prospect of work themselves. Many of the farmers who once employed them had recently sold their land to large timber companies which, once new plantations were established, had no further need of labour. We found these couples bewildered and depressed, not knowing which way to turn. They welcomed the DDT sprayers who would rid their simple homes of insects and thereby slightly ease day-to-day discomfort, but their future outlook was forlorn.

One day we called at a small building, more a shack than a house, and found an elderly black woman living there alone. She said (and looked as though) she was nearly 100 and had been a slave when a young child. Her surname was Phinizy, given to her and her family by the white family of the same name which lived in east Georgia during the Civil War. She had helped to raise two generations of white Phinizys who kept in touch with her for many years after she had become free. Then, as they died, married or moved away, their visits to her ceased and she was forgotten. She spoke not with bitterness, but nostalgia.

Meanwhile, my mother was busy lining up "events" which would quickly introduce Mary to small town life in Georgia. First, however, a shopping expedition to nearby Augusta was essential, for the weather was now exceedingly hot and even her thinnest British clothing left Mary perspiring. For one who was only 15 when the war started and had never known ration-free shopping, Mary found the Augusta outing a bewildering experience.

"(Here I was in) my first American shop," she wrote in her diary, "and I was quite overcome. It was stacked with clothing such as one sees in fashion magazines. All frocks had much larger shoulder pads than English ones. Sizes did not go by bust measurement, as in England, but by set numbers like 14, 16, 18 and so on. Eventually we decided I was size 18, but by then I was practically worn out by the heat and there was not a scrap of energy in my body. Still dazed, I was taken from shop to shop. Eventually I accumulated a few frocks, some underclothing, a hat and a pair of shoes. It had been necessary for me to have a complete outfit because my first social engagement was the following day. On departing from Augusta I thought I would die from the heat, but just then a mighty thunderstorm broke and it immediately became cooler."

Mary's "introductory party" the following day, although pleasant and instructive, was in some respects also an ordeal. About 15 or 20 Louisville ladies, some not much older than she, had gathered at the home of family friends of long standing. Again, Mary's diary entry best describes the impressions of this first social exposure to the United States.

"The party was set for 11 a.m. and although my host's house was only 100 yards away, I was taken there by car. I was attired in a new dress, a green and black striped affair, a huge black straw hat, elbow-length black gloves, and despised black patent shoes with terrific heels. The house had a screened verandah in which I saw a number of ladies waiting and more in the living room. At first they struck me as models, for all were dressed superbly and were beautiful. My hostess, whom I had not met before, graciously introduced me to each guest in turn. There were so many I feared I would remember very few of their names. Finally I sat beside a charming young matron who couldn't have been kinder and more understanding. She spoke in a very soft Southern drawl. Many things I couldn't understand, but I mumbled "Yes" and hoped for the best. Meanwhile, I knew she was having just as much trouble with me.

"In a short time refreshments were served by the hostess, aided by two friends. I was offered a large variety of food on a large plate – salad, savoury patties, tiny cakes, frozen titbits and many other things. I managed to eat a fair sampling, but with difficulty, for there was such a mix of sweet and savoury. The drink was ice cold Coca Cola. Soon after, the ladies started drifting away by car, some to houses almost next door. I saw no one walking. It was, however, a delightful occasion, for most of the ladies were my own age and I was struck by the gracious manner in which they lived – very much like the southern ladies I had heard and read about before leaving Britain."

After this introduction, Mary was invited to a series of lunches – some given in honour of the upcoming wedding of Elizabeth Plaxco, daughter of the Louisville Academy headmaster and, as well, the local Presbyterian minister. Mary's diary records one of these occasions:

"As before, the house was beautifully decorated with flowers throughout. There were about ten guests besides myself, among them Elizabeth and her mother. After chatting among ourselves for a while, the hostess announced lunch was served and we were led into the dining room. Each place was accompanied by an attractive name card. Very soon a smiling, neatly dressed black woman began serving us; she was as efficient and quick as any servant I had seen in Britain. The meal was meant for the weather – nothing hot, but thin slices of Southern cured ham, congealed salad patties on lettuce leaves and homemade potato chips. The colour scheme of the dishes and the table arrangements made for a beautiful presentation. I had my first piping hot scones, called 'biscuits' in the South, to which we added butter. After ice cream, we retired for coffee in the sun lounge overlooking green sloping lawns and blooming borders of flowers."

Gradually Mary was getting used to a completely new diet.

"The most popular dishes in the South," she observed, "seem to be fried chicken and barbecue. Chicken would be served two or three times a week, with a great range of vegetables. Instead of potatoes, we often had rice with very thick, but delicious, gravy. The chicken was prepared by cutting up the bird into pieces, shaking them in a bag of flour and salt and pepper, and then frying them in deep fat. One ate as much as one could with knife and fork, then took the remainder and nibbled it with fingers – perfectly acceptable, apparently. At first when I did this I remembered those English kings doing the same thing.

"Unfortunately we were not given finger bowls and everyone's napkin got in a terrible state. Barbecue I tasted only once in those first weeks. It was pig, although chicken barbecue is also very popular in the South. The pig was prepared on a spit some distance from the house over red-hot embers. I learned that many Southern homes had these brick barbecue "pits" where family and friends assembled, usually in the evenings, for barbecues and wiener roasts. Most have rustic tables and seats and outdoor lighting to facilitate *al fresco* eating."

Mary passes muster

My mother and Mary attended the wedding of Elizabeth Plaxco and her husband, a former US Navy Chaplain who, like me, had been discharged from active service recently. This, the first American wedding for Mary, became etched in her memory because of its dignity and simplicity.

"The wedding took place at 3 in the afternoon," Mary wrote in her diary. "The church, Presbyterian, was quite new compared with English ones. It was small, yet the architecture was very beautiful. On our arrival, about 30 minutes before the service was scheduled, we were escorted to our pew about half way down the centre aisle by one of four ushers in US Navy uniform. The church was decorated with white lilies, complemented by groups of lighted white candles on the altar and in the windows. The tallest candles were in the centre of these groups, the smallest at the ends of the arrangements. White carpets had been placed in the aisles and ribbons attached to those pews reserved for the families of the bride and groom. The organist played softly until the bride's father, the Reverend M.R. Plaxco, arrived. Then the relatives arrived, the ladies dressed elegantly, wearing hats and corsages. Just as it would have been at home in Wickham, the whole town turned out for the wedding. Eventually there was the usual wait for the bride, with the bridegroom and best man also waiting nervously at the altar, each glancing frequently toward the door.

"Finally she arrived and there was silence as everyone turned to get a look at her. She really looked a picture in her white gown and flowing veil. She walked alone, slowly and stately, up the aisle, followed by a tiny bridesmaid dressed in pink, about six paces behind. Then came two small pages in white, carefully keeping their distance from those in front. Each of the pages carried a white satin cushion bearing the two rings for the ceremony. The actual ceremony was quite short. I was delighted with the custom of playing soft organ music while the vows were being said. After the wedding the little bridesmaid walked ahead of the bride, solemnly sprinkling rose petals along her path. It was altogether the loveliest wedding I had ever seen."

While my mother was busy introducing Mary to customs of the American South, I concentrated on some of the broader aspects – rural life, the economy, education, local government, and the judicial system. As it happened, a session of the Superior (Regional) Court was scheduled shortly after her arrival in Louisville. Most interest was centred on a murder trial, which Mary followed with some apprehension.

The defence attorney asked the invalid sister of the accused to take the stand in support of her brother. Utterly devoted to him, she tugged the heartstrings of all present by saying what a good child he had been and how, if the court were inclined to be lenient, she was sure he would "go straight" hereafter. The jury, however, was not impressed and found the man guilty and the judge sentenced him to death in the electric chair.

The accused took the sentence calmly, but his crippled sister screamed and tried to prevent her brother from being led away by the officers. For Mary, coming from England where capital punishment was a rare event, this came as "rough justice" and made her realise homicides and death penalties were much more common in America.

One day I proudly took Mary to meet Virginia Price, editor of our weekly newspaper, the *News and Farmer*. The two got along famously. To our surprise and embarrassment, Mrs. Price praised Mary's good looks and personality in her next weekly column, "Blooming Beauties". In one paragraph she quoted Leslie Stuart's well-known line, "Tell me, Pretty Maiden, are there more at home like you?"

In another reference, Virginia compared Mary with Greer Garson, who had starred in the 1942 classic, "Mrs. Miniver". The film caused so many Americans to empathise with Britain's war effort that Winston Churchill equated it's "power" as being worth six divisions.

The annual graduation ceremony of Louisville Academy, my old high school, occurred within a few weeks of Mary's arrival and this she also attended. Some features of the American high school graduation ceremony, taken for granted by me, she found fascinating. She had associated caps and gowns mainly with Oxbridge and other British universities, and was unprepared to see 18-year olds wearing them at a graduation exercise in rural Georgia. Although the cap-and-gown custom had originated in Britain centuries before, she was impressed that the ceremony was conducted with great dignity in my home town.

At about the same time college graduations were also taking place all over the United States. By coincidence, my old friend and mentor since my university days – Kendall Weisiger – was on the Board of Governors of a small college (Piedmont) in the foothills of Georgia's Appalachian region.

I had kept him informed about Mary since we first met and now he invited us to be his guests at Piedmont's commencement service. She jumped at the chance to meet him for she knew he had inspired me during my university years. They had already exchanged several letters. At the start of her letters she had called him "Daddy Whiz" – a reference to his energy and wisdom.

We three sat together in the open-air theatre that accommodated Piedmont's graduates and their families. Occasionally I caught snatches of speeches and the award ceremonies, but wondered how Kendall could have taken in anything given his lively conversation with Mary.

"Don't worry about the speakers" he said, turning to me, "the Seniors won't remember a word they are saying. All they want is their diplomas."

At length the ceremony was over. As mothers and fathers rushed to take photographs of their newly graduated offspring, Kendall turned to me with a twinkle in his eye and said:

"Your Mary – she's a lulu!"

61
Mary dares to serve English food in America

About this time I learned that my alma mater, the University of Georgia, offered a scheme whereby the wife of a former serviceman could enrol with him without paying full tuition. I was aware that the university's school of home economics operated "home management houses" as a kind of finishing-course for four years of academic work. This special course, normally open only to senior students, was offered during the summer quarter which would fit perfectly with my plans. Would the university, I wondered, permit Mary to attend this final course even though she had done none of the preceding four years' work?

I hurriedly contacted my old freshman dean, William Tate, and other university officials. In a matter of days word came back that Mary would, indeed, be welcome to attend the home management course, provided, of course, I was also enrolled at the university. As I planned one day to study for a doctorate in which I hoped to learn another foreign language (French I already knew), I enrolled in the summer German course.

Mary was thrilled and somewhat bewildered that the home economics school was willing to accept her "on faith". The only drawback to this otherwise ideal arrangement was that we could not live together. Only single students finishing off their four years of study were admitted to the homes; a young married couple among them would have been out of the question.

Accordingly, I took a room in a nearby boarding house and was content to see Mary only at weekends. More frequent visits would have been disconcerting to other course members, all about Mary's age but unmarried. Thus, we went one fine summer's day to enrol in our respective courses. Mary's goal was to learn all she could about American homemaking in the space of one summer while I would concentrate on my German.

Those weeks spent in Home Management House "A" were memorable ones for Mary. Miss Matilda Calloway, the resident house faculty member, happily took Mary under her wing and filled in many gaps in her knowledge about the American way of running a house. The other young ladies were kind, sympathetic and, most of all, brave. Brave because each young lady in turn assumed the various responsibilities for running the house; this meant, at some stage, Mary would be obliged to choose their food and, most frightening of all, prepare it!

Mary was sometimes amused, but more often terrified at these various "jobs" which I heard about piece-meal during our weekend meetings. Only later, when she shared her diary with me, did I get a better picture of her adventures. Her initial entry was a description of Home Management House "A":

"The house, built of red brick and with green shutters at the sides of windows, looks rather ordinary from the outside. Although my stay was during the hottest part of the summer, many flowering shrubs were still in bloom. On the left of the house is a veranda which connects the living room and dining room. White rocking chairs and a low, white table adorned the veranda. On entering the large front door, one sees an attractive entrance hall. To the left, an archway leads to the living room; to the right another archway through which is a small study whose bookshelves are loaded with references on cookery, needlework, gardening and everything else associated with managing a home. The glass-covered desk, chair and bench in the study are all Early American style.

"At the end of the hall is a door leading to the kitchen, the like of which I have never seen before. Cream walls, white ceiling and cream and white mottled linoleum on the floor. Although quite small, it boasts of 'having a place for everything and everything in its place.' Two doors lead from it: one to the outside, the other, which swings in either direction, goes into the dining room. On one side of the kitchen is the cooking unit (a gas stove) with work tables the same height and a variety of cupboards mounted on the walls for storing cooking utensils, cutlery, glass and china. On the other side is a large double sink over which are windows looking out over the lawns to some of the university buildings.

"Miss Calloway's private bedroom is downstairs, excellent planning, since it allows the eight women students to have the upper floor to themselves. The 'heart' of the house and its largest room, is the living room. Two large windows look out over the front lawn and French doors open to the veranda. Although centrally heated, there is an attractive fireplace with logs neatly laid on the fire-dogs. The room is made up of three sections: the 'writing area' with a desk, the 'conversational area' with a love-seat and chairs and the 'recreational area' with a radio and small library. Dust jackets are left on books to add colour and interspersed among the books are pieces of pottery and copper plates made by previous students in handicraft classes.

"Upstairs are four bedrooms, each with twin beds and two bathrooms. All are similar, furnished again in Early American furniture. As each student provides her own bedspread, this gives a pleasant variation in colour to the rooms. Except for the living room, which employed concealed lighting, the house was lit by overhead light and table lamps. I found it both intriguing and practical that chimes announced someone at the front door, a bell someone at the back. Thus we never made a mistake of going to the wrong door."

Such was the physical description of Mary's "home" that summer in 1946, surroundings totally different from the medieval house at Frith Farm which she had known since childhood. But what of Miss Calloway and the other seven young ladies? Her diary describes her new "family".

"Miss Calloway, our house director, was a very attractive person who seemed in her forties. Always neat in appearance with not even a hair out of place, she always wore freshly laundered linen dresses – a sight that made me feel cool however hot the day. She had been director of House 'A' for some years and was greatly loved and respected not only within the university but throughout the state of Georgia where her 'old girls' had gone to live. Hardly a week passed but some former student would drop by to see her. Miss Calloway's most treasured possession was 'Dopey', an ancient black car.

"The seven young ladies were a fascinating lot. One, a striking brown-haired girl who had won a beauty contest, was also a gifted seamstress. On more than one occasion she was seen to depart early on a Saturday morning to buy dress material, return home and set to work and wear the completed dress for dinner that evening. Another girl, noted for her wit, kept us in fits of laughter at meal times. On her first night at the house, she arrived late and when told that I was British, rushed in and awakened me. Was my husband, she asked, related to Hope Mays? When I replied "Yes", it transpired she had been a roommate of Hope's while the two were students at Georgia State College for Women in Milledgeville.

"The third girl, youngest of us all, was a brilliant student who had taken the prescribed courses in less time than normally required. She was renowned for her exclusive clothing, especially night attire. Another student, slightly older than the average, had been teaching in Savannah where she had acquired a glorious tan. A lovely girl with a mass of light brown curls, she was much admired for taking additional courses to enhance her future career.

"The other girls were friends of several years' standing. In many ways they were alike, including their long hair which, it seemed, they were constantly washing to make the best impression on their boy friends who either telephoned or turned up almost daily. By the end of the three months semester, both had become engaged.

"The last girl, Eunice, was my roommate. She, I surmised, was 'assigned' to me by Miss Calloway because she could get along with anyone. Like Millie, she had already started teaching, but returned to the university each summer to earn more academic credit towards higher qualifications. Her Southern accent was wonderful and was remarked upon not just by me, but everyone who called at the house. This, coupled with her dry humour, delighted all who came in contact with her. She had a steady boyfriend about whom I heard much."

The testing time for young ladies in the home management houses came when they had to perform the several obligatory jobs, ranging in importance from Maid to Homemaker. Not only was every movement keenly observed by the other seven girls, but Miss Calloway's sharp eyes also were everywhere noting favourable or unfavourable points that would contribute to the course grade.

"Being totally ignorant about American food, place settings and customs," wrote Mary in her diary, "I was made Assistant Waitress as my first job. Eunice was Waitress and helped me enormously. We rose at 7 to lay the table for breakfast, always served punctually at 7:30. We also laid the table for lunch and dinner and served the various courses. After the meals we had to clear the table, polish it and leave the dining room in immaculate condition. In between meals we had to collect and launder the soiled napkins and place-mats.

"It took me some time to get used to the position of the American silver, especially the salad forks and iced tea spoons. And those wretched iced tea glasses which are unknown in England. All of us had courses to attend, morning and afternoon, so we had to be fast and efficient with our house duties. I took a two-hour food course in the morning and a home nursing one in mid-afternoon. Three times a week all the girls in the four home management houses gathered for a lecture on homemaking by Miss Calloway.

"Every nine days we took on new responsibilities. My next job was Maid, not as hair-raising as waitressing but nonetheless demanding. I had to sweep and dust both upstairs and down, including the staircase, keep the bathrooms spotless and the house stocked with fresh, attractive flowers. The flowers were a problem. Whereas at Frith Farm we had a large garden filled with many species, here I was obliged to visit the large 'curb market' and select suitable flowers for the house. Worse was to come, for I was also charged with arranging them.

"Happily for me, most of the girls were gifted at putting together the right balance of blooms and foliage and they kindly shared their knowledge. The Maid's job also included answering the telephone and notifying the girls that their respective boyfriends wished to speak to them. I had two problems: making myself understood and mustering enough energy to rush up and down the stairs seeking out this or that girl. It seemed to me that the phone in this small house was ringing from morn to night."

In July, about midway through Mary's course, I took her for a weekend to Blairsville in the Appalachian Mountains of northeast Georgia. While there I dropped in on the owner-editor of the local weekly newspaper, the *Union County Citizen*, who had earlier indicated he might be willing to sell the publication. Mary was stunned by the beauty of the wooded mountain ranges and the purple haze which often hung over them. Everywhere in that part of North Georgia wonderful Indian place names prevailed - such as Hiawassee, Unicoi, Testatee and Walasiyi – for this had once been the home of the proud Cherokee Indian nation.

Only a few days after this visit to Georgia's mountains, a remarkable coincidence occurred. The *Atlanta Constitution* and Davison-Paxon, one of Atlanta's large department stores, announced an essay contest to promote tourism in the state. I persuaded Mary to enter while memories of her travel to the mountains were still fresh. Miss Calloway graciously consented that Mary could be excused from her homemaking courses in the unlikely event (as we all thought) that she won.

She entered the contest and won. The prize was a week's tour of the state in a private plane, accompanied by a *Constitution* reporter – photographer. She was feted everywhere she went with lunches, dinners and parties and the newspaper carried daily accounts of the sights she saw – among them, the Little White House at Warm Springs (where President Franklin D. Roosevelt died), St. Simon's Island, the Okefeenokee Swamp, gracious old Savannah and a glorious sweep of North Georgia's mountains from Clayton to Rome. When the week was over, she returned to Athens where Miss Calloway and the seven girls gave her a rapturous welcome.

Mary's next house assignment was Head Waitress, a task she found not overly challenging – thanks to the earlier tutelage by Eunice. Serving as Housekeeper also proved an easy chore, the main duty being to maintain the large living room in perfect order. This meant cleaning the rug daily and making sure all doors in the house were locked at night. Mary "escaped" duty as Baker, this having been scheduled during her tour. Secretly she was relieved, for she told me she had been fearful about producing those hot, light biscuits and home-made cakes and pies for which Southern ladies are so renowned.

The Cook's job turned out to be a nightmare, as Mary's diary reveals:

"I was hopeless and at times wondered how the others could put up with me. Cook was responsible for the main dishes, the Assistant Cook vegetables and minor dishes. Salads were my responsibility and they almost drove me crazy. I had never mixed mayonnaise with apples or pears, or raisins with carrots and placed them on a lettuce leaf. Either I would use too much or too little of one ingredient. I was amazed that all the others liked the strange mix of savoury and sweet.

"Another horror came at breakfast when, it seemed, each girl wanted her eggs prepared a different way. At Frith Farm we all liked scrambled eggs cooked in a communal saucepan. The first morning I served scrambled eggs cooked in the English style, but hardly a soul touched them. Miss Calloway, anxious not to waste good food and also to speed up my American cooking knowledge, kindly gave me a helping hand. I learned that some people like their eggs fried hard, some soft, others scrambled and, a few, poached. It was both time-consuming and nerve-wracking getting the eggs just right. Fried chicken also was a new venture for me; roast chicken, English style, was not nearly so popular."

The position of Homemaker was made difficult because it entailed planning, budgeting and actual shopping with cash. Mary's words describe the onerous responsibility that befell her:

"A draft of menus for the next nine days had to be prepared and cleared with Miss Calloway. I was given a cheque for $45 (about £20 at that time) which was deemed sufficient to feed the nine house occupants for a week. Accompanied by Miss Calloway, I went to the bank and exchanged the cheque for cash; this incidentally introduced me to the American banking system. We then visited a large supermarket where Miss Calloway advised me about quality and quantity, constantly referring to our limited budget. At last, we had bought everything on the list and had a few pennies left over.

"In the days that followed I was given permission to prepare several English dishes. Naturally the first I chose was roast beef and Yorkshire pudding, with vegetables. Alas, my English recipe was in ounces and pounds, and the kitchen was equipped to measure only in cups and spoons. My estimates were not very accurate and by the time the Yorkshire pudding reached the table it looked quite dejected. By the time we served it with the beef, it had become so hard only a few brave souls could manage to chew it. For dessert I had prepared English treacle tart, but as golden syrup did not exist in the United States, I had to substitute the popular American "Karo".

"The end result was similar to that of the Yorkshire pudding. These setbacks, and others, caused me to spend all of the allotted $45 except 15 cents by the end of my tour as Cook, whereas most of the girls prided themselves on saving several dollars.

In the closing weeks of the term, the young ladies were required to organise a variety of social functions that would prepare them for similar occasions the rest of their lives. These ranged from a Sunday morning breakfast party to full scale dinners with written invitations, place cards and all the rest. The girls were allowed to invite their boy friends, which all did – resulting in the house being swamped with flowers for these social events. In addition, each of the four houses had to 'host' another house during the term, an exercise that required being good guests for a change. When House 'A's turn came, Betty suggested a watermelon feast to which House 'C' would be invited. Everyone thought this a great idea.

"Miss Calloway and Betty went to the Athens market," Mary recounts, "where they spotted a truck loaded with watermelons parked in the street. They set to work banging the melons with their fingers to see if they were ripe – an art, I am told. Amazingly, every one they chose turned out to be superb. The cutting was held on the lawn in front of the house. By eight o'clock when the guests arrived, the moon was shining brightly – most romantic for the girls and their boyfriends. Girls from the two houses led us in games for about an hour, and then we partook of the watermelons. A quarter of a whole one on a tray with a fork – very tasty, very sweet!

"Each girl was expected to contribute something 'creative' to the house or garden before the term ended. One made mats for the dining table, another tea towels, and still another repainted the small trays which we used often in the garden.

"For myself," Mary recounted, "I decided upon a herb bed in the garden, as I was such a chump at crafts. A suitable space was found which I dug and filled with a variety of herbs suitable for use in the kitchen. Unfortunately, August was not the right month to start a bed of any kind, so I had to water the plants constantly."

The memorable summer ended with Mary reeling from culture shock. Before her arrival in Athens she had barely been introduced to life in the American South; then, at the University, she had been tossed head-long into the home management course normally reserved for final-year students. Her lasting impression of that summer would be the overwhelming kindness extended to her. Her biggest adjustment was no longer adapting to American home-making, but coping with daily temperatures of 90 to 100 degrees which prevailed during most of the summer and early autumn months. The hot weather was no problem for me as I carried on with my study of German.

By the time Mary's courses ended I had acquired, after much soul-searching, the *Union County Citizen* in Blairsville. It was a weekly with a circulation under one thousand. Even with an increase in circulation and commercial printing, I could not hope for more than a 'holding operation' because the population base was so low. Like the young Buddhist committed to begging as a test of his faith, I had determined from my university days to commit a portion of my early life to the grand old state of Georgia, even if I could earn more working elsewhere. In addition, here was a chance, albeit of limited duration, to live in the Southern Appalachians – my favourite region of the American South. But was I right, I asked myself, to pursue my idealism at the risk of imposing austere living conditions upon the dear girl who had left her family and home in England to marry me? With typical enthusiasm, Mary said "Let's give it a try!"

It took a decade, however, to provide the answer to my moral dilemma. It was a difficult period for, like many servicemen returning to civilian life after the war, I found the world had changed drastically. I was to undertake five jobs – some in America and some abroad – before my restlessness was assuaged and my purpose in life became clearer.

Meanwhile I determined to make the most of my love affair with Appalachia – however short it might be.

62
Mary narrowly escapes the great Winecoff Hotel fire

Housing was impossible to find in Blairsville itself, but we heard that a small cottage – just over a mile outside the town – was available. We obtained directions, saw the house and decided on the spot to take it. It was unpretentious, but adequate for our needs. It overlooked Round Mountain, less than a mile away, which we once set out to climb. When Mary was attacked by angry hornets after we disturbed their nest, we promptly abandoned the trek. Almost within view was Georgia's highest mountain, Brasstown Bald (4784 feet), which we ascended many times by car during our stay in Union County.

Our simple home had one unusual feature we have not enjoyed before or since: a private water supply from a nearby mountain spring fed into the house by a half-inch pipe laid across the ground through the adjacent pine trees. Mountain water is delightful at any time, but those who – like us – had it piped into their homes were indeed fortunate.

Our immediate neighbours were the Foxes and the Bowlings and from them we learned a great deal about the ingenuity of mountain folk in providing most of their basic needs. Mrs. Fox seemed to have a child almost every year, judging by the "step-ladder" heights of her happy brood, but neither the child-bearing nor the child-raising appeared to dampen her energy and enthusiasm. Although slender in the tradition of mountain women, she was nonetheless hardy and we never knew her to have anything but a cheerful outlook on life. When the time came for making sorghum syrup, there she was pulling her weight with the men folk.

The Bowlings, while past the age of rearing children, nonetheless practised frugality and between them kept alive a host of old crafts and customs. Mrs. Bowling was not merely content to preserve home-grown foods, but made the family butter in an old fashioned urn in which the cream was stirred by a long-handled paddle. She took the wool (sheared from her husband's sheep) and spun it on her spinning wheel, afterwards knitting useful wear against the cold north Georgia winters. As well as providing the essentials for the family table, Mr. Bowling grew his own tobacco. We never failed to visit these neighbours without coming home the richer for the knowledge and wisdom they had proffered.

Within days of Mary's arrival in Blairsville, the Georgia tourist department asked her if she would undertake a speaking tour of the state based on her recent week-long trip and any other impressions. We discussed what seemed a wonderful opportunity for her to see more of the state and agreed a schedule that allowed one or two speaking engagements each week for the indefinite future. She began the tour but usually managed to join me at weekends to help with distributing the paper.

On one such weekend we made a trek which I had long dreamed of, a hike on the nearby Appalachian Trail. In England I had once humorously suggested we could walk the entire 1,900 mile route from Georgia to Maine as our honeymoon. Now, however, we set a more modest goal of less than 20 miles, the distance from Neel's Gap to either Testatee Gap or Unicoi Gap (depending on progress made) and return. Armed with the official handbook, indispensable for locating lean-to shelters, springs and other essentials, we set out the first weekend in October when the hardwood trees were in their autumn glory. We carried a pair of old Army sleeping bags, enough food for two days and a water bottle. I wore Army "fatigues", Mary her Land Army uniform. For added warmth, we each carried heavy jackets. As the forecast was for fine weather, we left raincoats behind – sometimes a foolhardy move in the Appalachians.

The route we had chosen was in the heart of Georgia's former "Cherokee country". At Neel's Gap, our starting point, we were reminded of this past by a marker which read:

"WALASI-YI. This gap, according to Cherokee myths, is the abode of Walasi – the "Great Frog" – leader of the ancient animal council. Until 1926 it was known as Frogtown Gap and was traversed only by the Frogtown Indian Trail. Blood Mountain, on the west, is the home of Nuunchi, friendly spirit folk of the Cherokee. Blood and Slaughter mountains form a traditional battle site upon which the Cherokees defeated the Creeks. (Now called) NEEL'S GAP. Elev. 3125 ft."

Our first objective was a mountain called Levelland because of its flat, bald summit. Its altitude was 3,942 feet, one of Georgia's highest. From its summit we could see many miles in most directions. We paused to take in the vast, beautiful peaks and valleys around us, forgetting the timetable we had set. We had climbed over 800 feet since leaving Neel's Gap, but it had taken longer than we planned. Unfortunately for our morale, we could see Cowrock, the next mountain we had to climb, ahead of us. It seemed only a mile away, but to get there we had to pick our way down Levelland, cross a gap and then climb again – a distance our handbook told us was three miles. Midway across the gap between the two peaks was a bare "knob" where we paused for lunch. Famished, we quickly gulped down our sandwiches and then stretched out on the sleeping bag to rest our tired bodies. In no time at all Mary was sound asleep. Cruelly, I shortly had to rouse her so that we could continue.

Our packs seemed twice as heavy as we began the ascent to Cowrock. We had already been introduced to "switchbacks" (in England, sometimes called "zig-zags") by which one constantly reverses direction in climbing or descending a mountain. Here were more, with metallic Appalachian Trail markers or the familiar phosphorescent paint smudges on tree trunks, to keep us on the path. Rustic wooden signs reading "H_2O" told us of nearby springs where we could replenish our water supply. We startled half a dozen pigs who no doubt used the gap area as a feeding ground. Eventually we reached the summit of Cowrock where I discovered a benchmark indicating a height of 3,867 feet, a fact I proudly announced to Mary.

"The altitude of Cowrock or any other mountain," she tersely wrote in her diary, "meant nothing to my tired and aching body at that time."

Shortly after this we came upon another H_2O sign, this time painted on a large rock on the ground. After much pleading, I got Mary to agree to stretch out on the ground with her tongue hanging out, as if gasping her last breath with an oasis in sight, for my camera. In later years, she was to tease me unmercifully for making her assume this "corny" pose.

We shortly arrived at Testatee Gap, through which ran the original road connecting points north and points south. Before the white man came to North Georgia, an Indian trail had also traversed the gap. Although the old route had not been in use for many years, its route could be clearly discerned because of its stunted tree growth.

By this time the sun had almost set and we knew, to avoid getting lost, we should find the lean-to shelter that our handbook said was close by. We found it not too far from the benchmark indicating the highest point of Testatee Gap. It was a superb structure, built by the US Forest Service, large enough to accommodate seven or eight people. It had two sides, a back and a roof, with the exposed side facing a handsome stone fireplace which we were honour bound to use to avoid forest fires. The builders of the fireplace had ingeniously added wings on either side of the fire-pit to reflect heat off the fire into the lean-to. Closer examination revealed an iron grill at the rear of the cooking area. Surely hikers could not wish for more!

Night was fast coming on and we had two urgent needs, firewood and water. Mary agreed to look for the wood and I retraced our steps on the trail to the point where we had seen the sign for a spring. The spring was there all right but badly silted and covered in leaves. Moreover, its low retaining wall had been broken on one side, possibly by an animal or previous hikers. It took me several precious minutes to clear the spring and rebuild the gap in the little wall. Fortunately I had taken a torch and so made my way back to Mary, arriving much later than planned. She had built a fire in my absence, having found a bountiful supply of fallen branches nearby. We had brought along an old coffee tin for making coffee. When we added coffee to the boiling water a few minutes later, a glorious aroma permeated the camp site. We placed potatoes, covered in mud, in the embers of the fire. It seemed to take ages for them to cook, but we were in semi-paradise and it didn't matter.

Sleep came easily until the cold mountain air descended upon us. Despite our sleeping bags, we found it difficult to keep warm without continuously stoking the fire. Fortunately Mary had collected plenty of firewood but it seemed we were getting up every few minutes to replenish the flames. At the crack of dawn I made another tin of coffee. After a hearty breakfast, we decided to forego the Unicoi Gap leg and began to retrace our steps to Neel's Gap. Amazingly the views seemed entirely different as we leisurely made our way back. Soon we were back at our little home, after a wearying but delightful variation in our lifestyles.

Mary's speaking engagements continued unabated. Sometimes she returned home at the weekend laden down with gifts from her hosts. For example, after she spoke at LaGrange, home of the famous Calloway Mills (and later Calloway Gardens), she was given enough towels and face cloths to last us a lifetime.

In late November Mary began to have periods of not feeling well. She seemed perfectly fit and had not, to the best of her knowledge, been near anyone with flu or a virus. This was worrying, for the most important talk of the series was scheduled for Atlanta in early December. Much planning had gone into this appearance by the state tourist agency organiser and Mary did not wish to let him down. As the December date approached, her condition fluctuated. On some days she felt miserable, on others normal.

She was booked to stay the night of December 6th in Atlanta's renowned Winecoff Hotel. When she was preparing to leave Blairsville for Atlanta earlier that day, she became extremely nauseated. Seeing she was unfit to travel, and definitely in no condition to speak the following day, I hastily telephoned the tourist agency organiser. He was devastated for there was no time to make alternative programme arrangements.

The next morning we awoke to hear on the radio that the Winecoff Hotel had been razed by a fire in which 119 people had lost their lives. To this day the Winecoff casualty total remains one of the world's greatest sustained in a hotel fire. Tragically, the dead included a large group of high school students who had come to Atlanta to take part in a mock exercise of state government. Among these was the daughter of Georgia's Lieutenant Governor. It was not until Mary and I had digested the horror of the fire, however, that it dawned on us that the tragedy could have affected our own lives. Was it possible, we wondered, that the room reserved for Mary was in the hotel's burnt out area?

With some foreboding because of our unpleasant telephone conversation the previous day, I called the state tourist director. This time he spoke in a measured, calm voice:

"Yes", he said, "your wife's room was on a floor that was completely gutted. Her sickness, whatever it was, saved her life."

63
The people of Appalachia

That day Mary saw Doctor Welborn who, after a few questions and a brief examination, pronounced her pregnant. Angela, at precisely the right moment, had begun her life, thereby saving her mother's.

Although Mary's morning sickness meant her days of travel and speaking were over for the time being, we had no regrets when we pondered how close she had come to losing her life in the Winecoff Hotel fire. Doctor Welborn calculated the baby would arrive during the first week of July. By that time I knew we would be obliged to move from Blairsville, given its distance to the nearest hospital and the jeopardy to which Mary and the baby would be subjected should an emergency arise.

Then came a sudden economic reason which put an end to my hopes for expanding the size of *The Citizen*, a plan that would have provided more income. My linotype operator, with only a week's notice, quit to join the Georgia state police. No local replacement could be found and the acute shortage of housing precluded hiring someone from a distance. I was thus obliged to have the newspaper printed in adjacent Fannin County, where two brothers, Luther and Lewin Cobb, generously agreed to produce my paper each week as soon as their own journal had come off the press. This drastic limitation to our future income potential plus Mary's pregnancy meant our days in Blairsville were numbered.

Nonetheless, while awaiting a new work opportunity, we determined to make the most of our remaining stay in one of the most beautiful areas of the Southern Appalachians.

During my pre-war work on the *Cobb County Times*, I had learned about the importance of rural correspondents to the success of country weekly newspapers. They were the eyes and ears of their respective communities, reporting both fact and gossip and, when it seemed appropriate, advice. If anything, the correspondents writing for *The Citizen* were even more alert and audacious, qualities that enhanced the liveliness of the paper's columns.

These snippets from the paper's correspondent in the hamlet of Coosa were of interest not just to residents of that community but also to our general readership:

"Wood cutting seems to be the order of the day in our section."

"A singing school began at the Baptist Church Monday night. If the cold weather only lets up, it is bound to be a great success."

"Quite a bad accident at Hemptown Saturday. Better be careful, boys; cars aren't made with wings."

The lady correspondent from another village, Choestoe (not far from Cowrock Mountain which Mary and I had climbed), gave this intimate report of community life toward the end of the summer:

"It seems we are all back on schedule again. Some have returned to school, some to farming, others saw-milling and some are away at occupations in other places."

"The cool nights and fine days are causing the fodder to turn brown and when it is pulled off and the bare ears of corn (maize) exposed, we realise autumn is here."

"The whooping cough epidemic in this area is subsiding somewhat now."

"Lots of good luck, everybody."

At that time Georgia's state school superintendent was M.D. Collins, a Union county native. He had many relatives in the county and the highlight of their social life was the family reunion, usually held every year or two in late summer. The correspondent from this rural community posed the dilemma of those who would like to attend the reunion, famous for its sumptuous food but whose links with the Collins family were tenuous:

"All the people in our locality", he wrote, "are trying to find some 'Collins blood' in their make-up so they can attend the Collins family reunion Sunday. Most of them won't have to search too far back, for many are kin."

Our county, Union, is in that part of northeast Georgia and the Southern Appalachians where many place names were assigned by the original American inhabitants, the Cherokee Indian tribe. They gave us such beautiful names as Hiawassee and Nacoochee. Then, in the early part of the 19th century came the pragmatic Scotch-Irish settlers who left their mark with no-nonsense names such as Dead Man's Creek, Roaring Fork and Briar Knob. Although the Cherokees were evicted by the state of Georgia to form the infamous "Trail of Tears", their distinctive place names survive to remind us that this was once their homeland. Only at a reservation in western North Carolina are the Cherokees to be found in substantial numbers in the South. Here they regularly enact a pageant depicting their forced exodus from the mountains.

The Southern Appalachian custom of employing verbs for nouns and nouns for verbs, or a combination of the two, still prevailed when Mary and I were in Blairsville. Horace Kephart, in his classic 1926 work, *Our Southern Highlanders*, gave examples such as "That bear'll meat me for a month" and "Josh ain't much on sweet-heartin'." I was surprised, when occasionally standing in as a substitute teacher, to hear variations of these speech forms from Blairsville high school pupils. For example, when a certain boy was absent one day, I asked if anyone knew why. A girl in the rear of the classroom promptly shouted: "Oh, he got bus-left."

Blairsville in particular and northeast Georgia in general have now become prime retirement areas for Americans, but in our day the area had not altered greatly from Horace Kephart's time. Poor roads and the absence of television combined to preserve the area's customs and traditions to a remarkable degree. Self-reliance was the driving force that enabled mountain families to eke out livelihoods from the rocky soil. Those who lived in valleys fared better. Some mountain families living near streams or springs built "springhouses" over them from local stone to preserve their eggs, meat, milk and other home produce.

Ed Mauney, a likable Blairsville character, knew the old ways of mountain living were fast disappearing and so set up a kind of museum in his home. His collection included an ancient fiddle, made in Blairsville 75 years earlier by William Lawrence; two fine steel knives from the time when the cutlery craft flourished locally and an ancient dulcimer, the "Queen" of Appalachian musical instruments. Ed's items were not confined to those that once belonged to Scotch-Irish settlers; he also had a fine assortment of Indian relics, among them bows and arrows and bats and balls used by the Cherokees in their version of baseball.

"Uncle Boney" Colwell, then 93, was another highly respected character who could remember events going back to the Civil War. Before automobiles were invented he would take 12 days to make the return trip to Atlanta (115 miles) to dispose of his wagon load of farm produce. Neither he nor his father believed in slavery. Union county was one of three in north Georgia that traditionally voted for the Republican party. Nonetheless, as he told me, not everyone in the county rushed to side with the North during the war: "I'm ashamed to say there was many a man who hid out in these mountains when it came time to fight."

Blairsville also had its village "smithy", Marion Jackson, during our time. He thought horses would last longer in the mountains than elsewhere because of the difficult terrain, but admitted his craft was already a dying one. He said this with a sense of nostalgia, for his father and grandfather had been blacksmiths before him. Of all the smithy's challenges, he said none equalled that of shoeing a club-footed animal. "Seldom are there ready-made shoes that will fit club-feet", he explained, "so we first have to take a pattern and then make shoes to order."

Another local personality was Jake Plott, member of a family of the same name found in many parts of the Southern Appalachians. Jake knew all about mountain animals and herbs and earned his living from selling hides and medicinal plants. In 27 years he had prepared and sold an estimated 200,000 skins. When I visited him, the cellar of his house was filled with drying racks containing pelts of the 'possum, muskrat, raccoon, mink, weasel and skunk. Among the medicinal herbs he found that ginseng, then rare but once found widely in the Southern Appalachians, was most in demand.

Tourism at that time was virtually non-existent. Industries were few and most were based on timber. One such was a small mill that made blocks of wood from which textile shuttles were fashioned. W.A. Owensby, who owned the local mill, told me he used only dogwood for making the shuttle blocks. I asked why.

"From long experience textile mill operators have found that dogwood is best for shuttles because, when they wear slick, they do not fuzz up the thread," he said. "A goodly number of my blocks wind up as shuttles for textile mills in England."

Unexpected drama came to our sleepy mountain village when a US Marine Corps fighter plane crash-landed in the mud flats adjacent to Nottely Lake, just outside Blairsville. The pilot, a handsome young major, hit the top of the bridge's railing as he was about to land, almost causing the plane to crash at that point. He nonetheless made a safe, if bumpy landing and emerged unhurt. His home base was several hundred miles away in eastern North Carolina, a distance which meant the Marine Corps's recovery team would take two days of tortuous driving over narrow mountain roads before it could reach Blairsville.

With nothing to do but wait, the major made himself at home under the shady trees of the hotel opposite *The Citizen*'s office on the town square. The hotel owner, Bob Christopher, provided him with a rocking-chair and before long the major was completely at home with the other townsmen addicted to the rocking-chair habit. For the best part of two days he thrived on his enforced leave. It was with a look of genuine sadness that he heard the approaching sound of mighty diesel engines lugging a heavy crane and other rescue gear into the square. The team soon set to work but it was late afternoon before the aircraft had been hoisted from the mud flats. This meant staying the night in Blairsville.

Word soon got around that the major and his rescue team, made up largely of handsome young Marine Corps sergeants, would be staying in the hotel that night. Eligible maidens rushed to the hotel to make unnecessary purchases in the hotel's little gift shop. Then came an invitation from a lakeside fishing camp owner for the entire party to be his guest for an evening of fishing and fun. The major was sorely tempted to accept but, if he did so, he knew there would not be the slightest chance of achieving the dawn departure already scheduled. To the dismay of the rescue team, the offer was declined. Next morning the major abdicated his temporary citizenship of Blairsville and departed with his glum rescuers.

One day Mary and I met Union County's most prominent literary figure, a young poet named Herbert Byron Reece. Soft-spoken and shy, he had already come to the attention of Ralph McGill (editor of the *Atlanta Constitution*) and academics at nearby Young Harris College. Dozens of his poems were published in literary journals nationwide and he seemed destined for greatness. Awards and honours followed and his fame continued long after Mary and I left Blairsville. Sadly he took his own life at the early age of 40.

Living in the mountains of northeast Georgia allowed Mary and me to visit and study much of the TVA (Tennessee Valley Authority) region, created in 1933 as part of President Franklin D. Roosevelt's massive public works programme. The project, encompassing a flood-prone area of about 50,000 square miles in seven states, saw several dams constructed across the Tennessee River and other large Southern Appalachian streams.

Besides helping to control floods, the dams generated electric power and, in the process, created large inland lakes for recreational activities. Unquestionably this massive project had improved the lot of millions residing in the TVA region.

64
For a difficult labour, try fresh peaches

Although it was a great emotional tug to think of leaving Georgia's most scenic area after such a short sojourn, I had no hesitation in accepting an offer to become editor of *Rural Georgia*, a new monthly magazine for members of Georgia's rural electric cooperatives. In the spring of 1947 I disposed of *The Citizen* to a nearby weekly newspaper and moved to the town of Monticello – not far from the geographical centre of Georgia. The town was a hub from which major roads led in all directions, a necessity because my work would entail travel to all parts of the state in search of model farmers about whom I could produce photographs and feature articles.

I entered upon my new editorial responsibility with zeal and enthusiasm. The goal of helping Georgia's farmers to enjoy a higher standard of living perfectly fitted with the ideals I had first developed at university; now I had the opportunity to put them into practice.

It was Henry Grady, the legendary editor of *The Atlanta Constitution*, who most inspired me. He coined the phrase "The New South", by which he meant a region no longer laid low by poverty, but one which would rise 'by its own boot straps' to new heights of progress and prosperity. I reproduced on *Rural Georgia*'s letterhead Grady's ambitious hope for Southern farmers:

"THE FULLNESS OF OUR DAY – wherever farmers in the South shall eat bread from his own fields and meat from his own pastures, and be disturbed by no creditor and enslaved by no debt; shall sit amid his teeming gardens and orchards and vineyards and dairies and barnyards, pitching his crops in his own wisdom and growing them in independence... getting his pay in cash and not in a receipted mortgage that discharges his debt, but does not restore his freedom – then shall be the breaking of the fullness of our day."

When my school of journalism at the University of Georgia was casting about for a name, Henry Grady readily came to mind not only as a great editor but an idealist who envisaged a South that would one day rise phoenix-like from the ashes of the Civil War. He did not live to see his dream come true but he inspired thousands of young people like myself to lead purposeful lives. Meanwhile, Mary and I had our present-day mentor, Kendall Weisiger, who was to rekindle our enthusiasm over the coming years by his ever-optimistic outlook and treasured advice.

From Monday to Wednesday for three weeks of each month I travelled with my Speed Graphic camera visiting farmers throughout the state. They had been recommended to me as "models" by their local REA (Rural Electric Administration) managers. The common theme of these features in *Rural Georgia* was to show how the coming of electric power to rural homes and farms had benefited farmers and their families. This was not difficult to document, for there was general agreement that, apart from cars and tractors, electricity had added more to the quality of American rural life than anything else.

Now it was possible to use labour-saving devices such as electric milking machines. In the farmhouse women and children now enjoyed benefits of electric stoves, home freezers, washing machines and other appliances. On returning home from these model farms I could prepare feature articles for the next issue based on the interviews and photographs I had obtained.

Mary, meanwhile, maintained the mailing list (tens of thousands) by deleting names of farmers who had changed addresses and adding those newly connected to the electric co-ops. Once a month she printed great rolls of labels on the addressing machine in our apartment. When my photographs were processed and the magazine's text and advertisements were edited, I set off to the printers where I spent the greater part of two days giving instructions and overseeing the preparatory work. The printers then took over the labelling and mailing of each issue.

In the course of these duties I was obliged to travel to most of Georgia's 159 counties. Always aware that the state was the largest east of the Mississippi River, I now lived that reality in my weekly travels. The long trips were wearying but they allowed me to see parts of the state not visited previously and to make many new friends. The greatest downside was leaving Mary alone so often.

On several occasions I was able to combine business with pleasure. One such time took me to an Atlanta convention of REA executives during which, in my spare time, I was able to show Mary some of the city's sights and also drop in on our dear friend, Kendall Weisiger.

Kendall did not drive but insisted on our taking several excursions together to some of Atlanta's attractions by street car. In those days the city's suburban housewives used the street car for their midday shopping and it was a common sight to see them returning home hours later laden down with parcels and bags from the city's department stores.

It was on such an excursion that Mary was subjected to a spell of good-humoured teasing the like of which she had not experienced before or since. A popular song of the day was "My Sugar is so Refined", in which the girl in question was referred to as "one of those high-class kind" who preferred to say "dress" instead of "frock" and so on. Seated beside Mary, Kendall began singing this song in a voice loud enough to be heard by all the lady passengers. Mary blushed coyly at first but when all the ladies fell silent and turned toward her she reddened deeply, protesting.

Unfortunately for her, Kendall knew all the verses and mercilessly persisted with his singing to the bitter end. When he finished, the lady passengers gave him a hearty round of applause while Mary buried her face in her hands. She was, of course, secretly delighted that Kendall had again lived up to her epithet, "Daddy Whiz", which was to remain his "family name" for as long as he lived.

The weeks and months flew by and I realised we had not yet made arrangements for the birth of our first child. As there was no hospital in Monticello, we decided the baby would be born in nearby Madison. This town is one of several in Georgia possessing a number of 'colonial style' homes dating from before the Civil War.

Because Madison was not on the route of General Sherman's march to the sea, most of its homes survived. Every year thousands of people came to see these gracious houses. Our focus in Madison, however, was on a small rural hospital owned by a Doctor McGeary. Located only a minute's walk from the town square, where old men and young boys joined in leisurely games of checkers under shady trees, the hospital served an area extending well beyond the town's borders.

Doctor McGeary had given us an estimated date of arrival for our first-born and I accordingly arranged my work schedule so as to be at home at the time. It had not occurred to me, however, that one of Mary's gastronomic adventures could affect the date.

Monticello's county, Jasper, at that time still produced delicious free-stone peaches, for which Georgia and other southern states are famous. The local packing shed and its associated plantations were largely operated by the Henderson family. Those peaches intended for shipment to northern states and other distant destinations could not be fully ripe, for they would deteriorate before reaching their markets. Hence a sizeable quantity of ripe, or over-ripe peaches were rejected each day. These were sold at bargain prices to local residents either during the late afternoon or "after hours" by the night watchman; those not sold were thrown away. Mary and I became regular customers of the night watchman

Mary soon became addicted (the only word for it) to these luscious free-stones marvels and could easily make a meal of them and still be hungry for more. Late one afternoon, after the day's packing was over and the rejected ripe peaches had been set to one side, Mary and I went round in the hope of picking up several for our evening meal.

To our delight, the night watchman explained that an unusually large quantity of ripe and over-ripe peaches had remained and that we could have an entire bushel for a token price. Overjoyed, we accepted his offer, returned home and immediately set to on the peaches – giving no thought to an evening meal. The peaches were so soft they easily pulled apart in halves after which the stone was lightly flicked away. The skin peeled off in one unbroken fabric. I was sated after only a few but Mary's appetite knew no bounds. She sat at the kitchen table, gulping the peaches non-stop and after half an hour we had devoured most of the bushel.

We needed no supper that evening and passed a contented night. Early the next morning, however, Mary complained of pains. At first we put them down to all those peaches, but as they increased in intensity and the time intervals shortened, we knew she had to be in labour. Although the baby was not due for several days, she felt the labour signs were unmistakable.

By midday Mary was in even greater discomfort. I telephoned Doctor McGeary and told him we were on the way. When we arrived at his hospital 25 minutes later, Mary's spasms seemed stabilised and I wondered if we had misjudged the urgency. Doctor McGeary suggested I return to Monticello and continue my work and that Mary remain for observation. If I came back in the late afternoon, he would make a judgement about whether she should remain in hospital or be released.

I followed his suggestion and duly returned about 5 p.m. to find Mary sitting up on her pillows with baby Angela in her arms! Apparently the birth came on so quickly there was no time to telephone me. I asked Doctor McGeary if Mary's meal of peaches could have triggered Angela's birth ahead of schedule. "Undoubtedly", he said, smiling. After that, we referred to Angela, with ample justification, as our "Georgia Peach".

Thirteen months later our son, Stuart, was born, but under totally different circumstances, albeit with another element of pre-natal drama. From the outset of her second pregnancy Mary thought the child would be a boy. Aware that no male child had been born in Frith farmhouse for over a century, she was determined that our second child be delivered there. At that time there was no way of determining a baby's gender before birth, but Mary said all "that violent kicking" could come only from a boy. She was not against hospitals in America or hospitals in general, but as her mother had been a nurse she felt sure of receiving the best care at home. Since my courting days at Frith Farm, I had been acutely aware of the deep sense of family history among the Roberts and so readily consented that our next child should be born in England. After all, the family had not yet seen baby Angela.

Mary was by then nearly eight months pregnant and, to our consternation, neither Cunard nor any American shipping line would accept her because of the risk of premature birth on the high seas. Then remembering that the French sometimes don't mind bending a rule to accomplish an objective, I telephoned the French Line's regional office in New Orleans to ask if they would accept Mary on the *De Grasse*, due to sail from New York within a fortnight. To my joy, the shipping agent immediately replied "Yes", adding the caveat that, for legal purposes, her stage of pregnancy should be listed as "six months". Mary and I readily agreed and two weeks later she sailed. As the ship moved away from the pier, a photographer captured me and my old Army friend, Bill Ehlert, looking pensively at the departing vessel.

Stuart's birth came off without a hitch at Frith Farm with Mary's mother, Rose, attending her daughter and grandson around the clock. Mary had not been able to keep her food down on the voyage and Stuart, a bundle of bones at birth, was promptly dubbed "the Belsen baby" by Mr. Roberts. In a short time, however, he became robust and ruddy – in part from passing most of his waking hours outdoors. When Mary returned with him to New York several months later, a chorus of 'oohs' and 'ahs' arose from the crowd of waiting relatives when they spotted the bonny Stuart as Mary and I proudly snaked our way through them.

65
Stuart's marbles steal the show

By this time we had moved into a small house on the edge of Monticello. Apart from giving us more room, it had a large garden. It was separated from the house next door by a hedge, thick everywhere except near our back door. Here it was apparent an opening had been deliberately made to allow communication between the two houses.

The occupant was "Miss Berta" Giddens, a widow who baked cakes to earn her living. Anyone who had a birthday or anniversary would get her to bake a cake for the occasion. Chocolate was her specialty. Even if there was no need for cakes, families would order them from Miss Berta – in part to give themselves a treat, but as well in recognition of her need for income.

The day we moved in, Miss Berta came around and said: "See that gap in the hedge? You must not allow it to grow back. For a generation people in your house and mine have used it to keep our friendship blossoming. We must always keep that gap open!"

We did. As the children grew older, Angela was content to play with her doll and other toys in our back yard but one day Stuart disappeared. At first we searched for him in the house, the garden and in the adjacent woods but always with no luck. Desperately Mary and I edged our way through the hedge to Miss Berta's back door to ask if she had seen him.

Grinning broadly but not saying anything, she motioned for us to come inside. We were greeted by that unique, seductive aroma which comes only from home-baking. She pointed to the space behind her trusty wood-burning stove where we saw an unconcerned Stuart quietly licking a great wooden ladle on which Miss Berta had deliberately left a generous amount of chocolate. Stuart was blissfully unaware that his face was half covered in chocolate. Thereafter, when he was missing, we went directly to the "chocolate source" and always found him there. Mary and I wondered, years later, if this was where he developed his "sweet tooth".

Life in Monticello, as in any small town anywhere in the Deep South, could be either leisurely or lively, depending on what the inhabitant put into it. There were four churches for Monticello's 2,000 residents, three for white residents and one for blacks.

Most county towns in the South have a courthouse in the centre of a large square, adapted from the village greens of England. The courthouse was usually the largest and grandest building in the county, apart from the local school. The other feature common to most county towns in the South was a monument to the Confederate war dead. Latterly memorials to the dead of World Wars I and II were added.

In 1949 Mary became eligible for American citizenship. It had been painful for her to switch allegiance after growing up in wartime Britain and in a home where her father placed great emphasis on patriotism. Nonetheless she assiduously studied the booklet of questions supplied by the US Immigration Service about the history of the United States and its Constitution.

When the day arrived for us to travel to Macon for Mary to be examined and, hopefully, be sworn in as an American citizen, we were all agog. The Federal judge of Georgia's "middle district" was appointed to preside over the testing of would-be citizens and administer oaths to successful candidates. Mary and I looked at each other apprehensively as we entered the impressive US Federal Court Building. Mary was not at all keen on being quizzed about the legal language of the US Constitution with its various Articles and Amendments and was sure she would fail to answer any question put to her.

On arrival we were ushered into an awesome chamber with a high ceiling, chandeliers and a white marble floor. To our surprise there were about 30 other aspiring citizens. Most, like Mary, were young and with babies and older children, some of whom were restless and noisy. Stuart, not quite a year old, refused to sit still, so Mary let him crawl around the floor with Angela.

There they played happily together until suddenly there was a slight uproar from nearby parents and children. Stuart, feeling the need to relieve himself, had discharged a long trail of faeces looking like marbles from his diaper. As Mary and I rushed to clear the floor, the judge – looking in our direction, got to his feet and called the gathering to order. Smiling, he said:

"Don't worry about the baby. It happens all the time!"

He then announced there would be no quizzing on American history or the Constitution, at which a great sigh of relief went up. Instead he gave a five minute talk on how America's greatness was derived from its make-up of people from many lands. He was sure, he said, that all the candidates for citizenship present would fully enter into the life of their respective communities and, above all, exercise their right to vote. Then everyone stood and recited the oath after him. It was all over in a matter of a few minutes but it was Stuart who had left his mark.

66
A frantic race to the hospital

During my four years as editor of *Rural Georgia* I witnessed a remarkable transition in the state's agricultural make-up. Although benefits of rural electrification by now extended to the remotest farms, the rural population was steadily decreasing.

This phenomenon was not peculiar to the South; all over the United States the number of people employed in agriculture had declined dramatically. In part this was due to giant harvesting machines that had replaced men. There were also improved varieties of grain, cotton and other crops that meant greater tonnages could now be produced by fewer workers.

The displaced workers, whether white or black (in the South), moved first to the nearest county towns, then to the cities. Many former black servicemen moved north to Detroit, Washington and New York. Suddenly agriculture in the South became an industry with emphasis on saving labour costs and meeting higher production targets.

It gradually dawned on me that the "New South" that Henry Grady envisaged had, in effect, arrived. That realisation left me feeling I could end my "mission" to help promote a prosperous way of life for Georgia's farmers and now - if I wished - to explore that other burning ambition: to serve my country abroad in some way.

The Cold War between the West and the Soviet Union was now a growing menace and the Korean War a terrible reality. I hoped my journalistic and military experience could be put to use in America's growing role in maintaining democratic values in the Western world. In Europe military alliances within NATO (North Atlantic Treaty Organisation) and other nations caused a dramatic expansion of US military bases in Europe and North Africa. Supporting the large troop population was a network of "post exchanges" - popularly known as PX's by those in uniform. Not only did these military shops provide many of life's necessities at reduced costs, but they also generated profits to pay for recreational and other morale-boosting services.

I applied for, and was accepted by the US Air Force as an information officer working first in London and later at the USAF Headquarters in Wiesbaden, Germany. My primary job was issuing an in-house magazine for post exchange managers and visiting PX installations to document the best practices - much as I had done with farming when with *Rural Georgia.*

For my work in London we chose to live in suburban Esher, a 22-minute ride by train to the capital. Angela and Stuart were happily enrolled in "Kingfishers", a small private school run by two gifted middle-aged ladies.

Esher made it convenient for us to see an Oxford-Cambridge boat race one year under conditions I shall never forget. We managed to park our car near a bridge of the Thames, not far from Kew Gardens, and then walked to a vantage point where we could see the rowers. The race over, we were making our way back on the bank of the river when suddenly the footpath flooded and was getting deeper by the minute. When we reached the ramp where we had left our car, we saw that all the vehicles parked there were rapidly being submerged by water. Two other cars parked beyond ours already had water up to the engine level.

A police constable attired in knee-length Wellington boots protecting his immaculately pressed trousers, saw my dilemma and offered to carry me on his shoulders, piggy-back style. His aim was to get me to my car so I could move it before the engine was flooded. Embarrassed, but grateful, I accepted his offer.

By this time a crowd of on-lookers had gathered. As the constable took each step into deeper water, the crowd shouted encouragement. The water edged ever nearer to the top of his Wellingtons. I, more than anyone else, hoped he could reach the car before the water spilled into his boots. Alas, he did not make it. One stride away from the car the rising water surged into his boots, at which the concerned on-lookers let out an agonising groan.

I was mortified, but the brave constable marched on, held me until I could unlock the car door and pushed me inside. Then the crowd erupted into a loud "Hurrah!" for, after all, the constable had accomplished his objective. I hastily extracted the car, unharmed, and we sped away as quickly as we could. That night, after telephoning around to discover the policeman's superiors, I wrote a thank-you note expressing my gratitude for the gallant officer's action. I secretly hoped he would be promoted.

Late in 1954 I flew to Frankfurt to take the US military train to West Berlin where I was to spend two weeks of Reserve duty in the US Army's public information centre. At a time when Allied military presence was beginning to be resented in some parts of West Germany, it was refreshing to experience the welcome that then existed in West Berlin.

The Soviets and the East Germans proudly flaunted their infamous Berlin Wall and it seemed there was little the Allies could do about it without risking war. One day the officer in charge of arranging tours to East Berlin for visiting American VIPs, detailed me to escort the editor of a leading American women's magazine to East Berlin. The itinerary included passing through the Wall at "Checkpoint Charlie" and continuing on to the flamboyant Soviet War Memorial.

These expeditions were useful to Allied foreign policy, for they enabled journalists and other influential people to see the Wall first hand, as well as the complete subjugation of East Germans to Soviet authority. These visits, however, were not without risk, for more than once the East Germans had stopped our Army sedans and detained their passengers. Experience had taught us that the East Germans either did not know what to do with their captives or else simply stopped cars to demonstrate a show of "authority". These impasses were resolved only when the "captives" demanded that a Soviet officer be summoned. Invariably, the Soviet officers allowed the cars to continue.

So, when setting out with my lady editor, I was instructed to speak only with a Soviet officer should our car be halted anywhere in East Berlin. In addition, by using the car's radio telephone every few minutes I could constantly indicate our location. The East German border guards glowered at us as we passed through "Checkpoint Charlie", but did not delay us. We wended our way through a residential area where young children, well coached in Communist party slogans, shouted abuse at us in English. Eventually we reached the huge war memorial, guarded by Soviet soldiers in immaculate uniforms.

My editor companion, now allowed to use her camera for the first time, took picture after picture of the memorial with its Soviet soldiers. Our return journey went without mishap and I breathed a sigh of relief when at last the editor thanked me and got out to file her story. Sadly, it would be more than three decades later and only after many fleeing East Germany had lost their lives, that the wall would be knocked down.

Esher's proximity to London sometimes allowed the family to partake of the capital's rich cultural and entertainment attractions. Mary and I saw to it that Angela and Stuart shared these pleasures. Once, after suddenly obtaining tickets for "Wind in the Willows", I realised Angela and Stuart did not know the story. Hastily grabbing the book, I rushed Mary and the children to the railway station to catch the next train to London. During the 22-minute journey to Waterloo and afterwards on Underground trains, we condensed the highlights of the tale - finishing only as we entered the theatre.

Luck also once allowed me to see a member of the Royal Family close up. Walking down Bond Street, I noticed a small crowd gathered outside a beauty salon. I was told by an excited lady, speaking in a low tone, that Princess Margaret had gone inside some time before and was due to appear at any moment.

Sure enough, her car and chauffeur were waiting. Almost at once Princess Margaret emerged, stepping into the narrow space left open by the line of spectators on either side. I am sure all the on-lookers, like me, hoped the princess would give us a glance, but if she did so, would it be to the right or the left? As she strode to the waiting car, she suddenly turned her head to the left, where I stood, displaying a more radiant smile than I had ever seen in her photographs. She was not quite 21 at the time; I always like to think of her as she appeared on that occasion - happy, confident and possessing great natural beauty and charm.

The outstanding event of our stay in Esher was the arrival, in 1954, of our third child, Melinda, who Mary promptly nicknamed "Pipkin". It was to become her preferred name to this day.

By this time the number of USAF bases and service men and women had grown to such an extent that my employers, the exchange service, decided to move its headquarters from London to Wiesbaden - the latter already USAF headquarters for Europe. Spared from Allied bombing raids because it had been pre-selected as the site for the US Air Force Headquarters in Europe, Wiesbaden was, and is, a beautiful city with fine buildings, sprawling parks and gracious avenues. Angela and Stuart were then of an age to enjoy the wide range of German fairy tales, many of which were screened weekly in Wiesbaden's cinemas. Angela was thrilled with German dolls and dolls' houses while Stuart played incessantly with his mechanical toys.

One of the most remarkable events of our Wiesbaden stay was the visit of the evangelist, Billy Graham. Aware that his service would be well attended, the Air Force command (USAFE) allocated the massive space in front of its headquarters building for the occasion. Everyone who could be spared from duties was allowed to come and they turned up in their thousands – servicemen not only from the Air Force but also nearby Army units – many with their families.

Mary and I attended and we marvelled how this Southern Baptist evangelist, son of a North Carolina dairy farmer, connected so magically with the military. They, like the police, had willingly entered professions in which laying down their lives was a daily possibility. They seemed to sense they were in the presence of a divine inspirer and so joined rapturously in the singing of hymns, always a feature of Graham's ministry. As he preached Graham seemed to draw strength from the very intensity of their devotion.

On the occasions when we could obtain baby-sitters, we toured Wiesbaden's museums and attended concerts. The city had received some of the rarer objects from Berlin at the outbreak of war for safekeeping; we were thus able to admire some of these, including the magnificent bust of Queen Nefertiti, before they were returned to Berlin.

Our stay in Wiesbaden was marked by a great scare from Pipkin. Only just past her first birthday, she was already learning to walk. Early one evening, while I was feeding her in her high chair, she keeled over unconscious after her first drink of milk. I reached to support her and found that her arms, legs and entire body had gone as limp as jelly. She had enjoyed robust health all of her young life; clearly something out of the ordinary was happening to her. Mary and I wondered if she had swallowed some object but there had been no indication of impaired breathing.

Then my eyes lit upon the coffee table where we kept a vessel of cigarettes for guests who smoked. At once I saw an open cigarette pack and the remains of one cigarette scattered nearby on the floor. I quickly telephoned the Air Force Hospital (the same one used years later to receive American hostages freed in Beirut) and explained the situation. The doctor on duty interrupted me.

"She probably has acute nicotine poisoning," he said tersely. "You can get her to us quicker than we can send an ambulance. Come as quickly as you can, but do drive with care."

We grabbed Pipkin without bothering to take additional clothing, raced to our car and sped through the night to the hospital. The waiting doctor and a team of nurses snatched her from our arms and disappeared while Mary and I, still stunned, attempted to complete the hospital admission forms. After nearly half an hour, the doctor emerged and told us he had pumped out Pipkin's stomach and that she was now conscious. We rushed into the children's ward to find the bewildered child crying amidst all the strange surroundings.

"Are we free to take her home now?" Mary asked.

"I'm afraid not," the doctor replied, feelingly. "To be on the safe side, she should remain here overnight. That way, she will be in good hands if complications set in."

We drove home slowly, giving thanks that Pipkin was going to be all right but rebuking ourselves for leaving the cigarettes within her reach.

67
In the steps of Robert Louis Stevenson

In the autumn of 1955 I asked Mary if she could manage without me if I obtained ten days leave to go to southern France and retrace the trek recounted by Robert Louis Stevenson in his *Travels with a Donkey*. I had been introduced to Stevenson at the age of eight when I went to hospital to have my tonsils removed. While recovering I read "The Land of Counterpane" in his *A Child's Garden of Verse*. It was so easy imagining my bed and its covers as Stevenson's counterpane; from that day onward he became my childhood favourite and I read everything of his I could find. To my great delight, his *Travels with a Donkey* was included in our high school English literature textbook. As soon as I had read it, I secretly resolved one day to repeat his journey.

Mary, knowing my enthusiasm, generously agreed to let me fulfil the long-held dream. Accordingly, I travelled by train to Le Puy and thence by bus to the nearby village of Le Monastier-sur-Gazeille where Stevenson had acquired the donkey, "Modestine", before starting his travels.

The mayor of Le Monastier, who owned the village wine shop, told me I was far from being the first person to retrace Stevenson's steps. Was I, he asked, going to use a donkey as Stevenson had done? I had only a large rucksack and saw no need for a donkey. Besides, my earlier enquiries in the village indicated there were no donkeys for miles around. So I told the mayor: "No donkey".

"Too bad," he replied, "Mademoiselle Singer had a donkey."

"Who is Mademoiselle Singer?" I asked.

"Oh, she is the English girl who passed this way a few years back, doing the same thing as you are planning." he said. "Only she did it the same way Stevenson did - *with* a donkey."

It was just as well that I was deflated at the outset of my adventure for almost everywhere I went thereafter local people told me about Mademoiselle Singer and her exploit. I tried in vain to find out more about this young lady but the only thing the villagers remembered was that she probably came from the Midlands - perhaps Birmingham. If she ever publicised her adventures, I never heard of it.

Armed with Michelin maps Nos. 176 and 180, I set off determined to follow Stevenson's route as closely as possible but knew that some new roads had been built while others had been abandoned. I soon learned that Stevenson had been modest about his daily mileage for he and the 'lazy' Modestine had gone at a rate I found difficult to match.

It had taken Stevenson until noon of his first day to reach the village of Goudet and I was pleased to have made the same progress. At the inn the host had showed Stevenson an engraving of his nephew, Regis Senac, acclaiming him "Professor of Fencing and Champion of the two Americas". That honour had brought the nephew a prize of $500 in New York's Tammany Hall in April, 1876. Dare I expect, 79 years later, that the same family might own the inn and possibly still have that engraving?

When I introduced myself and mentioned the purpose of my visit, the innkeeper smiled, said he was Emile Senac, grandson of the proprietor in Stevenson's day and, yes indeed, that engraving was still intact. He obligingly fetched it, then posed while I took a photograph. What luck and what a commentary on French village life that the local inn should remain in the same family for three generations!

Incredibly, another link with Stevenson's day came when I reached Bouchet St. Nicholas. The inn where he had stayed still bore its name, albeit badly faded, across the front. Entering, I found myself in a large room with an earthen floor. At one end near a stone fireplace was a lady I took to be the mistress of the house, chatting with another woman. She said nothing to me, but smiled and motioned that I should seat myself on the corner of a wooden table nearby. This I did while the two continued to chat away, plainly exchanging village gossip. After some minutes the visitor departed, having divulged all her most recent intelligence.

The lady then turned to me, offering a cup of coffee, which I gratefully accepted. Yes, this was the same hostelry Stevenson had stayed in and, yes, I was not the first to ask that question. In fact, she added, a Mademoiselle Singer had come that way only a year or two before and *she* (she emphasised the *she*) was accompanied by a donkey just as Stevenson had been. I mumbled something about not being able to find a donkey but the lady was not impressed. She told me that the village had not changed much since Stevenson's time except for the departure of young people to the cities. I thanked her and left. I now knew the spectre of Mademoiselle Singer was likely to hang over me for the remainder of my trek.

I continued on my way south, following as nearly as possible the route taken by Stevenson. There were a few occasions when he either became lost or had misjudged his direction and others where the tracks and roads had been changed. The countryside, sometimes beautiful, sometimes wild and desolate, always held interest. Then I realised that a large, well-built man had joined the road behind me. Was this pure coincidence, or did he have a sinister motive? Stevenson had come across a few hostile characters; was I in for the same fate? I decided not to leave it to chance but increased both my stride and pace. After a few minutes I had the road to myself and never saw the man again.

One place where Stevenson lingered for a while was the Trappist monastery, Notre Dame des Neiges (Our Lady of the Snows). I consulted my Michelin map and saw that it was clearly marked near the town of La Bastide-Puy Laurent, so at least it still existed. But, I wondered, was it much changed? I had never visited a Trappist monastery but now looked forward to seeing one.

As I turned off into the side road leading to the monastery I first saw tractors and a handsome barn on the left, then an elegant avenue of trees leading to the principal buildings. Certainly the place looked prosperous, but how could a few monks achieve this? I made my first enquiry at a building where many cars were parked, this in itself an omen of the 20th century. Inside I found a queue of people waiting to buy the monastery's wine, which a man from Paris told me was both good value and quality.

"But it's sad," he continued, "to see all these people coming here just to pick up a bargain. Not one of them bothers to enter the chapel."

He went on to say that he came to the monastery each year for a week's retreat. Away from the hectic pace of life in Paris, he could meditate and worship to his heart's content. He then showed me round the buildings, all of which seemed too new to have existed in Stevenson's time. In this community of brothers where the spoken word was prohibited, one monk was permitted to converse with the public.

When this monk had served the last of the wine-buyers, I asked which building Stevenson would have stayed in. He took me by the arm and led me a short distance, pointing to the shell of a building, long since razed by fire. The reason why I had not seen a modern-day Father Appollinaris toiling with his barrow (as Stevenson had described) when I arrived was that tractors had taken his place.

The monks received me graciously and gave me a simple room for the night. I noticed that above the door to each room was the name of a Saint instead of a room number. A friend once told me that there is a Saint for every day of the year in France, thereby guaranteeing every new-born child a Saint for his or her birthday.

That evening I joined my friend from Paris in the chapel service. He whispered that because their speech was restricted at all other times, the monks "let themselves go" with their evening chants. Certainly their harmonious incantations constituted the highlight of my sojourn at the monastery. Breakfast the next morning was a crust of baguette, butter and strawberry confiture, washed down by coffee drunk from a large bowl - continental style.

Leaving the monastery, I continued on my way, soon crossing a massive, barren mountain peak with no sign of civilisation except for a peasant with his bullock cart and goats. The next town was Pont de Montvert, described by Stevenson as the heart of the Protestant Cevennes. It was here, in the early 1700s, that fighting broke out between the Camisards (Protestants) and Catholics. Before the blood-letting ended, many atrocities were committed in the name of Christendom. It was also this region, during Stevenson's time, that supplied many British Protestant families with French nannies.

The churches I passed indicated the surrounding area was still dominantly Protestant. But was the fervour as great as it had been a century and a half ago and could Protestants still overtly proclaim their faith? Walking on, I had part of my answer when I came to the crest of a hill. To my right, a friendly "Bonjour!" rang out. There, almost hidden by trees, was a cottage with a neatly manicured lawn. Its owner was leaning over the front gate smiling at me. I went over, explained the purpose of my trek and found him willing to help with answers to my questions about the present state of relations between the areas Protestants and Catholics.

He said he was a schoolmaster and a Protestant. Most other families in the immediate region were also Protestant but no hostility now existed between people of the two faiths. He thought that Protestant families were more faithful in attending church than their Catholic brethren, possibly because of their historical necessity to stick together.

At that moment his daughter joined us and I noticed that she was wearing a gold pendant supporting a *colombe* (dove), where a Catholic might wear a cross. Her father saw my puzzlement and explained that the *colombe* was worn by devout Protestants in that region of France. He agreed that I could take a photograph of his daughter displaying the ornament with her fingers. I thanked them both for updating my scant knowledge of the Camisard country and pressed on southwards.

Stevenson had ended his travels at St. Jean du Gard and I planned to do the same. The sun was shining brightly when I arrived and I could see at once that the town was unspoiled by the ravages of tourism. I was taking photographs of pleasing corners and arches when I stumbled on a delightful little square where a collection of the town's elder citizens sat at tables, chatting, smoking and sipping coffee.

A scholarly looking gentleman beckoned me to join his table. I did so, explaining that the day was a momentous one for me, since it marked the completion of my travels modelled on Stevenson's original trek. The man had heard about Stevenson's little book but had never seen a copy in French or in English. I asked if he would like to see my English copy. When he said he would, I spent a quarter of an hour outlining the route Stevenson had followed but omitting the details of his adventures. When I finished, he said he must now go to his library and get the French version. He congratulated me on completing my odyssey and wished me a safe return home.

Stevenson had taken eleven days to cover the nearly 200 kilometres (about 115 miles) from Le Monastier to St. Jean du Gard. I had taken the same time, but without the encumbrance (as Stevenson would have us believe) of a Modestine. It didn't make sense; either he had travelled faster than his account led me to believe or I had spent more time talking to people along the way.

Time, however, had not been a factor for either of us. Stevenson's journey was only one of several in his short life, each being conceived as a cure for his tuberculosis. My motive was more simple – merely retracing the footsteps of an author whose writing had captured my boyish imagination three decades earlier.

PART IV

Flying the flag

1956-1970

68
Training for duty in Israel

Our stay in Wiesbaden came to an end early in 1956 when I joined USIA (the United States Information Agency) as an Information Officer.

My work with the US forces in England and Germany had been gratifying for it coincided with a rare post-World War II period when American military assistance was broadly welcomed in Europe. Although the war was a thing of the past, a future nuclear conflict was feared and country after country entered into military defence pacts with the United States. It was pleasant for the Americans to be regarded as friends and defenders and nowhere was this more evident than in West Berlin. Here the British and American airlift of supplies crucial to the city's survival gave Berliners hope for surviving the Cold War.

But the Cold War also left me wanting to be more broadly involved in world affairs. This could be achieved only if I joined the Foreign Service of my country, a responsibility that would place me in the front line of advancing the American cause abroad. That challenge was to be both daunting and exhilarating.

USIA officers worked in three fields: public affairs, culture and information. I was to join the ranks of the latter with my primary contacts being the media operatives of the country. Dealing with such varied and specialised professions obviously required a familiarity with the field and intense training. Because of my journalism experience I had no problem grasping the scope of my forthcoming responsibility. But the training was also to be my introduction to the life of a diplomat – sometimes referred to as "one sent abroad to lie for his country".

My class of young trainees reported to USIA headquarters in Washington and was told we had to undergo two months of intense training. None of us knew in advance where we would be sent; those decisions would be made only towards the end of the training.

Our "home" in Washington was the legendary Francis Scott Key hotel. Although several storeys high, it was more like an over-stretched boarding house than a slick, modern hostelry. For many years its primary purpose was to accept and look after, with tender loving care, foreign service families on short-term assignments or on leave in between assignments. This remarkable establishment was presided over by a genial man who had retired from his military duties as a Captain.

The moment we arrived Mary and I became downcast at the prospect of having to split our family of five into two groups – even for so short a stay as two months. The sympathetic Captain, seeing how depressed we were, took us to an upper floor where he opened the door to a large double room.

"Hmm," he said, "might be a little crowded, but if the children don't mind sleeping in cots, we just might manage to fit you all in."

"Cots! Cots!" cried Angela and Stuart in unison, "we'd love to sleep in cots!"

And so it was that they had cots on the far side of the room while

Pipkin, not yet two, was adjacent to our double. This was but the first of many kind acts by our host – a man who knew how important it was to provide agreeable living conditions for families uprooted from their former surroundings.

As Mary and I unpacked our belongings at the Francis Scott Key, our exhilaration was overwhelming. At last, I – supported by my young wife – was about to begin my long-held dream of representing my country abroad. For both Mary and myself, the two months of training made us acutely aware that what we knew, what we said and how we behaved would profoundly affect the way our foreign contacts would regard the United States.

"When you arrive in your country of assignment," our instructor said, "all eyes will be upon each member of your family. It will be as if you are in a goldfish bowl with hundreds of eyes constantly peering at you."

This was a daunting challenge for Mary and other wives of officers in my training class.

"But does that apply to young children?" one officer asked.

"The same goes for them," the instructor replied solemnly. "There have been cases when families have been sent home on short notice because their children behaved badly."

Mary and I glanced at each other. We could not imagine Angela, Stuart or Pipkin doing anything that would result in our family being disgraced. We noted, however, that this warning apparently sent shudders through some couples in our training class.

My preparation was perhaps more predictable, with lectures on American culture, economics and politics as well as a study of the Soviet Union, the Arab nations and countries of the "Third World". In the second half of the training, after my country of assignment was known, I would concentrate on its place in the contemporary world.

What neither Mary nor I had realised was that wives would also receive training. Mary's general introduction to homemaking at the University of Georgia had been of enormous help in adapting to American home life, but now experts from the State Department and other agencies came to lecture the wives on subjects ranging from the intricate business of calling cards and protocol to keeping an ear open for bits of information affecting American interests.

For both of us there were discussions about climate, diseases and medicines, clothing, children's schooling, religion, language and other information that would assist our daily life in the country of assignment. For me and other members of my entry class, the training was long and arduous. Facts were tossed at us so fast we could barely digest them. About halfway through the two month period, we were all told where we would be going and what our positions would be. I could hardly believe my good luck when I learned I was to be the next press attaché at the American Embassy in Tel Aviv.

Kendall Weisiger, who had long championed the cause of Arab-Israeli reconciliation, was thrilled when we told him of my appointment to

Tel Aviv. He had contacts there among both Jews and Arabs who, he was sure, would make us welcome. Once our place of assignment was announced, the emphasis of training narrowed to that part of the world. Because Israel and her neighbours were at war, of necessity I was obliged to learn a great deal about the whole of the Middle East, the emotions aroused in Jews and Arabs alike about the symbolism of Jerusalem, the perceived threat of the Soviet Union to the region and, of course, the importance of Arab oil to the United States and the West.

How could the United States walk that "tight rope" with confidence? How could our Middle East policy be seen as fair to Arabs given the influence of America's large, wealthy and articulate Jewish community? In particular, how could I, as the embassy's press officer, present a balanced American position without offending my Israeli contacts? That challenge proved to be the most formidable of all.

Some of my class members were going abroad as cultural attachés; others, like myself, were to be press attachés. One by one we were subjected to ruthless cross-examination by the faculty in mock social situations (a reception, dinner, a press conference in which we would be besieged by make-believe journalists, educators and other "opinion makers" about controversial aspects of American foreign and domestic policy. For 30 minutes or so each of us had to stand in front of the class while faculty members bombarded us with questions like American policy on Israel and her Arab neighbours, the seemingly slow progress of racial equality in the United States and other tricky topics.

At the end of each session we would emerge totally drained, for not only had we been obliged to come up with plausible answers, but the tones of our voices had to reflect confidence in what we said. In short, we had to keep cool and smile, however vicious the questions or accusations. With the possible exception of the "hot times" later experienced by American diplomats during the Vietnam war, those mock training sessions sometimes proved more trying than real-life situations we later confronted.

Our senior instructor advised us to erase any previous notions we may have held about the places we were going to and asked us to approach our assignments with open minds.

"Try and achieve an *understanding* of, not *empathy* with, the country that will be your temporary home," he urged.

The reading requirements for our training were greater than any of us had known for any single year of our university education. As the days were packed with oral and visual instruction, the only times left for reading were in the evening and at weekends. Two excellent texts for someone proceeding to Israel, I was told, were the Old Testament and the Koran, and a general familiarisation with both was advised. Then came an historical survey of the area from Turkish times right up to 1948

Two of the most important pronouncements had been made in the *Balfour Declaration* of 1917 and the *Palestine Royal Commission Report* of 1937. Ideally, if not realistically, they foresaw both Jewish and Arab "homelands" in Palestine. The critical question, it was suggested, would always be whether this objective was being pursued by each party when the state of Israel was born.without prejudice to the other. The reading list was finely balanced between "pro-Israel" and "pro-Arab" works, with a few historians trying to take an objective view somewhere in between. We were also warned that there were both pro-Jewish and pro-Arab lobbies in Washington anxious to influence us if given half a chance.

We were told that the Semites (i.e. Arabs and Jews) had existed together in Palestine in Biblical times and in the centuries since under many rulers, sharing Jerusalem and other centres of population while generally respecting each other's religion and customs. The Jewish population had been relatively small, concentrated mainly in Zionist settlements and in some larger towns where it was mainly engaged in commerce and crafts. The Arabs were mostly farmers and small shopkeepers.

We learned it was Charles Lindbergh who, when he first heard that large numbers of Jews planned to settle on land in Palestine, had famously asked: "On whose land?" Sharing land and water would be the key to a lasting peace between Jews and Arabs, our training officers said. This seemed a simple enough goal to my ears in faraway Washington, but our advisers had no answers for resettling the million or so Arabs already displaced and how to deal with the problem should Jewish immigration continue to grow. One thing was certain, my senior adviser said, failure to resolve the land / water issue fairly would lead to a state of permanent conflict between Jews and Arabs.

69
Don't mix circumcision with meat sandwiches

On a hot day in April 1956 our plane landed at Tel Aviv. We were met on the airport ramp (unheard of now, but common in those relaxed days of security) by my superior, Joe Bennett, and his Chinese-American wife, Nancy. Joe was a quiet, studious officer with a penchant for analysing and correctly predicting the outcome of complex political situations. He had met, and eventually married, Nancy during his work in China a decade earlier. A vivacious young lady of great charm, she readily agreed to become Mary's unofficial tutor in our first diplomatic assignment.

The other member of our USIA trio at the American Embassy was Dr. Thomas McGrail of Roxbury, Massachusetts. A bachelor and a lieutenant colonel in the Second World War, Tom spoke with a typical New Englander accent. He had a room in one of Tel Aviv's large hotels but greatly missed New England cooking - especially his favourite, Boston baked beans. Several times during our two-year stint he was to approach Mary with a tin of beans and ask her to prepare them for him in authentic New England style. The first time he did the cooking himself, but thereafter she was on her own. As our friendship with Tom ripened we learned he had a great fear of flying. Usually he was able to persuade the American government to send him from one point to another by ship.

Jack Haggerty was the director of the American aid programme to Israel. I was later to assist him with publicising certain aspects of American economic assistance to Israel. Haggerty was one of those rare individuals who had accumulated such a vast stock of stories that he could instantly come up with one to meet any situation. I accompanied him on several field trips into distant parts of the country where he constantly kept his Israel government counterparts in fits of laughter. A typical one:

"I attended my first Brith Millah (circumcision ritual) the other day. Everything was all right until they served the meat sandwiches."

Our ambassador, Edward Lawson, was a fellow southerner from Tennessee who looked to our USIA staff to prepare most of his speeches. In our initial meeting we agreed that I would incorporate Old Testament place names, quotations and references into his remarks whenever possible. I did not then own a concordance of the Bible, but now quickly bought one and found it indispensable thereafter.

With new immigrants arriving daily in Israel, housing for diplomats was a great problem. After several weeks in a hotel in a Tel Aviv suburb, however, we at last found a small apartment in the centre of the city. We were grateful to be offered the most modest of accommodation, even if we had to convert the living room into a bedroom for Angela and Stuart each evening. This meant opening out the sofas each night and changing them back the following morning.

Two disadvantages arose from this: first, Mary and I were obliged to use the dining room for our evening discussions or planning; second, when we entertained, we were obliged to put Angela and Stuart into our beds, there to remain until midnight or thereabouts. Only when the last guest had departed could I carry them (usually sound asleep) to their converted beds in the living room.

The apartment was round the corner from one of Tel Aviv's largest cinemas. We soon learned that the last showing ended just before midnight and that it was no use retiring before then, for the noise of exiting movie-goers - some walking and talking excitedly, others in cars - was bound to awaken the heaviest sleeper.

There was only one school in which English was the principal language of instruction, Tabeetha, operated by the Church of Scotland. This school was in Biblical Jaffa, once an all-Arab metropolis before Tel Aviv was founded but now largely overshadowed by Tel Aviv after many Arabs fled to refugee camps in Jordan and Lebanon. Most American and British embassy children attended Tabeetha, being transported there by bus. Schlomo, the bus driver, was an amiable character and a great favourite of the children. He had only one annoying habit: shaking the ash from the end of his cigarette while driving and scattering it down the front of the children's shirts and dresses.

Don't mix circumcision with meat sandwiches

With so many English-speaking children in the diplomatic community, Angela and Stuart attended parties virtually every week. We soon heard about the exploits of one Zaporah, a talented circus artist who was well-known in Berlin before the holocaust and since had become a legend among diplomatic families serving in Tel Aviv. Dressed in colourful circus attire, she had a vast repertoire of stunts and tricks. A favourite of the children was her cowgirl routine in which she made her lasso perform incredible shapes and antics.

For baby-sitting, required often because of official functions in the evenings, we found a gem in Sarah. She became so fond of the children that she would bring them small gifts paid for out of her own earnings. We did not learn until we left the country that part of her attraction for the children was the narration in great detail of the latest gory movie she had seen. Sarah thought nothing of treating the children to an ice cream or strawberries when taking them to the zoo, park or seaside. Long after our departure from Israel we kept in touch with Sarah, providing news of the children's development.

Most Protestant English-speaking families attended the Anglican church in the Jaffa district of Tel Aviv and it soon became our family place of worship, too. It was a unit of the Church of England's "Ministry among Jews", and, as such, was not welcomed by the orthodox Jewish community. The Church operated a small hostel nearby, inhabited by a few Jewish Christians. The Reverend Roger Allison, whose brothers became Bishops of the Sudan and of Winchester, was in charge of our international congregation, of whom the British ambassador was the most prominent member.

Dependency on a small, mainly transient congregation meant the church was in constant need of funds for essential maintenance and repairs. When lightning struck the steeple and left the spire dangling precariously and pointing earthwards, Roger was in deep despair for there seemed no way of raising the money needed for repair. We put our heads together and decided to ask someone from each embassy represented in the congregation, to write appeals to all diplomats who had once been posted to Tel Aviv. As it happened, some of the former Americans gave such generous donations that the spire was soon righted.

One day, when the Sunday service was over and the congregation was making its way to the car park, the British ambassador saw, to his horror, that his Rolls Royce had been scratched from one end to the other with a metal object. The Israeli government was embarrassed and said it would mete out appropriate punishment if the culprit could be caught. Nonetheless the incident meant that Her Majesty's ambassador had to forego use of his prestigious transport until complete repainting was done.

Roger Allison was the first clergyman Mary and I had known who arranged special services for New Year's Eve. His philosophy was simple: if you are grateful to be alive now that another year has come and gone, and if you have reason to think you will need help in the year ahead, then let the stroke of midnight find you on your knees giving thanks, and asking for Divine Guidance. Most of his usual Sunday congregation took his advice, eschewed revelry and saw in the new year in prayer.

It was only a few months before I was invited to join the Tel Aviv Rotary Club. It had over a hundred members and included several American embassy officers. Rotary at that time chose its members on the basis of "classification", that is, inviting to membership only *one* leading member of each profession or trade. This limitation often brought criticism to Rotary Clubs, for its sister clubs (Kiwanis, Lions, etc.) have never hesitated to include two or more members from the same profession or trade. In recent times, Rotary has broadened its classification system so as to accommodate additional members within the same general group, but the Tel Aviv club was miles ahead with a generous arrangement of its own.

I welcomed the chance to join, for among the club's members were many of the most prominent political, commercial and professional men in the country. Whereas an embassy officer might spend untold hours contacting such important figures individually, here they were, gathered regularly in an informal atmosphere, in one place. By changing my seat from one meeting to the next, I could sit beside several people able to provide me with information useful in my work as press attaché.

Before coming to Israel Mary and I had been reluctant to use the word "Jew" in public discussion, lest we seem anti-Semitic. Now in Israel generally, and in the Rotary Club particularly, I discovered everyone using the term the whole time. Moreover, Israelis expected foreign diplomats to use the term freely.

"Are you a Jew?" I was asked by a neighbour, as I sat down at the Rotary Club for the first time. Before I could reply, a member to my right interjected:

"There's no need to ask him if he's a Jew; if he will come with me to the men's room, I'll be able to tell you."

Apocryphal stories which would be regarded as portraying prejudice outside Israel were related frequently at the club. One such concerned a successful businessman anxious to instil basic business principles in his young son whom he expected to follow in his footsteps. Taking the boy to his back garden, he put him on top of the tool shed and asked him to jump.

"But will you catch me?" asked the frightened boy.

"Certainly, am I not your father?"

The boy prepared to jump, then hesitated again.

"Are you *sure* you will catch me?" he asked.

"As sure as I am standing here."

As the boy jumped, the father stepped back. The boy fell heavily upon the ground. Unhurt but badly shaken, he got to his feet and, with a pained look, said: "But you are my own father, and you promised to catch me, and you didn't"

"Ah," said the father, quietly. "That's the first lesson in business, my son. You don't trust anybody."

Don't mix circumcision with meat sandwiches

Another Rotary story, this one also apocryphal, revealed the length to which a certain young man went to avoid Israeli military service. By distorting the truth he had managed to fail his eye test. Celebrating his "victory" over the optometrist, he decided to treat himself to a movie. The optometrist, still clad in his white coat, suspected the young man of trickery and followed him all the way to the cinema. As he sat down to enjoy the film, the young man noticed in the corner of his eye that he had been joined by the very man who had just examined him. He knew he was destined for military service unless he quickly came up with some ingenious excuse. So he turned to the man, squinting behind his cupped hand, and asked:

"Can you tell me if this is the right bus for Jerusalem?"

The president of the Tel Aviv Rotary Club was Pierre Gilbert, the French ambassador to Israel. Gilbert, who had lost a lung while fighting in Vietnam, was immensely popular in Israel because he had been instrumental in providing French "Mystère" jets for the Israel Defence Forces at a time when other countries were not so forthcoming. For this act, he was promptly dubbed "Mystère" Gilbert.

"Understand, but don't empathise." my tutor had repeatedly urged members of my entry class, and understanding Mary and I were determined to achieve. As Israel was a theocratic state, our first task was to get a broader knowledge of Judaism and, after that, try to see how religion affected the people and government.

Before leaving Washington I had acquired a book, *My Promised Land,* by a Canadian Jewess, Molly, who had moved to Israel. She and her Dutch husband assumed the Hebrew name of Bar David. Adoption of Hebrew family names was much encouraged by the government, although some of the older settlers already with Hebrew names took a dim view of newcomers who instantly acquired Hebrew names.

I telephoned Molly to say I had read her book and she immediately invited Mary and me to join her family at their next Sabbath. We did so and it soon became clear that the old saying was true: "More than Israel kept the Sabbath, the Sabbath kept Israel." Here was one of the great Jewish rituals, one that brought together all family members at the end of the working week to celebrate spiritual joy.

It was not an overly sombre occasion, as I had earlier expected. Here was a spotless white tablecloth, white candles, the best china and silverware and a profusion of flowers. Everyone was dressed in their Sabbath best and a dignified celebratory atmosphere pervaded the room. Molly's husband, Jaap, began the service by reciting in Hebrew a simple prayer: "May the good Lord keep thee and bless thee on this, our Sabbath day." Then we shared the food, some of it (twisted loaves of bread and sweet white wine, for example) intended mainly for this special day. At intervals, Molly and Jaap would explain the significance of customs or food. By the end of the simple observance Mary and I agreed we had received a most moving introduction to Judaism.

Another Jewish festival, Succoth, is the ancestor of the British "Harvest Festival" and the American "Thanksgiving Day". When possible, it is celebrated in or near the home. If circumstances do not permit this, the synagogue or some other communal building is used. Mary and I had met a young Jewish Rabbi and his wife who kindly invited us to their "place of thanksgiving", a *succah*, in our apartment building. Their *succah* was extremely simple, consisting of a partially enclosed balcony with no roof, for it was necessary that we see the sky. Two other essentials were a palm branch, preferably tied with myrtle and willows, and a citron (or lemon). As this is a festival of thanksgiving, it is customary to decorate the *succah* with seasonal fruit, grain and flowers - much as a Protestant home or church would appear in the same season. After traditional blessings, which all referred to the gathering in of the year's harvest and the hope that next year's will also be plentiful, we shared a simple meal with the Rabbi and his wife.

At another time we viewed Tel Aviv's Purim parade, held annually to mark Queen Esther's and Mordecai's cunning in thwarting the evil intentions of Haman to slaughter the Jews of ancient Persia. This turned out to be more of a carnival than a religious festival. Here we saw people in costumes, gaily decorated floats and other features not dissimilar to carnival parades in Christian countries. There seemed to be no prescribed rites or symbolism, only universal joy to celebrate the escape of those ancient Jews from the dire fate intended for them.

Little by little Mary and I realised that Israel, theocratic or not, experienced the same pattern of religious disaffection that has marked Christian nations in recent times. On the occasions when we attended synagogues, we found them sparsely attended although throngs of people were circulating noisily on the streets outside. Again, as with Christians, Jews come in hues of several colours ranging from the orthodox to the "reformed", with the conservatives in between. Israel's strict orthodox Jews neither used automobiles on the Sabbath nor allowed anyone else near them to do so. We learned that some newly arrived diplomats had strayed unwittingly into orthodox areas, only to have their cars stoned or barred from entry.

The state of Israel has suffered inordinately from political instability because its government is fragmented by many political and religious parties. This situation often leads to coalitions in which a very small party, such as that representing the orthodox Jews, can exert disproportionate power. Hence we saw the government, having made a "deal" with a small religious party, obliged to enforce strict orthodox Jewish demands at the expense of the rest of the population.

We soon realised that the orthodox Jews tolerated the conservatives, but regarded the reformed Jews as having been tainted by Protestantism with their instrumental music and equal treatment of women. Some of our Jewish friends told Mary and me that they, and probably thousands of others, would regularly attend reformed services in Israel, had they been held.

This point came to the fore when Dr. Nelson Glueck, a leading American Jew of the reformed wing, came to Tel Aviv to report on his archaeological work in the Negev Desert. Glueck was widely respected in the Middle East by both Arab and Jew, for he had been director of the American School of Oriental Research in Jerusalem and Baghdad before the state of Israel came into being. He was also professor of Bible studies at Cincinnati's Hebrew Union (reformed) College. It was his latter position which caused the Israeli government some anxiety, for if Glueck spoke to the public, could he be counted on to distinguish archaeological truths from his reformed beliefs?

Mary and I attended Glueck's "lecture", accompanied by Jewish friends, in a large Tel Aviv park where several thousand people had gathered. In a brilliant and lengthy address, frequently interrupted by applause, Glueck detailed the dramatic archaeological discoveries he had made, frequently punctuating them with quotations or moral truths taken from the Old Testament. The "congregation" was spellbound. When he had finished and the last of the lengthy applause had died away, one of our Israeli friends turned to me and said: "Our people have been hungry for this kind of message; what a pity we can't have it more often. Our government is simply a captive of our orthodox brothers."

70
Southern Baptist Arabs

I soon became aware that it was not enough for a newly arrived diplomat to strive for an objective view of the Arab-Israeli conflict. "If you are not with us, then you must be against us," summed up one of my radical media contacts. One woman columnist who enjoyed a national following, methodically listed each newly arrived diplomat as being "Pro-Israel" or "Anti Israel". I did not understand this rather crude approach until Teddy Kollek, later to become a long-serving Mayor of Jerusalem, explained to me:

"You must not be offended when you discover Israelis trying to fathom your feelings about our country. Our very existence depends on support from abroad, especially from the United States. For that reason, you must not be surprised if people go to any extreme to learn what you think about any subject affecting our people."

How right he was. When my friend, Kendall Weisiger, sent me a list of his Jewish and Arab contacts in Israel, I set about meeting them. The Jewish ones posed no problem, but when I attempted to visit a young Arab lady who had been educated at an American university, I found I could see her only with the knowledge and consent of the Israeli Defence Forces. This was because she resided in an Arab "pocket". Given the prevailing Israeli view that any Arab was a potential security threat (the United States regarded its Japanese-Americans similarly during World War II), I could understand the precautions.

As my car, bearing CD (diplomatic corps) plates, approached the area, I was stopped at an Army post. After producing the name and address of the lady, I was allowed to proceed. I noted, however, that the guard did not take my word for, in my rear view mirror, I saw he had jumped into his jeep and followed me at a discreet distance all the way to the lady's house. The lady was overjoyed to meet a friend of Kendall Weisiger and I was able to convey the latest news of him and his work with students of many nations.

Although she had received advanced training in the United States in her field of study, she was not permitted by the Israelis to work among Jews. This visit and another to a Nazareth Arab friend of Kendall's and my occasional enquiry about long-range Israeli plans to resettle Arabs living in the large refugee camps of Lebanon and Jordan, must have caused some Israelis to feel I was anti-Israel.

One Sunday when we were randomly exploring Arab villages on the West Bank, we came upon a sign which read "To the Baptist Church". Baptists in the Holy Land, Mary and I asked ourselves, how could this be? Eventually we found a small building, more of a hut than a church, with several people inside.

We stopped the car, got out and discovered a tiny congregation of Arabs singing Southern Baptist hymns! They stopped in mid-verse and gave us a warm welcome, explaining they were few in number and, sadly, with little prospect of future growth. When the service was over, they insisted I take away one of their Southern Baptist hymn books – the very ones I had known in Georgia in my youth. I was overcome with humility.

Inside the front cover of my copy was a purple rubber stamp, rectangular in shape, reading:

> "THE NEAR EAST MISSION OF THE
> SOUTHERN BAPTIST CONVENTION, USA
> *BEZALEEL DISTRICT*
> Jerusalem, Palestine"

I flipped the pages to see what was on the inside of the book front cover and lo! - there were pencilled numerous hymns and their page numbers. Above these was the notation: "Responses 200", an indication that the tiny congregation had striven for respect and dignity in its services.

But what most interested me were the dozen or so "favourite hymns" marked out in pencil. Would these devout Baptists, thousands of miles away from the American South, have chosen any of my old favourites? At the top right was No. 284 – "Lead Kindly Light". Beneath it was No. 8: "The Lord is My Shepherd". Others I instantly recalled were "Into My Heart" (No. 255) and "I Would Be True" (No. 266).

Some of the little band's favourites were unknown to me. I especially wondered about the one given prime position at the top left hand side. It was listed as "Tread Softly" (No. 261), written by Fanny Crosby, one of the great American hymn composers. I did not know it. Why, I wondered, had it so appealed to these Palestinian Christians?

The four verses urged the singer to "Be silent, be silent". The second verse explained why: "For holy this place". But it was the words of the chorus which filled me with awe: "Tread softly, tread softly, the Master is here." How heart-breaking this hope must have been for them in the years of strife that lay ahead.

By the autumn of 1956 it became clear to many Israelis, and to those in our embassy concerned with intelligence, that Israel was on the brink of some military adventure. There was an enemy to the east (Jordan), two to the north (Lebanon and Syria) and one (Egypt) to the south. If Israel attempted a pre-emptive strike, would it be against only one of these neighbouring countries, or more than one?

World attention was now focused on Hungary, where an attempt to throw off the Soviet yoke would prove short lived. For the man-in-the-street in Europe and America those events in Hungary would largely obscure preparations by France and Britain to join with Israel in attacking Egyptian forces along the Suez Canal.

For the Israelis, it was a tricky business to play a cat-and-mouse game with the Americans. Moshe Dayan, in his *Diary of the Sinai Campaign*, described his country's predicament when he said: " Israel, wishing and needing to maintain close ties of friendship with the United States, finds herself in the difficult position of having to keep from her – and being evasive about – her real (military) intentions".

The best informed American in Israel during the crucial month of October was our military attaché, Colonel Dan Querry. His intelligence pointed to action in the south, which could only mean the Suez Canal region. That Israel might have allies in any such endeavour seemed confirmed by the covert arrival in Israel of French air force planes and crews. Despite this, however, there always remained the possibility that some Israeli units might be deployed into Jordan, Lebanon and Syria. If Israel invaded any of these four countries, especially with the assistance of France or Britain, the implications for the United States would be enormous.

Angela and Stuart were vaguely aware that war was imminent for a large anti-aircraft gun suddenly appeared in the garden of the house opposite our apartment block. It was just as well that we did not have to use our air raid shelter, for the children discovered a snake had taken over the tenancy.

My family and I unwittingly helped Colonel Querry to rule out any Israeli action against Lebanon and Syria. It was our custom to pass some part of each weekend at the ancient Roman site of Apollonia located a few miles north of Tel Aviv and overlooking the Mediterranean. Adjoining the Roman site was an Israel Defence Force communications post whose task obviously was to monitor any activity on the beach and the adjacent stretch of the Mediterranean. The post observers thus would have known about the regularity of our recreational visits.

One day, as the Israeli build-up in the south was gathering momentum, we started home after the usual pleasant day of pottering about on the beach and among the ancient ruins.

When we reached the main Tel Aviv – Haifa road, the principal route to the north of the country, a small column of antiquated half-tracks and other vehicles emerged from a side road and turned north. The "coincidence" seemed incongruous, but nonetheless I decided to tell Colonel Querry about it.

"Your regular visits to Apollonia and the convoy's turn to the north just as your car reached the main road," he said, "indicate only one thing – the main Israeli strike will be in the opposite direction – south. This also coincides with our intelligence."

He was correct. When the so-called "Sinai Campaign" was over, the Pentagon would acknowledge Colonel Querry's analysis of events leading up to the fighting as being extremely accurate. Sadly, he was to die from a heart attack not long afterwards. The strain from closely monitoring the Israeli preparations for several weeks, often with little sleep or rest, had proved too much for his constitution.

Partly to punish Israel for its deception in joining ranks with Britain and France over the Suez issue and partly because the operation was a blow to reconciliation efforts with Israel's Arab neighbours, the United States decided to evacuate most of its staff in two stages. First would go the wives and children, later the officers.

On a few hours' notice Mary and I had to pack suitcases with only the minimum of clothing for herself and the three children. Then we crowded into our Morris Oxford and joined a convoy of about a dozen American cars, all driven by husbands of the families, bound north to Haifa. We had strict orders to keep the convoy closed up, that is, so close that there would not be space for an overtaking "hostile" (that had to be Arab) car to insert itself among our number.

Embassy contingency planners had not reckoned with the inability of our low-powered Morris Oxford keeping up with the larger American cars which made up the rest of the convoy. The coastal road from Tel Aviv to Haifa may appear on a map to be flat, but our heavily laden car was unable to cope with one hill after another. As we approached each one, however small it might be, the Morris lost speed dramatically. That resulted in the cars in front of us disappearing out of sight and those behind us bunching up in a tight group. If there had been hostile Arab intruders along the way, we would have been sitting ducks. Once I cleared a hill, I would race as fast as I could to catch up with the cars in front, only to fall behind again at the next hill. Mary and the children soon developed "helpful" grunts ("ahh, ahh, *aaahh*!") to nudge the little car forward, but inevitably the gaps in the convoy developed again.

We heaved a great sigh of relief, but perhaps not so great as those of our other convoy members, when at last we reached Haifa docks. There waiting for us was a small Italian coaster whose master had hoped to sail with a cargo of Israeli citrus fruit. It transpired that Washington had authorised our ambassador to approach the Italian embassy in Tel Aviv and charter the ship for taking our dependents out of the war zone. Stepping through the mass of fruit crates on the quayside, the wives and children hastily embarked and the ship sailed immediately.

The husbands who waved good-bye to their loved ones did not know that the vessel would shortly be sailing *into* a war zone. Off the coast of Israel ships of several nations were now deployed. When an Egyptian destroyer was seen in the area, it was immediately attacked by a patrolling French vessel which promptly put it out of action. Happily, the wives and children were unaware of the battle situation and their ship reached the port of Famagusta in Cyprus without incident. From there they went on to Venice and, eventually, Rome.

A few days later, a US Air Force plane arrived to take the embassy's officers. A few would remain to look after essential administration and communications. On the aircraft, which would fly us non-stop to Rome, I happened to be seated directly opposite our cultural attaché, Tom McGrail. I had no need to be reminded that he dreaded air flights, for he was trembling and in a state of deep anxiety all the way to Rome. One member of the plane's team of stewards called me aside and asked me if Tom was unwell. When I explained Tom's phobia, the sergeant said he had encountered it before but had never seen anyone show such extreme effects as Tom.

In Rome family members were happily reunited. Our Rome embassy and USIA staff took great pains to find accommodation for us, enrol children in schools and otherwise look after our needs and concerns. We were placed in a small pension where the friendly staff immediately adopted our three children as their own. Having Italian meals three times a day took some getting used to, but we soon adapted. It would be the many flavours of Italian ice cream, however, that we would most remember.

Our return to Israel was delayed while the American and Israeli governments argued about the freeze on US aid that had been imposed. Meanwhile, I was sent to Teheran for several weeks to help with the American nuclear exhibition, "Atoms for Peace", on which I had worked in Tel Aviv before the evacuation. I took a room in a small hotel run by an Armenian family. Although there was then some apprehension that the Shah would be toppled, I never dreamed that the embassy, from which I received my daily instructions and where I had my mid-day meals, would one day be seized and its officers held hostage by the Iranians.

The exhibition itself was popular and passed off without incident. The most exciting moment of my stay came in the middle of one night when my drip-dry shirt, hanging on a coat-hanger to dry, suddenly fell with a loud metallic ring. Then I realized my bed was moving and, so it seemed, the room itself. Then all became still and I turned over and went back to sleep. Next morning my Armenian hosts smilingly asked if the earthquake had interrupted my sleep. Amazed, I asked why the hotel's occupants hadn't been evacuated.

"Nothing to worry about," I was assured. "We have these little tremors frequently. The hotel is built to withstand much greater shocks. You might have been in greater danger had you run out into the street."

Thus passed my first and only earthquake experience.

71
The sad travail of Tom McGrail

Eventually, Washington and Tel Aviv reached an understanding over differences arising from the Sinai Campaign and our family returned to Israel. This time we enrolled Angela and Stuart in the only other Tel Aviv school offering some instruction in English, the Pensionnat des Religieuses de St. Joseph, a Catholic institution. It was to be the fifth school they would attend in the course of the academic year. Whatever advantages accrue to children of diplomatic families living abroad, normal schooling is not one of them.

Our programme of economic assistance to Israel, which had ground to a halt during the war and the impasse that followed, was now reactivated. It became my task to publicise the joint US-Israeli economic effort, one that brought me into contact with both American experts and their gifted Israeli counterparts. I frequently accompanied them to factories, schools, farms and *kibbutzim* to see the results of their schemes. For example, I saw the introduction of the larger and fleshier American chicken which was to revolutionise Israel's poultry industry.

Some of the American experts left behind valuable studies after completing their assignments in Israel. One, Dr. Henry Rosenfeld, undertook a painstaking scrutiny of the health and living conditions and family attitudes in the Arab village of Taiy'be. His highly readable report, when delivered to the Israeli Ministry of Health, was praised as being the most authoritative yet compiled in this area of public health.

Our aid mission to Israel had a large staff of Israelis who served as our assistants: secretaries, typists, translators, clerks, chauffeurs and so on. Like the population itself, they came from many parts of the world. Despite the government's campaign to promote use of Hebrew, Jews who came from Britain and the United States spoke English among themselves and read the *Jerusalem Post*. Jews who originated from Hungary, Poland, Romania, Spain and the Arab countries who had not yet fully learned Hebrew, read newspapers printed in their native tongues.

It dawned on me one day that the two or three Jews who worked most closely with my office actually resembled the popularly held facial stereotypes (French, Polish, Arab etc.) of the countries of their origin. But was this universally true? If so, it meant that one's national origin was the dominant feature in a Jew's appearance. Likewise, if national characteristics prevailed, the popularly held belief that all Jews look alike would be laid to rest.

My staff was fascinated with this question and enthusiastically joined me in a project to photograph several employees whose ancestral homes had been in countries represented by Israel's principal foreign language journals. Amazingly, we discovered that our French Jewess resembled any chic young lady from Paris; the same pattern held true for all the others in this small photographic survey. We concluded that first generation Jews in Israel facially resembled the residents of their country of origin; obviously, with subsequent intermarriage, this would not hold true for succeeding generations.

Many prominent Jews from other countries visited Israel during my tour of duty. All, of course, could have Israeli citizenship for the asking. As the embassy press attaché, I was often included in the welcome party for both prominent Jews and high-ranking official visitors at Tel Aviv airport and, occasionally, on their travels within Israel. On these occasions I frequently saw Teddy Kollek, then Israel's 'front man' for visiting foreign dignitaries.

When the American Secretary of Agriculture, Ezra Taft Benson, arrived for a visit, Israelis hoped he would bring news of a much needed grant. I ended up sharing the back seat of Kollek's car on the drive from the airport to Tel Aviv through a dairying area. As soon as he seated himself, Kollek turned to me and apologised, saying:

"The only way I can keep up my pace is to snatch a few minutes of sleep in cars, on an office couch, or whatever. Please excuse me if I drop off now."

With that he closed his eyes and instantly was sound asleep. Ten minutes later when we arrived at a model dairy farm and the car slowed its pace, he abruptly awakened. Leaping out, he was immediately his usual affable self with not the slightest hint of his recent slumber.

Benson, anxious to show off his knowledge of dairy animals, immediately climbed the nearby fence, dodged piles of manure and strode to the nearest cow and proceeded to examine her udder, back and sides. Now in his element, he praised the cow much as an auctioneer would at a cattle sale. Teddy Kollek and the rest of the Israeli party looked at each other with delight; the omens were good for that grant.

The visit over, Secretary Benson went on to meet his Israeli counterpart and to visit other farming areas. No one was surprised when the Secretary announced a substantial American grant. Kollek went on to become Mayor of Jerusalem, a post he would hold for many years and where he was held in great respect by Jewish, Arab and Christian residents.

Our embassy staff, from the ambassador down, groaned at the annual invasion of American Congressmen. Ostensibly on fact-finding missions about one or another world problem, most were on sight-seeing junkets financed by the United States government. If elections were scheduled shortly in the United States, they considered it a great advantage, while wooing influential American Jews, to be able to say "When I was in Israel recently….".

As my time in the foreign service lengthened, I learned that these jaunts were not unique to Israel; in fact, Congressmen travelled to every corner of the globe. At first I considered these overseas travels, in which nearly half the members of Congress participated, a great waste of public funds. I quickly learned, however, that many had never set foot outside the United States before, and that these trips, albeit brief, enabled them to look at global problems with a more informed eye. In truth, these travel costs represented good value. As the United States endeavoured to carry out its leading role on the world stage, her "actors" (i.e. members of

Congress) could now perform much better with their newly acquired knowledge.

Mary and I made the most of our own travel opportunities in our part of the Middle East. Twice we went to Beirut, as diplomats were entitled to do, for family shopping. The gracious, prosperous city at that time was unaffected by the terrorism that later tore it asunder. Its shops were filled with goods from all over the world and prices sometimes were lower than in Britain or the United States.

Beirut then had a small community of Jewish traders who lived and worked quite amicably with their fellow Lebanese. Although Lebanon always was regarded as the least hostile of Israel's neighbours, our Beirut embassy officers nonetheless felt it wise not to say aloud the word "Israel" in their conversations with us. Instead they would point to the south, nod knowingly and say, "Down in Dixie". The only unsettling aspect of the Beirut expeditions was the necessity to pass by the large refugee camps of Palestinian Arabs who had been dispossessed from their homes and lands. We did not visit the camps, but it was clear that their austere living conditions forced some Arab women, as we could see from our car, to cut wild plants on the side of the road for food.

On another occasion I joined a group of embassy officers and wives for a safari-type weekend at Petra in southern Jordan. Despite hours of travel over the then unimproved, dusty roads, we spent a glorious two days exploring the sights of the "Rose Red City" depicted so eloquently in the engravings of David Roberts in *The Holy Land*.

Mary and I were ever keen to see and learn more about Israel, often taking the children with us. Near Haifa a road leads to the B'hai Temple and the crest of Mount Carmel, one of our favourite picnicking spots. There were also jaunts to Safad, Tiberias (and the Sea of Galilee), Jerusalem, Beersheba and other towns. Once, south of Tel Aviv where bulldozers had started clearing away earth for a large building, Pipkin found a badly corroded coin. It had no value, but the thrill of finding a centuries-old coin was not lost on her; this insignificant discovery was the first sign of her subsequent interests in ancient history and numismatics.

One day, Tom McGrail, our bachelor cultural attaché, was asked to go to Eilat and discuss how it might have its share of American singers, musicians, actors, etc., who frequently visited Israel. Because of his fear of flying he passed up the offer of a one-hour flight from Tel Aviv to Eilat (170 miles) in favour of a two-day, body-racking ordeal by jeep. Although exhausted by the long trip south, he did not hesitate to repeat the land journey back to Tel Aviv, so great was his phobia of flying.

In our time, Israel was content to sustain a large number of *kibbutzim*, regardless of whether they were economically viable. Some became semi-military bases because of their proximity to borders of neighbouring Arab countries; others were occupied by staunch members of political parties. Most, however, were bustling agricultural enterprises with a variety of crops and farm animals, sometimes supplemented by small industries. A few were viable. Certain aspects of the *kibbutzim* life were then widely regarded in the West as socialistic (e.g., communal nurseries for children); in fact, these arrangements were the forerunners of the pre-school nursery movement now taken for granted in many countries.

Mary and I decided we could not leave Israel without personal experience of a *kibbutz.* After clearing it with the embassy, we arranged to pass a weekend at the Ha Maccabi *kibbutz* not far from Haifa. We stayed in a modest house, not much larger than a beach hut, and ate in the central dining hall. The meals were austere and almost vegetarian, but no one complained. Over the ensuing weekend we visited the various farm enterprises, the school, nursery and other centres of activity.

One evening the entire commune gathered to hear a report from a member who had gone to Eastern Europe to attend an international youth congress sponsored by the Soviet Union. As the United States was deeply concerned about the inroads being made on young minds by communist ideology, it followed press reports of the congress with great interest and no doubt the CIA had its own observers at the sessions.

Aware that the speaker might reveal useful information about the congress and that it would be tactless of me to make notes in public, I determined to make a mental record of everything that seemed significant. Thanks to the system I had learned at the Army's officers' candidate school for linking subjects with visual objects, such as "A for apple" and "B for box", etc., I was able afterwards to recall all of the pertinent observations made by the Ha Macabbi speaker. When we returned to Tel Aviv the next day I provided the embassy, and eventually Washington, with a first-hand account of the youth congress as seen by an Israeli intellectual.

During the first decade of the state of Israel's existence great pressure was put on its citizens to cast off their original names and adopt Hebrew ones. This was desirable because it would reinforce the country's identity with Biblical Israel where only Hebrew names were used. So great was the government's pressure on Israelis to adopt Hebrew names that, in some instances, the state refused to send its citizens abroad unless they adopted Hebrew names.

My fellow Rotarians told me how this policy caused chaos in the early days of Israel's modern statehood when the national football team first played abroad. The Israeli sports commentator desperately tried to make sense of the government's decree, but his running commentary of the game came out something like this:

"There goes Goldberg – oh, I mean Malchi – with the ball. Now he's passed to Silverstein – I mean Ben-Zvi – and now Rubin has it – he's now Tawil, I think – well he – whoever he is – he has now scored a goal!"

This hilarious charade went on for the whole of the game, with the poor commentator always speaking well after the action, so busy was he checking his cross-reference list of names for each player on the field.

Another story held that Levi Eshkol, then finance minister, was precisely the right man to levy taxes on Israelis, inasmuch as the Book of Genesis (Chap. 14:24), in reference to dealings involving one Eshkol and two other men, commanded: "Let them have their portion."

All three of our children relished exploring the ruins of the ancient Roman fortress at Apollonia on weekends. Although it was the beach there that had been recommended to us, the children's imagination always took over as they pretended to be Roman soldiers defending the site from maritime invaders.

One weekend, near the end of our stay in Israel, we had lingered longer than usual to allow the children to relive their pretended battles and skirmishes in the knowledge that, once we left the country, we were not likely to duplicate such an idyllic setting. Eventually Mary and I rounded up Stuart and Pipkin, only to discover that Angela was missing. We assumed she had taken the track up the cliff towards the spot where we had left the car and so started picking our way up the narrow, rough path. Rounding a large boulder, we suddenly came upon her deep in conversation with a soldier wearing a black eye-patch. As the man turned to greet us, we realised he was Moshe Dayan – then a national hero with the Israeli public because of his role in the Sinai Campaign. He smiled as we drew near, and said:

"What a wonderful daughter you have! She has been asking me about the history of Apollonia. I only wish more of our Israeli young people would be as interested."

Not far from Apollonia was one of Israel's largest hotels in whose grounds the embassy staged its annual Fourth of July party. These events ostensibly were for the leaders of government, business, religion, the arts and professions, but both American expatriates and visiting Americans expect, by right, also to attend.

Because many American businessmen have personal contacts with the White House, woe betide any ambassador who has the gall to turn away a fellow citizen on this, the national day of independence. At the same time, however, there were always Congressmen who deplored spending public money for "booze" and especially on Americans living abroad. Caught in the middle, our ambassador thus had to make sure he invited both prominent Israelis and visiting American VIPs.

For our final Fourth of July celebration Mary and I had gone early to the beach site overlooking the Mediterranean to offer our services. We were told that the Israeli catering staff had everything in hand and that our principal duty would be to introduce the country's media contacts to the ambassador. Several large tables, covered with white tablecloths, held an abundance of food and drink. The caterers mingled with the crowd, offering snacks and topping up drinks.

We had only one major concern: keeping an eye out for the arrival of the Chief Rabbi. The reason for our anxiety was that we offered delicious Virginia cured ham, which we knew to be popular with many Israelis, as an optional meat. Suddenly someone spotted the official car bearing the Chief Rabbi and there was a rush to grab the ham and hide it beneath the table where the overlapping tablecloth would afford concealment. The Rabbi emerged from his car, greeted the ambassador, envoys from other countries and Israeli government officials before briefly partaking of the food.

When he departed we all gave a sigh of relief that his visit had gone off without mishap. The caterers rushed to retrieve the ham from its hiding place, but lo, there was no ham to be seen. During the melee after it had been spirited off the table, it had somehow disappeared. Despite a thorough search among the tables and cases brought by the caterers, it was never found. Long live Virginia cured ham!

Our last, lingering memory of Israel was linked with the departure of our cultural attaché, Tom McGrail. He was immensely popular with the Israelis, having been instrumental in persuading Washington to send to Israel many leading American cultural figures on short visits. A few days before he was due to leave for Washington, he was honoured in a ceremony at the ZOA (Zionist Organisation of America) House. After receiving a certificate of gratitude awarded only rarely to Gentiles, Tom spoke movingly about the days when he used to sit on his mother's knee as she read him stories from the Bible. Now, he concluded, he was about to leave that Biblical land, which he had come to know as a child, after some of the happiest days of his life.

Sadly, that happy occasion at the ZOA House would not be the last newsworthy event Israelis would remember about Tom. After visiting his sister in Roxbury, Massachusetts, he went to Washington to learn of his next assignment. He was to be the next American cultural attaché to Burma, he was told, and shortly would be flying to Rangoon. Taking a ship was out of the question, his superiors said, for it was now less expensive to send an officer to a foreign country by air because of the travel time involved. Tom, with his fear of flying, no doubt had been horrified at this decision.

Pan Am, then the world's premier airline, operated a daily round-the-world flight. The organising of airport arrivals and departures, servicing of aircraft, catering for passengers and changing of crews was such a dramatic and complex affair that it once was the topic of a *Reader's Digest* feature. Not the least attractive feature of flying with Pan Am was its excellent safety record. None of these attributes, however, was likely to have impressed Tom as he boarded the flight for Rangoon,with several stops en route.

"Have you seen this news item?" an Israeli colleague asked me one day not long after Tom had left Israel. She handed me a copy of *The Jerusalem Post* stating that a Pan Am airliner was missing in the Pacific and that among its distinguished passengers was Dr. Tom McGrail, proceeding to Rangoon as the next American cultural attaché.

We could hardly believe our eyes. Israelis by the dozen telephoned the embassy to ask if we could confirm the report. We hastily telephoned Washington. "Yes," officials there said, "the plane disappeared without trace and there are no survivors as far as we know. Obviously we'll let you know if we hear good news of Tom." But there was none. Death had come to Tom in precisely the manner he had most feared.

72
Dealing with de Gaulle

Our memorable assignment to Israel came to an end in April, 1958 when I was appointed military affairs officer at the American Embassy in Paris.

France was then the only country in the world where the USIA stable included an officer dealing exclusively with military affairs. The reason was simple: the Cold War was raging and Paris, headquarters both of NATO and its military arm (SHAPE), would become the operational centre if a hot war broke out. The main problem was President de Gaulle, who sought to develop French national pride to the detriment of the North Atlantic Alliance. He became increasingly anti-American and anti-British both in his public pronouncements and his actions.

My mission was twofold: first, to foster good relations between our military forces and the French people and, second, to impress on French media NATO's vital role in defending Western Europe should the Soviet Union attack.

My superior was Bill Cody, a direct descendant of Colonel W.F. ("Buffalo Bill") Cody of Wild West fame. He was one of a handful of highly regarded USIA officers who strove to mould a favourable image of America immediately World War II ended. He was also renowned for his strong views and decisiveness. Foremost among the folklore about his methods was his lack of patience for anyone with a "problem".

"There is no such thing as a problem," he asserted, "everything in life is simply a matter of management."

I had been warned by friends that Bill wanted all his staff to live in central Paris so as to be convenient for entertaining French contacts. If I had a different idea, it was suggested to me, I should sign my rental contract before Bill knew about it. No doubt I would then face Bill's fury, but at least I would have a binding house contract.

After a few weeks of hotel life, we settled upon a villa in the suburb of Le Vésinet, about 20 minutes from Gare St. Lazare by rail on the line to St. Germain-en-Laye. It was large enough to provide a bedroom for each of the children and had an attic which could serve as a combination playroom and storage area. Only after moving into the house did we learn that Le Vésinet had been created as a model town similar to Finland's Tapiola, Britain's Welwyn Garden City and America's Reston.

The town, laid out in 1854, was the dream of one man, Alphonse Pallu, whose original home was opposite ours and now bore a plaque reading "Fondateur du Vésinet". It was in honour of his daughter, Marguerite, that the street on which we lived, was named. Pallu and his backers constructed a "Grand Lac" in the centre of the new town, with streets radiating in all directions. In the middle of the artificial lake was an island on which several buildings were erected. The complex came to be known as Les Ibis. Small canals wound along some of the streets andeven through some private gardens, including his own.

When we arrived in 1958, Le Vésinet had a population of about 17,000. Planning officials hoped to keep the population static by refusing permission to build additional houses in the spacious gardens, but even then the system was breaking down. We were fortunate to have lived there when it was possible to walk through parks and spacious tree-lined avenues from one end to the other, as Monsieur Pallu had envisioned.

The heraldic arms of Le Vésinet were strikingly beautiful, incorporating its ancient history, model town significance and wealth of nature. Topped by a crown signifying its one-time royal forest status, the arms' central motif is a shield bearing a hunter's horn, a pair of oak leaves and a marguerite (the French word for daisy) in honour of Monsieur Pallu's daughter.

At Douze Avenue de la Marguerite we inherited both maid and gardener from the previous occupants. Alice, the maid, was neither reliable nor happy in her work. She frequently left water taps running and her sight was so bad that teaspoons frequently went into the refuse pail along with scraps of food; only by methodically checking the pail after her departure were we able to preserve our set of silverware. Eventually we had to let her go.

André Chevallier, the gardener, however, was a gem. He always turned up with a smile, ready for his weekly chores. He had worked in the garden for years and knew every plant, shrub and tree. There was one caveat to his working agreement: we had to have a bottle of *vin ordinaire* ready for him on arrival, this a "perk" in addition to his wages. At first Mary had her doubts about the quality of André's performance as the day wore on but, although his face got redder by the hour, his energy flagged only slightly. If Mary saw problems in the garden, André did not. "Avec confiance, tout est possible", was his ready reply and, sure enough, he always found a solution.

André had seen service during the last war and looked forward each year to the Bastille Day parade of "ancient combatants" which terminated in the grounds of the local Mairie for a ceremony. His deep sense of loyalty also extended to our family.

When we subsequently went on home leave to the United States, we were cabled that our house had been burgled, and that we should immediately return. We did so, to learn that André, on arriving for work the day after the break-in and seeing the cellar door had been broken open, ran all the way to the police station a quarter of a mile away to report the crime. Fortunately, the thieves had taken only a few small objects and our insurance fully covered their loss.

Seizing the chance for the children to acquire a working knowledge of French, we initially enrolled all three in French schools. This left Mary free to shop for food in Le Vésinet's weekly marché. Meanwhile, I set off for Paris to begin my duties at the embassy's sprawling complex on the corner of the Place de la Concorde.

Here Bill Cody's first question was "Where are you going to live?" When I told him Le Vésinet because it was not as expensive as Paris and, in addition, was ideal for our family of five, he glared angrily. Then he smiled and said he agreed it was a congenial place for a family, even if its distance from Paris might prevent some of my contacts from accepting invitations to my social events.

He suggested I learn all I could about my work from Colette Gaudin, who had been my predecessor's secretary, and would now be mine. Colette, a strikingly beautiful brunette in her early thirties, was unmarried, although she had had several serious relationships.

She came from Marseille where her late father had earned hero status during the war for his work with the resistance. Colette was both bilingual and confident, so much so that she was as much at ease with a French cabinet minister and high ranking Americans as with a fellow secretary at the embassy. She was one of those rare individuals who could by-pass channels and go straight to the top with the greatest of ease. During her years at the embassy, she had established a network of contacts both in French government circles and at USIA in Paris and its Washington headquarters. In short, with few limitations and an excellent command of both French and English, she came close to being the perfect secretary.

When I arrived in France in the spring of 1958, the French government was very sensitive about the presence of so many American military installations on its soil. It mattered not that the Cold War was at its fiercest; President de Gaulle was determined to rebuild French national pride after, first, the humiliation of surrender to the Germans, and second, widespread collaboration during World War II. Now, 13 years after the war's end, France was still "occupied", and he and his party did not like it.

There were indeed several large US Air Force bases in France, a few small Canadian ones, as well as numerous US Army installations. At Orleans was the headquarters of the US Army's supply command which would direct war materiel to the whole of Western Europe in the event of a Soviet invasion. In the Mediterranean, the US Sixth Fleet also had anchorages.

De Gaulle, who had both the British and the Americans to thank for the prominence he gained during the war, now assumed an almost hostile attitude as he sought to develop France's independent nuclear capability ("force de frappe") and withdraw French forces from NATO's command. There was deep concern among Americans and Canadians that he might, on the least provocation, order the removal of all Allied installations from the country. If that happened, NATO's administrative headquarters, sited in a new "A" (for Alliance) shaped building in Paris, would become obsolete as might also the Allied military headquarters near St. Germain-en-Laye. Should such drastic actions one day occur, they would be a barrier to NATO's ability to respond quickly to a Soviet invasion.

This uneasy relationship existed for the whole of my Paris assignment. Once each month I had to draft the agenda for a Franco-American committee whose aim was to "Promote friendly relations between American forces and the French population". The committee represented the French foreign office, the US military, the American Embassy and USIA. The most important contribution of the committee was the creation of CRAs (Community Relations Advisers); they were French civilians assigned to all large US military bases in France.

These advisers sought to bring Americans and French together in activities such as wine and cheese tastings, tours to *chateaux* and historic sites, screening of French films and so on. They also were of great help to base commanders when there were accidents or incidents involving Americans. Each year we cited one of the CRAs for accomplishing some outstanding project. Ambassador Charles Bohlen, after presenting the award on one occasion, praised the CRA programme as "one of the most effective devices we have for bringing together French and Americans'"

Despite this endorsement at the highest level and the energy expended by many in community relations activities, it was difficult to impress the young servicemen. Most were in their upper teens or early twenties and often had only a high school education, very little knowledge of French and were likely to be Protestant. This background, combined with the traditional reluctance of the French to establish close relations outside their circle of family and friends, made it almost impossible for the two to communicate.

For sergeants and commissioned officers who were older and better educated, the position was only slightly better. Many of these were permitted to rent houses in towns and villages near their bases, and thus of necessity were thrown into contact with their French neighbours. But the majority of servicemen spent most of their time within the confines of their bases where they shopped in the American commissary and post exchange, saw American movies, played American sports and sent their children to the military school.

Meanwhile, De Gaulle continued his ambivalent stance: yes, French troops would be a part of NATO in a shooting war, but no, France would have its own nuclear capability, responsible only to itself. As theFrench public had little knowledge of how NATO would operate in the event of a war, I approached the US Air Force to see if they could provide a plane to take 20 French journalists on a week's tour of selected American NATO bases, first within France itself and the following year, in the whole of the NATO area. They agreed. I duly organised the tours and each journalist filed a daily feature, with photographs, describing the base being visited and how the US military would react to a Soviet attack.

The only hitch in the operation came when our group, originally cleared to visit the joint US-French air base at Chateauroux, was refused permission to disembark and the embarrassed French liaison officer was rapped on the knuckles by his superiors in Paris for originally agreeing to receive us. This was an ominous sign of things to come, but it may also have indicated that the NATO message was getting through to the French public because of the features being written by the touring journalists.

It was my privilege to work for several years with the American participants in the Paris Air Show, then and now the major aeronautics showcase in the world. When the publicity was favourable, such as revealing a sensational new aircraft, the American aviation industry was elated. When bad news unexpectedly occurred, as happened when an American plane crashed soon after having made a record-breaking Atlantic crossing, the negative effect was horrendous.

One year the American exhibition at the Paris Air Show emphasised the latest in spatial aeronautics. De Gaulle signalled his intention of visiting the American pavilion where, it was agreed, the two senior US Air Force officers and my secretary, Colette Gaudin, and I would be present to answer questions. As the centrepiece was at one end of the pavilion, we agreed that the two military officers would position themselves at one side, and the two civilians (Colette and I) at the other.

When the President entered with his aide, he ignored the two air force officers (blatantly, it seemed to me), took a quick look at the centrepiece and then came over to Colette and me, said "Congratulations!" and shook hands. We smiled and thanked him, whereupon he executed a sharp about-face and walked away without as much as a glance at the officers. I took this as one more example of de Gaulle's determination not to applaud the US military – or at least, not while they were on French soil.

73
Hot seat in Paris

On weekends and public holidays, our Paris embassy, in common with embassies worldwide, appointed a staff member to be "Duty Officer" to deal with any problems arising. Apart from London, Paris probably had more need of a duty officer on these occasions than most embassies, given the presence of huge numbers of American tourists and its sizeable expatriate colony. It was always sad to give up these weekends and holidays with the family but, on the other hand, there was a virtual guarantee that something exciting would happen. Some examples:

"Monsieur," began a voice one weekend on my telephone, "Nous avons ici un americain qui vient de mourir." The voice belonged to a hotel manager who had just discovered an elderly tourist dead in his bedroom. What, he wanted to know, should he do? There was no need for either the hotel manager or myself to panic. Thanks to an elaborate handbook developed over the years, the duty officer knew exactly what had to be done.

I at once telephoned one of the undertakers on the embassy's approved list; he said he would immediately take charge of the body and await further embassy instructions. Those instructions had to come from the consul, whom I called next. He would determine the dead man's next of kin from his possessions, make the necessary telephone calls to the

United States and then act according to the instructions they gave. All this was very straightforward, but nonetheless slightly daunting when undertaken for the first time.

On another occasion an embassy Marine guard escorted a long-haired young man of about 30 to my office. His was a sad saga. He had come to Paris several years ago, he said, attracted by its beauty and wealth of cultural attractions. Work was hard to come by, but his folks in the United States always baled him out. He was living in a small Left Bank hotel whose manager now threatened to turn him out unless he paid 30 francs rent immediately. Could the embassy lend him that sum? Fortunately the embassy always provided an experienced French secretary for the duty officer. I was in luck, for my secretary thought the young man's name rang a bell.

Digging into the duty officer file, she discovered a note saying he was a notorious borrower who already had swindled previous duty officers out of $50. Moreover, the note continued, his passport had been cancelled. The young man saw our whispered conference, sensed the game was up and mumbled several mild oaths.

I called the Marine guard to escort him off the premises and added another note to the logbook advising caution when dealing with this young man hereafter. (Some years later, when visiting Paris as a tourist, I saw this same young man near the American Legion building, detailing a hard-luck story to an innocent American visitor who, no doubt, he hoped would provide a useful hand-out.)

One Saturday a private in the US Army was ushered into the duty officer's room where he tossed a sheaf of travel documents on my desk and flopped down in a chair, exhausted. He said he was supposed to report for duty at a St. André "somewhere in France".

"I've been to one St. André," he said wearily, "and they had never heard of the United States Army."

Unable to converse with the French railways ticket agent, the private had been sent to a well known town of St. André in the Rhone valley. I knew the St. André he wanted was near the US Air Force base at Evreux, only an hour's ride from Paris. I had the French secretary type a note to the railway clerk, explaining the error. Attaching this to his travel warrant, I directed him to nearby Gare St. Lazare. He departed without thanking me, obviously not quite willing to believe his problem was over. The incident drove home to me the plight of the American serviceman who is obliged to travel alone in a strange country whose language he does not understand.

On another day an irate Parisian landlord shouted on the telephone that his American tenant had flown the coop without paying his rent. I asked if he knew the man's name and if he had his passport. Sadly, he knew nothing about the man, did not have his passport and therefore didn't know if the name signed on his register was an alias or not.

"Je regrette," I explained, after exhausting all efforts at learning the man's identity, "mais il n'y a rien à faire."

Hot seat in Paris

Two well dressed American ladies, clearly in distress, were ushered into the office one weekend by the Marine guard. I judged both to be in their upper sixties, or older. They were very, very lost and had been wandering the streets for hours. Questioning revealed they came to Paris the previous evening on their first visit abroad. They had spent the morning seeing nearby sights on foot, but when they became tired and wanted to return to their hotel, it was nowhere to be found. Their small tourist map of the city had been no help. They had no room key, hotel brochure or any other clue as to the hotel's name or address.

This was indeed, a "toughie". By asking more questions, I narrowed the hotel's likely location to a ten-block expanse along the Seine's right bank. Then, my persevering secretary set about telephoning small hotels in the area. On the 27th attempt, she located the hotel. When she repeated it, the ladies beamed and exclaimed in unison:

"Oh yes! That's it! We knew it all along."

I hastily drew them a map, more detailed than the one they had and they departed happily, thanking the secretary profusely for her efforts.

On another occasion an American with an urgency about his manner was escorted to the office. He showed me his credentials, confirming that he was with the US civil aviation agency in Paris. He must, he announced, fly to Rome at once to deal with a crashed American airliner. All the flights out of Paris were full, he said, but one airline was willing to "bump" a passenger if the embassy made an official request. He gave me the number of the airline's manager. When I explained that the embassy would be grateful if the official's travel could be facilitated, he readily agreed and said no further confirmation was needed. This problem took no more than five or six minutes to solve; one of the easiest of the day.

Occasionally there were tricky situations in which time was of the essence, as happened one Saturday when an irate American woman came on the telephone. At first she spoke so quickly and with such emotion that I couldn't understand a word. After quietening down slightly she said:

"I'm at the airport and am due to board my plane in 30 minutes. I've bought several bottles of expensive French perfume to take back as gifts and the French customs officials won't let me take them unless I break the seal on every bottle. Can't the embassy do something about this? After all, the French should be pleased I bought their perfume."

Hers was an all too familiar story and I was able to explain the position at once. To protect its American retail distributors, French perfume manufacturers would not allow certain brands bought in France to be exported to the United States unless the perfume was "used", that is, the seals of the bottles had been broken. French perfume sellers knew this and were supposed to advise buyers accordingly, but some didn't for fear of losing a sale. I told the lady she had two choices: she could miss her flight, go back to the shop in Paris and get a refund and then take a later plane, or she could, as the customs officials had suggested, open each bottle and catch her scheduled flight. At first she resisted the idea of taking home "used" bottles of perfume for her friends.

"But think what a story you can tell about how those bottles almost made you miss your flight!" I interjected.

There was a slight pause during which I could invisibly see her checking her watch. With a deep sigh, she said perhaps it didn't matter so much after all about the bottles being opened. She thanked me hastily and hung up.

A more complicated incident happened one Sunday late in August when a young American of about 20 was ushered into the office. He explained he was a university student who had been "doing Europe", including the Soviet Union, and had run out of money. His father, he explained, had twice sent him enough money for the return flight to the United States, but he had spent it all in Western Europe seeing more and more places that greatly interested him. He was afraid of his father's wrath and did not want to approach him again. Could the embassy lend him the $200 for a ticket to New York where he was shortly due to continue his studies?

It took me some time to convince him that a telephone call to his father was his only solution. And the cost of that call, I added, had to be reversed to his father. He was appalled at the suggestion and at first refused to accept it. I told him I had other things to occupy my mind for the moment and advised him quietly to think over this problem. After about five minutes he meekly agreed to make the call.

His father spluttered and objected furiously when told there was a reverse-charge call from his son at the American Embassy in Paris, but eventually agreed to accept it. His first question to the son must have been "What's this all about?" for the young man immediately went into a long story about "one thing leading to another", to which my secretary and I could hear the angry father's frequent oaths. The conversation ended with the son repeatedly uttering "Yes, sir," in a subdued voice.

"Everything all right?" I asked.

"I hope so," the student replied, "My father's ordering my ticket through American Express – he's not sending me the money."

At midday one Sunday the Marine guard escorted a prosperous-looking American of about 50 to my office. The man's story about losing his passport did not ring true. After a few questions, he admitted he had spent the night in the Pigalle district, noted for its women-of-the-night. Not only had he lost his passport, but his wallet and wrist watch as well. I told him the consul probably would issue a new passport on Monday.

On calling the police station nearest to the restaurant where the man's adventures began, I learned that the wallet had been found with its credit cards intact, but the money was missing. The man left the embassy reasonably mollified, grateful that he would shortly be "back in business again" with his credit cards and would get a fresh passport the next day.

On another occasion the telephone happily prevented confrontation between an unpleasant American and me. The secretary couldn't understand the obviously drunken man on the other end. She handed the phone to me, but the man said he would speak only with the ambassador. When I pointed out the day was Sunday and the ambassador was not in, he interrupted:

"But I demand to speak with the am-bas-sa-dor himself!" he shouted, slurring his every word.

I then explained that the ambassador's whereabouts were unknown, but if he had a message, I would be happy to pass it on to the ambassador's office. He relented and slowly his grievance came out.

He was the first mate of a small American cargo vessel unloading at a port not far from Bordeaux. The captain of the ship, he would have the ambassador know, was an unqualified so-and-so. Here his voice was almost drowned out by the din of the bar from which he was calling. An occasional "Yeah, yeah!" in the background indicated that other crew members were there to support him. I listened patiently, interjecting the odd "Really?" and "You don't say!" to show I was still listening. After several minutes, during which he kept repeating his message, the man realised the call was costing him a pretty penny.

"And you solemnly swear to let the ambassador know?" he asked.

"You can count on it," I lied, hanging up.

74
Ike "steals" an umbrella

Despite my daily involvement in what sometimes seemed a losing battle to help retain the American military presence in France, there were pleasant weekends and numerous French holidays when our family could relax together. On such occasions we were grateful to be in our normally quiet suburb. I say, "normally" for it seemed some activity was always under way at Douze Avenue de la Marguerite.

There was a small colony of English-speaking families in Le Vésinet and their children frequently made their way to our house for parties and amateur plays. Angela, 11 when we arrived in France, frequently organised "Grandes Fêtes" in support of local charities. In 1959 came an opportunity for her to raise funds for survivors of the most deadly flood in recent French history.

The tragedy occurred one day in December when the Barrage de Lampassat at Frejus burst. Only five years old, it was considered a masterpiece of French construction with its graceful, slim design. Nearly 200 feet high and 738 feet long, it was 22.5 feet thick at its base but only five feet at the top. It held back waters of the Reyan River to form a lake two miles wide and six miles long. Hailed as the world's thinnest dam, it struggled to hold back the water from several days of torrential rain.

On December 2nd the dam burst, propelling a wall of water 25 feet high speeding at 50 miles per hour. Some 500 people died, despite massive rescue efforts. The French government promptly issued a stamp overprinted FREJUS. Angela organised a fête which raised a small sum for the survivors. On this occasion, and others, she would deliver the receipts to the *Mairie* and, after a day or two, would receive a letter of appreciation from the *Maire.*

When the children staged their dramatic productions, they were held either in the spacious attic or at the top of the stairs leading from the French doors into the garden. Talent was no problem for there was a small international community in Le Vésinet and its nearby area. Most of the fathers in these families were diplomats, military officers assigned to NATO, journalists and executives of multinational business and professional firms. Family bonds always insured sold-out performances, for woe betide any parent who did not turn up to see his or her offspring on the stage.

Over the years Mary and I had the good fortune to know several members of the Christian Science faith. Lady Astor had been the first and in Monticello our best friends were members. In Le Vésinet we met two more such families whose children became acquainted with Angela, Stuart and Pipkin. By this time Mary and I were aware of the Christian Scientists' preference for their own medical practitioners and their dislike of alcohol and smoking.

On two occasions our children unwittingly involved youngsters from these families in activities that went beyond the pale. When we moved into Douze Avenue de la Marguerite we found a huge mountain of empty wine bottles in the cellar, accumulated over many years. I made enquiries about the salvage value of the bottles and discovered they would command a few pennies each, if cleaned and sorted by size and colour of glass. Stuart, with his budding interest in business, was eager to undertake the enterprise but needed a partner to tackle the mammoth task of cleaning and sorting. After explaining the project and its potential reward to his friend, Andrew Ellis, he thought the way was clear for the two to earn a small fortune. Andrew's father, Harry, was the *Christian Science Monitor*'s correspondent in Paris. When he learned about the venture, Harry decreed that Andrew most definitely would not handle those bottles which once had contained strong drink.

Pipkin, now nine, had a close friend in Marcia from another nearby Christian Science family. Mary and I always allowed our children and their friends to have the run of the house and garden, for both were large and appealing to youngsters. One day Pipkin said to Marcia: "I know where we can find some chocolate." She took Marcia to the cupboard containing toilet articles and a few patent medicines. Picking up what she thought was chocolate, she divided the squares with her friend and in a few moments they had devoured the lot.

A few hours later, after Marcia had returned home, her mother telephoned Mary to say that Marcia was having voluminous and continuous bowel movements. Had Marcia, she asked, when visiting Pipkin eaten any food that might cause this? Mary said not to her knowledge, but would ask Pipkin.

At that point Pipkin herself had an enormous bowel blowout.

Questioned, she said she and Marcia had eaten some chocolate taken from the bathroom cupboard. Mary rushed there to find an empty Ex-Lax package. She immediately informed Marcia's mother. While not amused, she nonetheless was relieved to know that her daughter's ailment was only temporary. It was to be several days before the insides of both girls were restored to their normal working order.

Sunday church services allowed Mary, myself and the children to enlarge our circle of friends. At first I was attracted to the American Church in Paris, at that time presided over by Dr. Clayton Williams. His sermons were well thought out and photocopied digests were made available after each service. His French wife, renowned for her cooking, edited a small book of her favourite recipes whose sale provided useful income for church funds. The church had a large membership and was also attended by many Americans visiting Paris.

For a short period I was a sidesman at the American Church. During this time former President Eisenhower, on a private visit to France, came one Sunday to worship. After the collection, when our team of sidesmen had gathered at the rear of the church preparatory to presenting the plates at the altar, one smilingly held up a $20 bill and said:

"This is what Ike put in the collection plate. I'm removing it and replacing it with one of my own. Just think, I'll be able to tell my children and grandchildren that this note once belonged to the President of the United States!"

As Eisenhower emerged from the church, a cloudburst descended. He stopped dead, not wishing to get drenched in the dash for his waiting limousine. When I saw his Secret Service agent was also stumped, I grabbed an umbrella from the stack just inside the door, opened it and led the former President to his car. He made it without getting wet. As he stooped to enter the car, he took the umbrella from my hand, entered the car and the agent slammed the door shut before I could say the umbrella was not his to take. The car sped away and I was left standing empty-handed. The worst part was that the poor owner of the umbrella was never to know it had become his gift to the President.

Increasingly our family found the American church too large and, at times, too impersonal to provide the intimacy which we were accustomed to in Sunday worship. We pondered over the other Protestant churches in Paris and eventually decided to attend the small Methodist church in Rue Roquepine. Established in 1862 under the aegis of the Methodist Missionary Society, it had long since become an international centre for Protestants of many nationalities and denominations.

The church's first minister, William Gibson, led the congregation for 30 years. During his ministry he had a line of six tablets erected in the apse bearing the passage from St. John: xiii: "A new commandment I give you, that you love one another; as I have loved you that you love one another." In deference to the church's international congregation, each tablet was inscribed in a different language: French, Italian, English, Latin, German and Hebrew. Church records indicate the hardworking

French artist had great difficulty transcribing the Hebrew characters.

Three times the church survived the rigours of war, occupation and liberation. During the two world wars it was attended by thousands of British and American servicemen based in France. The most fascinating member we met was a Madame Biaginni, an English lady whose late husband was an Italian. They risked their lives to befriend Allied servicemen and agents during the Second World War. To earn her keep, she translated American and British best-sellers into French for Paris publishers and sometimes approached me for help on Americanisms.

When our family started attending services at Rue Roquepine, the minister was James Edwards, previously a Methodist missionary in Jamaica. We had no idea he possessed musical ability until one day, when the organist failed to turn up, he calmly left the pulpit and played the piano, in a fast tempo, for all the hymns.

He explained, on remounting the pulpit, that he should be excused the fast tempo, for that was the way the Jamaicans had liked their hymns when he was among them. The habit, he added, had remained with him. Edwards was an extrovert with an endless supply of stories to inspire and amuse his multi-national and multi-racial congregation. The "American story" I liked best in his repertoire went like this:

"The climate in Florida had been perfect for so long that no one had died for decades. As funerals constitute an essential Christian rite, one Florida church decided it must stage a funeral so its congregation would know what it was all about. So they sent to California for the body of a pauper who could be buried without bother. The rare event was widely advertised and the church was filled to overflowing by people who had never been to a funeral service. In the midst of the minister's oration, there came a mighty popping and cracking, as the lid of the coffin suddenly burst open. The minister and the congregation waited, spellbound, as the pauper sat up, rubbed his eyes and exclaimed: "My, what this Florida sunshine does for a body!"'

Displaying both charm and tact, Edwards added, on completing the story:

"If any Californians present don't like the story, all you have to do is reverse the states."

75
Eleanor Roosevelt puts us at ease

The years in Le Vésinet were crucial ones in the early education of our three children. Angela and Stuart now required continuous secondary school preparation if they were to enter university. Although in theory both could enrol in French schools, their curricula would be a hindrance to gaining entry to an American university. The American and British schools in Paris either were over-crowded or difficult to reach from Le Vésinet. After much agonising we decided to enrol them in British boarding schools.

The wrench was as great for Mary and me as for the two children, but the decision proved to be a wise one in the long run for each child was able to complete secondary education in the same school. After a short spell in Le Vésinet's middle school, Angela eventually went to The Mount School in York, a Quaker institution, and Stuart to Queen's College in Taunton, a Methodist school. Despite our initial fears, both adapted well to boarding school life: Angela founded the school's chapter of Amnesty International, while Stuart excelled in both the classroom and on the sports field and eventually became head boy.

Pipkin's educational experience in Le Vésinet was to prove invaluable. She attended the local École Normale throughout our five year stay. Both the nursery school and the primary school buildings were on the same site, about 100 metres from our residence. Thus, unlike Angela and Stuart, she had no problem of adjustment or difficulty in reaching school. Between the school and our house ran one of Monsieur Pallou's canals lined with mature trees. Pipkin made this short trek every day, happily wending her way in and out of the trees. Mary and I marvelled at the ease with which Pipkin adapted to French schooling and increased her language competence. She frequently visited her French school friends in their homes and they, in turn, came to see her and play with "Miss Brown", our family dog.

Miss Brown was like a member of our family. Our previous postings had been for only two years; now – for the children's sake – we hoped we could stay put for at least twice that long. Aware that a child most needs a dog between the ages of five and twelve, we went to Au Printemps – one of Paris' great department stores - to see if they had a suitable dog.

Friends had told us they operated an adoption service for abandoned canines, some of whom had proven stunningly successful with their new owners. Miss Brown, we learned, originally had a litter of puppies, but now only one remained. The store assumed we would take the puppy. The thought of that left us looking downcast at the mother who, we felt sure, was imploring us to take her. We did.

She proved the perfect companion for Pipkin and gave endless hours of pleasure to us all. She loved the taste of caramel sweets, but took forever to masticate them. She would sit determinedly chewing and chewing, thinking the caramel would dissolve so she could swallow it.

But the caramel remained obstinate and refused to cooperate. As the dog despaired, tired and then gathered strength for another try, we would roll about in fits of laughter. Eventually, after perhaps fifteen minutes, she reduced its size sufficiently to get it down. Then she would collapse and look at us with lovely accusing eyes as if saying "What have you done to me?"

Miss Brown somehow managed to find boy friends who enabled her to have dozens of puppies during our stay. We disposed of them easily by taking them at their cutest stage to the large American military headquarters nearby just when small children were about to be taken to Saturday movies with their parents.

Each year a photographer came to take class pictures; we never could understand why, in these Le Vésinet pictures, Pipkin always looked like a little French girl. One of the proven concepts in foreign language learning is that a child who has the opportunity to spend the first years of schooling in a foreign country will retain elements of the new language for life. We had not fully appreciated Pipkin's facility until a French acquaintance, visiting us a decade later, said that he could not distinguish her speech from that of a French native.

As in Israel, Mary and I – during our stay in France – were to see or meet famous Americans who were in the country on official business. Senator James Fulbright, who founded the educational exchange programme bearing his name, visited the American Church during my time there as sidesman. Edward R. Murrow, the noted broadcaster who conveyed to millions of Americans the hardships endured by the British during the second world war, became director of our US Information Agency in 1960 and visited Paris shortly afterwards. Mary and I found him as charming to converse with as he had seemed during his wartime broadcasts.

The American we most enjoyed meeting was Eleanor Roosevelt. A reception was planned for her at the residence of the ambassador, Amory Houghton. As many prominent French leaders were also invited, embassy officers present were required to meet and introduce the French guests to those Americans we knew, or those the guests wished to meet. We worked hard to keep up with the rush of French guests who seemed to arrive at the same time.

To our consternation, Mary and I saw that Mrs. Roosevelt had been momentarily left alone in the middle of the large reception salon. Ambassador Houghton had not yet arrived, but we could easily imagine what his reaction would be if he learned of this unsociable situation. Mrs. Roosevelt's plight, for there was no other word for it, had been noticed by others but, either through fear or shyness, they dared not approach her. Obviously the question on their minds was "What can I possibly say that will be interesting to Mrs. Roosevelt?"

"Fools walk in where angels fear to tread", I whispered to Mary. "Shall we go and introduce ourselves?"

"Let's!" she responded, with the customary twinkle in her eye.

We strolled over, introduced ourselves, and started by saying we had previously served in Israel which we understood she had visited recently. She beamed and spoke warmly of the country and its people. I mentioned that I had read about her niece accompanying her on a visit to a Bedouin tribe which had presented her with a camel. Mrs. Roosevelt tossed her head back, laughed and said:

"Yes, that gift got us into trouble. The camel couldn't be imported into the United States because of foot-and-mouth regulations. On the other hand, we didn't want to offend the Bedouins. In the end, we had to leave it to the Israeli officials and our embassy to sort out."

By this time a small circle of onlookers had approached. Seeing that Mrs. Roosevelt was not at all the formidable lady they had imagined, they were now prepared to converse as Mary and I quietly withdrew.

Paris has long been a haven for American writers, artists and entertainers. This was true also in my time there. One of the most interesting was Tom Rowe, brother of a Hollywood producer. Tom himself had dabbled in motion picture work for several decades. At one time he produced short feature films about some of the expatriate American jazz musicians living in Paris. He attended the Cannes film festival every year, sending back daily articles to American screen journals. Like myself, Tom had been in the US Army during the Second World War, and we both were members of a reserve unit which met weekly and was called for active duty training for several weeks each summer.

Tom was then writing the script for a movie which he called "The Aristocats" which he hoped Walt Disney would accept. Each week, before and after our reserve meetings, he would try out the dialogue on several of the assembled reserve officers. Alas, we contributed nothing, for Tom was a master of the art of dialogue. Eventually Disney purchased the script and "The Aristocats" became a worldwide box-office hit.

Tom later alleged Disney had deprived him of certain subsidiary rights and also had added the name of another person as co-author of his story. "I'm suing Disney and Disney is suing me," he said, despondently. I never learned the precise details of the dispute or if he eventually received what he thought was due him.

My USIA boss, Bill Cody, for some years a widower, had recently remarried. He and his wife soon embarked on a pleasant but demanding challenge: a "secret" English-language guidebook to the best restaurants in Paris. Methodically they toured the eating establishments of the capital, making copious notes and adding even more copious pounds to their body weights. Aware that Bill cherished a good meal more than anything else in life, I asked him one day what he would dowhen his book was published and his "secret" haunts were crowded out by visitors. He laughed and replied:

"I'm keeping back my own secret list of the very best."

One day I had a shock when Zaporah, the popular children's entertainer in Israel, entered my office. She explained she was entitled to compensation from the (then) West German government for property lost during World War II.

"They won't pay me anything unless I turn up in person," she added, "and I've spent everything I have getting to Paris. Can you help me get to Germany?"

I recalled that our Embassy restaurant's manager was a Jew with many connections in Paris. When he heard Zaporah's story, he immediately went to work on her problem and soon she was on her way. As she left, she flashed the glorious smile that had so endeared her to the children of diplomats in Tel Aviv.

76
Missing! A gift for a Royal Wedding!

Nothing in my previous experience prepared me for the next problem which, if not resolved, could have led to a diplomatic blunder between the United States and a nearby European country where a royal wedding was about to take place.

For obvious reasons, when heads of state, royalty and high-ranking ministers of friendly countries announce wedding plans, each invited nation gives much thought to an appropriate gift. Often these are elegant and hand-crafted. Such was the case for the gift, a magnificent piece of Steuben glass, which the United States government planned to present to the royal couple. Delay in completing the glass, however, caused it to arrive in New York too late to catch the last direct flight to the capital where it was due to go on display with gifts from other world leaders the following day.

The first I knew about the impending catastrophe came when the embassy duty officer in the royal wedding capital telephoned. His ambassador was horrified at the thought of no gift appearing in the space reserved for the United States. My fellow duty officer said only one possibility remained; an Air France plane with the gift would leave New York shortly for Paris. If, and he admitted it was a big if, Air France could unload and clear the glass quickly through French customs, it could reach the wedding capital in time if – and this was an even bigger one – our Air Attaché could immediately depart with it in the US Air Force plane assigned exclusively for his use.

Fully aware of the difficulty of getting clearance for special flights, especially on short notice at weekends, not to speak of locating scattered crew members of the Air Attaché's plane, I told my colleague in the wedding capital that I could only do my best.

I thought the best chance of expediting the gift through the airport depended entirely on finding a sympathetic Air France executive with authority to act. After two or three false starts, I reached the senior supervisor who knew about Harry Truman's maxim, "the buck stops here". He listened patiently as I described the likely consequences if the gift did not arrive in the wedding capital on time.

I stressed the word "Royal" as often as I could, knowing the fascination with which the French regard royal events, they having long been deprived of their own. I told the supervisor that, in the meantime, I would be trying to arrange a US Air Force plane to take the gift on to the capital. He stopped me before I could continue.

"Pas de problème!" he said, in an authoritative voice. He went on to say that the airport operated an unscheduled cargo service to the wedding capital which departed at his discretion. As there was already a small amount of cargo waiting to be shipped, he would order the plane to take off as soon as the gift could be shifted from the incoming Air France flight. He promised to call me when the aircraft took off so that the embassy duty officer in the capital could arrange for pick up and delivery.

I telephoned the embassy duty officer and in a casual voice said:

"About that Steuben glass gift for the royal wedding. Well, I have arranged for a special Air France flight to fly it directly to you the moment it arrives in Paris".

Dead silence at the other end, followed by gasps of disbelief. True to his word, the supervisor called to say the cargo plane was now airborne and would arrive in the wedding capital within the hour.

The next day the world's media carried extensive photographs of the gifts. Only a few people, however, knew that the American gift almost didn't make it.

The Cuban Missile Crisis of 1962 threw up an unexpected ramification in France into which I was drawn. When Nikita Khrushchev decided to build missile bases on Cuba, the United States and Cuba may have been only hours away from initiating a nuclear war.

Special US Army units were hurriedly despatched to Florida, US Navy vessels in the Atlantic were placed on highest alert and US Air Force units in Europe and continental United States were put on standby. Among the designated Air Force units was a reserve group from Birmingham, Alabama. On short notice, its planes were readied and flown to a small US Air Force base in eastern France. Its commander expected a sudden order to join up with other USAF units in Germany for possible action against the Soviet Union.

When Khrushchev climbed down after President John F. Kennedy's ultimatum, there was understandable reluctance to withdraw the primed American military forces too quickly. Few expected the Soviets to renew their threats, but no one could be sure of their intentions. A certain degree of sagging morale set in, especially among members of reserve units who had been hastily called up from their civilian work.

One day I received a telephone call from Charlie Levy, our USIA regional officer for that part of eastern France where the Birmingham reserve unit was based. Speaking with great concern in his voice, he explained the officers and air crews had arrived expecting to see action and instead, with the missile crisis defused, they were now "sitting on their hands" with little to do. Worst of all, he added, some now doubted the value of coming to Europe in the first place. The situation was compounded, he added, by the impression given in the media that President de Gaulle did not welcome American bases in France – whatever role they might play in a shooting war.

"Can you come and talk to these men", Levy implored, "and give them some idea as to when they might be returning home and, more importantly, stress that their presence here is indeed worthwhile?"

This was a tall order, for I was fairly sure our American policy makers had not yet decided when to pull back the units previously designated for action. Rumours abounded that those units deployed to Europe (including the one in France) might be among the first to be returned. That I could pass on as a rumour – but nothing more. Convincing the crews that coming to France had been worthwhile would be more difficult. And France's seeming ingratitude towards the United States – how to explain that?

One ace I held just might prove useful. When World War II ended, I had stayed on in the US Army Reserve. As all the unit's officers and crew members also were reservists, I hoped this shared identity would allow me to engage with them.

These thoughts flashed through my mind as Levy elaborated on the problem. When he finished I agreed to go on condition that everything I said would be off the record. He was sure this would be no problem. When I arrived at the air base to speak, every seat in the movie theatre was filled. Ominously, I saw a smiling French liaison officer sitting near the front. I knew he would take careful note of every word I said, so I had to be ultra careful about any references to France.

After emphasising the need for my off-the-record stance I explained that I, too, was a reservist and understood their eagerness to see action when needed, and to return home when their services were no longer required.

When it came to explaining President de Gaulle's seeming ambivalence toward the United States, I suddenly hit upon the idea of comparing present day France with the American South following its defeat in the Civil War.

"Your parents and grandparents," I began, "like my own – long remembered the humiliation of losing the war and the ignominy of the Reconstruction Era that followed. It has taken the South a long time to recover the pride it once knew. France, too, has always been a proud nation, but it stills suffers from its defeat and occupation by the Germans.

"In my view, President de Gaulle sees himself as the one person who can restore France to its former role among the world's great nations. He may make hostile statements against the United States – the very country that helped propel him toward leadership during the last war. But we must not forget his driving ambition is to restore confidence in the French people and pride in being French."

So far the men listened with attention and respect - there were no questions although I had said they would be welcome. Now would come the most difficult part – explaining and, hopefully, convincing them that their presence in France was a small but important contribution to resolving the Cuban Missile crisis.

"Khrushchev's actions brought us to the very brink of a nuclear war," I began, "and we had to call his bluff. Our ultimatum to his threat was one thing, but our naval deployment and movement of troops to Florida and Air Force elements to Europe were visual and verifiable responses that left him in no doubt about our intentions. We had to call his bluff – and you were a part of that bluff – a bluff that may well go down in history for saving countless lives.

"So don't think for a moment your coming over was useless. It was exactly the opposite. About that rumour of your being sent home soon, well, I can't tell you anything about it. My hunch is it will be sooner rather than later. In the meantime, I suggest you continue your state of readiness and your excellent safety record of flight training for you never know if there are Soviet sympathisers who may pass on aspects of your proficiency to Moscow. As for your morale, let me point out that here in Eastern France you are almost in the geographical centre of Western Europe. The time you have left can be used to bring over your wives or girlfriends, allowing you to visit places you may have always longed to see."

I ended my talk with a reminder that everything had been off-the-record. The unit commander thanked me warmly and I left shortly afterwards. The next day Charlie Levy phoned to say the commander had called to thank him for my visit and that, for some reason, members of his unit had written an unusually large number of letters home the night before. Thus ended one of the most delicate tasks I ever attempted.

77
Dogs in restaurants – good!

Twice during my Paris assignment our family took home leave in the United States. These periodic stays of several weeks help the foreign service officer to keep abreast of the latest thinking, as well as technological, political and cultural developments, in the home country.

On one of these we took a large tent and camped for ten days in the Great Smoky Mountains National Park. Apart from meeting wonderful people from all parts of the United States, we had an exciting encounter with a mother bear and her cub one night in North Carolina. We foolishly had stored fresh food in our tent and the cub, standing on his hind legs, began sniffing out the prize.

I awoke the rest of the family and asked them to keep calm, for if the mother were to join her cub, we would be in deep trouble. After circling the tent, however, the cub decided to abandon the effort and slowly walked away. Next morning we were reprimanded by the park ranger for not hanging our food high on the limb of a nearby tree. While no one might have been hurt, he said, the adult bear could easily have ripped our tent to shreds in her quest for food. We just might have been injured in the resulting melee, he added.

The two periods of home leave came when the American South was adapting to the 1954 Supreme Court ruling, and others that followed, giving black people equal rights under the law. A brief incident demonstrates our family's learning process. While waiting for our plane at the Augusta airport Angela went over to a pair of water fountains marked "White" and "Coloured" and pressed the button to drink what she supposed would be coloured water.

When she compared it with the adjacent normal water, there was no difference. She wanted to know why, adding that she had never seen coloured water before. It was impossible to explain this anomaly to a child. The next time we passed through Augusta airport, both signs had gone and there was only one drinking fountain.

The 1960s saw drastic changes in public education in the South, including my home state. Two black students were admitted to the University of Georgia after some initial difficulty. One of them. Charlayne Hunter from South Carolina, enrolled in the school of journalism from which I had received my bachelor's degree two decades earlier. She got her degree in 1963 and went on to become a leading journalist and author.

State universities throughout the South increasingly accepted greater numbers of black students, although the proportion enrolled did not approximate the white-black population ratio. In part, this reflected the poor preparation many black students received in their high schools. On the other hand, the number of black athletes playing on university sports teams was sometimes disproportionate to the total number of black students enrolled. Despite these teething troubles, it was clear to me, returning to the South at intervals of two or three years, that enormous progress had been made towards racial equality since the 1954 Supreme Court decision.

Towards the end of our Paris assignment Mary's father visited us for a week. Thoroughly British in his outlook, he had little good to say of the French before arriving at our Le Vésinet home. His World War I memories were unhappy ones about futile battles in France, real or imagined mutinies by some French troops and, eventually, his capture and internment as a prisoner of war.

His stay with us converted him within the week. All his life a conservationist and lover of trees, he was amazed by the planning which had gone into Le Vésinet and the attention the city fathers had given to the town's tree-lined avenues and flower-filled parks. Accompanying Mary and Pipkin to the local market, he happily entered into the spirit of choosing delicious cheeses and other French delicacies. After this visit he never had a bad word to say about the French.

Our French sojourn had allowed me to fill in many gaps in my dormant love of classical music. By coincidence, the French national radio played a different work every morning just as I was bathing and shaving. Each piece was prefaced by seductive programme notes about the composer and the circumstances under which the opus was written or performed. The daily selections were listed in the Paris newspapers and, better still, several music shops made an effort to stock the "records of the week". Thus music lovers could instantly buy records of new pieces to which they were attracted. By the end of our five years, we had built up a sizeable collection which was to give our family great pleasure for years to come.

When I arrived home from work and changed into casual clothing, I sometimes stretched out on the sofa to relax before the evening meal. On many such occasions I put on Beethoven's Sixth (Pastoral) Symphony which usually had the effect of putting me to sleep within minutes.

After hearing Michel-Richard de Lalande's majestic "Concert de Trompettes Pour les Festes sur le Canal de Versailles" at a *son-et-lumière* performance at Versailles one evening, we adopted the piece as our family's welcoming music whenever a guest arrived for a stay or a family member returned from a stay abroad. Today I cannot hear this piece with its Baroque echo effect without recalling those frequent welcoming moments at Douze Avenue de la Marguerite.

All the family gained enormously from its stay in France. All three children were introduced to the French language; Angela and Pipkin were to make it one of their main areas of study in subsequent years. Mary was in "seventh heaven" with such a plethora of art galleries in the Paris area. Although she methodically visited all the galleries in the city and its suburbs, she never tired of revisiting the great impressionist paintings in the Jeu de Paume in the Jardin des Tuileries. On the other hand, I *did* tire of taking visiting friends to the Eiffel Tower. Seeing the Tower was one thing, but why did they always want me to climb it with them?

Whether my colleagues and I contributed anything toward a better appreciation of the United States and its goal of a strong Western Europe united through NATO is doubtful. While many French intellectuals thought it natural that NATO's headquarters should be based in France, de Gaulle did not like the American leadership built into the military structure. Oddly, this notion was contrary to the generally accepted thesis that the country which furnished the most troops in an international force should also provide the military leadership. While Britain and America had agreed to this principle in accepting Marshal Foch as the Allied leader in the First World War, de Gaulle insisted on putting French pride above American domination of NATO.

The United States was not the only target of de Gaulle's venom during my stay in France. The French president effectively kept Britain out of the Common Market for several years. I did not understand the anti-British stand frequently taken by de Gaulle and subsequent French leaders until a senior French foreign ministry official explained it to me at a reception:

"Where political, economic and military matters are concerned, you must not be surprised if my government frequently takes a stance opposite to that of Britain – even when there is no apparent justification. You see, over the centuries, France has often come off second best in its relations with Britain. You only have to read French school textbooks to understand how this long-standing resentment against Britain has been perpetuated. I don't think it will change in our lifetime."

De Gaulle was shortly to force NATO and its military headquarters out of France, necessitating their removal to Brussels. In fairness, one has to admit that de Gaulle had done much to restore pride to a France deeply traumatised by enemy occupation.

It is customary when a departing officer is about to end a tour of duty at the Paris embassy, that associates – American and French – club together to buy a small gift which is presented at an informal farewell party. As it happened, my French colleagues and acquaintances far outnumbered the Americans present and they decided to present Mary with a beautiful tray in pewter, a metal for which French craftsmanship is world renowned. We shared a bottle or two of champagne before I was thanked for my services by the senior officer present, John Mowinckel, who then presented the tray to Mary.

At this stage it is usual for the central figure to reply but, as neither I nor Mary particularly relished the task, we delegated the honour to Pipkin who, we knew, spoke far better French than either of us.

We warned her a few days in advance that she would be expected to say a few words about how much our family had enjoyed living in France but left to her the wording of her little speech. She had, in fact, decided to write a short poem reflecting her love both of dogs and the French people. Long since lost, the poem first extolled the French for various praiseworthy qualities. But they deserved thanks most of all, she said in her concluding lines, for allowing dogs into their restaurants.

Only nine at the time and speaking earnestly in impeccable French, she charmed everyone present. Her contribution was the perfect ending to our assignment in France.

78
The wisdom of "Daddy Whiz"

During our stay in France news came that our friend, Kendall Weisiger, had died in Atlanta at the age of 80. Mary and I were deeply saddened by the loss of this gentle Southerner whose influence was brought to bear on the whole of our married life and on mine since my university days.

We had corresponded frequently since I enrolled as a freshman, when I had heard about this "Grand Old Man" whose one great aim in life was to inspire young people to do their best.

Every letter from Kendall contained gems of wit and practical advice. One, which arrived in Israel at the time of America's Thanksgiving Day, was shared with friends on that most special of holidays. In part, it read:

> "For all the Blessings of Heaven and Earth
> For the Birds and the Bees
> For the Forests and the Flowers
> For the Bears and all the Beasts
> For the Moles and other under-earth critters – such as Prairie Dogs
> For the Fishes, rich in Iodine and Cobalt
> For Vitamins 12
> For Sunshine and Showers
> For Admiration, Affection and Love
> For little children, weak women and strong men
> For Jesus and Socrates and Sweitzer and Spinoza and Uncle Remus of Eatonton
> For Intelligence, latent and active
> For Purpose, Performance and Promise
> For Truth, Beauty and Goodness
> For Generosity, Kindness and Forgiveness
> And Lord, I hope I have not overlooked anything; if so you put it in for me, for I'm just a poor sort of soul, stomping around on your World doing the best I can to make it better for all your children."

When he learned my next assignment would be Paris, he was quick to offer his observations and advice.

"Paris," he said, "is a great city, laid out by a German, Hausmann. The part around the Arc de Triomphe I esteem to be one of the greatest monuments in the world."

He went on to record American ties with France. "Ben Franklin," he said, "visited Paris where he was well received and Thomas Jefferson acquired many of his ideas from France – especially equality, fraternity and liberty. Thomas Paine was made an honorary citizen and given a seat in the French Parliament. So in a way Paris is our Foster Mother."

Then, in a reference to my Baptist upbringing, he added: "If you have not learned to drink wine by all means do so now. Religion has nothing to do with it. A little wine is good for the stomach's sake." Always a staunch believer in learning foreign languages, he lost no time in stressing the point. "Learn all the French you can," he urged, "for it must become a part of your culture. Always ask 'combien' and then hold up your fingers – 'un, deux, trois, quatre, sank!' This is fundamental there!"

By now we had settled down in Le Vésinet and our letters reported how the children loved our more rural setting after the hectic urban life in Israel. His reply revealed that he, too, cherished the value of rural life. "One cause of our declining civilisation," he said, "is that so many men leave the rural areas to come to the city. No wonder God seems to be so far away. There is no contribution that can be made to the life of a man that is of more value than to have spent a part of his life in the country and being in touch with nature."

After we told Kendall we had acquired a magnificent mongrel, "Miss Brown", he never failed to inquire after her health. When we said she was expecting her first litter, he promptly sat down and wrote her a letter of "advice". For the (canine) family to become successful as an economic unit, the children should early be prepared for their respective occupations.

"The biggest pup – the one with the largest belly – should be chosen for the priesthood, but he need not be the smartest. You can name him Padre. The second one could become a store-clerk or a policeman. He should be named Carlos. The third – if he is smart – could drive a taxi. Name him Chiko. Of the girls, the least good-looking and most demure should be destined for a nunnery. Name her Joanne. The next could become a seamstress and, perhaps, some day will marry a rich man. She ought to be frisky and good-looking. Call her Gigi. And, finally, there is always, in Paris, a great demand for milliners. Call that one Mimi."

The year of 1959 was barely under way when Kendall informed us he had spent his birthday in hospital undergoing various tests. It was the first indication we had that his health was beginning to deteriorate, although he himself sought to make light of it. "I had a good time (in hospital)," he said, "for everybody was kind. My very competent physician says I'll have to walk the tight rope for the remainder of my days – no more salt in my food. What a comedown! From a gourmet to a salt-free oldster! I am now in my 80th year so I must make every one of my remaining days count for the most."

In August of the same year, he gave us a progress report. "I am somewhat better," he said, "though lacking in energy. I had thought that I would march right into Heaven in full strength – what vain creatures we are!" We had sent him a salt-free box of gourmet Dutch cookies which, he now told us, arrived safely. Thank you very much; the little Dutch cookies go well with Georgia peaches and ice cream. We shall enjoy them for a long time and think often of your generosity."

Two months later he reported great news about his students. "This (1959) has been our most rewarding year. 22 foreign students have received university degrees, of which 13 have earned advance degrees – four Africans among them!" Towards the end of this positive report he appended a note about his health. "The doctor agrees with me," he said, "that I am now almost back to normal after nine months of medication. At least I am running again on the main track."

Mary had written Kendall a letter while waiting for her hair to dry at the hairdresser's. "Mary," he wrote, "I was pleased you had thought of me while being reconditioned at the Beauty Salon. I should like to see how you appeared when you left the place." Then, in an aside he hinted again at my Baptist upbringing and my aversion to strong drink. "Donald," he said, "I know you will not approve, but I am now enjoying a slow sip of good whiskey, distilled at Bardstown, whence comes the best Kentucky spirits. It is made from the waters of the little stream passing by." Then he pointedly confided how he had come by the whiskey. "It was given me," he said, "by a Deacon who stands high at the Second Ponce de Leon Baptist Church."

On his eightieth birthday, Kendall wrote thanking us for the silk tie we had sent him from the renowned Hermes shop not far from our Paris Embassy. "My Christmas cravat is being worn today with nothing but admiration," he said. "My dear father always spoke of 'cravat' – where we now use the ordinary word 'neck-tie'. Thank you so much for it will represent you, the boulevards of Paris and the spirit of the Bon Vivant!"

His birthday was marked by many manifestations from admirers. "Cakes and wine and flowers and students and old friends have been pouring in all day," he said. "I wish Mary were here to be my Hand Maiden." He spoke only briefly about his health. "Day by day," he said, "I grow a little in strength and in Resolution – which is the key to everything. When a man has Resolution to back up his endeavours, he is Redoubtable! A French word, I believe. Over here (in the United States) we use an ugly word (guts) for it, but I give you Fortitude – from *fors, fortia*. Study Latin, boy, study Latin!"

His next letter revealed that Spring at last had come to Atlanta. "April in Atlanta is lovely," he said, "because of the blooming of the dogwood and the azalea, for all of which we are grateful – not only because of their great beauty, but because they show Winter has gone and Spring has truly come."

There was to be just one more letter and it betokened his failing health. His comments were brief – a single sentence only on several unrelated subjects – and, for the first time, there was no word of inspiration or advice. He ended by saying: "My love to the family – wish I could see you. Affectionately, Daddy Whiz."

Our enquiries revealed his condition then quickly deteriorated and in September my old friend on the *Atlanta Constitution*, Leo Aikman, wrote that Kendall was dead. Atlanta Rotarians were deeply saddened at the passing of the man who had helped bring hope to hundreds of young people of Georgia and the world. They had planned to honour him in October with a "Kendall Weisiger Day" but this was not to be.

Ralph McGill, the *Constitution*'s editor, summed up the thoughts of many when he paid tribute to the great man. "Kendall Weisiger," he said, "could say that his last years, when he had leisure to give to his fellow man, had been his happiest ... Young men and women whose lives he had touched and helped, kept in touch with him. For him this is a sort of worldwide immortality. Children yet unborn and their descendents will hear of this kindly man from Atlanta."

For many young people, Kendall Weisiger's legacy was the higher education they received during difficult times. For me and many others, it was his *joie de vivre* and optimism – perhaps best summed up in this excerpt from a letter written late in his life:

"Don't be fooled by the statement that new and better refrigerators will make a new and better world," he said. "It ain't so. Only Better People can make a better world." And who were these Better People? "The man for the new world," he said, "must not only be better ethically and spiritually but must also be a better co-operator – a man better able to get along with his fellows at home and abroad – a citizen of the new world."

79
Finland's struggles with "Big Brother"

Every American of my generation knows that little Finland, alone among several countries that borrowed sums from the United States during the First World War, repaid the instalments on her debt promptly. A grateful American nation decided in 1949 to employ the whole of those repayments in bringing Finnish scholars to study in the United States.

Then came the Second World War when brave Finland captured the imagination of the world with its resistance against massive Soviet forces during the "Winter War" of 1939-40. As track and field athletics was my favourite sport, I had an additional reason for admiring the Finns: on a population basis, they for many years outperformed the rest of the world in the Olympic Games.

Thus, when my assignment in Paris was nearing its end and I was told I would become the next press attaché at the American Embassy in Helsinki, my joy knew no bounds. Mary, who had accompanied me on a brief youth hostelling trip to Finland a few years before, was equally thrilled. Pipkin, at eight, was too young to appreciate our enthusiasm, but Angela and Stuart, coming up to 16 and 15, respectively, increasingly became excited as we drove the overland route from Paris through Denmark and Sweden and then crossed over from Umea on the Swedish east coast to the Finnish west coast city of Vaasa.

On the ferry voyage to Vaasa we met a lively Finnish family returning home after a holiday in central Europe. The couple's young son was about the same age as Stuart and the two boys immediately established a rapport, despite Stuart's knowledge of Finnish being limited to "*Hyvää päivää*" ("Hello" or "Good day") and "*Näkemiin*" ("Goodbye"). When we reached Vaasa and said farewell to the family, Stuart remarked:

"If they are a sample of the Finnish, then we are in for a happy time."

His prophecy was to hold true for our entire three and a half years in Finland.

At Vaasa we paused long enough to look back on the waters we had just crossed. We were told the west coast of Finland is gradually rising and that many years hence, the Gulf of Bothnia may gradually disappear. Already it is so shallow in parts, and so much constituted of fresh water, that it freezes over in the winter, allowing cars and even scheduled buses to cross over to Sweden.

But our goal was Helsinki, so we set out in a south-easterly direction on a route that would take us past some of Finland's renowned lake country. Many of the roads, even major ones, were not paved, and we could readily understand how Finland produced so many superb rally drivers. Thankfully the weather was fine, allowing us to avoid the slipping and sliding at which the professional Finnish drivers excel.

To relieve the monotony of vast expanses of forest and lakes, we devised a competition whereby those sitting on the right side of the car vied with those sitting on the left in counting saunas. We soon discovered every lakeside was festooned with saunas and that many were being used as we drove past. The tell-tale sign of smoke trailing up from a small hut on the water's edge could only mean a sauna in use.

At length we reached Helsinki and learned that we were to stay in the Hotelli Helsinki in the city centre until we could find housing. Warned that housing was difficult to come by, we philosophically settled into the hotel as our temporary home while the genial hotel staff reciprocated by making us a part of its "family".

The manager was from the old school of hoteliers who believed that customer comfort, rather than a large profit, should come first. As school was not yet in session, Mary and I were concerned lest the presence of three children cause our two rooms to be in a permanent state of untidiness. Moreover, there had to be some risk, if we were obliged to remain there for several weeks, of minor damage to the walls, carpets and furniture.

"Don't let it worry you," he said. "Let me tell you about another American family who stayed here a few years back. They had incorrigible children and it wasn't long before they were literally wrecking their rooms. To try and keep the children amused, the parents one day gave each of the children paint sets and artist's books. The parents then went out, house-hunting.

"When they returned, they found that the children, tired of the paint books, had decorated every wall in the family's two-room suite. The parents came to me, petrified with fear lest they had to bear the cost of redecorating the rooms. I went to their rooms and immediately realised that nothing short of total redecoration would make them habitable.

"I then explained to the couple that every year or so, the hotel took several rooms out of service and repainted them, and now it was time to re-do their rooms. Therefore, I said, you will not be charged anything. This was not strictly true, for their rooms had been redecorated only the previous year, but it was more important to keep the family happy and to retain the goodwill of the American Embassy."

At the hotel we were introduced to the glorious Finnish pancake with a strawberry filling, totally unlike the American breakfast pancake or the French *crepe*. It soon became our favourite and the waitress did not even have to ask what we wanted for breakfast after the first day. The children, meanwhile, learned that the harbour was only minutes away. Equipped with simple, newly bought fishing rods and lines, they caught small sardine-like fish, which bystanders told them were delicious.

Having been accepted as part of the hotel's "family", they walked proudly into the kitchen, confronted the chef and asked if the fish could be cooked for their next meal. The chef, reflecting his manager's philosophy, congratulated them on their catch and, yes, the fish would be served up in the proper Finnish manner at the evening meal.

That evening the lovely waitress, humming something like "Here Comes the Bride", approached our table with great dignity and solemnity, and uncovered the serving dish. There, for us all to see, were tiny golden brown fish, surrounded by small roast potatoes. The children were thrilled and it took some time to convince them that the busy chef – responsible for feeding everyone in the hotel – would not have time to prepare such a meal again.

Eventually we located an apartment, whose rental considerably exceeded our housing allowance, not far from the embassy and near the tram line which passed by our USIA offices opposite the Helsinki railway station. There was no garage with the apartment, which meant our car would have to remain outdoors in the sub-freezing temperature of the Finnish winters. But the apartment, overlooking one of Helsinki's great woodland parks, was ideally positioned for entertainment purposes and we decided to take it, even if it meant dipping into our income to pay the rent. We were not to regret being out of pocket.

During those first weeks in Helsinki we were introduced to an eating establishment which had become something of a national institution – the Kestikartano. Within its walls the visitor was simultaneously introduced to Finnish architecture, folk culture and, of course, authentic Finnish food. Some of its massive wooden beams and rustic furniture had been brought from Eastern Karelia, given up to the Soviet Union in its harsh treaty inflicted on the Finns. The waitresses were attired in folk costumes representing the several regions of Finland. There was always music, often by Sibelius and frequently included his haunting "Valse Triste" and "Karelia Suite".

If one was lucky, Martti Porkella, the country's foremost artist on the ancient *kantele*, played several pieces. Porkella had become a familiar figure during the heyday of ocean liners when he played the *kantele* daily aboard Scandinavian ships plying the Atlantic. A great *smorgasbord* table groaned under the weight of assorted meats, vegetables, salads and desserts. Our family favourite was "*Karjalkan paisti*", a paper-thin pasty of Karelian origin. The restaurant also served a delicious variety of *piirakka*, a rice dish to which we had been introduced at the hotel. In deference to its popularity with family groups, the restaurant did not permit strong drink on the premises, but instead served its own appetising speciality, *Kestijouma*.

No one can be long in Finland without being invited to a sauna. All hotels have them, as do many large apartment buildings. But the ideal sauna, we quickly learned, must be positioned on the shore of a lake. Owners of homes and farmsteads not lucky enough to have natural bodies of water, simply install cold water showers to provide the extremes of hot and cold necessary for a sauna experience. The best stones for heating in a sauna ideally come from the water's edge where they have been tempered by the weather over many centuries. A library of books has been written by sauna experts detailing just how to build and maintain a sauna.

Saunas, we learned, had long existed in Norway, Sweden, Finland and northern Russia but it was left to the Finns to give the steam baths their name and to make them into a national institution that has long since spread around the world. The concept of steam baths, generated by pouring water over hot stones, may have independent roots in various parts of the world, one Finnish expert told me. Even the Cherokee Indians in my own state of Georgia, he added, used this form of bath, but without the follow-up cold shock employed with saunas.

I heard many Finns discuss the pros and cons of possible heart risk to people taking saunas. Certainly, the transition of leaving a sweat-producing sauna for a freezing roll in the snow or swim in an icy lake can produce a severe shock to the human nervous system. Doctors apparently agree, even when the hot-and-cold process is repeated several times, that there is no risk to a person with a sound heart; however, for those people with a history of serious heart disorders the sauna is not recommended.

Stories about the sauna are legion. When a young Finnish couple married and acquired their barren farm, it was not the farmhouse but the sauna that was first built. This was because it contained the heat necessary for severe weather, washing and cooking facilities and a place where the first child could be safely born. There are also accounts about lost travellers, calling at a farmhouse for directions in sub-freezing temperatures of mid-winter, who are greeted by the nude farmer emerging from his sauna. Even if the temperature is 30 or 40 degrees below freezing, he can bear the cold for a minute or two because he has, through his sauna cycle, conditioned his body to the extremes of hot and cold.

Diplomats assigned to Helsinki were quickly urged by their Finnish acquaintances to try an authentic sauna, if they had not already done so. Mary and I were deluged with invitations to try them at one or another site in the Helsinki area where waterside saunas abounded. "Never think a hotel or home sauna equates to the real thing," we were told.

So many visiting American businessmen, professional leaders and politicians demanded to have a sauna that our Helsinki embassy considered installing one on its premises. When we looked at the regulations dealing with embassy improvements, it became apparent that the cost of installing a sauna would not likely be viewed as a legitimate expense by our Washington superiors.

Eventually our embassy's wise men sold Washington the notion that "enhanced recreational facilities" on the premises were in the best interest of the country, given government policy that its employees should keep fit at all times. So the sauna was built and it immediately became popular both with our Helsinki staff and the continuing stream of official visitors from the United States.

Carl Rowan, a black ambassador to Finland, arrived at his post almost at the same time as our family. Never regarded as an "Uncle Tom's black", Rowan, in a speech given not long after his arrival, pointedly reminded Finns that the ideology of Nordic pureness had originated in "this part of the world". He nonetheless commanded respect for his intelligence and frank speech. Once Rowan was taking a sauna with several other embassy officials, among them a North Carolinian, John Reddington, our administrative officer. When the time came for the mutual administering of the traditional birch twigs, Reddington lashed out with great gusto on Rowan's back, causing the ambassador to wince and utter one of his best remembered quips:

"John, by any chance was your great-grandfather a slave driver?"

Rowan was the American ambassador to Finland when President Lyndon B. Johnson visited the country. The President was so impressed with Rowan that he soon named him director of the US Information Agency. Rowan was followed by Tyler Thompson, a career diplomat who had been interned by the Germans during the Second World War. Before coming to Finland, he was ambassador to Iceland. Intensely fond of cross-country skiing, Thompson was jokingly accused of accepting diplomatic assignments only to those countries where he could enjoy the sport. In common with Finland's President Urho Kekkonen and other prominent Finns, Thompson thought nothing of cross-country skiing expeditions lasting the whole of a weekend.

Kekkonen was his country's president for 25 years (1956-71), a period in which Finland lived dangerously with its hostile neighbour, the Soviet Union. In the "Winter War" (1939-40) Finnish forces at first held back the Russian might, but eventually crumbled. During the "Continuation War" (1941-44) Finland appealed for assistance against the Soviets; except for Germany, which sent armed forces, only fine words came from other countries.

When the Soviet Union emerged victorious, Finland was subjected to one of the harshest treaty settlements in modern times. Apart from ceding Karelia and the Arctic port of Petsamo, Finland was obliged overnight to treat her German allies as enemies and expel them from her soil. Finnish military forces, including para-military units, were ordered to stand down. A seemingly impossible reparations bill of 300 million gold dollars was ordered to be paid within eight years. Finland's president, Risto Ryti, and several other national leaders were ordered to be arraigned as "war criminals". Overlooked by the Soviet treaty writers was Finland's civil aviation arm, which alone among the country's military and quasi-military forces, expanded greatly in the post-war years.

It was against this background that Kekkonen became president. With the Soviet Union reserving the right to station troops in Finland whenever it "perceived" Finnish actions to represent a threat, Kekkonen was left in the tricky position of appearing as a nationalist among his own people but, at the same time, dealing harshly with anyone who might rock

When I arrived in Finland in 1963 some Western journalists were using the term "Finlandisation", to imply Soviet domination over Finland in all but name. It was true that Finnish exports were largely geared to the boat with anti-Soviet speeches, articles and actions. Soviet demands and that the country relied on Soviet oil to power its factories and transport. The Soviet Union also operated an extensive cultural programme and covertly distributed funds to political parties it considered friendly. Despite these subversive measures, however, Finns established other markets and, little by little, managed to distance themselves somewhat from their powerful neighbours to the east. Kekkonen, ever the astute politician, did not hesitate to pass himself off as being indispensable to the Soviets, when anyone challenged him for the presidency.

80
Two Presidents leave their mark

Finland's President Kekkonen could quickly cast aside his political cloak and revealed his long-standing enthusiasm for sports. Twice national high jump champion in his youth, he turned to cross-country skiing in later life and frequently skied 100 kilometres or more over a single weekend.

Accordingly, when Brian Sternberg, a champion American pole vaulter became paralysed after a trampoline accident and came to visit Finland, Kekkonen readily agreed to receive him. When our small party was ushered into the presidential office, Kekkonen's face fell when he saw the youthful Sternberg, struck down in the prime of his sports career. As if imagining a similar fate might have afflicted him as a young athlete, he asked Brian to relate just how the accident had occurred and what hope, if any, he had for recovery.

The rest of our party winced at this direct, cruel questioning, but Sternberg did not flinch. Realising Kekkonen's sincerity and aware of his sports background, he calmly recounted how the tragedy had occurred after a split second's disorientation on the trampoline. He added that the odds were against a recovery, unless there was a breakthrough in the field of spinal injuries. Kekkonen choked with emotion and was unable to hide his grief. Our session broke up with his alternating words of pity and encouragement.

A national TV channel featured Sternberg on a programme that included Finland's top vaulter, Pentti Nikula. The most moving moment came when Pentti presented Brian with a Finnish blue-and-white track suit. As millions of Finns watched on their television sets, Brian was so visibly moved by the gesture that at first he was unable to speak.

So highly did Finns value their accomplishments in the Olympic Games that those athletes who had won a medal of any colour had formed themselves into an elite "Olympic Club". At one time the number of Finns who held membership in the club was quite large, but in recent Olympics the rest of the world has caught up and not many Finnish athletes come by Olympic medals so easily any more.

Paavo Nurmi was without doubt the greatest of the Finnish Olympians; some would say he was the greatest track athlete the world has ever known. A realistic statue of him stands near Helsinki's Olympic Stadium, a reminder to all who come to watch track and field athletics that Nurmi won six gold medals in the Games of 1920, 1924 and 1928.

Some sports writers claimed that Nurmi wore a wrist watch to pace his laps (perfectly legal) and that this pacing contributed to his success as a long distance runner. My son Stuart, a budding athlete in his English boarding school, wanted to ask Nurmi if the wrist watch report was true. He asked me if I thought the busy Nurmi, by now owner of several properties (including his own specialty tie shop in Helsinki), would have time to chat with a schoolboy. To Stuart's great joy, Nurmi agreed to meet him in his shop. He greeted him warmly and quickly confirmed he had indeed used a watch to pace many of his races. When their brief conversation ended, Nurmi wished Stuart every success in his own running.

One day Ambassador Thompson received an urgent message from George C. McGee, the American ambassador to (then) West Germany. McGee shortly was to visit Finland and he was most anxious to meet Paavo Nurmi, against whom he had raced in Texas during his student days. Chris Hellstrom, my Finnish assistant, contacted Nurmi (who had a reputation for avoiding public appearances) and asked if he would mind coming to the embassy to meet Ambassador McGee. Nurmi said he would be delighted to come, although he confided he didn't remember McGee from his touring days in America.

When our small party assembled at the embassy, McGee chatted away with Nurmi (thanks to the interpreting of Chris), praising the Finn for his superb running in the 1920s. Still McGee hadn't indicated why he had wanted to see Nurmi. Then, he suddenly sat back, laughed, and said to Nurmi:

"You possibly do not remember your appearance in a race in Texas at the time I was a university student. I was in that race, too."

Nurmi, slightly embarrassed, said he could not recall the event.

McGee, grinning broadly, quickly put Nurmi at ease and continued:

"Well, we did have something in common. When the race was over, you and I represented the two extremes of the placings: you were first and I was last!"

This time it was Nurmi who laughed heartily, a gesture not often forthcoming from this normally shy man.

Chris Hellstrom, my assistant, was a young man of great ability. Soft spoken and scholarly, he was a great admirer of Shakespeare and many a time came up with a quotation from the Bard to fit an occasion. About 10% of Finns are of Swedish stock; the remaining 90% are descended from the original Finns who inhabited the country before the Swedes settled, first in coastal towns and later, to a lesser degree, in inland communities. Chris, a 'Swedo-Finn', was fluent in Swedish, Finnish and English and was frequently pulled away from his normal duties to interpret for visiting Americans at press conferences, seminars and meetings.

As my own Finnish was rudimentary, I could not hope to understand the nuances and subtleties when conversing with Finns with little or no knowledge of English. Chris, Mary and I put our heads together and came up with a formula to overcome the problem. We learned that many Finns liked a succulent macaroni dish topped with Finnish cheese and rashers of lean Danish bacon.

With this standard dish as the centrepiece, I invited, one at the time, selected journalists to lunch, with Chris handling the interpretation when I was stuck (which was often). In this way I came to host the editor of the Finnish communist daily newspaper, an intelligent man who maintained that "national communism" had a place in Finland, quite apart from the Soviet Union's influence. Not everyone agreed with this distinction, but as the communists had long been a considerable force in Finland, it was valuable to hear the editor's point of view. At times he spoke more as a socialist than a militant communist. As usual, it was poor Chris who came off worst. Except for a few simple exchanges between the editor and myself, he was so busy interpreting that his food was virtually untouched when the visit ended.

When Lyndon B. Johnson became president after the assassination of President Kennedy, he quickly set in motion programmes to achieve those ideals which he had cherished as vice-president. His support of civil rights reforms is well known, but his concern for the poor whites in Appalachia, the depressed mountain area extending from western New York to northern Alabama, was less appreciated.

Johnson's aid-to-Appalachia programme immediately caught the imagination of people worldwide, including the Finns. It also struck a chord with George Ingram, deputy to Ambassador Thompson, and myself. George had started his government service with the Tennessee Valley Authority, the agency set up by President Franklin D. Roosevelt to bring better living conditions to those farmers living in the lands often flooded by the Tennessee River and its tributaries.

My own love affair with the Southern Appalachians had dated from my university days. George, our cultural attaché (Tess Mravintz) and I developed an "Appalachian Week" of activities that included an appearance of a folk-singing couple from the United States, an exhibition of photographs, Appalachian crafts, a slide show and several talks. Our "piece-de-resistance", if it could be pulled off, would be a visit by our secretary of state, Dean Rusk.

I knew that Rusk was born in Cherokee county in my home state of Georgia and that President Johnson's "officially designated" Appalachian area included Cherokee county. Rusk had been one of those students whose higher education was made possible by the Rotary fund started by my friend, Kendall Weisiger; in short, I felt I knew enough about the difficult economic circumstances in which Rusk grew up (not too dissimilar from my own) to feel he would accept our invitation to come to Helsinki.

He did so, and the success of our Appalachian week was thereby assured. Just before Rusk gave his address, I spoke to him about our common respect for Appalachia and our mutual regard for Kendall Weisiger. He said that Weisiger's assistance and his ideals meant a great deal to him during crucial periods of his life. Pausing a moment, he added: "There are hundreds of others who can say the same thing."

Rusk began his much-awaited speech with the words "I am a son of Appalachia", and went on to praise the region which has contributed so much to the United States, despite the deprived conditions under which so many of its inhabitants live. Later he and Mrs. Rusk visited the Helsinki open-air market on the waterfront in the shadow of the city's great white cathedral. Unrecognised by stall-holders, they went their separate ways unobstructed. Occasionally one of them would make a "find" and edge up to the other saying, "Look what I've got!"

When the United States moved from merely giving military aid to South Vietnam to direct involvement of its armed forces, American foreign policy in general and Secretary Rusk in particular came in for a rough time in Finland, and in other countries. As the embassy officer most in touch with the media, I came under fire almost daily as I attempted to explain or justify American actions.

My basic thesis at the time was that the United States never had aspirations to create an empire, as had several European countries a century or two ago and the Soviet Union later. We instead had been busy assimilating peoples from every corner of the globe and, though not a perfect democracy, had made great strides along that path.

I pointed out that America, having been the "under-dog" in its struggle for independence against Britain, naturally sympathised with those countries that later had been invaded or threatened (as in the two world wars) by powerful forces. In those conflicts hundreds of thousands of Americans had given their lives so these countries – as well as our own – could live without oppression.

I maintained that South Vietnam, like Britain and France in the two world wars, had asked for our help. Should we refuse it, I asked, merely because it was a poor, agrarian country where the United States had no economic interests?

The high profile then exerted by the Soviet Union in Finland meant that Soviet sympathisers had penetrated into almost every facet of Finnish life – the media, education, the arts and, to a lesser degree, the government itself. Because Finland had known a strong Communist following since the country's independence in 1917, the party had been active over the years in national politics.

Thus, while Americans were having doubts about the country's growing involvement in Vietnam, some Finns – having been influenced by the Soviet line – saw us as "invaders" of a small Asian nation. I found that some university groups to which I spoke, led by left-wing students, either believed that North Vietnam had no interest or involvement in South Vietnam or refused to admit it.

I did not realise that Soviet influence in the Finnish media was so strong until I offered the director of a Finnish TV current events programme a documentary about North Vietnamese support of South Vietnam's Vietcong. The film was given a verbatim Finnish sound track *except* for the last five words which the film processor deliberately left intact in English: "... the aggressors from the north". When this was aired, the wrath of those in high places descended upon the programme director and there were serious consequences.

Meanwhile, opposition against American involvement in Vietnam continued to grow in the United States. This was brought home to me one day when I was asked to speak to the newly-arrived contingent of American Fullbright educators who shortly would disperse to universities and other educational institutions throughout Finland.

I was tipped off by my superior officer that these educators were in a virtual state of rebellion, for most did not agree with US policy in Vietnam. Having been brought to Finland under the auspices of an American government programme, some thought they would be obliged to reflect official American policy. Would I, my boss asked, speak to them? I agreed.

I explained to the professors that America, and the rest of the world – including Finland – was deeply divided over Vietnam and that passionate, sincere views were held on both sides. I put forth my "help the under-dog" view which, coupled with the aim of preventing the spread of Soviet influence in Southeast Asia, was similar in many ways to our support of European countries through NATO.

"But," I added, "because you feel differently you should feel free to discuss your point of view with Finns as you develop friendships. I suggest, however, that whenever you speak publicly you make it clear that what you say is your private opinion and not that of the US government." The professors agreed that this seemed a reasonable arrangement and our session broke up amicably.

We in the embassy had mixed feelings when news broke that the United States no longer would be content with supplying military advisers to South Vietnam, but henceforth would engage in the fighting itself. Ourfirst staff meeting after the new policy was announced was marked by the optimism of those who felt American involvement would ensure a rapid end to the war and by the gloom of others who predicted a difficult period ahead with many American casualties. What none of us foresaw was that the fighting would last long enough for our teenage sons to be caught up in it and that the war's end would be both disastrous and traumatic for our country.

81
George Szell in the land of Sibelius

Finland was a superb vantage point from which to experience the Cold War on the propaganda front. Both the United States and the Soviet Union engaged in vigorous programmes to influence the hearts and minds of the Finnish people. In this battle of words I occasionally broadcast pro-American extracts from Finnish newspapers over the Voice of America.

An often-used Soviet technique was to invite Finnish journalists, artists, musicians, educators, industrialists and trade union leaders to Leningrad or Moscow with all expenses paid. They stayed in good hotels, were plied with excellent food and drink and saw what their hosts wished them to see, returning to Finland with glowing accounts of their adventures. Similarly, Soviet cultural figures toured Finland. Both official Soviet news agencies, TASS and Novosti, had extensive operations in the country. There was also a permanent Soviet trade mission among whose staff were KGB members. This massive presence, plus the proximity of Leningrad and Moscow, meant the Soviets could sustain a formidable propaganda offensive.

The United States had its prestigious Fullbright programme, which not only brought Americans to Finland, but also enabled Finns to undertake academic or travel study in America. Some Finns were not amused, however, when one of our exchange arrangements notoriously backfired. Finnish trade union leaders traditionally carried little weight because of their reputation for being easy-going and caving in to industrialists during negotiations for better working conditions. Alas, after the leader of the maritime workers' union returned from a visit to his militant trade union counterpart in the United States, he was a different man. When the next round of negotiations came, he plunged the shipping industry into chaos by calling out his men on indefinite strike. This continued for weeks before an agreement was reached; meanwhile, the general public, deprived of the benefits of international trade, pointed an accusing finger at the American embassy.

Fortunately there were other occasions when we were able to put forward the best of American culture and enterprise. One such event occurred during the 1965 Sibelius festival, organised to celebrate the centenary of the composer's birth. Herbert von Karajan came with his Berlin Philharmonic Orchestra and George Szell with his Cleveland Orchestra. Von Karajan had the advantage of being more widely known and was also the beneficiary of the natural disposition of European music lovers for orchestras based in Berlin or Vienna. Finns also knew about the great orchestras of New York, Philadelphia and Boston, but the reputation of the Cleveland Orchestra, conducted by Czech-born George Szell, was not then widely appreciated outside the United States.

There were a few in Finnish national television who sought to embarrass the United States because they were unimpressed by Szell's credentials. Consequently when an interview with George Szell was scheduled, they deliberately sent along a young lady whose knowledge of classical music was somewhat limited. She tearfully approached me minutes before the interview was due to begin in Szell's hotel, saying she knew next to nothing about Szell and the Cleveland Orchestra and had not been given any references or notes by her superiors.

While Szell was being briefed by the technicians and the final adjustments were made to the electric cables, I took her to a quiet corner of the hotel ballroom and explained that Szell, in spite of his formidable reputation as a conductor, was relaxed and easy to converse with on a personal level.

I added that I knew him to be a great admirer of Sibelius and his music and that he had recorded several of his symphonies. I then suggested five or six questions which I considered appropriate to ask from the Finnish point of view (e.g., how he regarded Sibelius' position among modern composers).

Reassured, the young lady, whom I knew from previous experience to be a gifted interviewer, recovered her aplomb. The resulting interview, sparked by Szell's warmth and witty responses, was highly acclaimed when it appeared on Finnish screens that evening. The reference which was to endear him most to Finnish listeners was the phrase proclaiming Sibelius "the last of the great composers". Next morning the Helsinki dailies joined in singing the praises of Szell.

This favourable impression of Szell may have caused some music lovers, who otherwise might have stayed away, to attend the Cleveland Orchestra concert. They were amply rewarded for, after the orchestra played one of Sibelius' rarely heard symphonies, they heard an encore, Dvorak's Slavonic Dances, that saw the superb strings of the orchestra reach heights of perfection. Now they understood why the Cleveland Orchestra, under Szell's direction, had come to be regarded as one of the world's finest.

During Szell's stay in Finland he asked to visit Sibelius' home, Ainola, where the composer's widow resided. Tess Mravintz, our cultural attaché and the person responsible for Szell's arrangements in Finland, had asked the aging Mrs. Sibelius if she could receive Szell briefly. She agreed. Just as Tess was about to join Mr. and Mrs. Szell in the official embassy car, she turned to me and asked if I would like to accompany them. "You have been a great help with the publicity," she added, "wouldn't you like this chance to be with Szell privately?" She did not realise that the alert Szell was listening to our conversation until he called out: "Yes, let Jim come."

Delighted at the unexpected adventure thrust upon me, I joined the Szells and we set out in a motorcade carrying all the orchestra members. The car immediately behind us bore the orchestra's administrative officer, charged with knowing Szell's whereabouts at all times.

Mrs. Sibelius greeted Szell warmly and the two immediately entered into an animated discussion about the great composer, his works and his beloved Ainola. She answered his many questions in great detail, after which she led him to her husband's grave nearby. With quiet dignity, Szell placed a wreath on Sibelius' tomb, took a few steps backward, paused a moment in contemplation and then thanked Mrs. Sibelius for her hospitality.

While members of the orchestra were saying their farewells to the composer's wife and taking photographs, Szell quickly called me to one side and asked:

"Is, by chance, that model town, Tapiola, anywhere near here?"

I replied that it was only some 20 minutes away.

"Good!" he exclaimed, "let's go there. I've been so tied down with the orchestra that I've seen little of Finland. Before I decided on a career in music, I wanted to be an architect. Maybe we can look inside a house at Tapiola!"

His enthusiasm was akin to that of a small boy. Mrs. Szell laughingly shared his zeal and before I could say anything Szell took me by the arm and led me toward the embassy car. Suddenly I remembered the orchestra's administrative officer and his responsibility for the conductor's whereabouts.

"Shouldn't you let him know where we are going?" I asked.

"Not on your life," Szell replied. "That's the last thing I want – being trailed around everywhere I go."

Our driver knew the most direct route to Tapiola and we were soon under way. Szell, looking at his wrist watch, observed that it was lunch time.

"Is there a place in Tapiola where we can have lunch?" he asked.

I told him there was a good restaurant, which our family had visited, on top of the water tower that every visitor to Tapiola climbed to get views of the model town.

"In that case," he replied in a commanding voice, "it is settled and you will be our guest for lunch."

For the best part of two hours George Szell was lost to the outside world. His aide didn't have a clue where he had gone. At first he had tried to follow us, assuming we were returning to Helsinki; eventually he lost sight of our car. I knew I would be blamed for not letting the orchestra members know where their leader was, but Szell assured me he would "take the rap", so there was nothing I could do but acquiesce to his wishes.

As soon as we reached the winding, irregular streets of Tapiola, Szell noticed how mature trees stood near many houses. I explained that when a Finnish family wanted a house built, they paid the builder a bonus *not* to injure or cut down existing trees.

"Amazing!" he exclaimed. "The first thing an American builder does is to flatten the landscape."

Then he saw many large boulders had been left where they had lain for thousands of years.

"I can't get over it," he continued, "everything that Nature has provided – trees, boulders, water – has been left intact and the positioning of the houses has become secondary to the preservation of what was here already."

At the water tower we entered the lift and were quickly whisked to the restaurant and observation tower high above the town. After ordering our meals we went outside to the circular ramp where Szell first admired the harmony of woodlands and water that stretched before us, broken only by the rooftops of houses. Then he turned his eyes to the area just in front of the water tower, a graceful U-shaped shopping centre, free of advertising and garish lights. In the centre was a flower garden, obviously tended with great care.

Then Szell spotted something I had not noticed on my previous visits to Tapiola.

"Look!" he called, "the houses are built in groups employing a single style of architecture, yet each group is set off from its neighbour by trees or water."

Over the meal I ventured to ask Szell if it had been difficult reaching the top ranks of conducting. He smiled, reflected for a second or two, and replied:

"Yes, terribly difficult. My great break came years ago when I was asked to be a guest conductor of an American orchestra. That single exposure brought me to the attention of the symphonic orchestra world and I have never looked back. So often in life, I have found, a helping hand can make the difference between success and failure."

But Szell did not want to talk about music; our Tapiola expedition was his "escape" and so he quickly changed the subject.

"Now, Jim," he said, looking at me squarely, "we have seen Tapiola from the ground and from a great height, but I must – I simply *must* - see the interior of a house. How are we going to do that?"

I gulped, wondering how we might intrude on some Finnish family, no doubt relaxing at home on Saturday after the father's week of work in Helsinki. Still pondering the problem as we descended in the lift, I suddenly remembered our naval attaché, Bill Campbell, lived in Tapiola with his lovely wife, Lillian, and two little girls, Karen and Heidi. Karen, in fact, attended the same German school as my daughter, Pipkin. I quickly concluded that it would be better to invade the Campbell's privacy than that of a Finnish family. I told Szell about the Campbells, adding that it would be considerate to give them a few minutes warning.

"Oh, they won't mind," he said, "let's go!"

When Lillian opened the door to me she was wearing an apron and holding a dustpan and brush. She looked aghast as I told her the purpose of our visit. Then nervously saying something about Bill not being dressed, she begged for a minute's preparation and quickly closed the door.

Szell, however, was impatient. Pushing me aside, he rang the doorbell. By now Lillian had discarded her apron and cleaning up implements. Her protestations again were smilingly ignored by Szell, who pushed his way forward into the living room.

While he shook hands with Lillian and introduced Mrs. Szell, the two little girls were frantically picking up their books and other belongings from the floor. Nowhere was Bill to be seen. Then, after greeting the girls, he asked to see the kitchen-cum-dining room. "Seeing the kitchen" to Szell, the would-be architect, meant pulling open every cupboard and standing in the middle of the room and stretching out his arms as if measuring his ability to touch any part of it from the centre. With each discovery, he exclaimed "Wonderful!" and "Marvellous!" as Lillian looked on amazed.

The kitchen-dining room thoroughly inspected, he turned on his heels, marched back into the living room and flung back the sliding wall that separated the living room from the downstairs bedroom. He instantly found himself face to face with Bill who, determined to be properly attired before meeting his distinguished "guest", had not quite pulled up his trousers. With one hand holding up the trousers, his other went out to grasp Szell's outstretched one as the conductor's confident voice boomed out, "Hello!" Bill quickly recovered his composure and led Szell through the remainder of the house. Lillian, meanwhile, chatted with Mrs. Szell, whose interests happily were more domestic than architectural.

All the way back to Helsinki Szell raved about the excellence of Tapiola's planning and the practical aspects of the Campbell's house. Sure enough, his aide was waiting in the foyer of the hotel. Furious that Szell had been "lost" and not knowing if he had been involved in an accident or some other mishap, the poor man had almost made himself ill with worry. As he was about to vent his wrath on me, Szell put up his hand and explained how the "kidnapping" was his fault and was due to his keen interest in architecture. I bade them a hasty good-bye and made an even hastier retreat.

82
Steinbeck and Glenn

In 1966 Finland held a bitterly contested parliamentary election, one that was of considerable interest to the United States and the Soviet Union because of the alignment of one or two Finnish parties with the Communists. There was little the United States could do except to observe as the left-wing alliance piled up a healthy majority. When I subsequently saw one of the known KGB operatives at the Helsinki hotel where journalists frequently gathered, he laughed and gloated over the result, intimating that even better things were in store for Finland.

Aware that dissidents were more active than ever in the Soviet Union, I looked him squarely in the eye and said:

"On the contrary, I predict that better things, in the form of free elections, will come to your country in your lifetime and mine."

This time he did not laugh, but grimly looked away.

At about this time the United States suffered an acute embarrassment when its glossy Russian-language magazine, *Amerika,* was refused entry into the Soviet Union because its cover portrayed the flag of the Republic of China (Taiwan) flying before the United Nations headquarters in New York. The Soviet Union considered its ally, the People's Republic of China, to be the only nation entitled to be called a Chinese republic.

Offended that Taiwan had been given such prominence on the cover of the official American magazine, the Soviets refused to allow the journal to be distributed unless the offending cover was removed. The distribution of a glossy Soviet magazine in the United States, and ours in the Soviet Union, had gone on for several years without a major hitch; now the agreement for mutual distribution was at risk unless a prompt solution could be found. We were anxious not to withdraw the issue as we had good reason to believe that most copies of *Amerika* never reached Moscow newsstands, but were eagerly and surreptitiously snatched up by bureaucrats – some high level ones. Might not they one day become leaders?

As the magazine was dated, our Washington headquarters had to find a rapid solution to the problem. The rejected copies of *Amerika* were held in Helsinki while we sought a printer who could remove the offending cover and attach a replacement one. In some countries such an operation would have posed no problem, but in Finland, where a posture of neutrality had to be maintained, a printer was needed who could do the job efficiently and discreetly so as to prevent embarrassment to his country as well as to the United States.

I approached Aatos Erkko, publisher of the Finland's largest daily, the *Helsingin Sanomat,* and asked if his firm could undertake the job. Erkko, whose father had been a much respected foreign minister who had sought to maintain Finland's links with the West during his country's earlier period of strained relations with the Soviet Union, readily agreed. The switch of covers was made quickly, professionally and without public knowledge so that the altered copies of *Amerika* reached Moscow only a week or so behind schedule.

On another occasion Erkko took a patriotic step which was not without some risk to himself and his publishing business. When an American Fullbright professor compiled a short history of the Finnish Communist party, the only one ever undertaken, I pondered how this study could be placed before the Finnish public. The reason why no history of the country's Communist party had yet appeared was because few people dared risk offending the Soviet Union with its all-pervasive links with Finnish Communists.

While Erkko would have an exclusive feature, at the same time it was inevitable that he incur the wrath of President Kekkonen who knew all too well that some of the sensitive disclosures in the history would reflect the Soviet Union's heavy hand. Nonetheless, Erkko spread the history over two full pages of the paper. Although promptly admonished by Kekkonen, he was privately applauded by most political leaders and, as well, by countless Finnish readers.

Happily, not all of my work entailed high profile activities that touched on Finland's delicate relationship with the Soviet Union. Especially welcome were the visits of prominent Americans with non-political agendas. Two of them, John Steinbeck and John Glenn, proved great favourites with both the Finnish media and the general public.

Steinbeck was the 1962 winner of the Nobel Prize for Literature. When the Finnish media first heard he was coming, they wanted separate interviews – impossible because of the author's brief stay in the country. The only fair solution was to arrange a press conference where all the media could be represented equally.

For the best part of an hour, the journalists fired questions at Steinbeck while his devoted wife, Elaine, sat quietly by his side. He joked, laughed and was so totally at ease that I wondered if he didn't have something in common with his questioners. My hunch was confirmed when, near the end of the press conference, a young reporter asked:

"Mr. Steinbeck, I have read several of your books and I am amazed to see how you can write so intimately about totally different characters and situations. What is the secret of your versatility?"

Steinbeck's smile revealed how much he liked the question.

"It all goes back to my days as a reporter in New York," he began, "when I was no older than the youngest of you around this table. There is always a great camaraderie among journalists in every large city, even if the newspapers they represent are deadly rivals. I don't have to tell you that many reporters also are heavy drinkers.

"You see, when half a dozen reporters went to the scene of a fire, an accident or some other tragedy, or interviewed a visiting celebrity, or whatever, it often happened that one of our group was so far gone with drink that he was incapable of filing his story. When that happened, it was understood that the junior reporter of our group would cover for him, writing the story which would then be delivered to the inebriated journalist's newspaper. This was no easy matter for a fledgling reporter, but he soon came to know – through reading and practice of writing – the style used by the tabloids, the middle-of-the-road papers, and the erudite *New York Times.* That's why I, at one time or another, came to write articles for virtually every paper in the city and no one was the wiser, except our close circle of reporters.

"We had a strict code of loyalty, for we did not want one of our number to lose his job because he had had too much drink at the crucial moment a major story broke. I found those youthful years, writing for my own paper and occasionally for others, a time of great challenge that forced me to write in whatever style the occasion demanded."

Another prominent visitor to Finland during our stay was John Glenn who, in 1962, had become the first American astronaut to orbit the earth. In the months that followed he was sent on an international goodwill tour that included Helsinki. As his "project officer" for the visit, I found him to be an able and charming man, as well as an excellent instructor. For several days, accompanied by his wife and teenage daughter, Lynn, Glenn met and talked with the country's leading scientists and technicians.

The highlight of the stay was his lecture on the United States' plan for landing on the moon. Held in a large auditorium in the country's leading technical institute, the lecture was enthusiastically received by hundreds of students and invited members of the general public. Speaking without notes and using models brought with him, Glenn held the audience spellbound as he confidently explained how the moon landing would be accomplished. When he concluded and asked for questions, budding scientists peppered him with so many questions we were obliged to call time to allow him to keep his next engagement. Had he not opted for a political career in the US Senate, Glenn, I am sure, would have made an outstanding educator.

Washington has its famous National Press Club and some other national capitals have clubs where journalists, diplomats and others gather regularly to hear prominent people speak on events of the day. In Helsinki such a club, embracing journalists and diplomats both from the West and the East, would have posed awkward problems, to say the least. Given the Finnish government's wish not to offend the Soviet Union, such a club in Helsinki undoubtedly would have become an unwelcome arena for weekly verbal battles of the Cold War.

In any case, as diplomats and news agency representatives of the Soviet bloc were constantly meeting and discussing their propaganda tactics in Finland, they should not have objected to Western journalists having a club of their own. It was under this cloud of controversy that the Western Foreign Press Club (WFPC) had been formed several years before my arrival in Helsinki.

Our club met weekly to partake of a light meal and liquid refreshment (usually beer, but I was allowed to drink *piima*, the Finnish equivalent of Georgia's grandoldbuttermilk). There was never a guest speaker or a set agenda, although if we had an out-of-town guest, we naturally asked him to say anything on his mind. The club was essentially a place where important news – political, economic, cultural – was exchanged.

The greatest visible achievement of the club was publication of a small but lively guidebook to the Finnish capital, *Helsinki à la Carte.* Some 35,000 copies had been printed in four English editions and somewhat smaller quantities in Swedish and German editions. Profits went to a local orphanage and to aid budding students of journalism. In my time the WFPC was chaired by Lance Keyworth, a brilliant Cambridge graduate. Married to a Finn, he operated a translation service and also was the *Financial Times* correspondent for Finland. Ulla, Lance's wife, taught skiing to children of Helsinki's diplomatic colony. Our Pipkin learned cross-country skiing in a matter of days under her tutelage.

The WFPC had use of an island in an archipelago off the Finnish south coast between Helsinki and Turku. (It was southwest of this archipelago that the ferry *Estonia* capsized in 1994 with the loss of many lives.) To reach the island from the mainland, one had to take a quarter of an hour's motorboat ride.

On this island a family could holiday for a weekend or longer, surrounded only by the sea and other islands. A large wooden building served as the island's social centre, and outbuildings provided living accommodation. The high point of the day was the arrival of the floating grocery, a fair-sized boat with an amazing variety of groceries, meat, vegetables and fruit.

Arranged supermarket style on tilted shelves, they were sold by a gorgeous young blonde attired in a spotless apron. Sadly for anyone who might wish to pass the time of day or admire her wares, she was very businesslike, pushing off to another island the minute she had supplied our provisions.

Our family spent many happy days on "The Island", relaxing and watching the ferries and other ships pass en route to or from Helsinki. There was a large supply of old 78 records and a hand-cranked player, both dating from before the Second World War, which we played over and over again. A fat photograph album contained pictures of men, women and children from those halcyon days when Finns had no inkling of the disastrous wars that were to follow.

83
A see-through dress outshines an Ambassador

We found the Finns to be very sociable. Although outwardly shy, they are warm-hearted and ready to extend every kindness once a bond of sincerity has been established. For example, when Stuart's fondness for athletics became known, he was invited to spend a week at the country's national training centre. Here he was able to observe the keenness with which Finnish athletes responded to expert training and he was also to make several enduring friendships.

Angela, after a disappointing first year in her American college, took a semester off to enrol at the University of Helsinki where she made many new friends. She was also able to share some adventures with former classmates from her English school, The Mount, when they visited Finland.

One summer Angela and another Mount "old girl" attended a student work camp in a rural area of northern Finland. A letter from Mary to her mother reflects the spirit of idealism which engulfed the youngsters at that impressionable age:

"Angela and Jane returned from the work camp last Saturday morning. They had three weeks there and it was really so worthwhile. These rural families are so poor, the men look so young and their wives so old and haggard. Their teeth are gone and everyone is overworked. Yet the girls said how very happy the children are, even with no toys and far from the nearest town. I think it did Angela and Jane a world of good.

"On Tuesday they went off to a totally different way of life – the Soviet Union – by bus. Just four days but we so wanted Angela to visit there before leaving for America. They return tomorrow night and, at the same time, four young men will be gathering: one from Norway, one from Israel, one from Egypt and one from Australia, to discuss politics. Goodness, what a lively lot!"

Pipkin, before going to The Mount, joined a unit of the Helsinki Brownies. As such, she entered into various local activities among which was a delicious visit to the country's largest chocolate factory (Fazer's) where, for once, her love of chocolate was more than sated.

Our apartment was typically Finnish in the sense that the bedrooms were unusually small by American or British standards, while the public rooms (living room and dining room) were correspondingly spacious. The psychology behind this, a Finnish friend told us, was simple:

"Your bedroom is unimportant so long as it is large enough for your bed; what counts more are spacious public rooms."

Our dining room accommodated a table seating a dozen people, useful because we could have a large number of guests for one meal instead of catering twice for a smaller number. The living room overlooked a large undulating park that was covered with snow in winter. The room was large and rectangular which allowed the easy separation of guests into at least two groups.

On one occasion this spaciousness proved a godsend. Unwittingly, Mary and I had invited two very beautiful ladies, both in their forties and prominent in Helsinki society, to the same reception. As soon as they caught sight of each other, we realised our dilemma. They edged their way to opposite ends of the room, each drawing with her a band of loyal supporters. Although the party was to continue for over an hour, no amount of coaxing could break up the opposing camps. Each lady and her orbiting friends held to their entrenched positions to the very end and managed to depart without seemingly being aware of the other's presence.

Finns are fond of drink and when couples were invited to a party, they often contacted another invited couple so four people could travel in the same car. Before setting out, they would draw straws to see who would do the driving, for drink-driving laws in Finland are severe. The unlucky driver knew he must drink moderately while his three companions had no such restraint. The hosts of a party, had they glanced out of their window five or ten minutes before the announced time, would see intending visitors circling the block so as to arrive on the dot of the appointed hour.

Occasionally we discovered that someone who had accepted an invitation to a reception did not turn up. When we made enquiries, we were told that he was engaged in some public works project such as "helping to extend the runway at Helsinki's airport". This was no excuse but the truth, for the penalty for driving while drunk, often was a period of labour. Unlike VIP drinkers in America or Britain who often manage to have their charges quashed, no one in Finland could escape a penalty. Thus, in our time, we sometimes heard of cabinet ministers and other prominent political and professional people who were sentenced to public work projects for short periods. The guilty ones made no attempt to get out of their drinking charges, for according to Finnish psychology, such manoeuvring would be thoroughly undemocratic.

One secret of entertaining, Mary and I discovered, was to invite people with contrasting views, whether political, cultural or social. In this way we were assured of sparkling conversation and sometimes, heated debate. For example, if among Mary's Helsinki friends there were ladies who were renowned for their unusual dress or hair styles, they were bound to create interest.

One humorous incident involving this deliberate attempt at a healthy mix of guests occurred not long before we finished our Helsinki assignment. One of my contacts had an extremely attractive young wife who, by now, had become a good friend of Mary's. She telephoned the very day of the party to tell Mary she had just acquired a fantastic see-through dress, but wasn't sure if it would be appropriate to wear it on this occasion, a reception to honour Ambassador Clare Timberlake, the chief American delegate to the Geneva disarmament conference.

"By all means wear it!" Mary dared her.

The dress more than lived up to its advance description. Not only did it have the see-through feature, but it also required its wearer to omit her bra. As the male guests arrived for the reception, they first did a double-take as they spotted Mary's friend, coyly standing to one side. Recovering, they assumed serious, dignified mannerisms as they were presented to Ambassador Timberlake.

As soon as they could politely extricate themselves from the ambassador's rapidly diminishing circle, they scurried, almost to a man, to the gorgeous young lady to get a closer look at the remarkable dress and all it disclosed. As she was exceptionally well proportioned, the converging male guests took some time to complete their reconnaissance. While ostensibly undertaking serious conversations, their eyes invariably wandered downwards.

"What a marvellous party!" all the men said, as they departed. Their wives smiled politely but did not repeat the compliment. Last to leave was the gorgeous lady who had been the centre of attention. She glanced apprehensively at Mary but she need not have been concerned.

"You were wonderful!" Mary exclaimed.

When everyone had departed, I looked at Mary and said wryly: "But Ambassador Timberlake thought the reception was in *his* honour."

84
Sisu – the Finns' indomitable spirit

Christmas in Helsinki was not merely the time for ingathering of one's family, but also an occasion to celebrate the peculiarly Finnish aspects of the season. Helsinki parents with small children were not content merely to tell their offspring about Father Christmas; Santa Claus had to turn up in person sometime during Christmas Eve. Given the thousands of families obliged to produce a Santa Claus, bookings had to be made well in advance of the Christmas season.

Even so, the streets of Helsinki were filled with hundreds of Santas cycling frantically from one home to another through the snow-laden streets. There was no need for Santa to take along a heavy coat, for every family he visited insisted on giving him a drink before he departed, thereby assuring him sufficient warmth to reach the next home. Given the large number of calls made that evening and the amount of drink consumed, it was perhaps just as well that Santa should navigate through the city by bike instead of car.

Finnish homes and shops, during the Christmas season, eschewed the coloured lights found in some Western countries, and opted instead for Scandinavian white lights or candles. One of the most memorable sights from my Finnish assignment was a visit to Helsinki's Hietaniemi Cemetery at Christmas.

The cemetery is the last resting place of hundreds of gallant Finns who lost their lives in the vain struggle against superior Soviet forces during 1939-1944. The tomb of the national hero, Marshal Gustaf Mannerheim, rests on a knoll overlooking the graves of his fallen comrades. At Christmas, and on other special occasions, each grave is lit by a candle, protected by a jar-like cover to prevent it from being extinguished.

Only at Christmas, however, does the haunting contrast of darkness, snow and candle light prevail. When Mary and I first visited the cemetery in 1963, some of Mannerheim's veterans were still alive. As we watched silently from a respectable distance, these old men, some with crutches and canes, hobbled to the place of honour beside Mannerheim's tomb, there to remain as erect as their frail bodies would permit, for the five or ten minutes allotted each veteran. Austin Goodrich, writing in *Helsinki à la Carte,* describes the scene:

"The sight of this huge cemetery with thousands of little flames of love burning for hours is not easily forgotten."

All Finns rejoice at the coming of spring, but none more so than university students. The first of May, known as "*Vappu*", and the night before are marked by festive events to celebrate the end of the academic year. Squares and parks in the university cities are filled with students dancing, singing and waving their white caps. On the evening of April 30th Helsinki's Market Square is filled with thousands of students awaiting the stroke of midnight. One of them is accorded the honour of climbing the statue of Havis Amanda, a gorgeous nude, and placing a large student cap on her head.

After an early breakfast, in which salted herring is an essential component, university students adjourn to a large park near the sea to continue celebrating the arrival of spring in songs and speeches. As our apartment abutted this park, we had a grandstand view of these festivities.

Undaunted by having a short season of warm weather, Finns long ago devised a simple but moving custom of anticipating spring by bringing greenness to their homes even when snow still lay thickly on the ground. This they accomplish by sowing grass seed on trays which are placed on window sills to capture the elusive rays of sunshine. As the days become longer and the warmth of the sun increases, these miniature gardens suddenly erupt in a frenzy of brilliant green – defying anyone to say that spring isn't just round the corner.

Church-going, I have always found, is all the more stimulating if the minister is a charismatic figure. William (Bill) Masters, the Church of England's "man in Helsinki", was such a one. Born of a humble family, he did not hesitate to refer to the austere circumstances of his youth when the opportunity arose. He was a big man in every sense, over six feet tall, and with an ample girth that betrayed his love of good food. A bachelor of the old school, he was in constant demand in Helsinki's international community for the pleasure he gave hostesses at meal times with his lively manner and great knowledge. In his younger days, he served with the British Forces in Palestine where he became a keen observer of Arab village and nomadic life.

When our family began attending his services in a small upstairs chapel in a residential area of Helsinki, we were at first startled almost out of our wits by his device to keep the attention of any member of the congregation about to doze off. In Palestine he had learned the shrill, guttural cry of the Bedouin shepherd attempting to keep his sheep under control.

If he spotted one of his "sheep" nodding – even a member of Helsinki's diplomatic corps – Bill would stop in mid-sentence, put his fingers to his lips and let fly his piercing shepherd's call. The dozing offender would awaken instantly, look around to see if he had been noticed and then give Bill a smile to signal his good-humoured acceptance of the reprimand.

When Bill came to our dinners he always brought us, in accordance with Finnish custom, some small gift – flowers or chocolates for Mary, or some item of British food (Bird's custard powder, Bovril, etc.) which he had obtained on his last trip to England and which he knew was not available in Finland.

He was a lover of classical music and had an extensive library of records, some of which he picked up at bargain prices in Leningrad or Moscow during his frequent visits there. His favourite was Schubert's "Unfinished Symphony"; Mary and I had standing instructions, on his arrival for a meal, to install Bill in our favourite wing chair and immediately put Schubert's work on the record player. There he would relax contentedly rejoicing in the master's music, while occasionally sipping sherry. His store of stories was so extensive that over three and a half years we never heard him repeat one at our dinner parties.

As the only Anglican minister in north-eastern Europe, Bill was frequently asked to hold services in Russia and other countries in the Soviet bloc. Following each visit he wrote a lively narrative which he shared with friends. These, combined with verbal notes, afforded valuable insights into living conditions in such remote areas as Outer Mongolia and Armenia.

His accounts of visits behind the Iron Curtain sparkled with wit. In one city he was assigned a pretty Intourist guide named Juliette. "She was very nice," Bill said, "but full of the party line – more often than not, I imagine, without being conscious of it. She plied me with endless statistics about Soviet achievements, all of which I promptly forgot."

Most Western diplomats who visited the Soviet Union waited for hours to have their meals served. Not so with Bill. Mary asked him how he managed to obtain prompt service. His technique was simple, but effective:

"I sent wine to the band and gave discreet but moderate tips to the waiters and was always looked after very nicely."

He did not say so, but I suspect his success was in part due to the "dog collar" he wore.

The Archbishop of York, Donald Coggan (later to become Archbishop of Canterbury), and his wife, Jean, visited Helsinki during our time. At a reception given in their honour, Mary mentioned that Pipkin had recently enrolled at The Mount School in York, which Angela had also attended earlier. Mrs. Coggan, ever the supportive wife, immediately reached into her handbag and withdrew a notebook.

"Give me her name," she said, "and I'll invite her to tea after we get back to York."

Mary did so and, sure enough, an invitation was sent via the headmistress for "Pipkin and one friend" to take tea with Mrs. Coggan at the bishop's palace. Unfortunately the rain poured as the two girls set out, first by bus and then by foot down the long drive to the palace. When they arrived they were soaked to the skin. Undaunted by the sight of a pair of drowned mice at her front door, Mrs. Coggan gave the girls a warm welcome and relieved them of their dripping coats. After meeting the Archbishop, they were shown round the palace before having tea. The only disappointment, Pipkin told us later, was the absence of a dungeon full of skeletons.

Random extracts from Mary's diary illustrate the Finns' love of festive occasions. The first was written after we attended a Christmas dinner in the family-friendly Kestikartino restaurant, Helsinki's temple of traditional Finnish food, folk music and costume:

"Fir branches everywhere decorated with small red apples. One large table with white table cloth with runners in blue (thus resembling the national flag). This covered with smorgasbord – breads of all descriptions, cheese, fish – both raw and cooked, smoked salmon, fruit salad, salads, cucumber, beetroot, boiled potatoes, stewed steak in gravy, a delicious macaroni and egg dish, liver pudding, Karelian pies – all washed down with a tasty mead. Children recite parts of the Kalevala, followed by a fashion parade of folk costumes worn by Finns down through the ages. A very lovely evening."

Our ambassador, Tyler Thompson, was determined not to be outdone by the Finns when it was his turn to host a Christmas party. Again, Mary's account:

"Eighteen people for dinner at the ambassador's residence. New pictures on loan from State Department very good conversation topic. During soup course ambassador welcomed each person, strictly following protocol order. Took care to say something specific about each guest. Very proud of him. Delicious fish, caught by Ambassador and Mrs. Thompson. Also Cornish Hen and stuffing, vegetables, gravy, salad, three wines. Finally, crepes come in flaming in orange sauce in same dish. Superbly brewed coffee followed by liqueurs. Really terrific evening!"

Ambassador Thompson had a winning way with the children of his embassy officers, as Pipkin found out one day to her acute embarrassment. She had "invented" a crude slot machine fashioned from an old shoe box which dispensed sweets when one inserted a coin. Having tried it out successfully on members of the family whose 10 penny coins had produced small sweets in return, she proffered it to Ambassador Thompson one day when he came to lunch with us. To her consternation, he pulled out his coin purse and started inserting mark pieces. A mark was considerably more than her weekly allowance.

Pip's embarrassment grew as she realised the ambassador had invested more than a dollar's worth of marks on sweets whose value was only a few pennies. She protested, but Ambassador Thompson smilingly insisted that she keep her newly gained riches. No wonder he was a favourite among embassy children.

The annual St. Lucia ceremony, observed with as much ardour in Finland as in Sweden, was held in Helsinki Cathedral. Mary's notes capture the spirit of the last St. Lucia rites we were to witness:

"As the clock strikes six, the Cathedral doors open and out walks slowly St. Lucia. An Army band meanwhile plays the old Italian melody. The St. Lucia 'queen' is dressed all in white – a long dress and also a long, white coat. She wears a red sash and carries red tulips and a sheaf of oats for the birds. Upon her head is a crown of green bayberry leaves and white candles. She walks slowly down the stairs, followed by ten girls in long, white dresses with tall hats, each carrying a white candle. Then comes Saint Nicholas and a large number of red-hatted elves who descend in snake-like fashion.

"They all then mount the floats nearby and the procession begins, led by a police car and flanked by policemen on white horses. They continue through the principal streets to a point where St. Lucia is given a golden necklace before presenting money and other gifts to the needy. Each of the floats bears children in white, well wrapped up for the evening, for it is a bitter night with the temperature minus 15 degrees!

We finish off the occasion at a journalist's home where we are treated to that wonderful Scandinavian Christmas drink, *gluggi,* a hot port and cabbage casserole accompanied by potato chips and concluded with a luscious peach dessert."

There had been only one truly sad event during our Helsinki assignment and that had nothing to do with the Finns. In common with many others, we would always remember November 22nd, 1963 as the date when President John F. Kennedy was assassinated. We had started a meal with our next-door neighbours when Natalie Mattison, the wife of our USIA chief, telephoned to say the president had been shot. She was busy calling members of the embassy and added that I should report at once to the USIA offices where our teleprinter would provide a running commentary on Kennedy's condition. I rose, apologised to my hosts, and left Mary to continue with the meal I had hardly touched.

When Kennedy died, the Finns quietly reflected the sorrow felt by peoples the world over. Most striking of the many manifestations was the simple display in the main window of Stockmann's department store. A framed photograph of Kennedy, flanked by a single white candle, told it all. A few weeks later a tribute to Jacqueline Kennedy, the "American Princess" appeared in book form. It was ironic that only through the death of the president would both Kennedys reach the pinnacle of their popularity.

The difficult but thoroughly enjoyable years in Finland came to an end in 1967. I had come to understand, first hand, that unique Finnish word *sisu* which has now found its way into dictionaries of several countries in the Western world. It can mean courage, stamina, determination, strength of heart, obstinacy, perseverance and a host of other exemplary qualities. Taken singly or together, they describe the Finnish national character. No other people, I think, could have achieved independence, and guarded it so carefully against the mighty Soviets next door. This was achieved despite an historically strong domestic Communist party, the need to gear the Finnish economy to meet Soviet bloc requirements and, at the same time, retain its democratic institutions, national culture and bonds with the West. That, indeed, is *sisu*.

85
"Washington's burning, Washington's burning!"

Although our family had visited the United States regularly on home leave, by 1967, when we returned from Finland, we had been away 17 years. We bought a modest home in Bethesda, the Washington suburb located just across the District of Columbia line in Maryland. We quickly learned that drastic changes in American society were taking place, little realising that we would be affected by them.

Angela and Stuart, by now university students, experienced the full force of the protest movements which dominated American student life in the sixties. The two principal protests grew out of US involvement in Vietnam and black Americans' struggle for equal rights. Hardly an institution of higher learning escaped the emotions, and sometimes the violence, arising from the two movements.

Mary and I were to see evidence of students' extremist actions when we visited Angela and Stuart on their respective campuses, but these were as nothing compared to events in Washington. The nation's capital was to share with Detroit, Newark and other places the wrath of young blacks who burned down many inner-city blocks, their own homes and businesses often among them.

The fuse that set the nation's capital ablaze was the assassination of Dr Martin Luther King on April 4th, 1968. Late that evening looting began. The next day feelings among the black inhabitants quickly led a crowd of 20,000 to assemble. At first the police were ordered to shoot looters on sight; later the order was rescinded but not before 12 men had been killed and other wounded. President Johnson ordered 15,000 Army and National Guard troops to take up positions in central Washington. By midday fires set by rioters spread rapidly. Firemen, vastly outnumbered and under attack by the arsonists, gave up.

The rioters came within two blocks of The White House before they were repelled. By early morning the extent of the destruction became clear. Over 1200 properties had been destroyed and cost of the damage was estimated at over $150 million. We were not to know until later that 100 American cities, among them nearby Baltimore, had been torched during the four days following Dr King's assassination.

From my office window on Pennsylvania Avenue, only five minutes' walk from the White House, I saw ambulance after ambulance conveying wounded black activists to nearby George Washington Hospital. They had been shot by police while setting fire to shops, or looting them. When the casualties from these incursions began to mount, public opinion caused the order to shoot to be lifted.

One day, in a week that had seen much violence and arson in Washington, our staff was ordered to leave off work early in the afternoon, as another evening of chaos seemed likely. As I rode home with a fellow employee through one of the burnt-out areas, we saw black men, women and children helping themselves to new clothing from mobile racks which had been spirited away from nearby department stores. The police, now operating under a "no shoot" policy, made no effort to arrest the looters.

Soldiers, quickly brought in from nearby military installations, stood on every corner in central Washington. The feared spread of violence from the dominantly black areas to the city's administrative dustrict did not, however, materialise. Gradually the capital returned to the uneasy calm that had existed before the mass acts of arson.

Many American colleges, previously slow to feature black history and culture in their curriculums, now hastily offered courses. Likewise, many more black students were now admitted to universities (and to the civil service), although some were to experience initial difficulty because their secondary school preparation had been so poor. Some white students, deprived of university places because of the intake of less well qualified blacks, successfully brought cases of discrimination against educational institutions.

Nonetheless, in spite of polarised attitudes which developed, the black protests spurred a shocked nation to make a painful reassessment of its civil rights progress, not just in the field of education but in industry, government and the professions. For example, when I visited my Washington bank, I discovered a black cashier had been installed at the first teller position. He was, however, the only black in a line of some six or seven tellers. This token integration, while welcomed by some initially, was eventually condemned because it often was the only integration practised by a firm.

The Vietnam protest movement was equally visible in Washington. At its height students broke into professors' offices, whether or not their universities had been engaged in some aspect of military research (the most common excuse for the rampaging), and destroyed valuable documents covering years of work – sometimes in medicine and other humanitarian fields.

In the process millions of dollars worth of damage was inflicted on the institutions' facilities in senseless raids. The government, unlike some countries in Europe, was unaccustomed to dealing with violent student protests. Thus an incredible debacle eventually occurred when National Guardsmen shot dead four students on the campus of Kent State University in Ohio.

During a lunch break from my work on Pennsylvania Avenue I witnessed students (and some who were not students) at George Washington University tossing out files randomly from upstairs windows to gleeful followers on the street who promptly set out shredding or burning them. During this anarchical stage, as with the arson in the inner city, the police were restricted in their ability to respond and so the pillaging frequently continued unchecked.

While I was exposed to these violent incidents in downtown Washington, Mary and the children experienced quite different aspects of the protest movements. When administrators of some black primary schools in Washington let it be known that they wanted their pupils to know more about the world beyond their violent Washington so much in the news, Mary and other foreign service wives volunteered to give talks about the countries they had lived in.

Mary had an advantage over some wives for she could talk not only about Britain in general but also its Royal Family. Once she got lost while trying to find the school where she was to talk and strayed into a district which was virtually a no-go area for whites. Two policemen in a squad car came upon her trying to locate the school on her Washington map. To her relief, they escorted her to the front door of the school half a mile away.

After a warm welcome, she gave her talk, illustrated with slides and photographs. A few days later she received a large, fat envelope bearing individual letters of thanks from the children. Most were decorated in watercolour and some portrayed the Queen wearing her crown. Mary concluded that America's black children, however caught up with civil rights activities, shared the same fascination for the British Royal Family as white Americans.

Pipkin enrolled in Sidwell Friends School in Washington, respected, like any Quaker school in Britain, for its mix of academic excellence and stress on social responsibility. Over the years Sidwell has been the school chosen by many US government officials (among them several Presidents) and foreign diplomats for educating their children. Here Pipkin fell under the spell of a superb Latin teacher, Rose Westbrook, who helped cement a growing interest in the classics. Sidwell, in common with many American high schools, invited guest speakers to talk about the civil rights movement at student assemblies.

Student activism was more strident at Stuart's college, Amherst (in Massachusetts) than at Angela's, the University of North Carolina at Greensboro. On a visit to Amherst Mary and I were startled by the contradictory demands of black students for both equal rights and a separate kind of student union building. The student newspaper, normally erudite and serious, was now an inflammatory journal filled with obscenities.

Some professors gained national attention by joining in the trendy themes, namely, unreasoned criticism of US domestic and foreign policies. We could not blame Stuart for being bewildered, after quiet, happy years at his Methodist school in Somerset. Angela, equally affected by protest movements in North Carolina, was spurred to help with a student 'workshop' at a nearby black university.

Despite the civil unrest which marked our time in Washington, my duties proved almost as challenging as those I had undertaken abroad. My first year was spent in the newsroom of our government information agency where I prepared news articles and features about contemporary American events for use by our information officers in embassies around the world. Much of this work was akin to that of the political reporter on a daily newspaper, the principal difference being that the finished article had to reflect official American policy. The Vietnam war was then at a critical phase and much of our output was aimed at justifying American involvement.

Perhaps the most dramatic event I witnessed was Secretary of State Dean Rusk's last press conference in 1969. By this time he shared the blame, along with President Lyndon B. Johnson, Defence Secretary Robert McNamara and the US military leadership, for prolonging a bloody war that had become increasingly unpopular with the American public. Would the Secretary, many journalists wondered, admit that the US rationale for participation in the war was in error and now argue for an orderly withdrawal?

Rusk did not, and instead repeated, in his quiet and measured voice, his often aired justification for American involvement, viz., South

Vietnam was a small, agrarian country threatened by a larger, more industrialised North Vietnam backed by unlimited resources of the Soviet Union. It followed, he added, that other small countries in the area could be taken over (the so-called "domino theory") if the United States and her allies refused to come to South Vietnam's aid. So ended, effectively, the government service of an official who steadfastly believed that the US should continue to support South Vietnam.

Rusk, in his memoirs, admitted to underestimating the tenacity of the North Vietnamese and overestimating the patience of the American people. McNamara, in his memoirs, went further by saying the war was wrong and that American forces should have pulled out as far back as 1963. The debate as to whether the United States should have become involved in Vietnam is now over, for most of the leading "players" from President Johnson downwards are on record that the American action was a tragic mistake.

In hindsight we now know the South Vietnamese government was both weak and corrupt, that her people never understood the concept of Western democracy we attempted to foster and that the American people – shocked by the brutality of war depicted daily on TV sets in their homes – had no stomach for seeing their young men slaughtered in a remote part of Southeast Asia where no United States interests existed. The greatest irony came when returning servicemen, almost all conscripts, were pilloried by the public. To this day the Vietnam war remains a blight on the American conscience. Perhaps it may deter future American governments from committing troops to fight abroad when justification is not clear.

Not long after Rusk's last press conference I was sent to Laos as a member of an inspection team to assess the US information programme there. Vientiane, the capital, had been laid out by the French as a kind of Paris in miniature, complete with its own Etoile and Arc de Triomphe. From our hotel on the banks of the Mekong River it was possible to walk to Bhuddist temples and other sites of the city.

One evening I ended my walk just as dusk was falling by strolling along a street filled with many small shops. Suddenly I found myself before one bearing Chinese characters and realised it belonged to one of a handful of Chinese families barely eking out a living in the precarious economic conditions of the capital. The front door had been left ajar to allow the last rays of sunlight to penetrate the interior. I glanced inside quickly and saw a family seated on the floor in a circle, with a lantern in their midst. An elderly Chinese, whom I took to be a grandfather, was earnestly instructing two young children while their parents looked on. The memory of that moving scene has remained with me as an indication of the high regard with which Asians in general, and Chinese in particular, place on learning and respect for their elders.

Our ambassador to Laos explained to us inspectors that an uneasy truce existed among the three factions attempting to control the country: Communists (known as Pathet Lao), conservatives and neutralists. From the ambassador's briefing it was easy to understand how this land-locked country could fall to the Communists if American involvement in South Vietnam and other areas of Southeast Asia ended. The Pathet Lao were so strong that they could assassinate and terrorise almost at will.

One of the bravest couples I have ever met was a young Irish-American and his wife, posted to a remote, hostile area of Laos where the Pathet Lao was never far away. My fellow inspector and I almost felt a sense of guilt when we were asked to visit the information officer and see the conditions under which he and his wife lived. Even the pilot of our CIA-operated plane had misgivings about flying us to the lonely airstrip near where the couple lived.

The young officer met our plane and immediately took us to the village bistro where we had a bottled drink. The bistro was ominously empty except for the three of us. Our host explained there was more “activity” in the evenings. We did not tarry long and adjourned to the officer’s modest home.

Here he and his wife quickly put on records of Irish reels and danced vigorously together for half an hour, seemingly oblivious to the presence of their guests. This remarkable absorption, my fellow inspector and I agreed, was the couple’s escape from the reality of the peril that overshadowed every moment of their lives. As far as I was able to ascertain, they survived their assignment. Laos eventually succumbed (1975) to Pathet Lao control.

86
How does one inspect nuclear facilities?

Another time I was despatched to East Africa and Madagascar with a fellow American inspector. The contrast between Tanzania and Kenya was striking. The foyer of the national museum in Dar-es-Salaam featured nothing associated with Tanzania’s culture, but contained a model of a Chinese commune donated by the Chinese government. I wondered: did this betoken a time when the Chinese would exert greater economic control of Africa than the states themselves? Clearly socialism was the order of the day as my fellow inspector and I soon saw from touring the capital and parts of the countryside where much of industry and agriculture was state owned.

We made a side-trip to Zanzibar where a goodly part of the world’s cloves is produced. On a coconut plantation small boys of about twelve scurried up tall trees and dislodged coconuts. These were hastily gathered up and taken to a slicing post, about three feet high and imbedded in the ground. Here a muscular native, bare to the waist, raised his machete and then sliced the coconut, mounted on the post, neatly into two halves. I shuddered to think of other uses to which the machete had been put in the revolutionary purge of 1964 after the Sultan of Zanzibar was deposed. In the chaos that followed numbers of Arabs were slaughtered within a few days.

Although Christians, Moslems and those holding traditional African beliefs each make up about a third of Zanzibar's population, I found the little Christ Church Cathedral empty and in need of maintenance. Only the wall plaques in memory of departed soldiers, civil servants and others bespoke of a former British presence. It seemed with the departure of the Sultan and foreigners, this little piece of Christendom had fallen upon hard times.

During the flight from Dar-es-Salaam to Antananarivo, the capital of Madagascar, our plane crossed over the Mozambique Channel which separates the island from the African mainland. As a lover of geography, I had always been fascinated by the fact that Madagascar had broken away from the mainland and that little imagination was needed to see how neatly the island had once fitted into the coast of Mozambique. Now, at 35,000 feet, I saw another aspect of this geographical phenomenon: the relatively shallow waters of the Mozambique Channel were clearly apparent from the height of our plane.

Although Madagascar had once been part of Africa I was amazed to find that it had none of the larger African animals (elephants, lions, rhinoceroses, etc.); crocodiles, however, abounded. The country, I found, is noted instead for its extensive range of brilliantly coloured fish and insects, some of which are depicted frequently on its postage stamps. More interesting still, the bulk of the population is of Malayo-Polynesian origin with a small infiltration of African and Arab blood.

At the time of our inspection Madagascar was struggling to throw off the French rule that had existed since Queen Ranavalona was dethroned in 1897. At one time or another in the past century French troops had quelled insurrections, causing deep-seated bitterness among the inhabitants. The Chinese stepped into the vacuum thus created and were to exert increasing influence on the native peoples.

On a brief visit to the island's second largest city, my fellow inspector and I toured a district where a large Chinese community was well established. A few years after our visit, the islanders successfully threw off the French yoke, nationalised all French industries and, at the same time, also distanced itself from several other Western countries.

During the latter part of my Washington posting I was seconded to the US Arms Control and Disarmament Agency, the State Department agency concerned with helping curtail the proliferation of nuclear weapons and with reducing the sale of conventional weapons by industrialised nations. The Eighteen-Nation Disarmament Conference in Geneva was the forum where Western countries and the Soviet bloc mounted fierce debates about the issues at stake.

Foremost of the problems, and one that persists to this day, was how to inspect effectively the arms facilities of a country determined to continue its research and production in secret. Modern satellite intelligence can tell a great deal about a country's nuclear capability but only on-the-ground inspection can detect precise conditions. This remains the essential dilemma of disarmament, for there will always be some nations which *say* they don't have a nuclear weapon capability when the truth is otherwise.

As there was then no spokesman for the Geneva Conference as a whole, it was left to each "side", i.e. the West or the Soviets, to explain to waiting journalists what had transpired in each session. As the press advisor to the American delegation, I had the tricky task of presenting not only the US position but, at times, what I thought to be the position of other Western delegates. When there was general agreement, there obviously was no problem. Happily, during my time, Lord Chalfont was named head of the British delegation and he proved an able communicator of the UK position.

Apart from the crucial issues being debated, the disarmament conference provided an opportunity to meet delegates from all participating countries, some of whom were already, or later to become, prominent figures in their respective countries' governments. Aldo Moro, Italy's Minister of Foreign Affairs, sometimes attended. He was later to be brutally executed by the Red Brigade.

Mrs. Alva Myrdal, leader of the Swedish delegation, held the rank of Minister. She spent most of the latter half of her life advocating disarmament and in 1982 shared the Nobel Peace Prize for her work. In Geneva she gave a series of luncheon parties, enabling her to meet most of the delegates to the disarmament conference.

When my turn came, I told her that her late husband, Gunnar, a distinguished economist, had written one of the first studies about the American South at a time when little attention in the United States had been focused on the region's problems. It had, I added, made an indelible impression on me during my formative years. A warm glow came into her eyes as she thanked me for the modest tribute I had paid her husband.

87
Fun in suburbia

Mary and I were blessed with wonderful neighbours in Bethesda. Donald Hagner was involved in one of the many projects which had been spun off from the NASA space programme. His wife, Jane, one of Mary's best friends, soon introduced us to delectable Maryland Crab Soup, a speciality she had learned from her mother in Baltimore as a teenager.

For those gourmets who like an elegant seafood soup and have the patience to prepare it slowly, here is Jane's recipe:

"Fry in the soup kettle five strips of thin bacon until brown. Remove and save bacon. Cut up and fry until brown two large onions in the bacon fat. Add half a pound of ground (minced) beef, again cooking until brown. Then add two large stalks of celery (including the leaves), fine chopped. Also add small quantities of chopped parsley, diced carrots and other available vegetables such as corn (maize) and peas. Pour in water to cover ingredients and then add a large tin of tomato sauce - preferably the Spanish type with a green pepper taste. (If Spanish type sauce is not available, substitute a small quantity of chopped green peppers.) Drop in two beef bouillon cubes and let mixture simmer for two hours. Remove all traces of shells from one pound of crab meat, add to the soup along with a teaspoon of authentic seafood seasoning, such as Old Bay, and salt and pepper to taste. Let simmer for the rest of the day!"

Another neighbouring family was the Stowells, Jim and Helen. Jim was a copyright lawyer whose office was then in downtown Washington. His natural sense of humour caught me by surprise when I dropped in for a brief visit one day. Greeting me almost casually with only the tiniest trace of a smile, he waved me to a seat in front of his desk while he fished around in his desk for something. At last he pulled out a huge alarm clock which he proceeded to wind vigorously. As he set the clock down gingerly, it began to tick loudly. Then, with another flicker of a smile, Jim said:

"You must excuse my delay in welcoming you. In the legal profession we charge for time spent and the only way I can keep an accurate record is to set my clock when a client arrives. Now what is it you want to say?"

When Jim saw my initial look of incredulity, he instantly burst out laughing, put away the clock and extended his hand in welcome.

Jim's wife, Helen, was another of Mary's good friends. She and Jane, together with three or four other wives of neighbouring families, frequently organised parties and expeditions. Our children and those of our neighbours had their own activity "programmes", some bordering on the verge of mischief. More than once Mary and I awoke to see a large sign reading, "For Sale: Open Viewing 2 – 5 p.m." embedded in the grass on the edge of our front lawn. After getting over the initial shock, the problem was not so much removing the sign, but figuring out what to do with it. Sometimes it belonged two streets away, but none of our neighbours' kids "knew".

Aware that Mary was a "new American" intensely interested in national affairs, another family, the Griffins, went out of their way to involve her in exciting events. Robert ("Bob") Griffin was a US Senator from Michigan. Young and dynamic, he was the Republican party whip. "Marge", his wife had been a school teacher before her marriage; in Bethesda she was fully occupied supporting her busy husband and their several children. Despite the great demands on their time, they took the trouble to invite Mary to President Nixon's inauguration in 1969 and to join a group of VIPs on an inaugural flight of the Boeing 747 over the Washington area.

Bethesda was an artificial suburb without a community centre or "soul". Except for a shopping mall, library, a few churches and schools – all scattered along the major roads, there was little to bind families together. On the fourth of July and at Christmas a few families formed impromptu music groups and toured the area on floats (open-topped trucks) to generate seasonal spirit. In the main it was left to families to develop friendships among like-minded neighbours, if they were to have any communal spirit at all. In this regard we were lucky to have amiable neighbours on all sides.

At first Mary found it difficult to adapt to the American custom of no fences or hedges around one's front garden. For example, one moment she could be in the house cooking or cleaning and the next a brigade of neighbourhood children would sweep across the lawn (and everyone else's) engaged in a Wild West chase. The children, in effect, knew no boundaries and they never considered a lost ball during a sports game a problem. More than once Mary looked up from her work to see a strange child retrieving a football or baseball from our garden.

Eventually she came to accept this openness and decided to make a contribution of her own – communal making of dandelion wine. Armed with her mother's recipe, she gathered around her a dozen or so children and told them, for very little effort, they could produce delicious dandelion wine for their parents. Thus spurred, they scattered in all directions and soon returned with pails of plucked dandelions which Mary proceeded to simmer in boiling water. After several days of fermenting, the wine was ready for bottling.

Again the children scattered, shortly to return with bottles rescued from recycling bins at their respective homes. Although none of them liked the taste of the stuff, they had been briefly occupied with a cottage industry that lay at their doorsteps and was theirs to continue if their parents so wished. Of this "company" of budding brewers, at least one went on to make it his career. On reflection, Mary wondered if some parents had disapproved of the venture. If they had, they were kind enough to keep their disapproval to themselves.

If Washington's theatre and symphonic orchestra did not at that time always win national acclaim, this could not be said for the capital's museums and art galleries. Thanks to a bequest of $500,000 in 1846 by an Englishman, James Smithson, the Smithsonian Institution became the world's largest museum complex. Although Mary and I made many excursions, sometimes with the children, we managed to visit only a few of the many Smithsonian museums.

The cultural centre we visited most often was the National Gallery of Art. Apart from many special exhibitions there, Mary, I and many others in the Washington area were drawn to the Gallery during the winter of 1969-70 for the screening of Kenneth Clarke's magnificent "Civilisation" series. Clarke became almost a cult figure and no one cared if he mistakenly pronounced Potomac as "Pot-o-mack". A number of ambassadors from Washington's diplomatic corps attended these scholarly screenings, along with ordinary mortals like us.

When, at last, the series was finished and viewers were offered copies of the British edition accompanying Clarke's series, we jumped at the chance. Over the years since, Mary and I took the volume from the shelf and, perusing its pages together, relived those winter weeks when we eagerly awaited the start of each new film. Her inscription on the fly-leaf tells all:

'To commemorate thirteen tremendous Sundays when, mid cold, rain, snow and a little sunshine, we stood in line with hundreds of others awaiting the opening of doors to the National Gallery of Art for these Civilisation lectures, November, 1969 – February,1970.'

88
The richness of American military history

Mary was also involved in various activities of the American Foreign Service Association (AFSA) in Washington. The ladies organised annual book sales which were eagerly attended by Washington's university professors, students and young foreign service officers anxious to acquire, at minimal cost, reference works and other volumes that had once belonged to diplomats serving in every corner of the globe.

Even more enjoyable for Mary was a small circle of women comprising the AFSA Writers Group. These were wives of serving or retired foreign service officers who were writing, or already had written, articles or books about every imaginable subject. Some foreign-born wives wrote about their upbringing in faraway places. Some wrote accounts of their overseas adventures. Others wrote fiction and poetry. At each meeting members read extracts from their writings. At one such Mary read an account of a festive Christmas spent at her grandmother's in rural Hampshire.

Mary never tired of visiting Washington with its many cultural and historical attractions. Despite the tensions arising from Vietnam and the racial unrest, she thoroughly enjoyed this first prolonged residence in the United States.

Since the end of the Second World War I had been a member of the United States Army Reserve. This had usually obliged me to go into uniform for periods of two weeks or longer annually at military installations in the United States or Europe. As the "Cold War" very much affected American military planning, the emphasis in my Reserve trainings dealt with countering any offensive the Soviet Union might initiate against countries in Western Europe or the United States itself.

Ironically, I was involved, on one hand, with concern for disarmament in my daily work and, on the other, with military preparedness in my Army Reserve training. The Reserve training culminated in graduation from two institutions whose history and traditions form a cherished niche in American military lore: the Command and General Staff College at Fort Leavenworth, Kansas, and the Army War College at Carlisle Barracks, Pennsylvania.

Both institutions were steeped in the lore of the United States

Army. Fort Leavenworth had been established by Colonel Leavenworth in 1827 to protect the old cross-country route, the Santa Fe Trail, from the Indians. General Sherman, in 1881, was mainly responsible for converting the post into the Army's staff college. Its importance became so crucial to the careers of staff officers that none could hope to progress far without being selected to study there. Almost all the great American generals of the two world wars received staff training at Fort Leavenworth.

In the late afternoons when our classes were over, I enjoyed strolling with fellow officers along the streets of the post whose elegant homes, constructed in the style of early military architecture, overlooked the mighty Missouri River. With the help of a guide, we relished the stories about high-ranking Army officers who lived there with their families while studying at the staff college.

Carlisle Barracks was also hallowed ground where many a noted general once studied but the post had an altogether different origin from Fort Leavenworth. It began (1879 – 1918) as America's only "off-reservation" school for Indians (native Americans). Drawing the best students from the country's many Indian tribes, it soon earned a niche in the annals of college football, sometimes defeating the best known universities in the land.

The sports star of that period was an Oklahoma Indian, Jim Thorpe, who was twice selected on the "All America" football team. Thorpe's achievements, however, were not limited to the football field. In the 1912 Olympics at Stockholm he won both the pentathlon and the decathlon, the gold medals being presented by the Swedish King. On receiving these, Thorpe is reputed to have said: "Thanks, King."

A few years later it emerged that Thorpe had played semi-professional baseball for a brief period and, because he was paid, he was not a "pure" amateur athlete. He was obliged to return his medals. Intoday's climate such a penalty would be unthinkable; in 1912 it was considered a disgrace. Long after Thorpe's death, Olympic officials reversed their earlier decision and presented the medals posthumously to his family.

Aware of the Thorpe story and the role the Indian School had played in the education of native Americans, I frequently visited the Indian cemetery situated in a distant part of Carlisle Barracks. I was fascinated by the Indian names that were meant to depict either physical characteristics or extraordinary feats of their bearers and how 144 of them had been buried there in the relatively short history of the school. Some 22 had perished in 1888, suggesting an epidemic of some kind. 15 died the following year and another 11 the year after. For the last 12 years of the school's existence, however, there were no headstones, an indication that either medical standards had improved or the school's enrolment had dropped.

Nearly 50 Indian tribes were represented among the dead. Some, like the Cherokee, Sioux, Cheyenne, Crow, Apache and Seminole were well known to me; others, such as Sax and Fox, Kickapoo, Niagotoc and Winnchaga, were new.

Most of all I was drawn to the beautiful surnames of these Indians, many of whom had died in the prime of their youth. So I repeatedly returned to study their headstones. I saw that James Fox Catcher had died on 2 June 1888 and that three years later, Ada Fox Catcher had followed him. Were they, I wondered, brother and sister? It took little effort to imagine either the appearance or physical prowess of Indians with names like Almeda Heavyhair, Matavito Horse, Percy Whitebear, Herbert Littlehawk, Young Eagle, Titus Deerhead, William Snake, Harry Greenbird, Blue Tomahawk, Fanny Charging Shield, Chief Swift Bear, Chief White Thunder, Jane Lumpfoot, Rebecca Little Wolf and Samuel Flying Horse. And how lovely Lucy Pretty Eagle must have been, I thought.

89
A university ceremony or a riot?

Back in Washington an unusual incident sharply reminded me that tension among the black population was far from over.

Howard University, one of the most prestigious black universities in America, was about to inaugurate a new president. These inaugural occasions are major events on the American higher education scene, with many other universities (including Oxford and Cambridge) being invited to send representatives to the ceremony. Institutions which are quite distant seldom send members of faculty but instead designate graduates who live in the vicinity of the inaugural site – in this case, Washington. Thus I was asked to represent my alma mater, the University of Georgia, whose charter dated back to 1785, making it the oldest chartered state university in America.

In the inaugural procession the delegates, attired in robes designating the degrees they held, marched in chronological order according to the years in which their institutions had been established. I had assumed that my university's 1785 charter would put me somewhere near the front, but suddenly there was a gorgeous American girl, an Oxford graduate, leading the way! She was followed, moreover, by a Cambridge graduate and after that came representatives from Harvard, Yale and other private universities whose founding dates antedated my own. It reminded me of a fact I had almost forgotten, viz., America's founding fathers had not waited long to introduce higher education into the Colonies.

I was warmly welcomed by Marion Mann, a native Georgian and prominent member of Howard University's medical faculty. Marion had been a fellow student at the Army War College at Carlisle Barracks where, at weekends, he would get into his cherished Rolls Royce and drive back to Washington to be with his family. On one occasion he also drove me home, where my family and neighbours much admired his "chariot", the first Rolls Royce I had ever ridden in. Marion later became the first member of our War College graduating class to become a General.

So many delegates and guests from all over the United States were in attendance at the installation of Howard's new president that there was not an empty seat to be seen. Occasionally during the ceremony I could hear students shouting outside, sounds I took as congratulatory shouts for the new president. When we began to emerge from the auditorium at the end of the installation rites, however, we immediately saw the students were hostile. They carried no weapons or objects that could be thrown at us, but clearly were greatly upset about something.

As we tried to mount the waiting buses that had been chartered to take us back to downtown Washington, they blocked our path. Only with great difficulty were we able to extricate ourselves and take our seats. The students, however, were unwilling to let us proceed. Some stood in front of the bus and others started rocking it, amidst a rising crescendo of racist shouts about "Whitey".

Fortunately for us, there was a young black professor from an Ohio university in our bus. He took it upon himself to try and resolve the impasse. At last he managed to quieten the unruly crowd and start a dialogue with its leader. The student, soft-spoken and intelligent, explained.

"Why is it that we, Howard University students," he asked, "have been deprived of attending the inaugural ceremony of our own university president?"

That was the first we visiting delegates had known about the dilemma facing the university. When so many educational institutions across America decided to send delegates to the ceremony, there were very few seats left for Howard students. We now understood the bitter disappointment of hundreds of others who had taken for granted their attendance. The professor from Ohio held up his hand and asked the crowd to listen to him.

"I understand your feelings. I probably would feel the same if I were in your shoes but there is another point that is terribly important. When Howard sent out invitations all over the country, and to universities abroad, they had no idea so many of them would want to share in this inaugural occasion. It is a tremendous compliment to Howard, its faculty and students, that you are held in such high regard that so many delegates have gathered here today. Surely you would not have wanted them to be shut out while you took the seats inside? All of us in these special buses wouldn't be here if we didn't have great respect for you and the university. It has been a memorable occasion for us. Surely you wouldn't want to spoil it by delaying our departure?"

The student leader and his companions smiled at us, with unashamed pride now radiant on their faces.

"We hadn't thought of it that way," the leader said. "Of course you are right. We thank you for being with us today. Please forgive our misunderstanding."

With that he waved away those who had blocked our exit. As we left the campus, we exchanged friendly waves. We delegates reflected on how a calm exchange of views had made all the difference between violence and understanding.

In 1970 came one of those periodic opportunities for senior American foreign service officers to retire early with enhanced pensions. For one, like myself, who had contemplated a second career sooner or later, the issue was thoroughly complicated because of my family's situation. Early retirement would mean a new residence as well as new work. An analysis of each family member's situation showed that we could, with some justification for each alternative, either continue residing in the United States, or move to Britain. Mary's father, now a lonely widower in England, was overjoyed when he heard that we could, in theory, be returning there. Both Angela and Stuart, on the other hand, were happy in their American universities and made it clear that Mary and I should not be influenced by their situations in making our decision.

For Pipkin it was a different story. As her interest in the classics grew she was determined to get into Oxford. This could best be achieved, however, by completing her secondary education in England. After a frantic exchange of letters with her old school (The Mount), the headmistress said she would welcome Pipkin back to resume her studies.

Most difficult of all was my own position. For many years I had accumulated notebooks, diaries, letters and references on history, topography, biography and numismatics – fields which I thought one day could blossom into books. Mary also had copious notes and diaries and hoped to join me in some of the writing. We considered our first duty was to our children – especially Pipkin, our youngest. For myself, a career of writing ideally would best be achieved either while teaching at a university or living in some quiet rural setting. As it is virtually impossible to teach at university level without a doctor's degree, I had earlier started evening classes at George Washington University. When the chance to retire early arose, however, I was only halfway through my doctoral studies.

As the question of our future abode had to be made quickly, attempting to go straight into higher education with only limited qualifications seemed a non-starter. On the other hand, all the signs indicated that a second career in writing, as well as the family's general welfare, could best be served by moving to England. Thus, the die was cast.

Mary and I were aware that our decision in all probability meant we would spend most of our remaining days in England. It was a great wrench, therefore, to say goodbye to our neighbours and friends in Bethesda, even if we knew we would see them on future visits to Angela and Stuart and to my family in Georgia. Our decision made, however, we turned our minds towards Britain and the opportunities it offered: the chance to monitor closely Pipkin's education, the solace that Mary could give her aging father and, for myself, the prospect of unimpeded research, writing and even publishing if I so wished.

As both Mary and I had been born in rural areas, we keenly looked forward to finding a village in southern England that would be our future home. It had to be in the south if Mary were to visit her father easily and if we were to see Pipkin frequently should she gain admittance to Oxford. But the south extended from Somerset and Gloucester in the west to Kent in the east and that stretch contained hundreds of villages. We asked ourselves as we flew to London, how quickly could we find *the one* that would come closest to our ideal?

PART V

Idylls of the New Forest

1970-1986

90
We buy a cottage in the New Forest

The Britain that existed in 1970 when Mary and I arrived in England was a far cry from that I had known in the Second World War.

Gone was the land of bicycles, for now almost every family boasted a car. Almost gone were the interminable queues for public housing following the ravages of the war and the austere building programme that followed. Virtually every town and village now had its public housing estate. Moreover, many families of modest means now started to acquire homes of their own.

With the launching of many new universities, the number of higher education spaces available to state school finishers had soared. A television set, although at first black and white, was now a "must" in every home. Higher wages and a long list of welfare benefits meant families in lower income brackets now enjoyed expectations undreamed of during the war. On the minus side, prices of houses, goods and services were rising steeply and inflation looked set to run rampant.

It was against this background that Mary and I arrived in the autumn of 1970. After spending a few pleasant days with Mary's father and visiting Pipkin at her school in York, we turned our attention to our most pressing need: finding a home, either temporary or permanent, so that we might resume a normal lifestyle.

Eventually we decided it would be best to rent a small cottage which could serve as a base while we undertook the hunt for our permanent home. Mary suddenly remembered that friends she had known abroad had turned to the pages of the highly regarded magazine, *The Lady*, when they wanted to find short-term accommodation in Britain.

She hurriedly obtained a copy and there found an advertisement for a cottage for rent at Burley in the New Forest. The location was ideal: almost dead centre in southern England and less than an hour's drive from her father's home in Wickham. We hurriedly contacted the owner, learned the cottage had not been taken and agreed to rent it over the coming winter.

"You'll find the key under the front door mat," the owner said. Although I had passed through Burley many times during the war, neither Mary nor I knew much about it. Eventually we found the cottage, situated next door to the house that had once been the manse for the local Congregationalist Church. After brushing away the leaves that covered the front door mat, there was the key just as we had been promised. Indeed, those were the days when burglaries were rare occurrences in villages.

Except for purchases of food, we had little contact then with the village. We used all our free time, Mondays to Fridays, viewing houses for sale across the southern quarter of England. By reading pages of *Country Life* and regional newspapers we learned who the principal estate agents of the area were. Soon dozens of circulars were tumbling through our letter box.

We quickly discovered we could not take at face value the glowing terms in which most properties were described. More than once we drove as far afield as Gloucestershire or Kent to view a house, glamorously described in itself but situated next door to a pig farm, a motorway about to be constructed or some other undesirable feature. No amount of pleading by telephone would make an agent admit to anything objectionable about the house or its location. The only way to learn the truth was to make a trip to the site, a costly and time-consuming exercise. At the end of the winter we still had no prospect of a home and, all the while, the prices of houses were rising sharply.

With the advent of spring we decided to move our base to West Sussex which, together with Hampshire, became our prime area of consideration. We took short-let cottages, first in Henfield and later in West Harting, again with no luck. By this time a new feature had reared its ugly head, the practice known as *gazumping*.

It was the opposite of the tradition that an Englishman's word was his bond. It simply meant the estate agent's word was only as good as the last price increase he was offered and hard luck to all those who had made previous offers. Several times we agreed verbal prices with estate agents but, by the time we could start the financing process, we were told someone else had offered more and the house was no longer on the market.

During our meanderings over southern England we took advantage of our travels to visit stately homes and historic sites adjacent to the areas of our search. We also enjoyed the food of country inns, visited vicarage fêtes as we happened upon them and attended local auctions.

Once in Wiltshire we halted briefly in a village where there was a viewing of household items that once belonged to "a gentleman". We soon found the gentleman's "home", the upstairs apartment of a converted barn. When we reached the apartment we were greeted quietly by a local lady, employed by the auctioneer to welcome viewers.

Mary and I were the only viewers at the time and, looking around the small apartment, we could see there was not much to interest anyone wishing to refurbish a home. As books were then, as always, my main interest, I went over and saw a dozen or so volumes, mainly reference works, that evidently had been selected by its owner for providing basic information in literature, history, the arts and music. Among them was a copy of the *Oxford Companion to Music,* a volume I had long wanted but whose new price was too much while we were committed to putting all our savings into a house. Then I noticed there was also a concordance of the Bible.

"Tell me," I asked the lady, "who is the gentleman whose possessions are being sold?"

The lady suppressed a look of what I detected to be grief and replied:

"He was our vicar – an enthusiastic young man just out of theological college. Ours was his first church. He had been here only a few months and had just come to know us all. We loved him and I'm sure he loved us in turn."

The lady paused as if finding it difficult to continue. Noting that she spoke of the vicar in the past tense, I asked:

"What happened? Why did he choose to sell his possessions?"

She pointed to the large open window that once had been the upstairs loading door of the barn.

"One day he was absent-mindedly strolling about this room no doubt deeply engrossed in thoughts about a forthcoming sermon or some parish activity with which he was involved. Without thinking he walked through the open door, no doubt believing he was on the ground level. He died instantly."

Mary and I were deeply touched by this tragedy. I decided against making an offer for the volume that interested me. I knew I could never open its pages without being reminded of the fate that had befallen its owner. We thanked the lady and quietly departed.

In December 1971 Mary and I returned to Totnes in Devonshire where we had honeymooned 25 years earlier. Happily, our honeymoon hotel, The Royal Seven Stars, was still flourishing and we were able to stay there. On the morning after our arrival, the sympathetic manager presented us with a bottle of champagne to mark the anniversary.

We could not bear to tell him, however, how the charm of the old panelled lounge had been destroyed by new fixtures, modern furniture and bright paint. Totnes itself had changed, too. Times were now better. Gone were the austere little shops with meagre war-time supplies; in their place were spacious plate glass windows filled with consumer goods of every description. We spent several happy days revisiting sites in Totnes and the nearby area, among them Dartington Hall, now a prestigious centre for the arts.

One welcome piece of good news during our otherwise frustrating period of house-hunting came one evening when Pipkin telephoned from her school in York. "Well," she said, quite casually, "I've been accepted by St. Anne's (then an Oxford women's college)." Mary and I were overjoyed that our youngest child was about to realise her dream.

We were sobered, however, when she reminded us she had gained admittance on her qualifications in French, while in her heart she was now drawn to the classics. Had she been dishonest, she wondered, and would the university authorities allow her to switch at some later date? We had no ready answers and so advised her to be grateful for being accepted and, once enrolled, to consult her tutors to see if they would grant her wish. (They did.)

Having had no luck at finding a house from our bases in West Sussex, we again rented the cottage in Burley. This time we determined not to rely only on agents' advertising but to attend auctions of desirable houses whenever we heard about them. By the time of this second sojourn in Burley we had come to know a few of its inhabitants and also started attending the local parish church.

One day I discovered in the cottage's book collection one written by a Miss Felicité Hardcastle of Burley. The volume was not just a local history, but also a compilation of notes about virtually every house in the village. I hastily checked the telephone directory, discovered that one "F. Hardcastle" was listed and telephoned her. She seemed a cheerful extrovert and promptly invited Mary and me to tea the very next day.

Over tea we learned that she not only was the village's unofficial historian but also had been its Cub Scout leader and was active in many other village activities. Except for the period embracing the Second World War, she had written a monthly "Nature Notes" column for the village magazine since the 1930s. A clue that she might also be an eccentric was the way she interrogated us, relying on a prepared list of questions on her table. She was eventually to become one of our most cherished friends.

The more we went away from and returned to Burley, the more we became attracted to the village. Could *this* be the village we were seeking? One overriding advantage we had by renting a cottage in the village was that we were likely, by word of mouth, to hear about a house coming on the market before the estate agents could grind out their publicity. That would give us a few days' advance time to assess the value and location of the property and determine the absolute maximum we could afford. We therefore came to a new conclusion: should an acceptable house become available in Burley, we would make a serious offer for it.

We had not long to wait. A small "forest cottage" with the usual two-up, two-down room arrangement, was going to be auctioned shortly as the heirs to the property wanted an immediate settlement and were not interested in stretching out the now all-too-common *gazumping* process. The cottage was really too small for us and was in need of major repairs. Still, we reasoned, if we obtained it for a fair price, we could make improvements gradually, as we could afford them.

With great expectations Mary and I jumped on our rusty second-hand bicycles and pedalled to the sprawling Burley Manor Hotel, whose ballroom had been booked by the auctioneers for the sale. Secretly we hoped the auction would be of little interest, for the fewer bidders – in theory at least – the lower the successful bid might be. As we cycled up to the hotel entrance, our hearts sank as we saw a large number of parked cars, including an elegant Rolls Royce. People were still filing in. We approached one man and asked if he knew who the Rolls belonged to. Yes, he said, everyone knew who that classy car belonged to; the owner was none other than a well-known property developer, reputedly a millionaire, who was frequently in the news.

Our spirits sank even lower. What chance had we against a wealthy man with unlimited capital? Mary and I held a hurried conference. We decided to sit in the back row so we could see all the bidding. That would allow us to observe the pattern of the bidding and, as well, to see if the wealthy developer, pointed out to us in the front row, always came in with a new offer just as the bidding was about to go against him. We also agreed that Mary, not I, would do the bidding, for her father had offered to lend us a small sum should our savings not be sufficient to cover a successful offer by us.

Hugh Pasmore, perhaps the best known person in the New Forest, was the auctioneer. In addition to being a chartered surveyor and auctioneer, he had been a member of the New Forest Verderer's Court for many years. As a commoner and long-standing member of several Forest organisations, he probably knew more about Forest life than any other person. He had even traversed the entire perimeter of the Forest while recharting its official boundary. For years he had written a lively column called "A New Forest Commoner's Notebook" that appeared in several newspapers in the New Forest area.

The ballroom fell silent as Mr. Pasmore read out the standard conditions for conducting the auction. One consoling point was that a deposit of only 10% of the house price need be paid at the end of the auction. I knew, however, that we would be liable for the other 90% in a month's time, so that we still had to take great care not to exceed what Mary and I had agreed beforehand to be our final figure. We instinctively clutched hands as Mr. Pasmore reached for his gavel to start the bidding.

In response to the auctioneer's opening question for a realistic starting bid, the property developer in the front row calmly offered a price that just exceeded the top amount that Mary and I had agreed we could make. Mary and I exchanged looks of consternation as sudden intakes of breath, low whistles and gasps met the absurdly high starting bid. After the initial shock passed, Mr. Pasmore proposed a higher figure. To the surprise of many, a determined lady, obviously with her heart set on acquiring the house, matched the auctioneer's new price. The property developer came back immediately with an offer several hundred pounds higher. The lady, crushed and clearly not wanting to commit herself to a financial obligation well beyond her means, fell silent.

Mary looked at me, horrified. Mr. Pasmore, gavel in hand, resumed his intonation for a higher offer. To my astonishment, Mary shouted out a figure substantially higher than that Mr. Pasmore had suggested! Again the room fell silent. Heads, including that of the wealthy developer, turned to see who had made that amazing, unrealistic bid. I looked at Mary, almost fearful that her bid would be accepted, for I knew the offer was well beyond our resources – even considering what we thought her father might contribute. Even the developer must have thought her bid mad, for he did not instantly react. We waited with baited breath as Mr. Pasmore's commanding voice called, "Going, going, GONE!"

The house was ours. Had Mary done the right thing? I had no chance to ask her, for she turned quietly to me and said: "I'm sure it will be all right; we'll just have to take longer to make the improvements."

After completing the paperwork and handing over our cheque for 10% of the house price, we noticed that the unsuccessful developer was still hovering about at the rear of the room keeping his eyes upon us. We realised we knew relatively few people in Burley and the Forest and that some curiosity about the successful bidder was natural, but why was this wealthy man lingering? Did he propose speaking to us, or did he have something else in mind?

As we shook hands with Mr. Pasmore and started to leave, the millionaire developer left the hotel and stood beside his Rolls Royce. When he made no attempt to speak to us, Mary and I suddenly realised his real interest now must be in seeing what kind of car *we* drove. As we mounted our two old bicycles and slowly cycled away, we glanced quickly towards the Rolls where we saw its owner standing, his mouth open in disbelief!

91
Fun at a country auction

When we told Miss Hardcastle about the cottage she immediately said:

"The first thing you must do is change the house's name."

She went on to say that the existing name, Westbury, had been given the cottage decades earlier, according to her research, by a couple who had spent a happy honeymoon in the Wiltshire town of the same name.

"What you must do," she insisted, "is find a name that relates to the village or the Forest."

When we asked if she had any suggestions, she pondered a moment and replied:

"Well, an old forester named John Piper once owned the land on which your house and the adjacent one rests. Your house, in fact, is in what was his orchard. You could call your house either Piper's or Piper's Orchard with equal justification."

We settled on Piper's. Later we learned that Miss Hardcastle, as the "human depository" of the village's history, frequently advised newcomers about appropriate names for their houses. Similarly, when the opportunity of naming new streets arose, she was quick to supply suggestions from her encyclopaedic store of village information. Would that every village, Mary and I thought, be blessed with someone so devoted to preserving its history and traditions as Miss Hardcastle.

It was almost three years before we could make all the necessary improvements to the cottage. The delay meant we could stretch out the heavy costs of adding a large living room below and more bedroom space above. At the same time we installed central heating. Mary went to great trouble to give the cottage a New Forest flavour by choosing both wallpaper and frosted glass with designs of leaves from trees of the Forest.

Our brick fireplaces were crafted by "Old Ted", a much revered Forest bricklayer from Fordingbridge. The wooden surrounds of the fireplaces were made by a retired Army major who took great pride in simple, classic designs. Over the ensuing years, I marvelled as Mary painstakingly went about choosing the fixtures, curtains and other features of our cottage that most appealed to her.

"You mustn't mind if I seem to be taking a long time," she explained, "but this is the first house in which we have had total freedom to express ourselves."

It was the same in the garden. She gathered plants and shrubs from a variety of nurseries and stately homes and from friends with whom she exchanged cuttings. Being much attracted to the house and garden mix favoured by Gertrude Jekyll and Sir Edward Lutyens, she strove to bring about a similar "flowing" of our garden right up to the cottage.

As the health of Mary's father was clearly in decline when we arrived in England in 1970, we tried to visit him weekly. So much did he look forward to our visits that he placed a chair in the kitchen where he could survey the drive at the back of the house and spot our car the moment it turned in. Just as I had seen how much his visits to elderly friends had meant to them in his younger days, so now I saw that he, in turn, looked forward keenly to our arrival.

Eventually Mary was obliged to employ a housekeeper to look after him. Then, in 1973, when he became terminally ill, Mary spent many weeks looking after him, returning to me in Burley only at weekends. She was with him when he passed away in November at the age of 84.

Many tributes came to Mary and her sisters from friends, as well as complete strangers, who had known Mr. Roberts through his work with Men of the Trees or who had bought A.E. Roberts, Ltd. plants from Woolworth stores all over Britain. At a memorial service during which young trees were planted in his memory around the perimeter of Wickham's sports field, Richard St. Barbe Baker, founder of the Men of Trees said:

"His buoyant personality was an inspiration to all who came his way. Like another Man of the Trees, the late Franklin D. Roosevelt, he will be remembered as a planter of trees, for 'He who plants trees loves others besides himself'."

Once the house extension and improvements were completed, I was able to turn my attention to researching several subjects which I had short-listed as being suitable for my first book. My interest in and knowledge of the New Forest was growing daily, but I realised I was not yet capable of producing a volume on any aspect of it. That "seed" I set aside to grow, adding to an already large file when I came across new information.

Spurred on by the abolition of Britain's centuries-old pounds, shillings and pence and the introduction of decimal coinage, I decided my first book should be about the social history of the shilling – easily the most engaging coin of the old series. After visiting the British Library in London and the Bodleian in Oxford, I was convinced that enough material existed to justify a slim volume. While much information could be gleaned from library references and correspondence with individuals, there remained much research to be undertaken. My format was simple: to present the shilling's story by dynasties, from the Tudors to the Windsors, highlighting the principal events of each reign as well as the customs and traditions associated with the coin.

It was not long before I was travelling again in southern England to seek information associated with the several reigns and their coins. As most of the house improvements were now complete, Mary joined me on many of these travels. While I pored over ancient tomes in provincial museums and libraries, she visited local art galleries and historic sites. Occasionally she spotted items that were useful to my research. As a diversion we visited virtually every stately home in the southern half of England. At some, for example, Petworth in West Sussex, there was common ground: I was delighted to learn about Edward VI's association with Petworth while Mary was thrilled to visit the house and grounds for their particular merit. (Edward VI's shillings were especially attractive.)

As we were still on the lookout for small articles for the house, Mary and I scanned the advertisements for auctions that disposed of contents of houses – especially those in rural areas. If the auctions were held at the actual houses, one could be reasonably sure that most of the items on offer belonged to the house. If the auction took place in a sales room, the odds were that articles from other sources had been added to the list. Thus we were thrilled one day to read in the *Hampshire Chronicle* of a sale in the village of Bishops Sutton of household goods belonging to a prominent citizen, recently deceased. As the house would not accommodate a large crowd, the village hall had been rented by the auctioneers for the occasion.

We previewed the articles the day before the sale and agreed to bid on three items: Mary settled on a small pair of opera glasses, fashioned in mother-of-pearl; we thought Pipkin might like a pewter ink stand with a small porcelain pot in the middle; my intention was to acquire a two-volume set by one John Nailson, printed in London in 1652, covering "Great Affairs of the State from the Beginning of the Scottish Rebellion to the Murder of King Charles". We agreed not to offer more than £18 for the three lots.

Next morning we could hardly find a place to park, so great was the press of intending buyers. When the car at last was safely parked, we just managed to squeeze into the back of the village hall. The selling started at the advertised time with three auctioneers taking it in turn. Well dressed antique dealers from London and elsewhere had positioned themselves near the front and soon were acquiring choice articles at prices which seemed high to most of us present, but which they knew to be bargains.

"Who'll start me? Will you, madam? Good!"

"Twenty – twenty, now thirty – thirty. Come now, who'll give me forty? The more you pay the more you will enjoy it!"

"You weren't bidding, were you sir? You were? Oh, dear, I thought you merely had cramp in your arm."

A beautiful Roman vase in perfect condition went for £15; a pair of Dresden vases, £80; a 19th century mahogany secretaire bookcase,£125; a collection of rat-tailed table silver, £160; and a Dutch marquetry card table, £310. Villagers attending the sale gasped in disbelief at the high prices; the antique dealers who bought them retained their stoic expressions.

There was an outburst of laughter, quickly followed by silence when a beautifully bound collection of Trollope's works went for the astounding sum of £370 and the buyer was asked for his name. With a straight face and no sign of embarrassment, he replied: "Foyles of London".

Mary and I could not believe our luck in acquiring all three items we wanted for just under the amounts we had set as our spending limit. Pipkin was thrilled to have the pewter inkstand for her desk and I was to spend many pleasant hours perusing Nailson's tomes. Mary had a wonderful idea for initiating the opera glasses: we would attend a London performance of "Vivat! Vivat! Regina."

92
Long live village shows!

Gradually both Mary and I were able to immerse ourselves in village activities. Burley was ever a caring village, so there were ample opportunities for Mary to help with Meals-on-Wheels, driving the elderly through scenic areas of the New Forest and, in general, keeping in touch with the infirm and lonely.

In December 1977 came an opportunity to give expression to two of her special interests, the British Royal Family and the Men of the Trees Society. She discovered one reason why the Forestry Commission could not replant more broad leaf trees in the New Forest was the high cost of erecting wooden "surrounds" to protect the seedlings from deer until they had reached sturdy growth. After consulting the Commission about costs, she collected enough money from friends to plant a small grove of trees near the village cricket ground to mark the Silver Jubilee of the Queen's reign.

She keenly wanted a proper tree-planting ceremony modelled on that followed by Men of the Trees, the society founded by her father's friend, Richard St. Barbe Baker. So it was that on a frosty December morning the Vicar, Norman Jones, began by intoning the words familiar to Society members:

"He that planteth a tree is a servant of God. He provideth a kindness for many generations and faces that he hath not seen shall bless him."

In quick succession thereafter, despite the penetrating cold, the trees were planted one by one by the chairman of the parish council, Miss Hardcastle, several elderly inhabitants and a group of Brownies.

When the earth was packed around the trees, the Vicar concluded:

"Lord, prosper thou the work of our planting and establish Thy Kingdom of love and understanding upon the earth."

Thanks to generous contributions by villagers, the tree planting committee had enough money left over to pay for a "super cup" to be awarded annually at the Village Show for the best overall entry. This trophy was duly purchased and named the Jubilee Cup.

As my circle of acquaintances grew I met the secretary of the Village Show, actually a federation of village clubs and societies who together staged annual summer and winter exhibitions of the best flowers, fruit, produce and crafts. The Show's history went back nearly a century, as attested to by the more than 20 cups and trophies donated by keen gardeners and others over the decades. The then secretary, an invalid with progressive disabilities, asked if I would take on his job.

I agreed on the condition that I should not be expected to know anything about flowers. Somehow, I had grown up knowing little about flowers. Once, after Mary had established the garden at Piper's, she asked me to remove all the weeds I could find. Because flowers bloom, I adopted as my weeding guiding principle: "If it's green, cut it down". When I finished my well-intentioned work, I invited Mary to view the huge amount of weeds I had removed. To her horror I had chopped down some choice green lilies planted against the hedge. She never asked me to do the weeding again.

On another occasion, because we both had been engrossed in particularly strenuous work since early morning, we sat down with keen appetites to partake of a hearty lunch Mary had prepared. After our usual grace, "For what we are about to receive may the Lord make us truly grateful", Mary asked me to look round the dining room to see if there was anything different before beginning our meal.

I checked the four walls to see if new pictures had been installed; I could see nothing. I looked on the sideboard; it seemed just the same. I even glanced at the carpet to see if there was anything unusual there, but there wasn't. I gave up.

Then she pointed to the centre of the dining table. There I saw, for the first time, a beautiful arrangement of flowers – all from our own garden. I could not explain my failure to notice them. Was it because she always had flowers in receptacles around the house and I took them for granted? Or was it because I had always regarded flowers as objects best grown and appreciated by women?

The Village Show committee took the gamble and agreed I need know nothing about flowers. What was really needed, the chairman said, was someone to organise the two big events of the year. I took the job and soon learned that the secretary's responsibilities were many: booking the village school or the Women's Institute hall for the two events, finding judges for the various classes; printing the annual schedules, entry cards and publicity posters; organising teams of workers to set up the exhibit tables and stalls; gathering in the cups and trophies from those who had won them the previous year (there was always one that turned up at the last minute); finding someone to make the presentations, give a talk and so on. When the show chairman told me, "I am only a figurehead", I realised how right he was.

Being secretary, however, had a few advantages. As I was anxious to meet villagers and learn where they lived, I jumped on my bicycle and delivered the entry cards daily in the run-up to the show days. In this way I met many people for the first time and, in the years that were to come, our friendships blossomed. It was a thrill to see so many village organisations involved in the show and that, for some people, the event was the highlight of their year.

Frankie Tanner, who lived alone in his cottage, had won the prize for best lettuce for years. What his secret was he never told me, but he could be relied upon to bring a magnificent head – dripping with water to keep it fresh – to the vegetable section at precisely one minute before the closing time for entries. We always had to mop up after him.

The ladies of Burley were renowned for creating ingenious exhibits of flowers, arranged by themes listed months in advance on the show schedule. Each exhibitor had to comply with high standards set forth in a handbook stipulating permitted accessories, space limitations and the like. These tableaux of floral art gained the praise both of the judges and visiting journalists.

Miss Hardcastle, ever the rebel, thought there should be a chance for the free-spirited lover of flowers, uninhibited by handbook constraints, to display an arrangement. So she established a cup for a winner who would not be determined by a judge, but by public vote. This proved immensely popular and, later, the village art club also adopted this voting technique for honouring the artist whose work was most liked by the public.

The only confrontation I encountered during my six years as show secretary came one year when the standard of home-produced wine was unusually high. As the show was nearing its end and exhibitors were removing their entries, a well dressed man – a newcomer to the village – stormed into the show office bearing his bottle of wine in one hand and waving his entry card with the other. He let me know that he had entered wine for many years in shows much larger and more prestigious than Burley's and had consistently come away with first prizes. How was it possible, he demanded, pointing to his third place label, for his wine to get 99 marks out of 100 and still be only third?

"Well," I replied, looking serious and making up my defence as I went along, "our villagers have long prided themselves on making wine of superb quality. Secret formulas passed along from one generation to another and that sort of thing. I feel sure, with your vast knowledge of wine, that you would have awarded the first two prizes to other entrants had you been the judge."

The man spluttered, tried to speak but couldn't and stomped out. Sadly he did not enter the wine class the following year. I later learned he had moved away but I trust his disappointment over his third-placed wine was not a factor.

93
The remarkable Constance Applebee

Although our village historian, Miss Hardcastle, had taken us to meet one of Burley's most prominent residents, Constance Applebee (introducer of women's hockey to the United States), we saw little of her because we were preoccupied with house-hunting and, afterwards, enlarging and improving our cottage. As the years went by, however, Mary and I got to know her better and quickly came to appreciate her remarkable qualities. She and Mary shared two things in common: both were English-born and had become American citizens and both retained an almost equal love for America and Britain.

"Apple", as her friends called her, was born in Essex in 1873. She decided on a career in physical education and soon obtained a diploma from the British College of Physical Education. While visiting an educational exhibition in Kensington, she came across material written by Dr. D.A. Sargent of Harvard University, a renowned authority on physical education. Dr. Sargent conducted an annual summer school at Harvard attended by physical education leaders from America and elsewhere. After an exchange of letters, he invited her to attend his 1901 school.

She proved a star pupil, both in class and on the sports field where she won two events in athletics. The latter feat caused Boston newspapers to hail her as "this amazing English girl". She was not interested in athletics, however, and instead was determined to meet Helen Ballintine, the highly regarded director of physical education at Vassar College. Her chance came one day when she and Miss Ballintine happened to be selected to play a game of musical chairs. Seeing Miss Ballintine eliminated early, Miss Applebee managed to dawdle and get herself eliminated in the next round.

She quickly engaged the Vassar director in general conversation in which the game of women's hockey soon arose. Did Miss Applebee know anything about this new British game, Helen Ballintine asked and, if so, could she arrange a demonstration for Dr. Sargent's school and, later, at Vassar College? Although her knowledge of hockey was scanty, Miss Applebee hastily organised a demonstration game. Delegates from the leading American women's colleges were much impressed and asked Miss Applebee to visit their campuses after fulfilling her initial obligation at Vassar.

That summer school experience sealed Miss Applebee's career. She returned to Britain, quickly acquired all available information on hockey from publications and physical education instructors and sailed back to the United States. American women's colleges and universities instantly took to the game. In 1904, at the age of 31 and largely based on her hockey coaching, Miss Applebee was chosen to direct the physical education programme at Bryn Mawr College near Philadelphia.

She once told Mary a humorous incident from her early days at Bryn Mawr. The college stood to earn a handsome commission if all its faculty members subscribed to a group annuity plan. Young and not altogether sympathetic to the scheme, she at first refused. When told her refusal would prevent Bryn Mawr from achieving 100% participation in the scheme, she relented.

"I feel so guilty," she remarked to Mary, "because I didn't want that annuity in the first place. You see, I've been drawing a pension from it for over 40 years!"

On another occasion, the Queen of Belgium visited the college. After an afternoon of touring the principal campus attractions, she was scheduled to see a demonstration of women's hockey. By the time she arrived at the sports field dusk had fallen and the players had great difficulty in seeing the ball. Not to be outdone by the approach of evening, Miss Applebee rushed onto the field and said:

"You silly asses! Lift your great feet and play! Act as if you had the ball!"

While at Bryn Mawr Miss Applebee established a hockey training camp, "Tegawitha", in Pennsylvania's beautiful Pocono Mountains. She also founded a magazine, *The Sportswoman,* which she edited for many years. On retirement in 1928, she gave more time to the summer camp and to coaching hockey at other women's colleges, notably William and Mary in Virginia. Her American friends claimed she could outrun many players at the age of 92. She remained a coach until her 97th year.

Constance Applebee firmly believed in the thesis that an athlete improves only if pushed to the limit by a competitor of superior ability. To that end, she imported for many years the best British players, as well as some coaches. In a remarkably short period, the standard of America's women hockey play improved so much that the national team could hold its own with the world's best.

Although she urged her best players to excel, Miss Applebee was convinced that hockey was good for all girls, whatever their physical or mental limitations. Thus she organised 54 teams at Bryn Mawr with 54 captains, affording virtually every able-bodied student a chance to participate. She evolved the motto of the "3 F's": "Fun, Fitness and Friendship", which she considered as worthy dividends resulting from hockey play.

Impatient with *prima donnas* on the sports field, Miss Applebee came up with "put-downs" to meet every occasion. When an egotistical athlete thought she could move downfield by herself and ignore fellow players, Miss Applebee halted play and reprimanded the surprised athlete:

"You like playing with the ball, lovey? Well, you just take another ball, go off the field and play to your heart's content."

She never took to the American custom of gum-chewing and would not allow it during sports. Once, when she caught a girl chewing in a game, she blew her whistle, called the girl to her and said:

"If you love your gum so much you have to chew it during play, just take it out of your mouth and put it on your hockey stick where you can admire it all the time."

Miss Applebee's work at Bryn Mawr was by no means limited to women's hockey. Fond of English country dancing, she instituted an annual maypole dance which became a cherished college institution. She followed keenly Cecil Sharp's search for old English folksongs in the Southern Appalachians where they had been kept alive long after having been forgotten in their country of origin. When Sharp died, Miss Applebee helped to raise funds in America for the permanent headquarters of the English Folk Dance Society, eventually named Cecil Sharp House in London.

During her long association with Bryn Mawr and her premier position in women's field hockey, Miss Applebee came to meet many of the great and near-great of the United States, including several presidents. The first was William Howard Taft, whose daughter was a Bryn Mawr student: the last was Richard Nixon.

After retiring from Bryn Mawr, Miss Applebee came to England with Mary Warren Taylor, her companion of many years, to seek a summer home to avoid the intense heat of the United States. They settled on the New Forest as both a pleasant area and one convenient to Southampton from which the great liners regularly plied the Atlantic to American ports. When passing by the post office in the village of Burley, they saw a photograph of a house that instantly appealed to them. After hastily viewing the house from a distance, they decided to buy it. Entering the post office, Miss Applebee said:

"I want to buy that house, The Withies, advertised outside. I've got the money here."

The sub-postmaster gasped. It took days, sometimes weeks, to complete the sale of a house, he explained. He added that both the estate agent and the solicitor lived in Ringwood and appointments had to be made with both before a sale could be contemplated.

"Appointments!" raged Miss Applebee, "I'm not interested in appointments. You have a house for sale and I have the money." With that she pulled out several hundred pounds in notes. "Do you want to sell that house or not?" she demanded.

The sub-postmaster gave up, telephoned the two principals in Ringwood and the sale was completed within the hour.

When Miss Applebee's American companion died, Emily Carpenter took her place. Emily had long helped with the household chores at The Withies; now she also became companion and adviser. Fastidious in her dress and person until the end of her life, Emily probably was the only person who could weather Miss Applebee's fiercely held views. Her technique was simple: hear out her mistress, then calmly tell her she was mistaken and that there could be merit in another viewpoint. Amazingly, Miss Applebee respected Emily's judgement, frequently reversed her decisions and ended by thanking Emily for helping her to "see the light".

The two were involved in many antics, as Emily later recalled:

"Once, on a cold March day, Miss Applebee got up the apple tree and couldn't get down. I was inside the house and I suddenly heard her calling, 'Help! Help!' Only then did I think of looking up and there she was at the top of the apple tree. I said, 'What are you doing up there? Why you look like an overgrown blackbird!'

"Miss Applebee did not think this funny and said she couldn't get down. I got the ladder, climbed it and twisted her feet until she could get a hold. Eventually she got down and I got her a little drop from the cupboard and she was all right. Why had she climbed the tree? Well, the gardener couldn't reach five juicy apples at the top of the tree and Miss Applebee was simply determined they should not go to waste.

"Another time – it was ever such a cold morning – she dressed me up in her old coat which came right down to my feet. She put on a little blue hat she liked to wear when gardening and her dirty old gardening coat. We worked in the garden for about half an hour when she said it was too cold to do any more. We started back towards the house, Miss Applebee carrying her broom and the two of us looking very much like witches. Just at that moment a pedlar came to the gate carrying brooms, polishes and all that sort of thing. He never spoke, but took one look at us, took fright and fled."

During the Second World War when Miss Applebee was temporarily stranded in Burley, she did not let Americans forget Britain. She helped to place evacuated British children with American families, backed the American food parcel scheme and encouraged American hockey players to provide three ambulances for Britain's beleaguered cities.

In 1946 she formed a club for the elderly in the village and, a few years later, one for young girls called the "Campden Community Club". A genius at organisation, she divided the youngsters into three groups: the "Lits" (5-7 years), "Robins" (7-10) and "Nightingales" (10-14). They engaged in a variety of social, religious and educational activities.

She erected at her own expense a clubhouse which also served as the first and only village library. Apart from books collected locally, she persuaded American friends to send additional volumes. Her club flourished for a decade and half, its impact being felt as far away as London's East Ham area whose St. Paul's church was "adopted" by club members. Apart from exchange visits, the Burley club regularly sent Forest evergreens to the East Ham church at Christmas and garden flowers at Easter.

Following a severe ulcer attack in 1969, Miss Applebee's doctor advised against further transatlantic travel. Her confinement to Burley in no way restricted her interest in hockey. By this time the American Field Hockey Association, which she helped to found, had become a national organisation and each summer dozens of its members – high school and university players, as well as older "girls", flew to England to visit "the Apple".

One day the president of Bryn Mawr, Harris Wofford, came to interview her for the college's alumnae journal. She spent several hours recalling the period when she reigned supreme as the college's physical education director.

During her final years in Burley, despite becoming blind and enfeebled, she never lost interest in the sport she had introduced to America and which now was played by tens of thousands from coast to coast. She went on to receive many sporting honours *in absentia*, one of the most prized being her election to William and Mary College's Hall of Fame.

A cherished memento for a Brit who reaches the age of 100 is a message from the Queen. Formerly it was a telegram - nowadays it is a personalised card.

For her 100th, Apple, British born but still an American citizen, received not only the Queen's blessings but hundreds more from admirers in the United States and the rest of the hockey world. She felt duty bound to reply to each one, but Mary and I pointed out it would be physically impossible. Instead, I asked her, why not send a photocopied letter of thanks to everyone? I added that we could include a picture of all the cards and another of herself reading one. She was thrilled to have her dilemma solved and so dictated to me what she wanted to say:

The Withies, Burley, Ringwood, Hants. October 1973

Dear Kind People,

How can I ever thank all of you for the wonderful birthday greetings received this summer and, above all, for the joy of all the happy memories they brought. Your greetings arrived in the hundreds and continued to trickle in long after my birthday. Although I am unable to see well, every one of them was opened and read to me.

You may be interested in some of the greetings which, although addressed to me, really belong to you. First, from the International Federation of Women's Hockey, representing 35 countries; the I.F.W.H. has spread the love of hockey right round the globe and I would like to share with you these words from their greeting: "Both young and old, the vision hold." In another greeting, President Nixon spoke of "the outstanding work of promoting field hockey", which again, is an achievement which has been shared by all hockey lovers. There was also a letter and plaque from the American Association for Health, Physical Education and Recreation which praised the work of hockey people in schools and colleges. Finally, there was a telegram from the Queen sent in recognition of the friendship which hockey has developed between English and American players. I was also touched by the greetings from many young players in high school and college. It was heartening that so many players spoke of the joy which hockey had brought them: "Happiness is hockey", as some young players described it.

If, in January of 1968, when I was sailing out of New York harbour and watching the Statue of Liberty pass – if I had known that I wouldn't be using my return ticket to the United States, I think I would have gone below and demanded that the pilot let me return with him. I almost returned this past spring when President Wofford of Bryn Mawr invited me over for the annual class reunion week in May. I was all for it, but the doctor took a dim view of the idea.

In the meantime I am living alone and attending to the usual housekeeping chores with a little outside help. I am also blessed with good neighbours. Thus, in spite of the infirmities and restrictions, I am finding old age to be a tranquil and joyful era. It is like a California poet once said: "You go slow, but you see more on the way." I was wondering how to thank you all for your greetings when along came an American family, the Mays from Washington, to live here in Burley while their daughter attends Oxford. They have very kindly suggested this letter, made the photographs and arranged for the printing. I'm darn lucky.

(Then, in her handwriting:)

With all my love, Apple

In her 104th year Miss Applebee was visited by the noted American portrait photographer, Bern Swartz. He had come to Britain to photograph prominent leaders and figures in the arts for a book to be published by Collins. Bern's wife, Ronny, had been a student at Bryn Mawr and there was no doubt in her mind that "Apple" belonged in this elite group. Working for most of an entire day, Swartz had Miss Applebee pose for over 50 sittings before he was satisfied.

When the book was launched in 1978 the portraits were exhibited at London's Colnaghi Gallery. Unable to travel to London, Miss Applebee asked Mary and me to attend the preview as her representatives. This we happily did. Although her eyesight was now greatly diminished, Miss Applebee could recognise some of the notables featured in the volume and gleefully asked why people like Lord Mountbatten, John Gielgud, Harold Wilson, Edward Heath, Archbishop Coggan, Prince Charles, Henry Moore and Rudolph Nureyev had come to be included in "my book".

Because of her semi-invalid state, Miss Applebee had been unable to go to London to renew her American passport. Although she held no hope of visiting her adopted land again, she considered it essential to maintain a valid passport, in her own mind equating the passport with her cherished American citizenship. I knew when applicants were unable to travel, their passports could be renewed by post. Accordingly I took her to Ringwood for a photograph, sent off the application form with the old passport to the London embassy and within the week her pristine new passport arrived. She was overjoyed.

As Apple's health further declined, Mary spent more and more time with her. Soon we both were visiting her daily, taking along a jar of freshly made "beef tea", her favourite nourishment. With no living relatives and now totally blind, she asked us if we would take control of her life and affairs. I was reluctant for Mary to become so intensely involved in another person's life, for I felt she had not emotionally recovered from her father's illness and subsequent death. She pointed out that Miss Applebee had no one else to turn to, adding: "Perhaps this (looking after the infirm) is my mission in life."

I went along with Mary's wishes. Soon we found ourselves organising three shifts of nurses daily, with all the attendant problems of directing them to Miss Applebee's somewhat remote house. More than once a first-time nurse, arriving in the evening, plunged her car into the deep ditch outside the house and had to be rescued. In theory the same nurses should have stuck continuously to their jobs; in fact every week we had to brief new ones who turned up without notice. I was obliged to assume power of attorney to pay their wages, as well as utility bills, rates, repairs and other expenses.

During her decline Miss Applebee received visits from old and new hockey friends from all over the United States. One former teaching colleague from Bryn Mawr brought her an American flag, a gesture which left her in tears. Those who could not make the trip to England flooded her post with cassettes bearing cheery messages and lively hockey songs. These helped to fill her lengthening days of disability.

Mary and I were concerned that Apple might not be up to celebrating her 107th birthday on 5 June 1980 for her sight was now totally gone, her energy flagging and memory sometimes faulty. We need not have worried, for she miraculously recovered most of her faculties in the nick of time, as Mary recorded in a letter to an old friend who had been unable to attend:

Thursday June 5th, 1980
Dear Miss C,

Do allow me to share with you Miss Applebee's birthday, Wednesday June 4th for it was such a happy occasion.

Two days before, the Apple had looked so ghastly and spoken hardly a word that truly we felt there was a good chance that she just wouldn't be with us for June 4th. Yet the day before, she suddenly caught the excitement of the occasion – the cake arrived – each year 'tis a masterpiece made by Miss Douglas (a Quaker friend who used to live next to The Withies but now is at Pennington, some eight miles away). This year, the wording was simple and to the point – THE GREATEST – 1873 – 1980, and in the centre, four hockey players poised with sticks and a ball. From that time on Miss Applebee has been in great form.

Yesterday was such a lovely day. We are having a heat-wave and the Apple was downstairs by 11 o'clock. The windows were flung open, azaleas, rhododendron and white lilac all in flower in the garden – the dining and sitting rooms all full of flowers and cards and an air of great happiness and contentment. The Apple sat in state whilst her old friends followed one after another to call upon her. Interrupted by telephone calls from great friends in America, she saw off the last visitor at 12.45 and then she paused for lunch. Then a nap, but it was interrupted by dear Dr. Wood who came, he said, to congratulate her, for she was his oldest patient - 107 years old. With that she rose up and said "Really – what a silly old fool!" She was so very gracious to him and thanked him many times for coming and bringing lily-of-the-valley from his garden which smelt so heavenly. She asked for news of his wife and her many horses and he gave her a full report. I mention all of this to show you how very well she is.

During the afternoon, Mrs. Witt came bearing one of her home-made cakes (I am sure you know her for she worked for years for Apple, sewing for her, writing letters etc.). Alas she can no longer work, but they had such fun talking of old times. After tea Ambassador Kingman Brewster's letter was read, as were a number of others, thanking her for the fun and happiness she had given them through hockey and reminding her of hockey adventures they had shared together – and their future plans as well. This gave her tremendous pleasure.

Then came Mr. and Mrs. Carpenter, now retired, Mrs. Carpenter having worked for Miss Applebee for 43 years. Mr. Carpenter also has a birthday on June 4th so it is a tradition that they both celebrate the occasion. Out came the precious Jefferson cups and first Miss Applebee's health was proposed followed by that of Mr. Carpenter. Gifts were exchanged, Mr. Carpenter being given a bottle of sherry and Miss Applebee a box of soft jelly candies. (This we have witnessed with delight for the past eight years.) Mrs. Carpenter told Miss Applebee the exciting news that their mutual friend, Mrs. Roberts, had regained her speech and hearing *the day before*, after over fifty years of silence. Mr. Roberts was Miss Applebee's gardener for many years and alas died last November. We so well *remember* each June 4th evening when Mr. and Mrs. Roberts would call on Miss Applebee bearing a pot plant, and the largest birthday card ever seen with the years of Miss Applebee's age stuck on in gold lettering. He was always so tender with his wife telling her in sign language what Miss Applebee was saying and how much the Apple adored their visits. She was utterly thrilled about this and remarked if only Mr. Roberts were alive to see this miracle.

The nurses who have served Miss Applebee then called to see her. She has difficulty telling one from another as she cannot see them, so she calls them all Mary and is utterly charming to them; they adore her. I tucked her into bed at 10.15 p.m., read her favourite Chapter, 1 Corinthians: 13, and bade her sleep well.

I really think it couldn't have been a happier day. And for all of us here – we shall certainly never forget this 107th birthday of a very great lady.

Yours sincerely,
Mary Mays

Miss Applebee died in January, 1981 and was buried in the Burley churchyard and, as she had requested, in the same plot as her companion of many years, Miss Taylor.
Without doubt, Mary's care had extended her life, but in the process how much had she put her own health at risk? I would never know the answer to this question and, indeed, it was academic, for concern and care – whether for her father, myself, Miss Applebee or someone else – was always at the heart of Mary's generous nature.

Apple's funeral was a simple affair, but some of her devotees in the United States, drawn from the more than 200,000 hockey players she had inspired, immediately started planning a memorial event.

It was to be no ordinary service, for they commissioned a stained glass window whose cost would be borne by high school girls, university players and her hockey 'old girls'. Some of the younger ones contributed only a few pennies, all they could afford; others gave in keeping with their means. Eventually enough was collected to enable the window to be commissioned by one of Britain's foremost stained glass makers. The result was a magnificent juxtaposition of many symbols associated with Miss Applebee's life, not least of which were an apple and a bee. The three true objectives of sport, as advocated by her – "Fun, Fitness and Friendship" – were also prominently displayed.

94
"How nice to do business with Hatchards!"

During Pipkin's undergraduate days at Oxford, Mary and I made numerous trips to the city, often sharing a meal with her at a roadside public house near Woodstock renowned for its good food. When time permitted, we continued our exploration of Oxford's colleges and churches and also saw some of the stately homes in Oxfordshire and the surrounding area.

One visit Mary particularly enjoyed was to the village of Elsfield, a few miles outside Oxford, where her favourite author, John Buchan, had spent some of the happiest years of his life. When we returned to the New Forest, Mary promptly sat down and wrote to Pipkin about that adventure:

"Daddy took me to see the manor house in which John Buchan once lived. It is in Elsfield, the dearest village with only a few houses, a church and a vicarage. J.B. said the modern world had passed over the village. It still has. We met the wife of the present owner and she very kindly showed us over the premises. The outlook over the fields at the rear was utterly pastoral. At the cemetery we saw the round stone under which Buchan's ashes were placed. Surrounding it are four yew trees which have now grown to a good size. Even though it was a bleak day, we so enjoyed this excursion."

After being admitted to Oxford for her French language studies qualifications, Pipkin was allowed to transfer to the classics, for her enthusiasm for Greek and Roman history, archaeology and numismatics, now knew no bounds. The switch, however, meant she would not get her B.A. degree until 1976. When the great day neared, I think Mary was as much excited as Pipkin, for of all things British, she most loved ceremonial occasions.

We knew the degree ceremony would take place in the Sheldonian Theatre which up to 1713 had housed part of the Oxford University Press. Circular at one end and rectangular at the other, the building seats 1,500 people and is ideally suited for university functions.

We were not overly surprised to learn that the degree ceremony would be conducted entirely in Latin.

Some of the degree candidates came forward in ranks of four, partly to speed up the proceedings and partly to allow the accompanying Latin commentary to be broken down into four equal segments. As the presiding officer moved from one candidate to another, he uttered a part of the commentary, bringing it to an end with the fourth.

When we saw this process in operation, Mary and I suddenly remembered an Oxford graduate from Burley who had been subjected to a surprising and amusing variation of the procedure. Somehow she found herself being the fifth person, instead of one of the customary four, when she advanced to the front. She was momentarily horrified as she wondered what the academic would do when he encountered her after having used up all the Latin commentary on the other four candidates. She need not have worried. When he spotted her, he hesitated only a moment and then said, in English, "In the name of the Father, the Son and the Holy Ghost."

There was no such hiccough in Pipkin's case. The candidates were marshalled in and out of the theatre in rapid succession, grouped according to the type of degree they were receiving. Pipkin had earlier given us a booklet about Oxford academic gowns, so that we could spot the many variations in dress. The tradition of academic robes, instituted by Archbishop Laud in 1636, has since spread to all corners of the globe. In the United States high schools follow the custom with as much decorum as institutions of higher learning.

Neither Mary nor I had seen Harold Macmillan during his political career. Now, as Oxford's Chancellor, he was nearing the end of his public life and presided over the degree ceremony with obvious pleasure. When the last of the degrees was awarded, the graduates joined relatives and friends outside the Sheldonian for congratulations and photographs. For Mary and me it was a special moment. Not only had our youngest obtained her degree, but she had done so in her chosen field, the classics, and at Oxford, twin goals she had set for herself while still in high school.

In 1978 there came an end to my military "career", a period stretching back to the Second World War and continuing into our stay in the New Forest. In total I had accumulated 36 years of combined active and reserve service. Like many another young man who suddenly found himself in uniform during the war, I – at one time or another – was bewildered, frightened, elated or saddened. Without a doubt these decades of military service enriched my life enormously, first, indirectly leading me to Mary's door and, second, opening my eyes to the wider world beyond the shores of the United States.

A particularly happy event for Mary occurred in 1981 when she organised a village fete for children of Burley to commemorate the wedding of Prince Charles and Lady Diana Spencer. The highlight of the day's festivities was the presentation by Miss Hardcastle of a limited edition Charles-and-Diana mug to each young person. These happened to be the first major productions of the newly opened Burley Pottery.

With Miss Applebee's passing there was time for me to pick up the threads of my first literary "brain-child". This was to be a social history of the shilling coin. My major concerns were spicing up the text with suitable illustrations, choosing a good title and overcoming numerous technical problems in printing.

It was no good looking to private collectors for photographs of the rarest shillings, for no one was likely to have a complete set from Henry VII to the present time. A quicker and less expensive solution was to approach the British and the Ashmolean museums and the Royal Mint. In all three instances, the keepers went to great pains to meet my needs. For likenesses of the relevant British monarchs I found that the National Portrait Gallery would supply photographs of all royal portraits.

Documenting the social history of the shilling was to prove far more exciting than I had ever imagined. Before the 20th century the shilling probably was the most useful coin in circulation. For many decades it was a good day's wage for the unskilled worker. It also had considerable purchasing power, even up to the time it was replaced by the decimal 5 pence piece. Thus economic records quickly indicated there was no problem in learning what a shilling could buy during any recent period of British history. In the field of English literature (including Shakespeare's work) I found so many references to the shilling that I could easily have compiled a volume containing these citations.

Joseph Addison, who together with Richard Steele had edited *The Spectator*, wrote an essay entitled "Adventures of a Shilling" for *The Tatler* in November, 1710. In it he doubted any human could experience the adventures a shilling coin had been engaged in. His lively account, which was reproduced in the Appendix to *The Splendid Shilling*, relates the many fortunes – some good, some bad – that befell the twelve-penny piece.

Nathanial Hawthorne's *The Pine Tree Shilling* reminded me that Colonial America had shillings in Massachusetts (and New England) and in Maryland. Hawthorne's story relates how Captain John Hull extracted from the authorities a payment of one shilling out of every 20 he minted – a commission which made him a wealthy man. Hawthorne invents an incident at the end of his tale when the mint master's plump daughter is married off to a fine young man who receives a dowry of shillings whose weight is equal to that of his daughter's.

Most fascinating of all, however, were the customs that had been associated with the coin. Charming and commendable was the custom of a young man presenting his sweetheart with a love token, often an engraved or a "bent shilling". Less than laudable, however, was the custom of recruiting officers who "enlisted" naïve young men by covertly passing them a shilling in a mug of beer, or those of tyrannical fathers who cut off their heirs with only a shilling.

In more recent times the Scout movement employed the shilling for its well known work project, "Bob-a-job". These customs and others assured the shilling's status as Britain's most engaging, if not most beloved, coin. But could I ever devise a title that would reflect all this?

In the Bodleian Library, pondering over almost endless references to the shilling in English literature, I came across the words "splendid shilling" by John Phillips, a 17th century poet unknown to me. I then obtained a volume of Phillips' works and found the words were taken from a verse reading:

"Happy the man, who void of cares and strife
In silken or leathern purse retains
A splendid shilling."

Mary and I agreed that we could not hope to improve on this reference and so settled on *The Splendid Shilling* as the book's title.

Our one remaining major problem was how to get the book published. I had never envisaged the volume as a best seller; indeed, the question was: was it attractive enough to cause any major publisher to accept it? In my heart of hearts I wanted to produce and publish the book myself, for this freedom offered several outstanding advantages.

Firstly, it would allow me to position the illustrations on the same pages as their relevant texts, whereas publishers often grouped them together to save printing costs. Secondly, I could choose high quality paper, even at some additional cost, to ensure good photographic reproduction. Thirdly, I could use my old "typographic friends", Baskerville type for the text and Bodoni for titles, which I had first come to admire as a university student. Most of all, however, I looked forward to the challenge of learning all aspects of the book publishing trade, starting with the manuscript and ending with promotion and marketing.

Being obliged to learn all about publishing would be time-consuming but at least I would be in total control of my product. I decided, therefore, initially to send an outline and sample chapters to three major publishers. If none of the three was willing to take a risk with the book, I would regard this as the signal to do my own thing. The three publishers replied in similar vein: the book was both timely and interesting, but probably not economically viable.

The message seemed clear: start your own family publishing firm, select the titles you like and produce the volumes according to your own standards of typography. Mary and the children, all of whom had assisted me in one way or another with the research and writing, shared my enthusiasm as we entered into one of the most exciting ventures of our lives.

Before we could officially launch our effort, however, we had to have a "house" name. As we were happily settled in the New Forest and hoped to publish at least one or two works on the Forest, Mary and I came up with the name, "New Forest Leaves". But what if someone had already chosen this?

Hurriedly I wrote to the Department of Trade's Registry of Business Names. They could not, or would not tell me, but pointed out I was legally bound to register our publishing business if it did not carry my name in its title. I filled in the required form and in due course received a certificate certifying "New Forest Leaves" was duly inscribed on the national register.

Not until the text of *The Splendid Shilling* was set up in type did we feel we were getting close to publishing. I was never good at proof-reading but Mary had the uncanny ability instantly to spot a typographical error on a page. Next we had to lay out the pages, taking care to place each illustration precisely where it belonged in the text. When this was done we would know approximately how many pages the book would contain. In addition, we had to allow several pages for the preface, table of contents, acknowledgements and index.

As I worked closely with the printers I was introduced to several new aspects of the trade that had somehow eluded me during my career in journalism. For example, I found that a "signature" was that part of a book printed on a single large sheet (back and front) by the press. If the press could print eight pages on one side of this sheet and another eight on the reverse, that signature contained 16 pages. Thus *The Splendid Shilling* had 192 pages, or 12 signatures of 16 pages each. In the years to come it was always a challenge, when laying out a book, to use up all the pages in a signature. Nothing was so unsightly or wasteful, it seemed to me, as having several blank pages at the end of a book.

Perusing book after book in libraries across southern England, I hoped to find an illustration suitable for the book's jacket. It was always possible to use an enlarged picture of a shilling, but this had little eye-catching appeal. Eventually Mary and I decided to use the inn sign of one of the many pubs called "The Volunteer", provided it was sufficiently attractive. As a minimum it should show a recruiting officer handing over the shilling to a young man who would shortly be in uniform. Although we found many pubs with volunteer signs, none met our need.

Then, one day after visiting the Brighton reference library, we reached a nearby corner of the block and saw a pub called "The Volunteer" with precisely the inn sign we had dreamed of! Enquiries revealed that it was the work of an elderly local artist. I visited him, explained my need and he promptly gave me written permission to use a photograph of the sign on the jacket.

Next came the problem of choosing the shade of red represented by the Army uniform. This proved a difficult task for we learned there are many shades of red. I eventually gave up but Mary persisted and eventually chose the "reddest red" that could be printed – one that not only most corresponded with the Army uniform, but was guaranteed to stand out in a bookshop.

At last, in May 1982, the book arrived from the printers with its bright red jacket showing the shilling being passed to a naïve country lad. It was an exciting moment for Mary and me and as well for the children who had all contributed something towards the final product.

We could not reflect too long on achieving our goal, however, for much remained to be done. Five copies had to be sent to the official distributor for the Copyright Libraries: Oxford and Cambridge universities, the National Library of Scotland, Trinity College in Dublin and the National Library of Wales. The British Library's copy went separately.

Failure to do this promptly might get us in trouble with the Copyright Act of 1911. A compensating fact: knowing the book would forever be available to library readers.

Coincidental with the copyright compliance was the need to get review copies to the media before copies of the book reached the booksellers. I soon learned that a publisher has to take a shotgun approach with review copies of a new book. They have to be sent to virtually all local newspapers, magazines, radio stations and television channels in the full knowledge that some will not bear fruit.

With national newspapers this game is even more of a lottery. A small publisher is lucky to get even one mention by the national press. With a mixture of expectancy and resignation we mailed off copies of *The Splendid Shilling* to media in Britain, the United States and the Commonwealth.

The reception of this, our first effort, brought us great joy. The local papers, as to be expected, made much of the "local author" angle. As the book was not, however, one of local interest (strictly speaking), we knew that sales would depend largely on national and international reviews. When the reviews began to appear, we were not to be disappointed.

London's *Sunday Express* called the shilling "maddening money", and the *Times Educational Supplement* carried an illustration from the book and said the volume "looks at the coin's entire history". Virtually all the major provincial papers carried favourable reviews. This nationwide publicity resulted in a great spate of orders from booksellers and libraries.

Several of the major London booksellers took the book. At this point Mary was asked for a copy by a dear friend. Instead of taking the volume from our general stock, she decided to make a small adventure of the request. On her next trip to London to view an art exhibition she planned also to drop into Hatchards, who had ordered several copies of *The Splendid Shilling*, and get her friend's copy there. She later recounted what happened.

"My good man," she said, straight-faced and dignified as she strode up to Hatchard's clerk, "I *know* you must have that marvellous book about the shilling that I have been reading about in all the papers. I would like to get a copy before they are all gone."

The man smiled automatically but it was clear he had never heard of the book.

"Yes, madam," he said, obviously wondering where to look for the exciting tome.

"Do excuse me, madam," he said eventually, "I'll just ask the manager what section the book is in."

He hurried off, chatted briefly with his lady superior and returned.

"I think it will be over here in British history," he said, leading the way for Mary.

Sure enough, it was. He took it from the shelf and handed it to her. As she glanced at the jacket and then thumbed through a few pages, she became increasingly animated.

"What a magnificent jacket!" she exclaimed. "And what lovely illustrations! I can see why everyone is raving about the book. May I have this copy?"

The clerk beamed in the reflected glory of his employer who had been so astute as to stock the book.

"You may count on Hatchards supplying all your book needs," he said. "Does madam wish to pay by credit card or cheque?"

Mary had anticipated a potential "trap" here, for either a credit card or a cheque would reveal her surname to be the same as that of the author.

"No," she said, "I will pay by cash."

When the transaction was completed, Mary carefully put the book in her bag, gave the clerk a smile and said:

"Thank you for your kind attention. I want you to know how nice it is to do business with Hatchard's."

"Thank *you*, madam," replied the man, "it has been a pleasure serving you."

I was asked to appear on regional radio programmes in London, Oxford and the Southeast. Soon we began receiving individual orders from people who had heard about the book by word of mouth. Perhaps the most moving of these came by telephone one evening from the young wife of a police constable in Wales. Her husband, she explained, had a small collection of shillings and was fascinated by the customs associated with the coin. It seemed, she added, that *The Splendid Shilling* would make the perfect birthday gift for him. The problem was, she went on, his birthday fell in just two days and there would not be enough time for her cheque to arrive and allow the book to be posted to her.

"Never fall for sentimental stories," we had been advised by other small publishers. We decided, nonetheless, to take the gamble and immediately sent the book by first class. The lady's cheque came the next day. A few days later a two-page letter of thanks also arrived: the young wife said her husband was ecstatic over the book. How wonderful it was, she said, that some people in this world still had trusting natures.

The review copies we had sent overseas took some time to arrive at their destinations, but eventually the foreign papers also gave a warm reception to the shilling's story.

The *New York Times* wrote: "a fascinating new book detailing the life and times of this long popular coin." Similar praise came from newspapers in Ireland, South Africa and New Zealand. The *International Herald-Tribune* sent its top feature writer to London to interview me; after her review appeared, orders came in from as far away as Hong Kong.

The ultimate accolade, however, came when the Royal Numismatic Society, based in the British Museum, selected the book for its Lotka Memorial Prize, an award made every two years for an outstanding numismatic work. Several years later, the Royal Mint also cited the book in its annual report.

Just as the excitement over the arrival of the first baby in a family is seldom equalled when subsequent offspring are born, so we found that the publication of our later books did not give us quite the same degree of elation as we had experienced with *The Splendid Shilling*. All, however, were to accord us great pleasure as we continued with our new career, leading me sometimes to wonder if we shouldn't have gone into publishing earlier.

95
Dolly Parton awakens me from a coma

In the summer of 1982 came an opportunity for a double treat for Mary: observing British pomp and ceremony and seeing Mary (now Lady) Donaldson, whose mother, Dorothy Warwick, had run the small "dame school" at Wickham that both Marys had attended as children.

The chance came when a Lyndhurst friend, aware of Mary's interests and also a past master of the ancient livery company, The Curriers, asked her if she would like to attend the Company's annual Livery and Ladies' Dinner. Mary eagerly accepted and the evening was to be one of the happiest of her later life.

Nearly 150 guests assembled in the Saddlers Hall for the dinner where Sir Christopher Leaver, the incumbent Lord Mayor of London, was seated beside The Curriers' Master. Also at the head table was Lady Donaldson, then Alderman and Sheriff, but on track to become Lord Mayor. In the course of the evening Mary savoured the pomp and ceremony of the occasion as well as learning about the educational and charitable activities of the ancient livery companies and those of The Curriers in particular.

At an opportune moment she approached Mary Donaldson and the two immediately launched into animated conversation, touching on their schoolday experiences and Lady Donaldson's present and future roles. Mary quietly rejoiced when she was told that Lady Donaldson's mother, who had died in 1979, had the satisfaction of knowing her daughter almost certainly would become the first woman Lord Mayor of London since the office was created in the 1100s. When Mary asked Lady Donaldson what it was like being Alderman and Sheriff, she replied:

"I always had a vague notion about the good works of the livery companies, but not until becoming Alderman and Sheriff did I realise how deep-rooted and extensive was their support for quality education, crafts training and a host of charitable works."

Then, with a slight shrug of resignation, she added:

"The only drawback is that the Alderman and Sheriff and, to a lesser degree, the Lord Mayor, are expected to attend the annual dinners and other functions of the livery companies. While these are enormously satisfying events for the knowledge one gains about the companies' good works, they also can be very demanding on the human constitution."

"For example," she added, laughingly pointing to the dinner table, "one is expected to partake heartily of the wonderful meals they serve on these occasions and it is impossible to do so all the time!"

Even before the shilling volume was published, I had started research on my second book. It was to be a biography of Nathanial Hawthorne, arguably the first great American novelist. His most popular works, *The Scarlet Letter, The House of the Seven Gables, A Wonder Book* and *Tanglewood Tales,* had won him many admirers both in the United States and Britain. Not until I read one of several biographies did I realise that he had been the American Consul in Liverpool. A little research revealed that no one had ever written in detail about his consulship.

Having spent years in the American foreign service, I was in a good position, it seemed, to assess how well Hawthorne had performed his consular duties. That he was a superb writer was not in doubt. But how well had he stood up to the glare of public attention, the challenges of resolving disputes and representing American interests at a time when some of Britain's political leaders were hostile to the United States?

The research on *The Splendid Shilling* required me to visit many places in Britain; I quickly discovered that the research on Hawthorne's consular career not only would permit me to make many visits to Liverpool and other places in England but to the United States as well. A trip to Washington allowed me to see copies of all the consular reports Hawthorne had filed during his four years in Liverpool. Another to New York's public library, where the original letters of Hawthorne's wife, Sophia, are held, enabled me to see the consul's activities from her point of view. Finally, there was an exciting trip to New England where I visited Hawthorne's grave in Concord, Massachusetts, consulted the archives of the Salem Institute and visited Hawthorne's alma mater, Bowdoin College in Maine. By this time I had virtually become Hawthorne's *alter ego*, so acutely could I identify with his emotions and actions.

Back in England, my research continued. I had known Liverpool briefly from my wartime days in Britain and the period immediately after. It was then a bustling port with consuls from several countries assigned to look after their nations' commercial and passenger interests. Most of the leading British and American shipping lines also had offices there. Nonetheless, the port's activity in no way compared with that which existed in August of 1853 when Hawthorne arrived to begin his duties as United States consul.

Liverpool already had earned an ignominious title as a leading slave port, with Gore Street housing many of the offices that directed the traffic. A large proportion of the immigrants who arrived in the United States in the first half of the 19th century also departed from Liverpool. It was, however, the port's cargo traffic that most interested Hawthorne, for he would receive a fee for every document he signed and there would be thousands.

A poor man despite the popularity of his books, Hawthorne had eagerly opted for Liverpool when his old Bowdoin friend (now President

Franklin Pierce) gave him his choice of consulships around the world. Hawthorne picked Liverpool for two reasons: the lucrative income it would provide and the opportunity to visit places associated with British writers, whom he greatly respected.

My research revealed Hawthorne to be a strong family man who always found time to play with his children. It also showed how he overcame his natural shyness to become an effective speaker on a number of occasions in Liverpool and London. Despite the sombre mood of his novels, he had a wry sense of humour. In short, I became so enthusiastic over each newly discovered morsel of information that Mary often found I was living in "Hawthorne's world" and took little notice of anything else.

When *Mr Hawthorne goes to England* appeared in 1983 it received warm praise on both sides of the Atlantic. Oxford University's *Notes and Queries* said the book "demonstrates Hawthorne's competence, intelligence and integrity." It also cited the illustrations, in particular one wonderful menu for a Lord Mayor's banquet at London's Guildhall.

Country Life pleased Mary when it wrote: "Mays has a happily rare way with the tongue." But how, I wondered, would the book be received in Liverpool itself? I need not have been concerned, for the city's *Echo* said the volume "paints a colourful picture of Victorian England and provides what must be one of the most informative records of … life on Merseyside in the middle of the last century."

America's *New England Quarterly,* one of the country's highly regarded literary journals, called the book a "lively and competent account of Hawthorne's four years of service in Liverpool," while the *Los Angeles Times Book Review* said: "(the author) invests the book with his considerable enthusiasm." Of the other American comments the *Foreign Service Journal* came close to echoing my own feeling for the work: "A well-written and beautifully illustrated volume which clearly is a labour of love."

Alas, that "labour of love" almost took me away. Any euphoria over the success of the Hawthorne book was suddenly tempered by an onset of tachycardia, a fierce and erratic pounding of the heart which can cause instant blackout. Mary rushed me to Southampton Western Hospital where the ailment was tentatively diagnosed. Because the precise nature of the attacks needed confirmation, it was necessary to see if they occurred during my sleep. If this were to be so, my life would be at risk becasue the wild swings of the heartbeat, if left uncontrolled, could cause instant death. For the next three days I had to wear a small tape recorder which would show if palpitations occurred while sleeping and if the extremes of heartbeats were life-threatening. Mary drove me to the hospital to return the tape and almost as soon as we returned home, the heart consultant telephoned to say I should return as quickly as I could.

I did not feel ill and nonchalantly strode down the hospital corridor. Spotting me a few yards away, the consultant rushed up and said I should not be walking so quickly. He then led me to the intensive care ward where I was at once put on a drip to regulate my heartbeat. I was then hooked up to a monitor. With the devices bleeping and the monitor flashing I must have presented a ghastly sight for I could read the expressions of horror on the faces of Mary and Angela (home for a brief visit) when they first visited me. After a few days my condition deteriorated and I fell into a deep coma.

When I regained consciousness I thought I must be in Heaven for I could hear the unmistakable sound of my favourite hymn, "Amazing Grace", being sung by an angel. As I focused my eyes, I saw that I was in the same hospital ward. Still that "angel" was belting out "Amazing Grace". Gradually I realised the sound was coming from the day-room behind my bed. A fellow patient in the next bed smiled and said it was the buxom country and western singer, Dolly Parton, singing on the TV set that had just been presented to the hospital by a wealthy American oil-worker from the Middle East after a successful heart by-pass operation.

Thereafter my recovery continued rapidly. I had no more serious palpitations, but was placed on a heart-regulatory drug for 18 months during which I was not allowed to drive. Mary dutifully drove me about as I slowly regained strength and pondered our next publishing move.

Having demonstrated that we could produce books that could attract acclaim both in Britain and abroad, we decided to undertake publishing works of other people. In this new outlook we adopted the original philosophy of the university presses, that is, many works deserve to be published as records of human achievement and experience, irrespective of their commercial viability. It is for this reason that some university presses receive grants to enable them to publish books in runs of only a few thousand copies. Thus it was that Mary and I agreed, should the opportunity present itself, to publish a book purely for its merit, even when there was only a prospect of minimal profit.

It was not long before such an opportunity arose. Grace Howard, the wife of our Burley general practitioner, showed us letters her parents had written during their stay in Peru as medical missionaries. Mary read the letters at one sitting, unable to tear herself away for meals or sleep.

She was in tears at the end, for this true story was more moving than many works of fiction. After I read the letters and saw some of the photographs made at the time, I agreed we had the makings of a little volume that could prove inspiring to both young and old. When Grace died suddenly after a tragic walking accident with her dog, her daughter Jenny devoted herself to the project and we were able eventually to publish the letters under the title, *Jessie's Journey*, with the sub-title, "Triumph and Tragedy in the Andes".

While the book was in its proof stage Mary's usual vivacity began to evaporate and at times she appeared listless and unable to concentrate for more than a few moments. She nonetheless eagerly awaited publication of *Jessie's Journey* and enjoyed reading with me the excellent reviews printed in provincial newspapers and religious journals, whose readers had been our primary targets. She and I were especially pleased when *The Times* listed it as one of the ten most interesting books received in the week the title was published.

By this time we had been living in the New Forest for almost 15 years and I had accumulated many notes and books about the Forest. I had in mind compiling an anthology, *The New Forest Book*, of the "most readable" extracts from the 600-odd books that had appeared on the New Forest. Although literary purists sometimes frown on an illustrated anthology, I felt I could be excused for breaking the rule because, above all, the Forest is a visual entity. The first step was to consult all the bibliographies that had ever been compiled on the Forest. Research showed that Southampton University's library contained several as well as a splendid collection of Hampshire local history and works on the New Forest.

Some of the most useful titles, however, were to be found only in the British and Bodleian libraries. This was maddening, for the time spent in travel to London or Oxford, plus the time required to locate and bring a rare title from underground storage areas, left me only two or three hours to peruse and photocopy extracts from the works before I had to take the train home again.

In this research stage Mary proved amazingly resourceful by locating several key books on the Forest not available outside London or Oxford. Methodically visiting second-hand bookshops in a large part of southern England, she asked to see titles on the Forest. In this way she came across a book detailing the life of Sarah Robinson, the "soldiers' friend" of the First World War, who had retired to the New Forest. In retirement she remained active, visiting many parts of the Forest and getting to know some of its fascinating characters. An invalid, she designed raised flower beds which she could tend from her wheelchair. Her "hut" was only five minutes walk from our cottage. Mary also found a copy of a rare English Civil War novel written by a vicar whose church was at Sopley on the edge of the Forest.

96
Mary's worrying lapses

During the early stage of our work on the anthology, Mary continued to have periods of unexplained loss of confidence and concentration. Once, after making minute plans to visit Angela, then working on her master's degree in French studies in the United States, she did not have the will to get out of bed on the morning of the flight when her taxi arrived. A hasty check-up with our local GP and hospital tests, however, revealed nothing abnormal.

Then came a series of unrelated memory lapses which, taken individually, did not seem unusual. Once or twice she left the tap water running after filling the kettle. On another occasion she left the tableware drawer open after taking out knives, forks and spoons for our meal. More disturbing, however, were other incidents reflecting loss of confidence.

One day she telephoned me to come to her rescue in a part of the village where she had parked the car near a tree on a piece of ground with a gentle slope. She said she was afraid of hitting the tree if she moved the car. When I arrived, I found neither the slope too sharp nor the tree too near the car and so had no problem in driving away. I was much puzzled why this minor difficulty should so shake her driving confidence.

Not long afterwards I had another message from her on a day when she had taken a group of "Over-70s" on a ride deep into the New Forest. A small band of drivers regularly took elderly villagers on excursions by courtesy of the Forestry Commission which provided keys to their gates from which tracks led into the forest. Mary had entered one of the gates and had progressed a mile or two along a trail where timber cutting had recently taken place. Stacks of logs and trees shorn of their branches lay alongside the track for 30 or 40 yards with no space for turning a car round.

As there was no point in continuing with her passengers into this area now bereft of its trees, Mary started to reverse the car. To her surprise, she found she was unable to reverse more than a yard or two without running into the logs on either side of the track. This, despite the fact that there was a verge of a yard or so on either side of the track. It was as if the presence of the logs on either side had triggered a kind of claustrophobia which shattered her confidence in reversing.

Her plight was relayed to me from a nearby Forest keeper's cottage. When a friend eventually reached Mary, it was clear to him that the problem could easily have been overcome by calm, patient reversing. That simple manoeuvre, however, was now clearly beyond Mary's present capability.

Although I insisted, for the time being, that I take over all driving, we continued our normal living pattern. This involved attending meetings of village clubs, going to church and occasionally seeing plays at Salisbury Theatre. We also continued to have friends in for meals and tea. One Sunday, when a couple had come to lunch, Mary seemed to be taking longer than usual with the cooking. I excused myself once or twice to see if there was any way I could help. Although somewhat agitated, she said there was nothing I could do. Some time elapsed when she suddenly came to the living room and tearfully asked if I could help her.

In the kitchen I found everything in order: the roast was done and all the vegetables had been cooked. Only the gravy remained to be made. When I asked what the problem was, she could not explain but merely said she wasn't able to carry on any longer. I took over and within minutes we served up the meal during which she showed no obvious sign of distress or feeling unwell. She was sensitive about discussing the episode afterwards and I did not press her. Nonetheless I was deeply concerned.

Mary had kept a diary since childhood, but now long gaps – some as long as two months – began to appear. I was not to be aware of this until years later but, in retrospect, I realise she had not felt well enough to write. Never inclined to write or talk about headaches, colds or even a serious illness, she always made it her rule to speak or write only positively. Nonetheless, she regretted not keeping her diary up to date, for she wrote in August of 1983: "For two months no entry in diary, yet such exciting happenings. Oh, shame!"

The American Thanksgiving Day that year fell on Thursday, 24 November and for the occasion Stuart flew over with his wife, Rebecca, and our first grandchild, Anna. It was the first time in many years that all three of our children were present for Thanksgiving. Despite the earlier gaps in her diary, Mary now recorded our joy:

"Oh happy day to have these three with us for this special occasion. With roaring fire in living room and dinner cooking away, *such* a happy time."

With increasing frequency of memory losses and the occasional loss of confidence, Mary's mind at times remained alert. When her over-active thyroid gland was diagnosed as being one possible explanation for her mysterious personality swings, the surgeon recommended that part of it should be removed. To this she readily agreed for she was at a loss to explain what was happening to her and wanted desperately to be her usual happy self.

When I suggested to Mary that travel, both within Britain and abroad, might prove just the therapy to restore her normal robust health, she concurred. We sat down and studied a guide to stately homes. When it became apparent that we had visited most of those in southern England, we decided to venture farther afield. One expedition took us to East Anglia, another to Lincolnshire and a third to the West Country. All these she thoroughly enjoyed but a curious development occurred: she was reluctant to be away from me for a moment, whether in a hotel, restaurant or sightseeing.

Having visited Venice twice before but under rather pressing circumstances, she now said she would like to go again, preferably on a conducted tour but only if a member of the family accompanied her. Pipkin, free at the time and also anxious to add to her knowledge of Venice, happily jumped at the chance to accompany Mary. The two had an interesting stay but were not prepared for the almost total dominance of ecclesiastical sites on the tour itinerary. Already acquainted with the magnificent churches on St. Mark's Square and along the Grand Canal, they were astonished as the tour guide led them daily to numerous other churches scattered all over Venice. For Mary and Pipkin it soon became a joking matter, but their guide was not altogether appreciative when some tour members eventually greeted her each morning with "What! Not more churches!"

Of all places in Britain, Mary liked Bath best and never tired of visiting it. One day, to my surprise, she asked if she could go there for a fortnight. Such a visit, she added quickly, might restore her health. She said she could manage alone, provided she was in a centrally located (preferably small) hotel. With some misgivings about her ability to cope alone, I agreed on condition she would telephone me at once should she not feel well. It turned out to be a thoroughly enjoyable stay, although she managed to write me only twice.

"Can you imagine," she wrote, "I have been trying to write you every day this week, but it just doesn't come off." She went on to say that she made a plan for every day, but was seldom able to keep it because "things keep happening."

"The Pump Room," she added, "is so agreeable, the music is delightful – the very same that the Georgians played in the same room – and everyone is so very happy." Outside she watched gardeners watering the flowers arranged in the square for the benefit of visitors. "The business people of Bath pay for them," she explained, "isn't that nice!"

She recounted her visits to Bath Abbey, Lansdowne Crescent, the Victorian Gardens and Bowood House and her conversations with several other visitors, ranging from an elegantly dressed lady from Lymington to "a dear old couple" she met at the bus station. "They were such pure, honest old people – can you see that I am enjoying every minute here?"

Admitting that she had been able to write only two pages a day, she ended the letter by announcing a pleasant discovery. "This morning," she said, "I was so thrilled to find the music to 'Bless this House' (whose words had always adorned the living room at Frith Farm) so that I can now send it to Stuart and Rebecca to learn." She then summed up her stay in Bath:

"I can only say this is the most happy place."

She was still ecstatic about her stay when I arrived the following Sunday to bring her back to the New Forest. I discovered that she had done a great deal of walking but sometimes had become lost. When I asked her why one knee was red, she explained she had walked off a curb without realising it and had fallen heavily in the road. A man nearby had rushed to help her up but she was not injured beyond the bruised knee. I now realised, despite the obvious pleasure Bath had given, that some memory loss still remained.

97
Last words of love

The frequency and seriousness of Mary's forgetfulness increased. One day when returning by train from doing research at the British Library, I chanced to read in my newspaper about a Hollywood star who had Alzheimer's Disease. I had never heard of the illness but as I continued reading, it occurred to me that the symptoms experienced by the movie idol were very similar to those Mary was displaying. This disease, I learned, was progressive and, worse still, incurable.

When I reached home I was determined to learn the truth of Mary's condition, so far as it was possible, for the article stressed that absolute diagnosis of Alzheimer's could be made only by autopsy. Whereas scans at Southampton Hospital had shown nothing abnormal, there was a recently installed super-scanner at Poole, our GP said, that might reveal more. We immediately arranged for scans there and, as we sat in the hospital waiting room, Mary turned to me and smilingly said:

"Isn't it wonderful! I was one of the Burley people who helped collect funds for the Poole scanner and now I must be one of the first to make use of it!"

Not long afterwards our GP called me to his office and said the various consultants had regretfully concluded Mary had Alzheimer's Disease. It had taken so long to make the diagnosis, he added, because they had hoped her illness had been due to other causes – hopefully treatable. One by one these other possibilities had been eliminated and now, sadly, only Alzheimer's was left.

Although not surprised, I was nonetheless shattered because I, like the consultants, had hoped her condition could be cured by either treatment or operation. After the news sank in, I sought to grasp the implications of the doctor's announcement. When I asked how long Mary might live, he replied he could not say with certainty, but as her condition was deteriorating rapidly, she was unlikely to live more than a year or two. He added that a relative of his had recently died of Alzheimer's at the age of 62.

I found it difficult to adjust to the concept that Mary's days were now numbered and that my role henceforth would be not just a devoted husband but a conscientious carer as well.

I immediately wrote to the children about the prognosis. All three were wonderful in their responses, uniformly pointing out that I must organise care of Mary in a way that would not be destructive of my own health. Each offered to help in any way I could suggest.

Stuart, from his home in Pennsylvania, rushed me two widely acclaimed books on Alzheimer's which detailed the pattern that I could expect Mary's illness to take. There would be minor and then major personality changes, aimless walking, picking up and dropping objects in the house, nightmares, inability to feed oneself, incontinence and growing inability to recognise family members and friends. Although it was helpful to know what was coming, it was nonetheless devastating to see Mary's bewilderment as her condition deteriorated rapidly.

"What is happening to me?" she implored, her eyes searching mine for an answer. I could not bring myself to tell her the truth. As she had once expressed some sympathy for euthanasia, I could not anticipate her reaction if she were told of her prognosis. So I lied, and said that the doctors still did not know the cause of her misery. I added that if the illness did not pass after a time, we would consider more tests.

Meanwhile more articles about Alzheimer's appeared in

newspapers and magazines and the disease was increasingly featured on radio and television. Some offered hope that a cure was just around the corner. I soon learned, however, that a cure was not likely in Mary's lifetime.

Despite the rapid and massive destruction of her brain cells, Mary could be amazingly lucid at times. Once she confronted me and said:

"I am dying. I know I am. Don't ask me how I know it, but it's true."

She did not ask me to comment. The best I could do was to say that everyone had to die sometime, but that I hoped she would be around a long time yet and that we still had each other, the children and grandchildren to enjoy. She was not reassured by my reply, however, and calmly repeated her point.

Only once, at least to my knowledge, did she contemplate suicide. If I were preparing meals or cleaning the house, I kept an eye on her as she moved from one room to another, sometimes sitting down, sometimes attracted suddenly to a picture on the wall, a book on a shelf or some other object. I had already removed objects that could be broken or those with which she could injure herself – or so I thought.

Suddenly missing her and not hearing her footsteps, I rushed upstairs and found her in the bathroom. The cupboard was open and she held the manicure scissors in her hand, pointed towards her chest.

"Shall I take my life?" she asked quietly, her voice tinged with despair.

I placed my hands gently on her arms and replied:

"I don't think so. That would make us all very sad."

I then slowly took the scissors, put them away and led her downstairs. In a flash she had forgotten the incident.

The nightmares came on gradually, as the books had predicted. Later they increased in frequency and eventually she was to suffer several in the course of the same evening. I soon developed a standard procedure. Turning on the light, which usually stopped the episode, I knelt down beside her bed and took her hands into mine, saying calmly with a slight trace of a smile: "You've had a horrible dream!"

When she grasped what I was saying, she usually repeated the words "horrible dream", and laughed aloud as if admitting to a childhood foible. Then I took her bottle of Yardley's Lavender Water and applied drops on her cheeks and forehead. The water had been her mother's all-purpose cure for anyone having difficulty with sleeping and Mary, in turn, had used it with our children when sleep would not come. Now she lovingly accepted my gentle ministrations, dutifully closing her eyes as I applied the water. Within a minute or so, she became totally relaxed and once more sleep returned.

As Mary's condition worsened I found it increasingly difficult to cope alone. Sooner or later I knew I had to face up to placing her in a nursing home or hospice where round-the-clock professional care could be provided. But so long as she had even a shred of her faculties I was determined – my health permitting – to keep her at home.

Angela, now teaching French in America, offered to come over. Pipkin, in a crucial phase of her doctoral studies at Oxford, thought she would be disloyal to her mother and our family if she did not also help. In the end I persuaded her to stick to her studies, cast aside any feelings of guilt she might have and allow Angela to join me. This Angela did and together we managed to cope until almost the very end.

The only way I could get sufficient sleep was to take a nap while Mary was resting. Thus it was that I stretched out beside her on our double bed after lunch each day, she beneath the covers and I on top of them. I always held her hand in mine, in case she realised my presence and found my touch reassuring. It had been many days, perhaps weeks, since Mary had spoken a word or shown a sign of recognition.

Suddenly my rest was broken as she turned toward me, her face aglow with her glorious smile of old, and said:

"I love you *so-o-o* much!"

I could not believe my eyes or ears. By what miracle had her few remaining brain cells allowed her to express her feelings so lucidly and movingly?

With tears streaming down my face I turned quickly toward her, saying that I, too, loved her – *very* much. Her eyes met mine in recognition, her wonderful smile continuing for an instant and then it disappeared. The entire episode lasted only a few seconds, but her words and expression more than repaid me for the care I was giving.

She never spoke coherently to me again. I did not mind. She had said it all on that memorable day.

Epilogue

Mary's funeral took place in our parish church on a crisp November afternoon in 1986.

Angela, permitted to decorate the church, made simple arrangements of flowers in blue, Mary's favourite colour. The prelude featured a medley of British and American folksongs. The hymns included "Who Would True Valour See", which had been favourites both of Mary and her father, and "O God Our Help in Ages Past". Instead of an address, we asked a friend to read one of Mary's often-quoted passages from literature, "Look to This Day", attributed to the Sanskrit dramatist and poet, Kalidasa:

With the strains of "Morning is Broken" wafting from the church, the children and I followed the pallbearers as they made their way towards the grave site, only a few yards from the last resting place of Miss Applebee. During the previous night someone had forgotten to close the gate to the churchyard and several Forest cows had entered, lost no time in munching the healthy growth of churchyard grass and deposited numerous heaps of shiny dung. These the pallbearers, and ourselves, gingerly dodged as we headed for the grave. Stuart sized up the occasion perfectly when he whispered softly to us:

"Knowing Mummy's sense of humour, she would have gotten a great kick out of the souvenirs the cows left behind."

Recalling Mary's fondness for John Buchan and how impressed she had been by the simple circular stone that marked his last resting place at Elsfield, I arranged for a similar, but smaller one to commemorate her life. It seemed to blend perfectly into the landscape of the churchyard corner overlooking the ancient manorial land of the village.

Adjusting to the loss of a loved one can be a traumatic experience for the next of kin, as Mary and I had often discussed. She always took a pragmatic approach to these situations based in part, no doubt, on how she felt after the loss of her father and, in part, from observing friends in our village. She came to adopt a simple, but useful, yardstick.

"I have observed," she told me some years before, "that it is the first calendar year that is most difficult for the principal survivor. You see, the date of the loved one's departure is indelibly stamped on the survivor's mind. Not until the first anniversary of the death is passed – and particularly the intervening Christmas, does the survivor realise that there are millions of other widows or widowers in the world and he or she is just one of them."

"But how," I asked her, "can the survivor cope during this year? A year is a long time to grieve."

"Ah" she said, "avoiding grief should be the constant objective of relatives and friends. The survivor must be kept busy. He or she should be encouraged to be active in community life, to travel, but above all to engage with people throughout the year."

Mary's point was illustrated a few years earlier when the husband of a dear friend was tragically killed in an automobile accident. Unknown to me, Mary had marked the date in her diary and invited the friend, a year to the day, to dine with us. For the best part of three hours we chatted, ate and sometimes laughed. Only later did I learn that the date had been chosen deliberately so that our friend was not left to grieve alone over the anniversary.

After our children returned to their respective duties and studies, I found the loneliness almost unbearable. Moving about the house I was reminded everywhere I looked of the "woman's" hand – the leafy wallpaper Mary had chosen to complement the New Forest all round us, the pictures she had so lovingly selected over the years and all the little touches which echoed her personality and love of simplicity. The print of Napoleon at the end of the passageway where the Emperor is pointing vigorously towards Pipkin's room ("What else would he be pointing at?" Mary asked). The snippets of flowers, cut from a wallpaper scrap, pasted on a panel holding the light switch. The heart-shaped dogwood leaf on the bathroom door and many other touches – all of these made our home unique and beautiful.

"Keep busy", had been Mary's advice and now I, too, adopted this strategy. I had completed only half of my anthology of the New Forest when Mary's illness obliged me to abandon the project; now I was resolved to resume it. At first I found it difficult to concentrate but gradually the need to conduct interviews, gather reference material and take photographs restored me to an almost normal pattern of life.

The book, six years in the making, appeared in 1989. With its large format and length (368 pages), plus colour plates, end papers and an embossed cover, it was by far our most ambitious and expensive title. I dedicated it to Mary, for she had not only helped at the outset but had greatly looked forward to accompanying me when I interviewed colourful New Forest personalities. She would have been delighted at the book's reception. Not only did it serve a long-felt need in the Forest but many regional and national libraries took copies for their sections of British topography.

Later I was to publish many extracts from Hugh Pasmore's "A New Forest Commoner's Notebook" which appeared earlier in several regional newspapers. Hugh, who was the auctioneer who had sold us our house, sat on the New Forest Verderers' Court for many years and was perhaps the best known figure in the Forest. His book, *A New Forest Commoner Remembers*, appeared in 1991 and was an instant hit. My second numismatic title, *Tokens of Those Trying Times*, appeared the same year. It was a social study of Britain's 19th century silver tokens which, for a brief period, largely took the place of the coin of the realm.

Producing these hard-cover books was very satisfying, but I also received tremendous pleasure from publishing a purely local booklet, only 40 pages in length, in 1988. This came about following the death of

Felicité Hardcastle, our local historian, naturalist and all-round village and New Forest "character".

Concerned that anecdotes about Miss Hardcastle should be collected before they were forgotten, I undertook to publish the slim volume. Our retired district nurse, Anne Powell, readily agreed to take on the editing. The result was a collection of lively stories reflecting the many aspects of Miss Hardcastle's life.

One of the most amusing accounts came from an old forester who revealed that Miss Hardcastle – who always made known her vegetarian preference – had been both a poacher and a meat-eater in her younger days. We all knew her as the staunchest of vegetarians, but as a young woman she made the best squirrel pie for miles around. The Lord Lieutenant of Hampshire, who presented Miss Hardcastle with her British Empire Medal a few months before her death, wrote to say he kept the little volume of anecdotes for bedside reading and several times reread the poaching / squirrel pie anecdote.

Publishing these works, plus lots of croquet play and travel over several years took me to places that had previously eluded me, among them New Zealand, Australia, South Africa and China. Each country held a particular fascination for me but New Zealand and China especially appealedt.

New Zealand, particularly South Island with its Milford Sound and fjords, lived up to its reputation as one of the most beautiful places on earth. An amusing incident happened when our small ski plane landed on Tasman Glacier adjacent to Mount Cook. The little aircraft had just completed its flight which took us, it seemed, perilously close to the peak which only that month had shed several metres of its height. As this breathtaking experience clearly called for some kind of celebration, one of the Japanese passengers whisked out a bottle of strong drink and demanded we all share it with him.

The pilot responded:

"Well, you have a choice. Either I have a drink and we spend the night here or I abstain and I fly you off the mountain now."

We decided the pilot should abstain.

I found the people of New Zealand extremely kind and still feeling close to "Britain, the Mother Country", despite a savage decrease in sales of agricultural produce because of the United Kingdom's obligations to its European Community partners. The courageous country has worked hard to replace this lost business by increasing its trade with Japan and other Pacific-rim nations.

My overwhelming impression of China was that chaos and corruption are so much a part of the Communist system that it will be difficult to eradicate them as the country strives to achieve a place among developed nations. From one day to the next members of our package tour were dispossessed of their hotel rooms, bumped off mid-morning flights and put on early ones and obliged to accept itinerary substitutions without notice or explanation. We eventually learned bribes were being passed from one tour group operator to another with hotel managers themselves sometimes sharing the "cut".

For example, when we arrived at Xian, we were shuffled off to a distant corner of the hotel lobby where the manager saw for the first time that our group had two single people (myself and a young secretary). Although we both had paid hefty single-room supplements, the manager insisted his hotel was full and we two singles must stay together.

Suspecting a scam, a Hong Kong member of our party slipped away to the reception desk, pretended to be a newly arrived Chinese-American, and asked if the hotel had rooms for the night. "Certainly," said the beaming receptionist, "how many do you want?" Both the secretary and I were then supplied with single rooms, but despite our telephone (and subsequent written) protests to our Beijing tour office (operated by the Chinese government), we never received either an explanation or apology. We concluded the manager and the tour operator hoped to coerce two single people to share a room so they could sell the freed room for several hundred dollars to a newly arrived businessman or tourist – perhaps pocketing the entire charge themselves.

En route back to Xian after seeing the terracotta army, our minibus driver, our group comprising four nationalities and the bus itself were incarcerated for several hours in a police compound because the driver allegedly did not have all the permits required. Whether this was the real reason or it was because he refused to pay the usual "bribe of passage" often extracted on Chinese roads, we never found out. Again there was no explanation or apology.

During the rare opportunities when we could speak privately with our English-speaking guides, we gained the impression that they were intelligent, hard-working and anxious to better their lot. More than one volunteered a secret wish to attend an American university and seek a new life abroad.

And so the years rolled by with travel as my primary therapy for the loss of Mary. Annual trips to the United States kept me abreast of Angela's and Stuart's careers in education. I combined these trips with visits to my sister, Hope, and brothers, Floyd and Harold.

Although I cannot agree with the wit who said there should be only grandchildren, not children, I am the first to admit that this Grandpa never ceases to marvel at his grandchildren, who surely must be the cleverest and liveliest ever born.

Supplementing travel, sport and social activity, I have often immersed myself in recalling Mary's spontaneity and *joie de vivre*. It has been especially comforting and inspiring to relive those moments in our marriage when Mary gave great pleasure to others, including members of our family, through her simple acts of kindness or gentle sense of humour, such as:

Early on Easter mornings when she furtively crept to neighbours' homes, leaving behind tiny baskets of eggs for the youngest children.

One day, when I was deeply engrossed in typing, she suddenly appeared behind me clad in her kitchen apron and with tears streaming down her face. "I want to go home to mother!" she cried, her expression perfectly matching her words. When she saw my horrified look, she broke into giggles and said: “I’ve been slicing onions.”

When two Jehovah’s Witnesses were entering the gate and were about to leave their literature, she quickly picked up the last remaining kitten from our litter. It was by now good-sized – almost a cat – and we were afraid that we might be stuck with it. Mary got in the first word as she handed the purring kitten to the wife while her husband looked askance. “That kitten just *loves* you,” she said convincingly. Before the husband could object, she added: “Wouldn’t it be wonderful if you could give it a nice Christian home!” A few minutes later the pair departed happily with their acquisition, having forgotten to leave behind the customary tracts. As we re-entered the house, Mary gave me a mischievous look and said: “You see, it really is more blessed to give than to receive.”

Once, years ago when we were in the midst of our nightly connubial bliss where concentration and timing are crucial to simultaneous success, she suddenly tapped me on the shoulder and in a grave voice said: “Guess what?” Taken aback by the interruption and fearing some catastrophic news, I replied: “What?” Then, while barely able to restrain her laughter, she burst out: “You’d never guess what I had to pay for fish today!”

Her pleasure in recounting how, one cold winter’s day when delivering “Meals on Wheels”, one grateful recipient told her: “I can do without the meal, but not your cheery visit.”

Her birthday cards to me, always amusing but never sentimental. If the printed card didn’t quite convey her feelings, she simply added what was required. My favourite, which she must have given me after 30 or 35 years of marriage, bore the printed message: ‘You are just my type.’ To this she appended: “I *think*”.

Index

The following abbreviations are used in the index:

JOM	James O'Donald Mays	Gen	General
MM	Mary Mays	GA	Georgia
AER	A. E. Roberts	NF	New Forest
Amb	Ambassador	Soton	Southampton